SOUTHERN PROGRESSIVISM

ᔰ *Twentieth-Century America Series*

Southern Progressivism

THE RECONCILIATION OF PROGRESS AND TRADITION

Dewey W. Grantham

THE UNIVERSITY OF TENNESSEE PRESS

KNOXVILLE

Twentieth-Century America Series
DEWEY W. GRANTHAM, GENERAL EDITOR

Library of Congress Cataloging in Publication Data
Grantham, Dewey W.
  Southern progressivism.

  (Twentieth-century America series)
  Bibliography: p.
  Includes index.
  1. Southern States—Politics and government—1865–1950.
  2. Progressivism (United States politics) I. Title. II. Series.
  F216.G73   1984   975'.04   82-25918
  ISBN 0-87049-389-2
  ISBN 0-87049-390-6 (pbk.)

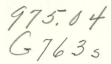
TO VBG

"Ni le temps ni l'hymen n'éteignirent leur flamme"

La Fontaine

Contents

Illustrations

MAPS

TABLES

Acknowledgments

IT HAS BEEN my good fortune to visit many libraries and archives in the South and other parts of the the United States while doing research for this book. I am indebted to the directors and staffs of these institutions, which include university libraries, state departments of archives and history, the Manuscripts Division of the Library of Congress, and the National Archives and Records Service. True to their professional calling, these men and women have facilitated my research in myriad ways and enhanced my satisfaction in using their collections. I am especially obligated to the librarians and archivists at Vanderbilt University and the Southern Historical Collection of the University of North Carolina, particularly to J. Isaac Copeland, former director of the latter repository. My search for illustrations was rewarded through the efforts of James C. Anderson of the University of Louisville Photographic Archives, Kay R. Beasley of the Vanderbilt Photo Archive, Claire Collier of the Rockefeller Archive Center, Robert G. Corley of the Birmingham Public Library, William G. Hauser of the U.S. Forest Service, Robert E. Snyder of the University of South Florida, and Michael Thomason of the University of South Alabama Photographic Archives.

Several fellowships and research grants have helped sustain my work on this undertaking. I am pleased to acknowledge this support and to express my appreciation to the John Simon Guggenheim Memorial Foundation, the Henry E. Huntington Library, San Marino, California, and the Social Science Research Council. I would also like to thank the University Research Council, the Institute of Research in the Social Sciences, and the Holland N. McTyeire professorship of Vanderbilt University for essential research assistance.

I am deeply grateful to my friend and colleague Jacque Voegeli for generously agreeing to read an earlier draft of the manuscript and for giving me the benefit of his critical acumen and profound understanding of southern history. I have profited as well from the criticisms and suggestions of Wayne Flynt and Jack Temple Kirby, who read the manuscript for the University of Tennessee Press. John M. Glen of Southwest Texas State University, who served ably as my research assistant during the years 1980–82, contributed in many ways to whatever merit this work may have. I want to thank him warmly for his help. It is a pleasure to acknowledge the aid and advice given me at various times by H. Franklin Brooks, Michael L. Carrafiello, James B. Gardner, Mary Egerton Higgs, William G. McBride, Patricia S. Miletich, Cheri Radford, Essie Wenar Samuels, Cecilia M. Stiles, Martha H. Swain, and Mary H. Wilgus. I am obligated to Anna B. Luton for her skill and good humor in typing the final version of the manuscript, and to Carese Parker for her proficiency in preparing the index. I am alone responsible, of course, for whatever errors and inadequacies this book may possess.

Portions of my essay "The Contours of Southern Progressivism," which appeared in the December 1981 issue of the *American Historical Review,* are included in this volume. I am indebted to the American Historical Association for permission to reprint this material.

I owe a special debt of thanks to Mavis Bryant, acquisitions editor, University of Tennessee Press, for her continuing interest in my project and for her unfailing cooperation and kindness. I shall always be grateful, in this venture as in so many others, to Virginia Burleson Grantham for her companionship and her example.

August 1982

DEWEY W. GRANTHAM

Abbreviations

The following abbreviations are used for frequently cited sources in the footnotes:

Annals   *Annals of the American Academy of Political and Social Science*

JSH   *Journal of Southern History*

La. Hist.   *Louisiana History*

SAQ   *South Atlantic Quarterly*

Introduction

DURING THE EARLY YEARS of the twentieth century, the American South experienced an extraordinary wave of political and social reform. The extent of this reformism was unprecedented in the South, and it contrasted sharply with two earlier reform movements. Unlike Radical Reconstruction, southern progressivism was largely an indigenous phenomenon, and in contrast to the Populist movement, it was both less disruptive and more successful in achieving its objectives. A series of progressive movements unfolded in the southern states as hundreds of politicians, newspaper editors, educators, and members of the emerging professions cast themselves in the role of reformers, launching scores of campaigns for public education, railroad regultion, more efficient agricultural methods, a more adequate welfare system, and so on. It is not altogether clear how this progressivism paralleled or differed from contemporary reform in other sections. The South's distinctive institutions, one-party politics, and perennial concern with the "race question" no doubt gave a special color to its social reform; but it is apparent, nevertheless, that the region shared in the national reform ethos and interacted with other parts of the country in developing its own brand of progressivism.

The origins of the progressive impulse in the South can be found in a confluence of internal and external developments in the late nineteenth century. Perhaps the most fundamental of these dynamics were changes in the economic and social landscape of the region, particularly the coming of industry, increasing urbanization, and the growing importance of a new middle class made up of business and professional elements. Southern progressivism was also given impetus by the restructuring of southern politics in the 1890s and early 1900s: by the overwhelming dominance of the Democratic party, the drastic shrinkage of the electorate, the persistence of agrarian protest and populist thought, and the dramatic enlargement in the part played by economic and professional organizations in the formulation and enactment of public policy. The growth of a stronger and more pervasive sense of social needs constituted a third source of progressivism in the South. Finally, the new social reform was rooted in the idea of southern progress. The idea was inherent in the longing for economic development and regional rehabilitation. It was promoted not only by the concept of economic development but also by a group of critics who wanted to improve life in the section by reforming various institutions and practices.

Southern progressivism was a wide-ranging but loosely coordinated attempt to modernize the South and to humanize its institutions without abandoning its more desirable values and traditions. Its spirit was probably more important than its reform accomplishments. Southern progressives were moderate, eclectic, and resourceful in their approach to social problems. In general they sought to impose a greater measure of social order, to foster economic opportunity and development, and to protect the weak and unfortunate in deserving cases. There was no typical progressive in the South, for no single "reformer" could have supported such a variety of corrective endeavors. But the most characteristic and significant of the region's progressives were middle-class men and women, inhabitants of the urban South and representatives of the new commercial and professional elements. They provided the leadership, created the new organizations, directed the reform campaigns, articulated the progressive rationale and mission, and gave the reform movements their distinctive tone and style.

In the ranks of the southern progressives were lawyers, editors, ministers, doctors, businessmen, agricultural scientists, demonstration agents, directors of the Young Men's Christian Association and Young Women's Christian Association, railroad commission experts, legislative lobbyists, and others. These types comprised the progressive coalitions in the South. Such coalitions usually involved what Sheldon Hackney has called "the politics of pluralistic interest groups."[1] The increasing resort to collective action by these professionals and specialists made them a powerful force in reform politics. Of course, the character and strength of these groups differed from state to state. Urban influences were obviously stronger in Tennessee than in Mississippi. Cultural traditions were more significant in Virginia than in Oklahoma politics. Farmer and labor organizations were better represented in the politics of the southwestern states than in the states of the Southeast. Despite the dominant role of urban leaders and groups, rural southerners played an important part in the South's progressivism, particularly in the mass support they provided such causes as disfranchisement, public education, railroad regulation, and prohibition. What distinguished the southern progressives was not only their effort to exert social and political power in their communities, states, and region, but also their search for accommodation and agreement as a basis for innovation and reform.

Although southern progressives were a rather disparate collection of social

---

[1] Hackney, *Populism to Progressivism in Alabama* (Princeton, N. J., 1969), 209. Hackney was speaking in the context of Alabama progressivism.

reformers, they were united in some measure by common goals and social values. They shared a yearning for a more orderly and cohesive community. Such a community, they believed, was a prerequisite for economic development and material progress. Its realization depended upon the effective regulation of society in the interest of ethical business practices and good government, and in the elimination of political corruption, machine politics, and the insidious power of large corporations and other special interests. This meant that the regulatory power of the state must be expanded. Social controls were also indispensable for the preservation of moral values, for the purification of social institutions, and for the protection of men and women from their own weaknesses. Underlying this coercive reformism was a substantial vein of self-righteousness and moral apprehension. Optimistic about future prospects but alarmed by the tensions and turmoil that pervaded the South in the late nineteenth century, southern progressives looked toward the creation of a clearly defined community that would accommodate a society differentiated by race and class but one that also possessed unity, cohesion, and stability. The search for community may explain the reformers' obsession with the virtues of rural life and with means of improving it.

Progressives in the South, like other American reformers in this period, talked about the virtues of "the people," identified morality with majority rule, and urged the desirability of preserving and expanding traditional democratic principles. But, characteristically, their concept of democracy was limited. The idea they invoked was that of *"Herrenvolk* democracy"—a democratic society for whites only.[2] Racial segregation and black disfranchisement, some white leaders claimed, were the touchstones through which the distinctions separating white men could be softened, white unity maintained, and a broader white democracy achieved. But well-to-do and middle-class southerners, including many social reformers, often revealed a deep distrust of the masses, whether black or white.[3] While the social critics and reformers in the early twentieth-century South worked for the education and uplift of the common man, they were fully aware of his prejudices and narrowmindedness, of his extreme sensitivity to criticism, obsession with the race question, and susceptibility to sentimentalism. Thus, southern progressives demonstrated a proclivity toward paternalistic solutions in dealing with many social problems. It is significant that progressives sometimes coupled education, which they em-

---

[2]See George M. Fredrickson, *The Black Image in the White Mind: The Debate on Afro-American Character and Destiny, 1817–1914* (New York, 1971), 256–82.

[3]If progressivism had a general theme in the South, J. Morgan Kousser suggests, it was hardly "democracy" or "the greatest good for the greatest number," but rather the stabilization of society in the interest of long-established powers and at the expense of the section's poorer elements (Kousser, *The Shaping of Southern Politics: Suffrage Restriction and the Establishment of the One-Party South, 1880–1910* [New Haven, Conn., 1974], 230). This interpretation slights the influence of other social values, including humanitarian concern and social justice, in the motivation of southern progressives.

phasized as an instrument of material progress and social control, with the need to cleanse the political process and limit participation to those who were prepared for responsible citizenship.

For all their stress on social order and their faith in social controls, many southern progressives displayed a strong commitment to social justice and the amelioration of human suffering in their communities. A growing number of southerners were genuinely worried about the consequences of industrialization for ordinary people, aware of the increasing need for social services, and sensitive to the social roles and responsibilities opening up to them as part of an emerging class of trades people, professionals, and experts. This humanitarian concern was also related to the pervasive influence of religion in southern life, both in its organized form and in its cultural manifestations. After the turn of the century the clergy spoke out with greater frequency against social evils, religious bodies showed a deepening interest in the possibilities of social reform, and all of the major Protestant denominations established social action agencies of one kind or another. The creative response of southern women to the plight of the disadvantaged was especially notable in the South's uplift campaigns. The cause of social justice in the South was also fostered by the monetary and moral support of northern philanthropists during the progressive era.

Most southern progressives were convinced that the South's social distress could be relieved through economic development. They accepted the basic assumptions of the New South program of regional progress through rapid economic growth, industrialization, and a more diversified economy. These objectives led directly to an emphasis on efficiency and rationality, not only in the production of goods, but also in such areas as education, the treatment of criminals, race relations, and the prohibition of alcoholic beverages. The theme of social efficiency was prominent, for instance, in the efforts of southern progressives to improve farm life, in their approach to industrial labor, in their municipal reforms and innovations, and in their advocacy of a larger role for state governments as promoters, regulators, and arbiters. The search for efficiency in these diverse areas of southern society, while not exclusively or even primarily a manifestation of social reform, was nonetheless a significant aspect of the progressive mentality and program in the South.

These social values—order, morality, humanitarianism, efficiency, and development—were not separate categories of progressive concern. Rather they were, as Hackney has written of the Alabama progressives, "interrelated facets of a single, economically self-interested, ethically shaped, middle-class attitude toward life."[4] These areas of social involvement were mutually reinforcing, and in seeking to give them effect southern progressives began to develop a broader view of governmental responsibilities and to advocate an

[4]Hackney, *Populism to Progressivism in Alabama*, 138.

array of public services. In other words, southern progressivism became "a movement for positive government."[5]

The progressive campaigns can be divided into three interrelated but fairly distinct categories. One group of reform efforts was primarily concerned with the imposition of social controls and state regulation in troublesome areas such as race relations. The white consensus on race that developed during this period reflected a widespread conviction that disfranchisement, segregation, and black proscription not only constituted a workable system of racial control but also promised less corruption in politics, more consideration of "real" political issues, and a greater degree of social stability and public calm. Prison reform, centering on efforts to abolish the leasing of convicts, to introduce prison farms, and to develop a new system of road work for prisoners, constituted another example of state regulation. Antimonopolism, of course, was yet another manifestation of the regulatory impulse. The movement to control railroads and other large corporations and to destroy their political dominance provided an important rallying point for progressive politics in the South. Big business, so often identified with powerful outside interests, entrenched political "machines," and the destruction of competition, seemed to demand effective regulation no less than did black workers, criminals, and alcoholic beverages. The concentrated attack of southern governors and legislatures upon railroads and other corporations in 1906 and 1907 soon spent itself, and much of the regulatory force during the next decade found an outlet in the antiliquor crusade, first in the drive for statewide prohibition and subsequently in the campaign for a national law. Prohibition offered a means of moral reaffirmation of traditional values, an assurance of cleaner politics, and a way to employ the power of the state in the pursuit of moral and social progress.

A second significant class of progressive campaigns in the South was dominated by the theme of social justice. One of these reform movements was devoted to the restriction of child labor. The child labor campaigns brought the section's social reformers together in a common cause, gave them valuable experience in organizing for reform purposes, and stimulated their interest in the creation of juvenile courts and programs for dependent children. No aspect of social reform in the South during the progressive era touched the immediate lives of more of the region's inhabitants than the great educational awakening soon after the turn of the century. It was the entering wedge and the sustaining focus for an unprecedented northern philanthropy, as well as a major element in the rationale of interracial accommodation that flourished during these years. It was almost always viewed by reformers as a redemptive force in the development of a better South. A third manifestation of social justice was the organized charity movement. By the end of the first decade of the twentieth century, social

---

[5] George Brown Tindall, *The Emergence of the New South, 1913–1945* (Baton Rouge, 1967), 32.

welfare in the South had begun to move away from the long-dominant emphasis on relief of the destitute and to put greater stress on casework, surveys, and organization. Organized activities inspired by social justice were closely related to "the woman's movement," which emerged more distinctly early in the new century. Feminine involvement in the campaign to regulate child labor, the educational crusade, and the prohibition movement, not to mention numerous community projects, indicates the distance the reformers had come since joining the missionary societies and the women's clubs in earlier years. As time passed, this feminist reformism tended to find greater focus in the drive for the suffrage.

The cause of social justice also included an embryonic movement to ameliorate the conditions of black people in the South. It is clear that white southerners during the progressive period, including most social reformers, were mainly concerned in their approach to the "race problem" with means of social control and social efficiency. Yet some whites sought to ease the terrible burden of racial injustice borne by Negroes. There was also a black approach to racial progress and better social conditions. Given sustenance by an emerging black middle class, it envisioned "an expanded concept of social justice, a more efficient pattern of living, and a greater emphasis upon local organizations."[6] Blacks, as John Dittmer has written, "built their own institutions behind the walls of segregation, preaching race pride and practicing self-help."[7] Negro civic organizations, boards of trade, public welfare leagues, and community betterment groups, particularly in the larger cities, labored to extract worthwhile concessions in education and other public services from the white system, to secure more adequate correctional facilities for black juveniles, to improve housing and sanitation in Negro areas, and to promote moral conduct, social order, and efficiency in the black community. The community work of Negro clubwomen was a prominent feature of this black progressivism.

Social efficiency, especially as it applied to economic development, was the most pronounced motif in a third category of reform movements in the region. A multifaceted attack on the ills of southern agriculture made up one such movement. Another was municipal reform in the South. It embodied all the major themes of southern progressivism in the early twentieth century—social control, humanitarian efforts to relieve social distress, and the drive for efficiency. Protective labor measures and other reforms affecting industrial workers provide still another example of the emphasis on social efficiency in southern progressivism. The progressive campaigns for efficiency in agriculture, municipal government, and industrial labor led to greater interest in scientific knowledge, expertise, and effective administration in the public arena. Similar pressures emanated from other reform campaigns such as the movements for

[6] Lester C. Lamon, *Black Tennesseans, 1900–1930* (Knoxville, 1977), 208.
[7] Dittmer, *Black Georgia in the Progressive Era, 1900- 1920* (Urbana, Ill., 1977), 50.

public education, good roads, and public health. The state was increasingly looked upon not only as the source of regulatory action but also as the provider of vital new services. Promoted by numerous pressure groups and specialized organizations of farmers, businessmen, industrial workers, and professional men and women, the steadily mounting demand for public services represented an important dimension of southern progressivism.

The reform movements unfolded more or less simultaneously during the first decade of the twentieth century, except for disfranchisement and the race settlement, which were well under way by 1900. Beginning as scattered and loosely organized efforts in the 1890s and early 1900s, the more significant reform movements soon moved to the creation of state organizations and campaigns. The incentives that underlay these reform movements were varied and overlapping. The campaign for public education, for example, was fostered by the reformers' interest in social order, efficiency, and economic development as well as social justice, though humanitarian concern seems to have been the most important at the outset. The pace of the campaigns varied from state to state, but in many cases they led to coordinated or parallel activities throughout the South, although the process was occasionally reversed, as in the launching of the southern education movement. Virtually all of these progressive campaigns had assumed a regionwide character by 1910, and they were promoted as "southern" reforms. A kind of progressive balance had emerged: the claims of numerous social groups were given a hearing, and tensions were modulated between classes, races, rural and city dwellers, South and North, tradition and innovation. In other words, progressives were able to create a strong sense of community as a setting for their pursuit of social reform.

By the time Woodrow Wilson assumed the presidency in March 1913, a new stage had arrived in the evolution of southern progressivism. Reform movements in the southern states, as in other sections, were increasingly influenced by national organizations, standards, and solutions. This tendency was evident in the formation of the Southern Sociological Congress, a regional civic organization established in Nashville in the spring of 1912. Characterized by a zeal for uplift and an evangelical spirit, the congress was intended to serve as a medium for the stimulation and coordination of various social reforms. The nationalization of reform after 1912 was also apparent in regulatory movements such as the effort to control railroads and the prohibition crusade. The inclination to look for national remedies was evident in numerous other progressive campaigns: in the child labor reform movement, in the demand by the Farmers' Union and other agricultural pressure groups for federal regulations, credit facilities, and farm demonstration programs, and in the willingness of organizations such as the Southern Commercial Congress to turn to Washington for assistance in dealing with problems like flood control. Meanwhile, southern politics showed signs of increasing involvement in the debate over national issues and elections. Southern interest in national politics rose to new heights with the nomination and election of Wilson as the nation's twenty-eighth president. Indeed, the region took a long step during the Wilson administration in the direction of a more positive role in national politics, but it did so in large part without surrendering its most fundamental cultural values.

In some respects the First World War weakened and redirected the currents of social reform in the United States, particularly after the nation entered the conflict in April 1917. But the war had a momentous effect on southern society. It contributed to the region's prosperity, brought an expansion in the functions of government, encouraged civic cooperation, enhanced the role of voluntary groups, and opened new avenues of social control, efficiency, and social justice. The mobilization of community resources for military purposes had important consequences for the development of new social services in the southern states. Several states took advantage of the wartime atmosphere to adopt more advanced social welfare legislation. The South was also involved in the drive for national prohibition and in the struggle to enfranchise women by amending the Constitution. During the war and its immediate aftermath, moreover, southern progressives intensified their search for a more constructive approach to the problem of race relations.

Nevertheless, the end of the war and the collapse of the Wilson administration in 1919 and 1920 weakened southern progressivism, disrupting its unity and changing its direction. Although progressivism continued to manifest itself in the promotion of economic growth and administrative efficiency and in the preservation of traditional morality, the social balance the progressives had nourished lost much of its vitality in the 1920s. Still, the approach, style, and social values of the progressives created an enduring design in the modern South. The synthesis that resulted from their efforts to reconcile progress and tradition survived for half a century as a compelling influence in the politics and social thought of the South.

This chapter in recent southern history has attracted a great deal of scholarly investigation, resulting in a large body of historical writing, particularly on state and local developments during this period.[8] The present study leans heavily on this impressive scholarship. My purpose has been to write a history of progressivism in the South as a regional phenomenon: to examine its origins, trace the evolution of the major reform movements, and evaluate the nationalizing influences of the Wilson era. I have also attempted to delineate the structure of southern progressivism—its organization, leadership, social base, and motivation—and to interpret the meaning of this regional reform from the perspective of modern southern and American history.

---

[8]For examples, see the works cited in Dewey W. Grantham, "The Contours of Southern Progressivism," *American Historical Review* 86 (Dec. 1981): 1035–59.

PART ONE

The Regional Setting

1

The Dynamics of Reform

A NEW SPIRIT was evident in the South during the early years of the twentieth century. After a generation of disruptive change, social disorder, and political uncertainty, southerners had reason to anticipate a more satisfying future. The structure of a revamped and more dependable politics was nearing completion. Social conflict had eased, and despite increasing fluidity and mobility in the social order, prospects for a more stable and harmonious society seemed good. Above all, returning prosperity had brightened the southern outlook. These circumstances and expectations reflected cumulative changes in the condition, behavior, and attitude of the southern people in the late nineteenth century. And underlying these alterations was a set of dynamics that proved to be the major determinants of southern progressivism.

ECONOMIC AND SOCIAL CHANGE

The historian Holland Thompson, writing in 1910 about the effects of industrialism upon the contemporary South, remarked that for twenty years "a silent force" had been transforming the section. "In fact," Thompson declared, "in almost every village in some sections of the South are one or more manufacturing enterprises which seek more than a local market for their products."[1] Another close observer noted a short time later that practically every southern industry was being put upon a more solid footing as a result of "better organization, expert management, or technical skill."[2] The growth of cotton manufacturing in the South, the Bureau of the Census reported in 1900, "is the one great fact in its history during the past ten years."[3] The region possessed a great

---

[1] Thompson, "Effects of Industrialism Upon Political and Social Ideas," *Annals of the American Academy of Political and Social Science* 35 (Jan. 1910): 136.

[2] Edwin Mims, "The South Realizing Itself: Remakers of Industry," *World's Work* 23 (Dec. 1911): 203.

[3] *Twelfth Census of the United States, Taken in the Year 1900.* William R. Merriam, Director. *Census Reports,* vol. 9. *Manufactures,* pt. 3: *Special Reports on Selected Industries* (Washington, D.C., 1902), 28.

railroad network, its textile industry had made dramatic progress during the past two decades, and its trade and finance were developing rapidly. By 1900, Alabama had more than $70 million invested in manufacturing enterprises and was producing goods worth $80 million annually—twice the value of its cotton crop. A decade later Tennessee had 123,754 workers in manufacturing and mechanical pursuits, out of a total of 855,546 gainfully employed persons.[4]

Increasing industrialization and the shift toward a more diversified economy brought greater entrepreneurial opportunities to the South. Within less than a generation, an impressive increase had occurred in the number of southern merchants, industrialists, and other businessmen. New and stronger economic interest groups were springing up. These groups became a significant factor in the progressive politics of the early twentieth-century South, supporting some reform causes, opposing others. But if economic change sometimes encouraged the drive for reform, the nature of the region's economy produced pressures of a quite different sort that also fueled progressive campaigns. Despite the regional trend toward industrialization and diversification, the South retained the principal elements of a colonial economy: an abundance of unskilled labor and undeveloped resources, inadequate capital, production of low-wage and low-value manufactures, and outside domination of the railroad trunk lines, large timber and mining properties, and much of the industrial and banking wealth. Sectional antipathy and resentment growing out of this situation, along with the aggressive jockeying for competitive advantage among the southern states, provoked a good deal of the reformism identified with southern progressivism.

Changes in social patterns and attitudes were perhaps more significant than the immediate material benefits resulting from the South's incipient economic transformation. These changes were reflected, for example, in the widespread enthusiasm for industrialism among southerners and in the vitality of the burgeoning entrepreneurial spirit. "To the Chambers of Commerce of many Southern towns," one scholar has written of this period, "the establishment of a cotton mill was the first essential step toward the desired industrialization and expansion of the town."[5] Even the little country newspapers devoted considerable space to the prospect of industrial salvation.[6] Scarcely less notable was the emergence of the businessman as a dominant figure in the political decisions and social life of the section, as well as his contributions to the mounting emphasis on organization, "scientific" techniques, and efficiency. Businessmen were most closely identified with the cities and towns, but they exerted

---

[4]Justin Fuller, "Alabama Business Leaders: 1865–1900," *Alabama Review* 16 (Oct. 1963): 280; William F. Donovan, Jr., "The Growth of the Industrial Spirit in Tennessee, 1890–1910" (Ph.D. diss., George Peabody College for Teachers, 1955), 156. Also see Victor S. Clark, *History of Manufactures in the United States*, 3 vols. (New York, 1929), vol. 3, pp. 171–76.

[5]Herbert J. Lahne, *The Cotton Mill Worker* (New York, 1944), 20.

[6]Thomas D. Clark, *The Southern Country Editor* (Indianapolis, 1948): 27–28.

increasing influence in all phases of southern life. According to a Vanderbilt University professor, writing in 1909, "The most capable business men, lawyers, doctors and preachers are practically all leaving the country for the town and the city." This meant that "the great centers of life and influence and authority" were shifting from the country to the city, and "as a result the city is more and more setting the pace of and dominating Southern life and Southern thought."[7] Economic and social innovations, including urbanization, subtly altered even the most basic of the region's institutions. The family, for instance, while remaining at the center of southern existence, gradually became "more limited in function, less authoritarian in character, and less romantic in sentiments." With the passage of time the "private aspects" of social life were less likely to be maintained at "the expense of the public sphere."[8]

Some southern cities grew with breathtaking speed. Birmingham's population increased from 38,414 in 1900 to 178,806 in 1920, Atlanta's from 89,842 to 200,616 and Richmond's from 85,050 to 171,667 in the same period, while the populations of Houston, Dallas, and San Antonio more than doubled during the first two decades of the century. The fabulous oil gusher brought in at Spindletop early in 1901 made Beaumont the "Queen of the Neches," causing its population to surge up from 10,000 to 30,000 within a few months. To the north, Oklahoma City grew from 10,037 in 1900 to 91,295 in 1920. As a whole the rate of urbanization in the South was proceeding at a considerably faster pace than that of the country as a whole, though the section remained overwhelmingly rural. North Carolina, which claimed almost three hundred cotton mills early in the twentieth century, contained not a single city with more than 25,000 people.[9]

The function of this embryonic urban South was, in the first instance, almost entirely economic, as in the tobacco and textile towns of the Piedmont, where the new mills sprang up, the transportation center of Atlanta, the Birmingham industrial district, the Gulf ports and their exports of cotton, lumber, petroleum, and other minerals. The process was also evident in the emergence of many small towns and cities as local centers of trade. But if the growth of the urban South mirrored the business and industrial development of the region, its implications went far beyond the organization and servicing of the economy. It was the southern city that manifested what one observer described as "radical

[7]Gus W. Dyer, "Social Tendencies in the South," in Julian A.C. Chandler, et al. eds., *The South in the Building of the Nation*, 13 vols. (Richmond, 1909–13), vol. 10, pp. 665–66. Hereinafter cited as *The South in the Building of the Nation*. See also Wilson Gee, "Qualitative Study of Rural Depopulation in a Single Township: 1900–1930," *American Journal of Sociology* 39 (Sept. 1933): 210–21.

[8]Rupert B. Vance, "Regional Family Patterns: The Southern Family," *Amer. Jour. Sociol.* 53 (May 1948): 426–29.

[9]Walter J. Matherly, "The Urban Development of the South," *Southern Economic Journal* 1 (Feb. 1935): 3–23; Holland Thompson, "Some Effects of Industrialism in an Agricultural State," *South Atlantic Quarterly* 4 (Jan. 1905): 71; Albert Bushnell Hart, *The Southern South* (New York, 1910), 26–29, 62–65, 292.

TABLE 1. *Urban Population of the South, 1900 and 1920*

	1900			1920		
	URBAN POP.	URBAN PLACES	% URBAN	URBAN POP.	URBAN PLACES	% URBAN
Ala.	182,448	27	10.0	509,317	39	21.7
Ark.	90,396	15	6.9	290,497	41	16.6
Fla.	87,414	12	16.5	355,825	30	36.7
Ga.	308,687	31	13.9	727,859	59	25.1
Ky.	423,646	34	19.7	633,543	51	26.2
La.	347,276	15	25.1	628,163	38	34.9
Miss.	82,099	22	5.3	240,121	32	13.4
N.C.	152,019	28	8.0	490,370	55	19.2
Okla.[1]	29,978	13	3.8	539,480	63	26.6
S.C.	157,111	20	11.7	293,987	32	17.5
Tenn.	285,886	22	14.1	611,226	47	26.1
Tex.	454,926	56	14.9	1,512,689	119	32.4
Va.	305,229	27	16.5	673,984	39	29.2

[1] Urban population in 1900 includes both Oklahoma and Indian territories.

NOTE: In this table an urban place in 1900 and 1920 is defined as one containing 2,500 or more inhabitants.

SOURCES: *Twelfth Census of the United States . . . Population*, part 1 (Washington, D.C., 1901), pp. lxv, lxxxiv; *Abstract of the Fourteenth Census of the United States, 1920* (Washington, D.C., 1923), 75, 80–83.

changes in the social tendencies" of the region: the spreading "spirit of American commercialism," the emergence of distinct "capitalist" and "laboring" classes, and increasing social differentiation based on wealth and business success.[10] Another contemporary noted that a kind of "shrewd, calculating, far-sighted, business man new to the section is being developed."[11] The South's growing towns and cities provided the setting for what a sociologist later referred to as "a hustling, urban type—the rising merchants, lawyers, and doctors."[12] These urban places contained a swelling class of railroad managers, supply merchants, and bankers as well as a broadening array of industrial entrepreneurs in the lumber, food, and textile industries.[13] They also attracted a stream of newcomers, many of them displaced and illiterate rural dwellers, and the southern towns and cities found themselves confronted with growing numbers of menial and casual laborers, domestic servants, and others poorly

[10] Dyer, "Social Tendencies in the South," 664–69.

[11] Thompson, "Some Effects of Industrialism in an Agricultural State," 75.

[12] Rupert B. Vance, *Human Factors in Cotton Culture: A Study in the Social Geography of the American South* (Chapel Hill, N.C., 1929), 63.

[13] Rudolf Heberle, "The Changing Social Stratification of the South," *Social Forces* 38 (Oct. 1959): 45–46.

equipped to get ahead on the urban frontier. The consequences of this urbanization were far-reaching, for the city, in the South as in other areas, sorted out people along economic and social lines, facilitated the formation of functional organizations, and fostered a heightened concern for social order, stability, and efficiency.

"Within the little islands of industrialism scattered through the region, including the old towns as well as the new," C. Vann Woodward wrote in analyzing social trends in the 1880s, "was rising a new middle-class society."[14] By the turn of the century, the size of that class had grown appreciably. The editor of the *South Atlantic Quarterly* asserted in 1903 that "the rise of the middle class has been the most notable thing connected with the white population of the South since the war." Another contemporary pointed to "the rise to power of a great 'middle class' . . . a class long existent, but only recently of such numbers as vitally to affect the whole social 'accent' of our civilization."[15] A striking illustration of the growth of the new middle class in the South is provided by Gastonia, a mill town in North Carolina. The introduction of industry into Gaston County helped create internal distinctions along occupational, residential, educational, and attitudinal lines. Three well-defined social classes arose in the county: farmers, millworkers, and an "uptown" group made up of owners and managers of mills, professional and commercial elements, white-collar workers, schoolteachers, independent artisans, and the like. Control of nearly every aspect of life passed progressively into the hands of the "uptown people," led by several hundred mill owners and managers. As the urban population grew, distinctively urban organizations and culture traits developed. The growth of "civic spirit," leisure time, and urban facilities was revealed in such agencies as a chamber of commerce, civic clubs, a private country club, music groups, garden clubs, parent-teacher organizations, and societies based on genealogy.[16]

This emerging urban-industrial system demanded a host of services and skills, including traditional professions such as law, medicine, engineering, education, and journalism. The significant thing about these older professions in the early twentieth-century South was the marked increase in the opportunities for their members and the professional organizations and standards they established. Modern economic and social organization called forth a wide range of newer specialties in industry, labor, and agriculture. New professions

[14]Woodward, *Origins of the New South, 1877–1913* (Baton Rouge, 1951), 150.

[15]"The Industrial Decay of the Southern Planter," *SAQ* 2 (Apr. 1903): 112; Edgar Gardner Murphy, "The Task of the Leader: A Discussion of Some of the Conditions of Public Leadership in Our Southern States," *Sewanee Review* 15 (Jan. 1907): 15–16.

[16]Liston Pope, *Millhands & Preachers: A Study of Gastonia* (New Haven, Conn., 1965), 49–69; originally published in 1942. See also David Carlton, " 'Builders of a New State'—The Town Classes and Early Industrialization of South Carolina, 1880–1907," in Walter J. Fraser, Jr., and Winfred B. Moore, Jr., eds., *From the Old South to the New: Essays on the Transitional South* (Westport, Conn., 1981), 43–62.

TABLE 2. *Occupations in the South, 1910*

	AGRIC. & RELATED (%)	MANUF. & MECH. (%)	TRANSPOR- TATION (%)	TRADE (%)	WHITE- COLLAR[1] (%)	DOMESTIC & PER. SERVICE (%)
Ala.	67.1	10.8	3.4	4.3	3.9	7.6
Ark.	70.4	9.9	3.7	4.7	4.4	6.3
Fla.	43.4	22.9	6.5	6.9	6.6	12.7
Ga.	63.3	12.3	4.0	5.3	5.0	9.8
Ky.	52.5	17.1	4.9	7.0	6.8	9.4
La.	51.3	17.3	6.0	7.1	6.3	11.8
Miss.	77.2	7.5	2.7	3.2	3.1	6.3
N.C.	64.6	16.7	3.1	4.1	3.7	7.5
Okla.	58.5	12.4	5.5	8.3	7.2	6.2
S.C.	70.4	12.9	2.4	3.5	3.4	7.4
Tenn.	54.9	14.5	5.1	6.9	6.3	10.4
Tex.	60.0	11.8	5.4	7.4	6.8	8.1
Va.	45.2	20.3	6.2	6.6	7.2	12.9

[1]"White-collar" occupations represent the combined percentages of public service occupations not elsewhere classified, professional service, and clerical work.

SOURCE: *Thirteenth Census of the United States . . . ,* vol. 4: *Population, 1910, Occupation Statistics* (Washington, D.C., 1914), 44–45.

arose in such fields as public administration, public health, social work, and recreational activities. In addition, there were many small merchants, sales-men, technicians, and clerical workers. These various groups were part of the somewhat amorphous but rapidly expanding middle class in the region.[17] A significant proportion of this new class identified itself with social change, joined in the creation of private organizations for civic improvement, and advocated the expansion of public services.

The organization of economic and social interests was also apparent among southern farmers. The agricultural organizations were dominated by farm editors, scientists, professional organizers, and commercial producers. These specialists constituted a rural counterpart of the urban bourgeoisie, with which they sometimes cooperated. Nothing did more to promote this organizational activity than the revival of agricultural prosperity at the turn of the century and the prospect of even better times in the years ahead. Feeling a new sense of confidence and optimism, farm leaders throughout the South turned to the organization of new associations, to the improvement of rural education, to the development of scientific agriculture, and to the task of securing more effective

[17]For a suggestive discussion of the new middle class in the United States in the late nineteenth and early twentieth centuries, see Robert H. Wiebe, *The Search for Order, 1877–1920* (New York, 1967), 111–32.

government regulation and assistance. They were committed not only to the expansion of agricultural prosperity and efficiency but also to the preservation of rural values and the traditional moralism associated with country life.

Changes in the South's economy and society during this period were not always beneficent in their effects. The extent of the section's poverty was actually increasing in the late nineteenth century, as thousands of yeoman farmers descended into tenancy or became textile mill workers, miners, or day laborers. By the early years of the new century, poverty had become institutionalized, not only for millions of black people but for a growing number of poor whites as well. Farm tenancy grew apace. The new industries were labor-intensive and exploitative. Economic growth and urbanization brought increasing social differentiation and greater class rigidity.[18] Consequences of this kind doubtless explain an undertone of anxiety and foreboding that recurs in the social thought of southern progressives. As one historian has recently written of the "town people" in South Carolina, "concern over what came to be known as the 'cotton mill problem' united ministers, journalists, teachers, club women, and businessmen in both a common desire for a more stable and better organized society and a common perception that one of the major barriers to its realization was a 'shiftless,' undisciplined operative class."[19]

Nevertheless, the members of the new middle class were moved to action, not despair. Although their vocational and professional concerns tended to isolate them from their local communities, these interests encouraged their organization on the basis of function and skill. Industrialists and other businessmen came together in trade associations, merchant organizations, banking groups, and chambers of commerce. All of the professions either reorganized older associations or created new ones with an eye to elevating professional standards and restricting admission. Farm leaders created a variety of organizations and pressure groups. While the proliferating organizations were primarily intent upon immediate entrepreneurial or professional advantages, many of them were naturally drawn into the larger arena of municipal and state politics, since they often sought public assistance or sanction, and since their desire to control the social environment in which they operated could be furthered through state action. These middle-class elements also provided recruits for the new civic clubs and improvement associations. As the professionals and specialists banded together in local, state, and sometimes national associations, they almost instinctively created Southwide societies, frequently with the announced purpose of promoting regional goals and reforms as well as the more limited ends of their particular business or profession.

[18] See J. Wayne Flynt, *Dixie's Forgotten People: The South's Poor Whites* (Bloomington, Ind., 1979), 33–63.
[19] David Lee Carlton, "Mill and Town: The Cotton Mill Workers and the Middle Class in South Carolina, 1880–1920" (Ph.D. diss., Yale Univ., 1977), 146.

THE NEW STRUCTURE OF SOUTHERN POLITICS

The origins of progressivism in the South can also be traced to the transformation of southern politics in the late nineteenth and early twentieth centuries. The most distinctive attribute of the new southern politics was the overwhelming dominance of the Democratic party and the broad agreement among whites on the basic structure of politics in the region. The bitterness and frustration engendered by the upheaval of the 1890s strengthened the widespread resolve to maintain political unity. Such unity must be achieved in the Democratic party—the party of Redemption, the party of state rights, the party of the white man. By the turn of the century, the Republican party in the South had declined to insignificant proportions, unable to offer effective opposition to Democratic control of state governments and so rare in most places as to be a curiosity in local politics. Consequently the competition for political leadership and public office, the formulation and discussion of political issues, the fate of reform movements, and the outcome of legislative action were all decided within the confines of one-party politics.

Within the consensus that developed among white southerners on the imperative need to maintain a one-party system existed a curious and somewhat paradoxical strain of political democracy. This democratic propensity, extending back to the early nineteenth century, was a palpable feature of early twentieth-century southern politics. It was apparent in the rhetorical emphasis on the common man and white democracy, in the introduction of direct-election procedures, and in the factional competition within the Democratic party. It was also evident in the invocation of Jeffersonian and Jacksonian traditions stressing the central role of ordinary people in community life, in the exercise of political power by new economic and social groups, and to some extent, in the growing acceptance by politicians of the desirability of making state and municipal governments more active.

Several features of the South's altered political system were especially significant in shaping southern progressivism. One of these was the drastic shrinkage in the electorate as a result of the restructuring of southern politics in the 1890s and early 1900s. Disfranchisement and restrictive election laws not only deprived most black southerners of the ballot, but in conjunction with the persistence of poverty, illiteracy, and cultural barrenness, sharply limited the political involvement of millions of whites.[20] Although other innovations gave the

---

[20]J. Morgan Kousser, *The Shaping of Southern Politics: Suffrage Restriction and the Establishment of the One-Party South, 1880–1910* (New Haven, Conn., 1974), 51–53, 72–76, 91–92, 126, 155, 166, 170, 175, 206–207, 246–47, 251–57, 261; Paul Lewinson, *Race, Class, & Party: A History of Negro Suffrage and White Politics in the South* (New York, 1932), 79–123, 214–17; Malcolm Cook McMillan, *Constitutional Development in Alabama, 1798–1901: A Study in Politics, the Negro, and Sectionalism* (Chapel Hill, N.C., 1955), 263–357; Francis G. Caffey, "Suffrage Limitations at the South," *Political Science Quarterly* 20 (Mar. 1905): 54–61; James W. Garner, "Southern Politics since the Civil War," in *Studies in Southern History and Politics: Inscribed to William Archibald Dunning* ... (New York, 1914), 372–73.

appearance of democratizing the political process, political power remained concentrated in the hands of the more affluent classes. In general the greater the economic power of an interest group, the greater its ability to influence political action to its own advantage. A recent study of political power in Birmingham, for example, finds that within each government function—taxation, allocation of revenue, and regulation—the higher the economic rank of a seriously contending group, the better its overall record of political success.[21] Indeed, the new structure of southern politics probably enhanced rather than diminished the relationship between economic power and political influence in the region.

The adoption of the direct primary and such democratic devices as the popular election of United States senators had a profound effect on southern politics in the early twentieth century. First adopted on a statewide basis in South Carolina in 1896, the primary system spread over the South during the following decade and by the end of the progressive era had been extended, by party regulation or public law, to the nomination of candidates at all levels of government in the section. "The South is the native soil of the direct primary," a writer for *Arena* asserted in 1903. "It has there a logical and necessary existence, the predominance of one political party making the primary the *de facto* election."[22] The popularity of the primary movement owed something to the widespread revulsion against the convention system, with its controlling cliques, chicanery, and unfair apportionment of delegates. Throughout the period 1876–1902, one scholar writes of the Mississippi situation, there was "a ceaseless clamor" against the evils of party conventions.[23] Dissatisfied elements, as well as ambitious politicians hobbled by the old convention system, turned to the direct primary as a mechanism of change and self-advancement. The primary was generally associated with the movement against "machine politics" in the South. It weakened the party role of conservative elites and served as a rallying point for many Democrats who reacted against the repression and corruption practiced by their party in the 1890s. The cry for a statewide primary system was one of the demands of Democratic reform factions in virtually every southern state, and most of the "reform governors" used the primary as a means of publicizing their programs and bringing together effective coalitions.[24] Primary elections institutionalized an element of competition within the one-party system.

The implications of these developments for social reform were ambiguous. The refashioned politics in the various southern states did not eliminate the political influence of the established elites, though the new system generally

[21]Carl V. Harris, *Political Power in Birmingham, 1871–1921* (Knoxville, 1977), 39–56, 243, 270.

[22]Edward Insley, "Primary Election Reform," *Arena* 29 (Jan. 1903): 74.

[23]Albert D. Kirwan, *Revolt of the Rednecks: Mississippi Politics, 1876–1925* (Lexington, Ky., 1951), 33.

[24]See, for example, Allen W. Jones, "Political Reforms of the Progressive Era," *Ala. Rev.* 21 (July 1968): 173–94.

diminished their power by responding to the pressures and needs of a wider range of groups and organizations. The reorganization of political affairs in the South did facilitate the emergence of interest-group politics and provide middle-class and professional elements with greater access to politics at the same time that their increasing resort to collective action was pointing in the direction of city councils, state legislatures, and administrative officials. Although the restructured system was restrictive and undemocratic in many respects, it nonetheless provided a setting for insurgent political campaigns, for the creation of coalitions, for broad appeals to the public, and for the formation and conduct of reform movements.

Southern politics in the progressive period was the product of many ingredients, most of which were rooted in experiences, traditions, and myths associated with the Civil War, Reconstruction, and the status of black southerners. Redeemers, silver Democrats, and Populists all contributed to the remodeled political edifice of the early twentieth century. Bourbonism was represented in the continuing influence of traditional, agriculturally oriented elites as well as the weight of the emerging industrial interests in the politics of most southern states. The Bourbons' emphasis on social unity and the integral role of different elements in the community, their effort to reconcile cultural traditions and economic innovations, and their paternalistic approach to matters of class and race were partially assimilated into the political culture of the early 1900s.[25] Democrats who opposed the Bourbons and became identified with the Bryan wing of the party also had a hand in shaping the new southern politics. They were primarily responsible for the reform posture among southern Democrats at the turn of the century, and they contributed to the formulation of a reform program by promoting railroad regulation, public education, the direct primary, and the like. Without leaving the Democratic party, they managed to take over a good deal of the Populist platform.

Populism also helped determine the structure of the South's politics in the new century. For one thing, the Populists provided a compelling example of the need for political solidarity, since they had not only rebelled against established political power in the region but also challenged social tradition and the integrity of the white community.[26] Yet in appealing for unity among whites, Democratic leaders were moved to make some concessions to erstwhile Populists, particularly in the rhetorical obeisance to the ideal of popular government. In earlier years Democratic leaders had frequently adopted third-party proposals as a means of overcoming the popular appeal of their insurgent opponents. The

[25] For various contributions of the Bourbons, see George Brown Tindall, *The Persistent Tradition in New South Politics* (Baton Rouge, 1975); Carl V. Harris, "Right Fork or Left Fork? The Section-Party Alignments of Southern Democrats in Congress, 1873–1897," *Journal of Southern History* 42 (Nov. 1976): 471–506; and James Tice Moore, "Redeemers Reconsidered: Change and Continuity in the Democratic South, 1870–1900," ibid. 44 (Aug. 1978): 357–78.

[26] See, for example, Carl N. Degler, *The Other South: Southern Dissenters in the Nineteenth Century* (New York, 1974), 330–31, 338, 366–70.

Populists were strong advocates of popular elections, and their proposals for stringent railroad regulation, liberal agricultural credit, abolition of convict leasing, and the development of public education became part of the reform agenda of progressives in the South.[27] Southern Democrats in the early years of the twentieth century increasingly accepted the Populist concept of the positive state—of a more active role of government in promoting economic growth and protecting society—and this notion found fertile ground in the new climate of interest-group politics.

The persistence of agrarian radicalism after the turn of the century had other consequences for southern politics. It helped nourish antitrust sentiment and the regulatory impulse. It contributed to the vigorous intraparty factionalism that emerged in the one-party South early in the twentieth century. It also played a part in the rise of a new generation of politicians who sought to identify themselves with the "common man." Progressivism in the South was not basically a mass political phenomenon, but several of the progressive campaigns in the region were couched in the language of the white masses and the uplift of the common people. Holland Thompson went so far as to say, in 1910, that the "rise of the 'wool-hat' man has had more influence [on the Democratic party in the South] than any other single force."[28] Another scholar complained in the same year of "a new school of politicians" whose principal appeal was to "the passions and prejudices of the masses by indiscriminate abuse of the negro, by dwelling upon his brutality, criminality and mental inferiority, by denouncing the Republican party for its sins . . . and by recounting and often magnifying the evils and humiliations of the reconstruction period and thus keeping alive and perpetuating old animosities that had better be forgotten."[29] Southern conservatives frequently alluded to the increasing influence of ordinary voters. Thus James C. Hemphill, editor of the Charleston *News and Courier,* wrote an editorial in 1906 lamenting "the political proletairism which has controlled the South" and the "Socialistic tendencies" which had "so largely affected the political activities" of the southern states.[30]

Comments of this kind suggest that politics in the South during the years after 1900 was not static. On the contrary, southern politics exhibited surprising vitality, movement, and conflict. To be sure, much of this energy was spent in debilitating factionalism and campaign demagoguery, while political debate and competition frequently served to belie the strong sway of special interests. The mechanisms and ideas associated with the one-party system no doubt helped sustain the section's political conservatism, as did the strength of the

[27]See Arthur S. Link, "The Progressive Movement in the South, 1870–1914," *North Carolina Historical Review* 23 (Apr. 1946): 172–95.

[28]Thompson, "Effects of Industrialism Upon Political and Social Ideas," 140.

[29]James W. Garner, "New Politics for the South," *Annals* 35 (Jan. 1910): 177–78.

[30]"The Conservatism of the South," Jan. 22, 1906, reprinted in Arthur S. Link and associates, eds., *The Papers of Woodrow Wilson,* vol. 16 (Princeton, N.J., 1973), 286–87.

South's traditional culture. But this conservatism was tempered as well as reinforced by the attitudes of the white middle-class community. The collective opinion of this middle register of southern whites embodied a number of common assumptions about the importance of social order, "good government," public service, higher voter standards, and the election of good men to office. These assumptions illuminate the political thinking of southern progressives.

Politics, of course, constituted an essential medium for the waging of progressive campaigns. In a broad sense political activities and government were not only necessary as the source of statutory authority, public support, and the implementation of reform objectives; they also formed a milieu that was immensely important for the promotion of reform causes. State and local governments were the primary agencies for the resolution of conflicts in the community and for the regulation of business practices and social behavior, as well as the source of public services. The South's economic growth and diversification—and its intense desire to further such "progress"—increased the demands on state and local governments for franchises, services, and regulations. Meanwhile, as transportation and communications facilities improved, the states steadily assumed functions that had once belonged to county and municipal governments. The trend toward professionalism and specialization in education, for instance, confronted state governments with responsibilities involving teacher certificates, normal schools, boards of education, graded schools, new curricula, and consolidated schools.[31] With the expanded role of government came a dramatic enlargement in the part played by economic and professional organizations in the formulation and enactment of public policy. Chambers of commerce, freight bureaus, farmers' organizations, labor unions, professional associations, and scores of other groups were soon participating in local and state politics throughout the region.

THE HUMANITARIAN IMPULSE

With the apparent resolution of the old divisive issues involving race, class, and party at the beginning of the twentieth century, there was greater scope for humanitarian efforts to ameliorate the harsher realities of southern life. The seeds of this humanitarianism had already begun to sprout in the changing conditions produced by industrial and urban growth, a developing middle class, and the fervent commitment to economic progress. An improving economic climate helped to nurture this new growth. The emergence of this concern reflected a broadening conception of Christianity, a more critical view of the way society was dealing with the weak and unfortunate, and a growing interest in the South's educational and social needs on the part of northern philanthropists and social reformers. In a broad sense, the major source of the

---

[31] For national trends, see Morton Keller, *Affairs of State: Public Life in Late Nineteenth Century America* (Cambridge, Mass., 1977), 477.

humanitarian spirit among southerners in the early years of the century was the church.

Historically, southern Protestantism had been a conservative force, resisting change and viewing the region's dominant social patterns uncritically. "The identification of Christ and culture," one historian has observed, "was so complete as to melt all tension."[32] Despite many sectarian quarrels, Protestants in the South had much in common, including an overriding interest in individual salvation, a fundamentalist theology, a strong revivalistic tradition, and relative lack of interest in social reform apart from the enforcement of moral conduct.[33] "Perhaps nowhere on earth to-day," the president of the Southern Baptist Theological Seminary remarked in 1909, "can be found so large a proportion of the ministry of all denominations who are skillful evangelists as in the South." The result of this "evangelistic tendency," he suggested, was a strong "doctrinal conservatism," relatively little emphais on "the ethical or moral contents of faith," and "the difficulty of making connections between the pulpit and social and civic life."[34]

Southern churches, rooted in a society that was overwhelmingly rural, culturally homogeneous, and religiously pietistic, were predisposed to resist the currents of liberal theology, the social gospel, and the institutional church. In a tour of the South early in the twentieth century, for instance, a northern religious writer attended a ministers' meeting in Charleston, South Carolina. The announcement of "Social Settlements" as the subject for discussion at the next meeting provoked several inquiries as to the meaning of the term; only one man seemed to know what the phrase really meant.[35] Apart from the natural conservatism of southern society, it was easy to identify religious modernism with the old distrust of a "political" church and with "Yankee fanaticism."[36] The preponderant Protestant character of southern religion had facilitated the growth of a civil religion that "blended Christian and southern values," including rituals and organizations identified with the Lost Cause. The religion of the Lost

---

[32]Robert Moats Miller, "Southern White Protestantism and the Negro, 1865–1965," in Charles E. Wynes, ed, *The Negro in the South Since 1865: Selected Essays in American Negro History* (University, Ala., 1965), 241.

[33]Kenneth K. Bailey, "Southern White Protestantism at the Turn of the Century," *Amer. Hist. Rev.* 68 (Apr. 1963): 618–35; Samuel S. Hill, Jr., *Southern Churches in Crisis* (New York, 1967), 5, 14–16, 26, 81, 113–14.

[34]Edgar Young Mullins, "Theological Education in the South," in *The South in the Building of the Nation,* vol. 10, pp. 319–20.

[35]Ernest Hamlin Abbott, "Religious Life in America. V.—New Tendencies in the Old South," *Outlook* 70 (Jan. 11, 1902): 133–35. Abbott did find evidence in his southern travels of "a larger liberty of thinking and a greater emphasis on the Gospel in relation to the social life."

[36]Referring to outside efforts to overthrow "the ideals of the South," one Methodist minister expressed the feeling that "the least need we have is to be Yankeefied" (Collins Denny to Warren A. Candler, Apr. 12, 1909, Warren A. Candler Papers, Emory University Library). See also, for sectional sentiment in the Southern Methodist Church, Hunter Dickinson Farish, *The Circuit Rider Dismounts: A Social History of Southern Methodism, 1865–1900* (Richmond, Va., 1938), 106, 126, 134, 147, 150, 153, 161.

Cause reinforced the bond between the section's churches and its secular culture.[37] A scholarly study of Southern Baptists during the thirty-five years following Appomattox reveals their increasing consciousness of the church's responsibility to society, but it also shows that Baptists conceived of that responsibility in terms of personal morality rather than social betterment. In general they were apathetic toward organized reforms, except for temperance and a few other movements with religious or moral implications for the individual or the denomination.[38]

Southern Protestantism unquestionably did more to conserve than to undermine the dominant culture of the region in the early twentieth century. Churches constituted a sturdy bulwark in support of existing institutions, class relationships, and cultural values in the South.[39] Yet the southern church was an agent of change as well as continuity. For example, some southern ministers, particularly those with middle-class and well-to-do congregations in urban areas, were articulate champions of the New South creed. Many of them embraced the idea of the South's modernization and its corollaries of business expansion, material prosperity, and social progress. The popular revivalist Sam Jones, for instance, while emphasizing the virtues of hard work, frugality, piety, and middle-class success, preached the gospel of the South's economic development through industrialization and agricultural diversification.[40]

An impressive number of ministers stood in the vanguard of social reform in the South, and when the social justice forces eventually organized on a regional basis, religious leaders dominated the movement. Journals such as the *South Atlantic Quarterly* and the *Sewanee Review,* which emanated from church-related institutions, provided much of the rationale and social commentary that sustained southern progressivism. Virtually all of the organizations used by southern women as an avenue into the broader fields of social reform were church-affiliated, and Christian ideals were in all likelihood the principal element in motivating their ameliorative endeavors. Social compassion, of course, transcended the organized churches. It was also fostered by the cultural force of religion in the everyday lives of many communicants.

One of the main roads leading to the involvement of church people in social action was the desire to uphold prevailing codes of moral conduct. Impelled by this puritanical urge, they began to advocate laws against gambling, prostitution, divorce, violation of the Sabbath, and the sale of alcoholic beverages. This

[37]See Charles Reagan Wilson, "The Religion of the Lost Cause: Ritual and Organization of the Southern Civil Religion, 1865–1920," *JSH* 46 (May 1980): 219–38, and *Baptized in Blood: The Religion of the Lost Cause, 1865–1920* (Athens, Ga., 1980).

[38]Rufus B. Spain, *At Ease in Zion: Social History of Southern Baptists, 1865–1900* (Nashville, 1967).

[39]See, for example, Frederick A. Bode, "Religion and Class Hegemony: A Populist Critique in North Carolina," *JSH* 37 (Aug. 1971): 417–38.

[40]Richard L. Wilson, "Sam Jones: An Apostle of the New South," *Georgia Historical Quarterly* 57 (Winter 1973): 459–74; Larry R. Hayward, "F.E. Maddox: Chaplain of Progress, 1908," *Arkansas Historical Quarterly* 38 (Summer 1979): 146–66.

tendency to turn to politics and governmental action, despite the Protestant fetish supporting separation of church and state, was justified in terms of the political corruption and influence of the "liquor lobby" and other immoral elements in the community. It was also viewed as a means of establishing social controls over race relations, urban crime, and violence. Thousands of men and women in southern churches found in alcohol the fundamental cause of the section's new social problems. They enlisted in the prohibition movement in growing numbers, first by concentrating on temperance as an individual matter and, in many cases, eventually becoming involved in interdenominational cooperation and political action. "The country preachers," wrote one Baptist minister in 1917, "have been the main force which has brought in the South the downfall of John Barleycorn."[41] Whatever their motivation, southern social reformers often attempted to blend private and public morality.

Religion was a pervasive reality in the South, and life itself was viewed by many southerners as a continuing and fateful struggle between the forces of good and evil. The result for a large number of people was a religious perception with weightier social implications than might be supposed. For one thing, the faithful were inspired to involve themselves in the struggle and to contribute what they could to the salvation of the community and the world beyond as well as to their own regeneration. Religious convictions sometimes narrowed the gap between personal ethics and social morality. The quest for Christian perfection, in the South as in other regions, led the churches not only to exalt personal piety but also to emphasize generosity and graciousness and increasingly to advocate community improvement and decency.[42] Even the fervent fundamentalism and mass evangelism so typical of southern Protestantism had begun to stress the need for some reform in contemporary society.[43] As might be expected, the middle-class churches in the cities and larger towns were most attentive to the social implications of their Christianity. They frequently appealed to the moral responsibility of the growing business and professional groups, and they succeeded in giving a kind of moral-religious tone to much of the South's social reform.

By 1900 the main Protestant denominations in the South were expressing greater interest in humanitarian causes, particularly where moral issues were

---

[41] Victor I. Masters, *Country Church in the South: Arranged to Meet the Needs of Mission Study Classes and Also of the General Reader* (2d ed., Atlanta, 1917), 26–27. Also see John Lee Eighmy, "The Social Conscience of Southern Baptists from 1900 to the Present as Reflected in Their Organized Life" (Ph.D. diss., Univ. of Missouri, 1959), 86–88.

[42] Hill, *Southern Churches in Crisis*, 111–12, 168, 171–72.

[43] For a useful study of the contribution of revivalism to social reform in an earlier period, see Timothy L. Smith, *Revivalism and Social Reform in Mid-Nineteenth-Century America* (New York and Nashville, 1957). The author points out that while northern evangelicals were making the law of love the key to the Scriptures and subjecting them to a Christian version of the doctrine of progress, proslavery preachers were "fatefully binding the conscience of the South" in the "strait jacket of literalism," thus conditioning later southerners to believe that "the good book was a shield against social innovation" (ibid., 219).

involved. The old introspective piety had begun to turn outward, and a missionary zeal directed both to foreign lands and to opportunities at home was manifesting itself. The increasing support of home missions testified to the changing priorities of many southern churches and reflected a heightened interest in the unredeemed and the unfortunate in their own midst. Although temperance was the social reform most vigorously promoted in the region's religious journals and ministerial associations, it was by no means the only social concern voiced by southern churchmen. Individually and in their various denominations, they spoke out against the inadequacy of southern education, the habitual resort to violence and crime, lynching and the mistreatment of blacks, and the neglect of the laboring classes, especially of women and children. Some churches were alarmed over their failure to reach the masses in the growing cities and attempted through missions and welfare work to help such people. Despite the tendency of the Baptists to rely on renewed evangelistic efforts in the face of new social problems, their home mission board in 1902 called attention to the "conditions of ignorance, congested population, over-work, child labor, and . . . personal shiftlessness" resulting from the industrialization and urbanization of the South.[44] The Protestant seminaries in the southern states had begun to offer courses on the social aspects of Christianity, and church leaders were contributing to the movement toward social criticism. Writing in 1912, the president of Trinity College, himself a Methodist minister, singled out what he regarded as two new and hopeful religious trends: the tendency to read the Bible "not slavishly according to the letter that killeth" but in "the light of the spirit that giveth life" and the tendency, "in recent times so pronounced, to shift the emphasis from correctness of creed to soundness of life."[45] Many preachers, a Kentuckian lamented in 1914, "are getting 'daffy' about social legislation."[46]

Methodists were the best equipped of the leading southern denominations to accommodate the South's traditions and folkways to the new currents of economic and social change. Possessing enough wealth and "culture" to enable it to exert great influence socially, the church's lack of particularistic doctrines and its fundamental accord with other major Protestant bodies in the South gave it great importance in the section's religious circles.[47] Growing rapidly in southern cities and towns, the Methodists evinced mounting interest in practical religion. In pulpit and press and deliberative bodies, southern Methodism dealt increasingly with problems of practical and social interest. The educator Harvie Branscomb recalled that his father, a Methodist minister in several

---

[44]Quoted in Eighmy, "The Social Conscience of Southern Baptists," 17–18.

[45]William P. Few, "Two Hopeful Religious Tendencies," *SAQ* 11 (Apr. 1912): 153–57. For a modern assessment, see John Lee Eighmy, "Religious Liberalism in the South During the Progressive Era," *Church History* 38 (Sept. 1969): 359–72.

[46]Frank M. Thomas to Warren A. Candler, Jan. 15, 1914, Candler Papers.

[47]Farish, *The Circuit Rider Dismounts*, 91–94.

Alabama towns during this period, took "great interest in social problems and political affairs, particularly the campaign against Demon Rum, and at times took positions that were unpopular."[48] Through the scores of colleges and secondary schools it operated and its support of the principle of universal education, the Methodist Episcopal Church, South, made a substantial contribution to the educational awakening of the region. Its advocacy of child labor reform, the improvement of working conditions for women, prohibition, and numerous civic reforms indicated a heightened awareness of the need to apply Christian principles to the solution of social problems. In 1910 the Southern Methodist General Conference reorganized its temperance committee into a standing committee on Temperance and Other Moral and Social Questions. Earlier it had joined in the organization of the Federal Council of Churches of Christ in America, and its general conference soon incorporated the liberal Social Creed of the Federal Council into its *Book of Discipline*.[49]

Numerically, the strongest religious group in the South was the Southern Baptist church. White Baptists, not all of whom were represented in the Southern Baptist Convention, were well entrenched in the rural areas whose social conservatism found ready expression in the democratic governance of that church. But the Baptists also discovered elements of relevance in the new social Christianity. Like most southern denominations, they tended to enter the arena of social reform by way of the prohibition movement. For a majority of the Baptists, perhaps, prohibition and certain other restraints on conduct took the church as far into politics as they were prepared to go. But having entered the field of social legislation, it was difficult to draw the line between legitimate and nonlegitimate religious concerns, since most issues seemed to involve moral questions. While stressing the conservative and evangelical character of Baptists and other southern Protestants, the president of the Southern Baptist Theological Seminary observed in 1909 that he could name communities in which ministers "have literally created sentiment for public schools as well as schools themselves and have thus transformed those communities."[50] Several of the denomination's state conventions created social service commissions in the second decade of the twentieth century, and in 1913 the Southern Baptist Convention established such a commission as a permanent agency. In its first report the commission defined the church as a social institution responsible for the solution of social problems. The church must

check private greed and compose class antagonisms. It must erect Christian standards in the market place, and insist that the labor of women and children be

[48]Branscomb, *Purely Academic: An Autobiography* (Nashville, 1978), 29.
[49]Farish, *The Circuit Rider Dismounts*, 104, 333–35; Kenneth K. Bailey, *Southern White Protestantism in the Twentieth Century* (New York, 1964), 28–29, 40–41.
[50]Mullins, "Theological Education in the South," 322–23. Also see William Louis Poteat, "Religion in Science," *SAQ* 6 (Apr. 1907): 147–64, and R.H. Pitt, "Denominational Accomplishment," in *The South in the Building of the Nation*, vol. 10, pp. 428–36.

TABLE 3. *Southern Religious Affiliations, 1906*

	TOTAL MEMBERS	BAPTIST	METH-ODIST	PRESBY-TERIAN	% PROT.	% CATH.
Ala.	824,209	452,559	254,373	30,722	94.3	5.1
Ark.	426,179	193,244	142,569	21,156	92.1	7.6
Fla.	221,318	91,988	82,262	7,051	90.3	7.9
Ga.	1,029,037	596,319	349,079	24,040	97.9	1.9
Ky.	858,324	311,583	156,007	47,822	80.3	19.3
La.	778,901	185,554	79,464	8,350	38.4	61.3
Miss.	657,381	371,518	212,105	22,471	95.4	4.3
N.C.	824,385	401,043	277,282	55,837	99.4	0.5
Okla.[1]	257,100	69,585	76,336	16,001	85.1	14.2
S.C.	665,933	341,456	249,169	35,533	98.2	1.5
Tenn.	697,570	277,170	241,396	79,337	97.2	2.5
Tex.	1,226,906	401,720	317,495	62,090	74.5	25.1
Va.	793,546	415,987	200,771	39,628	96.0	3.6
Totals	9,260,789	4,109,726	2,638,308	450,038		

[1] Oklahoma and Indian territories combined.
SOURCE: U.S. Bureau of the Census, *Religious Bodies: 1906* (Washington, D.C., 1910), vol. 1, pp. 46–47.

regulated . . . that the industrial system provide the minimum of necessary working hours with the maximum of wholesome life conditions, and that the workers have a fair share of the prosperity which they produce.[51]

Meanwhile, Southern Presbyterians, influential but much smaller in number than Baptists and Methodists, had shown some interest in practical religion despite their preoccupation with theology. In 1907 a laymen's missionary movement was launched in the Southern Presbyterian church to support work in home and foreign missions. Although they failed to establish a social service commission or to adopt the Social Creed of the Federal Council of Churches, the Southern Presbyterians joined in sponsoring the council, and in 1914 their general assembly issued a "United Declaration on Christian Faith and Social Service."[52] The region's Presbyterians, like the Episcopalians and several

[51] Quoted in Eighmy, "The Social Conscience of Southern Baptists," 31. For additional evidence of social reform sentiment among southern Baptists, see Wayne Flynt, "Dissent in Zion: Alabama Baptists and Social Issues, 1900–1914," *JSH* 35 (Nov. 1969): 523–42; Flynt, "Southern Baptists and Reform: 1890–1920," *Baptist History and Heritage* 7 (Oct. 1972): 211–23; and William Clemmons, "Volunteer Missions Among Twentieth Century Southern Baptists," ibid. 14 (Jan. 1979): 37–49.
[52] Bailey, *Southern White Protestantism*, 41, 118; Joshua Levering, "The Laymen's Missionary Movement in the South," in *The South in the Building of the Nation*, vol. 10, pp. 500–509.

TABLE 4. *Black Religious Affiliations in the South, 1906*

STATE	NO. BLACK CHURCHES	TOTAL MEMBERS	BAPTIST	METH-ODIST	PRESBY-TERIAN	CATHOLIC
Ala.	3,734	397,178	275,408	111,571	6,205	367
Ark.	2,094	146,319	94,464	47,449	467	—
Fla.	1,638	105,678	54,109	47,201	65	2,622
Ga.	4,834	507,005	342,154	158,102	2,263	1,303
Ky.	1,007	116,918	77,487	31,154	2,240	2,579
La.	2,085	185,918	134,163	41,748	195	8,967
Miss.	3,877	358,708	243,603	110,465	600	1,661
N.C.	2,813	283,707	165,503	96,465	9,765	54
Okla.[1]	618	29,115	17,102	10,841	536	214
S.C.	2,860	394,149	219,841	162,143	8,026	170
Tenn.	1,879	172,867	97,003	64,112	7,882	595
Tex.	3,047	227,032	146,158	72,848	2,136	3,700
Va.	1,983	307,374	270,219	30,492	2,088	503
Totals	32,469	3,231,968	2,137,214	984,591	42,468	22,735

[1]Oklahoma and Indian territories combined.

SOURCE: U.S. Bureau of the Census, *Religious Bodies: 1906* (Washington, D.C., 1910), vol. 1, pp. 542–63.

other significant groups, gave evidence in their pulpits and journals of broadening social horizons.

Before the United States entered the First World War, the major Protestant denominations in the South had officially endorsed an extensive list of social reform objectives. "Churchmen of the New South," one authority has written, "became more receptive to outside ideas, more responsive to social ills, and more involved in the Protestant search for secular relevance."[53] Religious currents of this kind were also being felt in black Baptist and Methodist churches, the dominant Negro denominations in the South.[54] The church was central to black culture in the early twentieth-century South, and it reflected many of the traditions and values evident in southern white Protestantism. But because of its vital institutional role in the lives of southern blacks, the church

[53]Eighmy, "Religious Liberalism in the South During the Progressive Era," 372. Also see Farish, *The Circuit Rider Dismounts*, 370; Bailey, "Southern White Protestantism at the Turn of the Century," 630; and Ronald C. White, Jr., "Beyond the Sacred: Edgar Gardner Murphy and a Ministry of Social Reform," *Historical Magazine of the Protestant Episcopal Church* 49 (Mar. 1980): 51–69.

[54]For the overwhelming numerical predominance of these two denominations, see U.S. Department of Commerce and Labor, Bureau of the Census, *Religious Bodies: 1906*, 2 pts. (Washington, D.C., 1910), pt. 1, pp. 542–65.

in the Negro community was even more directly involved in the gradual emergence of social action and social reform than was the case among white southerners.

The influence of religious liberalism in the South during the progressive era should not be exaggerated. The social gospel among southern Protestants was in considerable part a matter of conference and association rhetoric—of annual reports that often gave a superficial treatment of social problems. Liberal theology made slow progress even among the region's religious intellectuals. The social weaknesses of capitalism and the question of rights in the economic system, when discussed at all in religious circles, were usually treated in an abstract way. The institutional church, while manifesting itself here and there in urban centers, was later in its development and more limited in its tangible accomplishments than was true of that in the Northeast and the Midwest. Below the level of the conference, convention, and presbytery, Christian faith continued to center in the gospel of personal redemption. Two views frequently coexisted among southern white Protestants as to the church's social mission: that evangelism was "the cure for social problems" and that it was sometimes necessary to support social reform programs. Fundamentally, the South remained "a land of piety and tradition."[55]

One reason for this religious conservatism was the isolation and poverty of most southern churches, particularly those in rural areas. In 1917 one-fourth of the Baptist churches in the region had no Sunday school, two-thirds had no women's missionary society, and three-fourths were served by absentee pastors. The meager program of these small churches included little more than "the annual revival, the annual call of a preacher, and the lax habit of the monthly sermon by an absentee preacher."[56] There was clearly a democratic aspect to popular religion in the South. This was evident in the organization and control of thousands of southern churches, which offered their members evangelical zeal, the tradition of a "free gospel," and pastorates drawn from the common people. It was also apparent in the response of the masses to colorful revivalists such as Sam Jones, who assured his audiences that any sinner was worthy of salvation. The Baptists and Methodists often dwelt upon their responsibility to the poor and downtrodden. Yet even these churches reflected the old hierarchical view of social classes and roles. The paternalism of the textile mill villages, where the church served as a vehicle for social work and an

---

[55]Bailey, "Southern White Protestantism at the Turn of the Century," 635. Also see Eighmy, "The Social Conscience of Southern Baptists," 36, 85–86, 123.

[56]Masters, *Country Church in the South*, 163 and passim. See also Edmund deS. Brunner, *Church Life in the Rural South: A Study of the Opportunity of Protestantism Based upon Data from Seventy Counties* (New York, 1923); Edward W. Phifer, Jr., "Religion in the Raw: Cyclone Mack in Burke County, August-September, 1920," *N.C. Hist. Rev.* 48 (July 1971): 225–44; and J. Wayne Flynt, "Southern Baptists: Rural to Urban Transition," *Baptist History and Heritage* 16 (Jan. 1981): 24–34.

instrument for the personalizing of labor relations, provides an example.[57] The class basis of the established churches no doubt contributed to the numerous sects that sprang up in the early twentieth-century South. Their horizons were bounded by evangelism and personal salvation.[58]

Nevertheless, there was an active social gospel in the South. The movement for social justice in the region was largely a consequence of a humanitarian impulse originating in southern Protestantism. This humanitarianism was bolstered by the work of several religious groups outside the denominational churches. One example was the Protestant-inspired Men and Religion Forward Movement, a national interdenominational organization that enjoyed some success in southern cities. In Atlanta, for example, the movement worked with the city's Evangelical Ministers' Association to combat prostitution and other vices. During the years 1911–16 it supported prohibition, prison reform, care for unwed mothers, child labor legislation, and better treatment of industrial labor.[59] A more significant religious agency was the Young Men's Christian Association. By 1908 the YMCA reported 47 city associations in the South, with a membership of over 24,000. Its railroad department had 44 organizations in the region, the student "Y" boasted 187 chapters and almost 10,000 men in Bible classes, and the Negro department claimed 37 city associations. After Theodore Roosevelt's Country Life Commission issued its report in 1909, the YMCA joined with the state colleges and other interested parties in a movement to improve the country church and country life in the South. The organization was instrumental in 1911 in the establishment of an interchurch college in Nashville for the training of black and white specialists in moral, religious, and social work.[60] In the meantime, ministers, many of them connected with the YMCA, led the slowly developing movement to improve race relations in the South.

Women had traditionally served as a humanizing influence in the South by invoking the spirit of noblesse oblige and Christian compassion. It is not surprising that the more sensitive spirits among them, when given the advantages of education, travel, and some degree of social security, should have sought to express their individuality as human beings and to improve the social milieu in

---

[57]See Pope, *Millhands & Preachers*, 20–27, 29.

[58]Elmer T. Clark, *The Small Sects in America* (rev. ed., New York and Nashville, 1949).

[59]Harry G. Lefever, "The Involvement of the Men and Religion Forward Movement in the Cause of Labor Justice, Atlanta, Georgia, 1912–1916," *Labor History* 14 (Fall 1973): 521–35. See also Eighmy, "The Social Conscience of Southern Baptists," 65–67; Wayne Flynt, "Alabama White Protestantism and Labor, 1900–1914," *Ala. Rev.* 25 (July 1972): 192–217; Flynt, "Religion in the Urban South: The Divided Religious Mind of Birmingham, 1900–1930," ibid. 30 (Apr. 1977): 108–34; and Flynt, "Dissent in Zion," 525–26.

[60]W.D. Weatherford, "The Young Men's Christian Association in Relation to the Development of the South," in *The South in the Building of the Nation*, vol. 10, pp. 482–91; Masters, *Country Church in the South*, 30–31; "Interchurch College for Social Service," *Survey* 26 (Aug. 26, 1911): 749.

which they lived. What is notable—and sometimes startling to contemporaries—was the creative response an increasing number of southern women made to social justice causes. The church provided women in the South with their first real opportunity to become involved in the amelioration of social ills. Religion continued to be "a central aspect" in the lives of many southern women at the turn of the century, but its form gradually changed from "intense personal piety to a concern for the salvation of the heathen and for social problems."[61]

Women's organizations within the southern churches gave its members a degree of independence and experience. Among Southern Methodists the basic unit of organization was the missionary society of the local church. So rapid was the growth of these local bodies that in 1914 the church as a whole could report 3,884 home societies (with 90,801 members) as compared with 3,403 foreign societies (with 76,977 members).[62] Church work of this kind brought southern women into contact with social questions. The religious groups not only began to organize to improve social conditions but also provided many of the leaders for the welfare work being initiated by reformers outside the churches. In addition to the denominational organizations, the Women's Christian Temperance Union and the Young Women's Christian Association afforded women in the South an avenue to a broadened conception of social reform. Many women in the region doubtless shared the feeling of Belle Kearney, a Mississippi temperance leader, who described the WCTU as "the generous liberator, the joyous iconoclast, the discoverer, the developer of Southern women."[63] The club movement—literary and music societies, civic improvement leagues, and patriotic and professional organizations for women—grew rapidly in the South in the 1890s and early 1900s.[64] Like the WCTU and the missionary societies, these clubs sometimes permitted women to engage in respectable reforms, to educate themselves and the public, and in some instances to disguise attacks on chivalry. The observant wife of a Texas congressman noted in her diary as early as 1902 that women everywhere—including the South—were talking about things that were "progressive" and "altruistic."[65]

The humanitarian impulse in the South was also fostered by the support of northern philanthropists. Northern missionary and educational contributions to the advancement of southern blacks continued into the twentieth century, but

[61] Anne Firor Scott, "Women, Religion and Social Change in the South, 1830–1930," in Samuel S. Hill, Jr., and others, *Religion and the Solid South* (Nashville, 1972), 93.

[62] Noreen Dunn Tatum, *A Crown of Service: A Story of Women's Work in the Methodist Episcopal Church, South, from 1878–1940* (Nashville, 1960), 60–61, 70–72, 334.

[63] Kearney, *A Slaveholder's Daughter* (New York, 1900), 118. Also see Louisa B. Poppenheim, "Woman's Work in the South," in *The South in the Building of the Nation*, vol. 10, p. 635.

[64] Poppenheim, "Woman's Work in the South," 632–33.

[65] *Washington Wife: Journal of Ellen Maury Slayden from 1897–1919* (New York, 1963), 42.

the religious-centered philanthropy of earlier days was now overshadowed by the uplift work of several large foundations and a more comprehensive approach to the region's social problems. It was the quickening huanitarian consciousness of southern ministers, educators, and professional groups, however, that attracted the beneficence of outside philanthropists. Representatives of these groups served a key function as agents and intermediaries in this philanthropic work. Northern interest in the South represented more than the investments and donations of millionaires. It also involved a rising tide of social criticism, the "scientific" and factual analysis of southern problems by the new social sciences and the national welfare agencies, and the emergence of the South as a kind of regional laboratory for sociological experimentation. The scores of dedicated men and women who traveled south on Robert C. Ogden's special train to attend the annual Conference for Southern Education symbolized the mounting interest of well-to-do and middle-class outsiders in southern problems and their faith in education as the best way to solve them.

SOCIAL CRITICS AND THE IDEA OF SOUTHERN PROGRESS

By 1900, one historian has written, "a pattern of belief" had been established for many southerners in which they "could see themselves and their section as rich, successful, and just."[66] Most southern progressives shared in the assumptions that comprised this New South creed, which embodied a compelling vision of regional development. Enthusiasm for industrialism and faith in the gospel of material progress were not confined to publicists such as Henry W. Grady and Richard H. Edmonds, nor to industrialists such as Daniel A. Tompkins—the men who edited the industrial-minded newspapers and trade journals, who organized the industrial expositions, and who established the new industries in the South. These sentiments were also embraced by a host of other southerners and especially by the new middle-class and professional groups. Pinning their hopes on the promise of material advances, especially industrialization, they were optimistic about the future prosperity of the section. Indeed, the South's recent manufacturing growth seemed "as remarkable an industrial romance as the rise of New England."[67] Although southern progressives typically went beyond the prescriptions of the New South creed in their advocacy of legislative action and social reform, they were convinced that social progress could not take place without economic development.

The benefits to be derived from industrialization seemed boundless. "The surest hope for the southern rural schools," wrote a liberal southerner in 1904,

[66] Paul M. Gaston, *The New South Creed: A Study in Southern Mythmaking* (New York, 1970), 214.

[67] Douglas Southall Freeman, "Fifty Years from the Ashes," *Harper's Weekly* 61 (Aug. 14, 1915): 154. For other expressions of this kind, see Richard H. Edmonds, "The South's Amazing Progress," *American Monthly Review of Reviews* 33 (Feb. 1906): 177–90, and Samuel C. Mitchell, in *The South in the Building of the Nation*, vol. 10, pp. xix–xx.

"is in the building up of the industrial resources of the people."[68] An early
student of southern industrialization in this period concluded:

> All of our social gains in the South have been associated with the advance of
> industry—employment for the poor whites, urban growth with all the activity this
> implies, sound banking, establishment of a wage system, greater productivity of
> wealth and its more even distribution, larger tax yields, better schools and roads,
> improvement of farming methods, and the growth of many governmental ser-
> vices.[69]

Economic advances also promised to bring desirable cultural changes. Commenting in 1908 on "the exhilarated sense of prosperity" in the South during
recent years, a North Carolina professor expressed the conviction that the
"yielding to commercialism" represented a constructive spirit, "an heroic
effort to reconstruct a commonwealth that was wrecked." Business growth
would promote a larger view of the South, help diminish "prejudice and
emotionalism in Southern life," and further national integration.[70] "Nowhere
on this continent," the president of Trinity College asserted in 1909, "will you
hear a finer note of nationalism than you will hear in the humming wheels of a
Carolina cotton mill."[71] Southern industrialization, another contemporary declared, was "one of the mighty agencies for our intellectual and moral freedom."[72]

The idea of southern progress was promoted not only by fervent advocates of
economic development but also by a group of critics, who found an explanation
for their section's lag in certain "southern" attitudes and practices. Although
the New South creed was implicitly critical of many aspects of southern life, its
leading spokesmen had not articulated a thoroughgoing body of social criticism. Populism was a more important source of the critical spirit in the early
twentieth-century South. The wave of agrarian protest in the 1890s subjected
the South's economic and political institutions to harsh analysis, and Populist
thought continued to influence many southerners after the turn of the century.
But the members of the urban-based middle class, whose ranks were infused
with the New South ideology, had not generally joined the agrarian assault of
the nineties. Their challenge to the established order was stimulated by other
forces, most tellingly perhaps by the dynamics of their economic and professional roles. The church was also important in the rise of a more critical spirit in
the South, particularly in the writings and addresses of individual clergymen
worried about social problems in the section. There was, moreover, evidence of

---

[68]John Spencer Bassett, "How Industrialism Builds Up Education," *World's Work* 8 (July
1904): 5031.
[69]Broadus Mitchell, "Growth of Manufactures in the South," *Annals* 153 (Jan. 1931): 23–24.
[70]Edward K. Graham, "Culture and Commercialism," *SAQ* 7 (Apr. 1908): 121–23.
[71]John Carlisle Kilgo, "The Democracy and Fraternity of American Industrialism," *SAQ* 8
(Oct. 1909): 338.
[72]John E. White, "The True and the False in Southern Life," *SAQ* 5 (Apr. 1906): 109.

new intellectual currents and dissatisfaction with some aspects of provincial orthodoxy in southern scholarship by the end of the nineteenth century. Suddenly, it seemed, ministers, professors, writers, and publicists were singling out a variety of evils in southern life: in farm conditions, factory work, corporate practices, and political life. "There is a feeling," wrote a University of Arkansas professor in 1912, "that our education is not sufficiently related to the life of the people and that it is water-logged with traditionalism."[73]

There was also, of course, continued criticism from outside the South. One feature of this outside evaluation was the factual and "scientific" consideration of southern problems by the new social sciences and the national welfare agencies. A major focus of this scrutiny was race relations, which elicited both censure and sympathy from northern writers. Readers of such magazines as *Independent* and *Outlook* and even the large northern newspapers began to find in such publications a new awareness of the ramifications of race relations in the South. By and large, the northern press was extraordinarily tolerant of southern white social practices; seldom was there a strident note in their criticisms, or for that matter, any genuinely radical proposal for reform. "As the North has grown more tolerant and sympathetic," the chancellor of Vanderbilt University observed at the University of Pennsylvania in 1914, "the South has grown less sensitive and isolated."[74]

Meanwhile, a number of national associations and agencies were investigating southern problems and pointing the way toward regional progress through concerted action and social reform. The National Child Labor Committee, for example, launched a campaign in 1904 for effective state regulation of working children. The conferences, institutes, extension work, community surveys, and publications of the National Association of Charities and Correction, the Russell Sage Foundation, and *Survey* magazine did much to reveal the poverty and inadequacy of community programs, to stimulate the development of social work, and to mobilize the fight against disease and dependency in the South. The example and encouragement of northern settlement houses and the National Federation of Settlements contributed substantially to the modest success of early settlement-house work in southern cities. Southern problems were also investigated and attacked within a national context by such federal inquries and activities as the Commission on Country Life (1909), the White House Conference on the Care of Dependent Children (1909), and the program of the Children's Bureau beginning in 1912.

Mediating between the critics within the section and those residing beyond its borders were several southern expatriates. The most prominent of these was

---

[73]John H. Reynolds, "The State University and a National System of Education," *SAQ* 11 (Apr. 1912): 158.
[74]James H. Kirkland, abstract of address on "Southern Education and Southern Thought," delivered Feb. 27, 1914, in James H. Kirkland Papers, Vanderbilt University Library. Also see Hamilton Wright Mabie, "The New North," *SAQ* 4 (Apr. 1905): 109–14.

Walter Hines Page, a North Carolinian who edited several national periodicals in the 1890s and early 1900s. From the time he founded *World's Work* in 1900 until he relinquished its active direction in 1913 to become ambassador to Great Britain, Page maintained a constant interest in the development of his native region. He was quick to publicize its industrial and educational progress, and he spoke out against its political demagogues, racial barbarities, and religious and cultural intolerance.[75] Page and other expatriates were moderates who wanted to modernize the South through economic development and education but without major changes in its traditions and social arrangements. As intersectional emissaries, they were sensitive to the South's backward place in the nation and to its potential role as a constructive factor in American life. They tended to minimize the basic differences between North and South.

The voices of criticism that emanated from southern colleges and universities were especially significant, for they were the product of the region's first modern intellectual community. These voices differed in intensity, as might be expected. One of the sharpest of the academic critics was the historian William E. Dodd, a North Carolinian who received his Ph.D. degree from the University of Leipzig and taught for several years at Randolph-Macon College in Virginia before transferring to the University of Chicago in 1908. A zealous defender of democracy and a caustic adversary of economic privilege, Dodd sought in his interpretation of the southern past to revitalize the influence of Jeffersonian democracy and to elucidate the historic conflict between the forces and leaders contending for and against democracy.[76] His criticism of the limitations of southern education, of what he regarded as the subservience of many educational institutions in the section to monopoly capitalism, and his outspoken involvement on the antimachine side of Virginia politics provoked some controversy. "In the South, and particularly in the older section of it," Dodd wrote in 1904 in an essay on the difficulties facing the teacher of history in the region, "public opinion is so thoroughly fixed that many subjects which come every day into the mind of the historian may not with safety even so much as be discussed."[77] Dodd's role was diminished after he moved to Chicago, but few southern educators in this period were more forthright in their criticisms.

More influential in the gradual emergence of a critique of the South's

[75] Charles Grier Sellers, Jr., "Walter Hines Page and the Spirit of the New South," *N.C. Hist. Rev.* 29 (Oct. 1952): 481–99; John Milton Cooper, Jr., "Walter Hines Page: The Southerner as American," *Virginia Quarterly Review* 53 (Autumn 1977): 660–76; Cooper, *Walter Hines Page: The Southerner as American, 1855–1918* (Chapel Hill, N.C., 1977), 162–251.

[76] Robert Dallek, *Democrat and Diplomat: The Life of William E. Dodd* (New York, 1968), 3–92; Lowry Price Ware, "The Academic Career of William E. Dodd" (Ph.D. diss., Univ. of South Carolina, 1956).

[77] Dodd, "Some Difficulties of the History Teacher in the South," *SAQ* 3 (Apr. 1904): 117–22; quotation on p. 119. Also see by Dodd, "The Status of History in Southern Education," *Nation* 75 (Aug. 7, 1902): 109–11; "The Study of History in the South," ibid. (Aug. 21, 1902): 149–50; "Another View of Our Educational Progress," *SAQ* 2 (Oct. 1903): 325–33; and "History and Patriotism," ibid. 12 (Apr. 1913): 109–21.

shortcomings and dominant mythology was the work of a group of southern scholars and writers who disagreed with Dodd's distrust of the new industrialism. Many of these men were associated with Trinity College in Durham, North Carolina, and with its journal, the *South Atlantic Quarterly*, and several of them followed the intellectual leadership of Walter Hines Page. One of the Trinity professors was John Spencer Bassett, a young historian with a doctorate from Johns Hopkins University. From the mid-nineties until he left the South for a position at Smith College in 1905, Bassett was a courageous and provocative critic of southern life. He took the lead in launching the *South Atlantic Quarterly* in 1902, serving as editor of the magazine during its first three years of existence. Bassett and the other young men of Trinity saw monsters all about. As a later editor of the journal wrote:

> There were poverty and sloth, a tendency to whine that the South's troubles were caused by the Yankees. There were intolerance of dissent and other obstacles to the pursuit of truth. The South did little writing and reading; her schools were few and poor. Injustice to the Negro, fundamentalism, conservatism, demagoguery, child labor—there were hosts of wrongs to be righted. The young men of Trinity girded themselves. The *South Atlantic Quarterly* was their spear.[78]

In 1912 the editors could say with a note of satisfaction and pride that the *Quarterly* had taken "an effective part in the discussion of race questions, of the life and conditions of factory communities, of educational progress, of political independence, of ballot reform, of the betterment of health conditions, of improvement in agriculture, of the control of the liquor traffic, of road building, and of many other problems of rural and town life."[79]

Idealistic, somewhat puritanical, and Victorian in their cultural standards, the Trinity liberals were terribly in earnest. Insisting upon the central importance of southern industrialization, education, and the gospel of work, the *SAQ* writers were convinced that the most serious obstacle to progress lay in the ignorance and misconceptions of the mass of southern people, which sustained the demagogue. They set about enlightening public opinion. It was a delicate task and on occasion the enlighteners found themselves thrown from the comparative calm of the storm's eye into the lashing gale of its teeth. This was John Spencer Bassett's experience after the appearance of his assertion, in the *South Atlantic Quarterly* in 1903, that Booker T. Washington was "the greatest man, save General Lee, born in the South in a hundred years."[80] At about the same time, a University of Mississippi professor privately expressed his dissatisfaction because of "so much politics in our institution." At times, he noted, the

---

[78]William Baskerville Hamilton, "Fifty Years of Liberalism and Learning," in Hamilton, comp., *Fifty Years of the South Atlantic Quarterly* (Durham, N.C., 1952), 3–4.

[79]"Ten Years of the South Atlantic Quarterly," *SAQ* 11 (Jan. 1912): 2.

[80]Bassett, "Stirring Up the Fires of Race Antipathy," *SAQ* 2 (Oct. 1903): 297–305; Earl W. Porter, *Trinity and Duke, 1892–1924: Foundations of Duke University* (Durham, N.C., 1964), 96–139.

faculty felt as if it were "on the crater of a volcano."[81] There were other incidents from time to time, but on the whole the new critique developed with little fanfare or controversy.

The creators of this critique were careful to stress the authenticity of their credentials as southerners, and in so doing they sought sanctions from the section's past. Thus they invoked the example of Robert E. Lee, whose spirit and work, in the opinion of a Trinity College English professor writing in 1904, should be "a constant protest against passion and prejudice and provincialism." The Virginian's "magnanimity in defeat, his ready acceptance of the new order of things, his moderation and restraint under most trying circumstances, his steadfast hope in the future of his section, and his noteworthy effort towards the building up of an institution of learning, constitute the most glorious chapter in a very noble life."[82] Southern historians educated at Johns Hopkins, Columbia, and some of the European universities imbibed the passion for "scientific history," and many of them returned to their home states to train a generation of southern students in the new approach and to carry on their research in state and regional history. They rebelled against the sentimental and uncritical histories of Confederate brigadiers and other southern patriots. They hoped to foster a more realistic view of the southern past.[83] While there were emphatic over-tones of sectionalism in the scholarship of these historians, there were also strong nationalist themes in their work. Most of them were active members of the American Historical Association, which contributed to the development of the new history in the South and did much to effect what a later scholar described as the "national reunion in history."[84]

History, for many of the southern critics, became a field of reform as well as a branch of university training. Some of the historians and other intellectuals saw themselves as performing a social role by delineating the "true" history of the South, thereby helping to free southerners from their prejudices and provincialism. "A free estimate of our past and a frank realization and acknowledgment of its errors, where errors are found," one historian wrote in 1911, "will place us in position to assume the responsible duties that lie in the immediate

[81]Franklin L. Riley to Herbert B. Adams, May 8, 1901, in Charles S. Sydnor, ed., "Letters from Franklin L. Riley to Herbert B. Adams, 1894–1901," *Journal of Mississippi History* 2 (Apr. 1940): 109.

[82]Edwin Mims, "Five Years of Robert E. Lee's Life," *Outlook* 78 (Nov. 26, 1904): 782. Also see Mims, "General Lee's Place in History," ibid. 84 (Dec. 22, 1906): 978–82. Lee emerged as a national hero during the progressive era and by the time of World War I had become an important symbol of national reconciliation. See Thomas L. Connelly, *The Marble Man: Robert E. Lee and His Image in American Society* (New York, 1977), 101, 142.

[83]See Wendell Holmes Stephenson, *The South Lives in History: Southern Historians and Their Legacy* (Baton Rouge, 1955), for an evaluation of the first generation of professional historians in the South.

[84]David D. Van Tassel, "The American Historical Association and the South, 1884–1913," *JSH* 23 (Nov. 1957): 465–82.

and more distant future."[85] These interpreters found in the past a more progressive and national-minded South, one that was less prejudiced and less orthodox in outlook. Recalling the South's vital role in the early years of the republic, John E. White, a well-known Atlanta minister, explained that "something got in the way and sidetracked the South, shunted us on the wrong track and we have floundered in shallows and miseries."[86] In other words, another southerner observed, the contemporary South was the product of "an interrupted and broken past." The South originally was "progressive and prosperous," until "the deadly disease of slavery was early fastened on the body politic." Then came the tragedy of civil war, "the historical crime of reconstruction, followed by the tedious years of recovery." But, finally, the region was experiencing "a revival of prosperity and hope."[87]

The great concern of the Trinity liberals and of those like them was the creation of "a genuinely national spirit" and a "sound public opinion in the South." They looked to the day when southern politics would no longer be dominated by sectionalism and prejudice. "Champions though we have been of the policy of free trade in government," Edwin Mims warned in an essay stressing the constructive function of criticism, "we are in danger of putting a protective tariff on ideas."[88] Many of the new intellectuals and professionals wanted to get away from the never-ending absorption in the race issue. "The question for safe and sound citizenship," one of the progressives wrote, ". . . is the question of getting ourselves free from the thrall of one issue and of interesting the people in matters that stimulate life and that generate moral and intellectual energy."[89] This was a revealing comment. Although men like Bassett and Mims condemned lynching and called for just treatment of Negroes, the problem of race relations was not their point of attack or their primary objective. As a Trinity professor put it in 1905, "The problem is not so much what to do to elevate the inferior race as it is to save the whites from the blighting influences of narrow-mindedness, intolerance, and injustice."[90] Lurking in such critical comment was a cultural note that stemmed from a compulsion in some reformers to bring "culture" to the masses by way of good schools, public libraries,

[85]Enoch Marvin Banks, "A Semi-Centennial View of Secession," *Independent* 70 (Feb. 9, 1911): 300. For the uses of history as a guide to southern progress, see also Daniel Joseph Singal, "Ulrich B. Phillips: The Old South as the New," *Journal of American History* 63 (Mar. 1977): 871–91.

[86]White, "The True and the False in Southern Life," 103–104.

[87]William P. Few, "Conservatism and Progress," *SAQ* 9 (Apr. 1910): 194. See also Larry Kincaid, "Victims of Circumstance: An Interpretation of Changing Attitudes Toward Republican Policy Makers and Reconstruction," *Jour. Amer. Hist.* 57 (June 1970): 48–66.

[88]Mims, "The Function of Criticism in the South," *SAQ* 2 (Oct. 1903): 342. For a fuller treatment of Mims's liberalism, see Leah Marie Park, "Edwin Mims and *The Advancing South* (1894–1926): A Study of a Southern Liberal" (M.A. thesis, Vanderbilt Univ., 1964).

[89]White, "The True and the False in Southern Life," 106.

[90]William Preston Few, "Southern Public Opinion," *SAQ* 4 (Jan. 1905): 5.

and the chautauqua. To Mims, for example, literature was potentially useful and socially relevant. Literature, he declared, "does speak of life, it does teach moral ideas, it does give spiritual truth, it is the all of the religious element in man's nature—and it is only great when it is!"[91]

Social criticism in the early twentieth-century South was also expressed in newspapers and popular periodicals. As a matter of fact, the South produced its share of crusading journalists during the progressive years. None of the revelations of corporate abuse in the United States was more strident and unrestrained than that appearing in *Tom Watson's Magazine,* beginning in 1905, though the Georgian's growing preoccupation with racial and religious phobias weakened the force of his fierce attacks on big business and vested interests. While these writers were less well known than the muckrakers who wrote for the national magazines, they were very influential in the creation of reform sentiment in the southern states. A good example of the more thoroughgoing southern muck-raker was Claude L'Engle of Florida. During the decade before his election to Congress in 1912, L'Engle published a crusading newspaper, first in Jacksonville and then in Tallahassee, the state capital. He vigorously attacked local monopolies, political corruption, and state and local abuses. Although his views on blacks were typical of contemporary white thinking in the South, he was a staunch supporter of organized labor and an advocate of virtually all progressive reforms.[92] Few southern editors were as advanced in their advocacy of progressive measures, but every state in the region had at least one or two important newspapers dedicated to the practice of reform journalism.

From all these sources and others as well there gradually emerged a full-scale critique of contemporary southern society. As a whole, it presented the region in moderate and sympathetic terms; it sought to conserve the good and the valuable in southern life and reflected the middle-class values and aspirations of its authors. Most of the critics expressed an abiding faith in an industrialized South, in northern investments, in the developing middle-class and professional groups in the towns and cities, and in a new cadre of business and industrial leaders unfettered by politics and tradition.[93] The works of these middle-class critics reveal that they were eager to set the tone and pattern of regional life and to serve as the social conscience for the South, much as the old planter aristocracy had done. Acutely conscious of their own social ascent, they dwelt at length on the problem of uplifting and guiding the white masses. They were not

[91]Quoted in Michael O'Brien, "Edwin Mims: A Preliminary Estimate," unpublished paper (1970), in its author's possession. Also see O'Brien, "Edwin Mims: An Aspect of the Mind of the New South Considered: I," *SAQ* 73 (Spring 1974): 199–212, and "Edwin Mims: An Aspect of the Mind of the New South Considered: II," ibid. (Summer 1974): 324–34.

[92]Joel Webb Eastman, "Claude L'Engle, Florida Muckraker," *Florida Historical Quarterly* 45 (Jan. 1967): 243–52. Also see Herbert J. Doherty, Jr., "Voices of Protest from the New South, 1875–1910," *Mississippi Valley Historical Review* 42 (June 1955): 45–66.

[93]For a useful study of several of the new southern critics, see Bruce L. Clayton, "Southern Critics of the New South, 1890–1914" (Ph.D. diss., Duke Univ., 1966).

inclined to romanticize these denizens of their beloved South. As one of the liberals wrote in 1906, "Always there is the appeal to the illiterate masses, or to that solid phalanx of men who have inherited the passionate sectionalism of a generation of men who don't know that the war is over, or that they are living in a new age which teaches new duties and has to do with new problems."[94] Yet they spoke often of their confidence in the ordinary man, disclosing sometimes a sense of guilt over society's neglect of him in the past. Thus Walter Hines Page urged that the "forgotten man" (and woman) be rescued from the slough of ignorance and poverty. Edwin Mims suggested that "when moral issues can be clearly defined, and the best men of a community or a nation take an aggressive part in politics, the masses of the people may be counted upon to do the right thing." And Edgar Gardner Murphy asserted that "the masses of the people have been quick to respond to the appeal of every free and upbuilding purpose; and here lies the promise of the future."[95]

Southern social critics during this period were not always hopeful about the possibilities of regional progress. Disillusionment and sometimes cynicism fueled the blasts of a few southerners such as Tom Watson. Other reformers were pessimistic about the chances of improving race relations in the immediate future. Some critics were suspicious of cities and doubted that industrialization would be a good thing for the South. Edgar Gardner Murphy, for example, had reservations about the doctrine of material progress. Would it be possible, another southern intellectual asked in 1905, "to industrialize our society without commercializing its soul"?[96] Nor did southern reformers think the South had been or would be the beneficiary of any "immutable laws of progress." As an Atlanta minister said in 1906, "If any people in history have been taught no more again to rely upon fatuous confidence in fortune it is the Southern people. The solid and sober intelligence of the South knows that she is not the favorite of an indulgent and partial Providence."[97] To bring about social improvement required patience, courage, and well-directed energy, for, as a later writer observed, "progressiveness was always in conflict with established local order, and outside influences had to filter slowly through the social structure."[98]

Optimism coexisted with doubt in the minds of many southern progressives.

---

[94] Edwin Mims, "The Independent Voter in the South," *SAQ* 5 (Jan. 1906): 3–4.

[95] Page, *The Rebuilding of Old Commonwealths: Being Essays towards the Training of the Forgotten Man in the Southern States* (New York, 1902), 1–47; Mims, "The Independent Voter in the South," 1; Murphy, *Problems of the Present South: A Discussion of Certain of the Educational, Industrial and Political Issues in the Southern States* (New York, 1904), 170.

[96] Edwin A. Alderman, quoted in St. George L. Sioussat, "Should Idealism Perish in the Industrial South?" *Sewanee Review* 13 (Oct. 1905): 406. Also see David H. Overy, "When the Wicked Beareth Rule: A Southern Critique of Industrial America," *Journal of Presbyterian History* 48 (Summer 1970): 130–42.

[97] White, "The True and the False in Southern Life," 102–03. "The last fifty years of Southern history," White continued, ". . . reveals that the South has not been, and is not now, any great political, social or moral force in the world" (ibid., 104).

[98] Clark, *The Southern Country Editor*, 134.

Progress was alluring, but it was also threatening in its possible effects upon traditional values and moral standards. This may explain the reformers' emphasis on the concept of the "belated section," the idea that the South's institutional stability and Anglo-Saxon "purity" gave it a special opportunity to profit from the experience of other regions and even to perform a national mission. "Ours is a region unspoiled as yet by the too rapid and overwhelming set of foreign and material forces," Woodrow Wilson reminded an audience at the University of Virginia in 1895. "A region still of small towns and local community; of neighborhoods and friendships and admirations. A people preserved apart to recall the nation to its ideals, and to its common purpose for the future. What a sweet and noble revenge it would be could we save the nation we have been thought to hate!"[99]

Progressivism in the South unmistakably possessed a strong conservative cast. The historian Clement Eaton recalled long afterward how, as a student at the Univerity of North Carolina in the World War I years, he belonged to "a group of young liberals who felt that they had emancipated themselves from the shackles of old authority." Yet with all their "exhilarating sense of freedom," he wrote, "we accepted unconcernedly some of the ruling assumptions of the society in which we had been reared."[100] The assumptions that Eaton referred to were reflected in the basic approach of the southern progressives: in their moderation, desire for social order, and adherence to the cultural traditions and values of their region.[101] Extremism should be avoided in favor of change that was "gradual and slow." The progressives were intent upon the reconciliation of progress and tradition. "Conservatism and progress are not essentially antagonistic," one young scholar explained in 1904. "Conservatism need not be of the Bourbon type, never learning and never forgetting; the spirit of progress need not be exaggerated into radicalism. The conservatism of the South has in many things been of a distinctly liberal sort."[102] Still, the southern progressives were activists. "Man is himself the agent of all his improvement," a North Carolina educator declared in 1911. "And this improvement comes about

[99] Arthur S. Link and associates, eds., *The Papers of Woodrow Wilson*, vol. 9 (Princeton, N.J., 1970), 290. Also see H.I. Brock, "Contributions of the South to the Character and Culture of the North," in *The South in the Building of the Nation*, vol. 7, pp. 269–94, and Archibald Henderson, "Democracy and Literature," *SAQ* 12 (Apr. 1913): 97–108.

[100] Eaton, "Professor James Woodrow and the Freedom of Teaching in the South," *JSH* 28 (Feb. 1962): 16.

[101] Actually most southern progressives adhered to the basic values that combined to give American progressivism its distinctive ethos. These included Anglo-Saxonism, moral righteousness, popular elitism, and progress. See G. Edward White, "The Social Values of the Progressives: Some New Perspectives," *SAQ* 70 (Winter 1971): 62–76.

[102] Ulrich Bonnell Phillips, "Conservatism and Progress in the Cotton Belt," *SAQ* 13 (Jan. 1904): 2. For Phillips's progressivism, see William L. Van Deburg, "Ulrich B. Phillips: Progress and the Conservative Historian," *Ga. Hist. Quar.* 55 (Fall 1971): 406–16, and John Herbert Roper, "A Case of Forgotten Identity: Ulrich B.Phillips as a Young Progressive," ibid. 60 (Summer 1976): 165–75.

through individual initiative and individual effort."[103] The progressives were also conscious of living in a new age. John Spencer Bassett vividly recalled, for instance, the "high days of hope" that he and the other Trinity liberals had experienced during the early years of the twentieth century, "when we thought the redemption of the South was working in us till it was about to burst us with its expulsive power."[104]

The public mood at the turn of the century was itself a significant factor in the unfolding of southern progressivism. The hard times of the 1890s had finally come to an end, and the expansive potentialities of the southern economy were once again ascendant. "Go where you will," *World's Work* reported in June 1907, "the people are building homes, schools, and roads, and in the cities business buildings and factories."[105] The political turmoil of the nineties had passed from the scene, the "race question" was being resolved through disfranchisement and segregation laws, and the possibility of outside interference in the politics and social arrangements of the South appeared increasingly remote. It now seemed possible to facilitate regional rehabilitation through social change and social action. In the school, remarked an educational reformer, the South had discovered "the latent potency that will create industries, uplift the masses, adjust racial differences, and regain political prestige."[106] Such a functional view of education promised to open up undreamed vistas of progress. Whatever the mistakes and misfortunes of the past, economic development, the introduction of modern institutions and services, and a new enlightenment spread by socially conscious men and women would eventually bring a glad new day to the South.

[103]William P. Few, "Force and Right in the Government of the World," *SAQ* 10 (Oct. 1911): 321. "The way to improve society," Few emphasized, "is to train the minds and strengthen the characters of men, to increase the number of those who can think correctly and act in accordance with right." Ibid., 320.

[104]Quoted in Edwin Mims, "Early Years of the *South Atlantic Quarterly,*" *SAQ* 51 (Jan. 1952): 42–43.

[105]"The Arisen South," *World's Work* 14 (June 1907): 8925.

[106]S.C. Mitchell, "The School as the Exponent of Democracy in the South," *Sewanee Review* 16 (Jan. 1908): 18.

STATE POLITICS provided the basic arena for social reform in the early twentieth century. This was true for several reasons. For one thing, the expanding authority of state government made it a necessary consideration in virtually all reform campaigns, whether in behalf of regulatory laws, public services, municipal reorganization, or social welfare measures. The political system both promoted and accommodated itself to this larger role of state government. Evidence of this relationship can be found in the growing number of organizations and interest groups involved in politics, in the adoption of the direct primary in statewide elections, and in the governor's programmatic and legislative leadership. These developments made it easier for state politics to assimilate local and municipal political groupings. They also facilitated the use of state politics as building blocks in the creation of regionwide campaigns.

Although the one-party system soon became characteristic of every state in the South, the shape of factional politics was different in each state, depending upon such variables as the nature of the economy, intrastate sectionalism, class and racial consciousness, distinctive traditions, and the extent of Republican competition. The quality of a state's political leadership was also important. In Virginia, for example, the powerful faction led by Senator Thomas Staples Martin was the single most decisive element in that state's bifactionalism. In Mississippi, to cite a radically different example, a charismatic leader named James Kimble Vardaman did much to direct the course of politics in the progressive period.

There were, broadly speaking, three discernible groups of states in the southern political sphere during the progressive era. The Deep South, stretching from South Carolina to Mississippi, was dominated by a politics of race, disfranchisement, one-crop agriculture, and rural poverty. The Upper South, somewhat less concerned with racial issues, was more diversified economically and politically. The Republican party retained some strength in this subregion. The four states west of the Mississippi River constituted a third area with fairly distinctive political attributes, including a pronounced strain of agrarian

TABLE 5. *The Lower South: Population Statistics*

	POPULATION IN 1900	% INCREASE 1890–1900	% INCREASE 1900–10	% WHITE 1900	% BLACK 1900	% FOREIGN-BORN, 1900
Ala.	1,828,697	20.9	16.9	54.7	45.2	0.8
Fla.	528,542	35.0	42.4	56.3	43.7	3.7
Ga.	2,216,331	20.6	17.7	53.3	46.7	0.6
Miss.	1,551,270	20.3	15.8	41.3	58.5	0.5
S.C.	1,340,316	16.4	13.1	41.6	58.4	0.4

SOURCES: *Twelfth Census of the United States . . .* , vol. 1: *Population*, part 1 (Washington, D.C., 1901), pp. cxiv, cxviii, 2–5; *Thirteenth Census of the United States . . .* , vol. 1: *Population, 1910 . . .* (Washington, D.C., 1913), 32–33.

radicalism and more active involvement in political affairs by farm and labor organizations.

The tendencies of the new age in southern politics were clearly revealed in Mississippi. Indeed, developments in the Magnolia State seemed almost to caricature the main trends in the section as a whole. In no other state was preoccupation with the race question so complete, nor did any other part of the South offer more fertile ground for the cultivation of the mystique of the Lost Cause and the myth of Reconstruction misrule. Negroes were no longer able to vote, the Republican party had all but disappeared, and the dominance of the one-party system could scarcely have been more complete. Yet the political divisions among white Mississippians during the first part of the century were sharp, and the fierce conflicts of those years possessed a degree of economic and social relevance. In fact, Mississippi experienced a political upheaval and a kind of democratic triumph during this period.

Blacks made up more than half of the population, and they were spread over a considerable part of the state. Although Mississippians boasted that they were the first southerners to solve the "problem" of white supremacy by constitutional means, they nevertheless continued to torture the issue in their political campaigns. The black man, in a sense, still dominated the state's politics and there was still "a sort of Negro rule." It made no difference, observed one national journal of the Mississippi situation, whether a politician won power "by the votes of ignorant blacks or by denunciation of them"—the Negro was dominant in either case.[1]

Another basic influence in shaping Mississippi politics during these years was the state's overwhelming ruralism and its predominantly agricultural economy. A large part of the state still resembled a frontier, as was evident in the loneliness of the far-flung plantations, isolated hill farms, and vast timber tracts. Mississippi had no large cities, and its small towns functioned largely as

[1]"How the Negro Rules in Mississippi," *World's Work* 6 (Oct. 1903): 3941.

county seats and supply points for agriculture. Not only were most Mississippians dependent upon agriculture for their livelihood; they were also among the poorest of all Americans. Much of the land was thin and overcropped, and the upturn of farm prices in the late 1890s failed to bring a resumption of the agricultural prosperity of the antebellum period. Tenancy multiplied. Mississippi farmers developed a strong antipathy toward railroads, insurance companies, and the large lumber firms, which they associated with "trusts" and northern exploitation. "In the minds of the newly powerful hill people of Mississippi," a close observer later wrote, "the large corporations and 'trusts' became confused with their old masters, the delta folk."[2]

The pattern of factional politics that emerged in Mississippi soon after the turn of the century was rooted in physical and human geography. Geographical contrasts provided the foundation for a powerful intrastate sectionalism. The most favored section was the Delta, more than four million acres of fertile alluvial soil stretching two hundred miles from Memphis to Vicksburg. Overflows from the Mississippi and Yazoo rivers and their tributaries made this land extraordinarily productive, a rich and vibrant cotton empire.[3] There were also a few plantation counties along the Tombigbee River in the northeastern part of the state and in the central part of the eastern section, where the Alabama black belt extended into Mississippi. But in general the land beyond the Delta was poor and so were its farmers. Eastward from the Yazoo River lay a series of bluffs, rolling tablelands, and sand-clay hills. Much of the southern half of the state, except for the relatively small coastal terrace, was covered with timber, and the piney woods of the southeast were rapidly being felled by the great lumber companies. Although lumber provided the basis for a short-lived prosperity in parts of eastern and southern Mississippi, the plantation counties and particularly the Delta were the major scene of agricultural wealth and success during the first two decades of the twentieth century. In the Delta were concentrated the state's principal railroads, most of its capital, and much of its labor. It was hardly surprising that the poorer sections of the state should be envious and suspicious of the Delta's economic and political supremacy.

In Mississippi there was no substantial middle class to help bridge the gulf between the Delta planters and the hill farmers, and that no doubt partly explains the strong class consciousness that arose in the state. As William Alexander Percy said of his father's campaign for the United States Senate in 1910, "the undeclared issue had been the unanswerable charge against Father that he was a prosperous plantation-owner, a corporation lawyer, and unmistakably a gentleman."[4] Race served not only to reconcile Delta planter and hill

[2] Clarence E. Cason, "The Mississippi Imbroglio," *Va. Quar. Rev.* 7 (Apr. 1931): 235–36.
[3] Robert L. Brandfon, *Cotton Kingdom of the New South: A History of the Yazoo Mississippi Delta from Reconstruction to the Twentieth Century* (Cambridge, Mass., 1967), 21–31. For Mississippi geography in general, see John K. Bettersworth, *Mississippi: A History* (Austin, Tex., 1959), 1–20.
[4] Percy, *Lanterns on the Levee: Recollections of a Planter's Son* (New York, 1941), 146–47.

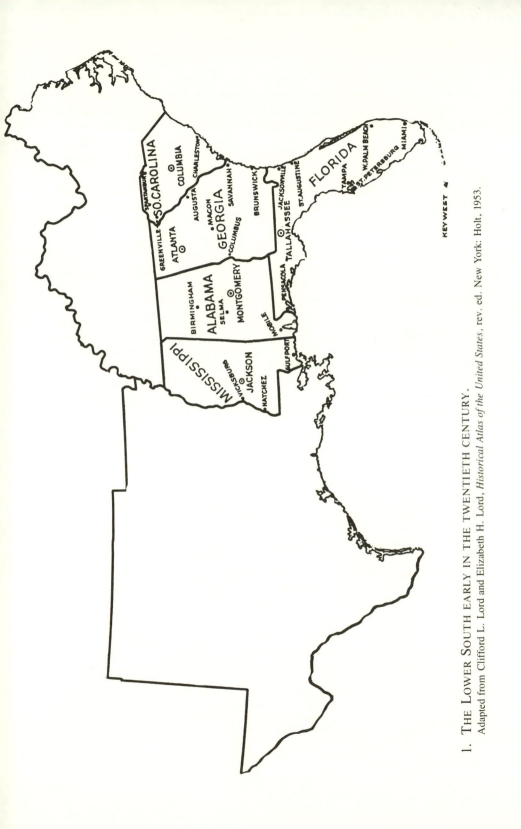

1. THE LOWER SOUTH EARLY IN THE TWENTIETH CENTURY.
Adapted from Clifford L. Lord and Elizabeth H. Lord, *Historical Atlas of the United States*, rev. ed. New York: Holt, 1953.

farmer but also to exacerbate their differences. The planter preferred the black laborer to the more intractable white, and the latter, seeing the Negro moving into the richest land and the best tenant shacks, viewed him as a symbol of planter domination. Finally, the cleavage between Delta and hills was a political matter, one that had manifested itself in earlier years in conflicts over representation in the legislature and state conventions, in the imposition of taxes, and in the allocation of school funds. Political sectionalism in Mississippi remained strong during the years after 1900, but the emergence of south Mississippi as a distinctive and self-conscious area complicated the old Delta versus hills polarity. As a rule, however, the planters of the Delta and black counties, in alliance with the business and financial interests, arrayed themselves against the small farmers of the hills and piney woods.

Populism enjoyed little immediate success in Mississippi, but it made a lasting impression upon the state's politics. Agrarian leaders such as Putnam Darden, Ethelbert Barksdale, and Frank L. Burkitt contributed to the class consciousness of the small white farmers in the 1890s, and the popularity of Populist doctrines and those espoused by William Jennings Bryan encouraged the rise of a reform faction in the Democratic party after 1896. Many former Populists joined the ranks of the Democratic reformers. One of them was Frank L. Burkitt, the Populist nominee for governor in 1895.[5] Burkitt became a reform leader in the legislature. Addressing his senate colleagues in 1912, he declared:

> I entered the People's Party in 1892, but the Omaha platform constitutes today the principles of the Democratic party. . . . At Ocala, twenty-two years ago, I wrote the planks which have since been indorsed by William Jennings Bryan, and the last Populist speech I ever heard was made by him here four years ago. I could see no reason for two parties with the same principles, and I don't care whether it is said I came back to the Democratic party or the Democratic party has accepted my principles.[6]

Still another factor of great importance in the development of early twentieth-century Mississippi politics was the part played by the primary election law of 1902. The primary undermined the Delta's control of Democratic state conventions and the party machinery, helped bring the "redneck" to political power, and set the stage for Mississippi's progressivism.[7] One of the leaders in the revolt against the old system of nominations, and the first statewide candidate to benefit from its adoption, was James K. Vardaman; his

[5] Albert D. Kirwan, *Revolt of the Rednecks: Mississippi Politics, 1876–1925* (Lexington, Ky., 1951), 94–102.
[6] Quoted in Charles Granville Hamilton, "Mississippi Politics in the Progressive Era, 1904–1920" (Ph.D. diss., Vanderbilt Univ., 1958), 238. See also ibid., 24–25.
[7] Martha Bigelow, "Mississippi Progressivism," *Jour. Miss. Hist.* 29 (Aug. 1967): 202–209; Clyde J. Faries, "Redneck Rhetoric and the Last of the Redeemers: The 1899 McLaurin-Allen Campaign," ibid. 33 (Nov. 1971): 283–98.

leadership more than that of any other Mississippian determined the course of the state's politics during the first decade and a half of this century.

A lawyer whose penchant for politics led him to edit several small newspapers, including the Greenwood *Commonwealth*, Vardaman served several years in the state legislature and ran unsuccessfully for governor in 1895 and 1899. He went to Cuba as an officer during the Spanish-American War but saw no military action. A long-time champion of prohibition, Vardaman had been sympathetic with many Populist demands and had become an exponent of Bryanism. He was increasingly critical of the convention system of making nominations, particularly after his defeat in 1899. Following the enactment of the primary law in 1902, he began a long campaign that culminated in his nomination as the Democratic choice for governor in the runoff primary of 1903. He shrewdly capitalized on the political awakening of the white masses and the smoldering racial antagonisms that lurked just below the surface of the social order.[8]

The state had never experienced a campaign like that conducted by James K. Vardaman in 1902 and 1903. Casting himself as a champion of the common man, Vardaman demonstrated an extraordinary ability to stir the masses. A magnificent actor, he looked the part—tall, erect, with long black hair that contrasted with the solid white attire he habitually wore. He projected a magnetic personality on the platform, and his swelling oratory lifted his audiences out of themselves. His speeches were impassioned, evangelical, and filled with glittering rhetoric. When he spoke, "the White Chief," as he came to be known, exhorted, wheedled, and taunted his audiences with marvelous effect. He combined an attack on the trusts and special "interests" with an assault on the hapless black man. As one student of Mississippi politics has written, "equalitarianism came to mean for him, as for the average voter of his state, equality for whites maintained by war on two fronts: against Negroes and against planters who sought to use Negroes."[9] In his incendiary speeches on the race question, Vardaman drew a graphic picture of black aggressors being misled by the policies of such leaders as Theodore Roosevelt, whom the Mississippian denounced as a "coon-flavored miscegenationist." Vardaman advocated the distribution of the school fund between the races according to the taxes paid by each. His attacks put the Delta on the defensive, since some planters feared that such racist assaults would encourage Negro migration out

---

[8] For biographical details, see A.S. Coody, *Biographical Sketches of James Kimble Vardaman* (Jackson, Miss., 1922), and William F. Holmes, *The White Chief: James Kimble Vardaman* (Baton Rouge, 1970). Also see Kirwan, *Revolt of the Rednecks, 144–61*.

[9] Hamilton, "Mississippi Politics in the Progressive Era," 80. Also see "Two Pleas for Negro Rights in Mississippi," *Outlook* 74 (May 16, 1903): 152–53; "The Negro Issue in Mississippi Primaries," ibid. (Aug. 22, 1903): 959; "Vardaman Chosen in Mississippi," ibid. 75 (Sept. 5, 1903): 1–2; James Wilford Garner, "A Mississippian on Vardaman," ibid. (Sept. 12, 1903): 139–40; and Harris Dickson, "The Vardaman Idea," *Saturday Evening Post* 179 (Apr. 27, 1907): 3–5.

of the state and jeopardize the supply of good labor. Vardaman demanded the repeal of the Fourteenth and Fifteenth amendments, and he was not averse to defending the practice of lynching. He also employed sectional themes, referring to the "malevolent North" while making dramatic appeals to Confederate veterans and the toiling masses of the "glorious Commonwealth of Mississippi."[10]

The people heard Vardaman gladly, in 1903 and in the years that followed. "Vardaman Day" was always a red-letter day. Mississippians long remembered "the Great White Chief riding the hounds of an eight-wheeled log wagon pulled by twenty yoke of steers, his face swarthy under the white sombrero, a red string about his neck to show the boys he was a redneck too, his long black locks flowing free; and the keening, drunken yells, 'Hooray for Vardaman!'"[11] A Pontotoc County man, writing to a critical editor, revealed something of the ordinary white man's loyalty to Vardaman: "You had just as well go to church anywhere in Pontotoc . . . get up in the pulpit and tell the people that Jesus Christ is a bastard as to say anything against . . . Vardaman to the people here."[12] When LeRoy Percy was heckled by Vardaman supporters on one occasion in 1910, he referred to them as "cattle" and "rednecks." The White Chief was quick to identify himself with the downtrodden and to use such epithets to his own advantage.

Vardamanism was based upon long-time sectional and socioeconomic divisions among white Mississippians. A contemporary writer stated the matter in succinct terms: "The small farmers of the hills, differing fundamentally in their environment and interests from both the wealthy planters of the black counties and the professional and business classes of the towns, and constituting the bulk of the white citizenship of the State, must in time come to realize their power and, given a leader, seek to make themselves effective in the affairs of the State."[13] Vardaman was such a leader, and for more than a decade after he came to power his leadership divided Mississippians into the ranks of those who supported him and those who opposed him. As governor between 1904 and 1908, Vardaman displayed a strong and growing interest in social reform, and the progressive accomplishments of his administration, while modest in comparison with those that followed, provided the impetus for many of the public improvements of later years. Seeking to move up to the United States Senate, the Mississippi leader was narrowly defeated in 1907 and again in 1910, the second time as a result of a secret legislative caucus that aroused great resent-

---

[10]Eugene E. White, "Anti-Racial Agitation in Politics: James Kimble Vardaman in the Mississippi Gubernatorial Campaign of 1903," *Jour. Miss. Hist.* 7 (Apr. 1945): 91–110; George C. Osborn, "A Country Editor Finds Himself: James K. Vardaman Champions Reform," ibid. 8 (Apr. 1946): 81–93.

[11]Arthur Palmer Hudson, "An Attala Boyhood," ibid. 4 (July 1942): 152.

[12]Quoted in Kirwan, *Revolt of the Rednecks*, 227.

[13]John M. Mecklin, "Vardamanism," *Independent* 71 (Aug. 31, 1911): 463.

ment among his followers. In 1911 the White Chief won an overwhelming victory in a Senate primary, and for the next few years his political power in Mississippi was at its peak.[14] But his absence from the state and the emergence of new issues and new leaders eventually weakened his influence, and by 1915 he was beginning to lose his dominant position. Three years later he was defeated in his bid for reelection.

Although Vardaman helped create the bifactionalism in Mississippi politics after 1903, he did not fashion an enduring political organization. His following was a highly personal one, even though it sometimes moved at the polls and in the legislature with considerable unity. Edmund F. Noel and Earl Brewer, the governors elected in 1907 and 1911, respectively, were reformers in their own right. While less strident in their campaigns and broader in their appeals to middle-class and business interests, each of these leaders endeavored to create his own contingent of supporters in the legislature and among the voters. Neither man proved to be a "Vardaman governor," but both expanded the progressivism introduced by the Vardaman administration.

To some extent this was also true of Theodore Gilmore Bilbo, who succeeded Brewer as governor early in 1916. But Bilbo, a young politician from the piney woods county of Pearl River, rose to prominence as an ardent Vardaman man, first as one of his lieutenants in the state senate and then as lieutenant governor. A diminutive dynamo, Bilbo was a skillful stump speaker, a master of invective and scurrility who delighted in the rough-and-tumble of Mississippi politics. One of his harshest critics described him as "a pert little monster, glib and shameless, with that sort of cunning common to criminals which passes for intelligence. The people loved him. They loved him not because they were deceived in him, but because they understood him thoroughly; they said of him proudly, 'He's a slick litle bastard.' He was one of them . . . ."[15] Yet Bilbo did not exploit the race issue during this period of his career, although, like Vardaman, he was a reformer and indubitably a man of the people. Made notorious by his ambiguous role in the secret caucus of 1910,[16] he campaigned during the next few years as a martyr for clean government and the "toiling masses." By the time he became governor, a coolness had developed between Vardaman and Bilbo, and as the state's chief executive the latter gradually

---

[14]Kirwan, *Revolt of the Rednecks*, 191–210; Holmes, *The White Chief*, 177–266; Heber Ladner, "James Kimble Vardaman, Governor of Mississippi, 1904–1908," *Jour. Miss. Hist.* 2 (Oct. 1940): 175–205.

[15]Percy, *Lanterns on the Levee*, 148.

[16]Soon after Vardaman's defeat as a result of the secret caucus, Bilbo created a sensation by claiming that in order to entrap Vardaman's opponents and reveal their unsavory methods, he had accepted a bribe of $645 from the opposition to vote for LeRoy Percy, who was eventually nominated. In the furor that followed, Bilbo was censured by the senate and almost expelled from that body. The trial of the accused briber resulted in the man's exoneration. Although Bilbo stuck to the essential points in his story, there were several discrepancies. For the details of the secret caucus and Bilbo's part in the whole affair, see Kirwan, *Revolt of the Rednecks*, 191–210, and Holmes, *The White Chief*, 196–229.

supplanted the former as leader of the rednecks. Bilbo proved to be a constructive governor, but he was defeated in 1918 when he tried to win a congressional seat.[17] The next governor, Lee M. Russell, was another representative of the same basic constituency that had controlled Mississippi politics since 1903.

The late nineteenth and early twentieth centuries brought significant changes to Mississippi pollitics. A period of "almost incessant agrarian revolt" finally engulfed the state.[18] The primary election law of 1902 and other changes revolutionized political campaigning, facilitated the rise of new leaders, and created a new and more competitive factionalism in the state's Democratic party. The number of white voters increased, at least in primary elections, and such democratic procedures as compulsory primaries, direct election of United States senators, the initiative and referendum, and an elective judiciary were adopted by the state's lawmakers. These developments broke the domination of the black counties in statewide elections, though without greatly diminishing their influence in the legislature. In the altered political setting of the early 1900s, organized farmers, businessmen, teachers, and prohibitionists brought new issues to the fore and frequently succeeded in obtaining their particular objectives. Political reform was pervasive for a decade and a half after 1903. A series of reform governors developed legislative programs and secured the enactment of a number of significant progressive measures: a new penal system, more effective railroad regulation, educational improvements, aid to farmers, a bank guarantee law, tax equalization, abolition of the fee system for county officials, public health programs, and statewide prohibition. But if the reformers shared power and enjoyed some legislative success, they failed to build durable political organizations, and their programs usually lacked coherence as well as sustained support. Their conservative opponents, meanwhile, managed more often than not to defeat progressive proposals in the legislature and to weaken the implementation of progressive statutes.[19]

[17] Kirwan, *Revolt of the Rednecks,* 241–58; Larry Thomas Balsamo, "Theodore G. Bilbo and Mississippi Politics, 1877–1932" (Ph.D. diss. Univ. of Missouri, 1967); A. Wigfall Green, *The Man Bilbo* (Baton Rouge, 1963), 3–66; Reinhard H. Luthin, *American Demagogues: Twentieth Century* (Boston, 1954), 44–55; John R. Skates, Jr., "Journalist vs. Politician: Fred Sullens and Theodore G. Bilbo," *Southern Quarterly* 8 (Apr. 1970): 273–85; Wilmuth Saunders Rutledge, "The John J. Henry-Theodore G. Bilbo Encounter, 1911," *Jour. Miss. Hist.* 34 (Nov. 1972): 357–72.

[18] Kirwan, *Revolt of the Rednecks,* 103, 309.

[19] See Charles Granville Hamilton, "The Turning Point: The Legislative Session of 1908," *Jour. Miss. Hist.* 25 (Apr. 1963): 93–111. The same author's "Mississippi Politics in the Progressive Era," cited above, provides a useful summary of progressive measures enacted during the period. Also see Nannie Pitts McLemore, "The Progressive Era," in Richard Aubrey McLemore, ed., *A History of Mississippi,* 2 vols. (Hattiesburg, Miss., 1973), vol. 2, pp. 29–58; Lester M. Salamon, "Protest, Politics, and Modernization in the American South: Mississippi as a 'Developing Society' " (Ph.D. diss., Harvard Univ., 1971), esp. 292–343; Ralph L. Kloske, "Was Mississippi More 'Progressive' Than Wisconsin?" paper presented at annual meeting of the Social Science History Association, Nashville, Tennessee, Oct. 1981; and John R. Skates, "Mississippi," in David C. Roller and Robert W. Twyman, eds., *The Encyclopedia of Southern History* (Baton Rouge, 1979), 832–33.

Mississippi's neighbor to the east, Alabama, typified the Lower South's economic, ethnic, and political attributes. One of the dynamics in its politics, like that of Mississippi, was a hardy and enduring sectionalism. Stretching across the south central part of the state were about a dozen counties known as the black belt, an area of rich soil and a heavy concentration of Negroes. On the south the black belt sloped off to the sand hills and the coastal plain, while on the north it was absorbed by rising foothills and, in the northeast, mountains. The seat of Alabama's plantation system in the antebellum period, the black belt continued in the twentieth century to be the center of the state's social and political power.[20] The conservative black belt leaders were astute politicians, dedicated to the maintenance of their own power and that of their area. While forced to make some concessions to the white counties in the constitutional convention of 1901, they were able to preserve the "rotten borough system" of apportionment in the state legislature, which heavily overrepresented their counties. And the legislature refused to reapportion itself following the census of 1910, despite the constitution's explicit stipulation.[21]

The Piedmont and hill section to the north, as well as the wiregrass country of the southeast, had long distrusted and opposed the black belt. Having fewer black inhabitants and less fertile land, these sections had resisted secession, provided strong support for agrarian radicalism in the 1890s, and stubbornly opposed many of the suffrage changes finally pushed through by black belt leaders. Although northern Alabama was the most rapidly growing part of the state in the late nineteenth and early twentieth centuries, the black belt frequently allied itself with the industrialists and financiers of Birmingham—the so-called "big mules"—as a means of dominating the state's politics. Sectional conflict, however, was only one of the determining factors in Alabama politics. The development of urban and middle-class groups, motivated by entrepreneurial and professional concerns and a growing interest in solving social problems, injected a new element into the crucible of political decision-making. A study of the roll-call votes in the constitutional convention of 1901 suggests that the basic policy differences in Alabama early in the progressive era were far more than a matter of sectional conflict, that a considerable number of delegates in the convention were sensitive to urban values and to the need for social reform, and that a successful challenge to the state's existing political arrangements would require a coalition of groups and interests whose political outlook sometimes differed.[22]

The intense factionalism of the 1890s, which reflected the state's sectional

[20]Renwick C. Kennedy, "Black Belt Aristocrats: The Old South Lives on in Alabama's Black Belt," *Social Forces* 13 (Oct. 1934): 80–85; and Kennedy, "Alabama Black Belt," *Alabama Historical Quarterly* 2 (Fall 1940): 282–89.

[21]Malcolm C. McMillan, *Constitutional Development in Alabama, 1798–1901: A Study in Politics, the Negro, and Sectionalism* (Chapel Hill, N.C., 1955), 307–309.

[22]Sheldon Hackney, *Populism to Progressivism in Alabama* (Princeton, N.J., 1969), 209–27.

cleavages, was carried forward in attenuated form into the twentieth century. Although the distinctions were broad and imperfect, one wing of the Democratic party was oriented toward agrarian reform and such causes as free silver, primary elections, and railroad regulation. Its leader was Joseph F. Johnston, a "half-way Populist" in the eyes of his contemporaries, who served as governor from 1896 to 1900. The two governors who followed Johnston tended to be more conservative and to represent the old Bourbon faction of the Democratic party. Yet several factors served to modify the Bourbon-agrarian reform bifactionalism of the late nineteenth century: a number of Populists went into the Republican party rather than returning to Democratic ranks, the Alabama economy was becoming more diversified, and many Alabamians, perhaps a majority of them, were committed to the New South ideas of economic development and thus were reluctant to endorse radical agrarian proposals.[23]

Progressivism in Alabama, while strongly influenced by populism, did not build directly on the earlier movement. Sheldon Hackney has argued that "Progressivism, the alternative to Populism, was a substantially different reaction by a separate set of men to the same enemy Populism faced—the dominant industrial wing of the Democratic Party."[24] Even so, the events of the 1890s had a marked impact on the emergence of Alabama progressivism. There was, in the first place, a widespread reaction against the turmoil and corruption in the state's politics, as well as against the lack of responsiveness by the Democratic party hierarchy. The progressives promised to change this situation. They also adopted a number of the reforms demanded by the Populists and Democratic reformers, including railroad regulation and election reforms.[25] In addition, they took over much of the democratic rhetoric expressed by the agrarian radicals in the 1890s.

Three factors contributed most directly to the development of new factional patterns in the state's Democratic party. One of these was the institutional changes in the electoral system effected by disfranchisement and the adoption

[23]Ibid., 112–13, 116–18, 122–25, 137–44; McMillan, *Constitutional Development in Alabama,* 251; David Alan Harris, "Racists and Reformers: A Study of Progressivism in Alabama, 1896–1911" (Ph.D. diss., Univ. of North Carolina, 1967), 28–109; Karl Louis Rodabaugh, "Fusion, Confusion, Defeat, and Disfranchisement: The 'Fadeout of Populism' in Alabama," *Ala. Hist. Quar.* 34 (Summer 1972): 131–53.

[24]Hackney, *Populism to Progressivism in Alabama,* 122. See also ibid., 116, 278–82. William W. Rogers, in *The One-Gallused Rebellion: Agrarianism in Alabama, 1865–1896* (Baton Rouge, 1970), challenges Hackney's status-anxiety view of the Populists and reasserts the importance of real economic problems in the movement and the positive, rational issues and objectives of the agrarian reformers. Also see John B. Clark, *Populism in Alabama* (Auburn, Ala., 1927), 176–81. Allen W. Jones, "Political Reforms of the Progressive Era," *Ala. Rev.* 21 (July 1968): 173–75, and Rodabaugh, "Fusion, Confusion, Defeat, and Disfranchisement," 152–53, find a closer relationship between populism and progressivism than Hackney, particularly in their common emphasis on certain issues.

[25]Hackney, *Populism to Progressivism in Alabama,* 123–25; Allen W. Jones, "Political Reform and Party Factionalism in the Deep South: Alabama's 'Dead Shoes' Senatorial Primary of 1906," *Ala. Rev.* 26 (Jan. 1973):3–32; Jones, "Political Reforms of the Progressive Era," 173–94.

of the direct primary. Disfranchisement virtually wiped out the black vote and deprived many poor whites of the ballot. The primary system, despite its restrictive features, eroded the political power of the black belt, gave reformers a better chance to influence party action, and tended to force candidates to assume popular positions on the issues. A second factor of great significance in the evolution of Alabama politics was the emergence of railroad regulation as a key issue. Railroad mileage in the state more than doubled between 1885 and 1905, and the carriers, which were intimately involved in the development and exploitation of valuable mineral holdings, exerted enormous influence in politics. They were associated with outside capital and with political manipulation to ward off public regulation. As one reformer declared in 1905, there were "too many railroad attorneys and too much railroad lobby in our State House."[26] Railroad regulation in Alabama during the progressive years, as in most southern states, was not merely a struggle between agrarian reformers and large industrial concerns. It was in considerable part a movement of business groups seeking to maintain a delicate balance between effective intervention by the state and entrepreneurial freedom that would further economic growth. Still, there was no mistaking the mounting hostility toward the railroads in Alabama, and the demand for regulation became a catalyst for broader reform activity. The real significance of the accelerating campaign in Birmingham for freight rate reform, one historian has written, "is that it was the breeding ground of a great movement of liberalism in Alabama in the first decade of the new century."[27]

The third factor in reshaping Alabama politics was a political newcomer named Braxton Bragg Comer, an independent and aggressive leader who plunged the state into a period of stormy controversy. Although Comer came from a planter family, he achieved success as a grain merchant and textile mill owner in Anniston and Birmingham. His business interests led him, about 1890, to become interested in better railroad rates, and throughout the 1890s he sought to get favorable action from the state railroad commission. By the end of the century, Comer had become a zealot on the question of rate reform, and he gradually assumed leadership of the incipient movement to secure more effective regulation of the railroads. He urged the constitutional convention of 1901 to take action to facilitate the regulatory movement and joined with others in 1902 in an effort to elect sympathetic legislators. After the next legislative session provided for the popular election of railroad commission members, an

---

[26]Braxton B. Comer, quoted in James F. Doster, "Alabama's Gubernatorial Election of 1906," *Ala. Rev.* 8 (July 1955): 169.

[27]James F. Doster, *Railroads in Alabama Politics, 1875–1914* (University, Ala., 1957), 101. See also Doster, "Railroad Domination in Alabama, 1885–1905," *Ala. Rev.* 7 (July 1954): 186–98.

[28]Quoted in Doster, *Railroads in Alabama Politics,* 140. See also Doster, "Alabama's Political Revolution of 1904," *Ala. Rev.* 7 (Apr. 1954): 85–98.

insistent demand of the reformers, Comer made a successful race in 1904 to become president of the commission. His campaign divided Alabamians into opposing camps, and his election, in the opinion of the Montgomery *Journal*, which had opposed him, was "a revelation and a revolution. All the old politicians were, as a rule, against Mr. Comer."[28] Most of the leading newspapers also opposed him. In railroad regulation, Comer had found an issue that could bring together "the interests of Black Belt planters, substantial farmers, town merchants, small manufacturers, and the professional men who identified with these groups. . . ."[29]

Despite his efforts as president of the railroad commission, Comer was unable to bring about the rate reductions he sought. He soon decided that he must run for governor. Thus, at the age of fifty-eight, "rich in background, training, achievement, and this world's goods, Comer flung himself into a heated fight for the governorship."[30] He made himself a martyr in a popular cause, waging a crusade to free the people from what he called the alien and arbitrary rule of railroads. He and his campaign spokesmen talked a great deal about popular government and self-rule. And they won a smashing victory in the Democratic primary, receiving impressive support in the urban centers and the black belt. Comer's forces gained control of the party machinery and committed themselves to a broad program of reform. In a gesture filled with symbolic anticipation, they struck "conservative" from the official name of the Democratic party of Alabama. The new governor moved vigorously and with considerable success in 1907 and 1908, but well before the end of his four-year term a new issue—statewide prohibition—replaced railroad regulation as the center of reform controversy. Comer became a champion of prohibition, and while there was a general correspondence between the supporters of that reform and those seeking stronger railroad regulation, the issue provoked great confusion and bitterness. It also brought setbacks to "Comerism," in 1909 in the defeat of a constitutional amendment providing for prohibition, in 1910 in the defeat of the prohibition candidate for governor, and in 1914 when Comer himself failed in an attempt to win a second term as governor.

Nevertheless, the leadership of Braxton B. Comer was the single most important factor in Alabama politics during the decade after 1904. Although Emmett O'Neal, Comer's successor as governor, was not a supporter of the reform faction, the former governor's policies tended to give Alabama politics a strong bifactional character. This was less true following Comer's defeat by Charles Henderson in 1914, although a prohibitionist named Thomas E. Kilby

[29]Hackney, *Populism to Progressivism in Alabama*, 254.

[30]Rupert B. Vance, "Braxton Bragg Comer, Alabama's Most Audacious," *Southwest Review* 19 (Apr. 1934): 245–64; quotation on p. 248. The discussion that follows is based largely on Hackney, *Populism to Progressivism in Alabama*, 288–323; Doster, *Railroads in Alabama Politics;* and Allen Johnston Going, "The Governorship of B.B. Comer" (M.A. thesis, Univ. of Alabama, 1940).

was elected governor in 1918. Most of the state's congressmen, including Oscar W. Underwood, the most prominent among them, were conservative and instinctively opposed the reform program advocated by Comer. At the same time, they usually avoided open involvement in factional struggles not directly related to their own campaigns, and this contributed to a multifactional politics in the state quite different from the political pattern in such states as Mississippi and Virginia.

Legislative reforms in Alabama during this era were concentrated in a few widely separated years, in part because the general assembly ordinarily met in quadrennial sessions. There were stirrings of reform in the session of 1903, and a few progressive measures, including a child labor act, were passed. But the first major reform enactments of the period came in 1907 during the Comer administration, which witnessed the approval of a series of railroad controls, the regulation of other business enterprises, the creation of a tax commission, the adoption of a general municipal code, and larger appropriations for education and other public institutions. Another series of progressive measures was enacted in 1915, when several important educational bills were passed, in addition to statewide prohibition, a primary election law, a juvenile court statute, a tax revision law, and the establishment of a public service commission. Four years later, during the Kilby administration, the legislature made several additions to the record of progressive reforms in Alabama. "The forces of social and governmental reform coming up out of forty years of action and reaction, and made more kinetic by the World war," wrote one Alabama historian, "rushed upon them [the governor and legislators] like a mighty tidal wave."[31] The result was reform of the state's finances and revenue system, creation of a child welfare department, enactment of a workmen's compensation act, and increased support for education, public health, and highways.

Somewhat paradoxically, Alabama politics became more open and more competitive after 1901, notwithstanding disfranchisement and the restriction of the electorate. This was true, at least, for the property-owning, professional, and middle-class elements. The "cliques, caucuses, and rings" of earlier years[32] tended to lose power. Although a coalition of black belt and urban-industrial interests—the big mule-black belt alliance—frequently exerted controlling influence in early twentieth-century Alabama politics, the exercise of political power was not monolithic.[33] The introduction of a state primary

---

[31] Albert Burton Moore, *Alabama and Her People*, 3 vols. (New York and Chicago, 1927), vol. I, p. 953.

[32] Allen J. Going, "Critical Months in Alabama Politics, 1895–1896," *Ala. Rev.* 5 (Oct. 1952): 270.

[33] Jonathan M. Wiener argues, in *Social Origins of the New South: Alabama, 1860–1885* (Baton Rouge, 1978), 222–27, that a coalition of planters, industrialists, and small-business progressives controlled Alabama politics after 1900. Carl Grafton, "Community Power Methodology and Alabama Politics," *Ala. Hist. Quar.* 38 (Winter 1976): 271–90, also emphasizes the continuing dominance of planter and industrial elites in the state's politics.

system, including the popular election of United States senators, paved the way for new political leaders and encouraged the consideration of diverse issues by the white electorate. Many business and urban groups, as well as black belt planters and organized farmers, now found it possible to advance their own legislative concerns and to join in the the pursuit of broader "reforms." The cement that held these elements together in loose and shifting combinations was their common commitment to organizational tactics and a measure of state intervention, as well as their growing acceptance of the idea that social institutions needed to be modernized and made more efficient. It was in this context that Alabama progressivism unfolded.

None of the states of the Lower South displayed more vigorous factionalism in Democratic party politics than Georgia. The personal factionalism that characterized that state's politics during the first part of the twentieth century revolved around an aggressive and ambitious lawyer from Atlanta named Hoke Smith. Although he had been identified with the conservative element of his party in the 1890s, having served as Secretary of the Interior in Grover Cleveland's second administration, Smith had emerged by 1905 as the leader of a popular antirailroad movement, and in 1906 he was swept into the governorship on a reform platform that included Negro disfranchisement. Despite the fact that the silver wing of the Democratic party had become dominant in the mid-1890s and Georgia Democrats had apparently become rather thoroughly Bryanized, the state administrations in the late nineties and early years of the new century were basically conservative. The intense factionalism that disrupted the party for a decade after 1905 was encouraged by the rivalry between the Atlanta *Journal*, which Hoke Smith owned and published from 1887 to 1900, and the Atlanta *Constitution*, whose editor, Clark Howell, was an influential legislative leader, a long-time member of the Democratic national committee, and a gubernatorial aspirant. Smith and Howell had opposed each other for years, and in the campaign of 1906 they found themselves locked in a bitter struggle for the Democratic gubernatorial nomination.

Although Howell suffered a humiliating defeat in the primary election of 1906, his factional battle with Smith was carried on by Joseph M. Brown, son of the Bourbon leader Joseph E. Brown. The younger Brown turned back Governor Smith's bid for reelection in 1908, but two years later Smith won another term by narrowly defeating Brown. The Atlantan defeated Brown again in the Democratic senatorial primary of 1914. Yet the anti-Smith faction enjoyed its share of victories. In 1912 it was successful in the gubernatorial primary, thereby recapturing control of the party machinery, and its candidate won the preferential primary held in connection with the Democratic presidential nomination that year. Nevertheless, Smith's determined quest for power shattered the complacency of the state's established hierarchy, brought a surge of excitement and anticipation to the ranks of the electorate, and forced most Georgians into two Democratic factions. His leadership was also associated with the growing demand for reform, and he eventually advertised his own program as one of "Progressive Democracy." After he went to the Senate, his faction was unable to replace him with an effective leader on the state scene. Neither of the two major factions, it seemed, could secure complete control of Georgia politics.[34]

One reason for this inconclusive struggle and for the blurring of Georgia's Democratic bifactionalism after 1914 was the role of Thomas E. Watson, the state's most important Populist in the 1890s. In 1905, Watson began to exert a decisive influence on the course of Georgia politics, first by throwing his support to Hoke Smith and later by endorsing "Little Joe" Brown. Thousands of former Populists remained loyal to Tom Watson and returned with him to the Democratic party; in close elections like that of 1908 his position was sometimes the determining factor in the outcome. As one of the reform Democrats acknowledged in 1904, while urging the Populist leader to return to the Democratic party, "The old populist party of Georgia can to-day almost turn the wavering balance. Their present incorporation into the democratic party, coupled with that great body of democrats who always sympathised [*sic*] in many of your populist views, and the ever growing increment of those who are disciplines of the new ideas . . . give assurance that such a leader as yourself, acting within the democratic, or rather the white party of Georgia, can accomplish uncountable good for this state. . . ."[35] Watson and other Populists were also instrumental in popularizing various "reform" issues such as railroad regulation, abolition of the convict-lease system, and Negro disfranchisement. An early student of Georgia populism noted that "the popular faction" of the Democratic party in this period "has advocated reforms along the general lines of those urged by the Populists in the nineties."[36] After 1908, Watson was an implacable enemy of Smith, and by 1912 his influence in the Democratic party was so great that few statewide politicians dared oppose him. He made and unmade governors. He seized upon such events as the tragic case of Leo Frank[37] to demonstrate the enormous extent of his appeal to the Georgia

[34] For the general political situation in Georgia, see William F. Holmes, "Part Five: 1890–1940," in Kenneth Coleman, ed., *A History of Georgia* (Athens, Ga. 1977), 257–308, and Dewey W. Grantham, *Hoke Smith and the Politics of the New South* (Baton Rouge, 1958), 131–237.

[35] Hooper Alexander to Watson, Aug. 1, 1904, Thomas E. Watson Papers, Southern Historical Collection, University of North Carolina.

[36] Alex Mathews Arnett, *The Populist Movement in Georgia: A View of the "Agrarian Crusade" in the Light of Solid-South Politics* (New York, 1922), 212–28; quotation on p. 213. See also Barton Carr Shaw, "The Wool-Hat Boys: a History of the Populist Party in Georgia, 1892 to 1910" (Ph.D. diss., Emory Univ., 1979).

[37] In 1913, Leo Frank was indicted and tried, allegedly for assaulting and murdering 13-year-old Mary Phagan, an employee of his pencil factory in Atlanta. Tom Watson led the outcry against Frank, whom he described as "the typical young libertine Jew." Watson's virulent charges probably contributed to Frank's conviction and subsequent lynching at the hands of a mob in 1915. See C. Vann Woodward, *Tom Watson: Agrarian Rebel* (New York, 1938), 435–49; Leonard Dinnerstein, *The Leo Frank Case* (New York, 1968); and Clement Charlton Moseley, "The Case of Leo M. Frank, 1913–1915," *Ga. Hist. Quar.* 51 (Mar. 1967): 42–62.

masses, and he further confused the state's politics by lashing out at the Wilson administration and picturing himself as a martyr who dared to challenge the national government's wartime restraints. In the troubled postwar period, Watson was elected to the Senate by defeating Smith and Hugh M. Dorsey, a man the old Populist had helped make governor in 1916.

If the tyranny of racism was somewhat less complete in Georgia than in Mississippi and South Carolina, it was equally as intense and all-encompassing during certain periods. The state had a large black population (46.7 percent in 1900), and its lynching record for the years 1888–1903 (241 Negroes) was second only to that of Mississippi.[38] Frustrated and embittered by the treatment meted out to the Populists, agrarian insurgents such as Tom Watson were disposed to join other southern politicians after 1900 in urging the Negro's proscription. The issue was an effective one in appealing to ordinary white men, and its skillful use by such agitators as Watson and Smith not only contributed to the terrible race riot of 1906 in Atlanta and the resort to disfranchisement in 1907–1908, but also helped produce the average Georgian's deep-seated and distorted complex of racist fear and hypersensitivity.[39]

Sectional conflict, which found expression in occasional charges in the southern part of the state that the more industrialized and urbanized region to the north got more than its share of statewide offices, was not a major theme in Georgia politics during the progressive era. More important was an urban-rural conflict and a cleavage between the more populous centers and the rural counties. Georgia's commercial and industrial growth after 1880 and the neglect of its large farm population sharpened the impact of the agrarian revolt in the state. In Georgia's county-unit system of making party nominations, Tom Watson and other politicians found a device that reduced the power of the cities and increased the influence of the state's many small counties in primary elections. When the Smith faction endeavored to scrap the county-unit system, Watson stirred up the country people by predicting that Atlanta would soon dominate the state's political life. The issue was one that could be invoked repeatedly, even after the county-unit scheme had been safeguarded by legislative act in 1917.[40] There was also an institutional barrier to reform. The general assembly was large and cumbersome. Much of its annual session was taken up with purely local legislation, and it was difficult for the governor to push many measures through the two unwieldy bodies.

[38] Clarence A. Bacote,"Negro Proscriptions, Protests, and Proposed Solutions in Georgia, 1880–1908," *JSH* 25 (Nov. 1959): 478. Also see W.E. Burghardt Du Bois, "Georgia: Invisible Empire State," *Nation* 120 (Jan. 21, 1925): 63–67.

[39] For Watson's racial views, see C. Vann Woodward, "Tom Watson and the Negro in Agrarian Politics," *JSH* 4 (Feb. 1938): 14–33, and Eugene R. Fingerhut, "Tom Watson, Blacks, and Southern Reform," *Ga. Hist. Quar.* 60 (Winter 1976): 324–43.

[40] Watson claimed with considerable justification that he held the balance of power in the rural counties and that they ruled the state. Albert B. Saye, "Georgia's County Unit System of Election," *Journal of Politics* 12 (Feb. 1950): 93–106; V.O. Key, Jr., with the assistance of Alexander Heard, *Southern Politics in State and Nation* (New York, 1949), 118–20.

Politics and political reform in Georgia were strongly conditioned by the introduction of the primary election system, the development of a fierce bifactionalism in the Democratic party, a substantial infusion of agrarian dissatisfaction, the anomalous role of Tom Watson, and the challenging leadership of Hoke Smith as a self-styled progressive. Urban pressures, particularly in Atlanta, and organizations like the Atlanta Freight Bureau were also important in state politics early in the century. The result was a somewhat more open and competitive politics than that of earlier years, one in which new issues arose and a variety of interests emerged. Although party factions and interest groups were constantly shifting during this era, the demands on state and city government steadily increased and the pressure for reform mounted. Several progressive measures were enacted during the latter part of Joseph M. Terrell's administration, in part as a consequence of Hoke Smith's reform campaign for the governorship. The session of 1906 produced Georgia's first child labor law, made the railroad commission elective, and established a number of agricultural schools. Smith's first term as governor, from 1907 to 1909, brought the greatest concentration of progressive enactments of the period, including a stronger railroad commission, statewide prohibition, abolition of the convict-lease system, the establishment of juvenile courts, corrupt-practices legislation, and the ending of free railway passes. In 1911, during Smith's second term, the state's educational administration was reorganized, an antilobbying law was passed, and a department of commerce and labor was set up. While no single year or administration stands out as notably progressive after 1911, some significant reforms were adopted: a tax equalization law in 1913, stricter child labor controls in 1914 and 1916, compulsory education in 1916, a state system of highways in 1919, a workmen's compensation act in 1920, additional educational improvements in 1918 and 1919, and the creation of a children's code committee in 1922.[41]

South Carolina politics also embodied the main characteristics of the Deep South pattern. Underlying the clash and clamor of politics in the Palmetto State were sharp sectional, class, and racial differences. Sectionalism was an old phenomenon, emerging in its earliest form in colonial times with the demand of the back country for self-government and equality with the dominant coastal region. In time a fairly clear-cut division developed between the coastal plain and the Piedmont Plateau, which stretched in a northwesterly direction from the fall line to the foothills of the Blue Ridge Mountains. Although the state's economy was basically agricultural, the low country was more dependent upon farming than the upcountry, which steadily became more industrialized and more urbanized. Population and wealth had been shifting toward the northwest for a long time, and such Piedmont counties as Anderson, Greenville, and

---

[41] Alton DuMar Jones, "Progressivism in Georgia, 1898–1918" (Ph.D. diss., Emory Univ., 1963), and "The Administration of Governor Joseph M. Terrell Viewed in the Light of the Progressive Movement," *Ga. Hist. Quar.* 48 (Sept. 1964): 271–90.

Spartanburg experienced a great textile expansion during the 1890s and early 1900s. But the state's sectional cleavage also mirrored the divergent traditions and attitudes of low-country gentry and upcountry farmers and workingmen. In a way these differences represented the distinctions between cavalier and puritan, between high church and fundamentalist sect, between Charleston's moral permissiveness and the Piedmont's compulsion toward moral absolutism.

South Carolina's sectional cleavage reflected but did not altogether coincide with a hardy strain of class antagonism. This hostility had its orgins in the social distance that separated the plantation aristocracy and the ordinary farmer and mechanic. During the latter decades of the nineteenth century, it was perpetuated and in some ways intensified by the continuing influence of the old aristocracy, in combination with the rising financial and industrial interests, on the one hand, and the growing farm dependency and mushrooming factory working class, on the other. By 1900 three out of every five farmers in South Carolina were tenants, and by 1914 one-fourth of the state's white population lived in textile mill villages. Before the 1890s the aging Bourbon elite that dominated political affairs, blinded by its own narrow interests, seemed to lose touch with the masses.[42] As a leading politician observed in 1916, "We have a goodly number of Bourbons in this State—who 'learn nothing and forget nothing.' They still believe that they are divinely commissioned to rule the State, and the people, of course, resent their insolence."[43] The agricultural depression of the nineties made the Bourbons vulnerable to attack by new and more vigorous political leaders.

The political upheaval of the 1890s in South Carolina, like that in Mississippi, was quickened by a pervading consciousness of the Negro's presence. Other questions might distract politicians and voters for a time, but year in and year out blacks and "the race problem" remained a never-ending source of public discussion and political conflict.[44] Negroes comprised over 58 percent of the state's total population in 1900, and they were spread over most of the state, except for a few counties in the extreme northwestern section. They provided a highly visible symbol of the planter's political domination in antebellum days, of "black rule" during the Reconstruction period, and of Bourbon manipulation and repression in more recent years. When the old order was disrupted, the black man was turned upon by ordinary white and Bourbon alike; but it was the new leaders of the common man who made the most spectacular use of white supremacy campaigns in the years that followed.

[42]David Duncan Wallace, *The History of South Carolina*, 4 vols. (New York, 1934), vol. 3, pp. 343–45, 350–51, 492.

[43]Benjamin R. Tillman to W.H. Glenn, Sept. 13, 1916, in "Notes on Tillman Manuscripts," Francis Butler Simkins Papers, Southern Historical Collection, University of North Carolina.

[44]For illustrations see Francis Butler Simkins, "Ben Tillman's View of the Negro," *JSH* 3 (May 1937): 161–74, and Ronald D. Burnside, "Racism in the Administrations of Governor Cole Blease," *The Proceedings of the South Carolina Historical Association, 1964* (Columbia, S.C., 1964), 43–57.

The first of these leaders was the redoubtable Benjamin Ryan Tillman, the principal architect of disfranchisement in South Carolina. A rude and one-eyed farmer from the upcountry county of Edgefield, "Pitchfork Ben" Tillman, as he was called, was a leader of skill, audacity, and explosive energy. He led the embattled farmers to victory in 1890, aroused the upcountrymen against the Charleston aristocracy and government by "gentlemen," and provoked the bitter hatred of financial, business, and professional men. Most of them shared the dismay of Narciso G. Gonzales, editor of the Columbia *State*, who felt that "the integrity of the commonwealth was threatened by the hegemony of the back country proletariat."[45] Tillmanism, in its leadership and constituency, cut across economic, social, and even family lines. While emphasizing the real hardships of South Carolina farmers, it offered no radical solutions, avoided third-party politics, and busied itself with capturing control of the Democratic party.[46] Tillman overturned Bourbonism in South Carolina but left intact many of the Bourbon traditions. As one scholar has written, "The holiness of the Democratic party and the white race together with reverence for the Confederacy and conviction of the horror of Reconstruction have, with the Protestant faith, formed the basic creed of the white Southerner."[47] Still, Tillman sponsored some reforms, and he caused South Carolina Democrats to assume two clearly defined factions in the 1890s. Though slow to adopt the direct primary, he was responsible for enlarging the official hustings so that all Democratic candidates for statewide office had to face each other in every county.[48] After serving as governor for four years, Tillman entered the United States Senate in 1895, remaining there until his death in 1918.

Although Tillmanism left a strong imprint upon South Carolina politics and Tillman remained invulnerable in his own campaigns, the senator gradually lost his dominant position in state politics. The old factionalism was also thrown into disarray by the acrimonious controversy surrounding the state dispensary established during Tillman's governorship to handle the whiskey problem. Conservatives won U.S. Senate contests in 1896 and 1897, and in the elections of 1902 assumed control of the legislature once more. Two former anti-Tillmanites served as governor during the years 1903–11. Meanwhile, Tillman himself was growing more conservative, finally appealing to his old factional

---

[45] Lewis Pinckney Jones, "Carolinians and Cubans: The Elliotts and Gonzales, Their Work and Their Writings" (Ph.D. diss., Univ. of North Carolina, 1952), 286.

[46] William J. Cooper, Jr., *The Conservative Regime: South Carolina, 1877–1890* (Baltimore, 1968), 17, 142, 203–207; Lawrence Goodwyn, *Democratic Promise: The Populist Moment in America* (New York, 1976), 215–16, 337–39.

[47] Cooper, *The Conservative Regime,* 15. For the career of a conservative South Carolina journalist during this period, see John Daniel Stark, "William Watts Ball: A Study in Conservatism" (Ph.D. diss., Duke Univ., 1961).

[48] According to the editor William Watts Ball, "The real revolution in South Carolina was the introduction of the primary system and it antedated Tillman" (Ball to W.K. Tate, Feb. 23, 1915, Ball Papers, Duke University Library).

opponents to help reelect him in 1912. As his biographer writes, in winning reelection he had joined forces with "the very persons it had been his mission in life to teach the common people to despise."[49]

The first decade of the new century was a period of relative calm in South Carolina politics. Duncan Clinch Heyward, a rice planter from Colleton County, served as governor from 1903 to 1907. Although he was identified with certain forward-looking proposals, his administration was not notably success-ful in achieving a progressive record. Neither was the administration of the next governor, Martin F. Ansel, though the legislature did end the dispensary sys-tem during his first year in office. Most South Carolina governors found it difficult to establish a constructive record, for the legislature was very powerful (it met annually) and several of the state's administrative officers were popu-larly elected and thus could be independent of the chief executive. Neverthe-less, social reform pressures were present in the state even if they were largely inchoate and ineffective. South Carolina reformers were active in campaigns for public education, prison reform, child labor legislation, prohibition, and municipal improvement. N.G. Gonzales and his brothers used the Columbia *State* as a weapon against lawlessness, lynching, and the convict-lease system, while promoting education, industrial and urban development, and other "progressive" advances.[50]

In 1910 the political calm was shattered by the gubernatorial triumph of a flamboyant upcountry politician named Coleman Livingston Blease. A pro-fessed heir of "Pitchfork Ben," Blease had been a Tillman leader in the legisla-ture and an ardent champion of the state dispensary. In general he appealed to the same elements that had supported Tillman, but there were some differ-ences. Many of the state's more prosperous farmers who had followed Tillman did not support Blease. On the other hand, the new leader was extraordinarily effective in winning the loyalty of textile mill workers, a group Ben Tillman had contemptuously called that "damned factory class."[51] Ambitious and op-portunistic, a man of forceful personality and colorful oratorical style, "Coley" Blease appealed to the racial, religious, and class prejudices of the South Carolina masses. Blease, in the words of a contemporary newspa-perman, "articulated the poor man's unexpressed emotions, ambitions and disgruntlements; did it garishly, did it sentimentally, did it courageously."[52] He exemplified the "hell of a fellow" complex. When the time came for Blease to speak at a political rally, a wave of animation would spread over the expectant crowd. Someone might shout, "Tell 'em about it, Coley!" "Goddermighty

---

[49]Francis Butler Simkins, *Pitchfork Ben Tillman: South Carolinian* (Baton Rouge, 1944), 499.

[50]See Lewis Pinckney Jones, *Stormy Petrel: N.G. Gonzales and His State* (Columbia, SC. 1973).

[51]Simkins, *Pitchfork Ben Tillman*, 485; Ernest McPherson Lander, Jr., *A History of South Carolina, 1865–1960* (Chapel Hill, N.C., 1960), 49.

[52]James C. Derieux, "Crawling Toward the Promised Land," *Survey* 48 (Apr. 29, 1922): 178.

ain't he a man," another might say.[53] "I'd put my vote in fer Coley if I was a-standin' knee-deep in Hell," boasted a cotton mill worker on one occasion.[54] Following Blease's renomination in the primary of 1912, one South Carolina politician admitted that he was "utterly unable to diagnose the case." Governor Blease, he wrote, "had against him almost every prominent public official, at least seventy-five per cent of the women of the state, an almost solid ministry, and practically the united public press and at the close of the campaign the influence of Senator Tillman."[55] But he still managed to win.

Blease's four years as governor were among the most tempestuous in the state's history. He fought with the legislature, a majority of whose members opposed him, and kept things in constant turmoil with his controversial actions in such areas as law enforcement, higher education, and use of the pardoning power. His administration accomplished little of a positive nature. As one scholar has written, "He mesmerized the mill workers, the tenant farmers, and the poor whites, while at the same time opposing governmental programs to benefit them."[56] Yet Bleaseism was also a protest movement generated by social conditions. Tillmanism, as it turned out, did little to relieve the discontent of the poorer farmers, and it largely eschewed the needs of industrial workers. Cole Blease directed his invective at the enemies of the common man, appealed to his strong sense of individualism, and aroused the political consciousness of the millworkers for the first time. A recent interpreter concludes that the upcountry insurgent brought to a focus "the sharpest class confrontation between white men" ever to appear in South Carolina. Millworkers were devoted to Blease because he was *not* an innovator, or even a conservative, but because, rather, he was an "obstructionist."[57] Fearing the effects of such reforms as child labor restrictions and compulsory education, mill people tended to view Blease's opposition to progressivism as a defense of their own interests. However negative his philosophy and program may have been, he expanded the meaning of white democracy in South Carolina. His leadership brought, at least for a few years, a dramatic increase in the voting participation of white South Carolinians. His personality, moreover, was a forceful element in creating pro- and anti-Blease factions in the state's politics. "There are now two distinct factions in the Democratic Party," an anti-Bleaseite warned in 1916, "and we may as well recognize it and act accordingly."[58] In Charleston,

[53]Ibid., 176. For Wilbur J. Cash's treatment of Blease, see *The Mind of the South* (New York, 1941), 245–53.

[54]Clarence N. Stone, "Bleaseism and the 1912 Election in South Carolina," *North Carolina Historical Review* 40 (Jan. 1963): 71.

[55]Mendel L. Smith to T.I. Jones, Sept. 10, 1912, Mendel L. Smith Papers, South Caroliniana Library, University of South Carolina.

[56]Key, *Southern Politics*, 144.

[57]David Lee Carlton, "Mill and Town: The Cotton Mill Workers and the Middle Class in South Carolina, 1880–1920" (Ph.D. diss., Yale Univ., 1977), 268, 272.

[58]Thomas F. McDow to William Watts Ball, Sept. 13, 1916, Ball Papers.

meanwhile, John P. Grace, spokesman for the working class and sometime ally of Blease, had become mayor and had introduced an important new element into city and state politics.[59] Blease's candidate for governor was defeated in 1914, and Blease himself suffered a setback in his campaign for a Senate seat.[60] But he and his faction remained important in South Carolina.

Richard I. Manning, an anti-Blease leader who was elected governor in 1914, had none of his predecessor's platform dash or boisterous personal qualities. A low-country planter, businessman, and lawyer, he was a descendant of several South Carolina governors and was an experienced legislator. He was more like "a benevolent patron," says a contemporary historian, "rather than one who could become the darling of the people."[61] In his inaugural address Manning evoked "the vision of a people reunited," and sought to identify his administration with "progressive Democrats."[62] As governor he became a crusader against lawlessness, something of a social reformer, and unquestionably the state's most constructive governor during the first two decades of this century.[63] Following Manning's four-year administration, Governor Robert A. Cooper continued the progressive approach to the state's problems pursued by his predecessor. In the meantime, Bleaseism as an organizing factor in South Carolina politics slowly lost its effectiveness, as had Tillmanism in earlier years.

In contrast to several other southern states, South Carolina failed to produce a dynamic progressive governor early in the twentieth century. Tillman remained powerful for a time, but he demonstrated little interest in social reform. A few progressive measures were adopted during the Heyward and Ansel administrations such as the state's first child labor law and the first legislation providing public support for high schools. Blease enlivened state politics and aroused the interest of many ordinary South Carolinians, but he was not an advocate of a reform program or of new public services, although he did urge changes in the state's prison system. There was still no effective reform coalition in South Carolina: political leadership was lacking, the rural and industrial elites were generally reactionary and defensive, and the middle-class and professional elements in the cities and towns were not yet well organized. The reform

[59]John Joseph Duffy, "Charleston Politics in the Progressive Era" (Ph.D. diss., Univ. of South Carolina, 1963).

[60]See Ronald Dantan Burnside, "The Governorship of Coleman Livingston Blease of South Carolina, 1911–1915" (Ph.D. diss., Indiana Univ., 1963); Daniel W. Hollis, "Cole Blease: The Years Between the Governorship and the Senate, 1915–1924," *South Carolina Historical Magazine* 80 (Jan. 1979): 1–17; Stone, "Bleaseism and the 1912 Election in South Carolina," 54–74; and Carlton, "Mill and Town: The Cotton Mill Workers and the Middle Class in South Carolina," 258–315.

[61]Wallace, *History of South Carolina*, vol. 3, p. 424.

[62]W.K. Tate, "After Blease—A New Program for South Carolina," *Survey* 33 (Feb. 27, 1915): 577.

[63]Robert Milton Burts, *Richard Irvine Manning and the Progressive Movement in South Carolina* (Columbia, S.C., 1974), 70–203.

breakthrough did not come until the Manning administration, when the new governor succeeded in broadening support for change and a more positive program based on expanding state services, greater administrative efficiency, and the modernization of social institutions. The legislative achievements of the Manning administration included the establishment of a board of charities and corrections, creation of a state tax commission and a highway department, increased appropriations for education, and passage of a compulsory school attendance law, child labor legislation and other labor statutes, a measure to regulate fire insurance companies, and a primary election law. Governor Cooper's administration, from 1919 to 1923, provided further support for education and established a budget system for state finances.

Florida was a natural component of the Lower South during this period, not only in a geographic sense but culturally and politically as well. Thus Florida remained a rural state during the first two decades of the century; 43.6 percent of its inhabitants were blacks in 1900; it was the scene of a large number of lynchings; and it was completely dominated by the Democratic party. The state's leaders spoke in the political idiom of the Deep South, and its people were heavily influenced by sectional traditions and images.

It was difficult to form a statewide political organization in Florida, in part because the governor shared many administrative powers with certain other state officials who were commonly regarded as independent officers rather than administrative aides of the chief executive. Under the constitution of 1885, these officials were popularly elected, and unlike the governor, they could succeed themselves in office. Furthermore, as a result of legislative action, they shared with the governor various collective functions in supervising ex officio boards and commissions. All of this reduced the governor's power and diminished the patronage at his disposal. Although the state's population was small—only slightly more than half a million in 1900—its geography did not facilitate rapid communication or easy assembly of people on a statewide basis.[64] Innumerable lakes and marshes made travel difficult, and distances were very great. It was 500 miles from the Georgia border to the Florida Keys and, in the north, 350 miles from the Atlantic Ocean to the Perdido River. The state had no less than 1,200 miles of coastline.

Florida's population increased by 42 percent between 1900 and 1910, and its rate of growth during the next decade was 29 percent, twice the national average. Much of this growth was the result of immigration from other states and regions, and many of the newcomers moved into the undeveloped central and southern areas of the state. The development of citrus-fruit and winter-vegetable farming was rapid after 1900, and the peninsular section also became the center of such industries as lumbering, fishing, phosphate mining, live-

[64]Herbert J. Doherty, Jr., "Liberal and Conservative Voting Patterns in Florida,"*Journal of Politics* 14 (Aug. 1952): 403–405; Wilson K. Doyle, Angus McKenzie Laird, and S.Sherman Weiss, *The Government and Administration of Florida* (New York, 1954), 4–6, 23–24, 84–87.

stock, and tourism. While it was only a subdued note in the clash of factional politics before 1920, a distinctive sectionalism was emerging in Florida. It was a north-south cleavage, in which the older section, bordering on Georgia and Alabama, was opposed by the growing peninsular region. The first had been the center of Florida's plantation system, and it continued to have close ties with the rest of the South. It provided most of the state's political leadership. This Old South area possessed the highest percentages of blacks in Florida. It tended to be conservative on social questions, even though it had given the strongest support for agrarian reform in the 1890s. The newer and less developed areas to the south were more diversified in their economy than north Florida, less "southern" in population, less traditional in outlook, and more obsessed with the New South approach to development.

Because of the state's obvious transportation needs and the spreading en-thusiasm for the development of the central and southern parts of the peninsula, legislators and administrative officials were reluctant to apply stringent regula-tions to railroads and other corporations. Most Floridians applauded the work of railroad entrepreneurs such as Henry B. Plant and Henry M. Flagler. Fol-lowing Reconstruction, the "developers" established close ties with the Bour-bon Democrats, who dominated the state government; they were rewarded with generous subsidies and tax exemptions. Railroads and land companies were granted more than eleven million acres of state land between 1879 and 1901.[65] These corporations were extremely influential in public affairs, and their critics singled them out as the chief source of political corruption in the state. Opposi-tion to the political role of the railroads and to the favored treatment they received from the state government began to develop as early as the 1880s. It was a major theme of the complaints voiced by the Populists and reform Democrats in the 1890s. And while the People's party enjoyed little success in Florida, "a line of Populist thought" ran through the consideration of public questions well into the twentieth century. Indeed, a discernible cleavage de-veloped between conservative and liberal Democrats during the nineties, and contemporaries referred to these elements appropriately as "corporation" and "anticorporation" groups. Manifestations of Democratic reformism appeared with the passage of a railroad commission act in 1897 and a primary election law in 1901, in the efforts of Governor William S. Jennings to recover large amounts of public land claimed by railroad companies, and in the vigorous attacks upon corporation abuses made in the Senate primary of 1903.[66]

[65]J. E. Dovell, "The Railroads and the Public Lands of Florida, 1879–1905, "*Florida Histor-ical Quarterly* 34 (Jan. 1956): 236–58. See also Edward C. Williamson, *Florida Politics in the Gilded Age, 1877–1893* (Gainesville, Fla., 1976), and Dudley S. Johnson, "Henry Bradley Plant and Florida," *Fla. Hist. Quar.* 45 (Oct. 1966): 118–31.

[66]Kathryn T. Abbey, "Florida Versus the Principles of Populism, 1896–1911," *JSH* 4 (Nov. 1938): 462–75; William T. Cash, *History of the Democratic Party in Florida, Including Bio-graphical Sketches of Prominent Florida Democrats* (Tallahassee, 1936), 77, 84, 94–97; Wayne Flynt, *Duncan Upshaw Fletcher: Dixie's Reluctant Progressive* (Tallahassee, 1971), 7–58.

In the amorphous and kaleidoscopic milieu of southern politics, wrote V.O. Key in 1949, "only the most able—or spectacular—personality can function effectively in the organization of a stable following."[67] Such a personality was Florida's Napoleon Bonaparte Broward, who created the most significant and enduring faction among the state's Democrats in the period. Broward was a reformer with a vivid personality and a genuine program. A descendant of a plantation family impoverished by the Civil War, Broward, like James K. Vardaman of Mississippi, became a hero of the common man, a champion of the "crackers" against the railroad interests and "land pirates," and more than that, a colorful and picturesque steamboat captain who achieved fame as the leader of filibustering expeditions to aid the Cuban revolutionaries in the nineties. The captain came out of the turbulent and faction-ridden politics of Jacksonville and Duval County, which he served for several years as sheriff and represented for a time in the state legislature. He became a forceful leader of the anticorporation faction and the reaction against the "developers," being identified with the Bryanization of his party, with the demand for a system of primaries, and with the movement for stronger regulation of railroads. He agreed with William S. Jennings, who declared in 1900 that the trusts were "sapping the lifeblood of the country and should be speedily suppressed or controlled by the Government."[68] Broward was elected governor in 1904, after winning a narrow victory in one of the state's most intensely fought primary contests.

Napoleon B. Broward's leadership precipitated a violent factional struggle in Florida. The Broward administration launched the Everglades drainage program and sponsored an impressive number of reforms, leading its opponents to condemn the governor as a demagogic radical whose innovations would frighten badly needed capital away from the state. One of the governor's critics was the *Florida Times-Union*, whose editor complained at the end of the legislative session of 1907 that "Never in the history of Florida, perhaps, has there been so much cheap demagoguery and reckless motives in legislation. . . ." It was a "sad lesson" for "the conservative men of Florida."[69] Broward's reform program was only partly successful, and in 1908 he was defeated in a race for the United States Senate. Two years later, however, he won another Senate campaign but died suddenly in October 1910 before assuming his new office. Broward's influence continued after his death, both because of the impetus his leadership had given to a bifactional grouping of the voters and because of the way it had encouraged progressivism in the state's politics. Park Trammell, an old friend and lieutenant of Broward, was elected governor

[67]Key, *Southern Politics*, 103.

[68]Quoted in Samuel Proctor, *Napoleon Bonaparte Broward: Florida's Fighting Democrat* (Gainesville, Fla., 1950), 164. See this work generally for Broward's public career and impact on Florida politics. Also see Joel Webb Eastman, "Claude L'Engle, Florida Muckraker," *Fla. Hist. Quar.* 45 (Jan. 1967): 243–52.

[69]*Florida Times-Union*, May 31, 1907. See also ibid., Apr. 11, May 1, 5, 1907.

in 1912, and his administration established a more comprehensive record of constructive reform.

By the time Trammell left office early in 1917, the Broward era was clearly drawing to a close. The old factional lines were disappearing, the anticorporation movement had lost much of its force, and new issues and leaders were beginning to occupy the political stage. The most prominent of the new leaders was Sidney J. Catts, a Baptist minister, insurance salesman, and political unknown who was elected governor as an independent in 1916. Catts was a colorful figure and an eloquent pulpit orator, and he conducted an unorthodox but effective campaign. He capitalized on prohibitionist sentiment, fear of what he called the "Catholic menace," opposition to the enforcement of the state fish and oyster conservation law, and the controversial Democratic primary that denied him the party nomination in 1916. The stormy Catts, disrespectful of the established political order and of social pretensions, in the manner of Coleman L. Blease, plunged the state into four years of turmoil. His following was a highly personal one, but he brought a new alignment of the Florida electorate. As governor he made full use of the spoils system and fought with the legislature and the press. Yet Catts was a reformer who, while flawed, improved public administration in such areas as education and the penal system. He had an undeniable appeal to the little man and to those who were disgruntled over the conduct of public affairs in the state. Catts was unable to perpetuate his influence in Florida politics, however, and he suffered an overwhelming defeat in an attempt to win a Senate seat in 1920.[70] Politics in the Peninsular State thereafter became calmer but also more conservative.

Progressivism in Florida initially gained momentum and direction early in the twentieth century during the governorship of William S. Jennings, who launched a program of land recovery and conservation. But it was Napoleon B. Broward who ushered in the era of reform politics and who first identified his leadership with a broad progressive agenda. Broward secured the creation of a board of drainage commissioners to implement his vision of reclaiming the Everglades, and he won legislative approval of laws designed to restrict child labor, guarantee the purity of foods and drugs, reorganize the state system of higher education, and regulate public utilities.[71] Under Broward's successor, Albert W. Gilchrist, the state's first farmers' cooperative act was passed and a juvenile court system was authorized. During the Trammell administration

---

[70]Wayne Flynt, *Cracker Messiah: Governor Sidney J. Catts of Florida* (Baton Rouge, 1977); John R. Deal, Jr., "Sidney Johnston Catts, Stormy Petrel of Florida Politics" (M.A. thesis, Univ. of Florida, 1949). Also see Stephen Kerber, "Park Trammell and the Florida Democratic Senatorial Primary of 1916," *Fla. Hist. Quar.* 58 (Jan. 1980): 255–72; Robert B. Rackleff, "Anti-Catholicism and the Florida Legislature, 1911–1919," ibid. 50 (Apr. 1972): 352–65; and David P. Page, "Bishop Michael J. Curley and Anti-Catholic Nativism in Florida," ibid. 45 (Oct. 1966): 101–17.

[71]See the evaluations by David R. Colburn and Richard K. Scher, *Florida's Gubernatorial Politics in the Twentieth Century* (Tallahassee, 1980).

progressive measures were enacted to strengthen the railroad commission, regulate primary elections more closely, outlaw corrupt practices, promote conservation, and establish a bureau of vital statistics, a state tax commission, and a highway department. The Catts administration could also point to some reform accomplishments: statewide prohibition, an industrial school for vocational education, and a mother's pension law. In the early 1920s, Florida established a central budget commission and finally moved to abolish the convict-lease system.

Politics in this unfinished state was less conducive to progressive action than was true of certain other southern states. Most Floridians were strongly committed to the economic development of the state and correspondingly reluctant to inhibit the activities and investments of outside corporations. But at the same time a current of agrarian radicalism carried over into the new century, and an anticorporation bias provided a rallying ground for political reformers. It is hardly surprising that so sparsely populated a commonwealth should have failed to generate diversified and well-organized interest groups or that urban and middle-class elements should have found it hard to create reform coalitions. Many reformers, moreover, became increasingly concerned with efforts to legislate morals in such areas as prohibition and anti-Catholic measures. Nevertheless, a number of progressive leaders rose to prominence in Florida politics, a competitive bifactionalism existed during this period, and the state's approach to social reform was much like that of the Lower South as a whole.

3   *Patterns of State Politics: The Upper South*

THE FOUR STATES of Virginia, North Carolina, Tennessee, and Kentucky made up a subregion that differed in many respects from other sections of the South. The economy of Virginia, for example, was that of a border state. Except for tobacco, which was a major staple in the southern part of the state, Virginia was not extensively involved in the South's cash crop agriculture. Tenancy was actually declining in the state during the years after 1900, and such diversified activities as livestock production and truck farming were growing rapidly. Although Virginia was still overwhelmingly rural, it was well equipped with railroads, was undergoing substantial industrial development, and was achieving noticeable urban growth. But if the Old Dominion's economy was dynamic and diversified, its characteristic social and political outlook was thoroughly traditional. Indeed, no other southern state was so dedicated to cavalier and aristocratic ideals—to the notions of personal honor, gentility, and paternalism. To the concepts of limited government, state rights, and white supremacy was added a widespread conviction that government was the responsibility not of ordinary men but of the best families. Style was important in politics, and a measure of decorum was expected. In Virginia, the home of Robert E. Lee and of the Confederate capital, there was a special veneration for the heroes of the Lost Cause, and this too blended into the nostalgia for the great days of the past.[1]

Historically, the eastern part of Virginia, where the plantation system had its origins, was the most artistocratic and conservative section, while the shifting west was the most democratic and progressive area. East and west, as in many other states, formed the bases of a strong intrastate sectionalism in politics, and despite the secession and statehood of West Virginia, this was still true to some extent in 1900. Moving from east to west, or more precisely, in a southwesterly

---

[1] Allen W. Moger, "Industrial and Urban Progress in Virginia from 1880 to 1900," *Virginia Magazine of History and Biography* 66 (July 1958): 307–36; Marshall W. Fishwick, *The Virginia Tradition* (Washington, D.C., 1956).

TABLE 6. *The Upper South: Population Statistics*

	POPULATION IN 1900	% INCREASE 1890–1900	% INCREASE 1900–10	% WHITE 1900	% BLACK 1900	% FOREIGN-BORN, 1900
Ky.	2,147,174	15.5	6.6	86.7	13.3	2.3
N.C.	1,893,810	17.1	16.5	66.7	33.0	0.2
Tenn.	2,020,616	14.3	8.1	76.2	23.8	0.9
Va.	1,854,184	12.0	11.2	64.3	35.6	1.0

SOURCES: *Twelfth Census of the United States*, vol. 1: *Population*, part 1, pp. cxiv, cxviii, 2–5; *Thirteenth Census of the United States*, vol. 1: *Population*, 32–33.

direction, one encountered the familiar geographical belts of the Southeast—Tidewater, Piedmont, and mountains. The plains of the Tidewater gave way, in the north, to rolling hills and, in the south, to the Southside, a crescent-shaped black belt whose base extended for a long distance along the North Carolina border. Farther west lay the Blue Ridge Mountains and beyond them the great Valley and the Allegheny highlands. In the southwest, where the state thrust to the south of West Virginia toward Kentucky and Tennessee, was a large upland area that reached into the very center of the Appalachians. Each of the state's main subregions had its own particular interests, but in general the political sectionalism of the early twentieth century reflected a cleavage that ran along the line of the Blue Ridge Mountains. The richest farm land, largest cities, principal concentration of Negroes, and greatest Democratic strength lay to the east. The area to the west, on the other hand, was largely one of small farms, few blacks, and the bulk of the state's Republicans. The political concerns of the western uplands frequently diverged from those of the larger and more populous east, as was evident, for instance, in the deliberations of the constitutional convention of 1901–1902.

Democratic supremacy in Virginia was almost complete in the years after 1897. Nevertheless, the Republican party remained a potential threat. Despite Democratic control of the state offices, the legislature, and the election machinery, Republicans dominated the southwestern highlands, perennially elected at least one congressman, were represented in the state legislature, usually polled one-third or more of the votes in presidential elections, and as a rule nominated candidates for the statewide races.[2] The Republican presence had a strong disciplinary effect on the state's Democrats. Had the Republicans

[2] See Gordon B. McKinney, *Southern Mountain Republicans, 1865–1900: Politics and the Appalachian Community* (Chapel Hill, N.C., 1978), 63–72, 99–108, 114–17, 129–31, 176–82, 219–20; William C. Pendleton, *Political History of Appalachian Virginia, 1776–1927* (Dayton, Va., 1927), 445–571; Guy B. Hathorn, "C. Bascom Slemp—Virginia Republican Boss, 1907–1932," *Journal of Politics* 17 (May 1955): 248–64; and Curtis Carroll Davis, "Very Well-Rounded Republican: The Several Lives of John S. Wise," *Va. Mag. Hist. and Biog.* 71 (Oct. 1963): 461–87.

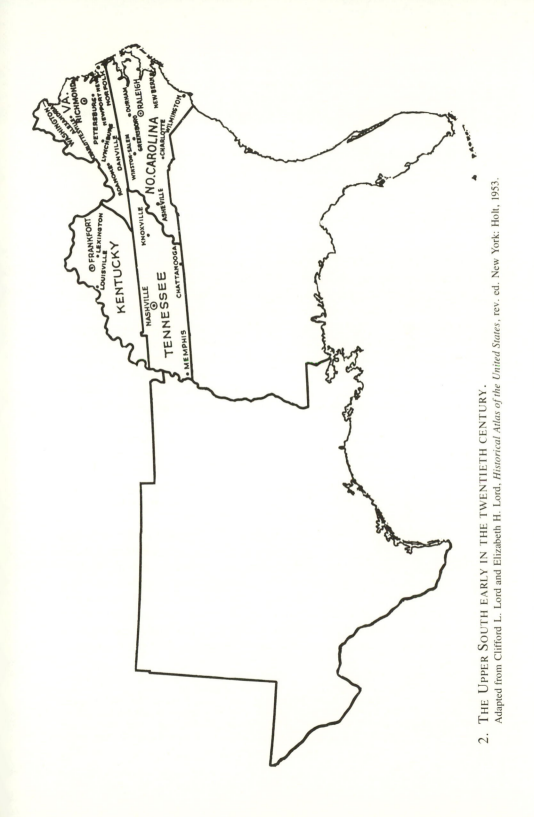

2. THE UPPER SOUTH EARLY IN THE TWENTIETH CENTURY.
Adapted from Clifford L. Lord and Elizabeth H. Lord, *Historical Atlas of the United States*, rev. ed. New York: Holt, 1953.

been able to count on blacks for support (they made up 35.6 percent of the state's population in 1900), they might have provided a stern challenge to the Democrats in the new century. But disfranchisement cost Virginia Republicans white as well as black votes, and they were further weakened by internal conflicts and a steady trend toward "lily-whiteism." Still, the Negro as an issue did not disappear from the state's politics. The Democrats would not surrender such a potent weapon, and from time to time they would drag the issue out and smite the ancient enemy—and occasionally each other—by invoking the horrors of "black rule."[3]

The continued efficacy of the "Negro question" in Virginia politics even after formal disfranchisement was the consequence not only of an irreducible Republican minority but also of the shattering impact of political insurgency in the last quarter of the nineteenth century. The manner in which the Readjuster movement of the 1880s was curbed left an especially bitter heritage in race relations.[4] It also left an indelible imprint upon the minds of the more independent Democrats, most of whom were careful to stay within the confines of the traditional party. At the same time, the methods employed by Democratic leaders in putting down Readjusters, Populists, and Republicans—their electoral machinations and crude alliances with railroads and industrial corporations—made them vulnerable to criticism from within the party and set the stage for a regrouping of the state's Democrats.

One of the most notable aspects of Virginia politics in the progressive era was the existence of two fairly well defined factions in the Democratic party. The basis of this bifactionalism was laid in the 1890s by Thomas Staples Martin, a little-known railroad lawyer and supporter of John S. Barbour, the organizer of the conservative Democrats' victories in the 1880s. Making effective use of railroad support, Martin was elected to the United States Senate in 1893, where he remained until his death in 1919. Unpretentious and diffident, a conservative but above all else a political pragmatist, Martin was a skillful organizer and an able tactician. His leadership was strengthened by a cadre of shrewd and dedicated lieutenants, chief of whom were Representative Henry D. Flood, a master of political arrangements and details; Claude A. Swanson, an extremely effective campaigner and one of the state's most popular leaders; and Richard E. Byrd, a leader in the general assembly.[5] Martin and his political

---

[3] Andrew Buni, *The Negro in Virginia Politics, 1902–1965* (Charlottesville, Va., 1967), 50–89.

[4] The Readjusters, who rebelled against the political dominance and conservative policies of the Bourbon Democrats, represented the most conspicuous of several independent movements in the South during the 1880s. See Charles C. Pearson, *The Readjuster Movement in Virginia* (New Haven, Conn., 1917), and Nelson M. Blake, *William Mahone of Virginia: Soldier and Political Insurgent* (Richmond, Va., 1935).

[5] Allen W. Moger, "The Origin of the Democratic Machine in Virginia," *JSH* 8 (May 1942): 183–209; James Adam Bear, Jr., "Thomas Staples Martin: A Study in Virginia Politics, 1883–1896" (M.A. thesis, Univ. of Virginia, 1952); Paschal Reeves, "Thomas S. Martin: Committee

allies created an "organization" or "machine" whose unity was sufficient to force all Democrats into a coherent two-faction system.

The Martin organization was a disciplined hierarchy whose sources of control included the legislature, Democratic party machinery, and strong outposts at the city and county levels. Although the legislature normally met only every other year, it was a powerful institution in Virginia, not least because it appointed the members of the state's several courts. The county and city court judges in turn appointed a number of local officials, including the electoral boards. The Martin organization also worked closely with the important elective officials of the various counties, who looked to the machine's control of the legislature for protection against governmental changes that might affect their authority or compensation, and these courthouse "cliques" or "rings" were usually able to furnish votes to the state machine. The organization enjoyed great strength in the rural areas, and with the small electorate after 1902, the local leaders were strategically placed to provide the margin of victory in most district and state elections. Martin and his lieutenants were skillful in the use of state and federal patronage, and particularly in the early years, they relied upon the financial support of railroads and corporations. While the organization was supremely practical in its view of politics, its oligarchical power was rooted in the social structure of Virginia, and its leaders saw themselves as guardians of the state's culture, which was basically rural, homogeneous, and traditional. Yet the machine was not unresponsive to the shifting winds of change.[6]

Although organization leaders weathered the agrarian storm of the mid-nineties and gradually adjusted to the consequences of William Jennings Bryan's candidacy in 1896, they encountered increasing opposition from other Virginia Democrats after 1897. The circumstances surrounding Senator Martin's controversial election in 1893 and the election tactics used by the regular Democrats in the campaigns that followed inspired a growing number of "independents" to demand clean elections, a party primary system, and stricter regulation of railroads and industrial corporations. They also urged the development of public education and a system of good roads. In 1897 a governor and an attorney general were elected without the endorsement of the state organization. In 1899, Representative William A. Jones, a strong critic of the Democratic hierarchy, and other independents arranged what became known as the "May Conference," a well-attended meeting that denounced the state's

Statesman," *Va. Mag. Hist. and Biog.* 68 (July 1960): 344–64; Burton Ira Kaufman, "Henry De La Warr Flood: A Case Study of Organization Politics in an Era of Reform" (Ph.D. diss., Rice Univ., 1966); John A. Treon, "The Political Career of Henry De La Warr Flood: A Biographical Sketch, 1865 to 1921," in University of Virginia History Club, *Annual Collection of Essays in History* 10 (1964–65): 44–64.

[6]For the character of the Martin organization, see Herman L. Horn, "The Growth and Development of the Democratic Party in Virginia Since 1890" (Ph.D. diss., Duke Univ., 1949); Key, *Southern Politics*, 19–35; and Allen W. Moger, *Virginia: Bourbonism to Byrd, 1870–1925* (Charlottesville, Va., 1968).

Democratic oligarchy, attempted to launch a movement for the adoption of a Senate primary, and lent support to those who advocated a constitutional convention in order to effect election reforms and to reorganize the state government. Carter Glass and other antimachine spokesmen wanted to "rid the State of a corrupt, costly, and intolerable domination of an office-holding clique."[7] The independents failed to prevent the reelection of Senator Martin in 1899, but the following year they took the lead in persuading the legislature to authorize a referendum on the question of calling a constitutional convention. The constitutional convention of 1901–1902 provided a means of consolidating the Democratic party of Virginia behind the forces of reform. And in 1901 one of the reformers won the governorship in a vigorous campaign against the machine.[8]

The man who was elected governor in 1901 was Andrew Jackson Montague, Virginia's most famous progressive. A Southside lawyer, the "red fox of Middlesex" was descended from a prominent Tidewater family. He made his influence felt in party circles as an eloquent speaker and staunch Cleveland Democrat, with an old-fashioned dedication to public service and lofty purposes. He was elected to the office of attorney general in 1897, and soon afterward joined other young party liberals in the reform movement. With his election as governor in 1901, it appeared that the independents were on the verge of a complete victory over the regular Democrats. Montague's administration was identified with the revival of public education and with the adoption of primary elections and the good-roads movement in Virginia. The governor's constitutional power was limited, however, and he had difficulty getting his reforms through the more conservative legislature. Nor did Montague perfect an organization of his own. The reformers were weakened by conflicting ambitions and an inability or unwillingness to cooperate. Montague himself was defeated by Martin in the Senate primary of 1905, and the organization's candidate for governor, Claude A. Swanson, was also elected that year.[9]

The "independent versus machine" struggle continued during the years 1905–12, but the regulars won the governorship again in 1909, and two years later, in a bitter campaign for two Senate seats, turned back the challenges of

---

[7]Glass, quoted in William Larsen, *Montague of Virginia: The Making of a Southern Progressive* (Baton Rouge, 1965), 84. See also Allen Moger, "The Rift in Virginia Democracy in 1896," *JSH* 4 (Aug. 1938): 295–317; Victor Duvall Weathers, "The Political Career of Allen Caperton Braxton" (M.A. thesis, Univ. of Virginia, 1956); Harry E. Poindexter, "The Virginia Democracy in 1897: Silver-Plated Conservatism," in University of Virginia History Club, *Essays in History* 2 (Winter 1955): 5–27; and Raymond H. Pulley, "The May Movement of 1899: Irresolute Progressivism in the Old Dominion," *Va. Mag. Hist. and Biog.* 75 (Apr. 1967): 186–201.

[8]Ralph Clipman McDanel, *The Virginia Constitutional Convention of 1901–1902* (Baltimore, 1928); Wythe W. Holt, Jr., "The Virginia Constitutional Convention of 1901–1902: A Reform Movement Which Lacked Substance," *Va. Mag. Hist. and Biog.* 76 (Jan. 1968): 67–102; John Ritchie, "The Gubernatorial Campaign in Virginia in 1901," in University of Virginia History Club, *Essays in History* 2 (Winter 1955): 53–70; Raymond H. Pulley, *Old Virginia Restored: An Interpretation of the Progressive Impulse, 1870–1930* (Charlottesville, Va., 1968), 92.

[9]See Larsen, *Montague of Virginia*, 113–215, for a comprehensive treatment of Montague's governorship.

William A. Jones and Carter Glass.[10] There was a certain irony in these electoral losses suffered by the independents, for the very election reforms that had served as their original rallying point had, after the ballot restrictions of 1902 became effective, probably hurt them far more than they impaired the organization. Despite the enmity between the two Democratic factions, they were not divided by sharp ideological disagreements. The progressives themselves were basically conservative, defenders of Virginia's peculiar cultural values, intent upon restoring social order and morality following the chaos and trepidation of the late nineteenth century.[11] Equally important, a consensus on progressivism gradually developed among Virginia Democrats during the early years of the twentieth century. That helps explain the apparent anomaly of the Martin faction's being identified with and sometimes sponsoring reform legislation. Furthermore, the organization demonstrated a surprising capacity to adapt itself to the progressive currents of the day. It gradually accepted and then successfully used the primary as a means of making party nominations. Governor Swanson's administration from 1906 to 1910 was much more successful with the legislature than Montague's had been, and it obtained an impressive number of reform enactments. The organization became less dependent upon corporation support, identified itself with the farmer's phase of the progressive movement, and after much soul-searching, slowly shifted to a position of outright support of prohibition, thus securing the backing of the Anti-Saloon League and its powerful spokesman in Virginia, James Cannon. The Martin faction also proved adept at neutralizing or absorbing its enemies. In 1912 it decided not to oppose former governor Montague's campaign for a congressional seat, thereby removing him as a major antimachine leader. Henry C. Stuart, another independent, was allowed the nomination for governor in 1913 and was brought into the organization. And the neutralization of and eventual alliance with Carter Glass was begun with his election as national committeeman in 1916. Meanwhile, after opposing Woodrow Wilson's nomination in 1912, organization leaders emerged as champions of the new Democratic administration in Washington. By this time the once vigorous bifactionalism had lost much of its vitality.

Democratic opponents of the organization were discouraged, but they did not abandon the field of battle. In 1914 they organized the Virginia Progressive Democratic League, with a renewed attack on the machine and an effort to popularize a broad reform program. But prospects were not very good. Though

---

[10]Robert A. Hohner, "Prohibition and Virginia Politics: William Hodges Mann versus Henry St. George Tucker, 1909," *Va. Mag. Hist. and Biog.* 74 (Jan. 1966): 88–107; Harold Gordon Wheatley, "The Political Career of William Atkinson Jones" (M.A. thesis, Univ. of Virginia, 1953); Charlotte Jean Shelton, "William Atkinson Jones, 1849–1918: Independent Democracy in Gilded Age Virginia" (Ph.D. diss., Univ. of Virginia, 1980).

[11]See Pulley, *Old Virginia Restored*, 67, 92–93, 187–88. See also William Larsen, "Virginia," in David C. Roller and Robert W. Twyman, eds., *The Encyclopedia of Southern History* (Baton Rouge, 1979), 1286–89.

antimachine Democrats usually arranged themselves in one opposing group, the regular wing of the party had won statewide primaries with monotonous regularity since 1905. But in 1917 the Martin organization suffered a defeat. It was careless in approaching the gubernatorial primary that year, allowing a three-man race to develop and giving its endorsement to a notorious "wet" who was forced to campaign on a prohibitionist platform. The winner was Westmoreland Davis, who slipped into office by defeating both the machine and independent candidates. A descendant of southern planters, Davis had left Virginia for New York as a young man, becoming a successful and well-to-do corporation lawyer. Returning to Virginia in 1903, he purchased a colonial plantation on the Potomac and proceeded to make it into an agricultural showplace. Davis eventually became the leader of the progressive farming movement in the state, assuming the presidency of the Virginia State Farmers' Institute in 1909 and becoming the owner and publisher of the Richmond-based *Southern Planter* in 1912. The energetic and ambitious Davis was a bitter opponent of the Martin regulars, and as governor he attempted to build up an organization to compete with the machine. Stressing the need for economy and efficiency in state government, the Davis administration enjoyed some success. But the governor had trouble with the organization-dominated legislature, failed to capture control of the party machinery, and was overwhelmingly defeated in a race for the United States Senate in 1922.[12] Following Senator Martin's death, the organization seemed to be momentarily adrift, but after a brief period of transition, it acquired a new pilot in the person of Harry Flood Byrd.[13]

The constitutional convention of 1901–1902 set the stage for progressivism in Virginia. The convention provided for a strong corporation commission, and that agency's work in later years was an important feature of state regulation. The Montague administration achieved a modest list of legislative reforms, including an employer's liability act, a child labor law, and the foundation for better public schools. But the most concentrated period of progressive legislation came during the governorship of Claude Swanson when several significant education measures were enacted, state aid to roads was inaugurated, a board of charities and corrections was created, a maximum railroad rate law was passed, pure food and drug legislation was approved, and the state's public health program was improved. In 1912 a comprehensive primary election statute was passed, and in 1914 a legislative reference bureau was set up and a prohibition referendum was authorized. Among the innovations introduced during the

[12]Jack Temple Kirby, *Westmoreland Davis: Virginia Planter-Politician, 1859–1942* (Charlottesville, Va., 1968).

[13]Henry C. Ferrell, Jr., "The Role of Virginia Democratic Party Factionalism in the Rise of Harry Flood Byrd, 1917–1923," in Joseph F. Steelman and others, eds., *Essays in Southern Biography*, vol. 2 of *East Carolina College Publications in History* (Greenville, N.C., 1965), 146–66.

Davis administration were an executive budget system, new state tax sources, a state highway system, a central purchasing commission, prison reform, and a children's code commission. This review suggests that progressive politics and social reform in Virginia were characterized by a kind of moderation that reflected the widespread commitment to social harmony and cultural traditionalism in the state. The hegemony of the Democratic party in the Old Dominion was strongly influenced by the potential challenge of the Republicans, by the greatly restricted electorate resulting from the constitution of 1902, and by the organization created by Thomas S. Martin. The "independent" or progressive faction of the Democratic party was also important; while it won few political battles, it was a major factor in forcing the Martin organization to broaden its program and assimilate a number of reform measures.

North Carolina was also an Upper South state. Less involved in the plantation economy than most southern states, its economic life was correspondingly more diversified. Although its inhabitants were less restrained by regional traditions than Virginians or South Carolinians, their politics returned again and again to the explosive issue of race. The black man's part in the fusion movement of the 1890s, an upheaval that brought Republicans and Populists to power in 1894 and 1896, had a traumatic effect upon many white North Carolinians. Fusion and the white supremacy campaign that led to its overthrow revived all of the old Reconstruction myths and strengthened the white resolve to eliminate Negroes from all participation in politics. The events of the late nineties were too vivid in the minds of North Carolina whites to permit the abandonment of the race question in the years after 1900.[14] Contemporary spokesmen liked to think otherwise. Thus a leading historian of the state, writing in 1909, asserted that Negro disfranchisement had produced "a distinctly liberalizing effect" upon politics. "Political issues are slowly changing," he declared, "and the leading questions between the parties in the future will be more of an economic nature than they have been since the War of Secession."[15]

One-third of the state's population in 1900 was made up of blacks, but they were concentrated in the eastern section. Their uneven distribution was, in fact, one of the aggravating factors in North Carolina's long-time political sectionalism. In antebellum times the plantation system was centered in the coastal plains, and that area proved to be far more ardent in advocating secession than the western region, where farms were small and few slaves were held. Unionist sentiment and Republicanism became strong in the extreme western counties.

---

[14]See, for example, Robert F. Durden, *Reconstruction Bonds & Twentieth-Century Politics: South Dakota v. North Carolina (1904)* (Durham, N.C., 1962), 145, 240–59. For the fusion movement, see Helen G. Edmonds, *The Negro and Fusion Politics in North Carolina, 1894–1901* (Chapel Hill, N.C., 1951), and Jeffrey J. Crow and Robert F. Durden, *Maverick Republican in the Old North State: A Political Biography of Daniel L. Russell* (Baton Rouge, 1977).

[15]Joseph Gregoire de Roulhac Hamilton, "North Carolina, from 1865 to the Present Time," in *The South in the Building of the Nation*, vol. 1, p. 508.

The most rapidly growing section in the late nineteenth and early twentieth centuries was the Piedmont, which served as a transition area between plains and mountains and, after disfranchisement, between Democrats and Republicans.

With the collapse of fusionism in 1898 and ratification of the disfranchisement amendment two years later, the Republican party in North Carolina no longer had any real chance of winning statewide elections. Nevertheless, the minority party continued to attract at least a third of the voters, and in some of the western counties it dominated local government.[16] The existence of a substantial opposition party in North Carolina, as in Virginia, affected the behavior of the Democratic party. If the Democrats became too divided among themselves, there was always a possibility that Republicans might attract enough dissidents from the majority to win a statewide election. Unfortunately for the Republicans, their internal squabbles were almost as violent as those of the Democrats, and despite some indications of a GOP revival during the period after 1905, the Democratic dominance of the Old North State continued without serious challenge.[17]

An inchoate bifactionalism characterized North Carolina Democrats in the nineties, with a rough cleavage being manifest on such issues as the regulation of corporations, free silver, and Bryanism. By 1898, when the climactic struggle with the fusionists was under way, conservative Democrats were ascendant. The chairman of the Democratic state committee and the srategist who led the party to victory in the white supremacy campaigns of 1898 and 1900 was Furnifold M. Simmons. An able organizer but no reformer, Simmons was elected to the United States Senate in 1900. Although he failed to create a disciplined machine in the manner of Thomas S. Martin in Virginia, he headed a group of powerful politicians who generally directed the party's course during the first quarter of the century. Simmons bound many Democratic politicians to his faction by strong ties of personal loyalty, particularly in counties where Republicanism was strong and Democrats looked to the state organization for help. Another important source of support for the regular Democrats in North Carolina was their rapprochement with the financial and business elite. The state's impressive industrial growth gave business interests an influential voice

---

[16]For the Republican party in North Carolina in the late nineteenth century, see McKinney, *Southern Mountain Republicans*, 48–50, 62–63, 65, 67, 69–71, 96–99, 119–21, 158–66, 190–91, 195–96, 199–201, 217, 219.

[17]Joseph F. Steelman, "North Carolina," in David C. Roller and Robert W. Twyman, eds., *The Encyclopedia of Southern History* (Baton Rouge, 1979), 922–24; Steelman, "Republican Party Politics in North Carolina, 1902: Factions, Leaders, and Issues," in *Studies in the History of the South, 1875–1922*, vol. 3 of *East Carolina College Publications in History* (Greenville, N.C., 1966), 119–50; Steelman, "Jonathan Elwood Cox and North Carolina's Gubernatorial Campaign of 1908," *N.C. Hist. Rev.* 41 (Oct. 1964): 436–47; Steelman, "Republicanism in North Carolina: John Motley Morehead's Campaign to Revive a Moribund Party, 1908–1910," ibid. 42 (Apr. 1965): 153–68; David C. Roller, "Republican Factionalism in North Carolina, 1904–1906," ibid. 41 (Jan. 1964): 62–73.

in the making of public policy and made the issue of corporation regulation both delicate and volatile.[18] According to Aubrey Lee Brooks, a liberal Greensboro lawyer, the Simmons "machine was perfected integrated and abundantly financed by the railroads, trusts, liquor interests, and other big business."[19] It was not always possible to separate Simmons and anti-Simmons partisans on the basis of their attitudes toward business corporations,[20] but the rising agitation against the railroads and tobacco companies during the first decade of the century was used by "liberal" Democrats in their campaigns against the Simmons organization. As one of the state's most dedicated reformers reminded William Jennings Bryan in 1913, progressives had been forced to make a long fight "in order to keep the extreme reactionary machine politicians from absolutely controlling" North Carolina politics.[21]

One reason for the success of Simmons and his faction was the fact that they were identified with a group of young and able leaders who came to the fore in the party battles of the late nineties. The most significant of these new men was Charles Brantley Aycock, a politician of great eloquence and popularity who was elected governor in 1900. Aycock was one of the most effective speakers in the disfranchisement movement, but he became a champion of universal education, a folk hero, and an evangel of moderation and progress.[22] He gained a reputation as North Carolina's "educational governor," and it was during his administration that a spirit of self-examination in public affairs began to bring significant changes in the state. The Aycock administration, like that of Andrew J. Montague in Virginia, made some modest gains of a progressive nature, including the passage of the state's first child labor act in 1903 and the decided impetus given to the development of public education.

After 1905 the reform movement in North Carolina quickened, and the "machine" was the object of sharp criticism during the years 1908–1913.

---

[18]Dwight B. Billings, Jr., *Planters and the Making of a "New South": Class, Politics, and Development in North Carolina, 1865–1900* (Chapel Hill, N.C., 1979), makes a case for the centrality of the antebellum landed elite in shaping the state's postwar industrialism and points up the weakness of North Carolina progressivism in the early twentieth century.

[19]Brooks, *A Southern Lawyer: Fifty Years at the Bar* (Chapel Hill, N.C., 1950), 61. For additional evidence of business and industrial influence in North Carolina politics during this period, see Edmonds, *The Negro and Fusion Politics in North Carolina*, 138–40, 151–54, and Joseph Flake Steelman, "The Progressive Era in North Carolina, 1884–1917" (Ph.D. diss., Univ. of North Carolina, 1955), 162–64, 197–202, 247, 308–10.

[20]For an example of a North Carolina progressive who consistently worked with Simmons, see John Robert Moore, *Senator Josiah William Bailey of North Carolina: A Political Biography* (Durham, N.C., 1968), 8–21.

[21]According to Edward J. Justice, 75 percent of the Democrats in North Carolina "are sincerely progressive, or could be made so by presenting for their action issues that clearly draw the line of cleavage between the progressives and the reactionaries." See Justice to Bryan, March 28, 1913, Walter Clark Papers, North Carolina Department of Archives and History.

[22]"This man, a politician, a man of the common people, fighting an issue based on prejudice, emerged by rising as far above prejudice as it has proved possible for any native-born Southerner to go" (Rupert B. Vance, "Aycock of North Carolina," *Southwest Review* 18 [Apr. 1933]: 288). For a comprehensive treatment of Aycock's career, see Oliver H. Orr, Jr., *Charles Brantley Aycock* (Chapel Hill, N.C., 1961).

The legislature of 1907 enacted several measures designed to regulate railroads more stringently, abolished free railway passes, established a state board of tax equalization, and increased appropriations for education and eleemosynary institutions. The voters approved statewide prohibition in a referendum the following year. In 1908 an anti-organization Democrat named William W. Kitchin defeated the man Simmons endorsed for governor. Progressives such as Walter Clark, Josephus Daniels, and Edward J. Justice demanded a reorientation of the state party along more liberal lines.[23] But Simmons easily won reelection against these progressive opponents in 1912. Nonetheless, the administration of Locke Craig, the "machine candidate" in 1912, proved to be one of the most progressive of the entire era. In his inaugural address Craig spoke of a "new era" having dawned and of a "spirit of progress" having pervaded the nation. He attacked discriminatory freight rates in North Carolina and urged stricter regulation of public service corporations; he also recommended adoption of an employer's liability law, a statewide primary system, and compulsory school attendance.[24] Nevertheless, the reformers failed in 1914 to secure the ratification of several progressive amendments to the state constitution. By the time Craig left office in 1917, the old factionalism in the Democratic party seemed to be dying out, and the antitrust and antimachine issues were losing their potency.[25] Even when the independent Democrats won the governorship, as in 1908, it proved impossible for them to build a strong and durable organization, in part because the governor's powers were too limited to permit control of the state's politics.[26]

Despite the setbacks and frustrations of its reformers, North Carolina acquired a progressive image early in the twentieth century. "I go nowhere, North or South," the educator Edwin A. Alderman told a Tarheel audience in 1903, "that I do not hear praises of North Carolina."[27] The state's improving image rested on the leading role that Governor Aycock and an inspired band of educational reformers had assumed in the South's public school movement. But it was also related to the vigor of other progressive campaigns in North Carolina, including those for railroad regulation, prohibition, social welfare programs, and the presidential nomination of Woodrow Wilson. An array of progressive bills was enacted, much of it during the years 1907–1908, 1913–1915, and 1919–1921. In 1913, for example, the general assembly passed a series

[23] Aubrey Lee Brooks, *Walter Clark, Fighting Judge* (Chapel Hill, N.C., 1944); Joseph L. Morrison, *Josephus Daniels Says . . . An Editor's Political Odyssey from Bryan to Wilson and F.D.R., 1894–1913* (Chapel Hill, N.C., 1962); Joseph F. Steelman, "Edward J. Justice: Profile of a Progressive Legislator, 1899–1913," *N.C. Hist. Rev.* 48 (Apr. 1971): 147–60.

[24] *Inaugural Address of Governor Locke Craig of North Carolina* (Raleigh, N.C., n.d.). Pamphlet in Craig Papers, Duke University Library.

[25] See Steelman, "The Progressive Era in North Carolina," and "The Progressive Democratic Convention of 1914 in North Carolina," *N.C. Hist. Rev.* 46 (Apr. 1969): 83–104.

[26] The governor did not possess the veto power, and he shared the administrative functions of the state government with several elective officials.

[27] Quoted in Richard N. Current, "Tarheels and Badgers: A Comparative History of Their Reputations," *JSH* 42 (Feb. 1976): 9.

of railroad and business control laws, a corrupt-practices act, and an employer's liability law, while introducing certain court reforms, providing a six-month school term, and approving a weak compulsory education bill. The state's progressive image was also associated with the ideas and activities of such committed and well-known reformers as Walter Clark and Josephus Daniels. These men were part of a discernible progressive faction that was emerging by 1905.[28] But if Democratic factionalism in North Carolina was real and intensive, there was never a clear-cut correlation between the two wings of the party and a fixed position on social reform.

Political affairs in North Carolina during the progressive era bore the heavy imprint of the race issue, disfranchisement, a restricted electorate, and a long-established Democratic hierarchy. Even so, North Carolina's one-party system operated in a distinctly different milieu from that of many other southern states. The continued existence of a minority party, ineffective as it was, brought a degree of discipline and coherence to state politics. Important also was the diversified nature of the economy, which fostered the emergence of a variety of interest groups, including organized shippers, the Farmers' Union, and social welfare elements. A vigorous group of progressives arose in the Democratic party, seeking political power and forcing concessions from the regulars who usually managed to control the party. The reformism of the Wilson administration also contributed to progressive successes in North Carolina, though the Simmons faction found it possible to embrace the New Freedom without jeopardizing its control.[29] Ultimately, Tarheel progressivism was shaped by the support of shifting coalitions that changed with different issues and circumstances, by the rough consensus on popular reforms that developed among political leaders, and by the state's basic conservatism.

None of the southern states was more diversified than Tennessee, whose narrow territory stretched more than five hundred miles from the mountain town of Bristol in the extreme northeast to the Delta city of Memphis on the Mississippi River. The state was marked off into three grand divisions that were set apart from each other by distinctive geographical, cultural, and political characteristics. East Tennessee, a land of mountains, plateaus, and valleys, had not been suitable for slavery and the plantation system. An area of small farms and increasing industrialization in the late nineteenth century, it had opposed secession, supported the Union, and become Republican in its politics. The western division, lying between the Tennessee River and the Mississippi, was the center of the state's cotton production and heaviest concentration of blacks. Although it contained the largest city in the state, West Tennessee was the most rural of the three divisions. It had been ardent in its support of secession and war, and was strongly wedded to the Democratic party. Middle Tennessee was

---

[28]See Steelman, "The Progressive Era in North Carolina," 280–358.

[29]See, for example, Joseph F. Steelman, "Origins of the Campaign for Constitutional Reform in North Carolina, 1912–1913," *N.C. Hist. Rev.* 56 (Oct. 1979): 396–418.

comprised of the highland rim and the central basin, a region that extended from the Cumberland Plateau in the east to the Tennessee River in the west. It was dominated by Nashville and the fertile bluegrass basin in which the capital city was located. Middle Tennessee had also shared in the antebellum plantation system, but its economy was more varied than that of West Tennessee. It had supported the Confederacy, however, and had become strongly Democratic in politics.[30]

The Republican party was an institution of greater consequence in Tennessee than in any of the other ex-Confederate states. Although the party was strong in a few counties along the highland rim of West Tennessee, most of the state's Republicans were located in the east, where antisecessionist and Unionist attitudes had spawned a strong devotion to the party of Lincoln. Indeed, the Republican party controlled a majority of the county governments and usually won two congressional districts in the eastern division. But the party was sometimes weakened by vexatious internal strife over federal patronage and control of the state organization. Democratic strength in middle and western Tennessee gradually undermined Republicanism as a competitive force in statewide elections after Reconstruction, and despite the minority party's strong showing in the gubernatorial election of 1894, when it may well have received a plurality of the votes, the GOP was seldom able thereafter to meet the Democrats on equal terms.[31] The Republican party in Tennessee, as in other states of the Upper South, remained a potential threat to the dominant party; but in determining the affairs of state government and in deciding the outcome of presidential elections, one-partyism had become the rule.

Despite the fact that by the turn of the century the race question was no longer a salient issue in statewide campaigns, the Republican party still suffered by being identified with Reconstruction and black participation in politics. As one historian has observed of the 1890s, "The state's strong Republican party was a convenient and familiar symbol for convincing voters that political disruption would bring social upheaval and Negro rule."[32] The operation of the poll tax, the registration laws, and the Democratically controlled election system also hurt the Republicans and diminished voter participation in general.[33] The

---

[30]Frank Bird Ward, "The Industrial Development of Tennessee," *Annals* 153 (Jan. 1931): 141–47.

[31]McKinney, *Southern Mountain Republicans*, 31–41, 63–64, 77–86, 132–37, 140, 143–50, 184–86, 197–98, 200; Gordon B. McKinney, "Farewell to the Bloody Shirt: The Decline of the Houk Machine," *East Tennessee Historical Society's Publications* 46 (1974): 94–107; Verton M. Queener, "The East Tennessee Republicans in State and Nation, 1870–1900," *Tennessee Historical Quarterly* 2 (June 1943): 99–128; Queener, "The East Tennessee Republican Party, 1900–1914," *East Tenn. Hist. Society's Pubs.* 22 (1950): 94–127.

[32]Roger L. Hart, *Redeemers, Bourbons, & Populists: Tennessee, 1870–1896* (Baton Rouge, 1975), 223.

[33]The largest vote in the five gubernatorial elections between 1906 and 1914 was 256,475 ballots—46 percent of the voting age males—in 1910. Joe Michael Shahan, "Reform and Politics in Tennessee: 1906–1914" (Ph.D. diss., Vanderbilt Univ., 1981), 22–23.

Democratic party had also contained the Populist challenge in the 1890s. Although Democratic leaders were confronted by a mass movement of Tennessee farmers, the rebellion was not very fruitful, either in the form of the Farmers' Alliance or the People's party. After 1896 the Democrats were once again in firm control.[34]

The relative weakness of agrarian radicalism in Tennessee no doubt reflected the pervasive enthusiasm and yearning for industrial development among the state's inhabitants. While Tennessee continued to be predominantly agricultural and rural, its urban-industrial progress was rapid in the late nineteenth century. Railroads and other business concerns exerted great influence in affairs of state, through both political parties. An industrial, New South element in the Tennessee Democracy had frequently clashed with the party's Bourbon leadership, which disdained the New South creed and remained loyal to a Jeffersonian philosophy and to Old South traditions. The New South Democrats, according to one study of late nineteenth-century Tennessee politics, encouraged economic modernization and the social changes that would come with it. They championed purification of society through businessmen's government, prohibition, and immigration restriction.[35]

Thus there were divisions among Tennessee Democrats in the late nineteenth century. Such issues as free silver, railroad regulation, and the direct primary split the party's ranks, though in a vague fashion. Yet "liberal" and "conservative" factions of the sort that developed in Virginia and some other states did not emerge in a clear-cut way in Tennessee during the early years of the new century. Instead, the Democrats entered a period of political calm, led by a series of traditional governors and having little to fear from either the Republicans or dissidents in their own party.

This harmonious scene began to change in 1905. The sudden death of Senator William B. Bate in March 1905 and the manner in which his successor was chosen precipitated a burst of factional maneuvering in the Democratic party, and the conflicts growing out of this situation were exacerbated by the party nominations of 1906. Two years later Edward Ward Carmack, a former senator who had been defeated in his bid for renomination in 1906, and Governor Malcolm R. Patterson engaged in a fierce struggle for the Democratic gubernatorial nomination. Carmack was defeated and a few months later was killed on the streets of Nashville by one of Governor Patterson's friends. These events divided the state's Democrats into two hostile camps. Since Patterson and his followers controlled the governorship and the party machinery, many of the Carmack partisans, calling themselves independent Democrats, refused to participate in regular party affairs and endorsed the Republican candidate for governor in 1910. He was elected and managed to win reelection two years later

---

[34]Hart, *Redeemers, Bourbons, & Populists*, 107–223. See also Daniel Merritt Robison, *Bob Taylor and the Agrarian Revolt in Tennessee* (Chapel Hill, N.C., 1935).
[35]Hart, *Redeemers, Bourbons, & Populists*, pp. xv, 56, 222–25, 232.

with the support of the independent Democrats. By 1914 this period of schism in the majority party was about over, and in that year a reunited and chastened Democratic party came back into control of the state government.[36]

Independent and regular Democrats sometimes disagreed over such matters as "machine rule," the need for a primary election law, and the nomination of Woodrow Wilson for president in 1912. But the most telling issue in separating independents and regulars and the one that served as a catalytic agent in creating the factional alignment of Tennessee Democrats for a decade after 1905 was the prohibition of alcoholic beverages. Long an issue in Tennessee politics, prohibition became increasingly divisive after 1903. The question of statewide prohibition was the major point of difference between Carmack and Patterson in their violent contest of 1908, and according to a Methodist journal published in Nashville, by that time the state was "in the grip of a machine which proposes to give no quarter to temperance sentiment."[37] Carmack's death made him a martyr to "the holy cause of prohibition," and in 1909 the legislature passed a statewide prohibition bill over Governor Patterson's veto. The issue was far from dead, however, and the difficulty of enforcement added fuel to the fires of party disagreement and bitterness. The whole problem continued to dominate Tennessee politics until the election of 1914 finally persuaded the regular Democrats to accept prohibition and to nominate a genuine "dry" candidate for governor.[38]

The most prominent progressive to come out of this period of political turmoil in Tennessee was not a Democrat but a Republican—Ben W. Hooper. An East Tennessee lawyer and a vigorous opponent of the "whiskey evil," Hooper led a movement that possessed some of the aspects of a religious crusade. The exigencies involved in heading an administration based on the fusion of independent Democrats and Republicans would have tried the patience and capacity of even the most gifted leader, and the Republican governor was not always master of the situation. The situation was further complicated by the role of Mayor Edward H. Crump of Memphis, whose organization made him a formidable protagonist in Democratic politics and state government.[39] The legislative sessions of 1911 and 1913 were attended by bitter strife, and in the latter year the governor was forced to call two extra sessions before getting the legislators to approve the principal features of his program. Hooper's inflexible determination to enforce the prohibition laws weakened the force of his

[36]Will Dunn Smith, "The Carmack-Patterson Campaign and Its Aftermath in Tennessee Politics" (M.A. thesis, Vanderbilt Univ., 1939); Paul E. Isaac, *Prohibition and Politics: Turbulent Decades in Tennessee, 1885–1920* (Knoxville, 1965); Arthur S. Link, "Democratic Politics and the Presidential Campaign of 1912 in Tennessee," *East Tenn. Hist. Society's Pubs.* 18 (1946): 107–30.

[37]*Christian Advocate*, quoted in Isaac, *Prohibition and Politics*, 154.

[38]See Isaac, *Prohibition and Politics*, 81–261, for a good account of the role of prohibition in Tennessee politics during the progressive era.

[39]See William D. Miller, *Mr. Crump of Memphis* (Baton Rouge, 1964), 106–15.

broader reformism, and his efforts to perpetuate the fusion movement proved unavailing in the face of traditional partisanship. Nevertheless, Hooper's administration introduced some significant changes in public policy and forced the regular Democrats to adopt a more liberal position on many issues.[40]

Tennessee progressives, according to a recent history of their activities, sought to adapt their society to the changing circumstances of twentieth-century life by embracing the concept of state intervention in behalf of the public welfare. They closed the saloons, laid the foundation for a modern system of public education, expanded and strengthened public health laws, began to protect the rights of labor, and endeavored to make business more responsive to the public's needs. They also wanted to make state government more efficient and the electoral system fairer.[41] The most productive period of progressive legislation began in 1907. During the Patterson administration, 1907–11, the general assembly created a state board of elections, a state reformatory for boys, and a state highway commission; enacted a general election law, a pure food and drug act, and a comprehensive education statute; adopted statewide prohibition; and passed legislation to regulate the labor of women and children. The Hooper administration extended many of these reforms and pioneered in the introduction of others.

The intense controversy surrounding the prohibition issue and the disruption of the Democratic party in Tennessee make it difficult to relate the social reformism of this period to political and factional divisions in the state. There was, in fact, increasing support for "reform" from both parties and from various segments of the Democratic party after 1905. Thus Malcolm Patterson, a "regular" Democrat, was identified with the success of several progressive measures during his governorship. While lacking a militant antirailroad campaign like that of Alabama and North Carolina, Tennesseans were nonetheless quite responsive to "the rhetoric of reform."[42] Although the state's progressivism was indelibly marked by prohibition and political confusion, it embodied the essential ideas and objectives of most southern reformers, including the demand for public services whose approval was promoted by organized interest groups and social reform elements.

Kentucky, one writer has observed, "waited until the war was over to secede

[40]See *The Unwanted Boy: The Autobiography of Governor Ben W. Hooper*, ed. Everett Robert Boyce (Knoxville, 1963); Russell L. Stockard, "The Election and First Administration of Ben W. Hooper as Governor of Tennessee," *East Tenn. Hist. Society's Pubs.* 26 (1954): 38–59; Stockard, "The Election and Second Administration of Governor Ben W. Hooper of Tennessee as Reflected in the State Press," ibid. 32 (1960): 51–71; and Paul E. Isaac, "The Problems of a Republican Governor in a Southern State: Ben Hooper of Tennessee, 1910–1914," *Tenn. Hist. Quar.* 27 (Fall 1968): 229–48.

[41]Shahan, "Reform and Politics in Tennessee," 382–83. For the progressive record in Tennessee, see ibid., passim, and James A. Hodges, "Meliorative Legislation in Tennessee, 1900–1920," unpublished paper dated Apr. 1957, in possession of its author.

[42]J.M. Shahan, "The Rhetoric of Reform: The 1906 Gubernatorial Race in Tennessee," *Tenn. Hist. Quar.* 35 (Spring 1976): 65–82.

from the Union."[43] There was considerable truth in this hyperhole. The Democrats swept the elections of 1866 and for a generation Kentucky was virtually a one-party state. Though more southern than northern, it was a border state. Its subdivisions were similar to those of Tennessee: the mountains in the east, the Bluegrass region in the middle, and the generally flat farming area of the west. After the Civil War, many of the former Whig slaveholders, who were mostly located in the Bluegrass country, moved into the Democratic party, where they joined with the small farmers of western Kentucky to give their party a dominant position in state politics.

The conservative leadership of the Democratic party also reflected the political leverage of the rapidly growing industrialists in Kentucky. This New South element made the party solicitous of the railroad, coal, liquor, and racetrack interests, and the business community had few political complaints until the agrarian upheaval of the 1890s threatened the control of the Bourbon dynasty. When the Democratic party in Kentucky embraced free silver and William Jennings Bryan, the business interests, including the powerful Louisville and Nashville Railroad, began to support the Republicans. The severity of the depression of the nineties, the appeal of the nativist and anti-Catholic American Protective Association, and the increasing disunity within the Democratic party enabled the Republicans in 1895 to elect a governor for the first time in Kentucky history and to carry the state for William McKinley in 1896.[44] So acrimonious was the conflict among the Democrats that it can be argued that Kentucky had become a three-party state—with two fiercely competing Democratic factions and the Republicans.[45]

Beginning in 1895, the Republican party in Kentucky became a serious competitor of the Democrats, always ready to take advantage of the majority party's factionalism. Kentucky Republicanism was strongest in the east, where the Whig party and Unionist sympathies had centered. The state's blacks, who comprised about 13 percent of the population in 1900, were also staunch Republicans, and in Kentucky they were not disfranchised. In the late nineteenth century, moreover, the GOP was attracting more support in the growing urban areas. Although Republicans controlled many of the local governments in the eastern part of the state, they were unable to dominate the legislature at any time during the progressive era. But the Republican party apparently won the governorship in the hotly contested election of 1899, and its gubernatorial candidates

[43] E. Merton Coulter, quoted in Joseph Frazier Wall, *Henry Watterson: Reconstructed Rebel* (New York, 1956), 76.

[44] John Edward Wiltz, "The 1895 Election: A Watershed in Kentucky Politics," *Filson Club History Quarterly* 37 (Apr. 1963): 117–36; Thomas J. Brown, "The Roots of Bluegrass Insurgency: An Analysis of the Populist Movement in Kentucky," *Register of the Kentucky Historical Society* 78 (Summer 1980): 219–42.

[45] This theme is well developed in John H. Fenton, *Politics in the Border States: A Study of the Patterns of Political Organization, and Political Change, Common to the Border States—Maryland, West Virginia, Kentucky and Missouri* (New Orleans, 1957), 14–64.

were successful in 1907 and 1919. There were usually one or two Republican representatives and occasionally a senator from Kentucky in Congress during this period.[46]

If the conservative Democrats were challenged by the Republicans in the 1890s, they were also opposed by a coalescing group of dissident Democrats. The struggle that ensued was both ideological and organizational. It was a conflict between the conservative planters of the Bluegrass counties and their corporate allies in the cities, on the one hand, and the populistic western farmers and urban workers, on the other. The issues involved the money question, the regulation of corporations, and new election laws, but the immediate stake was control of the party. The first phase of this internecine strife culminated in 1900 with the assassination of William Goebel, a leader of the reform Democrats. Goebel was a lawyer from northern Kentucky, an experienced legislator, and a political organizer of rare skill. Tacturn and ruthless, this son of German immigrants appealed to small farmers and urban workers by promising to reorganize the Democratic party and by dealing harshly with such "trusts" as the L & N Railroad and the American Book Company. When Goebel managed to win the nomination for governor in the tense Democratic convention of 1899, a conservative element in the party bolted and nominated an independent candidate. In the hectic campaign that followed, the Republican candidate, William S. Taylor, won a narrow plurality and was inaugurated as governor, despite charges of fraud by the Goebelites and their efforts to contest the election result. Early in 1900 the reform Democrats turned to the legislature, which they controlled, and moved to unseat the Republican governor under a controversial election law Goebel had engineered in 1898. Before they could complete this maneuver, their leader was fatally wounded on the capitol grounds by an unknown assailant. He died five days later, having been sworn in as governor following the legislature's hasty decision to declare him the winner of the election of 1899.[47]

No other single event had a greater effect upon Kentucky politics during the progressive period. In the tumultuous aftermath of this spectacular incident, Goebel became a martyr in the eyes of many Kentuckians; his lieutenant governor, John C.W. Beckham, became chief executive; and a stringent law to regulate the state's railroads was quickly enacted.[48] But the bifactional groupings that emerged after 1900 were less distinct than they were at the height of Goebel's leadership. Beckham, who served as governor for almost eight years,

---

[46]For Kentucky Republicanism in the late nineteenth century, see McKinney, *Southern Mountain Republicans*, 50–56, 63, 91–96, 119, 125–26, 128–29, 140–41, 166–76, 186–88, 198–200.

[47]Thomas D. Clark, "The People, William Goebel, and the Kentucky Railroads," *JSH* 5 (Feb. 1939): 34–48; Nicholas C. Burckel, "William Goebel and the Campaign for Railroad Regulation in Kentucky, 1888–1900," *Filson Club Hist. Quar.* 48 (Jan. 1974): 43–60; James C. Klotter, *William Goebel: The Politics of Wrath* (Lexington, Ky., 1977).

[48]Klotter, *William Goebel*, 126–31; Burckel, "William Goebel and the Campaign for Railroad Regulation," 59–60.

soon made his peace with the Bluegrass conservatives and the business interests (the L & N supported him for reelection in 1903). Other politicians, such as J. Campbell Cantrill, Ollie M. James, and Augustus O. Stanley, were more representative of the agrarian radicalism in Goebel's program, and in general they carried forward much of the fallen leader's reformism. Beckham's administration and that of his Republican successor, Augustus E. Willson, were confronted by a tense and drawn-out crisis in the dark-leaf tobacco district of southwestern Kentucky. This so-called Black Patch War, though charged with antimonopoly resentment and organized activity, did little to clarify the confused currents of the state's politics or to advance progressive efforts.

Former governor James B. McCreary, a more reform-minded Democrat than Beckham, won the governorship in 1911. McCreary sponsored election reforms, more effective regulation of public utilities and corporations, a workmen's compensation law, and other liberal legislation. When he left office in 1915, one historian has concluded, he "had established the most progressive record of any chief executive in Kentucky up to that time."[49] McCreary was succeeded by Augustus Stanley, who had earlier become prominent as a spokesman for the dark-leaf tobacco farmers of Kentucky and Tennessee against the monopolistic practices of the American Tobacco Company. He had also spearheaded a well-publicized investigation of the United States Steel Corporation in 1911 and 1912.[50] Yet the anticorporation campaigns of agrarian leaders such as Stanley did not mean that the industrial and commerical interests were curbed in the Bluegrass State. In general, the conservative Democrats of the middle section and the Republicans in the eastern part of the state dominated Kentucky politics after 1900, just as the Bluegrass and western regions had combined to control public affairs before the crisis of the 1890s. The L & N continued to wield enormous influence in politics, conservative Democrats usually managed to control their party, and when they lost, the Republicans were waiting in the wings to take over. Other issues also arose to distract the reformers, most notably prohibition, which the Beckham faction tended to support.

Although the legislature added a strong railroad regulatory law to the statute books in 1900, Kentucky was not very successful in dealing with corporation excesses during the progressive years. Nor was it conspicuous in the passage of progressive legislation generally. William Goebel was a transitional figure in Kentucky politics, but no other political reformer of equal power followed him during this period. Even so, there were progressive tendencies in Kentucky, particularly among social reform leaders and organizations, and the state legislature did approve a direct primary system, greater controls over corporations,

[49]Nicholas C. Burckel, "From Beckham to McCreary: The Progressive Record of Kentucky Governors," *Reg. Ky. Hist. Soc.* 76 (Oct. 1978): 285–306; quotation on p. 305.

[50]Thomas W. Ramage, "Augustus Owsley Stanley: Early Twentieth Century Kentucky Democrat" (Ph.D. diss., Univ. of Kentucky, 1968).

modest labor and prison reforms, increased support for schools and highways, and a modicum of tax reform. Kentucky had, as a recent study suggests, "come a long way toward adopting progressive reforms."[51] But at the same time the diverse nature of the state's economy, the great power exerted by railroads and other business interests, and the shifting nature of Democratic factionalism probably served to limit progressivism. Like the other states of the Upper South, Kentucky differed significantly from the political patterns that characterized the Deep South and the Southwest.

[51]Burckel, "From Beckham to McCreary," 306.

Forms of State Politics in the Southwest

THE OTHER STATES of the early twentieth-century South lay west of the Mississippi River. While their individual distinctions and eccentricities were easily
discernible, they differed as a subregion from other parts of the South. For one
thing, agrarian radicalism continued to manifest itself in the Southwest, and
agricultural and labor groups exerted a good deal of influence in economic and
political affairs. The black man as a political issue was less important than in
the Lower South. The Republican party maintained a precarious existence,
though it was of much less consequence than in the Upper South. Although
three of the four states had joined the Confederacy (Oklahoma did not become
a state until 1907), the trans-Mississippi South blended its southernism with a
western outlook.

Arkansas was perhaps the least characteristic of the four-state group. At the
turn of the century it was an overwhelmingly rural and agricultural state. Its
largest city, Little Rock, contained only 65,000 people as late as 1920. The
state's frontier-like character was intensified by poor roads and inadequate
communications. Arkansas had already begun to acquire an image of poverty,
of slow economic development, of what one of its historians later referred to as
"recalcitrant backwardness and resistance to change."[1] It was divided, geo-
graphically and to some extent culturally, into two major sections. A line drawn
diagonally from the northeast to the southwest, passing through Little Rock in
the middle of the state, would separate the northern and western highlands from
the southern and eastern plains. One part of the state consisted of hills, mountains, and valleys, while the other was made up of delta, prairie, and flatlands.
One was the habitat of small farmers and mountaineers, the other of cotton
planters, black tenants, and rice growers. Despite the cleavage between the
highlanders and the residents of lowland areas, political sectionalism in Arkansas was less pronounced than in many other southern states.

[1] Lee A. Dew, " 'On a Slow Train Through Arkansaw'—The Negative Image of Arkansas in
the Early Twentieth Century," *Ark. Hist. Quar.* 39 (Summer 1980): 125–35. See also Foy
Lisenby, "A Survey of Arkansas's Image Problem," ibid. 30 (Spring 1971): 60–71.

TABLE 7. *The Southwest: Population Statistics*

	POPULATION IN 1900	% INCREASE 1890–1900	% INCREASE 1900–10	% WHITE 1900	% BLACK 1900	% FOREIGN-BORN, 1900
Ark.	1,311,564	16.3	20.0	72.0	28.0	1.1
La.	1,381,625	23.5	19.9	52.8	47.1	3.7
Okla.[1]	790,391	—	109.7	84.8	7.1	2.6
Tex.	3,048,710	36.4	27.8	79.6	20.4	5.8

[1]Includes Oklahoma and Indian territories; percentages of white, black, and foreign-born are averages.

SOURCES: *Twelfth Census of the United States*, vol. 1: *Population*, part 1, pp. cxiv, cxviii, 2–5; *Thirteenth Census of the United States*, vol. 1: *Population*, 32–33.

The Republican party was strong in several northwestern counties, but it offered no serious challenge to the majority party. Although the Republicans usually put up a slate of candidates for state offices and elected a handful of legislators, they seldom polled more than 25 or 30 percent of the total vote.[2] While Negroes made up 28 percent of the Arkansas population in 1900, they were largely eliminated from any part in politics by stringent election laws, the poll tax, the white primary, and Republican lily-whiteism.[3]

The course of Arkansas politics after the Civil War mirrored the familiar sequence of Reconstruction, Redemption, and Bourbon control. But by the mid-1890s, conservative Democrats were beginning to lose their hold on the state's politics. The opposition to their leadership came largely from within their own party. Although populism made little headway in Arkansas, the force of agrarian protest ran strongly in Democratic channels. The free-silver movement swept the state, William Jennings Bryan was immensely popular, primary elections were instituted, and a wave of antitrust sentiment began to manifest itself by the late nineties. Then, at the end of the century, a new and spectacular leader emerged to articulate the state's agrarianism and to shape its politics for more than a decade. "In the State of Arkansas, as it developed from 1875 to 1900," wrote one historian, "it was certain that, sooner or later, some local politician was bound to arise who would capture all the discontent aroused in the backwoods agrarians by the spectacle of the bargain struck between the Northern industrialists and the conservative Democrats. Such a man need have but a single idea, the idea that the Northern corporations were bleeding

[2]William Orestus Penrose, "Political Ideas in Arkansas, 1880–1907" (M.A. thesis, Univ. of Arkansas, 1945), 137–42; Marvin F. Russell, "The Rise of a Republican Leader: Harmon L. Remmel," *Ark. Hist. Quar.* 36 (Autumn 1977): 234–57; Willard B. Gatewood, Jr., "Theodore Roosevelt and Arkansas, 1901–1912," ibid. 32 (Spring 1973): 3–24.

[3]John William Graves, "Negro Disfranchisement in Arkansas," *Ark. Hist. Quar.* 26 (Autumn 1967): 199–225.

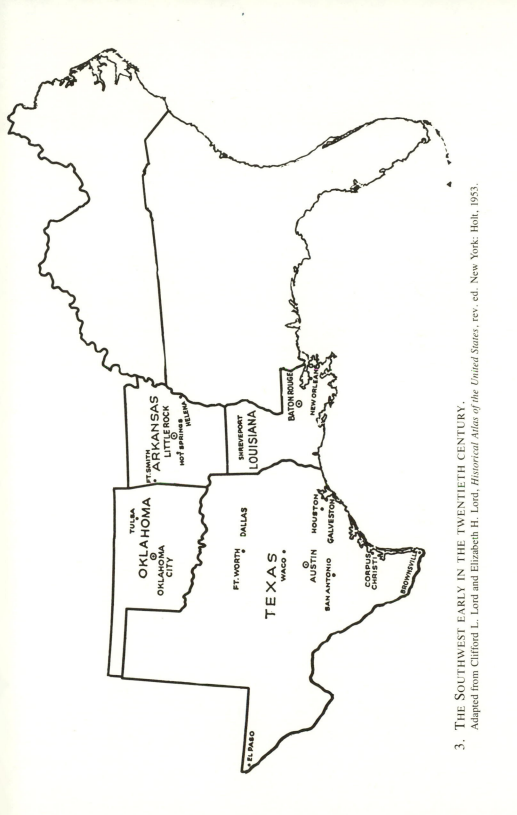

3. THE SOUTHWEST EARLY IN THE TWENTIETH CENTURY.
Adapted from Clifford L. Lord and Elizabeth H. Lord, *Historical Atlas of the United States*, rev. ed. New York: Holt, 1953.

Arkansas white and that the thing to do was to get rid of all corporations."[4]

Jeff Davis, a boyish-looking lawyer from Russellville, proved to be the man. He first achieved prominence as state attorney general, an office he was lucky enough to win in 1898. He also identified himself with the growing enthusiasm for a system of primary elections. Seizing upon a populistic antitrust law passed by the legislature soon after he took office, Davis created a sensation by launching a host of antimonopoly suits against insurance companies and other corporations. Although his antitrust campaign was frustrated in the courts, the young attorney general had found an issue that catapulted him into the governorship in 1900. He was twice reelected and in 1907 was elected to the United States Senate. In his campaigns, the fiery Davis pictured himself as a defender of "the people" against the machinations of "the trusts and the corporations." He spoke of being opposed by "every railroad, every bank, two-thirds of the lawyers, and most of the big politicians."[5] Thoroughly at home with the white dispossessed, he was, in the words of a contemporary writer, "surcharged with personal magnetism. He makes the people think he is persecuted for their sake, and stands between them and oppresssion."[6] No politician had ever aroused the Arkansas proletariat like this "Karl Marx for Hill Billies," for he "evoked a hierarchy of angels and demons in which there were no neuters." He set the "red necks" of the backwoods against the "high-collared crowd" of the city.[7] There was a strain of irreverence as well as an element of the comic and bucolic in his makeup (he habitually wore a frock coat and hat of Confederate gray and thereby heightened the effect of his celebrated name). His governorship, which found him frequently at odds with the general assembly (whose members tried to impeach him in 1903) and other state officials, produced few reforms. He eventually succeeded in getting the legislature to amend the antitrust law along the lines he recommended, but the prosecution of the corporations was largely abortive. And in the Senate the Arkansas leader quickly became an anachronism.[8]

[4] John Gould Fletcher, *Arkansas* (Chapel Hill, N.C., 1947), 286. For the persistence of Populist ideas in Arkansas, Louisiana, Texas, and Oklahoma, see James R. Green, *Grass-Roots Socialism: Radical Movements in the Southwest, 1895–1943* (Baton Rouge, 1978), 12–86.

[5] Charles Jacobson, *The Life Story of Jeff Davis: The Stormy Petrel of Arkansas Politics* (Little Rock, 1925), 60. Also see Paige E. Mulhollan, "The Issues of the Davis-Berry Senatorial Campaign in 1906," *Ark. Hist. Quar.* 20 (Summer 1961): 118–25.

[6] "The Gentleman from Arkansas," *Public Opinion* 40 (Apr. 21, 1906): 488.

[7] Rupert B. Vance, "A Karl Marx for Hill Billies: Portrait of a Southern Leader," *Social Forces* 9 (Dec. 1930): 180. Also see Richard L. Niswonger, "A Study in Southern Demagoguery: Jeff Davis of Arkansas," *Ark. Hist. Quar.* 39 (Summer 1980): 114–24.

[8] Nevin Neal, "Jeff Davis and the Reform Movement in Arkansas, 1898–1907" (M.A. thesis, Vanderbilt Univ., 1939); George James Stevenson, "The Political Career of Jeff Davis: An Example of the Southern Protest" (M.A. thesis, Univ. of Arkansas, 1949); Cal Ledbetter, Jr., "Jeff Davis and the Politics of Combat," *Ark. Hist. Quar.* 33 (Spring 1974): 16–37; David Y. Thomas, ed., *Arkansas and Its People: A History, 1541–1930*, vol. 1 (New York, 1930), pp. 267–78.

Although Davis and his friends dominated the party machinery during the early years of the century, they were unable to perpetuate their control. Such influential figures as Senator James P. Clarke and Representative Joseph T. Robinson were arrayed against Davis.[9] While the electorate tended for a time to divide itself into two camps on the basis of Davis's dramatic politics, it soon lapsed into an amorphous and shifting factionalism with little coherence or continuity. Nevertheless, the Russellville politician had done more than any other person to change the style of Arkansas politics. He broke the custom of organizing state campaigns around courthouse cliques and took his electioneering to the voters at the grass roots. Meanwhile, other Arkansas political leaders, more moderate and respectable than the irreverent Jeff, took up the reform banner. Governor George W. Donaghey (1909–13) identified his administration with a series of progressive measures: penal reform, establishment of a juvenile court, creation of a public health department, and expansion of public education.

Near the end of the progressive era a new face came to the fore. It was that of Charles H. Brough, a professor of economics and sociology at the University of Arkansas. Brough held a Ph.D. degree from Johns Hopkins, where he had taken some work with Woodrow Wilson. Before entering politics, he had become well known as an orator, Baptist layman, and genteel advocate of better race relations and other social reforms. In his campaign for governor in 1916, the professor took advantage of a widespread feeling that the political structure of the state was controlled by a few professional politicians. Brough's four years as governor resulted in a modest reform record somewhat like that of Richard I. Manning in South Carolina. Although Brough failed in his effort to secure the adoption of a new state constitution, he directed a major fiscal reorganization and a notable extension of state activities. His administration yielded a new election law, the reorganization of the railroad commission, a compulsory school attendance act, and the establishment of a variety of new boards and bureaus, including a board of charities and corrections and a commission on illiteracy.[10]

Arkansas progressivism was thoroughly consonant with the broader pattern of political and social reform in the South. Early in the period, to be sure, there was extravagant protest, a compelling new political leader, and a boisterous assault on railroads and insurance companies. But these economic interests—as

---

[9]See Emmett B. Fields, Jr., "The Senate Career of James P. Clarke of Arkansas, 1903–1916" (M.A. thesis, Vanderbilt Univ., 1949), and Stuart Towns, "Joseph T. Robinson and Arkansas Politics: 1912–1913," *Ark. Hist. Quar.* 24 (Winter 1965): 291–307.

[10]Charles Wann Crawford, "Charles H. Brough: Educator and Politician" (M.A. thesis, Univ. of Arkansas, 1957); Crawford, "From Classroom to State Capitol: Charles H. Brough and the Campaign of 1916," *Ark. Hist. Quar.* 21 (Autumn 1962): 213–30; Charles Orson Cook, "'The Glory of the Old South and the Greatness of the New': Reform and the Divided Mind of Charles Hillman Brough," ibid. 34 (Autumn 1975): 227–41; Calvin R. Ledbetter, Jr., "The Constitutional Convention of 1917–1918," ibid. 34 (Spring 1975): 3–40.

well as the lowland planters—remained strong in the state's politics. Arkansas voters were reluctant to jeopardize future opportunities for agricultural and industrial development, and most of their political leaders were sensitive to this ambivalence. There was, undeniably, a stream of agrarian radicalism in Arkansas politics; this was evident in Jeff Davis's campaigns and in the later adoption of the initiative and referendum in state government. This grass-roots democracy, however, was offset by a drastically restricted electorate after the mid-nineties, by the entrenched position of local elites, and by the basic conservatism of executive and legislative leaders in Little Rock. Thus, despite occasional breakthroughs such as the initiative and referendum, several labor-protection laws, and an increase in public services, the state's progressivism was both limited and mild.

Louisiana was another of the southwestern states. While sharing many characteristics of the Deep South, Louisiana differed in several respects from the states to the east. It produced two great cash crops, contained a large French and Catholic population, was the most urbanized state in the region, and had a powerful urban machine. New Orleans, its metropolis, was the biggest and most cosmopolitan city in the South. Much of the state was made up of river bottomlands, lakes, and swamps. Flowing south the Mississippi and Red rivers eventually joined to form a Y-shaped drainage basin. Most of the northern part of the state, except for the alluvial river bottoms, was comprised of hilly lands whose inferior soils were cultivated by poor white farmers and tenants. North Louisiana was cotton country, the most productive of which was the counterpart to Mississippi's Delta—a land of rich soil and many blacks. Another staple was produced in south Louisiana, in the flood plain between the Red River and the Gulf; this was sugar country, the scene of a capitalistic and large-scale planting economy. Late in the nineteenth century still another staple crop—rice—was successfully introduced to the prairies of southwestern Louisiana. Commercial lumbering was important in many parts of the Pelican State, and the production of petroleum became significant in the second decade of the new century. The pattern of the state's politics revealed three distinctive components: north Louisiana, south Louisiana (more precisely the triangular-shaped area from Lake Charles in the southwest to New Orleans in the east to Alexandria in the north), and Orleans Parish (with the city of New Orleans).[11]

The political divisions of north, south, and New Orleans reflected but did not coincide with a class cleavage that historically had separated the planter and the poor farmer.[12] At the turn of the century, economic disparities were greater

[11]Allen E. Begnand, "Louisiana," in Roller and Twyman, eds., *Encyclopedia of Southern History*, 733; Fred Kniffen, "The Physiognomy of Rural Louisiana," *Louisiana History* 4 (Fall 1963): 291–99.

[12]See Roger W. Shugg, *Origins of Class Struggle in Louisiana: A Social History of White Farmers and Laborers during Slavery and After, 1840–1875* (Baton Rouge, 1939), and Perry H. Howard, *Political Tendencies in Louisiana, 1812–1952* (Baton Rouge, 1957).

than ever. Louisiana had the highest illiteracy rate in the nation—almost 22 percent of the population ten years of age and over as late as 1920.[13] Although the conservative Democrats who ruled the state were plagued by sharp factional divisions, they carried out the wishes of the planters, the commercial and financial interests centered in New Orleans, and the railroad and lumber corporations. Resentment at this state of affairs fanned the fires of agrarian radicalism in the 1890s, but such evidence of class conflict was countered by the Bourbon Democrats' resort to an aroused racial animosity. Negroes constituted slightly more than 47 percent of the population in 1900. There was also a religious and cultural contrast—between the Creole-Catholic south and the Anglo-Protestant north—that cut across economic and social lines. Perhaps, as a noted scholar wrote in another connection, "the religious, linguistic, cultural division of the people itself made it difficult for a leader to arise who understood both groups, who constituted a common denominator capable of giving full-throated voice to the common unhappinesses and aspirations of both peoples in rip-roaring political campaigns—after which everyone could go back to work."[14]

The 1890's were a time of crisis for Louisiana's Bourbon Democrats. In the early nineties the party was disrupted by a fierce controversy over the question of rechartering the Louisiana State Lottery Company, a dominant factor in the state's politics.[15] The Populists, who joined with antilottery Democrats to defeat the recharter proposal, posed an even greater threat. The third party was strong in the hill parishes of north Louisiana, and in the state elections of 1894 and 1896 it undertook a fusion campaign with the Republicans, themselves a renewed threat to the majority party following a decade of steady decline. To make matters worse, the Wilson-Gorman Tariff Act of 1894 and the free-trade tendencies of the Cleveland administration caused some Democrats from the sugar parishes to abandon the Democratic party in favor of William McKinley's Republicanism. The regular Louisiana Democrats managed to win both the state and national elections in 1896, but they were forced to make some concessions to their opponents. They moved swiftly to prevent a recurrence of the Populist-Republican challenge. The weapon they employed was disfranchisement. As Governor Murphy J. Foster warned in 1894, it was imperative that "the mass of ignorance, vice and venality without any proprietary interest

---

[13] T. Lynn Smith and Homer L. Hitt, *The People of Louisiana* (Baton Rouge, 1952), 88–89.

[14] V. O. Key, Jr., with the assistance of Alexander Heard, *Southern Politics in State and Nation* (New York, 1949), 160. Another scholar has found that in a majority of the gubernatorial contests between 1879 and 1924, New Orleans working-class voters and north Louisiana planters and small farmers were aligned against south Louisiana voters in predominantly Catholic parishes. See Matthew J. Schott, "Class Conflict in Louisiana Voting Since 1877: Some New Perspectives," *La. Hist.* 12 (Spring 1971): 149–65.

[15] For evidence of the lottery's pivotal role in Louisiana politics, see Sidney James Romero, Jr., "The Political Career of Murphy James Foster, Governor of Louisiana, 1892–1900," *Louisiana Historical Quarterly* 28 (Oct. 1945): 1140–60, and T. Harry Williams, *P.G.T. Beauregard: Napoleon in Gray* (Baton Rouge, 1955), 292–303.

in the State" be deprived of the ballot.[16] A new election law enacted in 1896 and constitutional disfranchisement carried out in 1898 did the trick. Black registration dropped from 130,344 before the new suffrage changes went into effect to 5,320 in 1900. White registration also shrank, though much less drastically.[17] The dispirited Populists melted away, while the Republicans quickly lost the statewide strength they had acquired in the mid-1890s. Louisiana Republicanism was also enervated by a lily-white movement, led by sugar producers and New Orleans businessmen, that opposed control of the party by professional politicians.

Although the People's party soon died out and most of its members returned to Democratic ranks, populism left its mark on the majority party. By the end of the century the Democrats had pledged themselves to such reforms as free silver and the direct election of United States senators, abolished the convict-lease system and established a railroad commission, and adopted the Australian secret ballot and other election reforms. Disfranchisement and the introduction of the statewide primary, moreover, altered the relative voting strength in favor of New Orleans and the white upland parishes, at the expense of the alluvial planters, who were no longer able to dominate party nominations and statewide elections.[18] Yet, unlike its immediate neightbors to the north and east, Louisiana failed during the progressive era to produce a powerful champion of the poor whites and rednecks in the manner of Jeff Davis or James K. Vardaman.

One reason for this failure was the prominent role of New Orleans in the state's politics. The city had a population of almost 300,000 people in 1900, and Orleans Parish normally accounted for nearly one-fourth of the electorate and representation in the general assembly. Political affairs in the city were dominated by the Choctaw Club, an organization directed by ward leaders. The Choctaws, who controlled New Orleans from 1900 to 1920, were led by Martin Behrman, a traditional political boss and mayor for almost two decades after 1904. Behrman and his colleagues ran a disciplined machine and one that got out the immigrant and lower-class vote, worked closely with financial and corporate interests, and assumed a "let live" attitude toward gambling, drinking, and prostitution. While the Behrman machine became a consistent obstacle to labor legislation and the effective regulation of business, it combined an element of progressivism with machine politics. Behrman was responsive to

---

[16]Quoted in William Ivy Hair, *Bourbonism and Agrarian Protest: Louisiana Politics, 1877–1900* (Baton Rouge, 1969), 234.

[17]Paul L. Haworth, "Negro Disfranchisement in Louisiana," *Outlook* 71 (May 17, 1902): 163; Hair, *Bourbonism and Agrarian Protest*, 268–79; William Alexander Mabry, "Louisiana Politics and the 'Grandfather Clause,' " *N.C. Hist. Rev.* 13 (Oct. 1936): 290–310.

[18]Henry C. Dethloff, "Populism and Reform in Louisiana" (Ph.D. diss., Univ. of Missouri, 1964), 28–29, 284, 320, 322, 344–45; Dethloff, "The Longs: Revolution or Populist Retrenchment?" *La. Hist.* 19 (Fall 1978): 401–12; Lucia Elizabeth Daniel, "The Louisiana People's Party," *La. Hist. Quar.* 26 (Oct. 1943): 1055–1149.

many of the demands for civil improvement, and there was a constructive side to his record. Since parish and municipal governments were limited in their functions by the state constitution, the Choctaws were compelled to keep the peace with the governor and to prevent the rural factions from uniting against them. The part played by the New Orleans organization in statewide elections, in the distribution of patronage, and in the enactment of legislation made it a potent force in Louisiana politics. The Choctaws pulled Democratic factionalism in the direction of bifactional groupings and contributed a degree of coherence and stability to the state's politics.[19]

There was a rural-urban conflict in Louisiana, and the rural elements, particularly in the northern section of the state, feared and distrusted the economic and political power of New Orleans. But the most telling opposition to the Choctaws came not from the rural parishes but from within the city itself. A group of urban reformers had opposed the old machine that controlled the city before the Choctaws appeared in the late 1890s. Led by well-to-do businessmen, these reformers in the eighties and nineties worked against the corruption typified by the state lottery, advocated such political changes as the Australian ballot, fused with the Populists to fight the Democratic machine, and won a new city charter and the mayor's office in 1896. The city reformers also contributed to the leadership of the Gold Democrats in the campaign of that year. Like the Populists and other agrarian rebels, they had a part in liberalizing the Democratic party in the 1890s. A historian of Louisiana progressivism has noted that these urban reformers "held themselves apart as a better element in the community." Moralistic and self-righteous, "they equated good government primarily with the virtues of honesty and efficiency expressed in terms of a mixture of patrician and capitalistic values."[20]

The reformers' hopes for a civic transformation in New Orleans proved illusory in the nineties, and they were unable to offer a serious challenge to the Choctaws during the first decade of the twentieth century. But in 1910, John M. Parker, a prominent planter and New Orleans cotton factor, took the lead in organizing the Good Government League, which was instrumental in securing a commission form of government for the Crescent City. While the league helped elect a reform governor in 1912, it was unsuccessful in its effort to defeat Mayor Behrman in his campaign for reelection that year. Despite their elitism and their distrust of popular democracy, the New Orleans reformers were champions of electoral improvement, more efficient government, and purification of the city's politics. The comprehensive reform program advocated by the

---

[19]George M. Reynolds, *Machine Politics in New Orleans, 1897–1926* (New York, 1936); Robert Webb Williams, Jr., "Martin Behrman, Mayor and Political Boss of New Orleans, 1904–1926" (M.A. thesis, Tulane Univ., 1952); Allan P. Sindler, *Huey Long's Louisiana: State Politics, 1920–1952* (Baltimore, 1956), 21–25.

[20]Matthew J. Schott, "Progressives Against Democracy: Electoral Reform in Louisiana, 1894–1921," *La. Hist.* 20 (Summer 1979), 258. See also Dethloff, "Populism and Reform in Louisiana," 286, 360–61.

Good Government League had an important bearing on Louisiana's progressivism, and the conflict between the Choctaws and their upper-class critics was a salient theme in the state's politics for more than a decade after 1910. The climax of this urban progressivism came in 1920, when John M. Parker was elected governor and Martin Behrman was defeated in this effort to win a fifth term as mayor.[21]

Progressivism in Louisiana generally found expression in the Democratic party. Despite the sectional, class, and cultural divisions that set Louisianians apart from each other, Democratic leaders managed to retain the allegiance of most voters. A flare-up of radicalism among some of the old Populists and lumber workers in the hill region led to a Socialist vote of over 5,000 in the election of 1912, but this rustic rebellion soon subsided.[22] In the same year, John M. Parker launched a more significant assault on the Democrats by organizing the Progressive party in Louisiana as a part of Theodore Roosevelt's new third party. Parker ran for governor on the Progressive ticket in 1916, polling 37 percent of the total vote and carrying sixteen parishes.[23] As for the Democrats, most of the governors before Parker's election in 1920 were conservatives. Only one of them, Luther E. Hall in 1912, ran without the endorsement of the New Orleans Choctaws. And Hall disappointed the urban reformers by cooperating with Behrman and agreeing to water down his progressive program. The Parker administration came to power with the truest progressive credentials (Parker had returned to the Democratic party by this time), but its accomplishments were limited by intraparty squabbles, the emergence of the Ku Klux Klan as an issue in Louisiana politics, and the governor's ineffectiveness as a reform leader.[24]

Even so, a surprising amount of progressive legislation emerged from Baton Rouge during the first two decades of the century. A primary election law, a permanent registration statute, a corrupt-practices act, short ballot and anti-lobbying legislation, and a recall law were passed by the legislators. They also passed pure food and drug, child labor, workmen's compensation, and mechanic lien laws. They established a state board of charities and corrections, a department of forestry, a board of tax equalization, and a public utilities commission. They adopted a compulsory school attendance law, a series of

[21]See Matthew James Schott, "John M. Parker of Louisiana and the Varieties of American Progressivism" (Ph.D. diss., Vanderbilt Univ., 1969), and Howard, *Political Tendencies in Louisiana*, 107–23.

[22]Grady McWhiney, "Louisiana Socialists in the Early Twentieth Century: A Study of Rustic Radicalism," *JSH* 20 (Aug. 1954): 315–36.

[23]In 1916 the Progressives elected a congressman, 13 state representatives, and 5 state senators. See Matthew J. Schott, "John M. Parker of Louisiana and the Bull Moose Progressive Party in State and Nation" (M.A. thesis, Tulane Univ., 1960). For the Progressive party in the South, see Paul D. Casdorph, *Republicans, Negroes, and Progressives in the South, 1912–1916* (University, Ala., 1981).

[24]See Schott, "John M. Parker and the Varieties of American Progressivism," 350–495, for a more favorable appraisal of Parker's governorship.

antimonopoly acts, several conservation measures, and legislation permitting parishes and municipalities to establish commission government.[25] There was an urban flavor to much of this legislation, which derived from the influence of New Orleans reform organizations and professional groups as well as the machine that dominated the city's politics. This influence, along with an evolving political consensus on the necessity for a minimal reform program, goes far to explain the moderate and respectable character of Louisiana progressivism.

Texas had been a Confederate state, was dominated by the Democratic party, and had a substantial black population (about 20 percent in 1900). It was clearly a part of the South, but the Lone Star State was also characterized by a western outlook that set it apart from its neighbors to the east. This orientation was encouraged by the rapid development of the western part of the state, a vast region of treeless and semiarid plains and plateaus that contrasted sharply with the plantation and timbered areas of East Texas. Although it was still overwhelmingly agricultural and cotton remained its most valuable product, Texas had a more diversified economy than most other southern states, and the pace of its industrialization was noticeably quickening. The spectacular oil discovery at Spindletop early in 1901 opened the petroleum era in the Southwest and broadened the base of the state's economy still further.[26] Despite the considerable concentration of blacks in East Texas, the race question did not as a rule assume great importance in state politics. The population, moreover, was somewhat more heterogeneous than that of the average southern state. In a dozen or more counties south of Austin, nineteenth-century German immigrants gave a distinct cast to one part of Texas. Farther south, along the Rio Grande, a large number of Mexican-Americans provided another ethnic variation. Ethnic-religious voting blocs were formed by persons of German Lutheran and Catholic ancestry and of Mexican Catholic background.[27] The state's remarkable growth in the late nineteenth century and its vision of future economic development inevitably influenced its politics. Texas, one writer observed in 1906, "is all alive and awhir with a buoyant business progressiveness." Yet this observer was also struck by the force of tradition among Texans; from their conversation one might think that "the massacre of the Alamo

---

[25]In 1898, Louisiana had 44 state departments and boards. The number increased to 57 in 1912 and to 94 in 1924. State expenditures increased from $7,355,785 in 1912 to $21,223,477 in 1923. See Matthew J. Schott, "Progressivism in Pre-Long Louisiana: An Introduction," unpublished paper, dated May 10, 1966, in my possession.

[26]Fred Rathjen, "The Physiography of the Texas Panhandle," *Southwestern Historical Quarterly* 64 (Jan. 1961): 315–32; B.P. Gallaway, "Population Trends in the Western Cross Timbers of Texas, 1890–1960: Growth and Distribution," ibid. 65 (Jan. 1962): 333–47; Edwin L. Caldwell, "Highlights of the Development of Manufacturing in Texas, 1900–1960," ibid. 68 (Apr. 1965): 405–31; "The Growth of Southwest Texas," *American Monthly Review of Reviews* 33 (Feb. 1906): 206–11.

[27]Alwyn Barr, *Reconstruction to Reform: Texas Politics, 1876–1906* (Austin, Tex., 1971), 250.

happened last month, that the Mexican War occurred last week, and that the Civil War was a tragedy of yesterday."[28]

The Texas economy may have been more diversified than that of other southern states, but it was scarcely less colonial in nature. The foreign capital that nourished the corporate exploitation of railroad transportation, lumber, mining, and, after 1901, oil, when coupled with the depressed conditions among farmers, helps to explain the agrarian rebellion that swept over the state in the 1890s. Texas, the original home of the Farmers' Alliance and the scene of a robust Populist movement, produced one of the most notable political leaders of the period in the person of James Stephen Hogg. A popular campaigner with a pronounced anticorporation bias, Hogg was elected governor in 1890, the same year that Benjamin R. Tillman came to power in South Carolina. Hogg managed to steer a middle course between the Populists and the conservative Democrats who preceded him as party leaders. During his four-year administration a railroad commission was created and legislation was enacted to prevent the establishment of landholding companies, the watering of railroad securities, and the indiscriminate issuance of municipal securities. Hogg, a "reform Democrat" but no agrarian radical, was a forerunner of the early twentieth-century Texas progressives, many of whom served their political apprenticeship in his campaigns. He built up a sturdy political organization, and his forceful leadership momentarily compelled the state's Democrats to divide into Hogg and anti-Hogg factions.[29]

The legacy of James S. Hogg's politics was an important element in the eventual revival of political and social reform in Texas. But there were also other factors involved in the resumption and broadening of the state's reformism. Populism, for one thing, contributed to the liberalization of Texas politics during the progressive years, first by forcing the Hogg Democrats to move to the left and subsequently by providing part of the reform program and leadership. Nor did the farmers' movement disappear after 1900. A new organization—the Farmers' Union—was formed in 1902, and it soon became a vehicle for the promotion of innovative public policies. Agricultural distress and dissatisfaction continued, however, as was evident in the mounting rate of farm tenancy (over 50 percent by 1910) and the appearance of a radical organization in 1911 called the Land Renters' Union of North America. Organized labor was also becoming more influential in the state, and for a time agricultural and labor organizations were able to work together in the interest of common political objectives.[30] Meanwhile, support for greater use of state power came

---

[28] M.G. Cunniff, "Texas and the Texans," *World's Work* 11 (Mar. 1906): 7269–70.

[29] Robert C. Cotner, *James Stephen Hogg: A Biography* (Austin, Tex., 1959); Lawrence Goodwyn, *Democratic Promise: The Populist Moment in America* (New York, 1976), 25–94, 211–21, 234–38, 328–33, 463–69, 477–79, 508–10, 651–52n.

[30] See, for example, James R. Green, "Tenant Farmer Discontent and Socialist Protest in Texas, 1901–1917," *Southwestern Hist. Quar.* 81 (Oct. 1977): 133–54.

with telling effect from professional groups and organized businessmen whose numbers and influence grew with the economic development and urbanization of Texas.

How to handle corporate wealth and how to restrain the power of the railroads, lumber companies, and oil corporations became the central public issue in Texas during the first decade of the new century. Indeed, the debate over governmental policy toward business and industry raged almost continuously from 1890 to 1918. The problem was exacerbated by the pervasive yearning for economic growth, on the one hand, and the colonial character of capital investment and the enormous influence of the corporations, on the other. "The impression is going abroad everywhere," former governor Hogg declared in 1903, "that by means of free passes and other doubtful favors, the Texas Legislature has been subordinated to the will of the corporations. It is commonly asserted here upon the streets [of Austin] and in every section that whatever the corporations want now they can get done by the Legislature."[31] The focus of the antimonopoly movement after 1900 shifted from the railroads to the oil companies, and during the decade following 1905 a large number of these concerns and other corporations were prosecuted under the state's antitrust law. Somewhat related to the corporation issue was the controversial leadership of Joseph Weldon Bailey, a United States representative and senator from 1891 to 1913 and, after Hogg's retirement from politics, the most prominent politician in Texas. Bailey was employed by some of the large corporations and became identified in the public mind with the Waters-Pierce Company, an affiliate of the Standard Oil Company, in its unsuccessful efforts to avoid being driven from Texas. Despite the notoriety this case brought him, the senator managed to win reelection in 1906. But by that time "Baileyism" had become a fiery issue in Texas politics, one that divided Democrats for the remainder of the progressive era. Another important issue was prohibition, which soon rivaled Baileyism as the central political problem before Texans. The question presented itself in one form or another as a major concern in every state election and legislative session between 1908 and 1918.[32]

Although the political order was thoroughly shaken by the agrarian revolt, the tensions in Texas politics subsided in the late 1890s. The People's party withered away, the war with Spain brought an exhilarating display of patriotism, and the upturn of farm commodity prices heightened the promise of good times in the future. Though still somewhat divided, the Democratic party in Texas reigned supreme. The Democrats' flexible party organization, understanding of the state's varied economic and cultural interests, and willingness to

[31] Robert C. Cotner, ed., *Addresses and State Papers of James Stephen Hogg* (Austin, Tex., 1951), 511.

[32] Sam Hanna Acheson, *Joe Bailey: The Last Democrat* (New York, 1932); Seth Shepard McKay, *Texas Politics, 1906–1944, With Special Reference to the German Counties* (Lubbock, Tex., 1952), 20–101.

provide at least a measure of state and federal action helped them retain the loyalty of a majority of the Texas voters. The Republicans could offer little resistance. While they usually put up a ticket for state offices, they made no real effort to win such elections. The long-time division between the "lily white" and the "black and tan" factions continued, along with the distribution of federal patronage, to preoccupy party leaders.[33] There were also other hindrances. Republicans and potential third-party campaigns suffered a severe blow in the "reform" of the Texas electorate early in the twentieth century. The adoption of the poll tax as a prerequisite for voting, the institution of the white primary on a statewide basis, and the enactment of stringent new election laws served both to restrict the electorate and to allow the Democrats to make crucial election decisions in their primaries.[34] "The real purpose of the political leaders who supported the poll tax amendment and enactment of the Terrell election law," the Dallas *News* asserted in 1905, "was to disfranchise poor people, or else to compel them to pay large poll taxes to lighten taxes on property."[35]

Conservative elements dominated the Democratic party as the new century began. Joseph W. Bailey's political star was in the ascendancy. Two ex-Confederate soldiers, with the help of Edward M. House, a powerful behind-the-scenes figure in Texas politics, and a small clique of insiders, occupied the governor's office from 1899 to 1907. The trend toward business regulation slowed and the legislature approved a large number of railroad consolidation measures during this period. Even James S. Hogg seemed to have lost some of his reformist zeal, for he had become an enthusiastic advocate of outside investments in Texas and had entered the oil business himself.[36]

But the reform movement had only taken a holiday. In 1905 an impressive number of reformers appeared in the state legislature and a new attorney general launched a vigorous antitrust attack. The following year brought an exciting gubernatorial campaign and the election of Thomas M. Campbell, who became the state's outstanding progressive governor. Campbell was reelected in 1908, and during the four years of his administration a large number of legislative reforms were adopted. Among these measures were several laws for the regulation of corporations, a comprehensive insurance-control act, important tax reforms, a bank deposit guarantee law, a pure food and drug act, abolition of the convict-lease system, the establishment of a bureau of labor statistics, and

---

[33]Theodore Roosevelt's Progressive revolt so disrupted the GOP in Texas that the Socialist party, with more than 25,000 votes, momentarily assumed the position of second party in the state in the presidential election of 1912. By the end of this period, Texas Republicans had managed to restore a measure of harmony within their party. In 1920 they elected a congressman. Paul Casdorph, *A History of the Republican Party in Texas, 1865–1965* (Austin, Tex., 1965), 58–123.

[34]Barr, *Texas Politics, 1876–1906*, pp. 199, 201, 205–208.

[35]Quoted in James Aubrey Tinsley, "The Progressive Movement in Texas" (Ph.D. diss., Univ. of Wisconsin, 1953), 197.

[36]Rupert Norval Richardson, *Colonel Edward M. House: The Texas Years, 1858–1912* (Abilene, Tex., 1964); Richardson, "Edward M. House and the Governors," *Southwestern Hist. Quar.* 61 (July 1957): 51–65; Barr, *Texas Politics, 1876–1906*, pp. 209, 218–19, 228.

various acts designed to aid farmers.[37] The tide of progressivism weakened in 1910, when Oscar B. Colquitt, a more conservative leader, was elected governor. Even so, the state's aggressive antitrust prosecutions were continued during his governorship, and workmen's compensation, a "blue sky" law to protect the public against fraudulent securities, and other progressive measures were enacted in the period 1911–15. The progressives demonstrated their greatest strength in rallying to the cause of Woodrow Wilson in 1911 and 1912. They dominated the state convention in the latter year and sent a solid Wilson delegation to the Democratic national convention. During the decade after 1906, the pattern of Democratic politics in Texas revealed a distinct bifactional configuration. Although the division shifted from one issue to another, the "progressive" faction tended to support stricter regulation of corporations, to oppose Senator Bailey, to champion prohibition, and to be identified with the presidential campaign to nominate Wilson.[38]

After 1911 the "liquor question" became the most divisive issue among Texas Democrats. The relentless controversy over prohibition dominated the state's politics for several years, generally aligning drys and progressives. Then, in the gubernatorial primary of 1914, a new actor appeared on the political stage. He was James E. Ferguson, a farmer, lawyer, and small-town banker who had never before run for office. A colorful campaigner, "Farmer Jim" made a strong appeal to the state's poor farmers, and his first important legislative accomplishment was an act to put a ceiling on farm tenancy rentals. Ferguson was easily reelected in 1916. But he ran into trouble in his second term and in 1917 was impeached and removed from office for misapplying public funds and interfering arbitrarily in the affairs of the state university. "Fergusonism" now became an issue in itself, and Ferguson's personal following was destined to make him an important factor in Texas politics for almost two decades. Fergusonism and the events of World War I disrupted the progressive pattern of the state's politics, and, as in other southern states, the old bifactionalism rapidly disintegrated.[39]

Texas progressivism, to a greater extent than was true of social reform in most other southern states, represented the response of the state's major leaders and organizations to rapid economic growth and the dominant position of outside capitalists. The state's response was ambiguous, since many elements of the Texas elite were identified with or approved of the developmental role of

[37]Janet Schmelzer, "Thomas M. Campbell: Progressive Governor of Texas," *Red River Valley Historical Review* 3 (Fall 1978): 52–63.

[38]For a coverage of Texas politics during the progressive era, see Tinsley, "The Progressive Movement in Texas"; Seth S. McKay and Odie B. Faulk, *The Saga of Texas, 1901–1965: Texas after Spindletop* (Austin, Tex., 1965); Lewis L. Gould, *Progressives and Prohibitionists: Texas Democrats in the Wilson Era* (Austin, Tex., 1973); and Arthur S. Link, "The Wilson Movement in Texas, 1910–1912," *Southwestern Hist. Quar.* 48 (Oct. 1944): 169–85.

[39]Gould, *Progressives and Prohibitionists*, 120–221; Key, *Southern Politics*, 263–64; Reinhard H. Luthin, *American Demagogues: Twentieth Century* (Boston, 1954), 153–65.

railroads, insurance companies, and lumber firms. At the same time, the diversity of the state's physiographic, economic, and cultural interests encouraged the emergence of a variety of organized pressure groups intent upon shaping public policy. The pattern of Texas progressivism, one scholar has noted, was highlighted by "well-organized urban middle class pressure groups loosely coordinated at times with farmer, labor, business, or professional organizations on a variety of individual issues. . . ."[40] The Democratic party played a significant role in the formulation of this progressivism, for it attracted the support of most voters and usually managed to maintain a workable accord among the conflicting interests and politicians in the state. Democratic leaders also reduced the electorate, thereby weakening the Republican party and limiting the possibility of mass protest at the ballot box. Still, an identifiable liberal faction developed in the Democratic party led by such figures as James S. Hogg and Thomas M. Campbell. There were also outstanding reform Democrats in the legislature like Thomas B. Love and in Congress like Morris Sheppard. Finally, a number of salient issues helped define and stimulate progressivism in Texas, including business regulation, tax reform, and prohibition.

Of the thirteen states that seem to warrant inclusion in the South early in the twentieth century, the least "southern" was Oklahoma. The frontier was everywhere in evidence in this unfinished state, which did not enter the Union until 1907, and in many ways it was as much western as southern in its attitudes and behavior. The white population was diverse in origin, there was a large Indian minority, and Negroes made up only a little over 8 percent of the inhabitants in 1910. Although the economy was predominantly agricultural, it was based in part on the production of wheat, on mining, ranching, and lumbering, and on oil, of which it produced one-fourth of the national output by 1913. Nevertheless, Oklahoma felt the pull of strong centripetal forces that bound it to the South. Many of its inhabitants were natives of other southern states, and southerners, whose influence was pronounced in the eastern and southern sections, dominated the early years of statehood.[41] Southern attitudes on race were much in evidence, and the state quickly devised a means of disfranchising its black voters. The state also shared the cotton culture of the eastern South, and the staple spread during this period from the southeastern section to the central and southwestern areas.

A latent radicalism—manifesting itself as twentieth-century populism—burst into bloom by the time Oklahoma became a state. Nowhere in the United States was agrarian protest more conspicuous. The Farmers' Union and organized labor exerted great influence in the new state's politics. William Jen-

[40]Barr, *Texas Politics, 1876–1906*, p. xiii.

[41]Seventy-five of the 112 delegates to the constitutional convention of 1906–1907 were natives of other southern states, and a majority of the members of the first general assembly were migrants from the older South. Arrell M. Gibson, *Oklahoma: A History of Five Centuries* (Norman, Okla., 1965), 334.

nings Bryan was the idol of the Oklahoma masses.[42] The hazards of farming in Oklahoma, the increasing percentage of farm tenancy (over half by 1920), and the role of large corporations in exploiting the state's resources fostered a populistic spirit among the people. This radicalism was reflected in the Democratic party, but it was expressed more dramatically in third-party action, primarily in the Socialist party of America. The Oklahoma party had more paid-up members than any other state by 1910, and in 1914 its state ticket received more than 52,000 votes. Before the war decimated their numbers, the Socialists had become an alarming specter to the Democrats and tangible evidence of the desperate conditions surrounding many Oklahomans.[43]

By 1906, a student of Oklahoma progressivism writes, "common experiences with corporate arrogance, political irresponsibility, and social inequality had given rise to a body of reform notions as pervasive as they were robust."[44] The state's first constitutiton, which was drawn up just at the time the currents of reform were gaining strength in the South, became a repository for progressive concepts. The framers seemed to be inspired by the vision of a new political order. "The common suspicion of corporation management and fear of corporate wealth," a contemporary journalist wrote of the new constitution, "the more or less prevalent distrust of representative government and even of the judiciary, the growing belief in the effectiveness of pure democracy, the resentment against the saloon element and its political activities, all are embodied in its provisions."[45] The document contained a set of specifications for the practicing of direct democracy. Its formulation having been dominated by a farmer-labor bloc, the constitution included elaborate safeguards for the protection of workingmen and the public welfare. It also reflected a "thirst for corporate righteousness," devoting nine thousand words to the problem of controlling large business enterprises.[46] The ideological tone of this remarkable document conditioned Oklahoma politics for many years.

The Democrats were primarily responsible for the constitution of 1907, which proved to be immensely popular, and they were given power to organize

---

[42]See Norbert R. Mahnken, "William Jennings Bryan in Oklahoma," *Nebraska History* 31 (Dec. 1950): 247–74; Donald K. Pickens, "Oklahoma Populism and Historical Interpretation," *Chronicles of Oklahoma* 43 (Autumn 1965): 275–83; and Terry Paul Wilson, "The Demise of Populism in Oklahoma Territory," ibid., 265–74.

[43]Green, *Grass-Roots Socialism*, 9, 12–14, 23–25, 36–39, 57–63; George Brown Tindall, *The Emergence of the New South, 1913–1945* (Baton Rouge, 1967), 28–29; Oscar Ameringer, *If You Don't Weaken: The Autobiography of Oscar Ameringer* (New York, 1940), 227–80.

[44]Danney Goble, *Progressive Oklahoma: The Making of a New Kind of State* (Norman, Okla., 1980), 186. This study illuminates the origins of progressivism in Oklahoma.

[45]"Oklahoma's Radical Constitution," *Outlook* 87 (Oct. 5, 1907): 229.

[46]"Oklahoma's Constitutional Innovations," *World's Work* 14 (May 1907): 8826–27. See also J.H. Reynolds, "The Oklahoma Constitution," *SAQ* 7 (July 1908): 232–41; Charles Wayne Ellinger, "The Drive for Statehood in Oklahoma, 1889–1906," *Chron. Okla.* 41 (Spring 1963): 15–37; and C. Vann Woodward, *Origins of the New South, 1877–1913* (Baton Rouge, 1951), 387–88.

the new state government. Oklahoma became a Democratic state. In addition to their attack on the Republicans for opposing ratification of the constitution, the Democrats derisively identified the GOP with "the Carpetbagger, the Corporation, and the Coon."[47] The Republicans were weak at the grass-roots level, and they were hurt by the disfranchisement of blacks in 1910. Yet the party was a substantial threat to the dominant Democrats. It was strongest in the northern third of the state and generally in the western section. The party's gubernatorial candidates obtained over 40 percent of the votes in the elections before 1920, and as early as 1908 showed its promise by winning three of the five congressional seats (it relinquished one of these in 1910). The first real Republican breakthrough, however, came in 1920, when the party carried the state for Warren G. Harding, elected a United States senator, won five of the eight congressional seats, and elected a majority of the members of the state house of representatives.[48]

In 1905 a nucleus of Oklahoma's Democratic leadership had been formed at the Muskogee convention that drafted the so-called Sequoyah Constitution, an Indian Territory proposal that foreshadowed the constitution of 1907. Many of the delegates to the Muskogee convention also served in the 1906–1907 convention that met in Guthrie. Most of the leaders of the constitutional convention were from the Indian Territory in the eastern half of the proposed state, and they dominated the early politics of the new state. Among these leaders was William Murray, a native of Texas and a youthful advocate of James S. Hogg. "Alfalfa Bill," as he came to be called, migrated to Indian Territory in 1898, married an Indian girl, and became a lawyer for the Chickasaws. He was a member of the Muskogee convention in 1905, served as president of the constitutional convention of 1906–1907, and was elected as the first speaker of the house of representatives.[49] Another participant in the Muskogee and Guthrie conventions was Charles N. Haskell, a dynamic railroad promoter and politician from Ohio, who became Oklahoma's first governor. A third leader was Robert L. Williams, who with Murray and Haskell formed a powerful triumvirate in the constitutional convention. A native of Alabama, Williams became a member of the state supreme court and in 1914 was elected as Oklahoma's third governor.[50] A fourth political leader from the Indian Territory, but not a member of the constitutional convention, was Robert Latham Owen, the state's senior

---

[47]James Ralph Scales, "Political History of Oklahoma, 1907–1949" (Ph.D. diss., Univ. of Oklahoma, 1949), 67. See also George O. Carney, "Oklahoma's Territorial Delegates and Progressivism, 1901–1907," *Chron. Okla.* 52 (Spring 1974): 38–51, and Garin Burbank, "The Political and Social Attitudes of Some Early Oklahoma Democrats," ibid. 52 (Winter 1974–75): 439–55.

[48]Scales, "Political History of Oklahoma," 127–31, 149, 209–19.

[49]Keith L. Bryant, Jr. *Alfalfa Bill Murray* (Norman, Okla., 1968).

[50]Edward Everett Dale and James D. Morrison, *Pioneer Judge: The Life of Robert Lee Williams* (Cedar Rapids, Iowa, 1958).

U.S. senator and perhaps its most popular politician during the progressive period.

Democratic leaders, being prominently identified with the constitution of 1907, got the new government off to a good start. The Haskell administration achieved an impressive legislative record, including the passage of many progressive measures. But the triumphant Democrats were unable to maintain party harmony very long. Differences between Democrats from Indian Territory and Democrats from Oklahoma Territory did not completely disappear after statehood. More important was the rivalry that soon developed between Haskell and Murray, both of whom had large personal followings. In 1910, Lee Cruce turned back Murray's bid for the governorship, and "Alfalfa Bill" was forced to content himself with a congressional seat two years later. Oklahoma Democrats were also badly split over their party's presidential choice in 1912, and in 1914 Robert L. Williams won the Democratic nomination for governor despite the opposition of Governor Cruce and former governor Haskell. Williams, a pugnacious and domineering politician, was succeeded by James B.A. Robertson, the first governor from the western part of the state. By that time the old factional alignments based on the personal followings of the founding fathers were disappearing from the political scene. The bitter rivalries within their party weakened the Democrats, as did the Socialist upsurge before the war and the Republican challenge during the postwar reaction against Wilsonism.[51]

The first legislative session under the new constitution met from December 1907 to May 1908. It proved to be the busiest and most progressive session of the whole period, and with the other two sessions of the Haskell administration constituted the most concentrated time of reform in Oklahoma during this era. During these formative years the general assembly enacted a comprehensive labor code, several antitrust laws, corporation and income taxes, a bank guarantee deposit act, an oil and gas conservation law, and a compulsory school attendance statute. It also abolished the county fee system and created a state corporation commission and a textbook commission. The flow of reform legislation diminished thereafter, but the record of progressivism in the Sooner State was impressive.

Populism, Bryanism, and rural socialism influenced the shape of progressivism in Oklahoma, along with farm organizations, organized labor, and various social reform groups. The emergence of an interest-group politics was a key factor in facilitating the organization of reform campaigns and the enactment of progressive legislation.[52] Although the Republican party retained some strength, the Democrats controlled the state's politics and government.

---

[51]Scales, "Political History of Oklahoma," provides a good treatment of Oklahoma politics during this period. See also Monroe Lee Billington, *Thomas P. Gore: The Blind Senator from Oklahoma* (Lawrence, Kans., 1967), and Gilbert C. Fite, "The Nonpartisan League in Oklahoma," *Chron. Okla.* 24 (Summer 1946): 146–57.

[52]Goble, *Progressive Oklahoma*, 145–65.

They succeeded in disfranchising many Negro voters, and their policies neglected—and sometimes exploited—the black and white poor and the Indian.[53] Despite their commitment to democratic procedures and governmental intervention, Oklahoma progressives emphasized economic development and entrepreneurial opportunities for middle-class and professional people. The state's politics served to accommodate the interests and ambitions of the most advantaged elements. In this respect its progressivism was quite similar to that of other southern states.

The pattern of state politics in the early twentieth-century South had a good deal of uniformity, despite the individuality of the various state designs. The Democratic party dominated every state in the region. Most of the southern states enacted election "reforms" around the turn of the century which included some form of Negro disfranchisement, the poll tax as a voting prerequisite, and tough election laws. These so-called reforms, whatever their effect in preventing fraud, created a new and greatly restricted electorate in every state. At the same time, the introduction of state systems for the conduct of primary elections brought an increase in the number of political candidates and encouraged bifactional groupings among Democrats in the individual states. The primaries also provided an arena for interest groups and reform causes. Intraparty competition, along with interest-group politics, contributed to the rise of a group of colorful and influential reform governors, the most successful of whom served as focal points for progressive coalitions and assumed a new role as legislative leaders. Meanwhile, the state legislatures were becoming more important, with the development of numerous progressive campaigns and the increasing demand for state regulation and public services.

State politics, in the South as in other sections, constituted the essential context for southern progressivism. The early reform campaigns, such as those in behalf of public schools and child labor restrictions, looked to the general assemblies for enabling measures and appropriations. Politics in the separate states remained the most crucial consideration for southern progressives even when their causes acquired regionwide organization and, to a large extent, even when their reform endeavors assumed a national orientation, as they often did after 1912. By 1906, reform leaders and reform factions had achieved a measure of political power in almost all of the southern states, and during the next two or three years they were responsible for the first outpouring of progressive legislation in the region. Thereafter, the strength of the progressives in the South waxed and waned irregularly, in response to the vigor of their various campaigns, the salience of particular issues, and the vagaries of each state's factional politics.

[53]See, for example, Angie Debo, *And Still the Waters Run* (Princeton, N.J., 1940), 159–256.

PART TWO   *The Reform Movements*

5	*Regulation*

ONE OF THE MOST POWERFUL MOTIVATING FACTORS in the reform efforts of early twentieth-century southerners was a desire to expand the regulatory function of the state in behalf of economic opportunity and to apply more effective social controls in the interest of an orderly and cohesive community. The movement to restrict the electorate and revise the electoral system reflected this desire, as did the widespread antitrust feeling and the growing demand for stringent railroad regulation. The regulatory impulse derived a good deal of its strength from the agrarian radicalism of the 1890s, but it owed even more to a broad middle-class concern over the economic and social effects of industrialization and urbanization, to entrepreneurial pressures and aspirations, and to the activities of a variety of groups and organizations intent upon controlling the entry into and the conduct of particular vocations and professions. There was also another consideration. Southern progressives were, for the most part, middle-class and professional people convinced of the desirability, indeed the necessity, of their region's industrialization, economic diversification, and urbanization. New statutes and public regulations would be necessary to facilitate these developments, particularly in helping shape a social order that would encourage the South's economic transformation.

Use of the state as an instrument of social control was urged for other reasons as well. The regulation of behavior and morality through such reforms as prohibition represented one type of social control. But there were others, some of which mirrored the progressive assumption that human beings were malleable and could be improved if their social environments were modified.[1] Many progressives in the South, as in other sections, were motivated by altruism. Despite their paternalistic approach and the central role they assigned themselves in the creation of this new social environmentalism, some of these middle-class southerners exhibited genuine concern and compassion for the groups whose social control they worked to effect.

[1]For this theme generally, see John Chynoweth Burnham, "Psychiatry, Psychology and the Progressive Movement," *American Quarterly* 12 (Winter 1960): 457–65.

Although southern progressives differed among themselves as to the areas in which the state's regulatory power should be exerted, the theme of state intervention was a conspicuous feature of several important reform movements in the region. "The enormous growth and influence of the power of the trusts," asserted the Florida Democratic platform of 1900, "challenges the attention of the people, chokes the prosperity of the masses of the people, threatens the integrity and permanency of our institutions, and next to imperialism, presents the most vital question which must be settled at the coming election." The solution proposed by Democratic leaders was the expansion of state government, the development of more effective control mechanisms, and "the nomination of all candidates for office, both state and county, and of United States Senators, by a majority in white Democratic primary elections, held under the provisions of law which shall provide all possible protection against fraud, intimidation and other vicious influences. . . ."[2] Regulation as reform was exemplified in the disfranchisement of southern blacks, in the movement to regulate railroads and other corporations, in the campaign for a more effective and humane penal system, and in the prohibition crusade. Many of the advocates of such restraints were narrowly concerned with one or two issues to the exclusion of broader progressive objectives. But, even so, the role of the state as regulator, arbiter, and instrument of social control was at the very heart of southern progressivism.

DISFRANCHISEMENT AND REFORM

There was a pervasive belief among white southerners at the turn of the century that blacks were losing ground, that they were increasingly undisciplined, ignorant, and immoral, and that they were steadily becoming less efficient as laborers. Since most black Americans lived in the southern states, this degeneracy, white southerners declared, made it more difficult for the region to compete industrially, added to its crime rate, imperiled its health, and disrupted its race relations. White spokesmen argued that new and stronger race controls were needed not only for social peace and stability but also for black progress. Disfranchisement of Negro voters was early perceived by white leaders as a crucial step in the control of black behavior. White southerners generally viewed disfranchisement as a "reform," in part because it removed some of the alleged excesses of Reconstruction and struck at black lawlessness. It was also thought to be a sure way of causing blacks to forget about politics and concentrate on economic activities. Proponents of disfranchisement maintained that by removing the black man as a pawn in elections, southern politicians would no longer have to resort to intimidation, trickery, and fraud at the polls. With the race issue removed from politics, white southerners could freely debate

[2]Quoted in William T. Cash, *History of the Democratic Party in Florida: Including Biographical Sketches of Prominent Florida Democrats* (Tallahassee, 1936), 174–80.

the issues and divide as they saw fit. In addition, disfranchisement would help bring political peace and stability to the region.[3]

The campaign to disfranchise Negroes in a legal manner began, appropriately enough, in the most "southern" of the region's states, Mississippi. A movement to call a constitutional convention in that state succeeded in 1890, and a new instrument was drafted to replace the Radical constitution of 1868. The constitution of 1890 included several franchise provisions: a literacy test, a cumulative poll tax, a long residence requirement, registration four months before an election, and disqualification for a list of crimes. An alternative to the literacy requirement was devised for illiterate white men—to "understand" and give a "reasonable interpretation" of any section of the constitution.[4] In 1895, South Carolina followed Mississippi's course in adopting disfranchisement features as part of its new constitution. Louisiana, which resorted to constitutional disfranchisement in 1898, invented the "grandfather clause" as a temporary alternative to its literacy requirement. This provision exempted from the literacy test those who were entitled to vote on January 1, 1867, together with their sons and grandsons. North Carolina, acutely conscious of the actions of Mississippi, South Carolina, and Louisiana, adopted wide-ranging disfranchisement provisions in the form of a constitutional amendment in 1900. Alabama took a similar step by approving a new constitution in 1901, and Virginia followed suit the next year. Georgia added a comprehensive suffrage amendment to its constitution in 1908. Oklahoma, in 1910, was the last state to enact constitutional disfranchisement.[5]

Though the other southern states refrained from amending their constitutions to disfranchse black voters, all of them except Kentucky approved restrictive measures in one form or another. Tennessee, for example, took action in 1889 and 1890 by adopting a harsh registration act, a poll tax requirement, and a secret ballot law.[6] About the same time, Florida enacted registration, poll tax, multiple-box, and secret ballot laws designed to deprive black and independent

[3]See Claude H. Nolen, *The Negro's Image in the South: The Anatomy of White Supremacy* (Lexington, Ky., 1967), 26–28; Walter L. Fleming, "The Servant Problem in a Black Belt Village," *Sewanee Review* 13 (Jan. 1905): 1–17; Edgar Gardner Murphy, "The Task of the Leader: A Discussion of Some of the Conditions of Public Leadership in Our Southern States," ibid. 15 (Jan. 1907): 1–30; Lawrence J. Friedman, "The Search for Docility: Racial Thought in the White South, 1861–1917," *Phylon* 31 (Fall 1970): 313–23; Friedman, *The White Savage: Racial Fantasies in the Postbellum South* (Englewood Cliffs, N.J., 1970); and Guion Griffis Johnson, "The Ideology of White Supremacy, 1876–1910," in Fletcher Melvin Green, ed., *Essays in Southern History* (Chapel Hill, N.C., 1949), 124–56.

[4]William Alexander Mabry, "Disfranchisement of the Negro in Mississippi," *JSH* 4 (Aug. 1938): 318–33; Albert D. Kirwan, *Revolt of the Rednecks: Mississippi Politics, 1876–1925* (Lexington, Ky., 1951), 58–63, 68–71, 79.

[5]J. Morgan Kousser, *The Shaping of Southern Politics: Suffrage Restriction and the Establishment of the One-Party South, 1880–1910* (New Haven, Conn., 1974); James Ralph Scales, "Political History of Oklahoma, 1907–1949" (Ph.D. diss., Univ. of Oklahoma, 1949), 47, 127–30; "The Grandfather Clause in Oklahoma," *Outlook* 96 (Nov. 26, 1910): 655–56.

[6]J. Morgan Kousser, "Post-Reconstruction Suffrage Restrictions in Tennessee: A Look at the V. O. Key Thesis," *Political Science Quarterly* 88 (Dec. 1973): 655–83.

TABLE 8. *Suffrage Restriction in the South*

YEAR	STATE	PROVISIONS
1889	Fla.	poll tax, multiple-box
1889, 1890	Tenn.	poll tax, registration, secret ballot
1890	Miss.	poll tax, secret ballot, lit. test, underst. clause
1891, 1892	Ark.	poll tax, secret ballot
1893, 1901	Ala.	poll tax, registration, secret ballot, lit. test, prop. test, grandfather clause
1894, 1895	S.C.	poll tax, registration, lit. test, underst. clause
1894, 1902	Va.	poll tax, secret ballot, lit. test, prop. test, underst. clause
1897, 1898	La.	poll tax, registration, secret ballot, lit. test, prop. test, grandfather clause
1899, 1900	N.C.	poll tax, registration, multiple-box, lit. test, prop. test, grandfather clause
1902, 1903	Tex.	poll tax, secret ballot
1908	Ga.	poll tax (1871 and 1877), lit. test, prop. test, underst. clause, grandfather clause
1910	Okla.	lit. test, grandfather clause

SOURCE: Adapted from J. Morgan Kousser, *The Shaping of Southern Politics: Suffrage Restriction and the Establishment of the One-Party South, 1880–1910* (New Haven, Conn., 1974), 239.

voters of the ballot. By 1904 every southern state except Kentucky and Oklahoma had made the poll tax a prerequisite for voting. In several cases disingenuous registration and voting acts paved the way for formal constitutional disfranchisement by restricting the electorate, particularly Negro and poor white elements. The white primary was also a powerful disfranchising weapon. In the early years of the twentieth century most of the Democratic state committees or conventions introduced statewide primaries which excluded blacks.[7] Francis G. Caffey, a lawyer who lived in Montgomery at the time of the constitutional convention in Alabama, contended that the system of white con-

[7]Kousser, *The Shaping of Southern Politics,* 72–76, 91–92; John William Graves, "Negro Disfranchisement in Arkansas," *Ark. Hist. Quar.* 26 (Autumn 1967): 199–225.

ventions and primaries had largely eliminated the Negro as an active factor in the state's politics before the adoption of formal ballot restrictions.[8]

While it is difficult to determine which of the disfranchisement provisions was most effective, it is clear that the complicated franchise regulations prevented most blacks and a large number of whites from voting. In Louisiana, for instance, the total number of black registrants dropped from 130,344 on January 1, 1897, to 1,342 in 1904. The white registration declined from 164,088 to 91,716 during the same period.[9] Whereas almost 80,000 blacks were registered to vote in fourteen Alabama black belt counties in 1900, the number had plummeted to 1,081 by 1902. The number of white men on the Alabama registration lists dropped by more than 40,000 between 1900 and 1903.[10] "It is good bye with poor white folks and niggers now," wrote a Negro editor in Alabama, "for the train of disfranchisement is on the rail and will come thundering upon us like an avalanche, there is no use crying, we have got to shute the shute."[11] One contemporary observer summed up the impact of disfranchisement in Louisiana in these terse words: "the Negroes, who are almost all Republicans, feel that it is useless to vote; while the whites, who are almost all Democrats, feel that it is unnecessary."[12] In short, public regulation of voting requirements and election procedures proved to be a significant factor in limiting the suffrage, restricting political choices, and restructuring the political system of the various southern states.[13]

Disfranchisement was a striking manifestation of the South's "capitulation to racism" during the 1890s and early 1900s.[14] In general the movement was supported most strongly in the black belt areas, the historic centers of political power in the South, and opposed most vigorously by the upland sections, where few blacks resided and many disadvantaged whites feared that the new suffrage qualifications would strip them of the ballot. "We warn the white people," read a resolution of the Populist executive committee in North Carolina, "that this amendment will disfranchise approximately as many white men as it will negroes in this state, and will leave the Negro still a factor in

[8]Caffey, "Suffrage Limitations at the South," *Pol. Sci. Quar.* 20 (Mar. 1905): 53–67.

[9]Allie Bayne Windham Webb, "A History of Negro Voting in Louisiana, 1877–1906" (Ph.D. diss., Louisiana State Univ., 1962), 239–40; Paul Lewinson, *Race, Class & Party: A History of Negro Suffrage and White Politics in the South* (New York, 1932), 214; C. Vann Woodward, *Origins of the New South, 1877–1913* (Baton Rouge, 1951), 342–43.

[10]Malcolm Cook McMillan, *Constitutional Development in Alabama, 1798–1901: A Study in Politics, the Negro, and Sectionalism* (Chapel Hill, N.C., 1955), 352–56; Lewinson, *Race, Class & Party*, 216–17.

[11]Quoted in Sheldon Hackney, *Populism to Progressivism in Alabama* (Princeton, N.J., 1969), 179.

[12]Paul L. Haworth, "Negro Disfranchisement in Louisiana," *Outlook* 71 (May 17, 1902): 163.

[13]See Kousser, *The Shaping of Southern Politics*, esp. 5.

[14]C. Vann Woodward, *The Strange Career of Jim Crow* (New York, 1955), 51–74.

politics. . . ."[15] Alabama seems to provide an example of a political revolution perpetrated by conservative Democrats, a kind of Bourbon coup d'état.[16] Although Populists and Republicans offered the main resistance to suffrage restriction in most southern states,[17] the movement elicited increasing support from white southerners generally. The reasons for this emerging white consensus varied, but an important circumstance throughout the section was the way in which long-standing internal cleavages, the agrarian revolt, and white supremacy as a political issue combined to create a powerful dynamic in the drive to limit the suffrage. White Republican leaders were eventually persuaded by the rising tide of Negrophobia to diminish the role of blacks in most southern states and pursue the chimera of a "lily-white" policy.[18]

The exclusion of blacks from politics exerted a seductive appeal to southern whites in the wake of the upheaval of the mid-1890s. It was a "reform" that promised to banish the corrupt elections, political disorders, and bitter divisions of the nineties.[19] Democratic leaders were quick to see disfranchisement as a means of rehabilitating their party in the aftermath of the shattering experiences of the 1890s. If conditions were not changed, warned Carter Glass, the editor of the Lynchburg *News*, in 1900, they would "arouse a feeling of resentment that will break in a fury and wreck the Democratic party."[20] Even though the Negro's role in the state's politics had been greatly reduced following the defeat of the Readjusters in 1883, it was easy for white Virginians of almost all persuasions to fasten on the black man as the source of the Old Dominion's electoral immorality. As a Republican member of the constitutional convention caustically remarked, the Negro vote "must be destroyed to prevent the Democratic election officers from stealing their votes. . . ."[21] To think of disfranchisement as a reform, as "a cleansing of the electoral process," one historian

[15] Quoted in William Alexander Mabry, "'White Supremacy' and the North Carolina Suffrage Amendment," *N.C. Hist. Rev.* 13 (Jan. 1936): 16.

[16] For a broader treatment of this concept, see V. O. Key, Jr., with the assistance of Alexander Heard, *Southern Politics in State and Nation* (New York, 1949), 533–54.

[17] Kousser, *The Shaping of Southern Politics,* 126, 166, 170, 175, 206–207, 246–47.

[18] See, for example, Helen G. Edmonds, *The Negro and Fusion Politics in North Carolina, 1894–1901* (Chapel Hill, N.C., 1951), 213; "The Southern Republican Elimination of the Negro," *World's Work* 4 (Oct. 1902): 2591; Gordon B. McKinney, "Southern Mountain Republicans and the Negro, 1865–1900," *JSH* 41 (Nov. 1975): 510–15.

[19] Woodward, *The Strange Career of Jim Crow,* 66–68; Nolen, *The Negro's Image in the South,* 90–95; Lewinson, *Race, Class & Party,* 79, 88–91; C. Vann Woodward, "Tom Watson and the Negro in Agrarian Politics," *JSH* 4 (Feb. 1938): 14–33; Eugene R. Fingerhut, "Tom Watson, Blacks, and Southern Reform," *Ga. Hist. Quar.* 60 (Winter 1976): 324–43.

[20] Quoted in William C. Pendleton, *Political History of Appalachian Virginia, 1776–1927* (Dayton, Va., 1927), 421. Also see Harold Wilson, "The Role of Carter Glass in the Disfranchisement of the Virginia Negro," *Historian* 32 (Nov. 1969): 69–82.

[21] Quoted in Charles E. Wynes, *Race Relations in Virginia, 1870–1902* (Charlottesville, Va., 1961), 62. The Richmond *Times* expressed the opinion that "It is more courageous and honorable and better for public morals and good government to come out boldly and disfranchise the negro than to make a pretense of letting him vote and cheating him at the polls" (quoted in Ralph Clipman McDanel, *The Virginia Constitutional Convention of 1901–1902* [Baltimore, 1928], 33).

has written, "was a rationale that allowed whites to do what they wanted to do and feel good about it."[22]

Many of the more progressive elements in the Democratic party associated the election frauds of the 1880s and 1890s with the ascendancy of the Bourbons, and they sometimes turned to disfranchisement and other electoral "reforms" as a means of striking at the entrenched conservatives. In Virginia, for example, an independent or reform element in the party had begun to coalesce by the late 1890s in opposition to the dominance of Senator Thomas S. Martin's organization. "There is but one hope of salvation for the people of Virginia from the corrupt, costly and intollerable [sic] domination of an office-holding despotism," declared Carter Glass's Lynchburg *News,* "and that hope is a constitutional convention."[23] Disfranchisement and other constitutional changes seemed to provide a key for the introduction of institutional changes that would eliminate corrupt elections, corporation favoritism, and bossism associated with the Martin machine. Some Virginians, moreover, wanted to use the constitutional convention to streamline the state government and prepare the way for effective regulation of railroads and other reforms.[24] Other southerners maintained that disfranchisement would have a "liberalizing effect" upon state politics by giving greater priority to economic issues, by encouraging independent voting, and eventually by making possible a two-party system in the South.[25] Legal disfranchisement, the historian Ulrich B. Phillips wrote in 1904, "tends to lessen irritation and to enable the white people to follow their own judgments in questions of current politics and restore the South to its former national influence." Another contemporary intellectual saw disfranchisement as an illustration of the imperative necessity of "doing things by law." It represented "the first great result of . . . [a] return of social reason in the South."[26]

Advocates of political reform such as William Garrott Brown were inclined to subordinate the question of race relations to the ideal of a more competitive politics and to the yearning for a more important southern role in national politics. Brown looked upon disfranchisement as a reform, although he would have preferred to give the ballot to blacks who owned property and were educated. He contended that by settling the problem of Negro politics, disfran-

[22]Hackney, *Populism to Progressivism in Alabama,* 176–77.

[23]Quoted in Pendleton, *Political History of Appalachian Virginia,* 420–21.

[24]McDanel, *The Virginia Constitutional Convention of 1901–1902,* p. 24; Herman L. Horn, "The Growth and Development of the Democratic Party in Virginia since 1890" (Ph.D. diss., Duke Univ., 1949), 48; Allen W. Moger, *Virginia: Bourbonism to Byrd, 1870 to 1925* (Charlottesville, Va., 1968), 181–202.

[25]See, for example, Joseph Gregoire de Roulhac Hamilton, "North Carolina, from 1865 to the Present Time," in *The South in the Building of the Nation,* vol. 1, pp. 508–509.

[26]Phillips, "Conservatism and Progress in the Cotton Belt," *SAQ* 3 (Jan. 1904): 9; John E. White, "Temperance Reform in the South," in *The South in the Building of the Nation,* vol. 10, p. 578.

chisement would free white southerners to turn to more basic issues. Brown believed that once a two-party system emerged in the new political environment, race relations would automatically improve.[27] John Spencer Bassett, on the other hand, was far more skeptical about the potential benefits of disfranchisement. "When the railroad rates shall have been reduced to the point of diminishing returns," he wrote in 1908, "when the trusts shall have been 'busted' till the people are satisfied with the operation, and when prohibition shall have accomplished its utmost, there will still remain in the South the possibility that politicians will again stir the fires of race antipathy."[28]

There was apparently a reasonably close correlation between the rhetoric of political democracy for white men and the rising walls of racial discrimination for black southerners. Segregation and other forms of racial discrimination did enable whites to displace blacks in many skills and industrial jobs, although such proscription did not prevent industrialists from employing race as a means of dividing the labor force and slowing the advance of trade unionism in the South. The idea of *"Herrenvolk* democracy"—a democratic society for whites only—was widely diffused in the South during this period.[29] As a South Carolina professor pointed out in 1903, it was important that the population "of a self-governing democracy shall be approximately homogeneous in those fundamental tendencies of thought, traditions, and ideals, which bind men together in mutual comprehension and sympathy." But he also made the point that "the final power of determining public policies" must be guided by "intelligence, patriotism, and steadiness of purpose."[30] Mississippi, according to that state's *Official and Statistical Register* for 1904, was the first commonwealth "in the Union to solve the problem of white supremacy in the South by lawful means." The *Register* went on to note, "the Constitution of 1890 disfranchises the ignorant and vicious of *both races,* and places control of the State in the hands of the virtuous, intelligent citizens."[31] Despite the white supremacy rhetoric and the promises that no white man would be disfranchised, the suffrage restrictionists revealed a distrust of the electorate that did not stop at the color line. The antidemocratic motivation of many disfranchisers was scarcely concealed in their insistence upon such suffrage prerequisites as the poll tax, which deprived a large number of poor whites of the ballot.[32]

[27] Bruce L. Clayton, "The Racial Thought of a Southern Intellectual at the Beginning of the Century: William Garrott Brown," *SAQ* 63 (Winter 1964): 93–103.

[28] "Discussion of the Paper by Alfred H. Stone, 'Is Race Friction between Blacks and Whites in the United States Growing and Inevitable?'" *American Journal of Sociology* 13 (May 1908): 827.

[29] See George M. Fredrickson, *The Black Image in the White Mind: The Debate on Afro-American Character and Destiny, 1817–1914* (New York, 1971), 283–319, and Kenneth P. Vickery, "'Herrenvolk' Democracy and Egalitarianism in South Africa and the U.S. South," *Comparative Studies in Society and History* 16 (June 1974): 309–28.

[30] Joseph Alexander Tillinghast, "Race Heterogeneity in a Democratic Society," *SAQ* 2 (Apr. 1903): 153.

[31] Quoted in Lester M. Salamon, "Protest, Politics, and Modernization in the American South: Mississippi as a 'Developing Society'" (Ph.D. diss., Harvard Univ., 1971), 292.

[32] Kousser, *The Shaping of Southern Politics,* 70, 230, 251–57; Lewinson, *Race, Class &*

Indeed, a great many southern progressives emphasized the need to cleanse the political process and limit participation to those who were prepared for responsible citizenship.[33] The Austrailian ballot, which was adopted in eight southern states between 1888 and 1900, was championed by such typical middle-class "progressive" organizations as the New Orleans Reform League. As one might expect, the adoption of the secret ballot in the southern states revealed the same mingled motives of discrimination and reform that underlay the disfranchisement movement. The ballot reformers in New Orleans and elsewhere were dedicated to destruction of machine politics and to the establishment of clean government; it is not surprising that they were more interested in eliminating fraud than in safeguarding the rights of illiterates.[34] Furthermore, suffrage restriction was quite compatible with the progressive desire to rationalize the economy and the political system and to substitute public regulations for private agreements.

The convulsion of the 1890s and the forces that gave rise to disfranchisement and the reinforcement of the one-party system in the South also resulted in the widespread adoption and elaboration of the direct primary as a means of making party nominations. Primaries were used in some localities as early as the 1870s, apparently as a way to secure the nomination of white candidates, and by the 1890s they were being widely employed in nominating county officials. First adopted on a statewide basis in South Carolina in 1896, the primary system spread over the region during the next decade and by the end of the progressive era had been extended, by party regulation or state law, to the nomination of candidates at all levels of government. "The South is the native soil of the direct primary," according to a writer in *Arena* in 1903. "It has there a logical and necessary existence, the predominance of one political party making the primary the *de facto* election."[35]

In many respects the primary became the capstone in the southern structure of suffrage restriction and political solidarity. "If we can get an effective suffrage *article* in the new Constitution," wrote a Virginia leader in 1901, "the *primaries* will or can be made to be the real elections."[36] Disfranchisement dealt a

---

Party, pp. 82–83; Woodward, *Origins of the New South,* 346; Key, *Southern Politics,* 543; Frederic D. Ogden, *The Poll Tax in the South* (University, Ala., 1958), 23–24; Frank B. Williams, Jr., "The Poll Tax as a Suffrage Requirement in the South, 1870–1901," *JSH* 18 (Nov. 1952): 469–96. Whatever the claims of their advocates, the constitutional changes that accompanied disfranchisement did little to equalize the distribution of legislative power in the interest of white counties.

[33]See, for example, Nolen, *The Negro's Image in the South,* 118–52.

[34]Kousser, *The Shaping of Southern Politics,* 51–53, 155; L. E. Fredman, *The Australian Ballot: The Story of an American Reform* (East Lansing, Mich., 1968), pp. ix, 31, 71–82, 97; William H. Glasson, "The Australian Ballot—Why North Carolina Should Adopt It," *SAQ* 8 (Apr. 1909): 132–42.

[35]Edward Insley, "Primary Election Reform," *Arena* 29 (Jan. 1903): 74–75.

[36]William A. Anderson, quoted in Raymond H. Pulley, *Old Virginia Restored: An Interpretation of the Progressive Impulse, 1870–1930* (Charlottesville, Va., 1968), 128.

final blow to whatever lingering hopes the Republican party had in the South, and nomination in the Democratic primary soon came to be the equivalent of the "real election." Meanwhile, party rules prevented blacks from taking part in most Democratic primaries. They became *white* primaries. In South Carolina, for instance, every Negro "applying for membership in a Democratic club, or offering to vote in a Democratic primary election, must produce a written statement of ten reputable white men who shall swear that they know of their own knowledge that the applicant or voter cast his ballot for General [Wade] Hampton in 1876 and has voted the Democratic ticket continuously ever since."[37]

While closed to certain groups and to all who would not pledge themselves to support its nominees, the party primary was represented as a democratic instrumentality, a means of enhancing the ordinary white man's influence. The primary did undermine older political arrangements, and its adoption was a demand of Democratic reform factions in virtually every southern state. In Mississippi, for example, the enactment of the primary law of 1902 opened the way for James K. Vardaman's election as governor in 1903, enabled the rednecks to capture control of the party machinery, helped equalize the power of white voters in the state, and drastically changed the techniques of campaigning in Mississippi. Primaries in the early twentieth-century South customarily attracted more attention than the general elections, which were often uncontested, and frequently in strongly contested races more votes were cast in the former than in the latter. Yet the primary's claims as a democratic device were not very substantial. The voter turnout, even among whites, dropped sharply during the progressive period, and the rate of voter participation in most southern primaries was much below that in the general elections of states having more competititve parties. In Texas, to take one case, the vote in the Democratic primary during the first two decades of the century ranged from a high of over 40 percent to a low of about 20 percent of the potential electorate.[38] Even so, the white primary was immensely important as a symbol. It served, along with other means of racial discrimination, to remind all white southerners of the historic bonds of ethnicity that, their traditions held, had made them a distinctive people.

One aspect of the movement to establish a system of primaries in the South was the use of such contests to secure the popular election of United States senators. A favorite Populist proposal and one strongly favored by most Bryan Democrats, the direct election of senators was endorsed by a number of south-

---

[37] Quoted in "The Progress of the 'Direct Primary' Reform," *World's Work* 6 (Aug. 1903): 3715–16. Blacks were not barred from participating in Democratic primaries in Kentucky. While there were no statewide rules for the exclusion of Negroes in Florida, North Carolina, and Tennessee, blacks were usually prevented from voting in Democratic primaries in those states by local party rules. See Lewinson, *Race, Class & Party,* 111–12.

[38] Key, *Southern Politics,* 534–35; Woodward, *Origins of the New South,* 345–46; Kousser, *The Shaping of Southern Politics,* 205–209, 224–27.

ern legislators about the turn of the century. Long before the ratification of the Seventeenth Amendment in 1913, most southern states had secured the popular election of senators through Democratic party rules which bound party members in the legislatures to vote for the top man in special preferential primaries. In Arkansas, for instance, the Democratic state convention of 1904 decided to select the party's Senate candidate in the general primary of that year. The state committee then secured written pledges from the candidates and promises from most of the Democratic candidates for the legislature to abide by the result of the primary.[39] The winners of these primaries were not always the ablest candidates, as critics were quick to point out. In 1906, Democratic primaries in Arkansas and Tennessee brought the nomination of a "cheap demagogue" and a "popular buffoon," in the opinion of *World's Work*. "If popular elections send to the Senate this type of 'popular' politician from some states," lamented the editor, "and the great corporations control the legislatures that elect Senators in other states, we seem yet to be betwixt the devil and the deep sea when we come to this high task."[40]

The broadening sweep of public regulation, gradually bringing party primaries within its scope, soon came to cover almost all aspects of the electoral process. Most southern states enacted laws designed to limit and publicize the campaign expenses of candidates, to outlaw the issuance of free passes by railroads, and to restrict lobbying by corporations and vested interests. Thus an Alabama law of 1915 set limits to campaign expenditures and required each candidate to file an itemized statement of his expenses as well as a list of contributors and contributions to his campaign. Another statute, also enacted in 1915 and amended in 1919, sought to prevent corporation involvement in Alabama elections and to regulate all forms of campaign advertising. Many of these laws—Louisiana's corrupt-practices act of 1912, for instance—were not enforced.[41]

Proposals for the introduction of the initiative, referendum, and other forms of direct democracy made relatively little progress in the southern states. Several of these devices were popular in the Southwest, however, and in two states of that subregion they were adopted on a statewide basis. The Oklahoma constitution of 1907 authorized the use of the initiative and referendum at all

[39]"Direct Vote for a Senator," *Outlook* 82 (Apr. 14, 1906): 819–20. Also see George N. Haynes, "Popular Control of Senatorial Elections," *Pol. Sci. Quar.* 20 (Dec. 1905): 577–93.

[40]"Two Discouraging Examples of Popularly Elected Senators," *World's Work* 12 (July 1906): 7702.

[41]Albert Burton Moore, *Alabama and Her People*, 3 vols. (New York and Chicago, 1927), vol. 1, pp. 964–65; Arthur Ludington, "Ballot Laws in the Southern States," *SAQ* 9 (Jan. 1910): 21–34; Tom Finty, Jr., "Our Legislative Mills: IV. Texas Makes Haste," *National Municipal Review* 12 (Nov. 1923): 649–54; George M. Reynolds, *Machine Politics in New Orleans, 1897–1926* (New York, 1936), 87–90; Alton DuMar Jones, "Progressivism in Georgia, 1898–1918" (Ph.D. diss., Emory Univ., 1963), 135–61; Allen W. Jones, "Political Reforms of the Progressive Era," *Ala. Rev.* 21 (July 1968): 173–94.

levels of government in the state, and the legislature immediately formulated a
definite procedure for the operation of the system.[42] George W. Donaghey,
who was elected governor of Arkansas in 1908, advocated the initiative and
referendum in his campaign, and in 1909 the legislature approved such a plan as
a constitutional amendment. The Arkansas voters ratified the amendment in
1910 by a vote of 91,367 to 39,111. A revised system, first submitted in 1916,
was finally approved in 1920. One of the early measures initiated by the
Arkansas voters was a constitutional amendment providing for the recall of
state officials. But it was defeated by the voters, in part it appears because
frequent elections and brief terms of office made the recall less compelling than
the initiative and referendum.[43] There was considerable support for direct-
legislation machinery in Texas, particularly in the ranks of organized labor, the
Farmers' Union, and the Socialists. In 1913 the legislature approved the initiative and referendum in the form of a constitutional amendment, but the voters
failed to ratify it in the general election. Most of the commission governments
created for Texas municipalities between 1905 and 1911 did contain direct-
legislation provisions, and these procedures were used with some success. In
1912, Louisiana voters rejected a constitutional amendment authorizing the
referendum and recall, but in 1921 a recall law was adopted that applied to all
state, parish, and city officials. The initiative, referendum, and recall were
sanctioned for municipalities in Mississippi by legislation passed in 1914. Two
years later the constitution was amended to provide for the initiative and referendum at the state level, but the amendment was later ruled unconstitutional.[44]

Although this kind of direct legislation was occasionally granted to municipalities in other southern states and the idea received support from some of the
region's progressives, it did not become a popular reform in the South. Even in
Arkansas, there was strong opposition to the initiative and referendum on the
ground that the system was an instrument of radicalism. Critics of an initiative
and referendum plan considered by North Carolina legislators in 1913 argued
that the scheme would arouse the "mob spirit," and conservatives were afraid it

---

[42]The Oklahoma system was based on the famous Oregon plan. It provided that 8 percent of the
voters in the last general election could initiate a legislative measure by petition (then to be voted on
by the electorate), 15 percent of such voters could initiate a constitutional amendment, and 5 percent
could obtain a referendum on any act of the general assembly. Legislative acts, except general
appropriation laws, were not to become effective until 90 days after passage. Scales, "Political
History of Oklahoma," 19, 43; J. H. Reynolds, "The Oklahoma Constitution," *SAQ* 7 (July
1908): 233–36; Arrell M. Gibson, *Oklahoma: A History of Five Centuries* (Norman, Okla., 1965),
333.

[43]David Y. Thomas, ed., *Arkansas and Its People,* 4 vols. (New York, 1930), vol. 1, pp.
320–25, 329–32.

[44]Emmett O'Neal, "Distrust of State Legislatures—The Cause; The Remedy," *North Ameri-
can Review* 199 (May 1914): 684–99; James Aubrey Tinsley, "The Progressive Movement in
Texas" (Ph.D. diss., Univ. of Wisconsin, 1953), 201–203, 212–13; Matthew James Schott, "John
M. Parker of Louisiana and the Varieties of American Progressivism" (Ph.D. diss., Vanderbilt
Univ., 1969), 391; Charles Granville Hamilton, "Mississippi Politics in the Progressive Era,
1904–1920" (Ph.D. diss., Vanderbilt Univ., 1958), 274–75.

would lead to an avalanche of social legislation.[45] Writing in 1913, an Oklahoma editor noted that the initiative and referendum were supposed to serve as a safeguard for the people and as a means of circumventing an unscrupulous legislature. But "under existing conditions" in his state, he remarked, "the people are kept in a turmoil all the time by men who put their own ideas above public good or the real needs of the people."[46] Despite such misgivings, the initiative and referendum in Oklahoma did not reesult in hasty or radical laws. Oklahoma voters passed upon forty-five measures between 1908 and 1920, twenty-three of which were submitted by the legislature. Of the eighteen bills initiated by the people during that period, only five were ratified.[47]

However limited democracy in the early twentieth-century South may have been, the appeal to popular sentiment was an important feature of the region's progressive politics. There was no better illustration of this point than the juxtaposition of race and reform during this period. Commenting on one of Hoke Smith's campaign speeches in 1906, the Atlanta *Journal* observed, with no apparent irony, "Equal rights to all, special privileges to none, coupled with a stirring appeal to white supremacy and popular government, was the theme of Mr. Smith's address."[48] In a reference to Tom Watson's support of Smith in the campaign of 1906, C. Vann Woodward suggests that "the picture of the Georgia Populist and the reformed Georgia conservative united on a platform of Negrophobia and progressivism was strikingly symbolical of the new era in the South."[49]

If southern progressives were sensitive to the attitudes and prejudices of the white masses, they were no less attracted to the notion of regulating the electoral process in the interest of orderly procedures, "good government," and social stability. They were also concerned with appearances and with the views of outside observers. With respect to "the race problem," they were eager to help develop controls that would bring northern acquiescense. To substitute legal for extralegal methods of controlling politics might well "authenticate" the southern political system's legitimacy in the eyes of outsiders as well as native whites.[50] There was, in fact, little likelihood of outside intervention. While northern journals were sometimes critical of the southern suffrage schemes, they tended to be understanding in discussing racial problems, to

---

[45]Thomas, ed., *Arkansas and Its People*, vol. 1, p. 332; Joseph Flake Steelman, "The Progressive Era in North Carolina, 1884–1917" (Ph.D. diss., Univ. of North Carolina, 1955), 477–83.

[46]Byron Norrell to the editor of *Youth's Companion*, June 15, 1913, William Garrott Brown Papers, Duke University Library.

[47]There were only four referenda on legislative enactments during the years 1908–20. John H. Bass, "The Initiative and Referendum in Oklahoma," *Southwestern Political Science Quarterly* 1 (Sept. 1920): 125–46; Bertil L. Hanson, "Oklahoma's Experience with Direct Legislation," *Southwestern Social Science Quarterly* 47 (Dec. 1966): 263–73.

[48]Quoted in Jones, "Progressivism in Georgia," 275.

[49]Woodward, *The Strange Career of Jim Crow*, 74.

[50]Kousser, *The Shaping of Southern Politics*, 262–63. See also David W. Southern, *The Malignant Heritage: Yankee Progressives and the Negro Question, 1901–1914* (Chicago, 1968).

consider the question a matter for the southern states to handle, and to content themselves with a plea for fair application of the new voting requirements. The *Atlantic Monthly* conceded in 1901, for example, that the indiscriminate bestowal of the ballot upon the newly liberated slaves was "a most dangerous policy." There was no short cut to equality, the magazine's editors wrote— only "the painfully slow but certain path that leads through labor and education and mutual understanding and unimagined patience to the goal of full political privilege."[51] The permanent features of the South's suffrage plans were "just and right provisions," in the opinion of *Outlook*. If properly enforced, a writer in that magazine declared, the requirements would be "beneficent" to the Negro as well as to the white man, and he suggested that northern states might well "attach similar limitations to the suffrage."[52] Thus James H. Dillard, director of the John F. Slater Fund, could remind another southern progressive in 1915, "The Northern people for the past ten years have been growing less keen in their interest in the Race question, just in proportion as they have come to the conclusion that they had better leave it to the Southern people."[53]

Some of the assumptions and expectations of the disfranchisers were confirmed by subsequent developments. Others were not. Although Negroes in varying percentages continued to vote in Kentucky, Tennessee, Arkansas, and Texas, the great majority of black men ceased to take any part in political affairs after the new suffrage measures became effective. The prediction that elections would be purged of corruption was not borne out entirely, and disfranchising devices like the poll tax opened the door to widespread fraud. Disfranchisement facilitated and legitimized the Democratic party's dominance by strengthening its control of the electoral process. In some states, suffrage restriction reinforced the control of conservative party factions. In Virginia, far from helping to overthrow the machine, the constitutional changes of 1902 served to consolidate the power of the Martin faction.[54]

Disfranchisement was only a part, though no doubt the most vital part, of the broad wave of segregation and proscription measures directed at southern blacks during the progressive era. While the suffrage restriction drive was still running its course, a comprehensive array of Jim Crow laws began to emanate from state legislatures and city councils throughout the region, mandating

[51]"Reconstruction and Disfranchisement," *Atlantic Monthly* 88 (Oct. 1901): 433–37. Also see "The New Negro Crime Again Considered," *Harper's Weekly* 47 (Oct. 3, 1903): 1577, and L. Moody Simms, Jr., "Charles Francis Adams, Jr. and the Negro Question," *New England Quarterly* 41 (Sept. 1968): 436–38.

[52]"Suffrage Limitations in the South," *Outlook* 76 (Mar. 12, 1904): 632–34. See also "Negro Suffrage in the South," ibid. 74 (June 13, 1903): 399–403; "Changed Opinions on the Race Question," *World's Work* 5 (Mar. 1903): 3156–57; and "The Caste Notion of Suffrage," *Nation* 77 (Sept. 3, 1903): 182.

[53]Dillard to Charles H. Brough, March 22, 1915, Charles Hillman Brough Papers, University of Arkansas Library.

[54]See Wythe W. Holt, Jr., "The Virginia Constitutional Convention of 1901–1902: A Reform Movement Which Lacked Substance," *Va. Mag. Hist. and Biog.* 76 (Jan. 1968): 100.

segregation in virtually all public facilities and institutions, and extending to residential neighborhoods and some forms of employment.[55] Rigid racial separation was easily accommodated in the reformers' rationale of social control, and in some cases, such as Clarence H. Poe's grandiose proposal for rural segregation in North Carolina in 1913 and 1914, progressives became obsessed with the promise of white supremacy statutes.[56] Yet many of the reformers recoiled from the mounting incidence of racial violence. The mob violence, brutality, and mayhem manifest in such outbursts as the Atlanta race riot of 1906 strengthened the conviction of middle-class southern whites that thoroughgoing segregation was necessary for social stability and peaceful race relations.[57] Jim Crow, as one historian has written, "rescued the white South from the dark uncertainties of heterodoxy. Now, with order and orthodoxy, anything might be possible."[58]

The idea of increasing Negro degeneracy encouraged white southerners to believe that black progress was crucially dependent upon legal segregation, which would bring order and tranquillity to race relations, enable black people to develop their own institutions, and demonstrate to the whole nation that the South's social arrangements were workable. But segregation in the opinion of many reformers was needed for whites—particularly poor and illiterate whites in the cities and towns—even more than for blacks. It would lessen the chances of mob action and remove a tempting target of aggressive whites. This explains why most southern progressives placed such great emphasis upon education, not only as an instrument of individual development and economic progress but also of social control. Southern humanitarian progressives such as Edgar Gardner Murphy believed that the removal of white ignorance represented the best hope for improved race relations. Southern education reformers contended that to educate the white masses would make them more tolerant of blacks; on the other hand, a substantial increase in the education of blacks would only increase

---

[55]See Woodward, *The Strange Career of Jim Crow,* 81–87; Jack Temple Kirby, *Darkness at the Dawning: Race and Reform in the Progressive South* (Philadelphia, 1972), 24–25; Germaine A. Reed, "Race Legislation in Louisiana, 1864–1920," *La. Hist.* 6 (Fall 1965): 379–92; John Hammond Moore, "Jim Crow in Georgia," *SAQ* 66 (Autumn 1967): 554–65; John Dittmer, *Black Georgia in the Progressive Era, 1900–1920* (Urbana, Ill., 1977), 8–22; Charles E. Wynes, "The Evolution of Jim Crow Laws in Twentieth Century Virginia," *Phylon* 28 (Winter 1967): 416–25; I. A. Newby, *Black Carolinians: A History of Blacks in South Carolina from 1895 to 1968* (Columbia, S.C., 1973), 46–48, 134; Linda M. Matthews, "Keeping Down Jim Crow: The Railroads and the Separate Coach Bills in South Carolina," *SAQ* 73 (Winter 1974): 117–29; and Bruce A. Glasrud, "Enforcing White Supremacy in Texas, 1900–1910," *Red River Valley Historical Review* 4 (Fall 1979): 65–74.

[56]Gilbert T. Stephenson, "The Segregation of the White and Negro Races in Rural Communities of North Carolina," *SAQ* 13 (Apr. 1914): 107–17; Clarence Poe, "Rural Land Segregation Between Whites and Negroes: A Reply to Mr. Stephenson," ibid. (July 1914): 207–12; Kirby, *Darkness at the Dawning,* 121–30.

[57]For the Atlanta race riot, see Charles Crowe, "Racial Violence and Social Reform—Origins of the Atlanta Riot of 1906," *Journal of Negro History* 53 (July 1968): 234–56, and "Racial Massacre in Atlanta, September 22, 1906," ibid. 54 (Apr. 1969): 150–73.

[58]Kirby, *Darkness at the Dawning,* 25.

the anti-Negro hostility of ordinary white southerners. "Education," Murphy observed, "is the process by which the irresponsible are bound into the life of the responsible . . . by which a people is changed from a mob into a society."[59]

In the spring of 1900 a group of professional leaders, businessmen, and politicians convened a well-publicized conference on the race question in Montgomery, Alabama. The timing of the Montgomery conference was significant, for it coincided with the wave of disfranchisement campaigns, growing awareness of the racial implications of the nation's new imperialism, southern eagerness to facilitate regional economic development, and heightened concern among some white southerners over mob violence and harsh abuse of blacks. One scholar has aptly described the Montgomery meeting as "essentially an effort by the conservative, propertied interests of the South to reach an understanding through which the outstanding racial difficulties could be removed as impediments to the economic progress and political stability of the region."[60] Edgar Gardner Murphy and other leaders of the Montgomery conference had hoped to arrange another racial symposium in 1901 and to continue such discussions in later years. But no further meetings were held, and the attention of reformers like Murphy soon shifted to other causes such as the public education movement. Meanwhile, despite the hopes and expectations of progressives, worsening race relations, the prevalence of mob violence directed at black people, and the occurrence of numerous controversial incidents involving blacks were all borne along by the strong current of anti-Negro thought that welled up in the early years of the twentieth century.

Thus the racial settlement of the 1890s and early 1900s was a fundamental component of southern progressivism. The progressives shared in the widespread conviction among white southerners that disfranchisement, segregation, and black proscription not only constituted a feasible system of racial control but also promised a greater degree of public calm and social order. The new racial milieu, it was assumed, would make it possible for reformers to address themselves to a variety of other social problems. It might also encourage the development of a new national consensus on racial matters, a consensus based upon such themes as sectional reconciliation, greater appreciation of the South's "burden of race," and the possibility that the southern example could serve the nation as a whole.[61] There were differences, of course, among southern progressives on the "race problem." Political reformers, including racial

[59]Quoted in Daniel Levine, "Edgar Gardner Murphy: Conservative Reformer," *Ala. Rev.* 15 (Apr. 1962): 111.

[60]Hines H. Hall III, "The Montgomery Race Conference of 1900: Focal Point of Racial Attitudes at the Turn of the Century" (M.A. thesis, Auburn Univ., 1965), 2. Also see the letters exchanged between Edgar Gardner Murphy, Booker T. Washington, and other correspondents in Louis R. Harlan and Raymond W. Smock, eds., *The Booker T. Washington Papers,* vol. 5: *1899–1900* (Urbana, Ill., 1976), 406, 413–14, 432, 441–42, 475–78, 489–94, 513–17, 590.

[61]See, for example, Fredrickson, *The Black Image in the White Mind,* 298–99, 304, and F. Garvin Davenport, Jr., "Thomas Dixon's Mythology of Southern History," *JSH* 36 (Aug. 1970): 350–67.

extremists like James K. Vardaman of Mississippi, were usually, though not always, advocates of repressive measures aimed at blacks. Progressives of the humanitarian type such as Edgar Gardner Murphy, although no less committed to the search for social controls, tended to be more moderate than the politicians and sought to apply "understanding" and "reason" to race relations. A third group of southern reformers, which became apparent in the second decade of the twentieth century, was more aware of the need for new approaches to the South's racial dilemma and more hopeful about the future. While assuming that blacks were racially inferior to whites, they interpreted the Negro's position as the result of environmental conditions as well as heredity.[62] But whatever their differences over solutions to the "race problem," southern progressives were not social radicals; they were reformers within the framework of the established society.

THE ILLUSION AND REALITY OF PENAL REFORM

The prison system in the various southern states was one of the most notorious of the institutions that characterized the "backward South" at the turn of the century. The disruptive effects of the Civil War and Reconstruction, widespread poverty, hopes for economic development, and obsessive white concern with the control of blacks were all involved in shaping the region's penal arrangements. The criminal codes and legal systems in the late nineteenth-century South facilitated the use of convict labor by cities, counties, and states.[63] In addition to furnishing labor for economic enterprise, the ready availability of this supply of convicts encouraged public officials to rely on it as a source of revenue, or at the very least to use convict labor as a means of making the penal system self-supporting. The administration of prisons in the South was also a central instrument of social control, especially of racial supervision. As the editor of the Birmingham *News* remarked in 1906, "Anyone visiting a Southern city or town must be impressed at witnessing the large number of loafing negroes. . . . They can all get work, but they don't want to work. The result is that they sooner or later get into mischief or commit crimes."[64] Prisons provided a mechanism of social control well adapted to handle this problem.

[62]See the categories suggested by I. A. Newby, *Jim Crow's Defense: Anti-Negro Thought in America, 1900–1930* (Baton Rouge, 1965), pp. ix–x. Also see Fredrickson, *The Black Image in the White Mind,* 283–88; William Starr Myers, "Some Present-Day Views of the Southern Race Problem," *Sewanee Review* 21 (July 1913): 341–49; and Mark Aldrich, "Progressive Economists and Scientific Racism: Walter Wilcox and Black Americans, 1895–1910," *Phylon* 40 (Spring 1979): 1–14.

[63]In Texas, for example, the prison population during the thirty years before 1903 grew more than twice as fast as the state's population. Charles S. Potts, "The Convict Labor System of Texas," *Annals* 21 (May 1903): 426.

[64]Quoted in Carl V. Harris, "Reforms in Government Control of Negroes in Birmingham, Alabama, 1890–1920," *JSH* 38 (Nov. 1972): 567.

The mainstay of the penal system in most southern states after the Civil War was the leasing of state convicts.[65] The arrangement was simple, convenient, and potentially profitable. It disposed of prison inmates for long periods of time and relieved the states of providing public facilities and custodial personnel. It furnished a reliable source of labor for the rapid railroad construction of the 1880s and 1890s, as well as such varied operations as mining, large-scale farming, the turpentine industry in Florida, and levee building in Louisiana. Though several of the state leases were first made during the Reconstruction period, the system assumed definite shape under the Bourbon governments and embodied their emphasis on social order, frugality, limited government, entrepreneurial enterprise, and the industrial spirit of the New South. By the mid-1880s most southern states were realizing a profit from their convicts. Annual expenditures for the operation of the penitentiary system in Louisiana during the years 1874–1901 never exceeded annual revenues derived from convict labor.[66] The system was safeguarded through legislative support, the influence of its private beneficiaries, and a good deal of collusion between government officials and the lessees.

Although the convict-lease system was widely accepted in the South as an effective and remunerative arrangement, it was citicized on both humanitarian and economic grounds almost from its inception. The isolated location of the convict camps, the absence of state supervision, and the operators' determination to exact the ultimate amount of labor from each prisoner resulted in incredible conditions of cruelty, brutality, and degradation. An official of the Prison Reform Association of Louisiana estimated that the annual death rate per thousand prisoners between 1893 and 1901 in that state was over one hundred.[67] Sporadic protests were generated by legislative investigations and newspaper accounts of leasing abuses, and the system was also criticized by some ministers, physicians, boards of health, and reform-minded individuals. The Greenback-Labor party in the early eighties and the Populist party during the next decade denounced convict leasing, in part because of its barbarous features and in part because it seemed to reflect Bourbon favoritism toward corporations and the well-to-do. Industrial labor also protested against the practice because of competititon from convict labor. Though prison reform in the South was hardly an organized movement by the end of the century, those concerned with the amelioration of prison conditions had agreed to give priority to the abolition of the convict-lease system.

The leasing system was abolished in three southern states and weakened in

---

[65]John Davis Anderson, "The Southern Prison Lease System," *Independent* 51 (July 13, 1899): 1879–81; Fletcher Melvin Green, "Some Aspects of the Convict Lease System in the Southern States," in Green, ed., *Essays in Southern History*, 112–23.

[66]Mark T. Carleton, "The Politics of the Convict Lease System in Louisiana: 1868–1901," *La. Hist.* 8 (Winter 1967): 7.

[67]Ibid., 6.

several others during the 1890s. Somewhat surprisingly, the first state to outlaw the system was Mississippi, which had been leasing its convicts for private plantation work and railroad building since 1875. By the end of the 1880s, the leasing of convicts was being subjected to strong criticism in Mississippi. The system was resented by many small farmers, since it apparently served the interests of a few wealthy planters, and it was no longer a steady source of revenue for the state government. The constitution of 1890 introduced some improvements in the penal system, and it provided that convict leasing must be discontinued by the end of 1894. Although the worst aspects of the practice were eliminated by the mid-nineties, vestiges of the system survived, and the operation of the state penitentiary and farms was plagued by mismanagement, corruption, and cruelty in the treatment of prisoners. More thoroughgoing reform did not come until 1906, when the determined efforts of Governor James K. Vardaman were primarily responsible for the complete abolition of convict leasing and for the creation of a more efficient means of penitentiary management.[68]

Tennessee, the second southern state to abandon the leasing system, did so in large part as a result of vigorous labor opposition. During the 1880s, more than half of the state's prisoners were leased for long terms to railroad and mining corporations, including the Tennessee Coal, Iron and Railroad Company (TCI). Industrial workers, a growing component of the Tennessee labor force, protested against the employment of convicts by private firms. A series of disturbances by coal miners in 1891 and 1892 resulted in the freeing of the convict workers of TCI and other companies, and the burning of the prisoners' stockades. Meanwhile, the Farmers' Alliance and the Populist party condemned the leasing system, the two major parties pledged themselves to abolish it, and labor demonstrations demanding prison reform were held in various Tennessee cities. In 1893 the general assembly acted to resolve the mounting crisis by abolishing leasing with the expiration of the existing contracts in 1896, providing for a new penitentiary building, and introducing several other improvements in penal practices.[69]

Louisiana also moved against the leasing system in the 1890s. While criticism of the state's convict leases increased during the 1880s, the practice did not become a pressing political issue until the following decade. Governor Murphy

[68]John K. Bettersworth, "The Reawakening of Society and Cultural Life, 1865–1890," in Richard Aubrey McLemore, ed., *A History of Mississippi,* 2 vols. (Hattiesburg, Miss., 1973), vol. 1, p. 631; James P. Coleman, "The Mississippi Constitution of 1890 and the Final Decade of the Nineteenth Century," ibid., vol. 2, pp. 15–16; Kirwan, *Revolt of the Rednecks,* 167–75; William F. Holmes, "James K. Vardaman and Prison Reform in Mississippi," *Jour. Miss. Hist.* 27 (Aug. 1965): 229–48.

[69]Jesse Crawford Crowe, "Agitation for Penal Reform in Tennessee, 1870–1900" (Ph.D. diss., Vanderbilt Univ., 1954), 250–302; Randall G. Shelden, "From Slave to Caste Society: Penal Changes in Tennessee, 1830–1915," *Tenn. Hist. Quar.* 38 (Winter 1979): 462–78; Woodward, *Origins of the New South,* 232–34.

J. Foster helped secure the passage in 1894 of a constitutional amendment that would have ended the lease system in 1901. But the electorate failed to ratify the amendment in the chaotic election of 1896. Reformers, led by the Prison Reform Association, were more successful in the constitutional convention of 1898: Article 196 of the new constitution prohibited the leasing of convicts to private firms or individuals after the existing leases expired in 1901. A legislative act of 1901 implemented this directive, established a "new" penitentiary system, and introduced other prison reforms.[70] A close student of the state's penal system has concluded that "the practice of leasing convicts had been terminated in Louisiana—not primarily for humanitarian reasons nor because penal reformers had suddenly acquired genuine influence, but rather because the lessee (together with the lottery, black voters, and Populism) had become politically intolerable to the new ruling faction of the state Democratic Party."[71]

Although a decade passed before the next southern state ended its leasing policy, the system remained the focal point of prison reform in the region. As its notoriety increased, the leasing of convicts was both attacked by southern progressives and frequently cited in other sections as an illustration of southern backwardness. Those states that retained the lease system did attempt to supervise their leasing arrangements more closely and to remove some women and children from the prisoners let out by contract. While the system was still profitable to some state governments, it had economic as well as social and political flaws. The lessees were often behind with their rentals, and their contracts were sometimes canceled. The states were forced to pay rewards for runaway convicts and to support disabled prisoners. And convict labor competed with free labor.

Convict leasing was continued in Georgia until 1909, despite being attacked by Populists and other critics in the 1890s. But as the expiration of the current leases approached in 1909, a vigorous reform movement took shape, led by the Atlanta *Georgian and News* and such reformers as Dr. John E. White, an Atlanta minister, and encouraged by the progressive administration of Governor Hoke Smith. "Every one knows," one legislator conceded, "that the question of the convict lease system is so rotten that it smells to heaven."[72] When the legislature failed to act in the regular session of 1908, Governor Smith called an extra session and recommended abolition of the system. The disclosures resulting from an investigation of leasing practices by a joint legislative committee stimulated the demand for reform. Given a committee report filled with evi-

---

[70] Mark T. Carleton, *Politics and Punishment: The History of the Louisiana State Penal System* (Baton Rouge, 1971), 33–38; Carleton, "The Politics of the Convict Lease System in Louisiana," 5–25; Elizabeth Wisner, *Public Welfare Administration in Louisiana* (Chicago, 1930), 154–65.
[71] Carleton, *Politics and Punishment*, 58.
[72] Quoted in Dewey W. Grantham, *Hoke Smith and the Politics of the New South* (Baton Rouge, 1958), 173.

dence of leasing's abuses and with charges of "grave neglect of duty," and faced with an increasingly indignant public, the general assembly abolished the arrangement in September 1908 and reorganized the state's prison system.[73]

Georgia's example may have had some effect in Texas, as did the climate of social reform in the administration of Governor Thomas M. Campbell. In any case, a wave of critical publicity was suddenly directed at the prison system generally and the convict-lease policy in particular. This heightened criticism seems to have commenced with a series of articles written by George Waverley Briggs, a reporter for the San Antonio *Express,* in late 1908 and early 1909. Briggs's articles, based on a tour of the state's convict camps, emphasized the abuses in the prisons and their operation as part of the spoils system. The legislature responded to these exposures by authorizing an investigation of the penal system by an ad hoc committee. The committee's final report early in 1910 corroborated many of the publicized abuses, in state facilities as well as lessee camps. Meanwhile, a journalist named Tom Finty contributed to the campaign for prison reform in twenty-two articles on Texas penal conditions for the Galveston *News* and the Dallas *News.* The question became a political issue in the campaign of 1910. Governor Campbell, seeking to secure action before his term expired, called a special session of the general assembly in the summer of 1910. In September the legislators voted to end the convict leases as they expired during the next three years and to reform the penal system in various other respects.[74]

The last southern state to take decisive action against the convict-lease system before World War I was Arkansas. During the early years of the century the state's convicts were cultivating thousands of acres of land for planters and the leasing system was permeated with fraud, illegal business transactions, and brutality in the treatment of prisoners. Governor Jeff Davis (1901–1907) spoke out against the lease system, and various legislative committees recommended its abolition, but without noticeable effect. The movement against leasing entered a new phase with the election of George W. Donaghey as governor in 1908. Donaghey pressed the general assembly throughout his four-year term to abolish leasing and introduce other penal reforms. The legislature would not act. Near the end of his tenure the governor made a spectacular move. Influenced by the example of Governor Coleman L. Blease in South Carolina, Donaghey on December 17, 1912, abruptly pardoned 360 convicts. This sensa-

[73] Ibid., 173–74; A. Elizabeth Taylor, "The Convict Lease System in Georgia, 1866–1908" (M.A. thesis, Univ. of North Carolina, 1940): A. J. McKelway, "The Convict Lease System of Georgia," *Outlook* 75 (Nov. 7, 1903): 522–23; Alfred C. Newell, "Georgia's Barbarous Convict System," *World's Work* 16 (Oct. 1908): 10829–31; Atlanta *Georgian and News,* July 7, 1908; Jones, "Progressivism in Georgia," 12–34; Matthew J. Mancini, "Race, Economics, and the Abandonment of Convict Leasing," *Jour. Negro Hist.* 63 (Fall 1978): 339–52.

[74] Potts, "The Convict Labor System of Texas," 426–32; Tom Finty, Jr., "The Texas Prison Investigation," *Survey* 23 (Dec. 18, 1909): 387–91; Tinsley, "The Progressive Movement in Texas," 222–30.

tional act aroused great interest in and out of Arkansas, as did the publication at about the same time of *Story of the Arkansas Penitentiary*, a revelation of prison horrors by an ex-convict named William N. Hill. Much discussion of the prison problem and its possible solution ensued. Governor Joseph T. Robinson's first message to the legislature in 1913 recommended reorganization of the prison system. This time the lawmakers acted, abolishing the convict-lease system and creating a new penitentiary board.[75]

In the other southern states the status of the leasing system varied. Virginia, Kentucky, and Oklahoma had never made much use of a lease policy. North and South Carolina gradually abandoned their reliance on leasing arrangements in the late nineteenth century, adopting alternative means of employing their prisoners under state supervision. Florida and Alabama retained the convict-lease system throughout the progressive era, finally abolishing it in the 1920s. Beginning about 1910, a reform movement developed in Florida that resulted in the passage of a bill in 1911 abolishing the lease system. But the governor vetoed the measure, even though he advocated changes in the system.[76] In Alabama both the state and county governments leased their convicts to private firms, usually coal companies which used them as miners. Although the leasing practice provoked a good deal of controversy in the late nineteenth and early twentieth centuries, a vigorous and purposeful movement to abolish the system did not develop in Alabama until 1917.[77]

As leasing was gradually abandoned in the South, state officials were forced to devise new methods for the handling of their prisoners. However much southerners might condemn the evils of the convict-lease system, they were equally opposed to the expenditure of state money for their penitentiaries. They assumed that certain state institutions, among them the prisons, should be financially self-supporting. Thus they generally approved new arrangements to replace convict leasing that promised to bring revenue to the state treasury as well as to control the prison population effectively. By the turn of the century,

[75]Jane Zimmerman, "The Convict Lease System in Arkansas and the Fight for Abolition," *Ark. Hist. Quar.* 8 (Autumn 1949): 171–88; Thomas L. Baxley, "Prison Reforms during the Donaghey Administration," ibid. 22 (Spring 1963): 76–84; "A Governor, 360 Convicts and the Lease System," *Survey* 29 (Dec. 28, 1912): 383–84; George W. Donaghey, "Why I Could Not Pardon the Contract System," *Annals* 46 (Mar. 1913): 22–30. For Blease's role in South Carolina, see Donald Dantan Burnside, "The Governorship of Coleman Livingston Blease of South Carolina, 1911–1915" (Ph.D. diss., Indiana Univ., 1963), 173–94.

[76]The system was modified substantially during the administration of Governor Sidney J. Catts (1917–21), though it was retained on a county-option basis. See Wayne Flynt, *Cracker Messiah: Governor Sidney J. Catts of Florida* (Baton Rouge, 1977), 138–39, 210–12, 238–39. Also see Marc N. Goodnow, "Turpentine: Impressions of the Convict Camps of Florida," *Survey* 34 (May 1, 1915): 103–108.

[77]Hilda Jane Zimmerman, "Penal Systems and Penal Reforms in the South since the Civil War" (Ph.D. diss., Univ. of North Carolina, 1947), 315–21, 386, 391; Malcolm C. Moos, *State Penal Administration in Alabama* (University, Ala., 1942), 4, 11–12, 14–16, 20; David Alan Harris, "Racists and Reformers: A Study of Progressivism in Alabama, 1896–1911" (Ph.D. diss., Univ. of North Carolina, 1967), 65–83, 275, 375–85.

the southern states had experimented with plantations, road camps, and industrial prisons, all of which were used extensively in the region during later years.

A majority of the southern states acquired prison farms or plantations during the early years of the twentieth century. Texas, North Carolina, and Virginia tried separating women, children, and disabled inmates from the regular prison population and placing them on "asylum" farms. Agricultural work seemed to offer other advantages as well: it would enable prisoners to work in the open air and sunshine; most of them were already familiar with farm work and such training was considered suitable for those leaving the penitentiary for society; prison farms could produce valuable staples such as cotton and sugar cane in addition to the foodstuffs needed for state institutions; and agricultural work would not compete with industrial labor. Political leaders, penal experts, and prison reformers generally agreed that farm work for convicts represented a progressive approach. In 1906, Frederick H. Wines, a leader in the activities of the National Prison Association, was quoted as saying of the Louisiana prison farm system, "It is difficult to conceive of a more ideal method of dealing with prisoners, especially Negro prisoners, than this."[78]

Mississippi was the first state in the South to make extensive use of convict labor on state-owned farms. By 1910 the state was operating four farms, including a 15,000-acre plantation known as Sunflower, and the prison farms made a profit that year of $179,000. Louisiana also emphasized agricultural work when it ended leasing and reorganized its prison system in 1900. By 1906 the prison board of that state was able to use every able-bodied prisoner in farm or levee work. Profits were encouraging for several years; then the cotton yield declined as a result of bad conditions and the appearance of the boll weevil, low prices for lumber hurt the sawmill operation at the largest plantation, and devastating floods in 1912 severely damaged prison farm output. In Texas the state government had gradually acquired thousands of acres in widely scattered farm units, and the reform act of 1910 authorized the prison commission to buy additional land so that by the end of 1914 all state convicts currently working on share farms or contracts could become directly employed on prison farms or in shops within penitentiary walls. When Arkansas abolished convict leasing and reorganized its penal system in 1913, it adopted a policy of using all inmates on state farms. By 1915, 1,182 convicts in Arkansas were cultivating 5,500 acres of farm land.[79] Other southern states, notably North Carolina, also used prisoners to operate large farms, but such operations were not the core of their prison systems.

[78]Quoted in Jane Zimmerman, "The Penal Reform Movement in the South during the Progressive Era, 1890–1917," *JSH* 17 (Nov. 1951): 467. See also Blake McKelvey, "A Half Century of Southern Penal Exploitation," *Social Forces* 13 (Oct. 1934): 112–14.

[79]Zimmerman, "Penal Systems and Penal Reforms in the South," 313–14, 333–40; Carleton, *Politics and Punishment*, 88–93; Wisner, *Public Welfare Administration in Louisiana*, 113, 115–16; Ralph W. Steen, *Twentieth Century Texas: An Economic and Social History* (Austin, Tex., 1942), 183–202.

The prison farms, sometimes advertised as an "ideal" solution to such evils as convict leasing, did not solve the South's penal problems. For one thing, they were designed, like the lease policy, to be profitable, or at least to be self-sufficient. They failed, moreover, to end the mistreatment of convicts and other harsh features of the lease system and the old penitentiaries. But they did provide what a leading student of American penology described as "several of the bright spots" in the South's penal history.[80] In fact, the southeastern states might have concentrated on the prison farm had it not been for the good-roads movement and the increasing use of convict labor in the construction and maintenance of roads and highways. The spreading interest in good roads in the South prompted chambers of commerce and various other organizations to advocate the use of state and county prisoners for this purpose. One scholar has concluded that the most significant development in southern penology between 1900 and 1917 was the acceptance of the new system of road work for convicts.[81]

What came to be called the county chain gang grew out of penal systems developed in the post-Civil War period for the local control of certain prisoners, usually those with short sentences. A survey published in 1886 by the United States commissioner of labor revealed that a majority of the southern states, as well as many states in other sections, had already perfected a system of prisoners' working on the public roads. By 1896 the practice had grown to such an extent that the warden of the state prison in North Carolina listed it as one of the reasons for the decline in the number of state prisoners.[82] The superintendent of that state's prison, in his report for the years 1907–1908, called attention to the fact that about forty counties in North Carolina had organized chain gangs under special acts of the legislature. There were more than 1,200 prisoners in these chain gangs. According to the superintendent, the state "has granted to the counties absolutely and unconditionally the full management and control of these prisoners, and has endeavored to surrender its responsibility for them, not even reserving a supervisory or inspectionary authority."[83]

Most of the other southern states followed North Carolina's lead and passed laws permitting counties and municipalities to use convicts for road work. This scheme emerged as the heart of the penal system in several of the southeastern states, constituting what one contemporary described as a "perpetual road-mending club."[84] When Georgia abandoned the lease system in 1908, for example, it substituted a more comprehensive policy of contracting with the counties for use of state convicts on local chain gangs. The system flourished

[80] McKelvey, "A Half Century of Southern Penal Exploitation," 115.
[81] Zimmerman, "The Penal Reform Movement in the South," 467–68.
[82] Jesse F. Steiner and Roy M. Brown, *The North Carolina Chain Gang: A Study of County Convict Road Work* (Chapel Hill, N.C., 1927), 11, 18, 21, 33–34, 37.
[83] Ibid., 39–40.
[84] George Herbert Clarke, "Georgia and the Chain-Gang," *Outlook* 82 (Jan. 13, 1906): 77. Also see Joe Asher, "County Road Camps in Arkansas," *Annals* 46 (Mar. 1913): 88–89.

and eventually resulted in more than five thousand prisoners' working on the county roads.[85] Southern cities also resorted to the chain gang for road work. Birmingham, for instance, shackled its convicts in chain gangs made up largely of blacks, and these gangs cleaned and repaired the streets ten hours a day. This street work was financially important to the city, which had a low constitutional tax rate limitation and experienced chronic financial crisis during this period.[86]

With the passage of time, the chain gang came under attack by some prison reformers. Only in Virginia were convicts assigned to road work supervised by state rather than county authorities. Many of the chain gangs lived in small, scattered camps or cages where conditions were often unbelievably bad, where flogging and other mistreatment were daily occurrences, and where health and sanitary standards, as well as clothing and food, were extremely poor. The theory was that those convicted of felonies and given long terms should be sent to the state prison, while those guilty of less serious offenses, and especially misdemeanors, should be sentenced to shorter terms and lighter work upon the roads. Yet ironically, two historians of the North Carolina system have written, "it is strangely true that harsher and more vigorous punishment is inflicted upon the petty offender than upon him who commits the more serious crime."[87] The superintendent of the North Carolina prison concluded as early as 1908 that his state's chain-gang policy was "in every respect as defective and as full of possibilities for wrongdoing, cruelty and inhumanity as was the old convict-lease system, now long since abolished."[88] In 1914 the superintendent of the Virginia penitentiary conceded that the system did nothing to "reform a prisoner."[89]

While the Southwest was turning to the prison farm and the Southeast to the county chain gang as means of dealing with their convicted criminals, the Upper South was emphasizing a third alternative to the convict-lease system. Virginia, Kentucky, Tennessee, and Oklahoma increasingly relied upon the contract labor system, which had earlier been used extensively in the North and had been tried in the late nineteenth century by several southern states. Under the contract system private industries were operated within the prison walls; only the *labor* of the convict was let out, since the state remained responsible for guarding, disciplining, and caring for the prison workers. The contract arrangement in some states was combined with the public account and state use systems, whereby certain prisoners labored for the state or produced goods for public institutions.

[85] Zimmerman, "Penal Systems and Penal Reforms in the South," 322–32; McKelvey, "A Half Century of Southern Penal Exploitation," 118; Clarke, "Georgia and the Chain-Gang," 73–79.
[86] Harris, "Reforms in Government Control of Negroes," 582–83.
[87] Steiner and Brown, *The North Carolina Chain Gang*, 40.
[88] J. L. Mann, quoted in ibid., 41.
[89] "The Meetings at Memphis: Forty-first National Conference of Charities and Correction," *Survey* 32 (May 30, 1914): 237.

Alabama chain gang, 1909. *The Collections of the Birmingham Public Library*.

Virginia made greater use of the contract system than any other southern state, although it was an important feature of penal policy in the Upper South generally and was employed in several other states on a modest scale. In 1912 the Virginia prison board negotiated a new contract with the Star Manufacturing Company, letting out the labor of five hundred inmates of the state penitentiary at a rate of eighty-five cents per day for men and forty-five cents for women. Industrial contracts in Tennessee's Nashville penitentiary early in the century involved the production of such items as shoes and hosiery, which were not well-established manufactures in the Volunteer State. Between 1903 and 1917, Tennessee's mining operations at its Brushy Mountain coal mines brought in net profits of over $1.6 million.[90] The contract system was not without its evils, however, and it too came in for citicism by prison reformers.

The penal practices that were being institutionalized in the South during the first two decades of the twentieth century did more than confine, punish, and exploit the region's criminals. They also provided the ultimate support for the South's labor system. In effect a condition of involuntary servitude, resting upon a variety of state and local laws and on prevailing community attitudes, was widespread in the South at the turn of the century. Peonage, a form of involuntary servitude based on alleged indebtedness, made up only one part of a more comprehensive system calculated to force laborers, particularly those with black skins, to work. Measures that facilitated involuntary servitude included enticement statutes, emigrant-agent acts, and an assortment of contract-enforcement and "false-pretense" laws. There were also numerous broadly drawn vagrancy statutes which enabled police to round up idle men and which gave employers a coercive tool that could be used to keep workers on the job. Alabama's vagrancy law of 1903, which replaced part of its black code enacted in 1866, was directed at "any person wandering or strolling about in idleness, who is able to work, and has no property to support him; or any person leading an idle, immoral, profligate life, having no property to support him. . . ." All of the former Confederate states except Tennessee enacted similar vagrancy measures between 1893 and 1909.[91] When labor was scarce, the control mechanism went into operation. During a labor shortage in 1904, for instance, a report from Newton, Georgia, indicated that local emergency offi-

---

[90]McKelvey, "A Half Century of Southern Penal Exploitation," 114, 120; Zimmerman, "Penal Systems and Penal Reforms in the South," 340–47; F. A. Magruder, *Recent Administration in Virginia* (Baltimore, 1912), 107–13; Crowe, "Agitation for Penal Reform in Tennessee," 318–19.

[91]William Cohen, "Negro Involuntary Servitude in the South, 1865–1940: A Preliminary Analysis," *JSH* 42 (Feb. 1976): 31–60; quotation on p. 48. Also see Harris, "Reforms in Government Control of Negroes," 567–600; "The Case of Alonzo Bailey," *Outlook* 97 (Jan. 21, 1911): 101–104; Jerrell H. Shofner, "Mary Grace Quackenbos, a Visitor Florida Did Not Want," *Fla. Hist. Quar.* 58 (Jan. 1980): 273–90; and William F. Holmes, "Labor Agents and the Georgia Exodus, 1899–1900," *SAQ* 79 (Autumn 1980): 436–48.

cers had made "wholesale arrests of idle Negroes . . . to scare them back to the farms from which they emanated."[92]

Those hapless individuals jailed on charges of vagrancy or other petty crime were frequently entrapped by the operation of the criminal-surety system, which enabled the offender to sign a voluntary labor contract with his former employer or some other person who agreed to post bond. Those who had no surety often wound up on chain gangs, "which in effect were a state-sponsored part of the system of involuntary servitude."[93] Forced labor under nominal legal sanction sometimes led to peonage. It might result, for example, under a farming contract whereby the tenant was continually in debt to his landlord for supplies and cash advances and was held by threats and terrorism. "There is no doubt whatever," a contemporary critic wrote in 1907, "that there are scores, hundreds perhaps, of coloured men in the South today who are vainly trying to repay fines and sentences imposed upon them five, six, or even ten years ago."[94] While peonage and other forced labor arrangements exacted their greatest toll from black people, there were also white victims of such practices, including some foreign immigrants to the section.

As the attack on the convict-lease system gradually succeeded, as new penal methods were introduced, and as the states extended their direct control over their convicts, a movement for general prison reform gathered momentum. State prison associations played a vital role in this movement for broader penal reform in the South. The Louisiana Prison Reform Association (LPRA) was perhaps the most active of the southern organizations. It contributed to the adoption of the constitutional prohibition of 1898 against convict leasing and to the prison reorganization act of 1900. The association then began a campaign to reform the state's criminal law, to improve prison management, and to assist discharged prisoners. The LPRA brought Dr. Frederick H. Wines to Louisiana to make a study of the state penitentiary. Under the leadership of Michael Heymann, a prominent citizen of New Orleans, the association fostered the state board of charities and corrections. It was instrumental in securing state laws providing for a parole system and the suspended sentence. During the years before World War I the LPRA cooperated with the board of charities and corrections, working for the improvement of the Louisiana Training School

---

[92] Quoted in Cohen, "Negro Involuntary Servitude in the South," 50. Also see Dittmer, *Black Georgia in the Progressive Era*, 73–89.

[93] Cohen, "Negro Involuntary Servitude in the South," 34.

[94] Mary Church Terrell, "Peonage in the United States: The Convict Lease System and the Chain Gang," *Nineteenth Century* 62 (Aug. 1907): 313. See also "Peonage," *Outlook* 74 (July 18, 1903): 687–88; "Peonage: A Significant Mistrial," ibid. (July 25, 1903): 732–34; "Peonage," ibid. (Aug. 8, 1903): 890–91; "White Peonage in North Carolina," ibid. 87 (Oct. 19, 1907): 319–20; "A Blow at Peonage," ibid. 97 (Jan. 14, 1911): 47–48; "The Stamping out of Peonage," *Nation* 82 (May 10, 1906): 379; Hastings H. Hart, "Peonage and the Public," *Survey* 46 (Apr. 9, 1921): 43–44; Pete Daniel, *The Shadow of Slavery: Peonage in the South, 1901–1969* (Urbana, Ill., 1972); and N. Gordon Carper, "Slavery Revisited: Peonage in the South," *Phylon* 37 (Mar. 1976): 85–99.

for Boys at Monroe and the establishment of such an institution for girls, assisting released prisoners and extending aid to the wives and children of inmates, and agitating for the indeterminate sentence and the abolition of corporal and capital punishment. The Virginia association established and maintained private reform schools, in addition to working for general prison reforms. In a number of states the prison reform associations were joined by organizations like the Carolina Prisoner's Aid Society, the Texas Society for the Friendless, the Negro Reformatory Association of Virginia, the Ex-Prisoners' Aid Society of Virginia, and the Women's Christian Temperance Union.[95]

A related reform endeavor involved efforts to establish juvenile courts to regulate the treatment and control of delinquent, dependent, and neglected children. The juvenile court movement, which began with the creation of a children's court in Chicago in 1899, emphasized special facilities and techniques for the handling of juvenile delinquency, along with new methods of detention, probation, and rehabilitation. A few southern cities had introduced some form of juvenile court by 1905, and the movement gradually spread over the South during the following decade, first through special acts applying to particular cities and subsequently through the passage of general state laws. Federations of Women's Clubs, state conferences of charities and corrections, and individual reformers such as Kate Barnard of Oklahoma spearheaded these efforts. At the end of the progressive era the juvenile court system, while taking root in most southern cities, remained largely unknown in the small towns and rural areas of the region.[96]

One section of the Louisiana prison statute of 1900 stipulated that convicts between the ages of seven and seventeen should be separated from older prisoners. This provision had been recommended by the Louisiana Prison Reform Association.[97] It suggests the special concern that penal reformers in the South had for the treatment of youthful offenders. They sought in every state to secure the introduction of a classification system that would permit young prison inmates to be removed from the general penitentiary population and given special treatment. Thus reformers worked to establish and support reforma-

[95]Wisner, *Public Welfare Administration in Louisiana,* 180–81; Magruder, *Recent Administration in Virginia,* 114–17; Zimmerman, "The Penal Reform Movement in the South during the Progressive Era," 471–73; Zimmerman, "Penal Systems and Penal Reforms in the South," 352–54.

[96]"Juvenile Courts in New Orleans," *Charities* 14 (May 20, 1905): 758–59; "Spread of the Juvenile Court Movement—Probation," ibid. (July 1, 1905): 871–72; Herbert H. Lou, *Juvenile Courts in the United States* (Chapel Hill, N.C., 1927), 33, 37–38, 56, 62–64; Virginia Ashcraft, *Public Care: A History of Public Welfare in Tennessee* (Knoxville, 1947), 33–36; Joseph F. Steelman, "Progressivism and Agitation for Legal Reform in North Carolina, 1897–1917," in *Essays in American History* (Greenville, N.C., 1964), 92–93; Keith L. Bryant, Jr., "The Juvenile Court Movement: Oklahoma as a Case Study," *Social Science Quarterly* 49 (Sept. 1968): 368–76; Frank O. Alonzo, "The History of the Mississippi Youth Court System," *Jour. Miss. Hist.* 39 (May 1977): 133–53.

[97]Carleton, "The Politics of the Convict Lease System in Louisiana," 23.

tories and training schools for boys and girls. While many of the larger cities had established some kind of juvenile reformatory by the turn of the century, the states were slow in creating such facilities. In Louisiana, despite the authorization in the omnibus prison act of 1900, the legislature made no appropriation for a reformatory until 1906, and it was not completed until 1910. As late as 1917 some youths in Louisiana were being confined within the walls or on the farms—two Negro children under twelve and one white and thirty-one black boys between the ages of twelve and sixteen.[98] Although all of the southern states had established juvenile reformatories and training schools before World War I, they were inadequately supported and administered by untrained personnel. They almost always neglected the needs of black children and of white girls.[99]

Some improvements were made in the treatment of the general prison populations. Most of the southern states eventually adopted procedures that enabled penal authorities to classify and grade prisoners, separating young offenders from adults, women from men, and the sick and disabled from the physically fit inmates. Several state laws specified shorter hours and lighter working assignments for convicts. Boards of health and other agencies began to show greater interest in prison sanitation and the health of penitentiary inmates. Efforts were made to provide religious instruction and prison libraries, but as late as 1912 only five commonwealths in the region had enacted legislation setting up any kind of secular educational program for their prisoners.[100] Here and there a warden would experiment with the principle of the honor system or abandon the requirement that convicts wear stripes. When the Texas legislature abolished the leasing system in 1910, it outlawed the whipping of prisoners, limited the number of hours they must work per day, and provided that inmates whose terms were reduced as a result of good behavior should be paid at a rate of ten cents a day and that they should be paid for overtime labor. The prison commission was critical of these reforms, and following a legislative investigation of the large penitentiary debt in 1913, a new statute was enacted which permitted surpervised whippings and repealed the per diem compensation of prisoners.[101]

The South lagged behind other parts of the country in adopting modern release procedures, a circumstance that contributed to the wholesale issuance of

[98] Carleton, *Politics and Punishment*, 95–96, 99. The percentage of black youths in southern prisons was very large. A recent study of the Tennessee prison system found that between the 1890s and the 1920s about a third of the prison inmates were under the age of 20. At least three-fourths of these youthful prisoners were black. See Shelden, "From Slave to Caste Society," 472–77.

[99] Zimmerman, "Penal Systems and Penal Reforms in the South," 370–75; Thomas, ed., *Arkansas and Its People*, vol. 2, pp. 499–503; "Prison Labor," *American Labor Legislation Review* 1 (Oct. 1911): 128.

[100] Zimmerman, "Penal Systems and Penal Reforms in the South," 359–70; Zimmerman, "The Penal Reform Movement in the South during the Progressive Era," 481–84, 490.

[101] Zimmerman, "Penal Systems and Penal Reforms in the South," 296–300. Also see Robert G. Crawford, "Degradation by Design: Punishment in Kentucky Penitentiaries," *Border States: Journal of the Kentucky-Tennessee American Studies Association* 1 (1973): 72–84.

pardons by a number of southern governors during this period. Some progress came with the passage of commutation or "good time" laws that reduced a prisoner's term in accordance with his record of good behavior. Seven southern states had adopted such measures by 1915. Several states had introduced parole and probation systems by that time. The indeterminate sentence, on the other hand, made little headway in the South during the early years of the century.[102] In 1917 the North Carolina general assembly, responding to an advanced prison program formulated by the state Conference for Social Service, enacted legislation providing compensation to prisoners for their labor and some help for their dependent families, an indeterminate sentence and a system of parole, the "honor system," better physical surroundings and care for inmates, and restrictions on the use of stripes and flogging.[103]

In the states where the broader movement for penal reform made progress, it was frequently a consequence of the activities of the boards of charities and corrections. State conferences, which encouraged creation of the state boards, also promoted the drive for prison reform in the South.[104] The most notable effort by a state board to provide inspectional and central supervision for penal facilities was that of Virginia. Created by the legislature in 1908, the Virginia board was enjoined to examine at least once a year the state, county, municipal, and private institutions of a correctional or reformatory character. When Dr. Joseph T. Mastin, the board's first secretary, visited the state penitentiary in 1908, he found conditions deplorable. Under Mastin's energetic leadership, the board of charities and corrections immediately launched a drive for penal reform in the state. It resulted in several distinct improvements, including the prison act of 1912. Meanwhile, Major J.B. Wood, who had become superintendent of the state penitentiary in 1910, abolished flogging except as a last resort, introduced a system of honor grading and rewards, and established a recreational program for prisoners.[105]

By the end of the progressive era, the convict-lease system had been largely abolished except in two states. Stricter state controls had been provided, better classification schemes introduced, and improvements made in prison management. Facilities for youthful offenders, women, and the physically handi-

---

[102]Zimmerman, "The Penal Reform Movement in the South during the Progressive Era," 472, 486–89; Wisner, *Public Welfare Administration in Louisiana*, 169–71; Joseph P. Byers, "Parole in Kentucky," *Journal of Social Forces* 1 (Jan. 1923): 135–36; Orben J. Casey, "Governor Lee Cruce, White Supremacy and Capital Punishment, 1911–1915," *Chron. Okla.* 52 (Winter 1974): 456–75.

[103]Zimmerman, "Penal Systems and Penal Reforms in the South," 409–10; A. W. McAllister, "Parole in North Carolina," *Jour. Soc. Forces* 1 (Jan. 1923): 131–35; Wiley B. Sanders, "The North Carolina Prison Conference," ibid., 136–37.

[104]See, for example, Foy Lisenby, "The First Meeting of the Arkansas Conference of Charities and Correction," *Ark. Hist. Quar.* 26 (Summer 1967): 155–61.

[105]Arthur W. James, *Virginia's Social Awakening: The Contribution of Dr. Mastin and the Board of Charities and Corrections* (Richmond, Va., 1939), 4–8, 19–34, 98–111, 124–34, 137–43; Zimmerman, "Penal Systems and Penal Reforms in the South," 356–57, 379–80.

capped were slowly provided, and some of the more brutal aspects of prison discipline had been outlawed. Penal reform organizations existed in every southern state, and by the opening of the second decade of the century the region as a whole was becoming aware of penal conditions and practices as a social problem, even a "southern" problem. A few governors such as Ben W. Hooper of Tennessee had become identified with the new penology. Governor Hooper, one Nashvillian declared in 1912, was "showering untold blessings upon the boys in the prison here," and thus all of Tennessee "will be blessed, because these reformed men with new ideas of honor and fresh trust in man and in God are sifting back into the fabric of the state. . . ."[106]

Nevertheless, the successes of the prison reform movement in the South were limited. Knowledgeable contemporaries, including prison reformers, identified the major penal evils with convict leasing, and the remedies they advocated—penal farms and road work—proved illusory as reforms. Although the private entrepreneur had been replaced, the states continued to operate their prison systems on the basis of economic profit and the goal of self-sufficiency. Retributive justice remained compelling, along with the economic motive. Not far behind these guiding principles, as one scholar has said of Louisiana, was "the belief that because most convicts were black, little more than agricultural work and Sunday preaching needed to be provided to effect rehabilitation of the inmates."[107] Many states, moreover, had delegated their supervision over and responsibility for most criminals to local authorities and the chain gangs. Politics still intruded in the operation of the southern penal systems. Wardens, guards, and penitentiary workers were often political appointees, and they seldom had any professional training. Flogging was still being used in 1920 as a means of discipline, especially in the county chain gangs.[108] Thus the movement to develop new and more efficient methods in dealing with criminals, a major goal of southern progressives, was limited and illusory. Ameliorative steps and innovative techniques were introduced slowly and unevenly, and even the reforms were often ambiguous in their effect.

REGULATING THE CORPORATION

During the fifteen years after 1897 almost every southern state at one time or another became the scene of a sharp struggle between reformers and big business. Sometimes the object of the reformers' attack was northern insurance companies, sometimes it was the great petroleum concerns or the tobacco "trust," but most often it was the railroad, the most familiar example of indus-

---

[106]Frank Holt to Oscar B. Colquitt, Jan. 2, 1912, Oscar Branch Colquitt Papers, Texas State Archives.

[107]Carleton, *Politics and Punishment*, 87.

[108]See Frank Tannenbaum, "Southern Prisons," *Century Magazine* 106 (July 1923): 387–98, and N. Gordon Carper, "Martin Tabert, Martyr of an Era," *Fla. Hist. Quar.* 52 (Oct. 1973): 115–31.

trial might in the region. In 1907, when the business regulatory movement in the South was at its height, one writer declared that the states were "enacting laws creating railroad commissions, reducing freight and passenger rates, prohibiting discriminations and rebates, establishing penalties for delay in the transportation of goods, enforcing liability for damages to passengers, prohibiting free passes, reducing the hours of labor for railroad employees, requiring the introduction of safety appliances, prohibiting combinations and traffic agreements, and dealing with a host of other questions. . . ."[109] In a number of states it was the politics of railroad regulation, as one historian has written of the Comer movement in Alabama, that "united the liberals and against which the conservative opposition concentrated its defenses."[110]

Southern distrust of big business owed a good deal to the agrarian revolt and the campaigns of Populist candidates and insurgent Democrats. In Texas, for example, the leadership of James S. Hogg and other Democratic reformers in the 1890s ushered in a state railroad commission, the Stock and Bond Law of 1893 giving the commission supervision over railroad securities, and a series of antitrust suits against "foreign" corporations, one of which resulted in the revocation of the charter of a Standard Oil Company subsidiary. In Kentucky the anticorporation spirit flared up fiercely in the late nineties and, under the leadership of William Goebel, promised drastic reforms and a realignment of the state's politics. Goebel challenged the domination of Kentucky politics by the Louisville and Nashville Railroad, and his program emphasized the need to increase the authority of the railroad commission, to tax railroads more adequately, and to enact a new antitrust law. The Populist indictment of railroads and other "trusts" profoundly influenced the economic and political perceptions of southerners, despite their reluctance to leave the Democratic party.[111]

Antimonopoly feeling remained pervasive in the early twentieth-century South, particularly among farmers. The social disorganization of the nineties, which contributed to the radicalization of southern politics, found a partial outlet in the assault on corporate business. The agrarian regulatory proposals were frequently adopted by insurgent Democrats, and rural dwellers were strongly influenced by the rhetorical flourishes of anticorporation leaders such

---

[109]William H. Glasson, "The Crusade Against the Railroads," *SAQ* 6 (Apr. 1907): 174. Also see by the same author, "The Railroads and the People," ibid. 5 (Jan. 1906): 21–29.

[110]James F. Doster, *Railroads in Alabama Politics, 1875–1914* (University, Ala., 1957), 151.

[111]See, for example, "Progressive Tendencies in the South," *Gunton's Magazine* 12 (May 1897): 306; Kathryn T. Abbey, "Florida Versus the Principles of Populism, 1896–1911," *JSH* 4 (Nov. 1938): 462–75; Thomas D. Clark, "The People, William Goebel, and the Kentucky Railroads," ibid. 5 (Feb. 1939): 34–48; E. T. Miller, "The Texas Stock and Bond Law and Its Administration," *Quarterly Journal of Economics* 22 (Nov. 1907): 109–19; Charles Shirley Potts, "Texas Stock and Bond Law," *Annals* 53 (May 1914): 162–71; Robert C. Cotner, *James Stephen Hogg: A Biography* (Austin, Tex., 1959), 250–352; and Jeffrey J. Crow, "'Populism to Progressivism' in North Carolina: Governor Daniel Russell and His War on the Southern Railway Company," *Historian* 37 (Aug. 1975): 649–67.

as Tom Watson and James K. Vardaman. Disturbed by the all-conquering new industrialism, suspicious of the alien and unknown city where the corporation was domiciled, and infected by the virus of Bryanism, the men of the soil were inclined to believe that the iniquitous operation of the tobacco "trust" or the fertilizer "trust" or the cotton exchange depressed farm prices and caused all their troubles. The son of an Alabama farmer later recalled how his father's complaints about low cotton prices in the 1890s had produced, in the boy's vivid imagination, the picture of "a long line-up of top-hatted, frock-coated, pig-faced gentlemen up New England way walking off with great buckets full of money squeezed from the poor cotton farmers of the South, and I experienced a deep sense of wrong and oppression."[112] Farmers, asserted the *Carolina Union Farmer* in 1910, were "the most thoroughly trust-ridden people on the face of God's green earth."[113]

If southern hostility toward big business became less volatile after the turn of the century, it could still be mobilized for specific purposes. In Arkansas, for example, Attorney General Jeff Davis employed a new antitrust law in 1899 and 1900 in launching a series of sensational antimonopoly suits against insurance companies and other corporations. In C. Vann Woodward's words, Davis "tilted with the corporation monster at every crossroad in Arkansas and made trustbusting the favorite sport of the rustic barbecue."[114] Texas was also the scene of numerous antitrust proceedings in the late 1890s and early 1900s, many of them directed at oil companies. One of these suits, against a Standard Oil affiliate known as the Waters-Pierce Company, created intense controversy in the state's Democratic party. In North Carolina the American Tobacco Company was the main target of Tarheel reformers. The outbreak of night-riding depredations in the dark-leaf tobacco belt of Kentucky and Tennessee during the years 1905–1909 was precipitated by resentment against the tobacco "trust." Meanwhile, a Democratic faction identified with antimonopoly reform appeared in almost every southern state. And there were outspoken critics of the "trusts" throughout the South such as North Carolina's Walter Clark and Josephus Daniels.[115]

---

[112] Mitchell B. Garrett, *Horse and Buggy Days on Hatchet Creek* (University, Ala., 1957), 97. See also Willard Range, *A Century of Agriculture in Georgia, 1850–1950* (Athens, Ga., 1954), 136, 140, 145; J. Carlyle Sitterson, *Sugar Country: The Cane Sugar Industry in the South, 1753–1950* (Lexington, Ky., 1953), 301–302, 349–51; and Louis Galambos, with the assistance of Barbara Barrow Spence, *The Public Image of Big Business in America, 1880–1940: A Quantitative Study in Social Change* (Baltimore, 1975), 59–65, 86–91.

[113] Quoted in Charles P. Loomis, "The Rise and Decline of the North Carolina Farmers' Union," *N.C. Hist. Rev.* 7 (July 1930): 316.

[114] Woodward, *Origins of the New South*, 376. Also see "The Arkansas Case," *Independent* 51 (June 15, 1899): 1651–52, and George E. Bearn, "Anti-'Trust' Legislation," ibid. (Sept. 21, 1899): 2553–56.

[115] See Walter Clark, "How Trusts Can Be Crushed," *Arena* 25 (Mar. 1901): 264–70; Clark, " 'Aaron's Rod'; Or, Government by Federal Judges," ibid. 38 (Nov. 1907): 479–81; Nannie May Tilley, "Agitation Against the American Tobacco Company in North Carolina, 1890–1911," *N.C. Hist. Rev.* 24 (Apr. 1947): 207–23; and Joseph L. Morrison, *Josephus Daniels Says . . . An*

The big corporations were also attacked from another quarter. Warehousemen, dealers, and small manufacturers whose functions were being jeopardized by monopoly and organized merchants who were seeking to retain or extend their markets began to demand public regulation of the large business concerns. Small businessmen in the South tended, for instance, to be enthusiastic about President Theodore Roosevelt's trustbusting cases.[116] Railroads became the center of these attacks of businessmen upon businessmen. The railroads were widely condemned for the high level of local rates, for discriminating in favor of shippers in neighboring cities and states,[117] for maintaining artificially high rates on locally produced items, and for preventing the development of water transportation. "It has seemed to be the policy of the railroads," a typical complaint ran, "to take from Georgia's abundance and give to others."[118] Freight bureaus and boards of trade from Virginia to Texas were a potent force in the regulatory campaigns that swept the South. In Virginia's regulation of railroads, a recent scholar suggests, merchants were perhaps the major reform force in the state.[119]

Southern attitudes toward monopoly were in some measure a reflection of the region's subordinate economic position in the nation and of its hopes for more rapid growth. There was good reason for this consciousness of sectional subservience; by the end of the nineteenth century, for instance, "northern men, money and management" were in firm control of the South's railroads.[120] Thus large timber and oil companies were denounced for exploiting southern re-

---

Editor's Political Odyssey from Bryan to Wilson and F.D.R., 1894–1913 (Chapel Hill, N.C., 1962), 150–55.

[116]Robert H. Wiebe, *Businessmen and Reform: A Study of the Progressive Movement* (Cambridge, Mass., 1962), 43–45.

[117]Residents of Danville, Virginia, for example, complained vigorously about the high freight rates they paid as compared with such cities as Lynchburg and Norfolk, which enjoyed more competitive transportation facilities. The muckraker Ray Stannard Baker, who visited Danville in 1906, wrote that the people of the town were divided into "two opposing parties." The first was made up of "a very large portion of the population," including governmental officials, the Business Men's Association, and many prominent citizens. This antitrust group charged that the Southern Railway had "injured the growth and checked the prosperity of Danville." The second group was small in size but represented "the party of wealth and power." It stood with the railroad. Baker, "The Way of a Railroad with a Town: Story of the Struggle of Danville, Virginia, with the Southern Railway," *McClure's Magazine* 27 (June 1906): 131–45; quotations on p. 133. Also see Thomas S. Martin to John W. Daniel, May 19, 1905, John W. Daniel Papers, Duke University Library.

[118]Atlanta *Journal,* June 25, 1905. See also M. G. Cunniff, "Texas and Texans," *World's Work* 11 (Mar. 1906): 7267, 7278, 7286–88.

[119]Robert H. Sanders, "Progressive Historians and the Late Nineteenth-Century Agrarian Revolt: Virginia as a Historiographical Test Case," *Va. Mag. Hist. and Biog.* 79 (Oct. 1971): 484–92.

[120]John F. Stover, *The Railroads of the South, 1865–1900: A Study in Finance and Control* (Chapel Hill, N.C., 1955), 284. The South also suffered from a discriminatory rate structure that placed it at a distinct disadvantage in competition with other sections. See David M. Potter, "The Historical Development of Eastern-Southern Freight Rate Relationships," *Law and Contemporary Problems* 12 (Summer 1947): 416–48, and William H. Joubert, *Southern Freight Rates in Transition* (Gainesville, Fla., 1949), 8, 19–21, 105.

sources in the interest of "foreign" entrepreneurs, insurance companies were attacked for draining away local capital, and railroads were criticized for establishing rate schedules that favored other parts of the country. Even those southerners who subscribed to the New South creed were perfectly capable of pleading for outside capital while simultaneously attacking Wall Street, the "trusts," and the railroads for policies that tended to perpetuate the colonial status of the section's economy. The vigor with which many southern businessmen joined the assault on Wall Street and outside corporations was an indication of the lengths to which they would go in their efforts to improve their competitive position in the economy.

Politicians were quick to sense the advantages to be derived from campaigns against the corporations, and the attack on the railroads and other big businesses was given added impetus by the desire of local and state politicians to capture the liveliest issue in sight. According to a contemporary student of railroad regulation in the southern states, "The agitation against the railroads . . . was carried far beyond its proper bounds by the efforts of petty politicians, who, with an eye single to their own advancement, took advantage of the popular disaffection to sweep themselves into power as the champions of the people. They promptly proceeded to deal with the carriers in a most arbitrary manner, giving attention, not so much to the question of justice as between the roads and the people, as to the feathering of their own political nests."[121]

In 1907, Daniel A. Tompkins, an ardent advocate of a New South economy, publicly identified what he considered "the real grievances" against railroads in the region as discrimination, stock jobbing and stock watering, and lack of consideration for passengers. "In some cases," Tompkins wrote, "the corporations seem rather to train their men to insolence."[122] Railroad leaders and other corporation executives, exhilarated by their power and prestige, were often arrogant in their attitude toward the public and impatient and disdainful in tolerating government controls. Their effective use of highly paid lobbyists, subsidized newspapers, free passes, and other means of influencing public officials and public opinion, their successful resort to the courts to head off regulation, and the alliance they formed with the controlling faction of the Democratic party in most southern states apparently made their position impregnable.[123] "Whether warranted or not," declared an Atlanta newspaper following the upheaval of 1906 in Georgia politics, "the prevailing opinion is that the railroad and corporate interests doing business in this state have excercised too great an influence in the affairs of state government and in the settlement of legislative questions and political contests. The people believe that

[121] Maxwell Ferguson, *State Regulation of Railroads in the South* (New York, 1916), 53.

[122] Tompkins, "The Real Grievances Against the Railroads," *SAQ* 6 (Oct. 1907): 317–22; quotation on p. 319. See also Glasson, "The Crusade Against the Railroads," 175.

[123] The historian of the Louisville and Nashville Railroad, for example, emphasizes the company's reliance upon the press and generous use of free passes. See Maury Klein, *History of the Louisville and Nashville Railroad* (New York, 1972), 345–94.

these corporate interests have been unfair to them in the matter of freight and passenger rates, and . . . that the general policy of the corporations is inimicable to the public welfare."[124] In North Carolina, Josephus Daniels, who was furiously attacking "corporate tyranny," declared that "all sense of shame has been lost by the corporations."[125]

The drive to regulate railroads in the South was divided into three fairly distinct phases. The first took place near the turn of the century, from 1897 to 1902, when several states strengthened their railroad commissions or established such agencies for the first time. North Carolina, in 1899, created the first corporation commission in the United States, and three years later Virginia set up a similar body. This resort to regulation by commission was fundamentally a moderate response to the popularization of the antitrust question and the issue of railroad control during the agrarian revolt of the nineties. The southern regulatory efforts about 1900 were also associated with the disfranchisement movement, for the new constitutions written for that purpose in Alabama and Virginia expressly authorized the creation of strong regulatory agencies. Except for Kentucky, where the power of the state's railroads was at the heart of the bitter struggle between Goebel and his opponents, and Arkansas, where Jeff Davis conducted a spectacular assault on insurance companies, the reforms of this period were both mild and limited.[126]

This was not the case in the second phase of the anticorporation movement in the South, from about 1905 to 1909. A series of statewide campaigns against railroads took place during this period, a majority of the southern states reorganized and strengthened their regulatory commissions, and almost every state in the region moved to secure lower passenger and freight rates and to prescribe a uniform system of intrastate rate classification. A close observer reported in 1907 that eighty-three antirailroad bills were pending in the Texas legislature alone![127] This wave of regulatory activity rested upon the concerted campaigns of freight bureaus, boards of trade, specialized producing groups, and organized traveling men. It was promoted by the publicity given to the railroad control movement by such newspapers as the Atlanta *Journal* and the Raleigh

---

[124] Atlanta *News*, Aug. 23, 1906.

[125] Daniels, *Editor in Politics* (Chapel Hill, N.C., 1941), 213.

[126] Thomas Edward Gay, Jr., "Creating the Virginia State Corporation Commission," *Va. Mag. Hist. and Biog.* 78 (Oct. 1970): 464–80; Clark, "The People, William Goebel, and the Kentucky Railroads," 34–48; Nicholas C. Burckel, "William Goebel and the Campaign for Railroad Regulation in Kentucky, 1888–1900," *Filson Club Hist. Quar.* 48 (Jan. 1974): 43–60; Nevin Neal, "Jeff Davis and the Reform Movement in Arkansas, 1898–1907" (M.A. thesis, Vanderbilt Univ., 1939); Cal Ledbetter, Jr., "Jeff Davis and the Politics of Combat," *Ark. Hist. Quar.* 33 (Spring 1974): 16–37.

[127] Glasson, "The Crusade Against the Railroads," 169. Also see William H. Glasson, "State and Federal Governmental Regulation in Southern Industry and Commerce," in *The South in the Building of the Nation*, vol. 6, pp. 454–66; Ferguson, *State Regulation of Railroads in the South*, 37–54; and Robert Emmett Ireton, "The Legislatures and the Railroads," *American Review of Reviews* 36 (Aug. 1907): 217–20.

News and Observer. And it was given greater salience by ambitious politicians who recognized the issue's potential value in the creation of reform coalitions.

The surge of state regulation efforts subsided after 1909, leading to a third phase in the South's anticorporation activities. This phase was characterized by a shift from reliance on state regulation to national control, in part because of the interstate character of the corporations the states were trying to regulate. Thus the state commissions found themselves increasingly dependent upon rulings of the Interstate Commerce Commission and edicts of the federal courts. On the broader antitrust front and on the problem of banking reform, southern leaders were also turning more to Washington, drawn by such developments as the Pujo Committee's investigation of the "money trust" and the debate between Woodrow Wilson's New Freedom and Theodore Roosevelt's New Nationalism in the presidential campaign of 1912. In the years that followed, southerners looked as never before to national solutions, not only for the "trust" problem but for a variety of other public needs.

Although anticorporation sentiment existed broadly throughout the South and the campaigns to regulate corporate power were an important factor in the development of the bifactional groupings that characterized southern politics during these years, the monopoly issue proved to be less significant in some states than in others. In Virginia, Tennessee, and Louisiana, despite the emergence of anticorporation or antirailroad political factions, the passage of numerous regulatory acts, and the eruption of acrimonious controversies over railroad rates, the question was relatively unimportant in its bearing upon progressive politics. This can be attributed to the influence exerted by large corporations in the politics of those states, to the nature of their dominant party factions, and to the fear that drastic controls would inhibit industrial development. Louisiana, for example, established a railroad commission in 1898 and increased its powers in 1902. Yet regulation was slack and ineffective during the progressive years. The state was still trying to attract capital to extend its railroad network. The Louisiana constitution of 1898 provided limited tax exemption to all railroads that completed their lines before January 1, 1904, and this deadline was later extended for five years.[128]

Campaigns to control railroads and utilities were also limited in several other southern states. Following William Goebel's death in 1900, the reform movement in Kentucky lost its direction and momentum. The antitrust campaigns of Jeff Davis had an important effect on politics in Arkansas, but the Davis movement was narrow and left few accomplishments to show for all of Jeff's fulminations against the corporations. This was even more the case with Coleman L. Blease of South Carolina, who advertised himself as an anticorporation man and campaigned as a railroad rate reformer. While the state enlarged its

---

[128]Ferguson, *State Regulation of Railroads in the South,* 180–82; Magruder, *Recent Administration in Virginia,* 147–59, 175–78; Pulley, *Old Virginia Restored,* 134–35, 141, 148–57.

supervision of corporate enterprise during the first two decades of the twentieth century, the South Carolina railroad commission was conservative in its regulation of railroads, express companies, and communications corporations. James K. Vardamañ was a more constructive leader than Blease, and the movement he led in Mississippi was strongly antimonopolistic; yet the regulatory efforts were not notably successful in that state. The Oklahoma constitution of 1907 devoted nine thousand words to the subject of corporations, but efforts to regulate corporate wealth in the Sooner State during the following years enjoyed only limited success.[129]

The relationship between the anticorporation movement and progressivism was more significant in Alabama, Georgia, North Carolina, Florida, and Texas. In those states progressive political factions with definite antimonopoly objectives came to power. In Georgia a spirited antirailroad movement came to a climax in the campaign of 1905–1906 that swept Hoke Smith into the governorship. The legislature enlarged the authority of the railroad commission in 1905 and provided for an elective commission in 1906; the commission ordered a reduction in passenger rates early in 1907, and following Smith's inauguration later that year, a comprehensive railroad commission act was approved which included public supervision of railroad securities. Many of the reforms the Smith administration achieved were concerned with the regulation of corporations. The high-water mark of the progressive movement in North Carolina came during the years 1907 and 1908, when the corporations were the object of extensive legislation and a bitter railroad dispute dominated the state's politics. While less narrowly concerned with railroad regulation, the anticorporation movement proved to be an equally vital force in Florida progressivism. The corporate exploitation of valuable lands and other resources encouraged the rise of an antimonopoly movement in the state. Napoleon B. Broward, the outstanding progressive leader in Florida, championed a strong railroad commission, a state insurance system, and a conservation program designed to rescue millions of acres of land from large corporations.[130]

[129]Ferguson, *State Regulation of Railroads in the South*, 85–93, 112–27, 149–52; Samuel W. Moore, "State Supervision of Railroad Transportation in Arkansas," in John Hugh Reynolds, ed., *Publications of the Arkansas Historical Association*, vol. 3 (Fayetteville, Ark., 1911), 267–309; Thomas, ed., *Arkansas and Its People*, vol. 1, pp. 337–41; Albert Neely Sanders, "State Regulation of Public Utilities by South Carolina, 1879–1935" (Ph.D. diss., Univ. of North Carolina, 1956); John Joseph Duffy, "Charleston Politics in the Progressive Era" (Ph.D. diss., Univ. of South Carolina, 1963), 100–10; Kirwan, *Revolt of the Rednecks* 165–66, 175–76; John K. Bettersworth, *Mississippi: A History* (Austin, Tex., 1959), 393, 397–98; Robert L. Brandfon, *Cotton Kingdom of the New South: A History of the Yazoo Mississippi Delta from Reconstruction to the Twentieth Century* (Cambridge, Mass., 1967), 80–94, 166–97; William F. Holmes, *The White Chief: James Kimble Vardaman* (Baton Rouge, 1970), 146–48; Reynolds, "The Oklahoma Constitution," 239–40; Danney Goble, *Progressive Oklahoma: The Making of a New Kind of State* (Norman, Okla., 1980), 34, 110–11, 157–60, 166–76, 216–18.

[130]Ferguson, *State Regulation of Railroads in the South*, 95–107, 153–79; Jones, "Progressivism in Georgia," 86–105; Robert W. Winston, "The Passenger Rate War in North Carolina,"

Regulatory efforts in Alabama and Texas constituted the most sustained campaigns to bring big business under control in the South during the progressive period. At the the the turn of the century, Alabama politics was dominated by the state's principal railroads, which had close ties with large industrialists, and by influential black belt planters. The state railroad commission was of little consequence.[131] But the next few years witnessed the coalescence of reform forces and the steady emergence of railroad regulation as a central political issue. The constitution of 1901 empowered the legislature to apply broad statutory control over the state's railroads, the question of regulation became an issue in the primary elections of 1902, and the general assembly in 1903 provided for an elective commission with mandatory power. During the following year a statewide railroad control movement was begun under the leadership of Braxton B. Comer, a businessman who had long urged rate reductions. Strongly supported by commercial organizations in Birmingham and other cities and by many merchants and small businessmen, Comer waged a vigorous campaign for the presidency of the railroad commission. Despite opposition from Alabama railroads and other conservative interests, Comer was elected. After assuming office, he made a determined effort to have the railroad commission order freight-rate reductions, but he was unsuccessful, since the other two commissioners voted against reductions.[132]

Thwarted in his attempt to secure favorable action by the railroad commission, Comer decided to run for governor in 1906 and to seek direct legislative action in fixing lower railroad rates. Focusing on the railroad issue, Comer's long and hard-fought campaign in 1905 and 1906 resulted in a sweeping victory. This electoral success was based on an emergent reform coalition of urban and middle-class business interests and professional groups, supported by many black belt planters and other rural elements. In 1907, during the first year of Comer's governorship, the legislature dutifully approved almost every administration recommendation, including some twenty separate bills affecting the state's railroads. The railroad commission was authorized to equalize and limit

---

SAQ 6 (Oct. 1907): 342–47; Annie Sabra Ramsey, "Utility Regulation in North Carolina, 1891–1941: Fifty Years of History and Progress," *N.C. Hist. Rev.* 22 (Apr. 1945): 125–51; Hugh Talmage Lefler and Albert Ray Newsome, *The History of a Southern State: North Carolina* (Chapel Hill, N.C., 1954), 527–29, 575–76; Joseph Flake Steelman, "The Progressive Era in North Carolina, 1884–1917" (Ph.D. diss., Univ. of North Carolina, 1955), 280–92, 308–309, 526–62; Steelman, "Edward J. Justice: Profile of a Progressive Legislator, 1899–1913," *N.C. Hist. Rev.* 48 (Spring 1971): 147–60; Samuel Proctor, *Napoleon Bonaparte Broward: Florida's Fighting Democrat* (Gainesville, Fla., 1950), 183–202, 214–26, 240–66; Nelson Manfred Blake, *Land into Water—Water into Land: A History of Water Management in Florida* (Tallahassee, 1980), 88–95.

[131]James F. Doster, "Railroad Domination in Alabama, 1885–1905," *Ala. Rev.* 7 (July 1954): 186–98, and "The Conflict over Railroad Regulation in Alabama," *Business History Review* 28 (Dec. 1954): 329–42.

[132]For these developments and those described in the next three paragraphs, see Doster, *Railroads in Alabama Politics*, and Hackney, *Populism to Progressivism in Alabama*, 125, 133–34, 137, 209–14, 222–23, 230, 235–39, 252–55, 257–78, 281–99. Also see Jonathan A. Wiener, *Social Origins of the New South: Alabama, 1860–1885* (Baton Rouge, 1978), 222–27.

intrastate rates. Passenger rates were reduced to two and a half cents per mile, while 110 commodities were placed under the same freight classification and rates as those prescribed by the Georgia commission, a major objective of the Comer movement. Another act prohibited railroads that were doing business in Alabama from beginning a suit in a federal court or, in actions against them in state courts, from transferring cases to such a court, under penalty of forfeiting their Alabama charters. Twelve railroads, led by the Louisville and Nashville, immediately sought injunctions in a federal district court to prevent the enforcement of the new regulatory laws, and Judge Thomas G. Jones, a former governor of the state and a firm conservative, granted the restraining orders. After the state canceled the license of the Southern Railway Company for violating one of the 1907 statutes, the Southern came to terms, followed by several other roads. But five companies, under the leadership of President Milton H. Smith of the L & N, defied the state.

Governor Comer, undaunted and full of fight, called the Alabama legislature into special session in November 1907 to counter the railroads' defiance. The legislature, at the governor's request, quickly repealed all of the enforcement provisions of the regulatory measures enacted earlier in the year, in a calculated effort to invalidate Judge Jones's injunctions. The general assembly then passed a bill authorizing private citizens acting in the name of the state to sue for punitive damages when charged more than the legal railroad rates. The L & N and three other railroad companies went back to the federal court, and Judge Jones again obliged them by issuing restraining orders against certain shippers who had acted under the November statutes. After the federal judge invalidated the regulatory acts early in 1908, the state appealed the decision, finally winning its case in the higher federal courts in the spring of 1909.

Meanwhile, the public had tired of the railroad question, and prohibition had moved into the limelight. But the movement was not entirely dead. During the summer of 1909 the legislature overhauled the state's railroad control laws, repealing their harsher features and buttressing the powers of the commission. The federal courts eventually struck down the maximum rate act and the railroad classification law of 1907. The long fight between the state and the railroads finally came to an end in early 1914, when the two sides agreed to a compromise settlement. The railroad commission then reclassified the rates to reflect the settlement. In 1915 the commission was transformed into a public service agency, with the scope of its activities being enlarged.

The great public issue in Texas during the first decade of the twentieth century was how to deal with corporate wealth. The foremost corporations were of "foreign" origin, a fact that accounted for much of the resentment in the state against the colonial status of Texas. Business malpractices and foreign ownership, one authority has suggested, "made the railroads the chief target of anticorporate legislation."[133] The regulatory movement that began in the 1890s

[133] Tinsley, "The Progressive Movement in Texas," 14.

had its most conspicuous success during the progressive administration of Thomas M. Campbell (1907–11). During this period the Texas antitrust laws were strengthened, a long list of railroad regulatory acts was passed, corporation taxes were increased, a bank guarantee measure was adopted, and the famous Robertson insurance bill was enacted. Scores of antitrust cases were successfully prosecuted during the decade after 1905, against brewing companies, cotton oil concerns, meat packing and stockyard commission companies, flour and feed mills, and even the big oil companies. The corporations strongly resisted this wave of regulation. Railroads operating in Texas complained loudly about state controls, fought a strong railroad commission and challenged its rulings in the courts, and finally almost pleaded for federal regulation.[134]

After 1910 the railroad issue declined in importance as a factor in Texas politics. As in Alabama, the controversy over prohibition replaced it as the dominant issue in state politics. In a sense, moreover, the Shreveport rate decision of 1913 marked the end of the vital era of state railroad regulation.[135] With the enhanced role of the Interstate Commerce Commission and the expansion of federal controls came a corresponding restriction of the authority of state commissions and state laws. The federal government's operation of the railroads during World War I and the provisions of the Esch-Cummins Act of 1920 gave additional force to this shift. Still, the regulatory movement in the various southern states had some positive results. Unjust discrimination was greatly reduced and many railroad abuses were eliminated during the first decade of the twentieth century. Intrastate rates were fixed and railroad finances were scrutinized more closely. The activities of the southern regulatory agencies are illustrated in the record of the North Carolina corporation commission, which heard 4,230 complaints during the years 1899–1911 dealing with such matters as rate discrimination and poor freight service.[136]

Another focus of southern antagonism toward corporate wealth was the insurance company, which was scarcely less "foreign" or less exploitative in its operations than the great rail lines.[137] All of the southern states created

[134]For the regulatory movement in Texas, see ibid., 12–31, 75–89; Robert Lewis Peterson, "State Regulation of Railroads in Texas, 1836–1920" (Ph.D. diss., Univ. of Texas, 1960); Ira G. Clark, "State Legislation and Railroads of the Gulf Southwest," *Southwestern Soc. Sci. Quar.*, supplement to vol. 41 (1960): 277–81; Herbert N. Casson, "The Anti-Trust Crusade in Texas," *Independent* 65 (Nov. 5, 1908): 1057–59; Lewis H. Haney, "Railroad Regulation in Texas," *Journal of Political Economy* 19 (June 1911): 437–55; Dan Moody and Charles B. Wallace, "Texas Antitrust Laws and Their Enforcement—Comparison with Federal Antitrust Laws," *Southwestern Law Journal* 11 (Winter 1957): 1–26; and Janet Schmelzer, "Thomas M. Campbell: Progressive Governor of Texas," *Red River Valley Historical Review* 3 (Fall 1978): 52–63.

[135]This decision involved the rate structure of the Louisiana-East Texas region. In the *Shreveport Rate Cases* (1914), the Supreme Court sustained the ICC's decision and its authority to regulate intrastate rail rates. See 234 U.S. 342 (1914).

[136]Lefler and Newsome, *North Carolina*, 528.

[137]See, for example, B. Michael Pritchett, "Northern Institutions in Southern Financial History: A Note on Insurance Investments," *JSH* 41 (Aug. 1975): 391–96.

insurance departments in the late nineties and early years of the twentieth century. They passed laws subjecting outside life and fire insurance companies to taxation, licensing, agents' residence, deposit, and liability requirements, as well as defining other areas of company responsibility. Insurance commissioners such as Reau E. Folk of Tennessee, Fitz Hugh McMaster of South Carolina, and Henry R. Prewitt of Kentucky sought to invigorate their state systems of insurance regulation. In Florida, Napoleon B. Broward tried unsuccessfully to have the state provide insurance coverage for its citizens. The revelations of the famous Armstrong Committee concerning practices of the great New York insurance companies and the passage of a strong regulatory law by New York in 1906 stimulated state insurance regulation in the South and other parts of the country. A Texas Democrat indignantly declared following the New York investigation: "I have been paying premiums to the New York Life for ten years, and now find that it has been using my money to fight my people and my country."[138] The insurance commissioners of Kentucky and Tennessee joined their counterparts from three midwestern states in traveling to New York to conduct a joint examination of the large insurance firms.[139]

In 1907 and subsequent years southern legislatures strengthened their insurance departments and enacted additional regulatory statutes. The most notable of these measures was the Robertson Act of 1907, a Texas law designed to compel out-of-state companies to invest a portion of their Texas earnings in local securities or real estate. James H. Robertson, the sponsor of the legislation, said his purpose was "to stop the long continued practice of taking from Texas money belonging to Texas people, and hoarding it in New York to be there used by officials of the great insurance companies. . . ." As revised, the state's insurance code provided for compulsory local investment of life insurance reserves, increased taxes, and state supervision of fire insurance rates. Twenty-one of forty-six "foreign" insurance companies doing business in Texas immediately left the state.[140] Several southern states attempted to impose restrictions on the sale of fire insurance within their borders. South Carolina, for example, precipitated an angry controversy in 1916 and 1917 when its legislators tried to reduce the cost of fire insurance by weakening the role of the Southeastern Underwriters' Association in prescribing rates.[141] The affected

---

[138]Quoted in Morton Keller, *The Life Insurance Enterprise, 1885–1910: A Study in the Limits of Corporate Power* (Cambridge, Mass., 1963), 256. See H. Roger Grant, *Insurance Reform: Consumer Action in the Progressive Era* (Ames, Iowa, 1979), for regulatory action in New York, Wisconsin, Missouri, Kansas, and Texas.

[139]Keller, *The Life Insurance Enterprise,* 194–200, 209–11, 246–48, 255–59; Proctor, *Napoleon Bonaparte Broward,* 213, 229; Jones, "Progressivism in Georgia," 107–109; Rowland, *History of Mississippi,* vol. 2, p. 293.

[140]James A. Tinsley, "Texas Progressives and Insurance Regulation," *Southwestern Soc. Sci. Quar.* 36 (Dec. 1955): 237–47; quotation on p. 239.

[141]"South Carolina Law," *Independent* 86 (Apr. 10, 1916): 86–87; Robert Milton Burts, *Richard Irvine Manning and the Progressive Movement in South Carolina* (Columbia, S.C., 1974), 288–306.

concerns in cases of this sort sometimes made concessions, but they gave ground grudgingly.

Southern lawmakers, in state legislatures and in Congress, revealed a continuing suspicion of the mysterious and remote commodity speculator. Many southerners, particularly in rural areas, blamed depressed cotton prices and the ups and downs of the commodity markets on speculation in futures. A majority of the southern states adopted antifutures laws in the late 1890s and early 1900s, and about 1906 a regionwide campaign developed to close the so-called bucket shops, small gambling establishments operated on the hour-by-hour fluctuations in the commodity futures market. At approximately the same time, the American Cotton Manufacturers' Association initiated a movement, led by Lewis W. Parker, a North Carolina textile manufacturer, to secure federal regulation of the New York and New Orleans cotton exchanges. Although a bill designed to free the cotton market of speculators passed the U.S. House of Representatives in 1910 with strong southern support, it failed to reach the floor of the Senate. But pressure for federal action mounted during the next few years, and in 1914 Congress passed the Cotton Futures Act. While the law's regulatory provisions were mild, they did include the establishment of an official system of cotton grading.[142]

Laws aimed at preventing the sale of fraudulent securities were also popular in the South. The Texas Stock and Bond Law of 1893 required the state's new railroad commission to register and approve all railroad securities and to eliminate stock watering. The Georgia legislature in 1904 attempted to regulate the sale of certain types of securities, and in 1907 the railroad commission was given broad supervision over the issuance of railroad securities in the state. A North Carolina statute of 1911 attempted to regulate the sale of foreign securities in the Old North State. But the "Kansas Idea" of 1911 set the pattern throughout the United States for the regulation of stocks, bonds, and other securities. Most southern states enacted such "blue sky" laws during the years 1912–16.[143]

Still another area of state regulation was that of banking. All of the states in the region expanded their supervision over banking practices during this period, often in collaboration with bankers themselves, and two states—Oklahoma and Mississippi—enacted bank deposit guarantee laws.[144] Many southern bankers

---

[142]Cedric B. Cowing, *Populists, Plungers, and Progressives: A Social History of Stock and Commodity Speculation, 1890–1936* (Princeton, N.J., 1965), 26–27, 30, 37, 42–47, 65–73; Harold D. Woodman, *King Cotton & His Retainers: Financing & Marketing the Cotton Crop of the South, 1800–1925* (Lexington, Ky., 1968), 339; Schott, "John M. Parker of Louisiana," 53–55; Wiebe, *Businessmen and Reform*, 144; "North Carolina: Divorce Reform; Gambling in Futures; Liquor laws; Vagrancy, etc.," *Outlook* 79 (Mar. 25, 1905): 721; Jones, "Progressivism in Georgia," 110–13; Morton Keller, *Affairs of State: Public Life in Late Nineteenth Century America* (Cambridge, Mass., 1977), 415.

[143]John B. McFerrin, "Blue Sky Laws of the Southeastern States," *South. Econ. Jour.* 17 (Jan. 1951): 302–303.

[144]Joe Michael Shahan, "Reform and Politics in Tennessee: 1906–1914" (Ph.D. diss., Van-

and other businessmen became advocates of federal regulation. They tended to be suspicious of a political economy in which powerful eastern and midwestern entrepreneurs seemed to dominate both the national economy and governmental policies. Thus Daniel A. Tompkins opposed the Aldrich plan of currency reform as a scheme of "Mr. Aldrich, the Standard Oil Company, and the Steel Trust."[145] The notion of an informal money trust controlling the nation's finances and credit, reinforced by the Pujo Committee investigation of 1912–13, was widely accepted among southern businessmen. A sectional bias was evident in the activities of such groups as the Southern Commercial Congress and the American Cotton Manufacturers' Association, and businessmen in the South and West joined reform movements as a means of obtaining national favors and advantages. It was hardly surprising that southern businessmen should support the growing demands for federal warehouses, credit, and marketing controls. Country and small-town bankers were influential in shaping the financial legislation of the Wilson administration, and in 1915 the Cotton States Bankers' Conference was organized to promote regional interests that seemed to be hindered by the American Bankers' Association.[146]

The power of the state, in the South as in other sections, was increasingly used in this period to regulate a wide range of industrial and business operations, such as those in fertilizer, food, textbooks, and banking. By the turn of the century, state authority was being employed more systematically to license and regulate the practice of medicine and other professions. It was also exerted in a series of statutes designed to curb the political influence of big business and to free government from the taint of "vested interests" and political corruption. The "perception that privileged businesses corrupted politics" was an instrumental idea in the coalescence of reform and regulatory forces in the South.[147]

Three areas of this public regulation were closely related to the broader distrust of railroads and other large corporations in the South. The campaigns to control the railroads more closely were usually accompanied by demands for the outlawing of free passes and free services to public officials and politicians, passage of antilobbying laws, and enactment of corrupt-practices legislation. Legislatures in all the southern states enacted measures of this kind. The lobbying activities of railroad lawyers and special interest representatives, long notorious in the state capitals, made them an object of particular concern among

derbilt Univ., 1981), 53–56, 338–39, 346–47; Arrell M. Gibson, *Oklahoma: A History of Five Centuries* (Norman, Okla., 1965), 341–42; Alfred Benjamin Butts, *Public Administration in Mississippi,* vol. 3 of *Publications of the Mississippi Historical Society* (Jackson, Miss., 1919), 157–77.

[145]Wiebe, *Businessmen and Reform,* 77–78.

[146]Ibid., 10–13, 23–24, 113, 199–200, 214, 217; Vincent P. Carosso, "The Wall Street Money Trust from Pujo through Medina," *Business Hist. Rev.* 47 (Winter 1973): 421–28.

[147]See Richard L. McCormick, "The Discovery that Business Corrupts Politics: A Reappraisal of the Origins of Progressivism," *Amer. Hist. Rev.* 86 (Apr. 1981): 247–74, for an illuminating analysis of this theme in the nation as a whole.

southern progressives.[148] There were reports, for instance, that in the Arkansas legislative session of 1905, "boodling and lobbying" reached a new high, with the corporations spending $200,000 to block most of the measures they considered dangerous.[149] Several states adopted antilobbying laws requiring the registration of lobbyists, denying them access to legislative chambers, and restricting their contributions to the formulation and passage of legislation. Most of the southern states also enacted laws intended to limit and publicize the campaign expenses of candidates and to reduce the influence of corporations in elections. Thus an Alabama law of 1915 set limits on campaign expenditures and required each candidate to file an itemized statement of expenses as well as a list of contributors and contributions to his campaign. Another statute, also enacted in 1915 and amended in 1919, sought to prevent campaign advertising. Many of these laws were not enforced, however.[150]

Despite the political rhetoric and organizational energy expended in its behalf, the regulation of business in the South was piecemeal, limited, and often ineffectual. Railroad control legislation enacted by southern lawmakers in this period was "voluminous" but, as a contemporary scholar noted, it was incomplete and filled with "repetitions, redundancies, elaborations, and conflicting passages."[151] Important questions such as control of stock issues, intercompany combinations, comprehensive valuation of railroad properties, and treatment of workers were neglected or indequately covered. Regulation of the oil and gas industries in the Southwest was rudimentary before the First World War. Nevertheless, the new regulatory legislation was partially successful. Several of the major railroads, including the Southern, Seaboard Air Line, and Atlantic Coast Line systems, proved conciliatory and generally avoided resort to "defiance or retaliation." A number of the reorganized and strengthened railroad commissions were aggressive and frequently victorious in challenging the corporations under their jurisdiction and in working to advance the interests of shippers and businessmen in their states.[152] Organized businessmen in vari-

[148]The legislative influence of arrogant railroad leaders like Milton H. Smith of the L & N was galling to many reformers. "We are always on the watch, just like any other interest," Smith said of the situation in Kentucky. "We are watching the Legislature to see what they will do, and if there are any bills prepared or introduced that are inimical to us then we endeavor in the proper way to defeat them" (Smith, "Memorandum of Interview with Mr. C. P. Connolly," Oct. 6, 1913, p. 56). I am grateful to Professor Bennett H. Wall for providing me with a copy of this 116-page memorandum. See also Mary K. Bonsteel Tachau, "The Making of a Railroad President: Milton Hannibal Smith and the L & N," *Filson Club Hist. Quar.* 43 (Apr. 1969): 125–50.

[149]William Orestus Penrose, "Political Ideas in Arkansas, 1880–1907" (M.A. thesis, Univ. of Arkansas, 1945), 196.

[150]Moore, *History of Alabama and Her People*, vol. 1, pp. 964–65; Ludington, "Ballot Laws in the Southern States," 21–34; Reynolds, *Machine Politics in New Orleans*, 87–90.

[151]Ferguson, *State Regulation of Railroads in the South*, 26.

[152]Ibid., 30–31, 34–36, 39, 53, 204; Gabriel Kolko, *Railroads and Regulation, 1877–1916* (Princeton, N.J., 1965), 164–66.

ous southern localities were sometimes able to secure rate changes through the Interstate Commerce Commission. The Henderson, Kentucky, Commercial Club, for example, an association of local wholesale and retail merchants formed in 1908, played a key role in the long campaign that eventually persuaded the ICC to equalize the discriminatory rates of the Louisville and Nashville and the Illinois Central railroads.[153]

Still, unless aroused and brought sharply to bear on particular types of monopoly power, as in the case of the railroads in several southern states in 1906 and 1907, hostility toward big business usually remained dormant and rather innocuous. Besides, an increasing number of southerners were coming to view large corporations in a more positive light, as a source of needed capital, services, and employment. The recession of 1907, coming at the very height of the progressive wave in the South, dealt the antimonopoly movement a serious setback. The old fears, so often played upon by conservatives, that radical politics would discourage northern investments in the region were once again awakened. The reform program in Georgia, warned a conservative newspaper in that state, "virtually has as its basis THE DRIVING OUT OF ALL FOREIGN CAPITAL now doing business in . . . Georgia—capital which is building railroads, developing mines, creating new industries of every kind, and adding untold millions to the tax valuations of the state."[154] Although Richard H. Edmonds became critical of high railroad rates in the years after 1910, his *Manufacturers' Record* repeatedly spoke out against radical political movements, "political agitators," and railroad regulators, asserting that their campaigns would discourage the entrance of outside capital and impede the economic development of the South.[155]

Several states, including Florida, Tennessee, and the two Carolinas, approved laws that held out the possibility of compelling railroads to grant low rates as a means of encouraging infant industries.[156] Such compulsion was

[153]Lee A. Dew, "Henderson, Kentucky, and the Fight for Equitable Freight Rates—1906–1918," *Reg. Ky. Hist. Soc.* 76 (Jan. 1978): 34–44. Also see Dew, "The Blytheville Case and Regulation of Arkansas Cotton Shipments," *Ark. Hist. Quar.* 38 (Summer 1979): 116–30.

[154]Atlanta *Constitution,* Aug. 6, 1905. One Texan, noting that Texas still needed to develop its transportation facilities, wrote to Governor Campbell in 1907: "Now while other States are trying such radical and stringent laws, would it, not only be good business policy but the wisest statesmanship, to . . . hold out a friendly hand to railroad enterprises and get some advantage out of this agitation" (J. G. Witherspoon to Thomas M. Campbell, Aug. 25, 1907, Campbell Papers, Texas State Archives).

[155]Yoshimitsu Ide, "The Significance of Richard Hathaway Edmonds and His *Manufacturers' Record* in the New South" (Ph.D. diss., Univ. of Florida, 1959), 93–95, 101–108, 203–11, 221–35, 270–82. Governor Andrew H. Longino of Mississippi expressed a widely held view when he voiced the hope, in 1900, that "no more sentimental or prejudiced opposition to railroads or other corporate enterprises will find favor with the legislature, so that capital hunting investment will have no just cause to pass Mississippi and go to other states offering legitimate inducements" (quoted in Rowland, *History of Mississippi,* vol. 2, p. 280).

[156]Ferguson, *State Regulation of Railroads in the South,* 40.

seldom if ever used, however. Instead, the railroads themselves were usually seen as a vital industry. As the Virginia corporation commission observed in 1908, in upholding a railroad complaint in a rate case:

> since no large business interest can be injuriously affected without injuring the community as a whole, we believe that the failure of the railroads to prosper so forces the reduction of the number of their employees and their wages, so reduces the ability and disposition of the railway companies to enter into new contracts for extensions, betterments and improvements, so curtails their power to purchase supplies of many kinds, thus affecting many other enterprises whose prosperity depends upon the purchasing power of the railways, and so discourages the investment of capital in new as well as old railway enterprises, as to amount to a public misfortune.[157]

A Richmond publisher offered this aphorism as a guiding principle: "Corporations: The most efficient agents for the promotion of modern progress. If an evil, then a necessary evil, and they have some 'rights which a white man is bound to respect.'"[158]

This line of thought made sense to most southern progressives. Far from being hostile to business enterprise, they were thoroughly committed to the idea of economic growth, industrial expansion, and entrepreneurial opportunity. While suspicious of the economic power and political influence of railroads and other big corporations, the progressives were generally far more supportive than opposed to business in all its forms. Many of them were businessmen. They were sympathetic with the efforts of organizations like the Tennessee Industrial League, which campaigned against stringent regulation of corporations on the ground that it would jeopardize economic progress and worsen Tennessee's competitive position among surrounding states. As a group the South's reform governors were strong supporters of business initiative and economic development.[159] Furthermore, the public regulation of business, as an interpreter of Alabama progressivism points out, was largely "enlightened" business self-regulation. "It was not only a response to humanitarian pressure, nor was it solely an attempt of small businessmen to shackle big businessmen, though these were elements in its complex composition. It was also designed to bring stability, insure growth, and free businessmen from the necessity of acting unethically in order to compete."[160]

Even so, the business component of southern progressivism should not obscure the fact that antimonopoly sentiment helped generate and sustain reform movements in the region. That feeling provided much of the moral indig-

---

[157]Quoted in ibid., 82.

[158]Joseph Bryan to A. C. Braxton, June 16, 1902, Allen C. Braxton Papers, University of Virginia Library. Also see Galambos, *The Public Image of Big Business*, 87–91, 99, 128, 132, 135–36.

[159]William F. Donovan, Jr., "The Growth of the Industrial Spirit in Tennessee, 1890–1910" (Ph.D. diss., George Peabody College for Teachers, 1955), 58–76; Kousser, *The Shaping of Southern Politics*, 230–31.

[160]Hackney, *Populism to Progressivism in Alabama*, 309.

nation and reform fervor in the progressive campaigns. After all, the railroads and other big corporations were a palpable source of unfair discrimination and political corruption. While the movement to regulate business was seized upon by political opportunists and demagogues, it served nonetheless as a major rallying point for progressive politics in the South. Yet the regulatory campaigns also embodied the progressives' concern for economic development and opportunity and their efforts to construct reform coalitions on the basis of interest-group politics.

There was an element of coercion in most of the important reforms sought by southern progressives. This incentive was the dominant motif in the reform efforts to control blacks, criminals, and corporate enterprise. These movements were often interrelated, and their controlling assumptions had much in common. Public authority—the power of the state—was urgently needed to control dangerous and undesirable elements in society. The application of these social controls would lead to cleaner, healthier, and more orderly communities where economic progress would be encouraged, civic improvements made, and law observed. None of the movements to achieve these objectives offers a more revealing illustration of southern progressivism than the campaign for prohibition.

6

Prohibition and the Politics of Morality

WRITING IN 1908, William Garrott Brown called attention to the culmination of two processes of "sweeping legislation" in the southern states—the drastic regulation of railroads and the sudden prohibition of the traffic in intoxicating beverages. Brown thought the South had "recently come into that phase of democracy in which government stretches its authority to the uttermost in the endeavor to enforce absolute moralities" and that government had become "well-nigh puritanized."[1] The movement to prohibit the manufacture and sale of alcoholic beverages may well have been the most dynamic and passionately supported "reform" in the South during the progressive era. The vigorous campaign against the railroads and other corporations in 1906 and 1907 soon lost its force, and much of the regulatory propensity during the next decade found an outlet in the antiliquor movement, first in the drive for statewide prohibition and thereafter in the struggle for a national law. So powerful was its influence between the Potomac and the Rio Grande that prohibition leaders could describe the South, with considerable justification, as the "main-spring" of the movement in the United States, "the propagandic base" of the national agitation.[2]

The fight for prohibition in the South was a significant aspect of the region's search for social reform in the early twentieth century. This was true in part because the movement was widely regarded as a genuine reform, and also because it enlisted the strong support of most southern progressives. In addition to its inherent appeal to southern social reformers, prohibition became impor-

---

[1]Brown, "The South and the Saloon," *Century Magazine* 76 (July 1908): 462–63. See also "The Prohibition Wave Over the South," *World's Work* 14 (Sept. 1907): 9278; John Corrigan, "The Prohibition Wave in the South,"*American Review of Reviews* 36 (Sept. 1907): 328–34; "The War on the Saloon," *Nation* 85 (Nov. 21, 1907): 460–61; "Prohibition in Alabama," *Outlook* 87 (Nov. 30, 1907): 707; "The Saloon in the South," ibid. 88 (Mar. 14, 1908): 581–82; and Frank Foxcroft, "Prohibition in the South," *Atlantic Monthly* 101 (May 1908): 627–34.

[2]John E. White, "Prohibition: The New Task and Opportunity of the South," *SAQ* 7 (Apr. 1908): 130–42. Also see White, "Temperance Reform in the South," in *The South in the Building of the Nation*, vol. 10, pp. 567–81.

tant as a symbolic issue in the intense factional contests in the Democratic party; in several states the question submerged all other political concerns and completely disrupted the party. As a social reform, prohibition proved remarkably versatile in its effect upon southern sensibilities and yearnings, bringing together such varying tendencies as the countryman's suspicion of urban institutions, the puritanism of the evangelical churches, the humanitarian concerns of social justice reformers, the identification of the liquor traffic with corporations and special interests, the need to "purify" the political process, the desire to control the "undependable" and "criminally inclined" Negro, and the economic argument that the saloon "breeds disorder and crime and demoralizes the labor system." Prohibition may even have served the southerner's peculiar psychological needs, as Wilbur J. Cash suggested, by "the further widening of the old split in the Southern psyche between Puritanism and hedonism."[3] Whatever its origins, the prohibition movement was, almost from the beginning, a major feature of southern progressivism.

During the eighteen months between the summer of 1907 and early 1909, six southern states adopted prohibition. This "wave of reform" was in part the natural outgrowth of a long period of temperance work by the Women's Christian Temperance Union and other organizations whose local option campaigns had steadily enlarged the dry territory in the region. Ninety percent of Alabama's counties had banned the saloon by 1907, and even in the famous distilling state of Kentucky only about one-fifth of the counties were still wet by that time. The twentieth-century prohibition movement in the South—and in the nation—began in Georgia with the enactment of a statewide ban in August 1907. In September the voters in what would soon be the new state of Oklahoma approved a constitutional provision outlawing alcoholic beverages. Later that fall the Alabama legislature adopted a prohibition statute. Mississippi and North Carolina passed similar legislation in 1908, followed by Tennessee early the next year. Meanwhile, statewide prohibition was narrowly defeated in Florida and Texas. "On the 16th day of July 1909," Alexander J. McKelway wrote with only slight exaggeration, "the crow can fly from Cape Hatteras in a straight line through North Carolina, Tennessee and Arkansas to the farthest boundary of Oklahoma, and return by way of Mississippi, Alabama and Georgia to the starting point, through prohibition territory."[4]

Although the antiliquor movement in Georgia had made impressive gains through local option elections, it was the reform campaign of Hoke Smith in 1905–1906 that provided the catalyst for the adoption of prohibition in that state. Sensing an opportune moment for decisive action and linking control of the liquor evil with the heightened awareness of new mechanisms of racial control, prohibition leaders moved swiftly when the legislature convened in

[3] Cash, *The Mind of the South* (New York, 1941), 227.
[4] McKelway, "Prohibition in the Southern States," unpublished article in Alexander J. McKelway Papers, Manuscript Division, Library of Congress.

June 1907. The dry majorities in the general assembly responded by enacting a statewide prohibition bill after a sharp struggle. Enforcing the new law was another matter, however, and in 1908 the legislature made the task more difficult by permitting so-called near-beer and the use of lockers for alcoholic beverages in private clubs. It was also possible, under the prohibition statutes, to import alcoholic beverages from outside the state. Over the next decade the antisaloon forces sought to abolish these exemptions and to devise effective machinery for the enforcement of prohibition.[5] While the drive for prohibition in Georgia led to some tumultuous scenes and was seldom absent from the political stage during the progressive years, it did not dominate the state's politics or become a distinguishing issue in the factional struggles of its Democratic party.

The adoption of prohibition in Oklahoma was closely related to the formulation and ratification of the constitution under which that state entered the Union in 1907. The liquor traffic had been prohibited in the Indian Territory by congressional action in 1895, and prohibition through local option had made steady progress in Oklahoma Territory after its creation in 1890. The movement for statehood, which obsessed the inhabitants of the two territories by the turn of the century, and a pervasive awareness of the Indian intensified the controversy over liquor control. When Congress finally passed an enabling act permitting single statehood, the measure prohibited the whiskey traffic in what had been Indian Territory and on Indian reservations for twenty-one years. Prohibition suited the mood of most of the delegates to the constitutional convention, for it fit in well with their penchant for direct democracy, their determination to control corporate interests, and their faith in moralistic remedies. The prohibition advocates gained the support of several Democratic leaders in the convention and succeeded in making prohibition a constitutional principle. The voters approved the prohibition clause in a special referendum on September 17, 1907, by a margin of 130,361 to 112,258. In 1908 the first legislature provided for a system of enforcement.[6]

Prohibition sentiment in Alabama, as in most other southern states, had deep historical roots. Promoted by the agitation of the WCTU and the great Protestant churches, the antiliquor cause gained strength in the 1880s. During the

---

[5]See A. J. McKelway, "Local Option and State Prohibition in the South," *Charities and Commons* 19 (Jan. 25, 1908): 1452–53; *"The Saloon Must Go": Proceedings Sixteenth National Convention of the Anti-Saloon League of America, Atlantic City, New Jersey, July 6–9, 1915, With State Reports* (Westerville, Ohio, n.d.), 409–11 (cited hereafter as *ASL Proceedings, 1915*); E. Merton Coulter, "The Athens Dispensary," *Ga. Hist. Quar.* 50 (Mar. 1966): 14–36; Alton DuMar Jones, "Progressivism in Georgia, 1898–1918" (Ph.D. diss., Emory Univ., 1963), 183–207; and Dewey W. Grantham, *Hoke Smith and the Politics of the New South* (Baton Rouge, 1958), 162–63, 189–90, 217.

[6]Jimmie Lewis Franklin, "Prohibition in Oklahoma, 1907–1959" (Ph.D. diss., Univ. of Oklahoma, 1968), 1–42; Franklin, "The Fight for Prohibition in Oklahoma Territory," *Soc. Sci. Quar.* 49 (Mar. 1969): 876–85; *ASL Proceedings, 1915*, pp. 494–97.

TABLE 9. *Statewide Prohibition Laws*

	YEAR OF ADOPTION	AUTHORIZATION	MEANS OF ENACTMENT
Ga.	1907	statutory	legislature
Okla.	1907	constitutional	constitutional convention
Ala.[1]	1907	statutory	legislature
Miss.	1908	statutory	legislature
N.C.	1908	statutory	submission to electorate
Tenn.	1909	statutory	legislature
Va.	1914	statutory	enabling act
Ala.	1915	statutory	legislature
Ark.	1915	statutory	legislature
S.C.	1915	statutory	submission to electorate
Texas	1918	statutory	legislature
	1919	constitutional	submission to electorate
Fla.	1918	constitutional	submission to electorate
Ky.	1919	constitutional	submission to electorate

[1] Repealed in 1911.

SOURCE: D. Leigh Colvin, *Prohibition in the United States: A History of the Prohibition Party and of the Prohibition Movement* (New York, 1926), 345, 435.

1890s the legislature enacted several restrictive measures and, swayed by the establishment of a state dispensary in South Carolina and pressure from several temperance organizations, introduced the dispensary system to Alabama on the basis of local option elections. The Anti-Saloon League entered the state in 1904, with strong support from Baptists and other churches, and in 1906 the Reverend Brooks Lawrence began an influential tenure as superintendent of the state organization. He soon began to edit an ASL newspaper called the *Alabama Citizen*. As prohibition feeling increased, the politicians responded. In 1907 the legislature finally adopted a general local option law, passed an antishipping bill, and approved a resolution requesting Congress to prevent the interstate shipment of alcoholic beverages into dry districts. Moving quickly to use the new local option law, prohibitionists succeeded in October 1907 in banning saloons in Jefferson County, where Birmingham was located. By the end of the year only seventeen of the state's sixty-seven counties permitted liquor sales. In the words of the historian of prohibition in Alabama, "a great wave of temperance reform had started and nothing could stop it."[7] When Governor Comer called an extra session of the legislature in the autumn of 1907 to elaborate his program of railroad regulation, prohibition leaders saw their opportunity to enact a statewide prohibition law. A bill introduced by Speaker Archibald H. Carmichael in the house of representatives made its way through

[7] James Benson Sellers, *The Prohibition Movement in Alabama, 1702 to 1943* (Chapel Hill, N.C., 1943), 108.

the two houses of the general assembly, cheered on by fervent well-wishers in the galleries, and the governor added his signature on November 23.[8]

A strong prohibition movement developed in Mississippi during the 1880s, and a general local option law was adopted by that state in 1886. Prohibitionists were among the advocates of a constitutional convention to disfranchise blacks, for they contended that the "wet" counties, located mainly in the plantation districts, were prevented from abolishing the liquor traffic by "the negro vote."[9] By the turn of the century, a large majority of Mississippi's counties had outlawed the saloon. The movement for a statewide law gained momentum during the next few years, strengthened by the support of three governors between 1902 and 1908 and numerous complaints of liquor law violations. The town of Sumrall, one correspondent informed Governor Vardaman in 1907, was "infested with what is commonly known as Blind Tigers." He urged that something be done to "rid our town of lawlessness."[10] The quickening of reform currents during the administrations of Vardaman and his successor, Edmund F. Noel, as well as the examples of prohibition at the state level in Georgia, Oklahoma, and Alabama, prepared the way for action in the Magnolia State. When the legislature met in 1908, the prohibition elements were able to pass a statewide measure with little opposition.[11]

The movement against alcohol in North Carolina was more sustained and far more disruptive than it was in Mississippi. During the last two decades of the nineteenth century, the liquor-control advocates steadily advanced their cause through special elections at the local level. Local dispensaries, which were first permitted in North Carolina in the mid-1890s, were supported by some prohibitionists as a means of publicizing the temperance cause and weakening the political power of the whiskey interests. The campaigns for local prohibition in places like Fayetteville, where Alexander J. McKelway was an ardent dry champion, advertised temperance objectives. Josephus Daniels lent the telling influence of his Raleigh *News and Observer* to the rising interest in stronger statewide controls. The Anti-Saloon League was organized in North Carolina

[8] For the prohibition movement in Alabama, see ibid., 50–123; Sheldon Hackney, *Populism to Progressivism in Alabama* (Princeton, N.J., 1969), 235, 302–305, 316, 323; David Alan Harris, "Racists and Reformers: A Study of Progressivism in Alabama, 1896–1911" (Ph.D. diss., Univ. of North Carolina, 1967), 395–416; and J. C. Jackson, "The Work of the Anti-Saloon League," *Annals* 32 (Nov. 1908): 12–26.

[9] Albert D. Kirwan, *Revolt of the Rednecks: Mississippi Politics, 1876–1925* (Lexington, Ky., 1951), 61.

[10] W. H. Atkinson to James K. Vardaman, Aug. 28, 1907, Vardaman Papers, Mississippi Department of Archives and History.

[11] See T. J. Bailey, *Prohibition in Mississippi, or Anti-Liquor Legislation from Territorial Days, with Its Results in the Counties* (Jackson, Miss., 1917); Ernest H. Cherrington, *The Evolution of Prohibition in the United States of America: A Chronological History of the Liquor Problem and Temperance Reform in the United States from the Earliest Settlements to the Consummation of National Prohibition* (Westerville, Ohio, 1920), 267; Charles Granville Hamilton, "Mississippi Politics in the Progressive Era, 1904–1920" (Ph.D. diss., Vanderbilt Univ., 1958), 96, 124, 146–47, 151–55, 188–89, 330–32.

early in 1902, and its impact on the movement was apparent almost im-mediately. In 1903 the reformers managed, after a hard fight, to push through a new state law, the so-called Watts Act, which limited saloons to incorporated towns and introduced a more effective plan of local elections. Two years later the legislature tightened the system of control still further, and meanwhile the drive for local option elections enjoyed conspicuous success. More and more church groups joined the campaign, which was endorsed by an increasing number of Democratic leaders and was upheld by moral, economic, and social justifications. The prohibitionists found their chance to enact a statewide law early in 1908, when Governor Robert B. Glenn called a special session of the general assembly to deal with the problem of regulating railroad rates. "State prohibition is inevitable," proclaimed the *News and Observer*. "Why not wait?"[12] The legislature did wait: it submitted the issue of statewide prohibition to the voters in a referendum. The campaign that preceded the balloting on May 26 was a stirring one, but the prohibitionists won handily, 113,612 to 69,416.[13]

Last to adopt statutory prohibition in this period was Tennessee, where the issue was bitterly fought and eventually became the central controversy in political affairs. During the 1880s, reformers almost succeeded in securing prohibition by constitutional amendment, and the WCTU and the Local Option League kept up the fight in the 1890s. The Anti-Saloon League began to operate in the state near the end of the century. By the beginning of 1903, fifty-five of the state's ninety-six counties had made saloons illegal. Yet despite prohibition progress in Tennessee, the whiskey interests found a sanctuary in the largest cities. In Memphis, the state's most populous city, there were 504 saloons in 1903. Most of them were unsavory places, deeply enmeshed in politics and the focal point of lawlessness.[14] Prohibition groups were increasingly drawn into the struggle for control of the Democratic party that erupted in 1905 and 1906. Malcolm R. Patterson, an opponent of statewide prohibition and the successful candidate for governor in 1906, was able to block several antiliquor measures in 1907. But he did not openly oppose the so-called Pendleton bill, which ex-tended the privilege of recharter—and thus the opportunity to apply the Four Mile Law prohibiting the sale of intoxicants in the vicinity of schools—to the state's largest cities. By 1908 only Memphis, Nashville, Chattanooga, and LaFollette still held out against the dry movement.[15]

---

[12]Quoted in Daniels, *Editor in Politics* (Chapel Hill, N.C., 1941), 521.

[13]Prohibition in North Carolina is described in Daniel Jay Whitener, *Prohibition in North Carolina, 1715–1945* (Chapel Hill, N.C., 1945); Daniels, *Editor in Politics*, 401–404, 440–42, 520–24; and Hugh Talmage Lefler and Albert Ray Newsome, *North Carolina: The History of a Southern State* (Chapel Hill, N.C., 1954), 568–69.

[14]William D. Miller, *Memphis During the Progressive Era, 1900–1917* (Memphis, 1957), 88–89.

[15]Paul E. Isaac, *Prohibition and Politics: Turbulent Decades in Tennessee, 1885–1920* (Knox-ville, 1965); Grace Leab, "Tennessee Temperance Activities, 1870–1899," *East Tennessee Hist. Society's Pubs.* 21 (1949): 52–68; Leslie F. Roblyer, "The Fight for Local Prohibition in Knox-ville, Tennessee, 1907," ibid. 26 (1954): 27–37; Joe Michael Shahan, "Reform and Politics in Tennessee: 1906–1914" (Ph.D. diss., Vanderbilt Univ., 1981), 106–108, 140–66, 176–88.

Prohibition dominated the incendiary campaign for the Democratic gubernatorial nomination in 1908, in which the Anti-Saloon League endorsed former senator Edward W. Carmack against Governor Patterson. As one Tennessee newspaper observed at the time, "The party is disrupted, brother is fighting brother, church organizations are being split wide open, the women are being dragged into the filthy mire of politics and the children are being corrupted."[16] The acting superintendent of the Anti-Saloon League, on the other hand, declared that "We have back of us practically the united support of all church and moral forces. Step by step the Anti-Saloon League, together with the W.C.T.U. and other kindred organizations, have been moving on the enemy of The Home, The Church, [and] The School . . . ."[17] Carmack was defeated in the primary, but his assassination in November 1908 at the hands of two of Governor Patterson's friends made him a martyr to "the holy cause of prohibition." The legislature that convened in January 1909 rushed a statewide prohibition bill through both chambers. Patterson vetoed the bill, but the general assembly quickly passed it over his veto, and various other antisaloon measures were enacted during the same session. "Tennessee has been redeemed," declared the Nashville *Tennessean* on January 14, 1909. "The highest page in her glorious history is this triumphant victory of the people."[18]

By the time state prohibition went into effect in Tennessee on January 1, 1909, the movement had almost inundated the southern terrain. In less than two years, six of the region's thirteen states had adopted statewide prohibition statutes. Prohibition had become a major issue in most of the other states, and the dry advance was continuing through local option elections. But just as it appeared that the prohibitionists would conquer the entire section, their crusade suddenly encountered several severe setbacks, the result of widespread violations of existing laws and the determined opposition of antiprohibitionists. Five years elapsed before the southern reformers were able to add another state to the dry column.

In 1910, resolute antiprohibition governors were elected in Alabama and Texas, while Florida voters rejected a constitutional amendment providing for prohibition. During the following year the Alabama legislature repealed its prohibition law, and a constitutional amendment calling for prohibition was defeated by popular vote in Texas. In 1912, Arkansas voters defeated statewide prohibition.[19] Meanwhile, there were bitter controversies and charges that prohibition was not being enforced in the states that were already dry.

[16]Nashville *American,* June 28, 1908.

[17]W. R. Hamilton to Edward W. Carmack, June 26, 1908, Carmack Papers, Southern Historical Collection, University of North Carolina.

[18]Quoted in Isaac, *Prohibition and Politics,* 165–66. Also see Nashville *Tennessean,* Nov. 12, 1908, and Eric Russell Lacy, "Tennessee Teetotalism: Social Forces and the Politics of Progressivism," *Tenn. Hist. Quar.* 24 (Fall 1965): 227.

[19]For developments in Florida and Arkansas, see Cherrington, *The Evolution of Prohibition,* 256, 295–96, 302, 336, 345, 359, 361; *"The Saloon Must Go": Proceedings Fourteenth National*

"Prohibition in the South is a failure," one observer asserted, "not only because it does not prohibit, but because it is breeding a defiance of law and has set up in the place of licensed saloons illegal dispensers of liquor."[20]

A number of factors contributed to the strength of the resistance forces. The "liquor interests" were well established in several southern states and determined to turn back the prohibition wave or at least to force concessions that would permit the continued traffic in alcoholic beverages. The Texas Brewers' Association, for example, began in 1903 to assess its members "for the purpose of promoting anti-prohibition matters in Texas." Texas brewers spent a million dollars fighting prohibition between 1900 and 1911, and they joined with other enterprisers in organizing the Texas Business Men's Association as a means of protecting their mutual interests and preventing the passage of hostile legislation.[21] Lobbyists for whiskey dealers made effective use of the argument that prohibition would force the states and municipalities to raise taxes by depriving those authorities of high license fees and excise levies. Another source of antiprohibition support lay in the ties between the saloons and politicians, particularly in the largest cities. In New Orleans, for instance, a saloon owner named Tom Anderson was a powerful member of the state legislature and boss of the city's "red-light" district.[22] The liquor interests also played an influential role in state politics through their campaign contributions. Resistance forces were bolstered by the emergence of prohibition as an important issue in the factional struggles that characterized Democratic politics in the southern states during this period. Some of the antiprohibition leaders in these struggles, such as Oscar B. Colquitt of Texas and Emmett O'Neal of Alabama, were genuine local optionists who successfully appealed to personal liberty sentiment and opposition to statewide prohibition on constitutional grounds. Other skeptics, like editor Fred Sullens of the Jackson (Mississippi) *Daily News*, deplored attempts by "fanatical prohibitionists" to "legislate morals."[23] Finally, the initial enthusiasm many southerners felt over the adoption of prohibition turned to disenchantment in the wake of widespread violations and growing disrespect for law and authority.

Convention of the Anti-Saloon League of America, Washington, D.C., December 11-14, 1911, with State Reports (Westerville, Ohio, n.d.), 107–108; George Murrell Hunt, "A History of the Prohibition Movement in Arkansas" (M.A. thesis, Univ. of Arkansas, 1933), 132–35.

[20] R. E. Pritchard, "The Failure of Prohibition in the South," *Harper's Weekly* 55 (Mar. 18, 1911): 12.

[21] Alwyn Barr, *Reconstruction to Reform: Texas Politics, 1876–1906* (Austin, Tex., 1971), 231–32; James H. Timberlake, *Prohibition and the Progressive Movement, 1900–1920* (Cambridge, Mass., 1963), 109–10, 123; Nuala McGann Drescher, "The Opposition to Prohibition, 1900–1919: A Social and Institutional Study" (Ph.D. diss., Univ. of Delaware, 1964), 15, 23, 76–77, 140, 151–52.

[22] Timberlake, *Prohibition and the Progressive Movement*, 114. Also see Joy Jackson, "Prohibition in New Orleans: The Unlikeliest Crusade," *La. Hist.* 19 (Summer 1978): 261–84.

[23] John R. Skates, Jr., "Fred Sullens and Prohibition," *Jour. Miss. Hist.* 29 (May 1967): 83–94.

The difficulties that confronted southern reformers in carrying their prohibition crusade to a successful conclusion is well illustrated in the case of Texas,
where the issue dominated state politics for almost a decde. As early as 1905, a
small-town Texas businessman pointed out that "the position of public men
upon this question has invited or repelled their following more than their views
upon all other questions combined: when the issue becomes acute it dominates
every other issue."[24] Prohibition became, substantively and symbolically, one
of the principal rallying points for Texas progressives during the administration
of Governor Thomas M. Campbell. But it was evident by the autumn of 1910
that the campaign for a statewide law faced a number of handicaps. For one
thing, statutory prohibition would apparently require an amendment to the state
constitution, and experience had already demonstrated that such a process—
endorsement by the voters in the Democratic primary, approval by the legislature, and ratification in a special election—was cumbersome. Of more fundamental significance was the opposition by a large number of Texans to the idea
of drastic state action against the saloon. Many urban dwellers resisted prohibition. Strong antiprohibition sentiment existed in the southern and western parts
of the state, including some fifteen counties with heavy concentrations of German population to the east, south, and southwest of Austin and a substantial
number of Mexican-Americans and Negroes who tended to support the local
machines in cities like Houston and El Paso. Despite their defensive stance, the
liquor interests were effectively organized and exerted great influence in the
Democratic-dominated politics of Texas.[25]

Oscar B. Colquitt's administration as governor strengthened the antiprohibitionists. Colquitt himself, a bold and colorful figure, embodied many of the
fears and suspicions of those who opposed a statewide law—faith in localism
and individualism, antagonism toward state regulation of personal morality,
hostility toward "political preachers." In his successful campaign of 1910,
Colquitt promised Texans a period of "political peace and legislative rest." As
governor he vigorously opposed statewide prohibition, advocated local option
and law enforcement as the wisest aproach to the liquor question, and emphasized the losses in revenue and personal freedom that statutory prohibition
would bring. But in spite of antiprohibitionist efforts, the general assembly of
1911 approved a prohibition amendment to the state constitution and set July 22
as the date for a vote on the proposal by the electorate. A rancorous campaign

[24] T. W. Carlock to Oscar B. Colquitt, May 15, 1905, Oscar B. Colquitt Papers, University of
Texas Library.
[25] Lewis L. Gould, *Progressives and Prohibitionists: Texas Democrats in the Wilson Era*
(Austin, Tex., 1973), 28–57; Sam Woolford, "Carry Nation in Texas," *Southwestern Hist. Quar.*
63 (Apr. 1960): 554–66; James Aubrey Tinsley, "The Progressive Movement in Texas" (Ph.D.
diss., Univ. of Wisconsin, 1953), 235–48; Ernest H. Cherrington, comp. and ed., *The Anti-Saloon
League Year Book, 1909: An Encyclopedia of Facts and Figures Dealing with the Liquor Traffic
and the Temperance Reform* (Columbus, Ohio, and Chicago, n.d.), 54–55 (cited hereafter as *ASL
Year Book*).

ensued, resulting in the defeat of the amendment by a vote of 231,096 to 237,303. Although 168 of the state's counties were completely dry by this time, a statewide law seemed as unobtainable as ever. Governor Colquitt was reelected in 1912, notwithstanding the fervent opposition of prohibitionists, and two years later the reformers suffered a double loss when their gubernatorial candidate was defeated in the Democratic primary and the question of submission was disapproved by more than 20,000 votes.[26]

Alabama antiprohibitionists found in Emmett O'Neal a leader similar to Oscar B. Colquitt in Texas. The problem of enforcing Alabama's prohibition act of 1907 and the possibility that opponents might force its repeal led reformers in that state to propose a constitutional amendment. After being adopted by the legislature, the amendment was defeated by the voters in the autumn of 1909 at the end of an intensely fought campaign. The battle between prohibitionists and antiprohibitionists continued almost without letup in the Democratic primary of 1910, in which O'Neal defeated Hugh S.D. Mallory, a zealous dry leader who was closely associated with Governor Comer's administration. O'Neal was an opponent of Comerism, a leader of conservative Democrats, and a determined local optionist. During his vigorous campaign O'Neal pictured himself as a champion of personal liberty and an agent of peace and tranquillity who would bring an end to the bitter strife in Alabama politics. Following his election he declared that the "people have expressed their condemnation of that spirit of radicalism which has retarded our prosperity, checked investments, and made property rights insecure."[27] As governor, O'Neal spoke out forcefully for local option, and the general assembly of 1911 followed his recommendation by repealing the statewide law and reinstating a policy of local option, despite the efforts of the Anti-Saloon League and other dry organizations. In the local option elections that followed, several of the urban areas, including Birminham and Jefferson County, voted to permit saloons or dispensaries.[28]

Meanwhile, the prohibition cause was experiencing limited gains and a variety of defeats in several other southern states. In Virginia a strong local option movement made considerable headway, but efforts to secure passage of an enabling act authorizing a referendum on the proposed statewide law were defeated by the legislators in 1910 and again in 1912. The prohibition movement in South Carolina was crucially affected by the establishment of a state dispen-

---

[26]Lewis L. Gould, "Progressives and Prohibitionists: Texas Democratic Politics, 1911–1912," *Southwestern Hist. Quar.* 75 (July 1971): 5–18; Gould, *Progressives and Prohibitionists*, 45–57, 87–91, 123–26, 143–45; Seth Shepard McKay, *Texas Politics, 1906–1944, With Special Reference to the German Counties* (Lubbock, Tex., 1952), 20–59; *ASL Proceedings, 1911*, pp. 68–69, 71, 149; Cherrington, *The Evolution of Prohibition*, 298, 301, 308–309.

[27]Quoted in Albert Burton Moore, *History of Alabama* (University, Ala., 1934), 676.

[28]Sellers, *Prohibition in Alabama*, 132–75; Moore, *History of Alabama*, 672–77; Wayne Flynt, "Dissent in Zion: Alabama Baptists and Social Issues, 1900–1914," *JSH* 35 (Nov. 1969): 527–28.

Prohibition parade in Birmingham, November 28, 1909, sponsored by the WCTU. *The Collections of the Birmingham Public Library.*

sary system in 1893. The dispensary survived, amid heated conroversy and administrative scandal, until it was abolished by the legislature in 1907. Spurred on by the Anti-Saloon League, which was organized in South Carolina in 1908, the prohibitionists won a series of local elections in 1908 and 1909. But local dispensaries were permitted under the disestablishment law of 1907, and the number of such counties increased during the administration of Governor Coleman L. Blease (1911–15) to fifteen. Unique factors in Kentucky and Louisiana also weakened the force of the prohibition movement. In Kentucky, where the whiskey distillers were an influential element in the state's economy and politics, the legislature refused to pass a general local option law until 1912. Although the local option approach enjoyed a good deal of success in Louisiana, the cosmopolitan atmosphere of New Orleans and the French and Catholic culture of southern Louisiana proved resistant to the pressures for total prohibition. The work of the Anti-Saloon League was desultory in the Pelican State.[29]

In the states that had legally abolished the saloon, the task of enforcing prohibition proved to be difficult, controversial, and politically volatile. The prohibitionists and their opponents looked for evidence to support the contention that statewide prohibition did or did not work, that it encouraged or depressed economic activity, and that it reduced or furthered crime.[30] Although the first two governors of Oklahoma—Charles N. Haskell and Lee Cruce—were stalwart advocates of enforcement, prohibition proved to be both divisive and impossible to enforce in that state.[31] Under North Carolina's prohibition act of 1908, alcoholic beverages could still be imported and also bought by prescription from drugstores. The state permitted social clubs to sell liquor to their members, and its policy of taxing near-beer and similar beverages provided a shield for the illegal sale of stronger drinks. There were numerous

[29]C. C. Pearson and J. Edwin Hendricks, *Liquor and Anti-Liquor in Virginia, 1619–1919* (Durham, N.C., 1967), 210–70; Robert A. Hohner, "Bishop Cannon's Apprenticeship in Temperance Politics, 1901–1918," *JSH* 34 (Feb. 1968): 33–49; Hohner, "Prohibition and Virginia Politics: William Hodges Mann Versus Henry St. George Tucker, 1909," *Va. Mag. Hist. and Biog.* 74 (Jan. 1966): 88–107; Henry C. Ferrell, Jr., "Prohibition, Reform, and Politics in Virginia, 1895–1916," in *East Carolina College Publications in History*, vol. 3: *Studies in the History of the South, 1875–1922* (Greenville, N.C., 1966), 175–242; Allen W. Moger, *Virginia: Bourbonism to Byrd, 1870–1925* (Charlottesville, Va., 1968), 297–307; Niels Christensen, Jr., "The State Dispensaries of South Carolina," *Annals* 32 (Nov. 1908): 75–85; Ellen Alexander Hendricks, "The South Carolina Dispensary System," *N.C. Hist. Rev.* 22 (Apr. 1945): 176–97 and (July 1945): 320–49; John Evans Eubanks, *Ben Tillman's Baby: The Dispensary System of South Carolina, 1892–1915* (Augusta, Ga., 1950); Ronald Dantan Burnside, "The Governorship of Coleman Livingston Blease of South Carolina, 1911–1915" (Ph.D. diss., Indiana Univ., 1963), 105–35; John Joseph Duffy, "Charleston Politics in the Progressive Era" (Ph.D. diss., Univ. of South Carolina, 1963), 140–53, 254–59; *ASL Year Book, 1909*, pp. 32–35, 53, 57; *ASL Proceedings, 1911*, pp. 117–18, 145–46.

[30]See, for example, Pritchard, "The Failure of Prohibition in the South," 12; R. W. Simpson, Jr., "Near-prohibition in the South," *Harper's Weekly* 53 (July 10, 1909): 15; and Jones, "Progressivism in Georgia," 193–99.

[31]Franklin, "Prohibition in Oklahoma," 44–77; Orben J. Casey, "Governor Lee Cruce and Law Enforcement, 1911–1915," *Chron. Okla.* 54 (Winter 1976): 435–60.

reports of "moonshining" and other illicit activities in the state.[32] Prohibition in Tennessee was openly defied in the state's larger cities, and hundreds of social clubs were incorporated under state law. In Memphis, which had a well-earned reputation as a hard-drinking river town, Mayor Edward H. Crump consistently refused to enforce the law. Mayor Hilary E. Howse of Nashville was reelected in 1911 and 1913 in spite of his refusal to execute the prohibition statutes and opposition from two Nashville newspapers, the WCTU, and many church and educational leaders. After four years Tennessee was still racked by political turmoil over prohibition and related controversies. Twice during the tense political situation of 1913, the state legislature failed to deal adequately with the frustrating enforcement problem, though it did pass nuisance and antishipping laws that year.[33]

The years of failure and disappointment that frustrated southern prohibitionists after 1909 began to end in 1914. The resistance the prohibitionists encountered during this period actually prepared them for the successful campaigns of 1914 and later years, since they learned from painful experience just what constituted the requisites of victory in the recalcitrant states. This was most apparent in the activities of the Anti-Saloon League, whose state organizations grew steadily more influential among members of the great religious denominations and as a factor in state politics in the section. The antisaloon campaign had also transcended state lines, had in fact become a regional movement.[34] Indeed, it promised to become a genuinely national movement, and prohibitionists in the South were encouraged by the passage in 1913 of the Webb-Kenyon Act, a congressional measure that outlawed the shipment of alcoholic beverages from a wet to a dry state. Some southern reformers were even beginning to talk about the need for national prohibition.

Prohibition, in a peculiarly satisfying way, absorbed the yearnings for reform and fulfillment in the early twentieth-century South. It offered a means of moral reaffirmation of traditional values, the promise of cleaner politics, and an avenue to employ the authority of the state in the search for moral and social progress. The movement's comprehensive and dynamic character made it an important consideration in the factional alignment within the Democratic party and, to some extent, in the larger struggle for social reform in the region. The prohibition campaigns were also an expression of concern about personal im-

[32]Whitener, *Prohibition in North Carolina*, 171–77.
[33]E. E. Miller, "When Prohibition Fails and Why," *Outlook* 101 (July 20, 1912): 641; Isaac, *Prohibition and Politics*, 170–81; Shahan, "Reform and Politics in Tennessee," 352–59, 364–68; Miller, *Memphis During the Progressive Era*, 124–26, 173–74; Richard S. Daniels, "Blind Tigers and Blind Justice: The Arkansas Raid on Island 37, Tennessee," *Ark. Hist. Quar.* 38 (Autumn 1979): 259–70.
[34]By 1914, for example, a truth-in-advertising movement was gaining ground in the Southern Newspaper Publishers Association, and a number of the region's journals had reversed their policy of accepting liquor and patent medicine advertisements. See Walter C. Johnson and Arthur T. Robb, *The South and Its Newspapers, 1903–1953: The Story of the Southern Newspaper Publishers Association and Its Part in the South's Economic Rebirth* (Chattanooga, Tenn., 1954), 48.

morality and an instrument of social control with far-reaching class and racial implications. But prohibition was more than an attempt at social control. It was, in some measure, the manifestation of a desire for social uplift of the poor and of a zeal to promote social justice.

The movement was rooted in southern Protestantism. Most advocates of prohibition were churchgoing people. It was "the Methodist and Baptist pastor, aroused by the Anti-Saloon League," one historian writes, "who led the crusade for prohibition. He co-operated with the League, opened his pulpit to its field agents, distributed its propaganda, collected money to support its work, and preached prohibition to his congregation."[35] Many southern church members viewed strong drink as a source of social evil as well as personal immorality. Although acceptance of what came to be called the social gospel was hindered by the theological individualism of southern denominations, the region's churches slowly began to concern themselves with the new social problems, particularly in the cities.[36] Prohibition became their bridge between the old and the new, between those who wanted to reform individuals and those who wanted to reform society. There was, in other words, "a sense of social obligation" as well as an impulse toward moral coercion among the supporters of prohibition in the South. "The drunkard and the drunkard's interests," one of its champions wrote in 1908, "are not the chief consideration, though these are not lost sight of. It is the drinker as a husband, a father, a voter, a worker, a citizen—the man as a social factor, who is being considered." This writer thought that prohibition might bring "an alliance of conscience on all the South's problems."[37]

Not even the fundamentalist churches were altogether preoccupied with life in the next world. As Timothy L. Smith wrote in his study of mid-nineteenth-century revivalism, "The quest of personal holiness became in some ways a kind of plain man's transcendentalism, which geared ancient creeds to the drive shaft of social reform."[38] The spectacle of hundreds of revivalists pleading for

---

[35]Robert A. Hohner, "The Prohibitionists: Who Were They?" *SAQ* 68 (Autumn 1969): 494. "The country preachers," wrote one Baptist minister in 1917, "have been the main force which has brought in the South the downfall of John Barleycorn" (Victor I. Masters, *Country Church in the South: Arranged to Meet the Needs of Mission Study Classes and Also of the General Reader* [rev. ed., Atlanta, Ga., 1917], 26–27).

[36]Hunter Dickinson Farish, *The Circuit Rider Dismounts: A Social History of Southern Methodism, 1865–1900* (Richmond, Va., 1938), 305–24; Milton L. Baughn, "Social Views Reflected in Official Publications of the Cumberland Presbyterian Church, 1875–1900" (Ph.D. diss., Vanderbilt Univ., 1954), 164–202; John Lee Eighmy, "The Social Conscience of Southern Baptists from 1900 to the Present as Reflected in Their Organized Life" (Ph.D. diss., Univ. of Missouri, 1959), 20–26; Eighmy, "Religious Liberalism in the South During the Progressive Era," *Church History* 38 (Sept. 1969): 363–64; Henry Y. Warnock, "Moderate Racial Thought and Attitudes of Southern Baptists and Methodists, 1900–1921" (Ph.D. diss., Northwestern Univ., 1963), 104, 192–94; Flynt, "Dissent in Zion," 528–29.

[37]White, "Prohibition: The New Task and Opportunity of the South," 134–35, 141.

[38]Smith, *Revivalism and Social Reform in Mid-Nineteenth-Century America* (New York and Nashville, Tenn., 1957), 8.

moral regeneration by law and of men such as the Reverend Sam Jones person-
ally marching into the slums to close saloons and gambling dives suggests social
implications in even the most narrowly based moral reformism.[39] Thousands of
ministers in the South had become dedicated supporters of statewide prohibition by the early years of the twentieth century. The Southern Baptist Convention, for instance, resolved in 1900 that "in brief we favor prohibition for the
nation and the state and total abstinence for the individual, and we do believe
that no Christian citizen should ever cast a ballot for any man, measure or
platform that is opposed to the annihilation of the liquor traffic."[40]

Southern churches were sensitive to the way in which social dislocations
were threatening established modes of conduct and traditional moral standards.
The swelling volume and constant movement of landless farmers, the growth of
cities and towns, and the declining vitality of older communities and institutions
alarmed many ministers and civic leaders. New controls seemed to be necessary as an instrument of social progress. Governor Hooper of Tennessee put the
matter bluntly in 1911: "If the drinking of any liquor . . . destroys his [the
citizen's] moral stamina, reduces him to the level of a beast, and makes him a
menace to his fellow-man, the State has a right to restrain him . . . for the great
and righteous purpose of protecting society."[41] The road to prohibition, of
course, led inescapably to politics. In many places the defeat of the liquor
interests appeared to be an indispensable requirement for civic improvement.
The role of the saloon in municipal corruption, the power wielded by the
"liquor lobby," and the allegedly malign influence of whiskey dealers in resisting various social reforms encouraged prohibitionists to broaden their reform
programs. "I am not a temperance advocate particularly," one Tennessean
wrote in 1906, "but there are thousands of us who are not, that are getting tired
of this damnable whiskey influence that corrupts everything, even to politics."[42] The intensive activity of southern churches on behalf of prohibition was
primarily responsible for their mounting interest in child labor laws, better
prisons, and other social reforms.

Public action to elevate community morals was also evident in antigambling
laws, campaigns against prostitution, Sunday closing statutes, the banning of
prizefights, and opposition to numerous city bosses in the South. The prevalence of vice and immoral behavior, especially in the cities, was profoundly
disquieting to the religious faithful. "Our people dance, play cards,—and

[39]See, for example, William G. McLoughlin, Jr., *Billy Sunday Was His Real Name* (Chicago,
1955), 37–38, 144; Richard L. Wilson, "Sam Jones: An Apostle of the New South," *Ga. Hist.
Quar.* 57 (Winter 1973): 459–74; and Ray C. Rensi, "The Gospel According to Sam Jones," ibid.
60 (Fall 1976): 251–63.

[40]Quoted in D. Leigh Colvin, *Prohibition in the United States: A History of the Prohibition
Party and of the Prohibition Movement* (New York, 1926), 268.

[41]Quoted in Shahan, "Reform and Politics in Tennessee," 263–64.

[42]James C. Beck to Edward W. Carmack, May 14, 1906, Carmack Papers. Also see Timberlake, *Prohibition and the Progressive Movement*, 113, 164–65.

profane the Sabbath," a Huntsville, Alabama, minister lamented in 1910, "—and there seems to be no end to the disregard for the authority of the Church. And many who are called Christians seem to defy God,—self-indulgence and Self-will are uppermost now."[43] Goaded into action by the flagrant violation of liquor and gambling laws, a significant number of religious leaders and other concerned citizens buckled on the armor of civic morality. In Miami, Florida, for example, a Dade County Civic Association was formed in 1908 "to promote and encourage good morals, good government, temperance and civic righteousness." More than forty Oklahoma City churches joined Governor Lee Cruce in 1913 in a campaign against drinking and gambling.[44] In 1912, 1,600 men and boys took part in an eight-day crusade sponsored by the Charleston YMCA, which was intent upon doing something about the "corruption" of youth in the city's poolrooms and "blind tigers." Meanwhile, the ladies of the Charleston Civic Club were attacking the problem of prostitution and condemning local racetrack "abuse."[45]

Thus antisaloon activities promoted, sometimes incidentally, a number of other reforms. The progress of prohibition in the South, Alexander J. McKelway declared in 1909, was "only an indication of the onward march of other social reforms." He cited the enactment of child labor laws, abolition of bucket shops, repeal of special divorce statutes, reform of the convict-lease system, establishment of juvenile courts and reformatories, the "war" being waged against gambling and "the social evil," and other legislative advances in the region.[46] McKelway's juxtaposition of prohibition and social reform is not surprising, for the prohibition movement was intimately associated with progressivism in the southern states, perhaps more closely so than in any other part of the country. Almost without exception the leading progressives in the South gave strong support to prohibition.[47] In only one or two states, most prominently Virginia, where conservative Democrats endorsed prohibition and

---

[43]S. E. Wasson to W. A. Candler, June 15, 1910, Warren A. Candler Papers, Emory University Library. For the prevalence of vice in the early twentieth-century South, see G. Croft Williams, *A Social Interpretation of South Carolina* (Columbia, S.C., 1946), 203–204; Robert Webb Williams, Jr., "Martin Behrman, Mayor and Political Boss of New Orleans, 1904–1926" (M.A. thesis, Tulane Univ., 1952), 87–117; and James R. McGovern, "'Sporting Life on the Line': Prostitution in Progressive Era Pensacola," *Fla. Hist. Quar.* 54 (Oct. 1975): 131–44.

[44]See Paul S. George, "A Cyclone Hits Miami: Carrie Nation's Visit to 'The Wicked City,'" *Fla. Hist. Quar.* 58 (Oct. 1979): 150–59; H. T. Laughbaum, "Oklahoma," in *ASL Proceedings, 1915*, p. 497; Casey, "Governor Lee Cruce and Law Enforcement," 443–59; and Barr, *Reconstruction to Reform: Texas Politics*, 230–31.

[45]Duffy, "Charleston Politics in the Progressive Era," 249–52. Also see Grace Warren Landrum, "The Southern Puritan," *SAQ* 22 (Apr. 1923): 171–75; J. E. Ericson and James H. McCrocklin, "From Religion to Commerce: The Evolution and Enforcement of Blue Laws in Texas," *Southwestern Soc. Sci. Quar.* 45 (June 1964): 50–58; and Charles A. Bobbitt, "The North Memphis Driving Park, 1901–1905: The Passing of an Era," *West Tennessee Historical Society Papers* 26 (1972): 40–55.

[46]McKelway, "Prohibition in the Southern States." Also see Timberlake, *Prohibition and the Progressive Movement*, 122–23.

[47]The career of Richmond Pearson Hobson of Alabama provides a suggestive example of the

cooperated with James Cannon, Jr., did antisaloon leaders fail to ally themselves with the more reform-oriented factions, and in the Old Dominion progressives tended to support prohibition.[48] "Progressive Democracy in Texas,"
asserted one of that state's progressives in 1913, "is represented by Prohibition
Democrats."[49] Although a few liberal politicians opposed statewide prohibition because they adhered to old-time democratic principles, there was a strong
correlation between prohibition sentiment and progressive notions, on the one
hand, and opposition to prohibition and conservative predilections, on the
other.

Prohibition was also linked to the omnipresent race problem, and nothing
was more significant in the movement's emphasis on social control than the
treatment of blacks. Alcohol, many whites assumed, demoralized and de-
bauched black men, reduced their efficiency as workers, and fueled their secret
lust for white women.[50] The white ribboners frequently charged that saloon
operators and city machines relied upon black votes to defeat local and state
prohibition campaigns. Many dry leaders were convinced that prohibition
would prove morally and economically beneficial to Negroes. Black southerners, like their white counterparts, seem to have been divided over the issue,
though black community clean-up efforts often included attacks on saloons and
related evils. Booker T. Washington supported prohibition, which he characterized as a "moral movement" inspired by ministers, women, and church
people.[51]

Social control as a progressive motive was related to the evolving class
structure of the South's white population—to the presence of a depressed mass
of rural and urban working people and an emerging middle class increasingly
conscious of the need for social order and restraint.[52] For the middle class,

relationship between prohibition and progressivism in the South. See Richard N. Sheldon,
"Richmond Pearson Hobson as a Progressive Reformer," *Ala. Rev.* 25 (Oct. 1972): 243–61.

[48]Some Virginia progressives saw prohibition (before 1914) as a way of attacking the Martin
organization, which received substantial support from liquor and saloon interests. See Hohner,
"The Prohibitionists: Who Were They?" 501–502.

[49]Quoted in Tinsley, "The Progressive Movement in Texas," 231.

[50]Prohibitionists complained that whiskey distillers and dealers were deliberately inciting
southern blacks by exhibiting obscene pictures of nude white women in saloons that catered to
Negro men and by employing sexually suggestive titles and labels in their advertisements. Timberlake, *Prohibition and the Progressive Movement*, 119–20, 123. Also see Corrigan, "The Prohibi-
tion Wave in the South," 328–30; Charles Crowe, "Racial Violence and Social Reform—Origins
of the Atlanta Riot of 1906," *Jour. Negro Hist.* 53 (July 1968): 236–37; John Dittmer, *Black
Georgia in the Progressive Era, 1900–1920* (Urbana, Ill., 1977), 111–13; Hanes Walton, Jr.,
"Another Force for Disfranchisement: Blacks and the Prohibitionists in Tennessee," *Journal of
Human Relations* 18 (First Quarter 1970): 728–38; and Hanes Walton, Jr., and James E. Taylor,
"Blacks and the Southern Prohibition Movement," *Phylon* 32 (Fall 1971): 247–59.

[51]Washington, "Prohibition and the Negro," *Outlook* 88 (Mar. 14, 1908): 587–89.

[52]For prohibition as a movement of social status in the United States, see Joseph R. Gusfield,
Symbolic Crusade: Status Politics and the American Temperance Movement (Urbana, Ill., 1963),
and S. J. Mennell, "Prohibition: A Sociological View," *Journal of American Studies* 3 (Dec.
1969): 159–75.

moreover, prohibition was symbolic of a more influential social role. It was also a protean reform whose various guises seemed to accommodate the values of modernization as well as tradition. At the same time, prohibition transcended class lines. Indeed, it was to some extent a democratic and grass-roots movement, as was evident in the dry crusades of the fundamentalist churches, the campaigns to rid hundreds of communities of saloons and blind tigers, and the enthusiasm of the southern countryside for legal prohibition. Nevertheless, in its rationale and organization prohibition was essentially an urban movement and a middle-class phenomenon.[53]

The struggle for prohibition, like other important social movements of this period, attracted support for several different reasons. It reaffirmed the evangelical ideals of southern Protestantism. It was both a coercive reform with strong racial and class overtones and an expression of social concern for those victimized by the South's new urbanization and industrialization. The movement also attracted support as a means of ensuring greater industrial efficiency and more rapid economic progress. Its ramifications as a political reform were especially vital. The liquor traffic was attacked as a center of political as well as moral corruption. It was a key issue in the factional conflicts within the Democratic party, and in many cases a focal point in the coalescence of reform forces. Prohibitionists tended to identify the whiskey interests with the need for more comprehensive business regulation. And in urging the adoption of prohibition, dry advocates were calling for an expansion of state and municipal government. In short, prohibition tied together most of the reform strands of the progressive era and offered a simple, moral solution to disturbing social ills.

[53] One study of the social status of 314 WCTU leaders in Virginia cities during the years 1887–1916 found that the great majority came from the middle class. It is perhaps significant that more than half of these women were married to or otherwise identified with such lower-middle-class workers as sales clerks, bookkeepers, printers, grocers, and railroad conductors. They may have perceived prohibition as a means of expressing middle-class values and achieving middle-class status and respectability. See Hohner, "The Prohibitionists: Who Were They?" 497–500.

7

Social Justice

AMONG THE DISTINCTIVE THEMES of southern progressivism was a spirit of compassion and uplift that expressed itself in a number of organized reform endeavors early in the twentieth century. The apparent resolution of the old divisive issues involving race, class, and party encouraged a certain hopefulness and a sense of possibilities that had scarcely existed in the 1890s, particularly among middle-class elements in the towns and cities. These socially conscious southerners were also inspired by a broadening conception of Christianity, by a more critical view of the way society was dealing with the weak and unfortunate, and by the gifts and examples of northern philanthropists and social reformers. While continuing to accept the imperatives of the "southern" outlook, these humanitarian reformers were beginning to recoil at the spectacle of millions of uneducated white and black children, at the exploitation of women and children in the South's new industries, at the primitive character of the section's public institutions for the deprived and defective, and occasionally at the brutality and injustice evident in the treatment of black people. The reformers were neither very radical nor very original, but they exemplified an important dimension of progressivism in the South. An early manifestation of their concern was the abuse of child labor.

THE CAMPAIGN FOR CHILD LABOR LEGISLATION

Writing in the October 1901 issue of *World's Work,* an Englishwoman gave her impressions of a visit to a typical Alabama textile mill:

> Walking up the long, orderly building, deafened by the racket, yet fascinated by ingenious machinery, you become suddenly aware of a little gray shadow flitting restlessly up and down the aisles—a small girl, and with bare feet and pale face. She has a worn and anxious aspect, as if a weight of care and responsibility rested already on her baby shoulders. She either does not look at you at all or she turns her eyes but for a moment, unchildlike in their lack of interest, looking back immediately to the spinning frame. A thread breaks first at one end of the long frame, then at the other. The tiny fingers repair the damage at the first place and she walks

listlessly to the other. Something goes wrong above, and the child pushes forward a box to stand on [so] that she may reach it. With a great shock it dawns on you that this child is working.[1]

By the time this article was published, a number of sporadic and uncoordinated efforts were being made to persuade southern legislatures to deal with the problem of child labor in the South's new industries. This movement became one of the first major social justice campaigns in the South. It brought the region's social reformers together in a common cause, gave them valuable experience in organizing for reform purposes, and became an important objective in the larger search for social justice in the South and the whole country. The regulation of child labor in the southern states was, in a limited way, the result of organized labor's determination to protect itself through the exercise of economic and political power. But the movement's inspiration and rationale were essentially humanitarian.

It is not surprising that the exploitation of child labor should have been one of the earliest targets of southern critics. The employment of children had increased during the hard times of the 1890s, and in the early years of the twentieth century they were to be found in textile mills, tobacco factories, and fish canneries. They were an important source of labor in the region's burgeoning textile industry. An estimated 25 percent of the employees in southern cotton mills in 1900 were between the ages of ten and sixteen, and some workers were as young as seven or eight. They worked incredibly long hours for extremely low wages. The rate of illiteracy among these children was high, three or four times that of other children in the same states according to reformers. Yet the South, unlike the industrial states to the north, had enacted almost no legislation to prevent such abuses.[2]

Legislative proposals to regulate child labor in industrial enterprises in the South began to appear in the 1880s, usually under the sponsorship of organized labor and in company with measures designed to limit the number of hours of workers generally. The first child labor law enacted in the South during the industrial era was an Alabama statute of 1887. Virginia passed a law in 1890 limiting the hours of women and children in manufacturing work, while Louisiana and Tennessee adopted measures in the early nineties that prohibited the

---

[1]Irene M. Ashby, "Child-Labor in Southern Cotton Mills," *World's Work* 2 (Oct. 1901): 1290. For other contemporary descriptions of child labor in the South, see Leonora Beck Ellis, "Child Operatives in Southern Mills," *Independent* 53 (Nov. 7, 1901): 2637–47; Hayes Robbins, "The Necessity for Factory Legislation in the South," *Annals* 20 (July 1902): 181–88; Alfred E. Seddon, "The Education of Mill Children in the South," in *Child Labor and Social Progress*, supplement to *Annals* 32 (July 1908): 72–79; and Lewis W. Hine, "Child Labor in Gulf Coast Canneries: Photographic Investigation Made February, 1911," in supplement to *Annals* 38 (July 1911): 118–22.

[2]Elizabeth H. Davidson, *Child Labor Legislation in the Southern Textile States* (Chapel Hill, N.C., 1939), 11–16; Hugh C. Bailey, *Edgar Gardner Murphy: Gentle Progressive* (Coral Gables, Fla., 1968), 66–77; Robert Hamlett Bremner, *From the Depths: The Discovery of Poverty in the United States* (New York, 1956), 212–20.

Child labor in Georgia, 1913. *University of Georgia Libraries Special Collections.*

employment of children under the age of twelve. Nevertheless, after the repeal of the Alabama law in 1894, at the behest of textile entrepreneurs, none of the region's leading child labor states had any regulatory legislation. In the late nineties the American Federation of Labor attempted to strengthen itself in the South, and at that time organized workers in Georgia began to promote child labor reform. But the movement for regulation really began in Alabama, where a number of labor unions, women's organizations, and ministers were advocating a child labor law.

Samuel Gompers of the AFL then made an important contribution to the inchoate reform drive by sending a special agent in the person of Irene M. Ashby to work for the proposed legislation. Miss Ashby was a young Englishwoman who had gained some experience in the labor movement of her native country. During the winter of 1900–1901 she carried out the first thorough investigation of child labor in the South. Her report, based on visits to twenty-five Alabama textile mills, made clear the prevalence of child labor in these factories. She estimated that the plants she inspected employed 430 children under twelve years of age; they worked twelve hours a day for daily wages that ranged from fifteen to thirty cents. Miss Ashby's work, including her investigations of child labor in the state's cotton mills, became an important factor in the campaign for a new and stricter bill introduced in the legislature early in 1901. Seeking more support for the bill, which was generally understood to be a "labor" measure, she tried to enlist women's groups, civic reformers, and sympathetic ministers in the cause. Among those she contacted in the state capital was Edgar Gardner Murphy, the young rector of St. John's Parish in Montgomery. Murphy joined the campaign. Indeed, he more than any other person organized the reform movement in Alabama and became the most potent influence in the swift development of a regional campaign.[3]

Murphy was only thirty-one years of age when he first met Irene Ashby. Born in humble circumstances near Fort Smith, Arkansas, he had grown up in San Antonio, Texas, and had attended the University of the South on a scholarship. Under the influence of an Episcopalian minister in San Antonio and his professors at Sewanee, Murphy was drawn toward the ministry. After studying for a year at the General Theological Seminary in New York, he began work in 1890 at a small Episcopal mission near Fort Sam Houston, Texas. In 1893 he was given a church of his own in the border town of Laredo, where he served briefly before moving to a church in Chillicothe, Ohio. Following another move, in 1897, to Kingston, New York, Murphy became rector of the old and influential St. John's Parish. Although the young minister was fairly orthodox in his theological beliefs, had great respect for tradition, and tended toward the conservative side of Democratic politics, he was warm in personality and

[3] See Davidson, *Child Labor Legislation in the Southern Textile States*, 18–51, for the campaign in Alabama through 1903.

humanistic in approaching the work of the church. Profoundly affected by the Christian doctrine of brotherhood, Murphy was increasingly concerned about social problems and the role of the church in dealing with them.[4]

The Montgomery minister was deeply impressed by the evidence in Miss Ashby's study, and he began to work for the child labor bill then pending in the general assembly. He persuaded the local ministerial association to endorse the measure and was the chief spokesman for it at a joint legislative committee hearing held in February 1901.[5] After the bill was rejected by committees in both houses and a new proposal was introduced, Murphy was again the leading advocate of regulatory legislation. A representative of the millowners replied to Murphy's arguments with a vituperation that amazed the rector and helped convince him of the necessity of arousing public opinion before child labor reform could be achieved. There was one positive result of the Alabama contest over child labor in 1901: it led directly to the formation of the Alabama Child Labor Committee. Once again, Edgar Gardner Murphy was the decisive figure in taking action. Working with the same men who had joined him in arranging the recent Conference on Race Relations, Murphy created a committee to promote the cause of child labor reform in the state. He became secretary of the organization, which was composed, he wrote, of "representatives of the Church, the judiciary, the labor unions, and the mercantile and banking interests of the state."[6]

A report by Irene Ashby in the summer of 1901 confirmed Murphy's belief that northern owners of Alabama textile mills were primarily responsible for the failure of the reform bill of 1901. This led the minister early in the fall of 1901 to write "An Appeal to the People and Press of New England," which was signed by the executive committee of the Alabama Child Labor Committee (ACLC) and published in the Boston *Evening Transcript* and later as a pamphlet. Murphy appealed to New England for understanding and support, asserting that twice as many children under the age of twelve were working in the northern-owned mills of his state as in those operated by local capital. Murphy's "Appeal" brought a defense from representatives of New England companies with plants in Alabama and resulted in an exchange of open letters between businessmen and the Montgomery clergyman. While conceding the undesirable character of child labor, the textile men attributed the child labor bill in Alabama to a "skillful, female labor agitator," warned that it was the

---

[4] For Murphy's religious and social ideas, see Bailey, *Edgar Gardner Murphy*, 1–64, 109; Allen J. Going, "The Reverend Edgar Gardner Murphy, His Ideas and Influence," *Historical Magazine of the Protestant Episcopal Church* 25 (Dec. 1956): 391–402; and Daniel Levine, "Edgar Gardner Murphy: Conservative Reformer," *Ala. Rev.* 15 (Apr. 1962): 100–16.

[5] This account of Murphy's part in the movement for child labor reform in Alabama and the South rests heavily upon Davidson, *Child Labor Legislation in the Southern Textile States*, 26–51; Bailey, *Edgar Gardner Murphy*, 65–108; and Hugh C. Bailey, "Edgar Gardner Murphy and the Child Labor Movement," *Ala. Rev.* 18 (Jan. 1965): 47–59.

[6] Quoted in Davidson, *Child Labor Legislation in the Southern Textile States*, 33.

entering wedge of unionization, described Murphy as an "ill-advised humanitarian," and expressed the opinion that child labor legislation should be preceded by the enactment of a compulsory education law and that regulatory measures must be contingent upon action by other states. Murphy considered these replies to be distorted and disingenuous, and he sought to rebut them by contending that the reform movement in Alabama was indigenous in origin and was being directed by local forces.[7]

Edgar Gardner Murphy's first pamphlet, which was published in December 1901, attracted attention not only in Alabama but in other states as well. During the next few months he wrote nine other pamphlets to further the reform cause in Alabama. Published under the authority of the ACLC, they were widely distributed and constituted, as one scholar has written, "the first body of printed material of any considerable extent or value" in favor of child labor legislation in the South.[8] Murphy presented a powerful indictment of child labor in southern textile mills and attempted to answer every argument used in defense of the practice. He estimated that there were at least 32,000 children under the age of fourteen and more than 10,000 under twelve in the section's textile plants. He demonstrated the South's backwardness in dealing with the problem and held that the state had the right and responsibility to protect the child against unnatural labor. The young minister conceded that the South had reason to be proud of its industrial development, but he insisted that the region's main interest was "not in her factories, but in her children." He called attention to the terrible accidents that happened to child workers in the mills, described the "heartrending" scene of small children tending machines for long hours day after day, and condemned a system that resulted in "compulsory ignorance." Murphy made effective use of statistics and logic, and he knew how to render an emotional appeal.[9] "Of all the sections of this world," he reminded millowners, "the South—the land of chivalry, of tenderness, of homes—the land where, if we have learned anything, we have learned to suffer our ideals—the South is the very last place in which to laugh at sentiment, least of all at the sentiment which touches the promise and freedom of our children."[10]

Murphy's concern—and his arguments—went beyond the condition of working children. He feared the system's effects upon the whole of southern society. The employment of child labor would inhibit the technological advance of the South, lower industrial wages, keep out skilled labor, and create a "backward industrial class." In the long run, moreover, it might even disrupt the social order, the maintenance and improvement of which were among the

[7]Bailey, "Edgar Gardner Murphy and the Child Labor Movement," 51; "Child Labor in Alabama," *Outlook* 69 (Dec. 14, 1901): 957–58.

[8]Davidson, *Child Labor Legislation in the Southern Textile States*, 36.

[9]For a summary of the major points Murphy advanced in his pamphlets, see Bailey, *Edgar Gardner Murphy*, 69–83, and Davidson, *Child Labor Legislation in the Southern Textile States*, 33–40.

[10]Quoted in Bailey, *Edgar Gardner Murphy*, 78.

clergyman's most cherished commitments. As long as child labor continued, there would be a "sacrifice of the childhood of our poorer people, the repression of their best skills and their fullest intelligence and efficiency."[11] Child labor was also presented as a menace to peaceful race relations, since black advancement was held to depend upon white leadership and such leadership could not be developed if the white masses were not educated.

Although the Alabamian was bitterly attacked by textile representatives and other New South votaries, he was careful to arraign the child labor system and not to condemn the employers as a class or to attack their motives. Realizing that the millowners were widely regarded as public benefactors and regional developers, he sought to convince them that enlightened self-interest alone would justify the restriction of child labor. He also endeavored to win the active support of the more progressive businessmen. Murphy spoke out against voluntary agreements among the textile men to limit child labor, arguing that such arrangements placed honest operators at a disadvantage and pointing to the ineffectiveness of such agreements in several southern states. He warned millowners that federal controls were inevitable unless the states provided adequate regulation. While Murphy avoided the issue of organized labor, he concluded that, since the industry's profits were high, the real source of opposition was "the dread that any sort of restrictive or protective laws will further, in some way, the cause of the labor union."[12] Despite his calm approach and moderate tone, the Montgomery minister resented the claim by opponents of child labor legislation that they were representative southerners who spoke for the best interests of the region. He noted, in a letter to Oswald Garrison Villard of the New York *Evening Post* in November 1902, that the opposition was "making the most effective possible use of whatever seems to be sectionalistic criticism from the North."[13]

In one of his pamphlets, *Child Labor in the Southern Press*, Murphy tried to demonstrate the wide support of the reform movement in the section's newspapers by using excerpts from thirty-nine journals. He emphasized the point that criticism of child labor was being made by southerners and that advocates of regulation were "not confined to 'agitators' and 'reformers'" but instead expressed "the representative and conservative opinion of the South." In *Child Labor and the Public*, Murphy called for greater popular support of the reform movement: to organize local committees, put pressure on legislators, and cooperate with the Alabama Child Labor Committee by circulating its publications and supplying it with information on labor conditions. His pamphlets provided newspapers and the public with evidence and arguments to back the reform movement. He was, in the words of his biographer, "a social pioneer who

[11] Quoted in ibid.
[12] Quoted in ibid.
[13] Murphy urged Villard to criticize "the Northern men who have stock in the mills and who are quietly doing all they can to oppose us." Quoted in *ibid.*, 84. Also see Harriet L. Herring, "Cycles of Cotton Mill Criticism," *SAQ* 28 (Apr. 1929): 113–25.

perceived and attacked a major problem when few others recognized it or dared raise their voices against it."[14]

Despite the work of Irene Ashby and Edgar Gardner Murphy, prospects for the passage of a child labor act in the legislative session of 1903 were not encouraging. Opposition was strong, and some of those who sympathized with the reform campaign appeared to be uncertain allies. Thus Lillian Milner Orr, president of the Alabama Federation of Women's Clubs and member of a family with textile holdings, had supported a voluntary agreement among millowners in 1902 instead of a child labor law. Murphy was especially concerned about the danger involved in having the movement characterized as a "northern" and "labor" proposal. He and his colleagues welcomed the support of the labor unions, but they tried to restrain the American Federation of Labor from taking an active role in the campaign and to press their cause in the general assembly with local spokesmen using humanitarian arguments. When it became apparent that the bill they were backing could not be passed in 1903, the minister and two other reformers reached an understanding with representatives of the mills providing for a compromise law. But even this weakened measure was barely approved by the senate; it was saved from defeat by the support of the "most progressive" mill men, whom Murphy had worked hard to convert to the side of mild reform. Though the child labor act of 1903 fixed a minimum age of twelve for industrial labor, it was crippled by exemptions permitting the employment of children as young as ten if their mothers were widows or their fathers were dependent. Yet it was the first significant legislative accomplishment of the movement for child labor reform in the South.

In North Carolina the bureau of labor statistics, established in 1887, made a few investigations of child labor that contributed to the demand for legal control. Labor unionism, while weak in the Old North State, included the regulation of child labor among several labor measures it advocated in the 1890s. In the late nineties an awakening humanitarian interest began to separate the proposal for child labor reform from other labor planks, and the question began to receive attention from such people as Josiah W. Bailey in the State Baptist Convention's *Biblical Recorder* and Josephus Daniels in the Raleigh *News and Observer*. Although the mill representatives were very strong in North Carolina, the mounting interest in child labor reform persuaded them to make a small concession early in 1901. They adopted a voluntary agreement with a twelve-year limit, but it contained a broad exemption clause and applied only during the few months each year when schools were in session. The voluntary agreement did not satisfy reformers like Alexander J. McKelway, who edited the *Presbyterian Standard* in Charlotte. McKelway wrote a series of editorials in favor of reform, using Edgar Gardner Murphy's arguments, and helped persuade Governor Charles B. Aycock to join the movement for a state law.

[14]Bailey, *Edgar Gardner Murphy*, 108.

Samuel Gompers sent an AFL agent to promote the campaign, and the North Carolina Federation of Labor lent its support. An opportune decision by the state supreme court, which nullified the doctrine of contributory negligence in cases involving accidents to workers under the age of fourteen, encouraged some textile owners to accept regulatory legislation in 1903, when a compromise bill similar to the Alabama law was enacted.[15]

Meanwhile, child labor reform was being advocated in South Carolina by a few labor unions, the Columbia *State*, and the King's Daughters of Columbia. Regulatory bills were presented in the general assembly. In 1901 the reform leaders were able to get their proposed statute considered, even though it made no headway against the formidable opposition of the millowners and other sources of authority in the state. The legislature would not even authorize an investigation of child labor conditions. But the situation had changed somewhat by the time the next general assembly convened early in 1903. The state Democratic convention of 1902 had gone on record in favor of a law with a twelve-year age minimum, and the governor had endorsed reform. The United Textile Workers, an affiliate of the AFL, had developed some strength in South Carolina and was supporting child labor controls. The legislators then enacted a child labor law. It provided that, after 1905, twelve years would be the lower limit for employment in South Carolina factories, though orphans and children of dependent parents were not required to abide by these standards.[16]

Unlike Alabama and the two Carolinas, Georgia, the other leading southern textile state, failed to enact a child labor law in 1903. In the autumn of 1900 a house of representatives committee held hearings on a child labor bill at which strong opposition was voiced by textile spokesmen. A substitute measure recommended by the committee was overwhelmingly defeated, but the question aroused a good deal of interest in Atlanta and in the state press. The criticisms of labor unions, women's clubs, and clergymen were sufficiently disconcerting to persuade some of the millowners to enter into a voluntary agreement to maintain certain age limits in their employment policies. In the spring of 1901 a visit to Atlanta by Miss Ashby led to the formation of a committee modeled on the one recently organized in Alabama. Ashby returned to Georgia in the fall and in subsequent months divided her time between the campaign in that state and the one in Alabama. She induced the Georgia reformers to support a bill introduced in 1901 by Representative C.C. Houston, editor of a labor journal published in Atlanta. The Houston bill was unsuccessful in 1901, and another Houston measure was defeated in 1902, in part it appears because the proposal

[15] Davidson, *Child Labor Legislation in the Southern Textile States*, 102–21; Bailey, *Edgar Gardner Murphy*, 86; Joseph Flake Steelman, "The Progressive Era in North Carolina, 1884–1917" (Ph.D. diss., Univ. of North Carolina, 1955), 238, 264–65.

[16] Davidson, *Child Labor Legislation in the Southern Textile States*, 89–101. See David Lee Carlton, "Mill and Town: The Cotton Mill Workers and the Middle Class in South Carolina, 1880–1920" (Ph.D. diss., Yale Univ., 1977), for a discussion of the "mill problem" and the middle-class response to it in South Carolina.

was identified as "labor" legislation. Edgar Gardner Murphy made a stirring address on child labor at the National Conference of Charities and Correction, which met in Atlanta in May 1903. But the house rejected the reform bill by a vote of 75 to 89.[17] The regulatory movement in Georgia faced intense opposition which identified the proposed bill with organized labor and northern meddling. Though supported by a number of reform groups and such well-known leaders as Hoke Smith and Tom Watson, the movement had not yet developed organized strength.

By the end of 1903 the first phase of the movement for child labor reform in the South was over. Three textile states had enacted modest laws setting a twelve-year age minimum. Texas and Virginia had also adopted child labor laws in 1903, while Louisiana and Tennessee had earlier passed their first regulatory statutes. The legislation of 1903 encouraged southern reformers to believe that adequate regulation could be accomplished by forces from within the South and that public opinion in the region was steadily becoming more sympathetic to the campaign for legal controls. A note of exhortation ran through the arguments of the reformers. Their primary contention was humanitarian: the injurious effects of industrial labor upon underaged workers. The compelling need, declared the governor of Georgia in 1908, was to rescue the little children from the mills—the "flaxen-haired boys and girls growing up starved mentally, starved physically, starved morally and spiritually."[18] Though some critics conceded that there were employers who followed humane labor practices and accepted the desirability of public regulation, they argued that the main cause of child labor exploitation was the greed of the industrialists. The millowners' adoption of voluntary agreements, asserted the advocates of legislation, was an admission that child labor evils existed.

Reformers soon learned how difficult it would be to secure meaningful laws setting age limits, regulating hours, and providing better conditions for youthful workers. Their most immediate obstacle was the commanding position of their adversaries, the millowners. These southern industrialists were men of influence and authority, intimately involved in making the important economic and political decisions of their respective states and localities. Their energetic business activities helped them sustain a cultural image as community benefactors, regional developers, and even philanthropists. Southerners were proud of their section's industrial progress and potential, which tended to reinforce their

---

[17]"Child Labor Reform Rejected in Georgia," *Outlook* 75 (Sept. 5, 1903): 2–3; Davidson, *Child Labor Legislation in the Southern Textile States*, 69–88; Alton DuMar Jones, "Progressivism in Georgia, 1898–1918" (Ph.D. diss., Emory Univ., 1963), 43–55.

[18]Hoke Smith, "The Duty of the People in Child Protection," in *Child Labor and Social Progress*, supplement to *Annals* 32 (July 1908): 98. See also Davidson, *Child Labor Legislation in the Southern Textile States*, 56–58, 62–68. For evidence of southern church support of child labor legislation, see Kenneth K. Bailey, *Southern White Protestantism in the Twentieth Century* (New York, 1964), 40–42, and Wayne Flynt, "Dissent in Zion: Alabama Baptists and Social Issues, 1900–1914," *JSH* 35 (Nov. 1969): 535–37.

laissez-faire attitudes. They hesitated to handicap the operations of the mill-owners, who were caught up in a struggle with New England capitalists for dominance in the textile field. There was also the problem of public apathy toward reform. Much of the difficulty, an Alabama minister suggested in 1905, was "the unfamiliarity of the people with the new industrial conditions, the rural character of the population, the slow development of civic consciousness, and the fact that the conditions sought to be remedied are of such comparatively recent growth. . . ."[19]

The attitudes of the workers themselves complicated the task of the reformers. Most of them were poor and illiterate whites who had come to the mills from Piedmont and mountain farms. Their individualism and clannishness often made them suspicious of labor organizations, which they associated with strikes and lockouts. Their background predisposed them to accept the position of a disadvantaged class. Inured to long hours of labor and to low wages, they were glad to have work that employed all or a large part of the family unit and that brought a regular income. The paternalism of the millowners—their personal interest in the workers and their welfare services—strengthened the mill people in their resistance to public intervention. The textile owners exerted a pervasive influence over the lives of their employees, most of whom lived in company towns or self-contained mill villages.[20] In any case, textile workers in the South were not generally a significant element in the movement against child labor in industry; indeed, they sometimes spoke out against stricter controls in legislative petitions and public statements. They were motivated not only by economic considerations but in some instances by a belief that middle-class reformers were indifferent or hostile to their interests and actually were intent on imposing their own values upon the "mill people."[21]

Although the defenders of child labor rarely aswered critics of the system with straightforward laissez-faire arguments, relying instead upon paternalistic blandishments, they strongly resisted the reform movement and mounted an intense counterattack. As Alexander J. McKelway pointed out in 1910, "Those of us who are engaged in this reform sometimes grow sick at heart when we consider the fierce opposition that we meet with and the abuse and ridicule to which we are subjected." The reformer was called "an extremist, an agitator," and was accused of "exaggerating the conditions."[22] The textile executives were well organized in groups like the Georgia Industrial Association.

[19] Neal L. Anderson, "Child Labor Legislation in the South," *Annals* 25 (May 1905): 86. Also see Jerome Dowd, "Child Labor," *SAQ* 1 (Jan. 1902): 41–43.

[20] See, for example, Liston Pope, *Millhands & Preachers: A Study of Gastonia* (New Haven, Conn., 1965), 3–26, 195–97, and Herbert J. Lahne, *The Cotton Mill Worker* (New York, 1944), 103–24.

[21] For evidence of this attitude, see Carlton, "Mill and Town," 235–53.

[22] "Child Labor. An Address delivered at the Texas State Conference of Charities, November 28, 1910. First Presbyterian Church. Houston, Texas," typescript in Alexander J. McKelway Papers, Manuscript Division, Library of Congress.

McKelway declared, at the annual meeting of the National Child Labor Committee in 1911, that there had not been a legislative session in ten years in the southern textile states "in which the cotton mill men have not appeared as a powerful lobby . . . resisting every advance in child labor legislation, though frequently, when a compromise has been accepted, they have immediately posed as the successful advocates of child labor reform."[23]

One of the tactics employed by the millowners and their allies was an attempt to discredit the reformers. They made personal attacks upon the reform advocates and accused them of exaggerating the evils of child labor and being overly sentimental in their concern for the well-being of youthful workers. They referred to "the theoretical philanthropy of overheated faddists" and to "certain, from-the-Pullman-car window sociological tourists" of the South.[24] Richard H. Edmonds was so provoked by one of Murphy's pamphlets in 1902 that he wrote a six-column editorial for the *Manufacturers' Record* in an effort to refute the Alabamian's arguments, which he characterized as impractical, inflammatory, and "bryanesque."[25] In Edmonds's opinion, "This whole child-labor agitation originated in the purpose to cripple the textile industry of the South, that a small factor of that industry in New England might profit temporarily."[26] Opponents of regulatory laws also blamed the reform movement on organized labor, which was portrayed as a manifestation of northern intervention. As the sentiment for child labor reform spread over the nation in the early years of the twentieth century, it was reflected in and no doubt stimulated by articles in such magazines as *Gunton's, Charities, Outlook,* and the *American Federationist.* In some cases there were sensational pieces depicting children in the southern mills as virtual slaves. This literature, focusing on the South and sometimes distorting actual conditions, fanned the flames of southern sectionalism and stiffened the resistance to stronger legislation in the region.[27]

Even though some textile owners came to admit the essential validity of the charges made by the reformers, they tended to assume that their position gave them the right to make the key decisions involving the industry and the workers.

[23] A.J. McKelway, "The Cotton Mill: The Herod among Industries," in *Uniform Child Labor Laws,* supplement to *Annals* 38 (July 1911): 49–50.

[24] E.J. Watson, "Enforcement of Child Labor Laws in South Carolina," supplement to *Annals* 35 (Mar. 1910): 97; Bailey, *Edgar Gardner Murphy,* 80.

[25] Bailey, *Edgar Gardner Murphy,* 79.

[26] Quoted in Yoshimitsu Ide, "The Significance of Richard Hathaway Edmonds and His *Manufacturers' Record* in the New South" (Ph.D. diss., Univ. of Florida, 1959), 165. For the position of another stalwart opponent, see Howard Bunyan Clay, "Daniel Augustus Tompkins: An American Bourbon" (Ph.D. diss., Univ. of North Carolina, 1950), 64, 157–59, 178–80, 204–29, 238–60.

[27] Alexander J. McKelway, "Child Labor and Child Labor Legislation in the South," undated manuscript, McKelway Papers; McKelway, "The Mill or the Farm?" supplement to *Annals* 35 (Mar. 1910): 52–57; Davidson, *Child Labor Legislation in the Southern Textile States,* 54–62.

Millowners were also confident that they knew what was best for their employees and that they had their youthful workers' best interests at heart. They
attributed child labor to the poverty of the people and to the greed of parents,
who, they claimed, frequently deceived them as to the real age of their off-
spring. Even so, contended the owners, the work done by children in the mills
was "light," and it provided a healthier and more wholesome environment than
the depressed rural areas from which many of them had come. Furthermore,
millwork prevented children from being idle on the streets, taught them regular
habits, and kept them under the eyes of their parents. The millowners and their
defenders made increasing reference to the welfare and educational work being
carried on in the mill villages.[28]

Perhaps the most insistent opposition argument was the assertion that child
labor legislation would be ruinous to southern textiles and would make it
impossible for the region's mills to compete with New England. "There are
now about 300,000 spindles standing idle in Georgia for the want of laborers,"
declared the president of the Georgia Industrial Association in opposing passage of a child labor statute in his state in 1906, "and the enforcement of this bill
will stop the hum of another 300,000, if not more."[29] Another line of defense
was the contention that child labor reform would put a state's textile mills at a
disadvantage in competing with outside manufacturers. In resisting a proposed
child labor law in 1907, for instance, the Chattanooga chamber of commerce
urged the general assembly "not to pass any laws which may prove harsh or
drastic in their application to our textile industries . . . and other Tennessee
manufactories which are in sharp competition with those of other states."[30]

The owners contended that child labor was unprofitable to them, and that
they preferred not to use young workers under the age of twelve or thirteen.
Nevertheless, as support of the reform movement grew, there was a tendency
for the mill managers to conceal the number of child workers in their plants, and
it was difficult to secure reliable statistics, particularly during the interim
between federal censuses. This difficulty pointed up the larger problem of
adequate enforcement even when southern legislatures enacted laws that appeared to be reasonably adequate. As *Outlook* magazine observed in 1907, in
commenting on the child labor reform campaign in South Carolina, the state
had no department of labor, no bureau of labor statistics, no factory inspector,

[28]Thomas F. Parker, "The South Carolina Cotton Mill—A Manufacturer's View," *SAQ* 8 (Oct.
1909): 328–37; ibid. 9 (Oct. 1910): 349–57; William P. Few, "The Constructive Philanthropy of a
Southern Cotton Mill," *SAQ* 8 (Jan. 1909): 82–90; Ellison A. Smyth, "Child Labor in the South,"
Outlook 85 (Mar. 30, 1907): 769–71; Mrs. J. Borden Harriman, "The Cotton Mill as a Factor in
the Development of the South," in supplement to *Annals* 35 (Mar. 1910): 47–51; Lewis W. Parker,
"Compulsory Education, the Solution of Child Labor Problem," in *Child Labor and Social
Progress*, supplement to *Annals* 32 (July 1908): 40–56.
[29]Jeff Davis, quoted in A.J. McKelway, "Child Labor Campaign in the South," *Survey* 27 (Oct.
21, 1911): 1026.
[30]Quoted in William F. Donovan, Jr., "The Growth of the Industrial Spirit in Tennessee,
1890–1910" (Ph.D. diss., George Peabody College for Teachers, 1955), 137.

no compulsory education law, and no census of the school population or of industrial workers.[31] Small wonder that the reformers sometimes became discouraged in the long campaign to end the exploitation of children in the South's mills and factories.

After 1903 the sporadic efforts of child labor reformers in the various southern states were slowly transformed into an organized movement that assumed a regional character. The principal instrument in this transformation was the National Child Labor Committee (NCLC), which was created in the spring of 1904 through the initiative of Felix Adler of New York and other social justice leaders. Edgar Gardner Murphy played an important role in the formation of the new organization. He had emphasized the need for nationwide protest and united action in dealing with the problem of child labor in an industrial society. He was consulted by Adler in the early stages of the effort to create the national committee, delivered a major address on child labor just before the new organization came into being, and was one of the twenty-five members of the NCLC when it was established in April 1904. The committee hoped to assist local bodies in achieving child labor reform, to undertake investigations of its own, and to act as a clearinghouse for information and activities involving the child labor problem. Murphy served briefly as secretary of the National Child Labor Committee and was instrumental in shaping its early policies. He was responsible for the selection of Alexander J. McKelway as director of the NCLC's work in the South.[32]

If Murphy was the most significant figure in launching the movement to restrict child labor in the South, McKelway became the most influential leader in the expansion and promotion of the reform cause from 1904 until his death in 1918. In 1911, McKelway recalled how he had first become involved in child labor reform:

> I was an editor living in North Carolina and had thought very little about the child labor cause. I had seen the children working in the factories, and had taken it as a matter of course. We had read about the evils of child labor in England, had heard of them in New England and New Jersey; but hardly thought that these evils existed at all in the South. It was the agitation in Alabama, fostered by Mr. Murphy, that interested me first in the cause and that put before my mind the idea that something practical could be done for the elimination of child labor from industry.[33]

Though a Pennsylvanian by birth, McKelway was reared in Virginia, where he was influenced by the Christian precepts of his maternal grandfather. He was graduated from Hampden-Sydney College in 1886 and, having decided to enter the Presbyterian ministry, from the Union Theological Seminary in Richmond in 1891. After a brief period of service in home mission work in Johnston

---

[31]"Child Labor in the South," *Outlook* 85 (Apr. 27, 1907): 917.

[32]Bailey, *Edgar Gardner Murphy*, 86–90.

[33]"The Proceedings of the Seventh Annual Conference on Child Labor Under the Auspices of the National Child Labor Committee," in supplement to *Annals* 38 (July 1911): 223.

County, North Carolina, he began a five-year ministry in Fayetteville, resigning in 1897 to become superintendent of home missions for the North Carolina Synod. The following year the young minister was appointed editor of the *Presbyterian Standard*. He soon identified himself with a number of social reforms, including prohibition, but child labor became his primary interest after 1903. Essentially a journalist, McKelway was a vigorous and effective writer, an astute publicist, and a resourceful lobbyist. An ardent southerner, he appealed to "the old southern patriotism," cultivated the friendship of progressive politicians such as Josephus Daniels and Hoke Smith, and sharply attacked those who opposed the reforms he championed. He endeavored to make clear, in Murphy's words, "that the Southern man has a right to make a national alliance and to associate himself with great national forces."[34] On occasion he resorted to ridicule, and not infrequently his forceful attacks pricked the sensibilities of his opponents. "He was not particularly sensitive, not easily galled," a friendly journal noted at the time of his death, "and he did not make sufficient allowance for people of thin skin and fine hair."[35]

Upon assuming his new position as the National Child Labor Committee's chief agent in the South, McKelway made an energetic effort to prepare himself for the work ahead. He read extensively in the history of child labor in Great Britain and made a tour of New England textile mills to compare their conditions with those in the South. Locating his headquarters in Charlotte, he turned his attention first to the child labor problem in the major textile states, but in time he broadened the scope of his work to include other southern states and other industries, in addition to lobbying in Congress for federal legislation. He and his assistants secured statistics showing the widespread use of child labor in southern cotton mills. In 1905, for example, he estimated that at least sixty thousand children under fourteen years of age were employed in the region's textile industry.[36] A strong religious theme permeated McKelway's arguments in favor of regulatory legislation. He spoke of the "sacredness of childhood" and warned that continued abuse of little children would destroy the family and ultimately the state. The average cotton mill community, he observed, "is the poorest place in the world for training the citizens of a democracy."[37]

[34] Bailey, *Edgar Gardner Murphy*, 93. McKelway summed up his philosophy by saying: "Trust the people. Their hearts are always right. When their heads are wrong, education is necessary before any enduring legislation can be achieved" (McKelway, "Legislative Hints for Social Reformers," undated manuscript, McKelway Papers).

[35] *Presbyterian Standard*, May 1, 1918, in McKelway Papers. For biographical information on McKelway, see Herbert J. Doherty, Jr., "Alexander J. McKelway: Preacher to Progressive," *JSH* 24 (May 1958): 177–90; Betty J. Brandon, "A Wilsonian Progressive—Alexander Jeffrey McKelway," *Journal of Presbyterian History* 48 (Spring 1970): 2–17; and Robert Smotherman, "The Political Development of a Southern Social Reformer: Alexander McKelway's 1905 Campaign for Child Labor Reform in North Carolina" (Honors essay, Duke Univ., 1964).

[36] McKelway, "Child Labor in Southern Industry," *Annals* 25 (May 1905): 21.

[37] McKelway, "Child Labor and Its Attendant Evils," *Sewanee Review* 16 (Apr. 1908): 214–27; quotation on p. 222.

McKelway also emphasized the point that child labor promoted illiteracy. The young minister asserted that a clearly recognizable "factory type" had already made its appearance in the South, and he expressed fear that the use of child labor would lead to "race degeneracy," to the deterioration of "the purest stock" in America. This last argument was clearly an appeal to racism, for McKelway contended that black children, who were infrequently employed in textile mills, were able to lead healthy lives and to attend school while the mental and physical growth of many white children was being stunted by factory work.[38]

McKelway made use of sectional appeals as well. Early in his campaign he and the NCLC were accused of being an instrument of New England textile owners who were seeking to destroy their southern competition. McKelway, like Murphy, was quick to reply that New England owners of southern mills were, in fact, among the most active opponents of child labor laws in the southern states. McKelway argued that child labor was both expensive and wasteful, that it hurt the South by bringing it lower prices for textile goods comparable to those produced in northern mills. Despite the setbacks and slow progress during the early years of his work, McKelway remained optimistic. He was convinced that southern attitudes were changing and that public opinion was the key to the ultimate success of the child labor movement. The awakening of the South, he wrote in 1907, was first an industrial awakening. Next came "the educational awakening." And, then, "with the increase of wealth, . . . with the school teachers going into all corners that the people may be taught, there has begun what I conceive to be the most significant movement of this generation, . . . the advancement of those social reforms which are infinitely more important than the economic questions. . . ."[39]

North Carolina was the first southern state in which the newly organized NCLC sought to secure legislative action. McKelway drafted a measure, based on the model child labor law recommended by the National Consumers' League, that would strengthen the North Carolina law of 1903 by raising the age limit of girls employed in industrial work from twelve to fourteen, elevate the minimum age of boys and girls engaged in night work to sixteen, and reduce the hours per week of children under sixteen to sixty. But prospects for passage of a new law were not bright, and the bill was rejected by a legislative committee in 1905. A campaign in South Carolina was also unsuccessful. In that state an earlier movement for a ten-hour-day law, which was finally approved in modified form during the session of 1907, overshadowed the child labor bill and

[38]See, for example, McKelway's articles on "Child Labor in the Southern Cotton Mills," *Annals* 27 (Mar. 1906): 1–11, and "The Child Labor Problem—A Study in Degeneracy," ibid., 54–68.

[39]McKelway, "The Awakening of the South against Child Labor," *Annals* 29 (Jan. 1907): 12–13. Also see McKelway, "Child Labor in the Southern Cotton Mills," 9–10.

dissipated the energies of the reformers.[40] The situation in most other southern states was equally discouraging.

The National Child Labor Committee enjoyed its first legislative success in Georgia. That state's continued failure to act constituted a serious obstacle to the southern campaign, and in November 1905 McKelway moved his office from Charlotte to Atlanta. Working with his usual vigor, he reorganized the state committee, assumed the duties of acting secretary of the committee, tried to get the support of organized women, and attempted to work with organized labor, which had maintained an interest in the question after the defeat of 1903. The Georgia Industrial Association, representing the textile companies, contended that the voluntary agreement of 1900 was still being observed. McKelway and his allies produced evidence designed to prove that the agreement was a subterfuge and was not being enforced. The issue was heated and aroused considerable public interest. A measure introduced by Representative Madison Bell, the leading labor exponent of child labor reform in the house, passed the lower chamber in 1905 but failed in the senate. Yet sentiment had so changed by the time the general assembly convened in the summer of 1906 that the industrialists found it expedient to acquiesce in the passage of Bell's proposal, which established a twelve-year age limit for industrial labor. Attempts to improve the statute failed in 1908. And during the following year bills to amend the law and to provide for factory inspection were defeated, in large part through the efforts of Jack J. Spalding, president of the Georgia Industrial Association.[41]

In late 1906 another significant change occurred in the slowly developing child labor movement in the South. This came with the NCLC's decision in December to endorse Senator Albert J. Beveridge's congressional bill to outlaw child labor. A critical factor in the committee's decision was the failure of its efforts to promote state action in the South. In spite of McKelway's energetic campaigns, almost no legislative progress seemed to have been made. Few southerners were affiliated with the NCLC, and the chances of going beyond the ineffective statutes already enacted appeared slight. Edgar Gardner Murphy, whose political conservatism led him to oppose the idea of federal legislation from the first, immediately resigned from the national committee. But McKelway was a champion of federal action, and he was soon dispatched to lobby for the Beveridge bill. Meantime, the NCLC continued to support the

[40] Davidson, *Child Labor Legislation in the Southern Textile States*, 149–55, 178–81; Smotherman, "The Political Development of a Southern Social Reformer," 24; Bailey, *Edgar Gardner Murphy*, 93.

[41] Davidson, *Child Labor Legislation in the Southern Textile States*, 194–210; Alton DuMar Jones, "The Child Labor Reform Movement in Georgia," *Ga. Hist. Quar.* 49 (Dec. 1965): 396–406; "The Georgia Industrial Association in a Dilemma," *Charities* 14 (June 10, 1905): 827–28; "A Child Labor Law in Georgia," *Outlook* 83 (Aug. 18, 1906): 872–73; "The Proceedings of the Fourth Annual Meeting of the National Child Labor Committee," in supplement to *Annals* 32 (July 1908): 172–73.

movement for effective state laws, and with the failure of the Beveridge measure in 1907, it turned with renewed energy to the state and local campaigns. In the South the committee gradually expanded its work, strengthened its staff, and commissioned special investigations. McKelway still carried the burden of the NCLC's work in the South, although he spent a great deal of time in Washington after 1909 supporting the committee's program in Congress.[42]

One southern state that adopted stronger legislation was Alabama. By 1907 the state was filled with talk of political reform, particularly involving railroads, and the question of more adequate child labor controls had once again emerged as an important issue. McKelway had reorganized the moribund state committee in 1906, organized labor was supporting the demand for a better law, along with other labor measures, and the Alabama Federation of Women's Clubs had endorsed the need for state action. The new governor, Braxton Bragg Comer, himself a millowner and earlier a strong opponent of child labor legislation, had been embarrassed as a reformer by the issue during the gubernatorial campaign of 1906 and had pledged in the state Democratic convention's platform to enact a stiffer child labor law. The contributions of Edgar Gardner Murphy and the Alabama Child Labor Committee were even more important. Just before the legislature convened in the summer of 1907, Murphy sent each member an article entitled "A Plea for Immediate Action." In it he pointed out the severe limitations of the act of 1903, made a fervent appeal for legislative action, and challenged the manufacturers to accept an effective law for the sake of the state's children. While the reformers were forced to compromise, they succeeded in securing a law in 1907 that raised the minimum working age to twelve (with no exceptions), reduced the maximum number of hours for children under fourteen to sixty per week, prohibited night work for those under sixteen, and required children between twelve and sixteen to attend school at least eight weeks a year. The general assembly also provided for factory inspection.[43]

The North Carolina Child Labor Committee worked for several years after 1906 to strengthen the law in that state. The committee was assisted by the NCLC, which sponsored a series of investigations in the two Carolinas, and in time the reformers were able to exert greater pressure in behalf of new legislation. But North Carolina legislators were predisposed to side with the industrialists, who organized a Manufacturers' Association to resist the enactment of regulatory laws. In 1907, textile leaders themselves proposed a measure that would establish a thirteen-year age limit but exempt twelve-year-olds in an "apprenticeship capacity." The legislature passed this bill handily. Efforts to

[42]Davidson, *Child Labor Legislation in the Southern Textile States*, 129–41; Bailey, *Edgar Gardner Murphy*, 94–102; John Braeman, *Albert J. Beveridge: American Nationalist* (Chicago, 1971), 112–21.

[43]Davidson, *Child Labor Legislation in the Southern Textile States*, 215–23; Bailey, *Edgar Gardner Murphy*, 102–107.

raise the standards failed in 1909 and 1911. One recurring difficulty was the inability of the state committee to maintain a united position in pushing its program, since some members were inclined to follow the lead of the millowners. The NCLC employed Wiley H. Swift as a special agent in North Carolina in 1912, and his investigations and publicity campaign helped prepare the ground for another legislative assault in 1913. By that time there was more organized support for legislative action, including that provided by two or three daily newspapers, women's organizations, the Farmers' Union, a few labor unions, and the State Conference of Social Welfare.[44]

South Carolina, Alexander J. McKelway observed in 1908, had the worst child labor law in the South. Attempts to strengthen the statute in 1907 and 1908 were unsuccessful, despite numerous indications of its violation. In 1909 the general assembly provided for the employment of two factory inspectors, largely because of the efforts of Representative John Porter Hollis, who later served as secretary of the reorganized South Carolina Child Labor Committee. In spite of stubborn resistance by the state's textile interests and the indifference of Governor Blease, the committee was able to secure two new laws in 1911. One of these measures modified the exemption provisions of the existing statute and outlawed night work for children under sixteen. The second act forbade the employment of youths under fourteen in the messenger service of telephone and telegraph companies or in the delivery of goods, and restricted the employment of children in theaters and places of amusement. Yet, in winning these modest concessions from the manufacturers, the child labor reformers abandoned their own demands for a fourteen-year minimum.[45]

All of the other southern states adopted child labor restrictions in one form or another. Among the states that enacted comprehensive legislation was Oklahoma, where a uniquely favorable situation was created by the new state's strong Populist heritage, a powerful coalition of organized labor and humanitarians, and the dynamic leadership of a young social worker named Kate Barnard. By the time Oklahoma entered the Union in 1907, the dominant Democratic party was committed to a far-reaching social justice program, including the prohibition of child labor. The constitution adopted in 1907 forbade the employment of children under fifteen in dangerous, unhealthy, or immoral occupations, set a minimum age of sixteen for work in mines, and created three elective positions to enforce these standards and other labor laws. Miss Bar-

[44]Davidson, *Child Labor Legislation in the Southern Textile States*, 155–67; "Reports from State and Local Child Labor Committees," in supplement to *Annals* 32 (July 1908): 139–40; "Reports from State and Local Child Labor Committees," in supplement to *Annals* 38 (July 1911): 176–77.

[45]Davidson, *Child Labor Legislation in the Southern Textile States*, 181–90; John Porter Hollis, "Child Labor in the Carolinas," in supplement to *Annals* 38 (July 1911): 114–15; McKelway, "Child Labor Campaign in the South," 1024; Ronald Dantan Burnside, "The Governorship of Coleman Livingston Blease of South Carolina, 1911–1915" (Ph.D. diss., Indiana Univ., 1963), 255–60.

nard, who was elected the state's first commissioner of charities and corrections, was a fervent advocate of child labor reform. She sought to advance the cause in numerous speeches, wrote a newspaper series to promote it, and in the autumn of 1906 organized the Oklahoma City Child Labor League, which soon became affiliated with the NCLC. She was responsible for visits to Oklahoma by several well-known experts in social welfare work to assist in the preparation of reform legislation. These experts included Alexander J. McKelway, who assisted in drafting a child labor bill. According to McKelway, Kate Barnard "painted figures of the wrongs of childhood, of the sufferings of minors without the protection of law, of the needs of the orphans, of the iniquity of sending juvenile criminals to the jails and stockades, thrilling her vast audiences with her earnest eloquence. . . ." The child labor bill advocated by the Oklahoma reformers was passed in 1908, only to be vetoed by Governor Charles N. Haskell. Miss Barnard and her allies then conducted an effective campaign during the second half of 1908 that resulted in the enactment of a broad-gauged law in 1909. The statute prohibited children under fourteen from working in factories, bowling alleys, theaters, and poolrooms; set an eight-hour day and a forty-eight-hour week for workers under sixteen; contained several literacy requirements; and provided for a system of enforcement.[46]

By 1913, Tennessee, which had only a few textile mills but one of the strongest labor movements in the South, had established a fourteen-year age limit, forbidden children under sixteen to work in dangerous occupations and night messenger service, and instituted a system of factory and mine inspection. Virginia had set a minimum age of fourteen (with an exemption clause for children between the ages of twelve and fourteen) and enacted a ten-hour-day law for women and children. Louisiana had provided an age limit of twelve for boys and fourteen for girls, outlawed night work for boys under sixteen and girls under eighteen, and instituted a system of factory inspection. A Texas statute of 1911 set a fifteen-year age limit for factory and mill workers and a seventeen-year minimum for employment in mines and quarries. Kentucky legislated an age limit of fourteen, a system of factory inspection, and the issuance of certificates for all children between fourteen and sixteen employed in factories or mills. Mississippi required a fourteen-year minimum for girls, a twelve-year limit for boys, and an eight-hour day for boys under sixteen and girls under eighteen. Reformers in Arkansas, making use of that state's new initiative and referendum system, secured the ratification of a law in 1914 establishing a fourteen-year age limit, forbidding children under sixteen from

---

[46]Alexander J. McKelway, "'Kate': The 'Good Angel' of Oklahoma," *American Magazine* 66 (Oct. 1908): 587–93; quotation on p. 591; McKelway, "The Cotton Mill: The Herod among Industries," 50; "The Proceedings of the Fourth Annual Meeting of the National Child Labor Committee," in supplement to *Annals* 32 (July 1908): 174; Keith L. Bryant, Jr., "Kate Barnard, Organized Labor, and Social Justice in Oklahoma During the Progressive Era," *JSH* 35 (May 1969): 145–64.

engaging in dangerous or injurious occupations, and restricting the number of working hours for children under sixteen to eight per day and forty-eight per week.[47]

Florida was one of the region's most resistant states in the struggle for more effective child labor controls. Although there were no textile mills in the state, there were tobacco plants and seafood canneries, some of which employed children. According to McKelway, in 1909 there were more than a thousand children under fourteen working in the cigar factories of Tampa alone. These interests strongly opposed a stringent child labor law in Florida, and efforts to raise the minimum age (fixed at twelve by an act of 1907) were defeated in the legislatures of 1909 and 1911. The NCLC, hoping to encourage the movement in Florida, held its annual meeting in Jacksonville in March 1913. One result was the organization of the Florida Child Labor Committee and the drafting of a reform bill based on the Uniform Child Labor Law. The proposed law was severely criticized by the conservative Jacksonville *Times-Union* and resisted by the Western Union Telegraph Company and other business firms. McKelway, who was taking part in the campaign, helped arrange a compromise that passed both houses under pressure from the FCLC, women's clubs, and labor unions. The act of 1913 established a fourteen-year age minimum (with some exemptions) and a nine-hour day for children under sixteen; it also provided for the issuance of school certificates and a system of factory inspection.[48]

In the meantime, the child labor reform movement in the South was achieving a degree of interstate cooperation and regional unity. The idea of the South as a unique and clearly defined section was seldom absent from the statements of opponents or advocates of restrictive legislation. Another impetus to the development of a regionwide child labor movement was a series of southern conferences. The first of these conventions was held in Nashville in October 1907, pursuant to a resolution adopted by the Tennessee legislature. Although only a few states were represented, the gathering urged the southern states to

[47] Davidson, *Child Labor Legislation in the Southern Textile States*, 238–45; A.J. McKelway, "Fighting Child Labor in Three States," *Survey* 28 (Apr. 20, 1912): 121–22; McKelway, "Child Labor Campaign in the South," 1024–25; McKelway, "Arkansas Child Labor Law Secured by the Initiative," *Survey* 33 (Oct. 10, 1914): 44; "Reports from State and Local Child Labor Committees," in supplement to *Annals* 32 (July 1908): 127–30, 148; "Reports from State and Local Child Labor Committees," in supplement to *Annals* 35 (Mar. 1910): 164–68; "The New Child Labor Law for Louisiana," *Outlook* 90 (Nov. 7, 1908): 507–508; James Aubrey Tinsley, "The Progressive Movement in Texas" (Ph.D. diss., Univ. of Wisconsin, 1953), 139–41; "The Proceedings of the Fourth Annual Meeting of the National Child Labor Committee," in supplement to *Annals* 32 (July 1908): 167; Nannie Pitts McLemore, "The Progressive Era," in Richard Aubrey McLemore, ed., *A History of Mississippi* (Hattiesburg, Miss., 1973), vol. 2, pp. 45–46, 58; Nancy Pride, "Incidents Preceding the Louisiana Child Labor Law of 1912," *La. Hist.* 19 (Fall 1978): 437–45.

[48] McKelway, "Child Labor in the South," manuscript dated June 13, 1909, in McKelway Papers; McKelway, "The Leadership of the Child," in supplement to *Annals* 32 (July 1908): 26; McKelway, "The Florida Child Labor Campaign," *Survey* 30 (July 12, 1913): 497–98; Emily Howard Atkins, "The 1913 Campaign for Child Labor in Florida," *Fla. Hist. Quar.* 35 (Jan. 1957): 233–40; Davidson, *Child Labor Legislation in the Southern Textile States*, 246–48, 250.

establish a fourteen-year minimum for industrial labor, to provide other safeguards for working children and women, and to adopt compulsory school attendance laws. Another conference was held in New Orleans in April 1909, at the instigation of Jean M. Gordon, the Louisiana factory inspector. Some two hundred delegates, including McKelway, attended the meeting and passed a resolution endorsing the basic standards of the NCLC. A permanent organization was formed at this meeting, with Governor Jared Y. Sanders of Louisiana as president. A year later the Southern Conference on Women and Child Labor, as it was called, met in Memphis, while similar conferences were held in Atlanta in 1911 and Chattanooga in 1912. Despite the fact that the leading industrial states were seldom represented at these regional gatherings and the failure of the conferences to produce concrete results, their very existence reflected the mounting interest in and support for stronger state action.[49] The meetings also brought the outstanding child labor reformers from the South together, enabling them to share experiences and compare problems. In addition, the conferences encouraged the slowly evolving idea of a broad social justice organization in the South.

By 1910 all of the southern states had established a minimum age for employment, at least in manufacturing. Yet only four southern states[50] had a minimum age as high as fourteen for boys and girls, several state laws were vitiated by broad exemption clauses, and only three of them required documentary proof of a working child's age. Inspection and enforcement were notoriously indequate, even when written into the statutes. During the next few years southern legislatures gradually raised their minimum age standards and extended the coverage of their child labor laws. The National Child Labor Committee also broadened the field of its work in the South, moving beyond its early preoccupation with the textile industry to include night messenger service and street trades by 1911, and oyster and shrimp canneries on the Gulf Coast by 1913. The national committee increasingly concerned itself with the enforcement and administration of child labor laws and with the need for practical education opportunities. In 1914 the committee turned once again to federal legislation as the best solution to the child labor problem.[51] The ensuing struggle represented a new phase in the evolution of the movement against child labor in the South.

---

[49] Davidson, *Child Labor Legislation in the Southern Textile States*, 145–47; "The Proceedings of the Fourth Annual Meeting of National Child Labor Committee," in supplement to *Annals* 32 (July 1908): 164–67; "The Proceedings of the Seventh Annual Conference on Child Labor Under the Auspices of the National Child Labor Committee," in supplement to *Annals* 38 (July 1911): 218; Bryant, "Kate Barnard, Organized Labor, and Social Justice in Oklahoma," 162; Joe Michael Shahan, "Reform and Politics in Tennessee: 1906–1914" (Ph.D. diss., Vanderbilt Univ., 1981), 130–32.

[50] Kentucky, Louisiana, Oklahoma, and Tennessee.

[51] Davidson, *Child Labor Legislation in the Southern Textile States*, 249–52; John R. Commons and others, *History of Labour in the United States*, 4 vols. (New York, 1918–35), vol. 3, pp. 414–15, 421, 429, 438–39.

FEMINISM AND REFORM

Efforts to ameliorate human suffering and to promote social justice in the early twentieth-century South were heavily dependent upon the activities of southern women. Their great goal eventually became their own cultural and political emancipation, but along the way they made a vital contribution to the cause of social reform generally. The reform movements that enlisted their support included virtually all of the important humanitarian endeavors of the period. Writing in 1919, for example, a New Orleans feminist declared that women in Louisiana had been working for "mother's pensions, better babies, school hygiene, prison reform, care of the feeble-minded, prevention of blindness, laws to give women equal rights and opportunities, more money for schools, more playgrounds, cleaner movies, homes for working-girls, better markets, lower living costs, a single standard of morality, and, in short, a higher type of civilization."[52]

It took courage for southern women to become social reformers. They possessed no political voice, had few legal rights, and in order to broaden their social role were forced to challenge the tradition of chivalry, which paradoxically had elevated woman as an ideal while restricting her functions to the home. As this feminist reformism took shape, the amused tolerance and ridicule of the guardians of southern culture frequently turned to contempt and harsh opposition. Rebecca Latimer Felton, a crusader for women's rights and other social reforms in Georgia, recalled in 1910 that "the world of society" looked askance in the late nineteenth century "at a woman who should dare to go out on the public rostrum and plead for the safety of her people. . . . How many taunts and slanders, and covert insinuations that were thrust at me, eternity alone can discover. How many sneers were leveled at me, I perhaps will never know, but, as I look back at the struggles of that early period, I almost tremble to remember that I was the target of such entrenched power and influence. . . ."[53]

Yet the beginnings of the movement for women's rights in the South were so modest and respectable as to cause scarcely a ripple. The movement began in the women's organizations of the Protestant churches. These groups introduced thousands of southern women to "home and foreign mission work" while providing their members with a degree of independence and experience. The Women's Christian Temperance Union and the Young Women's Christian Association also familiarized many women in the South with the concept of social reform. No group, one historian has written of the WCTU, "did more to subvert the traditional role of women, or to implant in its southern members a

[52] Press release, Oct. 10, 1919, Ethel Hutson Papers, Tulane University Library. Miss Hutson was publicity chair of the Woman Suffrage Party of Louisiana at this time.
[53] Rebecca L. Felton to Mrs. Angsley, Oct. 3, 1910, Mrs. William H. Felton Collection, University of Georgia Library.

sort of unself-conscious radicalism which would have turned the conservative southern male speechless if he had taken the trouble to listen to what the ladies were saying."[54] The most comprehensive program of social uplift sponsored by church women was that of the Methodist Episcopal Church, South.

Southern Methodists established a Woman's General Executive Association as early as 1878, and in later years the Woman's Board of Foreign Missions and the Woman's Board of Home Missions were set up to direct missionary activities at the general conference level. The consecrated service and earnest appeals of the church's foreign missionaries and their wives had a profound influence upon the thinking of many Methodist women, and the increasing support of missions abroad undoubtedly encouraged the home mission movement. By the end of the century the Home Mission Society had pointed to the social needs in Appalachia, among blacks throughout the South, and among Orientals on the West Coast. Methodist women had inaugurated a city mission movement which took firm hold during the progressive period. Early in the new century they moved more vigorously to improve the conditions of southern Negroes. In 1910 the foreign and home mission boards were combined to form the Woman's Missionary Council, which became an organic part of the church's Board of Missions. A bureau of social service was soon established, and conferences, schools, institutes, and seminars for leadership training and inspiration were developed. Methodist women exhibited an expanding interest in industrial problems, and at the annual meetings of their organizations they were able to hear such distinguished speakers as Jane Addams, Shailer Matthews, and Graham Taylor, as well as outstanding southern leaders.[55] Their widening social concerns are illustrated in the program adopted by the Woman's Missionary Council in 1916. It urged (1) the adoption of a uniform law on vital statistics; (2) the enactment of uniform child labor laws; (3) the abolition of illiteracy, enactment of compulsory education laws, and lengthening of school terms; (4) the establishment of juvenile courts and reformatories; (5) the constructive censorship of moving-picture films; (6) the passage and enforcement of statutes regulating the sale of habit-forming drugs, liquor, and cigarettes; (7) the establishment of state institutions for the "feeble-minded"; (8) the abolition of legalized and segregated vice and legislation to require the reporting of "social diseases" to boards of health; (9) the abolition of the convict-lease system and adoption of modern principles of prison reform; (10) improved race

[54] Anne Firor Scott, "The 'New Woman' in the New South," *SAQ* 61 (Autumn 1962): 477. Also see Louisa B. Poppenheim, "Woman's Work in the South," in *The South in the Building of the Nation*, vol. 10, p. 635, and Sara H. Hoge and others, "Organization and Accomplishments of the Women's Christian Temperance Union in Illinois, Massachusetts, New York, North Dakota, Ohio, and Virginia," *Annals* 32 (Nov. 1908): 527–30.

[55] Noreen Dunn Tatum, *A Crown of Service: A Story of Woman's Work in the Methodist Episcopal Church, South, from 1878–1940* (Nashville, Tenn., 1960), 21–30, 60–61, 70–72, 96, 223–29, 241–93, 334; Bertha Payne Newell, "Social Work of Women's Organizations in the Churches. I. Methodist Episcopal Church South," *Jour. Soc. Forces* 1 (Mar. 1923): 310–12.

relations; and (11) close cooperation with the Southern Sociological Congress and similar organizations.[56]

Women's organizations in other southern denominations were also making the transition from a preoccupation with foreign missions to greater involvement in efforts to relieve social problems at home. None of these groups was as active in reform causes as Methodist women, but almost all of them provided support for prohibition and one or another of the various reform campaigns. Meanwhile, other church organizations, including the WCTU and the YWCA, were fostering an awareness of social ills and a spirit of social justice among women in the South, particularly among members of the middle class. Some of these groups encouraged the organization and social reform activities of black women in the region. The WCTU established a department for work among Negroes. Black clubwomen, educators, and social workers began to look to the YWCA as a means of coordinating and expanding their social reform efforts.[57] As southern women began to organize and gain experience in their church societies, they slowly lost their self-consciousness and fear of involving themselves in matters that were customarily outside their domain. They became more sensitive to their treatment at the hands of men, who sometimes wrote the constitutions for the women's organizations, nominated their officers, and made their policy decisions. The growing confidence and assertiveness of southern women were evident in their long battle for equal rights in the council of the Methodist church, which finally granted laity rights to women in 1918.[58]

Southern women found another avenue to social reform in the club movement that grew rapidly in the 1890s and early 1900s. Literary and music societies, civic improvement leagues, and patriotic and professional organizations for women began to spring up throughout the South in the last years of the nineteenth century. By 1908 about two hundred civic leagues were reported in Texas alone.[59] Not all of these organizations were interested in civic matters, and the more reform-minded sometimes complained about the "fads and frivolities" of club life and the little "circles & coteries" of those preoccupied with literature, music, and art. Others, however, spoke with condescension and occasionally with alarm of "chafing dish and church and missionary and serving and civic improvement and the Lord only knows what."[60] Yet the fact is that the

[56]Tatum, *A Crown of Service*, 350–51.

[57]Janet Wilson James, "Introduction," in Edward T. James, et al., *Notable American Women, 1607–1950: A Biographical Dictionary*, 3 vols. (Cambridge, Mass., 1971), vol. 1, p. xlvii; Henry Leon McBeth, "The Role of Women in Southern Baptist History," *Baptist History and Heritage* 12 (Jan. 1977): 3–25; Norman H. Letsinger, "The Status of Women in Southern Baptist Convention in Historical Perspective," ibid., 37–44, 51; Jacquelyn Dowd Hall, *Revolt Against Chivalry: Jessie Daniel Ames and the Women's Campaign Against Lynching* (New York, 1979), 82–83.

[58]Tatum, *A Crown of Service*, 37–40.

[59]Poppenheim, "Woman's Work in the South," 633; Olivia Rainer, "The Early History of Music Clubs of Troy, Alabama," *Ala. Hist. Quar.* 24 (Spring 1962): 68–96.

[60]See, for example, George Handy to Laura Clay, Nov. 4, 1903, Laura Clay Papers, University of Kentucky Library.

club movement did lift the social horizons of many women and contribute to their emancipation. Like the WCTU and the missionary societies, the clubs enabled the ladies to engage in respectable reforms, to educate themselves and the public, and in some cases to disguise their attacks on chivalry.

The newer types of clubs, while not abandoning the literary and cultural activities that had dominated women's organizations in previous years, began to emphasize the improvement of women themselves and the value of community service. For example, the objectives of the Ladies Improvement Association of Green Cove Springs, Florida, which was incorporated in 1899, were "to promote neatness and order in the city and do what ever may tend to improve and beautify the town as a place of residence, and keep it in a healthy condition."[61] Early in the twentieth century the newly formed Woman's Club of Raleigh, North Carolina, was interested in the Associated Charities, the Board of State Charities, a proposed reform school, and plans for a women's workroom. Southern clubwomen, one of their leaders wrote in 1909, were caring for "the afflicted and distressed," "beautifying the waste places," and teaching their children the "high ideals of American patriotism."[62] Among the subjects discussed by members of the Era Club in New Orleans in 1909–10 were "municipal embellishment," "public improvements," the "white slave traffic," a pure milk supply, reclamation of Louisiana lands, peace and arbitration, and equal rights for women in the Southern Methodist church.[63]

Numerous projects were undertaken by the clubwomen. Women's exchanges were organized in some southern cities, designed to provide women with an opportunity to help themselves. Several feminist journals, such as *The Keystone* of Charleston, were launched to promote the work of southern women. A visiting nurses program was initiated in many communities, frequently with the support of local circles of the King's Daughters. Even the United Daughters of the Confederacy, whose purpose was primarily commemorative, became involved in benevolent, educational, and social work.[64] The clubs were often active in behalf of public education. North Carolina provides a good example. In 1902 a small group of women students at the Normal and Industrial College of Greensboro, disturbed by the condition of the state's rural schools, took the lead in establishing the Woman's Association for the Improvement of Public School Houses in North Carolina. Within a few years the membership had grown to several thousand, and county associations

[61]Quoted in Kenneth R. Johnson, "The Woman Suffrage Movement in Florida" (Ph.D. diss., Florida State Univ., 1966), 148.

[62]Charles F. Weller, "Charity and Social Development in Two Southern Cities," *Charities* 13 (Feb. 11, 1905): 467; Poppenheim, "Woman's Work in the South," 637.

[63]Manuscript (typewritten) address by Judith Hyams Douglas, May 28, 1910, Judith Hyams Douglas Papers, Louisiana State University Archives.

[64]Poppenheim, "Woman's Work in the South," 627, 634, 636; Nellie Roberson, "The Organized Work of Women in One State," *Jour. Soc. Forces* 1 (Jan. 1923): 174–75; Darlene Rebecca Roth, "Matronage: Patterns in Women's Organizations, Atlanta, Georgia, 1890–1940" (Ph.D. diss., George Washington Univ., 1978).

had been set up in three-fourths of the state's counties. The associations raised money, beautified school grounds, cleaned up and painted schoolhouses, purchased equipment, and offered prizes for the school district making the most improvement in its buildings and grounds.[65]

Despite the varied objectives of the women's groups and their fragmented and local character, the club movement was able to achieve some unity and to wield a concerted influence. The vehicle for this transformation was the General Federation of Women's Clubs, with which many of the individual societies were affiliated. By 1906 every southern state except Virginia had a state federation, and two years later the number of organized clubwomen in the southern states was estimated at 45,000.[66] The development of the federation in the South is illustrated in the case of Florida. In 1895 five individual organizations in that state worked together to form the Florida Federation of Women's Clubs (FFWC). The new state organization adopted a constitution providing that the societies that affiliated with it must be "free from sectarian or political bias and must express the spirit of progress on broad and humane lines." Many kinds of clubs came into the Florida Federation during the next few years. In 1898 the FFWC became an affiliate of the General Federation of Women's Clubs, and by November 1916 it boasted 138 clubs with a membership of more than 7,000.[67]

Every federation had departments devoted to literature, art, and music—and the Texas Federation even supported a traveling art gallery. But the leaders of these state organizations gradually became interested in much more than belles lettres and culture. "The club women who used to study Shakespeare have been looking around them upon life's state," wrote a Georgia feminist in 1906. "They are finding through their study of civic conditions that an enormous number of life's players are performing their parts under adverse circumstances."[68] This was clearly evident in the broadening civic interests of the state federations of women's clubs in the South. The federations began to press for such social objectives as pure food laws, child labor legislation, the establishment of juvenile courts, compulsory school attendance statutes, and more adequate institutional care for the unfortunate. Their most notable work was probably done in the field of education. The state federations supported larger appropriations for public schools, sponsored schools for mountain children, helped establish state industrial schools for wayward boys, promoted kindergartens and playgrounds, and awarded scholarships and loans to deserving students in the region's normal schools and universities. Many of the federa-

[65]E.C. Brooks, "Women Improving School Houses," *World's Work* 12 (Sept. 1906): 7937–38.
[66]According to one contemporary source, there were 350,000 organized clubwomen in the United States in 1908. Poppenheim, "Woman's Work in the South," 632–33. See also Mrs. A.O. Granger, "The Effect of Club Work in the South," *Annals* 28 (Sept. 1906): 50–51, and Anne Firor Scott, *The Southern Lady: From Pedestal to Politics, 1830–1930* (Chicago, 1970), 151–63.
[67]Johnson, "The Woman Suffrage Movement in Florida," 70–71.
[68]Granger, "The Effect of Club Work in the South," 253.

Jefferson County, Alabama, bookmobile at the Sayre Commissary, about 1915.
The Collections of the Birmingham Public Library.

tions carried on library extension work, and Tennessee alone had more than one hundred traveling libraries supported by its women's clubs in 1906. Writing in the early 1920s, one North Carolinian suggested that at least 80 percent of all the libraries in her state had been organized and kept alive by clubwomen.[69]

The entry of black women into the club movement was an important stimulus to the organization of social reform activities among Afro-Americans. Little groups of educated and professional Negro women began to coalesce throughout the South even before the end of the century. In Alabama, for instance, Mary Margaret Washington organized the Tuskegee Women's Club in 1895. The clubs formed by black women undertook a variety of community improvement projects relating to education, health, housing, prison reform, facilities for youthful offenders, and the like. The Atlanta Neighborhood Union, inspired and led by Lugenia Burns Hope, originated in a movement to establish a playground for black children. In Virginia, to cite another example, Janie Porter Barrett, a black social welfare leader and first president of the Virginia State Federation of Colored Women's Clubs, was instrumental in that organization's sponsorship of the Virginia Industrial School for Colored Girls.[70] Meanwhile, the General Federation of Women's Clubs, eager to promote the growth of its white affiliates in the South, refused to admit black delegates to its conventions, turning the controversial matter of Negro membership over to the state federations.[71] In the South many of the black clubs formed their own state federations, which were usually affiliated with the National Association of Colored Women.

Although their vocational opportunities were still severely limited in the early 1900s, an increasing number of southern women were moving into new or revitalized professions. For some women this professional involvement supplied an arena in which they were introduced not only to the dynamics of their particular profession's development but also to the world of interest-group organization, political lobbying, legislative appropriations, and public regula-

---

[69]Ibid., 250–52; Roberson, "The Organized Work of Women in One State," 176. Also see Kate Hutcheson Morrissette, "Traveling Libraries in Alabama," *Sewanee Review* 6 (July 19, 1898): 345–48; Mary Cooke Branch Munford, "Woman's Part in the Educational Progress of the South," in *The South in the Building of the Nation*, vol. 10, pp. 638–45; and Mrs. Alex Caldwell, "The Tennessee Federation and Legislation," in Tennessee Federation of Woman's Clubs, comp., *Woman's Work in Tennessee* (Memphis, 1916), 77–79.

[70]Gerda Lerner, "Early Community Work of Black Club Women," *Jour. Negro Hist.* 59 (Apr. 1974): 158–67; Sadie Daniel St. Clair, "Janie Porter Barrett," in James, et al., eds., *Notable American Women*, vol. 1, pp. 96–97.

[71]A white woman, writing to Booker T. Washington from Chicago in 1900, expressed regret over the discriminatory treatment of black women by the Generation Federation of Women's Clubs. But she warned that to disregard the feelings of southern white women "would increase the bitterness and misunderstanding following the war, and would therefore be really a great national calamity, and I believe it would not help the negroes one bit, but rather postpone the time, we all long for, when a better relation shall exist between the Whites and the Blacks" (Alice Bradford Wiles to Mr. and Mrs. Booker T. Washington, Nov. 23, 1900, in Louis R. Harlan and associates, eds., *The Booker T. Washington Papers*, vol. 5 [Urbana, Ill., 1976], 680).

tion. Thus women were drawn into various reform endeavors—ranging from narrow professional objectives to broader regulatory and ameliorative movements—as a result of their vocational roles in primary and secondary education, home economics, social work, and journalism. The volunteer slowly gave way to the professional in charitable and welfare work. The professional possibilities were sometimes revealed in the careers of older women such as Julia S. Tutwiler, a teacher, educational administrator, and social reformer in Alabama, and Rebecca Latimer Felton, a Georgian who championed penal reform, prohibition, woman suffrage, and laity rights in the Methodist church. As a columnist for the Atlanta *Semi-Weekly Journal* between 1899 and 1920, Mrs. Felton won the confidence and devotion of thousands of rural readers in the Southeast.[72]

Those women who joined the ranks of the southern progressives tended to be quiet reformers. Most of them were religious, respectable, and "southern" in outlook. They were not at heart revolutionaries any more than their male counterparts. To be sure, their moderation and circumspection were in some sense tactical. While revolting against the traditional constraints that fixed woman's place in southern life, they were careful to preserve the image of the southern lady and to reassure their male contemporaries that they were not out to undermine the fundamental verities of southern civilization (indeed, they frequently implied that they were the ultimate conservators of that unique civilization). The woman suffrage leaders in Virginia, remarked an observer in 1918, realized that the success of their movement "depends upon showing their cause to be compatible with the Virginia tradition of womanliness, and both instinct and judgment have prevented the adoption here of the more aggressive forms of campaigning."[73]

A surprising number of women reformers in the South were members of distinguished southern families. Madeline McDowell Breckinridge, one of the most dedicated and successful social reformers in the South, was a descendant of two outstanding Kentucky families, a great-granddaughter of Henry Clay, in whose Lexington home she grew up, and the wife of a member of the famous Breckinridge family.[74] Lila Meade Valentine, a crusader for educational reforms and other worthy causes, moved easily among the First Families of

[72]See Anne Gary Pannell and Dorothea E. Wyatt, *Julia S. Tutwiler and Social Progress in Alabama* (University, Ala., 1961); Josephine Bone Floyd, "Rebecca Latimer Felton: Champion of Women's Rights," *Ga. Hist. Quar.* 30 (June 1946): 81–104; and John E. Talmadge, *Rebecca Latimer Felton: Nine Stormy Decades* (Athens, Ga., 1960).

[73]Orie Latham Hatcher, "The Virginia Man and the New Era for Women," *Nation* 106 (June 1, 1918): 651. For evidence of more radical feminism in the early twentieth-century South, see Neil K. Basen, "The 'Jennie Higgenses' of the 'New South in the West': A Regional Survey of Socialist Activists, Agitators, and Organizers, 1901–1917," in Sally M. Miller, ed., *Flawed Liberation: Socialism and Feminism* (Westport, Conn., 1981), 87–111.

[74]Sophonisba Preston Breckinridge, *Madeline McDowell Breckinridge: A Leader in the New South* (Chicago, 1921); Melba Dean Porter, "Madeline McDowell Breckinridge: Her Role in the Kentucky Woman Suffrage Movement, 1908–1920," *Reg. Ky. Hist. Soc.* 72 (Oct. 1974): 342–63.

Virginia; along with the aristocratic tradition she inherited a strong sense of social responsibility, which was intensified by study and travel.[75] Belle Kearney, a WCTU lecturer and suffragist leader, was the daughter of a Mississippi planter and slaveholder.[76] In a land where ancestral prominence and aristocratic connections counted heavily, the family name and assured social place of many socially concerned women vouched for their southernism and gave them a certain immunity from attack, even if such attributes did not always increase the reformers' influence. If one had the proper social credentials, a good deal of strange radicalism and reform enthusiasm could be overlooked or explained away!

But not all reform-minded women in the South were members of first families, and the humanitarian impulse from the distaff side went well beyond the noblesse oblige of the aristocratic tradition. More characteristically, the women who began to attain new vocational identities and who joined the missionary societies, literary clubs, and civic improvement leagues were part of the South's emerging middle class, whatever their family connections and upper-class pretensions may have been.[77] What made many of them incipient social reformers was not their place in society but rather the fact that they were reasonably well educated, a large number were talented, some had traveled, and increasing leisure allowed them time to read and organize and participate in reform activities. Through travel and the widening circles of their various organizations, they were brought into contact with magnetic leaders such as Frances Willard and Anna Howard Shaw and with the ideas and methods of advanced social reformers in the Northeast and Midwest. More than any other factor, perhaps, the disheartening experience of seeing one's talents lie idle, in a society with few opportunities for women to lead independent and creative lives outside the home, spurred a growing number of southern women to enlist in the quiet rebellion. As one of the feminists wrote in 1900, "There was born in me a sense of the injustice that had always been heaped upon my sex, and this consciousness created and sustained in me a constant and ever increasing rebellion."[78]

---

[75]Lloyd C. Taylor, Jr., "Lila Meade Valentine: The FFV as Reformer," *Va. Mag. Hist. and Biog.* 70 (Oct. 1962): 471–87.

[76]Belle Kearney, *A Slaveholder's Daughter* (New York, 1900).

[77]This characterization may not be valid for the top echelon of early twentieth-century women reformers in the South. Most of some 40 southern progressives selected for biographical treatment in the first three volumes of James, et al., eds., *Notable American Women*, came from prominent families. Typically their fathers were planters, businessmen, educators, ministers, or professional men.

[78]Kearney, *A Slaveholder's Daughter*, 108. Also see Clement Eaton, "Breaking a Path for the Liberation of Women in the South," *Georgia Review* 28 (Summer 1974): 187–99. For an interesting discussion of women in the Farmers' Alliance, see Julie Roy Jeffrey, "Women in the Southern Farmers' Alliance: A Reconsideration of the Role and Status of Women in the Late Nineteenth-Century South," in Edward Magdol and Jon L. Wakelyn, eds., *The Southern Common People: Studies in Nineteenth-Century Social History* (Westport, Conn., 1980), 267–87.

As the intensity of what was called "the woman's movement" increased, it found greater focus in the drive for the suffrage. With the growth of their organizations and the refinement of their methods, it was natural that women should turn to a domain in which they had suffered great discrimination—the denial of political equality. Enfranchisement was not only the supreme objective in the crusade for the emancipation of women; it also represented a pragmatic decision on the part of socially conscious women whose reform efforts in other fields had been consistently nullified or diminished because of their political impotence in the South. A biographer of Madeline McDowell Breckinridge wrote of that devoted advocate of social reform in Kentucky, for example: "It was inevitable that she should be an ardent suffragist, witnessing as she daily witnessed, the neglect of causes for which women have tacitly assumed and acknowledged responsibility, even when not demanding the power with which competently to deal with that responsibility."[79] Patty Blackburn Semple of Louisville remarked in 1911 that when the woman's club was organized in her city "three subjects were tabooed—religion, politics and woman suffrage. We kept the resolution for awhile but gradually we found that our efforts in behalf of civic improvements and the correcting of outrageous abuses were handicapped at every turn by politics."[80]

The enfranchisement of women in the South was first discussed publicly during the disruptive years following the Civil War, but the earliest suffrage clubs in the region were not organized until the 1880s. Nationally known suffrage leaders occasionally lectured in the South during the latter part of the century, and in 1892 the National American Woman Suffrage Association (NAWSA) established a committee for the southern states. Many women became interested in the suffrage movement as a result of their work in the Women's Christian Temperance Union, which recognized that its campaign could be advanced if women were armed with the ballot. The religious overtones that characterized the early quest for social reform on the part of southern women were frequently apparent in their commitment to the suffrage fight. Writing in 1906 following a setback in one of her campaigns, Laura Clay of Kentucky remarked that she had come to realize more than ever "that this work is God's cause, and He is the leader of all our campaigns."[81]

Though tiny woman suffrage groups existed in almost all of the southern states in the 1890s, they were feeble and most of them disappeared soon after the turn of the century. For a decade there was little concerted activity in support of the votes-for-women cause. In 1903, Kate M. Gordon, the corresponding

---

[79]Sophonisba P. Breckinridge, "Madeline McDowell Breckinridge: Herald of Community Service," in Howard W. Odum, ed., *Southern Pioneers in Social Interpretation* (Chapel Hill, N.C., 1925), 195.

[80]Ida Husted Harper, ed., *The History of Woman Suffrage*, vol. 5: *1900–1920* (New York, 1922), 312.

[81]Laura Clay to Harriet Taylor Upton, June 26, 1906, Clay Papers.

secretary of the National Suffrage Association, persuaded the officers of that organization to hold its annual meeting in New Orleans. Several southerners participated in the program, and the meeting seemed to be successful. But the suffrage idea did not catch fire in the South; the section was not yet ready for an organized movement. By the time the NAWSA next decided to hold its annual meeting in the South, in Louisville, Kentucky, in 1911, interest in woman suffrage was being manifested in many parts of the region. And two years later, following a lecture tour through Georgia and Tennessee, Laura Clay joyfully reported: "Everywhere I find the people ripe for our movement."[82]

Efforts to organize suffrage groups in Tennessee, Georgia, and Texas illustrate the gradual emergence of the movement for women's rights in the South. There was some interest in woman suffrage in Tennessee as early as the 1870s, and in 1883 a bill was introduced in the state legislature to provide limited suffrage for women. The first woman suffrage society in Tennessee was organized in Memphis in 1889 by Mrs. Lide A. Meriwether, a WCTU leader. By 1897 there were ten organizations in the state, and in that year the Tennessee Equal Suffrage Association was formed in Nashville, with Mrs. Meriwether as president. The TESA declined after 1900, however, and it was not reorganized until early in 1907, following a meeting of southern suffragists in Memphis. Progress was slow for several years. Memphis remained the only center of organized activity until 1910, when a suffrage league was created in Knoxville. The next year a group was organized in Nashville, and other cities in the state were soon represented. The Nashville league's membership jumped from 60 in early 1912 to over 1,000 in 1914. The movement had become statewide, but the strong factionalism among Tennessee feminists soon caused the Tennessee Equal Suffrage Association to split into two competing state organizations.[83] By 1915 other suffrage associations had appeared, including the Business and Professional Women's Equal Suffrage League and the Congressional Union for Woman's Suffrage, which had considerable strength in East Tennessee. The Tennessee Federation of Labor had endorsed woman suffrage as early as 1908, several of the state's major newspapers and leading politicians became advocates of the cause, and in 1916 both major party platforms in Tennessee contained woman suffrage planks. The Nashville *Tennessean* gave a capsule report of the public's evolving attitude: "Hostility in 1913, ridicule in 1914, tolerance in 1915, frank approval in 1916."[84]

---

[82]Quoted in Clavia Goodman, *Bitter Harvest: Laura Clay's Suffrage Work* (Lexington, Ky., 1946), 51. Also see Harper, ed., *The History of Woman Suffrage*, vol. 5, pp. 17, 55–57, 310.

[83]The Tennessee Equal Suffrage Association and Tennessee Equal Suffrage Association, Inc.

[84]Quoted in A. Elizabeth Taylor, *The Woman Suffrage Movement in Tennessee* (New York, 1957), 73. For the developments described in this paragraph, see ibid., 15–93, 138; Ida Husted Harper, ed., *The History of Woman Suffrage*, vol. 6: *1900–1920* (New York, 1922), 596–99, 607–11; James P. Louis, "Sue Shelton White and the Woman Suffrage Movement in Tennessee, 1913–1920," *Tenn. Hist. Quar.* 22 (June 1963): 172–77; and Grace Elizabeth Prescott, "The Woman Suffrage Movement in Memphis: Its Place in the State, Sectional and National Movements," *West Tenn. Hist. Soc. Papers* 18 (1964): 87–94.

Georgia's first woman suffrage organization appeared in Columbus in 1890, and from it developed the Georgia Woman Suffrage Association. The GWSA had a hand in bringing the National American Woman Suffrage Association to Atlanta in 1895 for its annual convention. During the years after 1900 the movement continued at a low ebb, with the state association managing to hold a few annual meetings and sponsoring an occasional project. On at least two occasions during the first decade of the century suffragists in Atlanta tried without success to secure limited suffrage rights from the state legislature. Meanwhile, the Georgia Federation of Labor and the state Prohibition party endorsed woman suffrage. Yet as late as 1912 the state association had fewer than a hundred members. Then the movement began to gain momentum; the GWSA reported 250 members in 1913, over 1,000 in 1914, and eleven affiliates by late 1915. Several other equal suffrage organizations were created in 1913 and 1914: the Georgia Woman Suffrage League, which grew out of the Atlanta Civic League; the Equal Suffrage Party, which claimed almost 2,000 members and branches in thirteen counties by 1915; the Georgia Young People's Suffrage Association; and the Georgia Men's League for Women Suffrage. In 1914 a group of women in Macon formed the Georgia Association Opposed to Woman Suffrage. The legislature paid little heed to the demands of the suffragists until 1914, when committees in both houses held hearings on suffrage measures before voting them down.[85]

In Texas the concept of woman suffrage received limited support in the constitutional conventions of 1868 and 1875. The WCTU endorsed the idea in 1887 and was active in suffrage work in the 1890s. Meeting in Dallas in 1893, forty-eight people organized the Texas Equal Rights Association; it affiliated with the National Suffrage Association, encouraged the formation of local clubs, and held two or three state conventions before ceasing to function in 1896. The Texas movement was revived in 1903 with the organization of equal suffrage leagues in Houston and Galveston and the establishment of the Texas Woman Suffrage Association. But in two or three years the movement in the Lone Star State once again lapsed. In 1908, Anna Howard Shaw gave a series of lectures in Texas under the aegis of women's clubs, and in these appearances she attacked sexual discrimination and strongly advocated woman suffrage. A small suffrage club was organized in Austin during the same year. In 1912 another suffrage group was formed in San Antonio "to create a public sentiment in favor of 'votes for women' and to enlist all progressive women in the cause." Other clubs were soon organized, state conventions were held beginning in 1913, and by 1915 Texas had twenty-one local societies and about 2,500

[85]Harper, ed., *The History of Woman Suffrage*, vol. 6, pp. 122–29, 139–40; Jones, "Progressivism in Georgia," 208–22; A. Elizabeth Taylor, "The Origin of the Woman Suffrage Movement in Georgia," *Ga. Hist. Quar.* 28 (June 1944): 63–79; Taylor, "Revival and Development of the Woman Suffrage Movement in Georgia," ibid. 42 (Dec. 1958): 339–54; Taylor, "The Last Phase of the Woman Suffrage Movement in Georgia," ibid. 43 (Mar. 1959): 16–21.

members. The Texas Federation of Women's Clubs endorsed equal suffrage in the latter year, and by that time the question had become a significant issue in state politics.[86]

While the state associations usually furnished the leadership for the woman suffrage campaigns in the South, much of the work was done by local organizations. They planned the regular club programs, recruited new members, raised money for the cause, and publicized equal suffrage arguments and activities. They sponsored dances, musical programs, bazaars, teas, and better-baby contests to obtain money for the suffrage work. They issued press releases and suffrage bulletins, wrote suffrage columns, held debates, sponsored essay contests, and conducted suffrage schools and classes in citizenship and parliamentary law. Suffragists sent letters and petitions to legislators and congressmen, and they gradually became experienced in the art of organizing and conducting effective lobbies for their movement. In the meantime, the suffrage groups and their allies were promoting other social reforms—legislation to raise the age of consent, to make women coguardians of children, to outlaw child labor, to admit women to state universities, and so on. In breaking down prejudice against women in New Orleans, Kate Gordon remarked during the early stages of the movement in that city,"we have had to combine a great deal of social work with our effort."[87]

Many factors gradually strengthened the woman suffrage movement in the South, including the growth of urban population, changes in the home, the increasing number of women taxpayers, the decline of chivalric ideas, and the emergence of new types of women's organizations. The suffragists themselves argued that women should not be discriminated against at the polls, since they obeyed the laws, paid taxes, were mentally and morally qualified to vote, and possessed the same natural rights as men. They were careful to stress their allegiance to the southern ethos. The granting of the ballot to women, suffrage spokesmen argued, would be more than an act of justice; it would also protect women, increase the security of the home, and benefit society as a whole. As a suffrage statement in Georgia put the matter in 1915, "The women need the vote to represent the home interests which are controlled by politics—the schools, parks, playgrounds, sanitary conditions, and the milk supply. The country needs the woman's vote to create the best conditions about the home. The working woman needs the vote to secure short working hours."[88]

There were strong overtones of class and caste in the ideas expressed by southern suffragists. In 1908, Jean Gordon of New Orleans, sister of the busy Kate, gave an address, "Noblesse Oblige," at the NAWSA annual convention.

---

[86]Harper, ed., *The History of Woman Suffrage*, vol. 6, pp. 630–32; A. Elizabeth Taylor, "The Woman Suffrage Movement in Texas," *JSH* 17 (May 1951): 194–209.

[87]Kate M. Gordon to Laura Clay, Jan. 1 (1905?), Clay Papers.

[88]Quoted in Taylor, "The Last Phase of the Woman Suffrage Movement in Georgia," 13.

She urged women of education, wealth, and leisure—"free as the winds of heaven to do as they wish"—to concern themselves with the administration of public affairs. "Instead of being regarded as only fitted for women of ordinary position and intellect," she declared, "all offices such as superintendents of reformatories, matrons and women factory inspectors, should be filled by women . . . [who] would be above the temptation of graft or the fear of losing their positions."[89] The southern campaign to enfranchise women, like the movement in other parts of the country, was essentially "a struggle of white, native-born, middle-class women for the right to participate more fully in the public affairs of a society the basic structure of which they accepted."[90] Most southern women, little interested in what went on outside the home, were indifferent to the arguments of the suffragists. Others were concerned about social and community problems but were unwilling to become involved in politics or to join the suffrage movement.

In general the southern suffragists were not as militant as their counterparts in other regions. "We have to 'go slow', in the South," a Georgia woman explained in 1915, "also put on the soft pedal, and beware of the muffler cut-out. . . . So, we have to feel our way along, and watch as well as pray. We may not at first do very big things and we are perfectly certain not to do spectacular things, but . . . *we are not dead!*"[91] Such caution is understandable in view of the intense opposition the equal suffrage movement aroused in the southern states. Many ministers, especially during the early years of the movement, accused the suffragists of defying the Bible. There was much ridicule of "short-haired women" and of the "long-haired men" who supported their cause. Suffrage groups were not always able to secure the help of the WCTU and the Federation of Women's Clubs. Outside the cities and towns the suffrage movement encountered extremely strong resistance. As an Atlanta woman remarked during one of the campaigns in Georgia, "We are working very hard but it seems almost impossible to reach the rural districts, & this population is such an ignorant & hopeless one—."[92] Many rural inhabitants suspected that the enfranchisement of women would give the city an unfair advantage over the country. And far worse in the opinion of a Florida legislator in 1913, votes for women would "bring on marital unhappiness, divorces, and disruptive domestic condition."[93] The *Arkansas Democrat* knew the source of the trouble: "It is the woman without home life, more often, who must needs have something to

[89] Harper, ed., *The History of Woman Suffrage*, vol. 5, pp. 231–32.

[90] Aileen S. Kraditor, *The Ideas of the Woman Suffrage Movement, 1890–1920* (New York, 1965), p. x.

[91] Madeline J.S. Wyly to Antoinette Funk, Jan 8, 1915, Woman Suffrage Collection, Georgia Department of Archives and History.

[92] Emily C. McDougald to Clara Savage, Jan. 28, 1915, ibid.

[93] A. Elizabeth Taylor, "The Woman Suffrage Movement in Florida," *Fla. Hist. Quar.* 36 (July 1957): 55.

Members of the Alabama Equal Suffrage Association about 1919 at work on a prosuffrage mailing. Those identified are (1) Lillian R. Bowron, (2) Mrs. H. E. Pearce, (3) Pattie R. Jacobs, (4) Mrs. Charles Brown, (7) Mrs. W. D. Nesbit, and (8) Mrs. John R. Hornaday. *The Collections of the Birmingham Public Library.*

employ her mind, and having tired of theater parties and poodles, her mind naturally reverts to the suffrage question."[94] Southern men frequently asserted that there was no real demand for equal suffrage and that most women did not desire it. Other cirtics called the idea socialistic and foreign. "The women who are working for this measure," one southern woman warned in 1914, "are striking at the principle for which their fathers fought during the Civil War. Woman's suffrage comes from the north and west and from women who do not believe in state rights and who wish to see negro women using the ballot."[95] There was also evidence that the liquor interests opposed the enfranchisement of women. When Kentucky feminists lost their campaign in 1910 to allow women to vote in school elections, Laura Clay declared that "the liquor interests are opposed to even this small fragment of women suffrage, and defeated the bill."[96]

The most troublesome charge made by antisuffragists was that the suffrage movement would revive the "settled" question of the Negro in politics and enfranchise a horde of black women. "Well, it seems we are never to be done with the negro," wrote a pro-suffragist Georgian in 1915. "All my life he has been held up as a bugaboo to scare people into putting small men in office. Now, just as we had almost gotten him buried here comes the poor old negro 'mammy'!"[97] Seeing the danger in the racial innuendoes of their opponents, the suffragists were quick to grasp the nettle and use it to advance their own cause. A point they made time and again was that black men could still exercise the ballot in some areas while white women could not. Rebecca Latimer Felton would never let southerners forget that the Fourteenth and Fifteenth amendments were designed to enfranchise Negro men. "I do not want to see a negro man walk to the polls and vote on who shall pay my tax money while I myself can not vote at all," Mrs. Felton declared at a legislative hearing in 1914. "Is this fair?"[98] Far from being a threat to the established political system in the

---

[94]Quoted in A. Elizabeth Taylor, "The Woman Suffrage Movement in Arkansas," *Ark. Hist. Quar.* 15 (Spring 1956): 31.

[95]Dolly Bount Lamar, vice-president of the Georgia Association Opposed to Woman Suffrage, quoted in Taylor, "The Last Phase of the Woman Suffrage Movement in Georgia," 18. See also Johnson, "The Woman Suffrage Movement in Florida," 160–66, and Louise Boyd James, "The Woman Suffrage Issue in the Oklahoma Constitutional Conventional," *Chron. Okla.* 56 (Winter 1978–79): 379–92.

[96]Press release by Laura Clay, March 29, 1910, Clay Papers. Also see undated report (ca. 1912) by Mary Latimer McLendon and Kate Koch, president and corresponding secretary, respectively, of the Georgia Woman Suffrage Association, in Woman Suffrage Collection, Georgia Department of Archives and History.

[97]Harry Stilwell Edwards to Mrs. William H. Felton, Feb. 18, 1915, Felton Papers. See also James R. Wright, Jr., "The Assiduous Wedge: Woman Suffrage and the Oklahoma Constitutional Convention," *Chron. Okla.* 51 (Winter 1973–74): 421–43, and Mrs. Guilford Dudley, *The Negro Vote in the South: A Southern Woman's Viewpoint* (New York, 1918).

[98]John E. Talmadge, "Rebecca Latimer Felton," in Horace Montgomery, ed., *Georgians in Profile: Historical Essays in Honor of Ellis Merton Coulter* (Athens, Ga., 1958), 294. See also New Orleans *Item*, March 19, 22, 1914, and Andrew Sinclair, *The Emancipation of the American Woman* (New York, 1965), 296–99.

South, the region's suffragists argued, the enfranchisement of women would ensure white supremacy. In 1906 a conference of suffragists meeting in Memphis pointed out that there were 600,000 more white women in the southern states than the combined total of black men and women. State senator Fred P. Cone of Florida introduced a measure in 1913 that included both woman suffrage and a grandfather clause; he claimed that his proposal would mean the replacement of black men by white women at the polls.[99] Democracy, the southern suffragists seemed to believe, should be limited by color but not by sex.

Southern suffragists did not confine their racial appeals to the men of the South. They also contended that the white women of the North shared their interest in maintaining the supremacy of the Anglo-Saxon American. This thesis was given full expression in an address Belle Kearney delivered at the NAWSA convention of 1903 in New Orleans. In recounting the history of slavery in the United States, she called attention to the complicity of the "Puritan of the North" as well as that of the "cavalier of the South." Northern civilization, she declared, was threatened by "the influx of foreigners with their imported customs; by the greed of monopolistic wealth and the unrest among the working classes; by the strength of the liquor traffic and encroachments upon religious belief." She went on to predict that the North would some day "be compelled to look to the South for redemption from those evils on account of the purity of its Anglo-Saxon blood, the simplicity of its social and economic structure, the great advance in prohibitory law and the maintenance of the sanctity of its faith. . . ."[100] Southern appeals of this sort evoked a sympathetic response from the rest of the country. By the early 1900s the national woman suffrage movement had broken with the abolitionist tradition and had become less egalitarian than in earlier years. One reason for the development of a national movement, in fact, was "the common cause made by Northern women who feared the foreign-born vote with Southern women who feared the Negro vote."[101] Nevertheless, suffrage leaders outside the South eventually found it desirable to broaden their campaigns in order to attract the support of immigrant and working women. The NAWSA, meanwhile, became increasingly committed to the strategy of concentrating upon an amendment to the U.S. Constitution as the most promising path for the suffrage movement.

These developments aroused suspicions among many southern suffragists. The most outspoken critic of these trends was Kate M. Gordon of Louisiana. Fearful of the influence black women might exert in the NAWSA, she became a vigorous opponent of the federal amendment plan, contending that it would

[99]Harper, ed., *The History of Woman Suffrage*, vol. 5, p. 330; Taylor, "The Woman Suffrage Movement in Florida," 55.

[100]Harper, ed., *The History of Woman Suffrage*, vol. 5, pp. 82–83.

[101]Kraditor, *The Ideas of the Woman Suffrage Movement*, 137. For a fuller discussion of the parallel between southern and northern arguments, see ibid., pp. xi, 40, 125–32, 163–68, 198–220.

allow the national government and probably the Republican party to control southern elections. She devised a plan to force the states in the region to enfranchise women by amending their constitutions, apparently assuming that when faced with the alternative of having southern women join a movement that would bring federal action and possibly lead to investigations of state suffrage controls, the section's politicians would be willing to act themselves. In 1913 the New Orleans leader was instrumental in organizing the Southern States Woman Suffrage Conference, which pledged itself to support "states' rights" and to campaign for woman suffrage through state action. During the next few years Gordon and other like-minded suffragists competed with the National Suffrage Association and the more militant Congressional Union for the support of women in the South.[102]

There was widespread support among southern women for Kate Gordon's position, but it was apparent at least as early as the end of 1915 that many suffragists in the South had serious doubts about the wisdom of relying solely upon state initiative to accomplish their goal. Indeed, an increasing number of them turned with their sisters in other regions to support the National Suffrage Association's campaign for federal action.

THE EMERGENCE OF SOCIAL WELFARE

The dispensing of relief to the needy in the South at the turn of the century was undertaken largely by churches, benevolent associations, and other private agencies, especially in urban places. The principle of public responsibility for those in need, based on the old English poor laws, was widely recognized in southern legislative enactments; but local officials, the dispensers of relief, were generally indifferent if not hostile to the expenditure of public funds for such purposes. The dominant commercial-civic elite in most southern cities during this period regarded municipal expenditures for welfare as a threat to individual initiative. Most rural counties and villages in the South provided no poor relief at all. A Kentucky statute of 1906, for example, reaffirmed familial responsibility for the care of aged paupers. As late as 1923, only six of Louisiana's sixty-four parishes maintained almshouses or poor farms, and the state board of charities reported that only six parishes appropriated funds for "outdoor" (home) relief.[103]

---

[102]Kate M. Gordon, "The Southern Woman Suffrage Conference," in Harper, ed., *The History of Woman Suffrage*, vol. 5, pp. 671–73; Kenneth R. Johnson, "Kate Gordon and the Woman-Suffrage Movement in the South," *JSH* 38 (Aug. 1972): 365–81; Kraditor, *The Ideas of the Woman Suffrage Movement*, 173–80.

[103]Elizabeth Wisner, *Social Welfare in the South: From Colonial Times to World War I* (Baton Rouge, 1970), 3–4, 7, 27, 31–34; Roy M. Brown, *Public Poor Relief in North Carolina* (Chapel Hill, N.C., 1928), 1–98; Constantine William Curris, "State Public Welfare Developments in Kentucky," *Reg. Ky. Hist. Soc.* 64 (Oct. 1966): 303; Blaine A. Brownell, "The Urban South Comes of Age, 1900–1940," in Brownell and David R. Goldfield, eds., *The City in Southern History: The Growth of Urban Civilization in the South* (Port Washington, N.Y., 1977), 154.

Almhouses and poor farms supported by counties and cities were the principal agencies of public welfare in the South. These facilities, where they existed, were almost entirely concerned with the destitute, which often included the aged, disabled, and feeble-minded. They were usually run by individuals on a contract basis, were generally inefficient and frequently corrupt, and more often than not provided residents with only a wretched hovel, filthy conditions, and inadequate food. Little distinction was made in the treatment of paupers and criminals.[104] The secretary of the Birmingham Associated Charities reported early in 1912 that a recent investigation of that city's almshouse—a rambling wooden structure he described as a veritable "tinder box"—disclosed seventy-one inmates of both sexes and races, seven of whom had tuberculosis. The so-called jail maintained in connection with the almshouse incarcerated four imbecilic men and women who had committed no crime other than "being poor."[105] The Tennessee legislature, to take a typical case, waited until 1911 to empower county courts to make contracts with local hospitals for the care and treatment of indigent sick or injured persons.[106] In a great majority of rural communities and counties there was no organized system of welfare services before World War I. The only notable exception was the care of Confederate veterans. All of the former Confederate states established pension programs for these veterans, and soldiers' homes received public and private support.[107]

State legislatures in the South tended, until the early years of the twentieth century, simply to authorize the counties and municipalities to provide for paupers, dependent children, and defectives through direct assistance and institutional care. The states themselves gradually enlarged their role, at first by attempting to develop institutions for the blind, the mentally ill, and other handicapped persons. They also moved to establish reformatories and "industrial" schools for delinquent boys and girls, though the facilities for black youths were almost always extremely inadequate or nonexistent. Most of these state institutions, particularly those for the mentally ill, employed procedures and standards that were far behind their northern counterparts.[108] All too often the operation of these poorly financed institutions was impaired by politics and patronage. None of the southern states had a strong welfare commission before the First World War, and at the outset of the war only six commonwealths had created welfare boards of any kind. Those that existed had virtually no super-

[104]Wisner, *Social Welfare in the South*, 42–47, 117–18.

[105]W. M. McGrath, "Conservation of Health," *Survey* 27 (Jan. 6, 1912): 1503–1504. For conditions in the Alabama black belt, see Glenn Sisk, "The Poor in Provincial Alabama," *Ala. Hist. Quar.* 22 (Spring and Summer 1960): 101–102.

[106]Virginia Ashcraft, *Public Care: A History of Public Welfare Legislation in Tennessee* (Knoxville, 1947), 11.

[107]William H. Glasson, "The South's Care for Her Confederate Veterans," *American Monthly Review of Reviews* 36 (July 1907): 40–47.

[108]Wisner, *Social Welfare in the South*, 109–15.

visory authority over state institutions and little or no influence on the administration of local relief or institutional care. According to Howard W. Odum, the
work of the North Carolina board of public charities, which was created in
1868, was "more or less desultory and largely palliative." The Louisiana
legislature established a state board of charities and corrections in 1905, with
the governor serving as ex officio president. The board was charged with the
duty of inspecting all state, parish, and municipal institutions of a charitable,
eleemosynary, correctional, or reformatory nature and to report biennially to
the governor and legislature. But no appropriation was made to finance its
work, and its only power was that of recommendation. Virginia established a
similar board in 1908, but its five members served without compensation and
were given only "visitorial and advisory" duties.[109]

There was a pronounced tendency in the South during this period, as one
scholar pointed out in 1928, "to center all social work and other welfare efforts
through the schools, church, and industry."[110] The charitable impulse found
expression in all of the region's large denominations through home mission
programs and the maintenance of orphanages, hospitals, and homes for the
aged. Individual churches in southern cities undertook a variety of social services. St. Vincent's Hospital in Birmingham, for example, a Catholic institution founded in 1901, carried on a regular program of charity work, including
the operation of a free dispensary open to both races. The Southside Baptist
Church in the same city attempted to become an "institutional church," providing reading rooms, baths, a gymnasium, a free kindergarten, an industrial
school to instruct children in cooking and sewing, and a "Goodwill Center" for
the Italian community. Birmingham's Episcopal Church of the Advent supported the Boys' Industrial School, the Mercy Home for Women, the Northside
Community House, and social work among blacks. Meanwhile, the Pastors'
Union formed "social ministries" to promote uplift endeavors.[111]

Other sources of organized charity during the years after 1900 included
programs undertaken by the Young Women's Christian Association and the
Young Men's Christian Association chapters and the Florence Crittenton Mission for unwed mothers. An increasing number of textile mills and large industrial firms sponsored volunteer community work, night classes and kindergartens, visiting nurses, and sanitation programs, and some of these companies

---

[109]Ibid., 116; Elizabeth Wisner, *Public Welfare Administration in Louisiana* (Chicago, 1930);
Howard W. Odum, "The North Carolina Plan," in Odum and D.W. Willard, *Systems of Public
Welfare* (Chapel Hill, N.C., 1925), 172, 201; S.P. Breckinridge, "History and Development of
State Systems of Public Welfare," ibid. 16; "State Boards and Commissions," *Charities* 14 (July
29, 1905): 949; F.A. Magruder, *Recent Adminstration in Virginia* (Baltimore, 1912), 116–17.

[110]Howard W. Odum, "How New Is the South in Social Work?" *Survey* 60 (June 15, 1928): 329.

[111]Wisner, *Social Welfare in the South*, 118–20; McGrath, "Conservation of Health," 1502;
Wayne Flynt, "Religion in the Urban South: The Divided Religious Mind of Birmingham, 1900–
1930," *Ala. Rev.* 30 (Apr. 1977): 108–34; Martha Carolyn Mitchell, "Birmingham: Biography of a
City of the New South" (Ph.D. diss., Univ. of Chicago, 1946), 142–57.

began to use paid welfare workers.[112] Such welfare work, a leading textile manufacturer observed, "blesses giver and receiver," for "it builds prosperity on an indestructible foundation of education, peace, and good will. . . ."[113] The growth of civic and commercial groups also contributed to the charity movement in the South, especially in the organization of emergency relief measures to deal with catastrophic accidents and unusual distress.

The era of private philantropy witnessed the establishment of Southern Appalachia as a home mission field. By the turn of the century this subregion was widely perceived as a "strange land" inhabited by a "peculiar people." Religious organizations, voluntary agencies, and northern philanthropists entered the field in the late nineteenth century, building churches, subsidizing the salaries of ministers, establishing industrial schools, supporting traveling nurses, and pioneering in the introduction of public health work. Some contemporaries criticized such uplift activities as "mistaken missionary work," contending that Appalachia's poverty and isolation could be relieved only if the mountaineers came down from the hills and took jobs in the textile mills and other industries.[114] But social welfare projects continued to expand in the southern mountains, and by 1912 the work was beginning to receive some coordination and overall direction. Starting about 1914 an interdenominational Conference of Southern Mountain Workers was held in Knoxville each year. Two leaders in the broader approach were John C. Campbell of the Russell Sage Foundation's Southern Highland Division and Warren H. Wilson of the Presbyterian church's Department of Church and Country Life. These men saw Southern Appalachia not only as an example of regional poverty in America but also as a legitimate indigenous culture.[115]

Southern women assumed an essential role in the early welfare movement, not only in the institutional activities of the churches but also in their other

[112]Lyda Gordon Shivers, "The Social Welfare Movement in the South: A Study in Regional Culture and Social Organization" (Ph.D. diss., Univ. of North Carolina, 1935), 111–25; Harriet L. Herring, *Welfare Work in Mill Villages: The Story of Extra-Mill Activities in North Carolina* (Chapel Hill, N.C., 1929), 10, 29, 67–73, 106–18, 129–33, 149–52, 159–70; Walter H. Page, "A Journey Through the Southern States," *World's Work* 14 (June 1907): 9031–32; Alice N. Parker, "The Kindergarten in the South," in *The South in the Building of the Nation*, vol. 10, pp. 380–86; Marlene Hunt Rikard, "George Gordon Crawford: Man of the New South," *Ala. Rev.* 31 (July 1978): 167–71; Katherine Gertrude Aiken, "The National Florence Crittenton Mission, 1883–1925: A Case Study in Progressive Reform" (Ph.D. diss., Washington State Univ., 1980).

[113]Parker, "The South Carolina Cotton Mill Village—A Manufacturer's View," 356. Also see David English Camak, "The Power of One Man for Good," *Methodist Review Quarterly* 56 (July 1907): 482–87; Few, "The Constructive Philanthropy of a Southern Cotton Mill," 82–90; and Carlton, "Mill and Town," 83–117, 193–95.

[114]See, for example, Thomas R. Dawley, Jr., "Our Southern Mountaineers," *World's Work* 19 (Mar. 1910): 12704–14.

[115]William Goodell Frost, "Our Contemporary Ancestors in the Southern Mountains," *Atlantic Monthly* 83 (Mar. 1899): 311–19; John C. Campbell, *The Southern Highlander and His Homeland* (New York, 1921), 20–21, 219–22, 270–73, 298–321; Marshall W. Fishwick, *The Virginia Tradition* (Washington, D.C., 1956), 67; Rupert B. Vance, "The Region: A New Survey," in Thomas

organizational work. The state branches of the International Order of the King's Daughters sponsored welfare projects, especially hospitals and homes for the aged. The General Federation of Women's Clubs in the various southern states was even more important. In North Carolina, for instance, the federation organized a Village Improvement and State Charities department. Several of the state federations actively supported a wide range of social legislation. Particularly noteworthy among the social uplift activities of church groups was the program undertaken by women in the Methodist church.

The organization of social work on a regional basis by Methodist women did not make much progress before 1900. But individuals and local groups among the Southern Methodists had begun in earlier years to formulate schemes for the relief of society's unfortunate. The women of the Home Mission Society of the First Methodist Church in Birmingham, Alabama, had started an industrial school for deprived children as early as 1877. The Trinity Home Mission of Atlanta was organized in 1882, dedicated to "the physical, mental, and moral elevation of the poor of the city, and especially of our own Church and congregation." A city mission board was created in Macon, Georgia, in 1896, with a day school for indigent children as its first undertaking; during the following year it opened the Macon Door of Hope, a project that continued for a generation.[116] The Southern Methodist Woman's Parsonage and Home Mission Society founded or assumed control of several mission schools and training schools during the 1890s. It also began to evolve other plans for social service. The work of the home missions, like that of the foreign missions, tended to become increasingly comprehensive and to encompass all aspects of human suffering and need.

In 1894 the general conference of the church authorized the creation of city mission boards, and such bodies were soon organized in several southern cities. By 1899, seventeen workers were employed in ten cities; their duties included friendly visiting, Bible reading, teaching in kindergartens and industrial classes, and "rescue" work. Mrs. R.W. MacDonell, who became general secretary of home missions in 1900, urged that those engaged in city mission work should live within the districts in which they worked. The result was the establishment of three pioneer settlements—in Nashville, Dallas, and Atlanta—and the opening of four others by 1904. Although the city mission movement encountered a good deal of suspicion and opposition in the church, it took firm hold during the progressive period. Most of the mission centers were located in industrial areas among underprivileged workers. They were operated by trained resident social workers, with the help of local volunteer aids.

R. Ford, ed., *The Southern Appalachian Region: A Survey* (Lexington, Ky., 1962), 1–5; Henry D. Shapiro, *Appalachia on Our Mind: The Southern Mountains and Mountaineers in the American Consciousness, 1870–1920* (Chapel Hill, N.C., 1978), 32–58, 133–56, 186–212.

[116]Tatum, *A Crown of Service*, 26, 242, 279.

The Methodist women also set up cooperative homes for working women and rescue homes for girls.[117]

The settlement house movement, influenced by famous examples like Toynbee Hall in London and Hull House in Chicago, began to reach a few southern cities by the turn of the century. The *Handbook of Settlements* published in 1911 listed some 45 settlement houses in the South out of a national total of 413. Not all of these southern settlements were resident houses, but most of them endeavored to provide regular neighborhood programs. Ten of the southern states were represented with at least one settlement house. No fewer than 25 of the 45 were founded or sponsored by religious groups.[118]

Southern Methodists supported about eighteen of these settlement programs, which were usually called Wesley Houses. Wesley House in Atlanta, founded in 1903, served the area around the Fulton Bag and Cotton Mills. It was maintained by monthly subscriptions from the Women's Home Mission Society of fifteen Methodist churches and various other contributions, including some support from the local textile mill. The settlement house sponsored an array of services: a day nursery and a kindergarten, nursing service and a clinic, a "penny provident bank," a library and reading room, shower baths, gymnastic work for boys and girls, domestic science classes, a sewing school, rooms for community organizations, religious services, and a Sunday school. Another Methodist settlement was Ensley Community House near Birmingham. Established in 1913 through the cooperation of the Woman's Missionary Council, the city mission board, and the Tennessee Coal, Iron and Railroad Company, the center was located in a community of Italian steelworkers. The project flourished. Many types of community service were provided, including the teaching of English to the Italians and the operation of a kindergarten, a playground, a clinic, and a mothers' club.[119] A few settlement houses or neighborhood centers were sponsored by Episcopalian, Presbyterian, Baptist, and Jewish organizations. Several of the settlements were located in the Appalachian Mountains. The Nurses Settlement of Richmond, begun by some young nurses in 1901, maintained a visiting nursing headquarters, a kindergarten, a mothers' club, a newsboys' club, a class in home nursing, and informal friendly visiting.[120]

The first permanently established settlement house in the South was Kings-

[117]Ibid., 96, 223–29, 241–93; Newell, "Social Work of Women's Organizations in the Churches," 310.

[118]Robert A. Woods and Albert J. Kennedy, eds., *Handbook of Settlements* (New York, 1911), 6–8, 35–36, 87–92, 149, 249–50, 289–99.

[119]Ibid., 35; Tatum, *A Crown of Service*, 243–44; Lawrence A. Cremin, *The Transformation of the School: Progressivism in American Education, 1876–1957* (New York, 1961), 64.

[120]Frances MacGregor Ingram, "The Settlement Movement in the South," *World Outlook* 27 (May 1937): 12–14, 38; John Lee Eighmy, "The Social Conscience of Southern Baptists from 1900 to the Present as Reflected in Their Organized Life" (Ph.D. diss., Univ. of Missouri, 1959), 16–20; Frederick W. Neve, "Social Settlements in the South," in *The South in the Building of the Nation*," vol. 10, pp. 614–22.

ley House in New Orleans. Founded in 1899 on the basis of a free kindergarten and a neighborhood program conducted by two Episcopal churches, the house was located in New Orleans' Irish Channel, a depressed area mainly inhabited by Irish and Italian ethnic groups. Named for the English reformer Charles Kingsley, the new social settlement was greatly influenced by the example of Jane Addams's Hull House and Graham Taylor's Chicago Commons. The dominant figure in the development of Kingsley House was a young Louisiana teacher and social worker named Eleanor McMain, who served as head resident of the settlement for more than thirty years. She was at least partly responsible for severing the enterprise's Episcopalian connection in 1902 and for creating the nonsectarian Kingsley House Association. Under her leadership the settlement promoted clubs and classes, established a playground, opened a medical clinic, stimulated interest in formal and folk art, and campaigned for child labor laws, a tenement house code, tuberculosis and yellow fever control, a municipal recreation program, a community chest, and a council of social agencies.[121]

By 1912 or 1913 the Home Mission Board of the Southern Methodist church had begun to operate a few neighborhood centers for blacks in certain cities. These social service programs were called Bethlehem Centers. There was also a handful of settlement houses in the South organized by blacks. An example was the Calhoun Colored School and Settlement in Alabama. Social welfare facilities for black southerners were likely to be found only in the larger cities, where Negro communities steadily expanded and became more complex, economically diverse, and socially organized. Black civic and service organizations grew apace during this period, along with the existing religious and fraternal groups. Many of these organizations supported social services among blacks. The Neighborhood Union in Atlanta, for example, organized in 1908 by church women in the vicinity of Spelman and Morehouse colleges, undertook a variety of projects, including recreation for black children, the operation of a health center, a program of home visits, and a systematic effort to promote health care.[122] The First Congregational Church of Atlanta, long involved in social welfare work, sought in the aftermath of the terrible race riot of 1906 to rebuild the black community. Educators also contributed to the embryonic social welfare efforts in cities like Atlanta. This was evident in the conferences

[121]Milton D. Speizman, "The Movement of the Settlement House Idea into the South," *Southwestern Soc. Sci. Quar.* 44 (Dec. 1963): 237–46; Wisner, *Social Welfare in the South*, 122; Allen F. Davis, *Spearheads for Reform: The Social Settlements and the Progressive Movement, 1890–1914* (New York, 1967), 15, 23–24, 44–45, 65–66; "The Work of Kingsley House During the Epidemic," *Charities* 14 (Sept. 2, 1905): 1034–35; Eleanor McMain, "Kingsley House, New Orleans," ibid. 11 (Dec. 5, 1903): 549–53; Bradley Buell, "Eleanor McMain: One of the Pioneers," *Survey Graphic* 65 (Jan. 1, 1931): 374–77, 402–403.
[122]Woods and Kennedy, *Handbook of Settlements*, 6–8; Brownell, "The Urban South Comes of Age," 140; Lerner, "Early Community Work of Black Women," 158–67; Edyth L. Ross, "Black Heritage in Social Welfare: A Case Study of Atlanta," *Phylon* 37 (Dec. 1976): 297–307.

on Negro problems and the Atlanta University *Publications* produced by William E.B. Du Bois in the years after 1897. A recent scholar has stated that one of these early conferences and publications "served as the first explicitly scientific excursion into the field of social welfare as defined and developed by the black population."[123]

The most conspicuous manifestation of the social service impulse in the South during the early years of the twentieth century was the organized charity movement. The movement, which began with the founding in 1877 of a charity organization society in Buffalo, New York, had little influence in southern cities until after 1900. Emphasizing the advantages of "scientific charity," the new societies set out to coordinate local relief, not by competing with existing agencies, but by careful investigation of individual cases, efficient organization of philanthropic resources in the community, and avoidance of indiscriminate almsgiving and casual benevolence.[124] The Associated Charities of Raleigh, North Carolina, for example, stated its purpose as being "to suppress street begging, to decrease uninformed almsgiving at the house doors, and to gather all general relief work of the community into a center of cooperative, intelligent administration."[125] Implicit in the organized charity movement was the assumption that the middle class and the well-to-do had a responsibility to help the needy. Scientific charity was also thought to embody a method of prevention and rehabilitation rather than merely continuing the relief of poverty.

A few associated charities had made their appearance in the South by the mid-1890s, but they were not well organized or effective. The impetus toward cooperative relief sometimes came from community disasters such as the yellow fever epidemic that struck New Orleans in 1897 and a terrible winter storm that brought intense suffering to poor people of Atlanta in 1905. But the progress of the organized charity movement in other parts of the country and the influence of the National Conference of Charities and Correction were more important factors. The annual meeting of the NCCC in 1903, which was held in Atlanta, encouraged the consideration of social welfare needs in the urban South. A local committee comprised of one hundred men and sixty women helped prepare for the meeting, and at its request the governor appointed committees in a hundred other Georgia cities and towns. In 1905 a field department of the Journal *Charities and the Commons* was created to promote the organization of charity societies and to serve as a national clearinghouse for the movement.[126]

[123]Ross, "Black Heritage in Social Welfare," 301.

[124]Wisner, *Social Welfare in the South*, 120–21; Roy Lubove, *The Professional Altruist: The Emergence of Social Work as a Career, 1880–1930* (Cambridge, Mass., 1965), 2–14; Walter I. Trattner, *From Poor Law to Welfare State: A History of Social Welfare in America* (New York, 1974), 83–93; Margaret E. Rich, *A Belief in People: A History of Family Social Work* (New York, 1956), 13–14.

[125]Quoted in Frank Dekker Watson, *The Charity Organization Movement in the United States: A Study in American Philanthropy* (New York, 1922), 350.

[126]Ibid., 248, 337, 347–48; Wisner, *Social Welfare in the South*, 86–88, 99–101; Ben J.R.

The Atlanta Associated Charities provided the first substantial demonstration of "the new view of charity" in the South. The leader in the successful launching of the charities society in Atlanta was Joseph C. Logan, a young lawyer who soon became secretary of the organization. When Logan attended his first NCCC meeting, in Philadelphia in 1906, he had not yet learned what a case record was. But he was a man of great warmth, ability in working with other people, and capacity for asking unconventional questions and adopting new ways of doing things. He was able to secure both financial support and enthusiastic cooperation from many Atlanta leaders and organizations, including the business community. He also acted as a "social missionary" in promoting the organization of associated charities in other southern cities.[127] The child labor reformer Alexander J. McKelway wrote Woodrow Wilson in 1912 that Logan had "done more for the enlightenment and redemption of Atlanta during the last seven years than any [other] man in it."[128]

Under Logan's resourceful leadership, the Atlanta society organized the city into districts, employed paid secretaries, and instituted case conferences and a program of friendly visitors. The society endeavored to work with older social welfare organizations and to provide relief in specific cases on the basis of individual subscriptions or allocations of funds from other agencies earmarked for particular needs. The charities society also sponsored a community program. It took the lead in developing a playground movement in Atlanta and operated several playgrounds until they were taken over by the city park department. It helped organize an Anti-Tuberculosis and Visiting Nursing Association and aided in establishing a dispensary for the treatment of TB patients. It created a "committee on physical welfare of school children," with representatives from various civic and philanthropic organizations, and conducted a class for the study of social problems. Logan and his associates supported the establishment of the juvenile court in Atlanta and helped secure a city ordinance authorizing a system of adult probation. They arranged a series of conferences of medical authorities and socially minded citizens in 1913 that led to the beginning of medical social work at Grady Hospital.[129]

Charity organization societies were emerging in a number of other southern cities at about the same time. The journal *Charities* reported in May 1905 that the organization of such societies was "especially noticeable" in the South. It

---

Altemson, "Impressions of the National Conference of Charities and Corrections, Held in Atlanta, Georgia, May 6, 1903," *Annals* 22 (Sept. 1903): 149–50; Lyda Gordon Shivers, "Some Variations in State Conferences of Social Work," *Social Forces* 12 (May 1934): 546–50; "Relief Work at Birmingham Following the Mine Disaster," *Charities* 14 (Apr. 22, 1905); 671–72; "Indigent Cases Taken Over by the Charity Organizational Society," ibid. (Sept. 2, 1905): 1034.

[127]Kendall Weisiger, "Joe Logan, Genius of Social Work in the South," *Atlanta Historical Bulletin* 4 (Jan. 1939): 3–16; Watson, *The Charity Organization Movement*, 348–50; Shivers, "The Social Welfare Movement in the South," 188–90.

[128]McKelway to Wilson, July 23, 1912, McKelway Papers.

[129]Weisiger, "Joe Logan," 3–16; Shivers, "The Social Welfare Movement in the South," 188–90; Watson, *The Charity Organization Movement*, 348–50.

cited recent steps toward "organized charity" in Atlanta and Augusta, Georgia; Richmond and Roanoke, Virginia; San Antonio, Houston, Dallas, Brenham, Palestine, and Beaumont, Texas.[130] Reformers in Richmond had earlier expressed a need for an adequately paid social worker "familiar with modern methods of charitable work in other cities, and capable of serving as a leader and organizer for the rapidly growing philanthropic activities of the city."[131] In some cases the field secretary of the charity organization department of the Russell Sage Foundation facilitated the formation of new societies. That was true of the Associated Charities of Savannah, Georgia, where an active group of women created a "Committee on Charities and Health" to combat tuberculosis in connection with a local display of the National Tuberculosis Exhibit. Out of these activities came the Savannah Associated Charities. The Women's Club of Jacksonville, Florida, after studying methods of dealing with dependency, organized a Charity Council, which led in 1910 to the creation of an Associated Charities for the city. The new societies usually employed full-time secretaries, in many cases provided the only outdoor relief available, and frequently headed campaigns like the fight against tuberculosis.[132] Alexander J. McKelway, noting the organization of an Associated Charities in Birmingham in 1909 and the formation of a state conference of charities and corrections a year later, observed that in Alabama "the community spirit is just beginning to assert itself in recognizing its responsibility toward the weaker members of society."[133]

The Memphis Associated Charities, organized in 1911, quickly became one of the most successful societies in the South. By the second year of its operation, the society had a budget of $33,000. In an unusual move, the Memphis agency consolidated relief-giving, dispensary services, and visiting nursing into one organization, in the belief that the three divisions "more than any other agencies must work together in solving the problems of dependent families." The new society contributed to "a civic awakening" in Memphis that resulted in a juvenile court system, an efficient health department, a municipal children's hospital, and a fresh-air camp for run-down and convalescent children and their mothers. In 1914 the society aided in creating the Memphis Neighborhood Nursery Association and in establishing a department of public recreation with a budget of $12,000. The Memphis Associated Charities also took the lead in setting up a Negro auxiliary known as the "Colored Federated Charities." In general, however, blacks were neglected in the associated charities of southern cities, and they seldom applied to these white agencies for help. It is significant

[130]"Organization in the Smaller Cities," *Charities* 14 (May 6, 1905): 701–702.

[131]Quoted in Watson, *The Charity Organization Movement*, 350.

[132]Ibid., 350–56, 358, 361.

[133]McKelway, "What Birmingham is doing for its Children," undated manuscript in McKelway Papers; McKelway, "Conservation of Childhood," *Survey* 27 (Jan. 6, 1912): 1515–26.

that there were no black representatives at the NCCC meeting of 1903 in Atlanta.[134]

By the end of the first decade of the twentieth century, social welfare efforts in the southern states had begun to move, ever so slowly, away from the long-dominant emphasis on individual economic dependency and "moral behavior." Social welfare increasingly reflected not only a more "scientific" approach in providing relief to paupers but also more concern with the entire family and its relationships and with environmental improvement as a means of ameliorating poverty, dependency, and disease. Greater stress was being placed on casework, surveys, and education. The new approach was encouraged by the activities of national organizations and foundations. The Russell Sage Foundation, for instance, carried out a survey of Atlanta in the manner of the famous Pittsburgh Survey, while the Charities Publication Committee and *Survey* magazine undertook a social study of Birmingham.[135] Six of the approximately sixty charter members forming the National Association of Societies for Organizing Charity in 1911 were southern societies.[136] The number of southern associated charities grew rapidly during the next few years.

The organization of associated charities in southern cities was a major factor in the formation of statewide conferences in the region. Virginia organized such a conference as early as 1900, when twenty-four physicians and superintendents of state mental institutions met to consider common problems. The Virginia conference supported a number of social reforms during its early years, but its most important work was in urging the need for a state board of charities and corrections, an agency established by the general assembly in 1908. Ably led by Joseph Thomas Mastin, the state board assumed an active role in the inspection and supervision of almshouses, jails, orphanages, and other institutions; worked to develop child-placing agencies, industrial schools for boys and girls, and a juvenile court system; and used its influence for the enactment of much regulatory and remedial legislation.[137] In Oklahoma the State Conference of Charities, organized in 1908, worked closely with Kate Barnard in advancing her wide-ranging social justice program as Okahoma's first commissioner of charities and corrections.[138] Kentucky formed a state conference of

[134]"Charity Organization Societies," *Survey* 32 (May 30, 1914): 247; Watson, *The Charity Organization Movement*, 356–58; William D. Miller, *Memphis During the Progressive Era, 1900–1917* (Memphis, 1957), 104–26; Ross, "Black Heritage in Social Welfare," 300–305.

[135]Nathan Edward Cohen, *Social Work in the American Tradition* (New York, 1958), 107; Bremner, *From the Depths*, 156–57; John M. Glenn, Lilian Brandt, and F. Emerson Andrews, *Russell Sage Foundation, 1907–1946*, 2 vols. (New York, 1947), vol. 1, pp. 177–81.

[136]They were Atlanta, Chattanooga, Fort Worth, Jacksonville, Pensacola, and Savannah. Watson, *The Charity Organization Movement*, 337–45; Rich, *A History of Family Social Work*, 177–78.

[137]For an account of Mastin's impressive work, see Arthur W. James, *Virginia's Social Awakening: The Contribution of Dr. Mastin and the Board of Charities and Corrections* (Richmond, Va., 1939).

[138]It is interesting to note that Barnard was committed to direct action as the way to achieve

charities and corrections in 1904, South Carolina in 1909, Alabama in 1910, Florida and Texas in 1911, Arkansas in 1912, North Carolina in 1913, Tennessee in 1915, and Louisiana in 1916. These statewide conferences enlisted the participation of social workers, still only a small number, and socially conscious clergymen, educators, lawyers, and businessmen.[139]

Arkansas illustrates the way in which the state conferences came into being. The Arkansas Conference of Charities and Correction, which held its organizing meeting in May 1912, was created through the efforts of the recently formed United Charities Association of Pulaski County (Little Rock) and other associated charities in the state. Those who planned the initial meeting invited delegates from the various charity societies, boards of state institutions, orphanages, YMCA and YWCA chapters, and interested individuals. The meeting was held in Little Rock, and Governor George W. Donaghey gave an address on "Prison Labor." Well-known national social workers were invited too. Dr. Hastings H. Hart, a former general secretary of the NCCC and an outstanding figure in child welfare work, also addressed the conference. Among other decisions the conferees adopted a constitution setting forth these objectives: to provide an opportunity for those engaged in social work to confer among themselves concerning needs and methods; to disseminate reliable information about charities and correctional activities; and to encourage cooperation among persons and organizations involved in charitable and correctional programs.[140]

The North Carolina Conference for Social Service, which held its first meeting in 1913, was one of the most active and progressive of the new state associations. Plans were made for the conference in 1912, when a group of physicians, state department heads, superintendents of church orphanages, and reformers held a meeting in Raleigh. At its organizational meeting the conference considered a large number of social problems, including the need for aid to dependent children, for child labor laws and their enforcement, for reformatories and juvenile courts, for better treatment of the feeble-minded, for the

---

reform. As she wrote to another reformer, "While most of the leaders in the Charity movement deplore the fact that politics should enter our field, I cannot agree with them. I believe that if our people would get out and help elect friends of our measures and defeat our enemies, we should accomplish a great deal more than we do by getting women's clubs, churches, etc., to pass resolutions and look wise . . ." (quoted in Bryant, "Kate Barnard, Organized Labor, and Social Justice," 159–60). Also see Kate Barnard, "Working for the Friendless," *Independent* 63 (Nov. 28, 1907): 1307–1308, and "Human Ideals in Government," *Survey* 23 (Oct. 2, 1909): 16–20.

[139] An early student of public welfare in South Carolina wrote of the conference of charities and corrections in that state: "This body discussed problems of public and social welfare, conferred about the conduct of institutions, and stimulated popular interest in these subjects" (G. Croft Williams, in W. H. Calcott, ed., *South Carolina: Economic and Social Conditions in 1944* [Columbia, S.C., 1945], 206). Also see Shivers, "Some Variations in State Conferences of Social Work," 546–50.

[140] Foy Lisenby, "The First Meeting of the Arkansas Conference of Charities and Correction," *Ark. Hist. Quar.* 26 (Summer 1967): 155–61.

uplift of the state's blacks, for the improvement of country life, and for strict enforcement of prohibition. Leaders of the conference hoped to establish a forum for welfare concerns and a means of concentrating pressure for legislative reforms. The organization soon adopted the habit of meeting in Raleigh during the sessions of the general assembly. By the end of the summer of 1913, the conference had enrolled more than five hundred members.[141]

Another example of social welfare organization on the state level is afforded by Alabama. The statewide group created in 1910 seems to have had little influence and to have become inactive after a year or two. But in 1913 a new organization known as the Alabama Sociological Congress came into existence. At its second annual meeting in May 1914, the congress established a state social service committee with ten locals, launched an antituberculosis campaign, and made plans for a child welfare movement. A special section of the congress was presided over by blacks. The meeting of 1914 adopted a reform program for Alabama that called for a workmen's compensation act, compulsory education, new child labor laws, a state health code, antituberculosis legislation, equal suffrage, equitable distribution of school revenues, a prison and convict probation system, remedial loan legislation, and a state housing code.[142] The Alabama congress, as well as a number of other state conferences, was part of a larger movement whose most notable expression was the Southern Sociological Congress established in 1912.

The regional and state organizations concerned with social welfare reflected and gave impetus to the slow emergence of social work as a profession in the South. Generally, however, the administration of social services in the early twentieth century was dominated by nonprofessional workers and volunteers. Except for a few urban commnities, the development of the technical and professional aspects of social work was scarcely apparent in the South before 1917. For the most part, as one scholar has observed, "the reflective, intelligent layman was the dominant figure in the broader, regional social program initiated in the earlier decades of the twentieth century."[143] Social work, particularly in the South, did not yet have a distinctive focus. It was, as Roy Lubove cogently writes, "a compound of casework, settlement work, institutional and agency administration, and social reform, and anyone, paid or volunteer, who enlisted in the crusade to improve humanity's lot claimed the title of social worker."[144] The values and ideals that eventually infused the framework of

---

[141]Shivers, "The Social Welfare Movement in the South," 169–70; Steelman, "The Progressive Era in North Carolina," 630–31; William Foy Lisenby, "An Administrative History of Public Programs for Dependent Children in North Carolina, Virginia, Tennessee, and Kentucky, 1900–1942" (Ph.D. diss., Vanderbilt Univ., 1962), 11–25.

[142]"Some State Meetings," *Survey* 32 (May 30, 1914): 247; "Conferences," ibid. 34 (June 12, 1915): 253.

[143]Lyda Gordon Shivers, "Twentieth Century South-wide Civic and Lay Organizations for Human Welfare," in Vera Largent, ed., *The Walter Clinton Jackson Essays in the Social Sciences* (Chapel Hill, N.C., 1942), 187.

[144]Lubove, *The Professional Altruist*, 119.

professional action—rationality, universalism, disinterestedness, and specific-
ity of function—remained inchoate among the small contingent of southern
social workers.

Even so, the recruitment and professionalization of social workers in the
South had made some headway. Social workers had begun to be aware of their
group identity, even though they looked for professional guidance outside the
South. The Sociological Society of Georgia, for example, was operating as
early as 1905. The National Conference of Charities and Correction, while not
composed exclusively of paid workers, provided an opportunity for those
involved in social service activities to meet together for the exchange of professional experiences. When the NCCC met in Atlanta in 1903, 96 of the 1,550
members in the United States came from eleven southern states. The number of
southern members had increased to 141 by 1908 and to 677 (about 10 percent of
the nation's total) by 1914.[145] The charity organization movement, with its
emphasis on full-time secretaries and caseworkers, clearly contributed to this
increase, as did the establishment of new and more specialized state institutions. Local welfare commissions and councils of social agencies were being
formed in the South on the eve of World War I. [146] The organization of state and
regional conferences having to do with social welfare was, initially at least, a
response to the introduction of more adequate and better administered welfare
programs, and also to the growing number of professional workers in the southern states. A few of the region's states had created boards of control to govern
their penal, reformatory, and charitable institutions, and the other commonwealths would take similar action during the next few years. These developments seemed to indicate that the social welfare movement in the South was
emerging from its formative stage.

INTERRACIAL HARMONY AND BLACK UPLIFT

The rising tide of Negro proscription and racial alienation in the South at the
turn of the century swept aside the feeble restraints, from blacks and whites,
that occasionally were expressed in protest or misgiving. Black powerlessness
and the acommodationism embodied in the Atlanta Compromise largely determined the behavior and outlook of Negroes in the South. Most white southerners, while disagreeing on details, shared in the consensus that the new race

---

[145]Frank J. Bruno, *Trends in Social Work, 1874–1956: A History Based on the Proceedings of
the National Conference of Social Work*, 2d ed. (New York, 1957), 145; "A Virile Georgia
Society," *Charities* 14 (July 15, 1905): 919; Odum, "How New Is the South in Social Work?" 329.

[146]In November 1916, for instance, a group of social workers met in Nashville to organize a
Social Service Club. "What Nashville needs," the group announced, "is not more societies or
organizations to carry on its social work— we need more public support, more co-operation, and
closer co-ordination of the societies and organizations we now have" ("Brief History of the
Council of Community Agencies," undated flier in possession of author). See also Marvin C.
Crittenden, "A History of the Welfare Commission of Davidson County, Tennessee" (M.S.
thesis, Univ., of Tennessee School of Social Work, 1955).

settlement was necessary and that blacks should be kept in a subordinate position. Many southern progressives were willing to use racist means in their efforts to accomplish political and social reforms, and even the minority of whites that criticized repressive measures against Negroes were often motivated by a concern for whites rather than blacks.[147] One scholar who has examined the attitudes of white Baptists in Virginia on the race question found many expressions of concern about the the spiritual and educational welfare of black people. But he concluded that white interest in education was inspired by expediency and fear as well as Christian humanitarianism. Another historian has noted that while southern churches were inclined toward "kindliness and paternalism," they "equivocated" in dealing with the race problem.[148] Southern Methodists during the progressive era were willing to address the issue "through a Christian love that allowed distinctions to be made between a 'black brother in Christ' and a 'white brother in Christ.'"[149]

White southerners in the early twentieth century were basically concerned in their approach to the "race problem" with means of social control and social efficiency, and with a desire for "black docility."[150] To be sure, some of them were also motivated by humanitarian considerations. Yet even the "moderate-liberals," to use Ulrich B. Phillips's phrase, were primarily intent upon ensuring racial peace and harmony. These well-meaning moderates condemned lynching, stressed self-help, supported Tuskegee-style industrial education, and wanted economic opportunities for blacks with special talents. Their program, as a recent writer has observed, was based on "an updated version of paternalism in which whites would offer blacks help, guidance, and protection in exchange for a commitment to the New South values of thrift and hard work, as well as a continued subservience."[151] Moderates such as Bishop Charles B.

[147]Dewey W. Grantham, "Southern Progressives and the Racial Imperative," in *The Regional Imagination: The South and Recent American History* (Nashville, 1979), 77–106.

[148]H. Harrison Daniel, "Virginia Baptists and the Negro, 1865–1902," *Va. Mag. Hist. and Biog.* 76 (July 1968): 340–63; I. A. Newby, *Jim Crow's Defense: Anti-Negro Thought in America, 1900–1930* (Baton Rouge, 1965), 85–86.

[149]John O. Fish, "Southern Methodism and Accommodation of the Negro, 1902–1915," *Jour. Negro Hist.* 55 (July 1970): 200–14; quotation on p. 210. Also see Harvey K. Newman, "Piety and Segregation—White Protestant Attitudes Toward Blacks in Atlanta, 1865–1905," *Ga. Hist. Quar.* 63 (Summer 1979): 238–51, and Robert Moats Miller, "Southern White Protestantism and the Negro, 1865–1965," in Charles E. Wynes, ed., *The Negro in the South Since 1865: Selected Essays in American Negro History* (University, Ala., 1965), 231–47.

[150]Lawrence J. Friedman, "The Search for Docility: Social Thought in the White South, 1861–1917," *Phylon* 31 (Fall 1970): 313–23. Also see Mrs. L. H. Harris, "A Southern Woman's View," *Independent* 51 (May 18, 1899): 1354–55, and "The White Man in the South," ibid. (Dec. 28, 1899): 3475–77; A Southern Lawyer, "Remedies for Lynch Law," *Sewanee Review* 8 (Jan. 1900): 1–11; Albert Bushnell Hart, "The Outcome of the Southern Race Question," *North American Review* 188 (July 1908): 50–61; A Southern Woman, "The Negro: A Portrait," *Outlook* 96 (Sept. 10, 1910): 77–80; and Chester T. Crowell, "A Message to the North," *Independent* 70 (May 11, 1911): 990–94.

[151]Daniel Joseph Singal, "Ulrich B. Phillips: The Old South as the New," *Jour. Amer. Hist.* 63 (Mar. 1977): 871–91; quotation on p. 881.

Galloway of Mississippi emphasized the progress that blacks had made since Emancipation, regarded education as the best means of improving the Negro's character, reminded white southerners of their obligations to blacks, and urged that the race problem be dealt with in a spirit of understanding, reason, and Christian sympathy.[152]

The Episcopalian minister Edgar Gardner Murphy provides a revealing example of the southern racial moderate. The Negro's place in southern life absorbed much of Murphy's thought and energy. As early as 1893, during his ministry at Christ Church in Laredo, Texas, he had organized a public protest against the lynching of a black man by a local white mob. After becoming rector of St. John's Parish in Montgomery, late in 1898, he became involved in efforts to help black churches and in mission work among white millworkers. Early in 1900 he took the lead in organizing the Southern Society in Montgomery and became the most active leader in planning the much-publicized Conference on Race Relations which the society sponsored in the Alabama capital later that year. He wrote extensively on the "race question," and race relations proved to be a pervasive theme of his two books, *Problems of the Present South* (1904) and *The Basis of Ascendancy* (1909).[153]

Murphy's moderation was evident in his advocacy of white restraint in the treatment of blacks, in his opposition to lynching and peonage, and in his work for interracial harmony and accommodation. Most black leaders in the South apparently regarded Murphy as a friend of their race. "The real South," the Alabama minister thought, "—the South of the businessman, the educator, the churches, the schools, the homes—is helping the negro today as never before since the moment of emancipation."[154] Murphy's racial humanitarianism was mirrored in these words from an article published in 1907: "Here is this colored man whom you and I know to be 'a good negro'—industrious, sensible, self-respecting. He is making his way. He counts for something. We know him and we know we can trust him. He is right here with us on the soil of the same State. Do we want him? We do. Do we want him to stay? We do. How shall we deal with him? Treat him justly. Give protection to his life and property. Give his children a chance. Let *him* vote."[155] If blacks were given economic and educational opportunities, if they were encouraged to develop their own self-sufficient social and cultural life, Murphy argued, they would demonstrate their latent racial genius, evolve a sound separate culture, and thus lose any desire they might have to amalgamate with whites. Education was basic to the cler-

---

[152]Newby, *Jim Crow's Defense*, pp. ix–x, 87, 100–101.

[153]Bailey, *Edgar Gardner Murphy*, 21–64, 109–37.

[154]Quoted in Bruce Clayton, *The Savage Ideal: Intolerance and Intellectual Leadership in the South, 1890–1914* (Baltimore, 1972), 197.

[155]Murphy, "The Task of the Leader: A Discussion of Some of the Conditions of Public Leadership in Our Southern States," *Sewanee Review* 15 (Jan. 1907): 11. Also see Ronald C. White, Jr., "Beyond the Sacred: Edgar Gardner Murphy and a Ministry of Social Reform," *Hist. Mag. Prot. Epis. Church* 49 (Mar. 1980): 51–69.

gyman's reform efforts. As he said, "Education is the process by which the irresponsible are bound into the life of the responsible . . . by which a people is changed from a mob into a society."[156] The answer to his rhetorical question about schools for the black southerner was obvious: "Shall we keep him in the condition which best fits him to follow vile leaders, with low appeals and evil passions, to bad government; or shall we guard him against that day by educating him enough to make him amenable to the influence of reason and right?"[157]

Despite his moderation and good will, Murphy's racial policy rested on his conviction that blacks were inferior to whites. This accounted for his fear of "racial fusion" and his emphasis on the maintenance of "racial integrity." He found no fault with segregation laws, the dual system of public education, or the legal disfranchisement of virtually all blacks. In theory the Alabama minister opposed unequal enforcement of the suffrage restrictions, which he regarded as establishing for blacks and whites an incentive to education and the ownership of property. But he eventually decided that some illiterate white men deserved the ballot, since, he asserted, the white man "excels the negro voter by the genius of his race, by inherited capacity and by a political training which has formed part of the tradition of his class."[158] Murphy's paternalism toward blacks, his fear of offending more racist southerners, and his pronounced sectional bias limited his effectiveness as an advocate of black uplift.[159]

Early in the century Edgar Gardner Murphy seemed to be optimistic about the chances of greater racial tolerance, interracial cooperation, northern assistance, developing black leadership, and Negro progress in the areas of economic enterprise and education. But through the years Murphy was less hopeful about the future than many other southern progressives. He distrusted the philosophy of material progress, did not consider education a social panacea, and had only modest expectations as far as the various reform movements were concerned. Indeed, his hopes were tinged with anxiety resulting from his feeling that a great crisis threatened the South, especially in race relations. These forebodings reflected his apprehension over the upsurge of the region's white masses, the exploitative character of the burgeoning industrial system, and the disappearance of the old restraints which he associated with the social order, self-discipline, and noblesse oblige of the Old South. Injustice toward blacks, Murphy warned, would harm whites by spawning hate and lowering the standards of southern social, economic, and political life. Aggression

---

[156]Quoted in Levine, "Edgar Gardner Murphy," 111.

[157]Quoted in Claude H. Nolen, *The Negro's Image in the South: The Anatomy of White Supremacy* (Lexington, Ky., 1967), 130.

[158]Quoted in H. Shelton Smith, *In His Image, But . . . Racism in Southern Religion, 1780–1910* (Durham, N.C., 1972), 288–89. See also Edgar Gardner Murphy, "The Freedman's Progress in the South," *Outlook* 68 (July 27, 1901): 721–24, and "Shall the Fourteenth Amendment Be Enforced?" *North American Review* 180 (Jan. 1905): 109–33.

[159]See "Editorial Note," in Louis R. Harlan and associates, eds., *The Booker T. Washington Papers*, vol. 5 (Urbana, Ill., 1976), 407n.

against the black man would destroy "not the negro, nor the white man only, but society itself,—society as a sufficient instrument of equitable and profitable relations."[160] Many others agreed with William Garrott Brown's judgment that "the main thing is not what to do for the negro, but what to do for the white man living among negroes."[161]

The failure of Murphy and other southern moderates to carry through with their original plans to perpetuate the Montgomery race conference at the turn of the century points up the impotence and indifference of even well-meaning white leaders in countering the powerful tide of anti-Negro sentiment in the South. During the first decade of the new century there was no significant organization of white southerners devoting itself to the amelioration of the black plight. In the wake of the Atlanta riot of 1906, a group of moderates in that city created a "Southern Commission on the Race Problem," as a means of investigating and disseminating "the essential facts of this great problem." Little came of these plans, however, and one of the participants, writing in October 1907, cited as an explanation "a natural inertia of the public mind on the subject of the negro."[162] Northern philanthropy, while still a major element in the operation of black schools in the region, had generally accepted the rationale of the white educators who led the southern education movement. Blacks themselves pursued a variety of self-help and social improvement schemes, but they had few resources with which to work, and they were for the most part committed to Booker T. Washington's philosophy of acquiescence and accommodationism. Whatever their sympathies for black people, southern white moderates usually spoke, as one historian has remarked, in "the most glittering of generalities." They "offered enthusiasm, pious phrases, and uplifting as substitutes for realistic reform."[163] Or, as Edwin A. Alderman said of the issue in addressing a northern audience in 1908, "The deeper one's knowledge goes, the greater one's desire for silence and patience."[164]

Nevertheless, there were faint stirrings of new and more liberal approaches to race relations in the South. Within the framework of segregation, a body of

---

[160] Quoted in George M. Fredrickson, *The Black Image in the White Mind: The Debate on Afro-American Character and Destiny, 1817–1914* (New York, 1971), 297.

[161] Quoted in Wendell H. Stephenson, "William Garrott Brown: Literary Historian and Essayist," *JSH* 12 (Aug. 1946): 327. The Atlanta minister John E. White expressed the opinion that limitation and denial of privilege to blacks constituted no barrier to true progress: "I believe that restrictive dealing, for the Negro is wise dealing, not because I dislike or fear him, but because he needs its discipline" (White, "The Need of a Southern Program on the Negro Problem," *SAQ* 6 [Apr. 1907]: 184).

[162] John E. White to Ray Stannard Baker, Oct. 7, 1907, Ray Stannard Baker Papers, Manuscripts Division, Library of Congress. Also see C.B. Wilmer, "Story of the Atlanta Race Riot of 1906," undated manuscript in Papers of the Commission on Interracial Cooperation, Atlanta University.

[163] Newby, *Jim Crow's Defense*, 186.

[164] Alderman, *The Growing South: An Address Delivered before the Civic Forum in Carnegie Hall, New York City, March 22, 1908* (New York, 1908), 10.

moderate thought on race was beginning to develop among white southern-ers.[165] Inchoate and unorganized, this thinking reflected a desire to moderate harsher aspects of white supremacy, to defend the right of blacks to education and legal protection, and even to enfranchise "qualified" Negroes. The most striking of the white liberals on the race question were ministers and church women, particularly in the Southern Methodist church.[166] Compassion and paternalism shaped the approach of these liberals, one of whom asserted in 1902 that "our lower classes must be made to realize, by whatever means, that the black man has rights which they are bound to respect. . . ."[167]

No white southerner was more closely identified with the new liberal spirit in matters of race than Willis Duke Weatherford, the International Student Secre-tary of the YMCA for the colleges of the South and Southwest. A native of Texas and a graduate of Vanderbilt, Weatherford was a man of deep religious convictions and a strong advocate of "social Christianity." After he became YMCA secretary in 1902, he traveled widely through the southern states. One of his mounting concerns was the treatment of blacks in the South. As a result he helped organize study groups among college students for the purpose of learning more about the problem. In 1908 he arranged an interracial conference of "Y" men to consider the need for cooperative study of the "race problem." The men who attended this conference assumed that knowledge about the problem and contact among the better elements of both races would result in better race relations. They persuaded Weatherford to prepare a textbook for use in YMCA home mission classes. This pioneering study, *Negro Life in the South: Present Conditions and Needs,* was published in 1910. It was a success, and two years later the author brought out a more comprehensive treatment under the title *Present Forces in Negro Progress.* During the next few years Weatherford spoke and wrote extensively on the race question, and he was also active in promoting various conferences and meetings dealing with aspects of black life in the South.[168]

[165]Clayton, *The Savage Ideal,* 77–103; Fredrickson, *The Black Image in the White Mind,* 284–305.

[166]See, for example, Charles E. Wynes, ed., *Forgotten Voices: Dissenting Southerners in an Age of Conformity* (Baton Rouge, 1967); Wynes, "The Reverend Quincy Ewing: Southern Racial Heretic in the 'Cajun' Country," *La. Hist.* 7 (Summer 1966): 221–28; Wynes, "Bishop Thomas U. Dudley and the Uplift of the Negro," *Reg. Ky. Hist. Soc.* 65 (July 1967): 230–38; Wendell H. Stephenson, "The Negro in the Thinking and Writing of John Spencer Bassett," *N.C. Hist. Rev.* 25 (Oct. 1948): 427–41; Henry Y. Warnock, "Andrew Sledd, Southern Methodists, and the Negro: A Case history," *JSH* 31 (Aug. 1965): 251–71; and L. Moody Simms, Jr., "Theodore Dubose Bratton, Christian Principles, and the Race Question," *Jour. Miss. Hist.* 38 (Feb. 1976): 47–52.

[167]Andrew Sledd, "The Negro: Another View," *Atlantic Monthly* 90 (July 1902): 65–73; quotation on p. 72. See also Quincy Ewing, "The Heart of the Race Problem," *Atlantic Monthly* 103 (Mar. 1909): 389–97.

[168]George Peter Antone, Jr., "Willis Duke Weatherford: An Interpretation of His Work in Race Relations, 1906–1946" (Ph.D. diss., Vanderbilt Univ., 1969); Wilma Dykeman, *Prophet of Plenty: The First Ninety Years of W.D. Weatherford* (Knoxville, 1966); Edward Flud Burrows,

Southern paternalism toward blacks, a dominant concept in the pattern of race relations in the early twentieth-century South, was "graduated between the extremes of benevolence and malevolence."[169] Weatherford's paternalism was heavily weighted toward benevolence but infused with traditional assumptions about blacks. He shared the southern white view of "the terrible results" of Reconstruction and tended to romanticize social relations in the Old South. He believed there was a definite Negro character and temperament, and he spoke of such black "weaknesses" as overindulgence in food, liquor, tobacco, and sex. On the other hand, he stressed such "virtues" as fidelity, generosity, kindliness, a sense of humor, and a peculiar aptitude for music and religion as ineradicable racial traits. Although Weatherford regarded blacks as a "belated race," he emphasized environmental conditions as a significant force in shaping the race's development. Black people, in Weatherford's opinion, were capable of progress. Writing in 1913, he noted the encouraging growth of "race pride and race consciousness" on the part of black southerners. "When the Negro has become economically efficient, intellectually more advanced, racially self conscious," he declared, "there will be far less friction, for he will then feel as the white man feels that racial integrity and social separation are best for both races. . . ."[170] The YMCA secretary had sharp words for southern demogogues — "these so-called defenders of the white man's honor and the white woman's virtue."[171] He thought most white southerners had good intentions toward blacks, and he was convinced that Negroes needed the "helpful co-operation" of white men in order to advance. Such help, Weatherford believed, was a matter of noblesse oblige and a burden that whites should assume in the interest of "a larger and truer humanity." At the same time, Weatherford emphasized the interdependence of all southerners, white and black. Southern progress, he felt, ultimately depended upon progress in race relations. Every welfare movement for whites must become a welfare movement for blacks as well.

Willis D. Weatherford's emergence as an active reformer in race relations was, in part at least, a consequence of the YMCA's slow but quickening concern about the South's "race problem." There were similar indications of humanitarian interest in black conditions among certain other religious organizations in the region, particularly among a number of women in the Southern Methodist church. Although some Methodist women had made efforts in the late nineteenth century to improve the condition of black people, it was not until after 1900 that a unified approach to the problem began to evolve. Moving

"The Commission on Interracial Cooperation, 1914–1944: A Case Study in the History of the Interracial Movement in the South" (Ph.D. diss., Univ. of Wisconsin, 1954), 1–43.

[169]Guion Griffis Johnson, "Southern Paternalism toward Negroes after Emancipation," *JSH* 23 (Nov. 1957): 483–509.

[170]Weatherford, "Race Relations in the South," *Annals* 49 (Sept. 1913): 164–72.

[171]Weatherford, *Negro Life in the South*, 12.

Class in "Negro Life in the South," Vanderbilt University, 1910–11. The course was not a formal part of the university curriculum and was probably sponsored by the YMCA. *Photographic Archive, Vanderbilt University.*

beyond moral pronouncements, the Woman's Home Mission Society in 1901 launched a concrete program of action. One of its projects was the construction of an annex at Paine College in Augusta, Georgia, to be devoted to industrial training for black girls. The money needed to build the annex was raised, and thereafter the project received the steady support of Methodist women. In 1911, Mary De Bardeleben, a young Alabamian who had been graduated from the Methodist Training School in Nashville, was designated as the first Southern Methodist missionary to American blacks. She began her work in Augusta and in 1912 took the lead in opening the church's first community center for blacks. Meanwhile, the annual meetings of the Woman's Missionary Council devoted increasing attention to racial affairs. The council reported in 1915 that 244 auxiliaries in twenty conferences were at work on specific undertakings among Negroes.[172]

There were several prominent activists in the race relations activities sponsored by Methodist women in the South. One of these leaders was Belle H. Bennett of Kentucky, who served for many years as president of the Woman's Home Mission Society and of the Woman's Missionary Council. Another Kentuckian who played an important part in this work was Mary Helm, editor of *Our Homes,* the official publication of the Home Mission Society. Estelle Haskin, a member of the faculty of the Methodist Training School, was the creative spirit in organizing Bethlehem House in Nashville and in developing its extensive program. There were many others, including Lily Hardy Hammond. Mrs. Hammond and her husband, a Methodist minister and educator, were advocates of greater church support of black education and especially of Paine College. Despite her poor health, Mrs. Hammond labored tirelessly through Methodist organizations and meetings to advance the cause of southern blacks. She was also a prolific writer. In 1914 she summed up her thinking on the social and religious aspects of the race problem in a book entitled *In Black and White: An Interpretation of Southern Life*. She portrayed the injustices of the South's system of race relations, urged equitable treatment of blacks, and sought to arouse a social conscience in the region. She was particularly concerned about the pitifully inadequate housing for southern blacks.[173]

Many of the Southern Methodist women were no doubt more interested in evangelical activities than in social work among blacks. But a missionary emphasis of this sort was more characteristic of Baptists than of Methodists in the South. The traditional policy of Southern Baptists stressed the moral and spiritual welfare of the individual black. Thus the Southern Baptist Convention gave little attention before World War I to the social problems of Negroes. The

[172]Tatum, *A Crown of Service*, 349, 355–57, 367–69, 388; Henry Y. Warnock, "Moderate Racial Thought and Attitudes of Southern Baptists and Methodists, 1900–1921" (Ph.D. diss., Northwestern Univ., 1963), 43–50.
[173]Warnock, "Moderate Racial Thought and Attitudes of Southern Baptists and Methodists," 50, 61, 69–72, 77.

Women's Missionary Union, an auxiliary of the Southern Baptist Convention, was slow in asserting itself in the field of social work, although it took a leading role in the operation of the "good-will centers" the church began to sponsor in 1912. Organized efforts among Southern Baptists to ameliorate the suffering of black people, like those of most other white churches in the region, were limited and relatively inconsequential until the war period and the 1920s.[174] Even so, a careful scholar concludes that for Baptist leaders in the South the first two decades of the twentieth century were in many respects, including racial thought, "a watershed that stood between traditional ideas of reform and new concepts being restructured under the impact of the contemporary technological, urbanized, business society."[175]

Thomas Pearce Bailey, a southern educator, published a book on "the Negro Question" in 1914 in which he reminded his fellow southerners that "all the fire" had gone out of "the Northern philanthropic fight for the rights of man." As a matter of fact, Bailey asserted, "the North has surrendered!"[176] Although the southern author's point was exaggerated and failed to take into account the embryonic development of a more militant spirit in the North, his statement was essentially valid for the early years of the century. Black expectations in the presidential leadership of Theodore Roosevelt and William Howard Taft had been dashed. Congress had made no concerted effort to guarantee black rights even within the subordinated social order set up by southern legislatures, courts, and private groups. The Supreme Court had, for the most part, acquiesced in the South's new racial dispensation. The northern press, including many erstwhile advocates of Negro rights, adopted a sympathetic attitude toward the racial policies and arguments of southern whites. Northern and western progressives were generally apathetic and sometimes hostile toward black uplift as a part of their reform agendas.[177]

Northern philanthropists, in their strong endorsement of the Tuskegee model in black education and in the compromise they struck with southern white educators, also contributed in subtle as well as direct ways to the implementa-

[174]Ibid., 201; John Lee Eighmy, "The Social Conscience of Southern Baptists from 1900 to the Present as Reflected in Their Organized Life" (Ph.D. diss., Univ. of Missouri, 1959), 14–17, 62–63.

[175]Henry Y. Warnock, "Prophets of Change: Some Southern Baptist Leaders and the Problem of Race, 1900–1921," *Baptist History and Heritage* 7 (July 1972): 183. For the ideas of several Baptist leaders, see Josiah W. Bailey, "Popular Education and the Race Problem in North Carolina," *Outlook* 68 (May 11, 1901): 114–16; Charles Hillman Brough, "Work of the Commission of Southern Universities on the Race Question," *Annals* 49 (Sept. 1913): 47–57; and Daniel W. Hollis, "Samuel Chiles Mitchell, Social Reformer in Blease's South Carolina," *S.C. Hist. Mag.* 70 (Jan. 1969): 22–23, 27–28.

[176]Bailey, *Race Orthodoxy in the South and Other Aspects of the Negro Question* (New York, 1914), 29.

[177]C. Vann Woodward, *The Strange Career of Jim Crow*, 2d rev. ed. (New York, 1966), 69–74, 102–104; David W. Southern, *The Malignant Heritage: Yankee Progressives and the Negro Question, 1901–1914* (Chicago, 1968); Dewey W. Grantham, "The Progressive Movement and the Negro," *SAQ* 54 (Oct. 1955): 461–77.

tion of the Atlanta Compromise of 1895. Penn School on St. Helena Island, South Carolina, provides a good example. First founded by white missionaries soon after Emancipation, this northern-supported institution for blacks was reorganized in 1900 and made into a normal, industrial, and agricultural school patterned after Hampton and Tuskegee. The school's sponsors wanted to train "both parents and children in better methods of farming, which will result in making farms pay," to teach them "industries needed in an agricultural community," and "to intimately associate religion with everyday life."[178] This kind of emphasis on self-help appealed to both white and black leaders in the South; it found expression in two distinct but frequently related efforts—to promote economic advancement and to encourage personal regeneration among southern blacks.

Booker T. Washington's activities as a social reformer mirrored these themes. He supported such reform causes as prohibition, antivice campaigns, and the southern education movement. Through farmers' conferences, the National Negro Business League, land-purchasing revolving funds, all-black towns, and countless public addresses and magazine articles, he sought to encourage economic and moral development and to foster racial pride, self-help, and personal autonomy among blacks. His concern for family organization, education, and improved community life was evident in his many schemes for black strength and mutual aid. Behind the scenes, Washington was sometimes more combative than conciliatory. Thus he privately opposed the disfranchisement laws and secretly directed court cases against segregated railroad facilities, peonage, and the exclusion of blacks from jury panels. He fought a hard but losing battle to stem the tide of the lily-white movement in the Republican party in the various southern states. In his correspondence Washington occasionally revealed his dissatisfaction with the "reforms" of southern progressives. "Much of the advance in the direction of white education," the black leader complained in 1909, "is being made at the expense of Negro education, that is, the money is being taken from the colored people and given to white schools. The conditions in some sections of the rural South so far as Negro education is concerned are pitiable."[179]

The self-help and developmental emphases of the annual Tuskegee conferences on agriculture found expression in similar gatherings throughout the South. Hampton Institute, for example, sponsored a yearly convention for the purpose of reviewing the progress made by black Americans. Five hundred black southerners—"doctors, lawyers, ministers, business men, proprietor

[178]Quoted in I. A. Newby, *Black Carolinians: A History of Blacks in South Carolina from 1895 to 1968* (Columbia, S.C., 1973), 104. See also Elizabeth Jacoway, "Education for Life: The Penn School Experience," *South Atlantic Urban Studies* 2 (1978): 89–103.

[179]Washington to George Foster Peabody, July 30, 1909, Booker T. Washington Papers, Manuscripts Division, Library of Congress. See also Louis R. Harlan, "The Secret Life of Booker T. Washington," *JSH* 37 (Aug. 1971): 393–416, and Grantham, *The Regional Imagination*, 94–96.

farmers, and teachers"—were reported in attendance at the conference of 1909.[180] In 1904, Arkansas Baptist College, an institution founded by a black leader named Joseph A. Booker, convened a conference of Negro farmers. The assembled farmers adopted a series of resolutions, recommending that "our people everywhere renew their effort to buy lands, beautify their homes, pay their poll tax, and steer clear of unnecessary debts"; that they "do all they can to support the public schools in their communities"; and that they do their best "to live on peaceable terms with their neighbors, of whatever color."[181]

This kind of approach to racial progress and better social conditions was critically dependent upon the examples of the most widely known black leaders. Washington was preeminent among these leaders, but in every state there were locally influential advocates of self-help. Some of these men and women organized improvement societies, civic associations, and Tuskegee "daughter schools" like Snow Hill Institute in Alabama and Utica Institute in Mississippi. Robert Lloyd Smith, for instance, founded the Farmers' Improvement Agricultural College in Texas. The Reverend Richard Carroll of Columbia, South Carolina, to cite another example, operated an industrial home for blacks, organized a number of race conferences, and attracted wide support from whites as well as blacks. According to the Columbia publisher William E. Gonzales, the black minister "speaks the truth as he sees it to both races, without fear or favor, and has respectful auditors. He is seeking the upbuilding of his people on moral and Industrial foundations; he preaches justice in the service of the Negroes to the Whites and justice in the treatment of the Negroes by the Whites."[182] Men like Carroll served as the focal point for the expression of black attitudes and aspirations.

In the late nineteenth and early twentieth centuries many southern black leaders, frustrated with the failure of Reconstruction and the intensification of Jim Crow, turned to the school and church as institutions in which their hopes for self-help, race pride, and separation might be realized. By 1915 the drive for black autonomy had resulted in 60 percent of the teachers being Negro in the secondary schools and colleges in the South founded by or receiving support from northern missionary sources, though the white influence was still paramount in the major colleges.[183] Such developments represented both an accommodation to and a protest against the dominant trend in southern race

---

[180]"Definite Progress Among Negroes," *Outlook* 92 (July 31, 1909): 770. For the Tuskegee conferences, see "The Tuskegee Conference," ibid. 79 (Mar. 11, 1905): 619; Harlan and associates, eds., *The Booker T. Washington Papers*, vol. 5, pp. 99–100; and Linda O. McMurry, *George Washington Carver: Scientist and Symbol* (New York, 1981), 114–18.

[181]"A Declaration by Negro Farmers," *Outlook* 76 (Mar. 19, 1904): 671.

[182]Gonzales to "My Friends, and Others Whom This May Concern," Nov. 1, 1905, Baker Papers. See also Newby, *Black Carolinians*, 163–84. For the career of another black leader, see David E. Alsobrook, "Mobile's Forgotten Progressive—A.N. Johnson, Editor and Entrepreneur," *Ala. Rev.* 32 (July 1979): 188–202.

[183]James M. McPherson, "White Liberals and Black Power in Negro Education, 1865–1915," *Amer. Hist. Rev.* 75 (June 1970): 1357–86.

relations during this period. The growth of a black middle class and an increasingly self-conscious professional status among Negro teachers and similar groups encouraged the process of institutional development. In Richmond, for example, "an interlocking network" of black men and women championed the interests of the Afro-American community. This network, one historian writes, included businessmen who preached the value of thrift, Baptist clergymen who often doubled as local entrepreneurs, educators, social workers, journalists, lawyers, and physicians.[184]

As time passed, a new mood of impatience and disillusionment was evident among a minority of black leaders and northern liberals. Much of this dissatisfaction centered on the leadership of Booker T. Washington. Oswald Garrison Villard, one of the founders of the National Association for the Advancement of Colored People, complained after the Tuskegean spoke at a Lincoln Day dinner in 1909: "It is always the same thing, platitudes, stories, high praise for the Southern white man who is helping the negro up, insistence that the way to favor lies through owning lands and farms, etc., etc.; all note of the higher aspiration is wanting."[185] Though Washington's philosophy undoubtedly represented "the basic tendencies of Negro thought" in the early years of the twentieth century,[186] the "new slavery" in the South was producing a revival of the antislavery impulse, and a "new abolitionist movement" was slowly emerging.[187] The most conspicuous manifestation of this impulse was the organization in 1909 of the NAACP. The new militancy was beginning to have some effect, by the opening of the second decade of the century, on the thought and behavior of the black middle class and professional people in the region. Three things ought to be done at once, William E.B. Du Bois asserted in 1907: black people "should be given good common schools," they "should be allowed to vote on the same terms as other people," and they "should be given humane treatment." William Jefferson White, black editor of the *Georgia Baptist,*

[184]Raymond Gavins, "Urbanization and Segregation: Black Leadership Patterns in Richmond, Virginia, 1900–1920," *SAQ* 79 (Summer 1980): 257–73. See also W.E. Burghardt Du Bois, "The Upbuilding of Black Durham," *World's Work* 23 (Jan. 1912): 334–38; August Meier, *Negro Thought in America, 1880–1915: Racial Ideologies in the Age of Booker T. Washington* (Ann Arbor, Mich., 1963), 121–57; August Meier and David Lewis, "History of the Negro Upper Class in Atlanta, 1890–1958," *Journal of Negro Education* 28 (Spring 1959): 128–39; John Dittmer, *Black Georgia in the Progressive Era, 1900–1920* (Urbana, Ill., 1977), 60–65, 145–62, 169–74; Linda O. Hines and Allen W. Jones, "A Voice of Black Protest: The Savannah Men's Sunday Club, 1905–1911," *Phylon* 35 (June 1974): 193–202; and Zane L. Miller, "Urban Blacks in the South, 1865–1920: The Richmond, Savannah, New Orleans, Louisville and Birmingham Experience," in Leo F. Schnore, ed., *The New Urban History: Quantitative Explorations by American Historians* (Princeton, N.J., 1975), 184–204.

[185]Villard to William Lloyd Garrison, Feb. 24, 1909, Oswald Garrison Villard Papers, Harvard University Library.

[186]Meier, *Negro Thought in America, 1880–1915*, p. 102.

[187]James M. McPherson, "The Antislavery Legacy: From Reconstruction to the NAACP," in Barton J. Bernstein, ed., *Towards a New Past: Dissenting Essays in American History* (New York, 1968), 126–57, and *The Abolitionist Legacy: From Reconstruction to the NAACP* (Princeton, N.J., 1975), 299–393. See also Southern, *The Malignant Heritage*, 55–66.

arranged an equal rights convention in 1906 that attracted several hundred black Georgians. The conference issued a statement of grievances containing this declaration: "We do not deny that some of us are not yet fit for the ballot; but we do affirm that the majority of us are fit—fit by our growing intelligence, our ownership of property, and our conservative law-abiding tendencies;—and in any case certainly disfranchisement and oppression will not increase our fitness, nor will they settle the race problem."[188]

Negro newspapers like the Nashville *Globe* and the Richmond *Planet* and pioneering research ventures such as the *Publications* directed by Du Bois at Atlanta University were important agents of black progressivism.[189] The Nahville *Globe* was the voice of black men who, being resigned to the white demands for a system based on caste, became advocates of a parallel black "system" with its own board of trade, self-sufficient business community, "equal" schools, segregated parks, and pride in its own race. The editors of the *Globe* recognized the depressed status of southern Negroes but rejected the idea of racial inferiority and dependence upon white paternalism. They were optimistic, aggressive in tone, and determined to stress the potential strength of the black population rather than its moral and economic weaknesses.[190]

One manifestation of such strength was a series of boycotts organized against Jim Crow streetcars early in the century. These protests, which frequently included legal challenges and efforts to establish alternative means of transportation, were organized in at least twenty-five southern cities between 1900 and 1906. Although overt resistance of this character seldom appeared after 1906, these protests were quite remarkable in view of the powerful sweep of southern proscription and northern acquiescence in the South's new racial settlement.[191] The black reform spirit was also apparent in such civic betterment bodies as Negro boards of trade, equal rights associations, ward improvement groups, and law and order leagues. These endeavors combined, in varying degree, such purposes as self-help, protest, racial pride, and black welfare. Indeed, despite

---

[188]William M. Tuttle, Jr., ed., "W.E.B. Du Bois' Confrontation with White Liberalism During the Progressive Era: A Phylon Document," *Phylon* 35 (Fall 1974): 251; "What the Southern Negroes Think of Themselves," *Public Opinion* 40 (Mar. 10, 1906): 305.

[189]Du Bois and a few other investigators were responsible for the beginnings of scholarly black studies in the United States, one result of which was the first significant alteration in the "static image" of black southerners. See George B. Tindall, "Southern Negroes Since Reconstruction: Dissolving the Static Image," in Arthur S. Link and Rembert W. Patrick, eds., *Writing Southern History: Essays in Historiography in Honor of Fletcher M. Green* (Baton Rouge, 1965), 340–44; Elliott M. Rudwick, *W.E.B. Du Bois: A Study in Minority Group Leadership* (Philadelphia, 1960), 34–36, 39–53.

[190]Lester C. Lamon, *Black Tennesseans, 1900–1930* (Knoxville, 1977), 14–19, 209–15.

[191]See the articles by August Meier and Elliott Rudwick: "The Boycott Movement Against Jim Crow Streetcars in the South, 1900–1906," *Jour. Amer. Hist.* 55 (Mar. 1969): 756–75; "Negro Boycotts of Jim Crow Streetcars in Tennessee," *Amer. Quar.* 21 (Winter 1969): 755–63; "Negro Boycotts of Segregated Streetcars in Florida, 1901–1905," *SAQ* 69 (Aug. 1970); 525–33; and "Negro Boycotts of Segregated Streetcars in Virginia, 1904–1907," *Va. Mag. Hist. and Biog.* 81 (Oct. 1973): 479–87.

the expanding social justice activities of white southerners, black uplift was largely consigned to the black community itself.

Welfare activities undertaken by black organizations included orphanages, old folks' homes, hospitals, day nurseries, and settlement houses. Self-help cultural societies also existed. Black women played a vital role in these reform activities. The nucleus of their relief and improvement projects was the local club or association. Eventually a personal and political network of educated black women was created, in part through membership in the National Association of Colored Women.[192] Meanwhile, a new national organization made its appearance. The National Urban League, which was formed in 1911 with the support of white philanthropists, was intent upon promoting the social welfare of blacks. George Edmund Haynes, a young black professor at Fisk University, became the league's director of southern field activities. Haynes quickly decided to set up a training school for black social workers and to use the league as a means of coordinating the welfare efforts of Negro women's clubs, the business efficiency programs of the boards of trade and business leagues, the morality crusades of the "colored" ministerial alliances, and the housing and school improvement appeals of other black community organizations. He tried unsuccessfully to establish a "State Wide City Community Betterment Organization" in Tennessee.[193]

Most black leaders in the progressive period were moderates who recognized the reality of racial segregation but hoped to curb racial violence and intimidation, promote justice for black people in the courts, build educational facilities for Negroes, enlarge economic opportunities for the race, and strengthen institutions and race pride. These spokesmen tended to be optimistic about Negro prospects and to think progress would result from hard work and a cooperative attitude on the part of blacks. The ideological narrowness and social conservatism of many Negro leaders, particularly in the black church, led to preoccupation with "other worldliness," individual regeneration, and stress upon the need for the good will of whites. Some black leaders were torn "between assuming the mantle of racial leadership and giving in to feelings of superiority" toward the black masses.[194] A certain ambivalence in the outlook of southern black progressives was a natural consequence of their race pride and their resentment over the discrimination they suffered at the hands of white

[192] Hall, *Revolt Against Chivalry*, 77–86.

[193] Lamon, *Black Tennesseans*, 214–30; Arvarh E. Strickland, *History of the Chicago Urban League* (Urbana, Ill., 1966), 18–24; Nancy J. Weiss, "From Black Separatism to Interracial Cooperation: The Origins of Organized Efforts for Racial Advancement, 1890–1920," in Barton J. Bernstein and Allen J. Matusow, eds., *Twentieth-Century America: Recent Interpretations*, 2 ed. (New York, 1972), 52–87.

[194] See, for instance, John Michael Matthews, "The Dilemma of Negro Leadership in the New South: The Case of the Negro Young People's Congress of 1902," *SAQ* 73 (Winter 1974): 130–44, and Dorothy A. Gay, "Crisis of Identity: The Negro Community in Raleigh, 1890–1900," *N.C. Hist. Rev.* 50 (Apr. 1973): 121–40.

southerners. They were forever confronted with pressures both overt and subtle to see themselves through the eyes of the dominant whites—as an inferior race and as a problem to the white society and even to themselves. The degree to which they resisted these pressures was a measure of their autonomy and self-respect.

By the time Woodrow Wilson entered the White House in March 1913, the social justice campaigns involving child labor, women's rights, organized charity, and to a limited extent race relations had all more or less reached a new stage in their evolution. Encouraged by the new middle class, by such groups as the General Federation of Women's Clubs, by growing concern in the churches about social problems, and by the emergence of specific organizations to promote reform, the social justice movements had begun to acquire a regional configuration. This was revealed in many ways but most clearly perhaps in the organization of state and regional associations dedicated to particular reforms. Yet it was also apparent, despite the peculiar sectional nature of these reform movements, that they had been significantly affected by "progressive" standards and procedures from outside the South. Indeed, a nationalizing trend was under way in several of the progressive campaigns. In some cases the South was influencing the rest of the country. A rising class of urban and professional southerners, for instance, had begun to formulate a more moderate racial policy that appealed strongly to white Americans in other regions. Broadly speaking, the South, like the Northeast and Midwest in earlier years, was struggling to find a means of organizing its resources in fields such as social welfare, first through voluntary and private channels and then increasingly through public facilities at the state and local levels. The process was graphically illustrated in the movement for public education in the southern states.

8

Education and the Southern Redemption

NO ASPECT OF SOCIAL REFORM in the South during the progressive era touched the lives of more of the region's inhabitants than the great educational awakening soon after the turn of the century. Nor did any other movement of uplift mirror more faithfully the varied ingredients in southern progressivism and the strengths and weaknesses of the reform spirit in the South. It elicited widespread support from southerners and was the beneficiary of extraordinary northern philanthropy. It provides a striking illustration of the way in which social action in the southern states almost automatically assumed a regional character. It absorbed the energies and devotion of the South's new middle class and professionals, while exemplifying what C. Vann Woodward has called "that mixture of paternalism and *noblesse oblige* which is the nearest Southern equivalent of Northern humanitarianism."[1] In the South, an attentive observer pointed out in 1913:

> the machinery for social amelioration is to a large extent educational. Whether it be the hook worm in South Carolina or bad housing in Texas that is attacked, efforts to make the South a better place in which to live emanate to a surprising degree from state departments of education, agricultural colleges, state universities, sectarian colleges, secondary schools, and—praise be!—one-room rural schools.[2]

The campaigns for education provoked discussion and controversy over the proper role of the state, the meaning of democracy, the most desirable kind of schooling, and the place of blacks in the educational system.

Although the upheaval in southern politics during the 1890s momentarily spurred the hopes of educational reformers in the South and promised to implement the dormant provisions of the Reconstruction school statutes, the section as a whole remained in the slough of public poverty and a rudimentary school system. Outside of the larger cities, there was really no system of public

---

[1]Woodward, *Origins of the New South, 1877–1913* (Baton Rouge, 1951), 401.
[2]Warren Dunham Foster, "Southern Schoolmen and the Circle of Life," *Survey* 30 (May 10, 1913): 216.

education worthy of the name, and the numerous private institutions were for the most part little better. The usual school term was only three or four months, with scarcely more than half the school population enrolled; attendance was poor, the expenditure per pupil was only a few dollars, teachers were insufficiently prepared and badly paid. Not only were educational expenditures limited by the prevailing philosophy of fiscal parsimony, but in many states the local units of government were limited by constitutional restraints on levying taxes for schools. The maintenance of publicly supported high schools was almost totally absent from state law, and in some commonwealths no annual appropriations were made for higher education. In several states the church colleges were actively opposing public education, especially at the college and high school levels.[3] The whole process of erecting an elaborate caste system and institutionalizing the Negro's inferior position was well under way, and no segment of that structure was fraught with more uncertainty or more unforeseen implications than the education of black children.

Ironically, concern for the education of southern blacks was the force that inspired the dedicated group of ministers and educators that convened at Capon Springs, West Virginia, in the summer of 1898 to launch the Conference for Education in the South. Conceived by Dr. Edward Abbott of Massachusetts, the conference quickly found its leader in Robert Curtis Ogden, a New York businessman who had long been identified with Hampton Institute in Virginia. Ogden served as president of the conference from 1900 until his death in 1913, and under his leadership the movement attracted the support of many influential northerners. Ogden and his associates soon agreed that the most pressing need in the southern states was an adequate system of education for white children. Meeting in Winston-Salem, North Carolina, in April 1901, the conference set in motion a spectacular campaign for the advancement of southern education. J. L. M. Curry, the most famous educational spokesman of the South, concluded his address at Winston-Salem by declaring that the new organization represented "the rising of a new sun with healing in his wings to flood the Southland with rays of glory and happiness."[4]

Following the Winston-Salem meeting, Robert C. Ogden organized the executive board authorized by the conference. This committee, which soon came to be called the Southern Education Board (SEB), worked out the general plans for the educational campaign and exercised overall supervision in the execution of the board's varied undertakings. Edgar Gardner Murphy of Alabama became executive secretary of the board; Charles Duncan McIver of

[3]See, for example, John Carlisle Kilgo, "Some Phases of Southern Education," *SAQ* 2 (Apr. 1903): 137–51; M.L. Brittain, "The Rural School Awakening," *World's Work* 7 (Nov. 1903): 4144–47; Paul Neff Garber, *John Carlisle Kilgo: President of Trinity College, 1894–1910* (Durham, N.C., 1937), 32–34, 39, 50–58, 61, 66–72, 196–97; and David L. Smiley, "Educational Attitudes of North Carolina Baptists," *N.C. Hist. Rev.* 35 (July 1958): 316–27.

[4]Quoted in Charles William Dabney, *Universal Education in the South*, vol. 2: *The Southern Education Movement* (Chapel Hill, N.C., 1936), 43.

North Carolina headed a regional campaign committee; and Charles William Dabney of Tennessee directed a "Bureau of Information and Advice on Legislation and Organization" established in Knoxville early in 1902. In order to encourage northern understanding and support, Ogden made it a practice to invite a large number of prominent outsiders to the annual conferences, bringing them as his guests on a special train. National periodicals like *World's Work* reported these excursions and other features of the movement with sympathy and mounting approval.

One of Ogden's guests at the Winston-Salem conference of 1901 was John D. Rockefeller, Jr., whose family had contributed in earlier years to the support of black schools in the South. Rockefeller interested his father in the southern education movement, and this new concern was one factor in the elder Rockefeller's organization in 1902 of the General Education Board (GEB) as a means of promoting the development of education in the United States. Between 1902 and 1909, Rockefeller gave $53 million to the GEB, and the donor expressed a "special interest" in southern education. The board carried out state-by-state surveys of education in the region, helped support the Southern Education Board, worked to improve elementary education in the rural South, aided in the creation of a system of high schools in the section, assisted in modernizing state educational systems, subsidized farm demonstration work and other efforts to improve farm life, and gradually expanded its contributions in the field of black education. The GEB was intimately associated with the Southern Education Board from the very beginning; Ogden, William H. Baldwin, Jr., the first president of the new board, George Foster Peabody, and several others were members of both boards. This interlocking directorate facilitated the planning of educational uplift campaigns and the distribution of philanthropic funds in the South.[5]

The Southern Education Board was not designed to expend money in assisting existing institutions but rather "for the purpose of stimulating public sentiment in favor of more liberal provision for universal education in the public schools." The board sought to arouse interest and help organize an educational campaign in each of the southern states. As a means of encouraging these campaigns, the annual spring conferences were held in different cities throughout the section. Thus the Winston-Salem conference of 1901 stimulated the incipient educational crusade in North Carolina, the Athens conference of 1902 spurred on the educational reformers in Georgia, and the Richmond conference of 1903 contributed to the organization of the state campaign in Virginia.[6] Few

[5]Ibid., 123–64; General Education Board, *The General Education Board: An Account of Its Activities, 1902–1914* (New York, 1915); Raymond B. Fosdick, *Adventure in Giving: The Story of the General Education Board, A Foundation Established by John D. Rockefeller* (New York, 1962), 3–78; John Milton Cooper, Jr., *Walter Hines Page: The Southerner as American, 1855–1918* (Chapel Hill, N.C., 1977), 140–50, 206–17.

[6]Conferences were held in Birmingham, Ala., in 1904; in Columbia, S.C., in 1905; in Lexington, Ky., in 1906; in Pinehurst, N.C., in 1907; in Memphis, Tenn., in 1908; in Atlanta, Ga.,

of the South's leading educators failed to attend at least one of the conferences, and hundreds of ordinary teachers were drawn to the meetings. At the Little Rock conference in 1910, for example, more than 1,500 men and women were registered. The most intensive campaigns were held in the southeastern states, but all of the southern states, beginning with North Carolina in 1902, conducted organized movements for public education during the following decade. In some states several campaigns were sponsored during the period. Tennessee launched a campaign in 1903–1904, another in 1906, and still others in later years. The activities of the SEB gave the educational crusade a regional orientation from the outset, and the impact that the major campaigns had in other states reinforced the reformers' consciousness of being involved in a Southwide movement.

A similar pattern unfolded in every state. The Southern Education Board attempted to work through local leaders and to enlist the cooperation of responsible educational officials in the various states. As a rule a campaign committee would be organized under the direction of the state superintendent of education or some other prominent educator. Each campaign was conducted independently, but the SEB offered advice, literature, and some financial backing. The Bureau of Investigation and Information in Knoxville also lent its assistance. Within a year of its organization the bureau was regularly mailing material to 1,700 newspapers in the region. It communicated the results of its surveys and investigations through bulletins, circulars, and a weekly publication called *Southern Education*.[7] Edwin A. Alderman, president of Tulane University and a guiding light in the movement, described his own heart's desire in waging the crusade by urging "the establishment in every state of a comprehensive system of educational campaigning, wherein, by the use of literature and competent, wisely directed public speakers, the public sense and public conscience could be enlightened and aroused."[8] Action by the people themselves would follow, Alderman and his associates confidently believed.

The most notable of the state campaigns was carried out in North Carolina, where the ground was prepared in the 1890s for an educational awakening. Several developments during that turbulent decade challenged the widespread indifference toward the primitive conditions of North Carolina schools. The Farmers' Alliance and the Populists had demanded better public schools, and

---

in 1909; in Little Rock, Ark., in 1910; in Jacksonville, Fla., in 1911; in Nashville, Tenn., in 1912; and in Richmond, Va., in 1913. For an account of these conferences and the work of the Southern Education Board, see Dabney, *The Southern Education Movement*, and Wickliffe Rose, "The Educational Movement in the South," in *Report of the Commissioner of Education . . . for 1903*, vol. 1 (Washington, D.C., 1909), 359–90.

[7] Dabney, *The Southern Education Movement*, 74–80.

[8] Alderman, "Northern Aid to Southern Education," *Independent* 53 (Oct. 10, 1901): 2411. Also see Dumas Malone, *Edwin A. Alderman: A Biography* (New York, 1940), 131–56, and Clement Eaton, "Edwin A. Alderman—Liberal of the New South," *N.C. Hist. Rev.* 23 (Apr. 1946): 206–21.

the fusionist government had adopted a forward-looking program for education. The fusionists had increased school appropriations and enacted a local tax law in 1897. Meanwhile, Edwin A. Alderman, Charles D. McIver, Philander P. Claxton, and other educators had attracted attention through their zealous efforts to popularize public schools in the state. Walter Hines Page, in a provocative address at Greensboro in 1897, spoke of "The Forgotten Man"—and woman—and indicted the state for its illiteracy. It was time for "a wiser statesmanship and a more certain means of grace," Page declared while noting the failure of North Carolina political leaders to deal with the problem. The people needed a public school system "generously maintained by both State and local taxation." When the Democrats took control of the general assembly in 1899, they repealed the fusionists' local tax law but still found it desirable to appropriate $100,000 for support of the public schools. And during their all-out white supremacy campaign in 1900, the party's gubernatorial nominee, Charles B. Aycock, pledged himself not only to disfranchise North Carolina Negroes but also to support universal education, for blacks as well as whites.[9]

At its organizational meeting in November 1901, the Southern Education Board decided to undertake "a vigorous educational campaign for the public schools of North Carolina." The campaign was entrusted to Charles D. McIver, president of the North Carolina Normal and Industrial College and a leader in the Conference for Education in the South. McIver, with the support of Governor Aycock, called a meeting at the state capitol in Raleigh on February 13, 1902. Forty-three of the state's leading educators were invited to the conference, which was welcomed by the governor. The conferees proceeded to adopt a "Declaration against Illiteracy," a statement of purpose addressed to the people of the state. They created a central campaign committee made up of Aycock, McIver, and state superintendent James Y. Joyner and arranged local conferences in many parts of the state. The ensuing campaign, featuring oratory and the printed word, was remarkable for its intensity and evangelical appeal. "Everyone is discussing questions of education," one teacher wrote that summer. "It is the talk on the cars, the theme of discussion on the streets, the gos[s]ip of the corner grocery. Our editors are pushing the interests of education. In every town of importance there are graded schools in construction or already constructed."[10]

Inspired by Aycock's talk of universal education and the tireless work of McIver, the educational crusaders struggled to obtain longer school terms, better schoolhouses, more money for teachers, and the consolidation of weak

[9]D.J. Whitener, "Education for the People," *N.C. Hist. Rev.* 36 (Apr. 1959): 187–96; James S. Ferguson, "An Era of Educational Change," ibid. 46 (Apr. 1969): 130–41; Louis R. Harlan, *Separate and Unequal: Public School Campaigns and Racism in the Southern Seaboard States, 1901–1915* (Chapel Hill, N.C., 1958), 45–74.

[10]Quoted in Harlan, *Separate and Unequal*, 115. Also see Bert E. Bradley, "Educational Reformers in North Carolina, 1885–1905," in Waldo W. Braden, ed., *Oratory in the New South* (Baton Rouge, 1979), 237–75.

school districts. But the focus of the North Carolina campaign was local taxation for schools, which was still negligible. The campaign was resumed during the summer of 1903, when more than 350 educational rallies were held in seventy-eight counties, in addition to the regular township meetings conducted by county superintendents. The movement in the Old North State continued in less organized fashion for several years, ending with a second brief campaign in 1913 in behalf of a six-month school term and a statewide attendance law. The cause was supported by numerous organized groups, including the North Carolina Teachers' Assembly, the Woman's Association for the Betterment of Public School Houses, the State Federation of Women's Clubs, and the Farmers' Union.[11]

The reformers' most impressive accomplishment in North Carolina was the growing local support of public schools. By 1913, local taxes for education were being levied by 1,534 districts, one-fourth of the state's total; the school revenue from such taxes rose from $3,000 in 1900 to $1.4 million in 1915, by which time local taxes made up almost a third of the total school expenditures from public sources. In 1907 the reformers successfully challenged a court decision of 1886 which had restricted public support of the schools. In the meantime, the legislature had increased state appropriations for public schools, adding a second $100,000 in 1901 to the annual state outlay. In 1907 the general assembly authorized the establishment of rural high schools, and within a year 157 such schools were begun in eighty-one counties. The old literary fund was reorganized in 1903, and a permanent loan fund was created from which local educational authorities were able to borrow money to build or improve schoolhouses. A modest compulsory attendance law was enacted in 1913,[12] and provision was made for a six-month school term and a state equalizing fund. Beginning in 1903, when the functions of the state superintendent were increased, the legislature enacted a modern school code that strengthened the state's role in the operation of the public schools.[13]

In Virginia the public school campaign also grew directly out of the activities of the Southern Education Board. From within the state other voices were beginning to arouse interest in educational reform: the state teachers' association, the Richmond Education Association, and newspapers such as the

---

[11]Dabney, *The Southern Education Movement*, 336–47; Edgar W. Knight, *Public School Education in North Carolina* (Boston, 1916), 330–37; Rose Howell Holder, *McIver of North Carolina* (Chapel Hill, N.C., 1957), 195–227; Oliver H. Orr, Jr., *Charles Brantley Aycock* (Chapel Hill, N.C., 1961), 296–334; Joseph Flake Steelman, "The Progressive Era in North Carolina, 1884–1917" (Ph.D., diss. Univ. of North Carolina, 1955), 484–525; Joseph L. Morrison, *Josephus Daniels Says . . . An Editor's Political Odyssey from Bryan to Wilson and F.D.R., 1894–1913* (Chapel Hill, N.C., 1962), 63–86, 159–62; Elmer D. Johnson, "James Yadkin Joyner, Educational Statesman," *N.C. Hist. Rev.* 33 (July 1956): 359–83.

[12]The law stipulated that children between the ages of 8 and 12 must attend school at least four months a year.

[13]Harlan, *Separate and Unequal*, 102–34; Knight, *Public School Education in North Carolina*, 110, 315, 332–40, 345–47; Whitener, "Education for the People," 191–92.

Richmond *Times-Dispatch,* which introduced an education department and began to report on the sad condition of the public schools. Governor Andrew J. Montague, an opponent of the dominant political faction in the Democratic party, became a convert to the cause, emerging as Virginia's "educational governor." The reformers organized the Cooperative Education Association to promote an educational crusade in Virginia, and in May 1905 they launched an intensive solicitation for popular support. The May Campaign developed into an extraordinary mass movement. Over a hundred men and women toured the state during the month, making some 300 speeches, while local leaders contributed 1,500 more. Professor Bruce R. Payne, the campaign's publicity director, was simultaneously flooding the weekly and daily newspapers with promotional literature. At the local level, more than three hundred community improvement leagues were championing educational reform by the end of 1905. The movement strengthened the educational forces in Virginia. In 1908, for instance, the school lobby was able to secure the enactment of no less than forty of the forty-three measures it recommended to the general assembly. During the first fifteen years of the twentieth century, total school revenues tripled, the average school term was lengthened, teacher salaries were increased significantly, school consolidation grew steadily, and many new school buildings were constructed. By 1915, Virginia could claim 572 high schools (196 with a four-year curriculum), 7 normal schools and numerous summer schools, and 10 county agricultural schools.[14]

Another of the spectacular state campaigns took place in Tennessee. Charles W. Dabney's contribution to the Conference for Education in the South and the SEB's propaganda bureau in Knoxville helped spark the Tennessee movement. In 1902, Dabney inaugurated "The Summer School of the South" in Knoxville, and between 1902 and 1907 that institution enrolled more than 11,000 students, mostly teachers, from all over the South. The Southern Education Board and the organizers of the school considered it a crusading weapon for the advancement of southern education. Meanwhile, Professor Philander P. Claxton of the University of Tennessee and other educational leaders had begun to organize a systematic campaign to promote public schools in Tennessee. A concentrated effort was made in East Tennessee in 1905, when educational rallies were held in thirty-six counties. This became a "testing ground" for a series of statewide campaigns during the years 1906–12. By the time the educational campaign era came to an end about 1913, the Tennessee reformers could cite some impressive gains. Among these were an act of 1907 replacing district school control with

[14]H.B. Frissell, "Educational Progress in Virginia," *SAQ* 2 (July 1903): 199–208; Dabney, *The Southern Education Movement,* 320–32; Harlan, *Separate and Unequal,* 135–65; Cornelius J. Heatwold, *A History of Education in Virginia* (New York, 1916), 306–18; F.A. Magruder, *Recent Administration in Virginia* (Baltimore, 1912), 22–76; Allen W. Moger, *Virginia: Bourbonism to Byrd, 1870–1925* (Charlottesville, Va., 1968), 239–58; Raymond H. Pulley, *Old Virginia Restored: An Interpretation of the Progressive Impulse, 1870–1930* (Charlottesville, Va., 1968), 132–44, 150–51.

county school boards; a general education law in 1909 allocating 25 percent of the state's annual gross revenue to the general education fund; broad reform of state school administration in 1911; and a statewide compulsory attendance statute in 1913.[15]

Educational campaigns supported by the Southern Education Board were also undertaken in most of the other southern states. A series of educational rallies sponsored by Georgia reformers in 1903 and 1904 contributed to the adoption of a constitutional amendment permitting local taxation for public schools. In Kentucky a "whirlwind campaign" was conducted during the autumn of 1908 and a second during the summer of 1909, setting in motion a general process of school reorganization and consolidation. In 1911 a Kentuckian named Cora Wilson Stewart began a campaign in Rowan County to teach adult illiterates. The movement spread, and the success of her "moonlight schools" paved the way for a statewide literacy program three years later. The campaign in Alabama, though aided by such groups as the Alabama Educational Association and the State Federation of Women's Clubs, failed to make a major breakthrough until 1915, when a large number of educational reforms were approved, including a local tax amendment and a compulsory attendance law. Although the educational crusade reached into all the southern states, in some cases the campaigns were sporadic and unproductive. In Louisiana, for example, the SEB helped create a central campaign committee in 1903, but its program was neither well organized nor sustained. The Conference for Education in the South did not extend to Texas, but there was a campaign for better schools in that state. A state conference for education was organized in 1907, and during the next several years it worked successfully to promote the progress of school taxation, the establishment of rural high schools, the consolidation of schools, and the enactment of a compulsory attendance law in 1915.[16]

[15]Dabney, *The Southern Education Movement*, 105–14; Andrew David Holt, *The Struggle for a State System of Public Schools in Tennessee, 1903–1936* (New York, 1938), 77, 91–275; Charles Lee Lewis, *Philander Priestley Claxton: Crusader for Public Education* (Knoxville, 1948), 112–67; James R. Montgomery, "The Summer School of the South," *Tenn. Hist. Quar.* 22 (Dec. 1963): 361–81; Alexander J. McKelway, "The Summer School of the South," *Outlook* 71 (Aug. 2, 1902): 894–96.

[16]Dabney, *The Southern Education Movement*, 348–60, 369–89, 392–401, 410–31; Harlan, *Separate and Unequal*, 170–247; Alton DuMar Jones, "Progressivism in Georgia, 1898–1918" (Ph.D. diss., Emory Univ., 1963), 228–63; Frank L. McVey, *The Gates Open Slowly: A History of Education in Kentucky* (Lexington, Ky., 1949), 175–215; "Kentucky's 'Moonlight' Schools," *World's Work* 26 (Sept. 1913): 506–508; Willie E. Nelms, Jr., "Cora Wilson Stewart and the Crusade Against Illiteracy in Kentucky," *Reg. Ky. Hist. Soc.* 74 (Jan. 1976): 10–29; David Alan Harris, "Racists and Reformers: A Study of Progressivism in Alabama, 1896–1911" (Ph.D. diss., Univ. of North Carolina, 1967), 296–303, 348–64; Martha Carolyn Mitchell, "Birmingham: Biography of a City of the New South" (Ph.D. diss., Univ. of Chicago, 1946), 219–53; Joseph B. Graham, "Current Problems in Alabama," *Annals* 22 (Sept. 1903): 280–83; John K. Bettersworth, *Mississippi: A History* (Austin, Tex., 1959), 479–89; W.O. Wilson, "Public Education" and "The High School and Other Developments," in David Y. Thomas, ed., *Arkansas and Its People: A History, 1541–1930*, 4 vols. (New York, 1930), vol. 2, pp. 465–82; Edwin A. Alderman, "The Southwestern Field," *Annals* 22 (Sept. 1903): 287–92; Robert B. Fulton, "Educational Progress in Mississippi," ibid., 304–309.

Improved rural school, Montgomery County, Alabama, 1914. *Rockefeller Archive Center.*

Although the response to the southern education movement was decidedly favorable, there was strong opposition to the various school reforms. Some southerners were suspicious of educational improvement schemes. As Walter Hines Page explained to another reformer in 1911, "The moment you use the word 'education' the lay reader puts on rubber heels and runs as if the devil himself were after him. He doesn't want any educational talk in his Christmas stocking. You have got to catch his attention by talking about training. He is interested in training horses or vines or men. . . ."[17] Educational gains were modest in a state like South Carolina, which contained powerful textile interests and a pervasive political conservatism. Opponents in most states warned of increased taxes, the danger of black schools, outside interference by northerners, and the political implications of the educational campaigns. A dozen or so prominent newspapers in the region mounted a barrage of criticism against the Conference for Education and the northern philanthropists who contributed to its work. The *Manufacturers' Record* was especially aggressive in its attacks on the Southern Education Board, referring to "obsequious hat holding officials of institutions of learning training their students to intellectual mendicancy." Some denominational leaders such as Bishop Warren A. Candler of the Southern Methodist church denounced the SEB as a pawn of northern capitalists and as subversive of southern traditions. Sectarian institutions raised the specter of secular evils and infidelity in public secondary schools and colleges. The race question was inevitably introduced. As late as 1906 the Charleston *News and Courier* was asserting that "the so-called Ogden movement . . . is for the negro primarily, and for the white man only to the extent that it can make the white man of assistance to the work of elevating the negro."[18]

Even so, most southerners showed a keen desire to share in the benefits of outside generosity. "It seems to me," an Emory College professor wrote in 1909, ". . . that the impulse on the part of Northern philanthropists to aid the South is a creditable one and that in so doing they will be but paying a debt which is owed, though they will scarcely view it in this light. I am not in favor of hindering Zaccheus if his repentance be indeed genuine and his reparation without any ulterior motive."[19] Writing in 1915 of the GEB's contribution, an appreciative southern woman concluded that "the Board's great work has been to invigorate and enrich the life and thought of the common people of the South,

[17] Page to Edwin Mims, Dec. 22, 1911, Page Papers.
[18] Quoted in James W. Patton, "The Southern Reaction to the Ogden Movement," in R.C. Simonini, Jr., ed., *Education in the South: Institute of Southern Culture Lectures at Longwood College, 1959* (Farmville, Va., 1959), 75. Also see ibid., 63–82; Dabney, *The Southern Education Movement*, 44–49; Yoshimitsu Ide, "The Significance of Richard Hathaway Edmonds and His *Manufacturers' Record* in the New South" (Ph.D. diss., Univ. of Florida, 1959), 258–66; Ronald Dantan Burnside, "The Governorship of Coleman Livingston Blease of South Carolina, 1911–1915" (Ph.D. diss., Indiana Univ., 1963), 198–232; and Alfred M. Pierce, *Giant Against the Sky: The Life of Bishop Warren Akin Candler* (New York and Nashville, 1948), 190–92.
[19] Rembert G. Smith to Warren A. Candler, April 15, 1909, Warren A. Candler Papers, Emory University Library.

to increase their resources, and to help them to open for themselves the door of opportunity."[20] For their part, the northerners were extraordinarily sympathetic and tactful in approaching the southern states. The General Education Board, recalled one of its presidents, saw the South as "an exceptionally blighted region. The glaring inequity it chose to wage war against was not that which existed between the two races, but that which distinguished the South from the other regions of the United States."[21]

The school campaigns in the early twentieth century did arouse the southern people. The spirit of the region's educational awakening was reflected in a letter of 1902 from the president of the State Normal School of Georgia:

> I am here in the woods, eight miles from the railroad, organizing a model country school that the Women's Clubs of the State have mothered. We have got nearly $1,000 out of this little village of 200 people for this school. Do you know of any more effective way to induce a community to help itself forward? We have a three-roomed school-house, weather-boarded and equipped with modern furniture. We are building an adjunct for cooking and shop work. I've promised to secure— Heaven knows how—forty gallons of white paint for the weather boarding and the ceiling. We opened the school yesterday with eighty-six pupils, and every mother and father in a radius of five miles was here. It was a "revival" occasion. Everybody "got happy" and "shouted" over his boys and girls.[22]

Scenes like this were by no means unusual. "Patriotism and education," *World's Work* suggested, "so support one another in this movement that the public man must champion popular education, and the schoolmaster must become a public character."[23]

Public schools, educational reformers asserted, were the "citadel of democracy" in the South. The educators frequently invoked Jeffersonian ideals in their campaigns. Jefferson, Charles W. Dabney declared, was "the first conspicuous advocate in this country of free education in common schools supported by local taxation as well as state aid to higher institutions of learning."[24] But Jefferson was appealed to not only as a champion of universal education but also as an advocate of intensive schooling of the select few for public leadership and the advancement of learning. In the thinking of these uplifters, there was clearly a strong infusion of noblesse oblige, a conception of the school as a means of spreading their own middle-class culture, and a desire to bolster the stability and vitality of the new social order that made their leadership possible. Yet this instrumental view of education was not narrowly self-centered, at least not in any conscious sense. The reformers were sincere

---

[20]Mrs. John D. Hammond, "The Work of the General Education Board in the South," *SAQ* 14 (Oct. 1915): 348–57; quotation on p. 349.

[21]Fosdick, *Adventure in Giving*, 324.

[22]Eugene C. Branson, "The Real Southern Question," *World's Work* 3 (Mar. 1902): 1891.

[23]"Patriotism and Education in the South," *World's Work* 8 (June 1904): 4839–40.

[24]Quoted in Merrill D. Peterson, *The Jefferson Image in the American Mind* (New York, 1962), 241.

when they talked about sacrifice and patriotism and educational statesmanship. Schools, in their eyes, did serve broad social functions.[25] Education, they believed with an almost childlike faith, would contribute directly to individual prosperity and well-being, to the economic development of the South, to a literate citizenry, to a more democratic society, and to the freeing of men and women from the bonds of prejudice and superstition.[26] Here, Page said of the developing crusade for education, "is a broad and free force," free from "political and church and sectional control" and conducted on "a level of sound economics and high statesmanship."[27]

During the decade and a half after 1900, the per capita expenditure for education in the southern states doubled, the average school term was substantially lengthened, teachers' salaries went up, thousands of schoolhouses were built, and the illiteracy rate among white children was cut in half. School laws were extensively revised, compulsory attendance measures were passed, and high schools spread over the region. Yet, if the number and quality of public schools had increased, the South still lagged far behind other parts of the country, handicapped by its poverty, excessive number of children, and dual school system. While noting the great educational progress North Carolina had made in recent years, state superintendent James Y. Joyner emphasized the limits of that progress in 1916: only one-fifth of the state's teachers had college diplomas and fewer than half of them had any special professional training; the annual school term was 122 days as compared with a national average of 158 days; and the average monthly salary of rural white teachers in the state was $40.74 and that of black teachers only $24.69. "There is much pathos & tragedy about it all," the educator Edwin Mims wrote in 1909. "With all the boasted educational awakening in North Carolina, the children have no fair

---

[25]Cora Wilson Stewart's *Country Life Reader* (1915), a book prepared for use in the Kentucky campaign against illiteracy, not only taught reading and writing but thrift, improved farming techniques, better health, Christian living, and personal and civic responsibility. See Nelms, "Cora Wilson Stewart and the Crusade Against Illiteracy in Kentucky," 25.

[26]Peterson, *The Jefferson Image in the American Mind*, 240–43; Bruce Clayton, *The Savage Ideal: Intolerance and Intellectual Leadership in the South, 1890–1914* (Baltimore, 1972), 107–29; David Lee Carlton, "Mill and Town: The Cotton Mill Workers and the Middle Class in South Carolina, 1880–1920" (Ph.D. diss., Yale Univ., 1977), 31–34, 210–16, 318–26.

[27]Burton J. Hendrick, *The Training of an American: The Earlier Life and Letters of Walter H. Page, 1855–1913* (Boston, 1928), 410. For the ideals of the reformers, see Walter Hines Page, "The Rebuilding of Old Commonwealths," *Atlantic Monthly* 89 (May 1902): 651–61; Charles B. Aycock, "Education and Service," *Vanderbilt University Quarterly* 3 (July 1903): 151–58; Edwin Mims, "The University in the South," *Annals* 22 (Sept. 1903): 261–65; S.C. Mitchell, "The Educational Needs of the South," *Outlook* 76 (Feb. 13, 1904): 415–19; William P. Few, "Some Educational Needs of the South," *SAQ* 3 (July 1904): 201–11; Few, "Education and Citizenship in a Democracy," ibid. 7 (Oct. 1908): 299–308; Few, "The College in Southern Development," ibid. 10 (Jan. 1911): 1–8; Edwin A. Alderman, "The Achievement of a Generation," ibid. 5 (July 1906): 236–53; Philander P. Claxton, "Educational Ideals and Tendencies in the South," in *The South in the Building of the Nation*, vol. 10, pp. 398–427; and C. Alphonso Smith, "Our Heritage of Idealism," *Sewanee Review* 20 (Apr. 1912): 245–47.

TABLE 10. *Southern School Statistics, 1900 and 1920*

| | ILLITERACY (10 YEARS OF AGE & OLDER) | | | | AVG. DAILY ATTENDANCE PER NUMBER ENROLLED | | AVG. LENGTH OF SCHOOL TERM (DAYS) | | EXPENDITURES PER PUPIL (PER CAPITA OF TOTAL POPULATION) | |
| | 1900 | | 1920 | | | | | | | |
	WHITE (%)	BLACK (%)	NATIVE WHITE (%)	BLACK (%)	1900 (%)	1920 (%)	1900	1920	1900 ($)	1920 ($)
USA	6.2	44.5	2.0	22.9	68.53	74.77	144.6	161.3	2.84	9.80
Ala.	14.7	57.4	6.3	31.3	79.10	64.49	78.3	123	.50	3.88
Ark.	11.5	43.0	4.5	21.8	62.10	67.48	77.5	126	1.04	4.40
Fla.	8.9	38.4	2.9	21.5	68.90	73.60	93	133	1.45	7.26
Ga.	11.9	52.4	5.4	29.1	61.80	67.60	112	145	.89	3.13
Ky.	12.8	40.1	7.0	21.0	61.51[1]	63.75	115.4[3]	123	1.41	3.36
La.	18.4	61.1	10.5	38.5	74.58	72.34	120	149	.82	6.32
Miss.	8.0	49.1	3.6	29.3	55.98[2]	62.89	105.1[4]	140	.89	3.06
N.C.	19.4	47.6	8.2	24.5	51.67	68.51	70.8	134	.50	4.75
Ind. Terr.	14.1	42.8								
Okla.	2.9	26.0	2.3	12.4	63.96	60.41	95.3	166	1.72	11.29
S.C.	13.5	52.8	6.5	29.3	71.43	69.33	88.4	110	.67	3.94
Tenn.	14.1	41.6	7.3	22.4	69.76	73.81	96	133	.87	4.34
Texas	8.5	38.2	3.0	17.8	68.09	72.00	108.2	156	1.46	7.21
Va.	11.1	44.6	5.9	23.5	56.72[2]	69.51	119 [4]	147	1.07	5.62

[1] In 1896–97
[2] In 1898–99
[3] In 1896–97
[4] In 1898–99

SOURCES: *Abstract of the Twelfth Census of the United States, 1900* (Washington, D.C., 1902), 75; *Report of the Commissioner of Education for the Year 1899–1900* (Washington, D.C. 1901), vol. 1, pp. lxviii, lxix; *Statistical Abstract of the United States, 1921* (Washington, D.C., 1922), 120–21; *Statistical Abstract of the United States, 1933* (Washington, D.C., 1933), 43, 110.

chance. . . . Here are all the resources of the State. It has all stirred me profoundly, and I have felt all over again the call of duty.''[28]

Southern blacks took little part in the regional crusade for schools and were
excluded from an equitable share of the educational benefits it brought. They
were never invited to the annual conferences. Some black educators and editors
criticized the Southern Education Board for ignoring their race's interests.
Booker T. Washington, while friendly toward the movement's leaders, wrote
privately in 1906 that the educational campaigns meant "almost nothing so far
as the Negro schools are concerned.''[29] The educators who directed the southern school campaigns declared themselves to be in favor of black education, but
as J. L. M. Curry asserted at the Winston-Salem conference of 1901, "there is
greater need for the education of the other race.'' Education, Curry and his
allies believed, would teach white southerners tolerance and skills which would
moderate the prejudice stemming from economic competition between the
races.[30] Edwin A. Alderman reasoned that the education of "one untaught
white man to the point where it is clear to him that knowledge and not prejudice
must guide his conduct, and that for the honor of his name and country and his
posterity he must deal with these people in justice and kindness, is worth more
to the black man than the education of any ten men of his own race.''[31] Robert
C. Ogden and other northern supporters of the southern education movement
acquiesced in this approach. They concluded that the solution of "the Negro
problem" lay within the white community of the South and in an indirect
challenge to racism through "good will, tact, and hard work.'' Ogden advised
black leaders to adopt a policy of "concession, moderation and patience.''[32]
Chancellor Walter B. Hill of the University of Georgia could reassure his
audience at the Richmond conference of 1903 that "the Nation has remanded
the solution of the Negro problem, including his education, to the South.''[33]

Nevertheless, southern educational leaders sometimes found themselves
precariously balanced on a tightrope. "To devise a school system which shall
save the whites and not the blacks,'' a friendly northern magazine observed in
1905, "is a task of such delicacy that a few surviving reactionaries are willing to

[28]Quoted in Leah Marie Park, "Edwin Mims and *The Advancing South* (1894–1926): A Study
of a Southern Liberal" (M.A. thesis, Vanderbilt Univ., 1964), 46. Also see Knight, *Public School
Education in North Carolina*, 369–71.

[29]Harlan, *Separate and Unequal*, 94. See also George-Anne Willard, "Charles Lee Coon:
Negro Education and the Atlanta Speech Controversy," in *East Carolina College Publications in
History*, vol. 3: *Studies in the History of the South, 1875–1922* (Greenville, N.C., 1966), 151–74.

[30]Rose, "The Educational Movement in the South," 368; Harlan, *Separate and Unequal*, p.
xi.

[31]Alderman, "Northern Aid to Southern Education," 2412. For the views of a more conservative southern leader, see L. Moody Simms, Jr., "William Dorsey Jelks and the Problem of Negro
Education," *Ala. Rev.* 23 (Jan. 1970): 70–74.

[32]Harlan, *Separate and Unequal*, 76, 78, 96; Dabney, *The Southern Education Movement*,
101.

[33]Quoted in Dabney, *The Southern Education Movement*, 101.

let both perish together on the pathless mountains. The fear . . . that misguided Northerners will enter like a serpent and destroy a Southern paradise by giving the negro the fruit of the tree of knowledge, is a factor still to be reckoned with in politics."[34] The educational reformers, reinforced by progressive politicians in the region, insisted that black students needed the right kind of schooling; they talked about "practical education" along the lines of Hampton and Tuskegee, education that would make the Negro "a home-maker, a farmer, a mechanic, and a good citizen."[35] Yet even when white authorities had good intentions, they frequently neglected black schools, or considered them only as a fleeting afterthought. Wallace Buttrick, the southern secretary of the GEB, told of visiting "the Negro school" in Auburn, Alabama, in 1902. Local authorities, he reported, had done "next to nothing for the Negroes, simply giving them $450 with which to erect a building and then leaving the whole project to the execution of a group of untutored and inexperienced Negroes." The result was "a building that is worse than no building at all, and a school equipment that for inadequacy beggers description."[36] It was a situation that could have been illustrated endlessly across the South.

Charles B. Aycock, North Carolina's "educational governor," and many others who joined in the school reform movement held aloft the ideal of universal education in the South, and some of them, including Aycock, did what they could to protect black schools from blatant discrimination, particularly the widespread legislative proposals to allocate state school funds in proportion to the taxes paid by the two races.[37] Although these extreme anti-Negro measures were defeated, sometimes by a narrow margin, discrimination against blacks in the section's state and local school systems was pervasive and methodical. At the local level, where taxation for public schools was one of the reformers' principal objectives, the disposition of funds was usually left entirely to local authorities. Customarily, black schools were given a pittance. Educational appropriations by the state were usually allocated to the counties on the basis of total school enrollments, which in practical terms meant that the minority white schools in the black belt school districts were handsomely supported at the expense of the more numerous Negro children. Lacking influence in politics, southern blacks had nothing to rely on in the making and

---

[34]"The Conference for Southern Education," *Nation* 80 (May 11, 1905): 369.

[35]Dabney, *The Southern Education Movement*, 101.

[36]Quoted in Fosdick, *Adventure in Giving*, 81–82. William K. Tate, South Carolina's first elementary rural school supervisor, reported in 1911 that "The negro school houses are miserable beyond description. . . . Most of the teachers are absolutely untrained and have been given certificates by the County Board not because they have passed the examination, but because it is necessary to have some kind of a negro teacher. Among the negro rural schools I have visited, I have found only one in which the highest class has known the multiplication table" (quoted in Ernest McPherson Lander, Jr., *A History of South Carolina, 1865–1960* [Chapel Hill, N.C., 1960], 128).

[37]See, for example, Edwin A. Alderman, "Education for White and Black," *Independent* 53 (Nov. 7, 1901): 2647–49, and William E. King, "Charles McIver Fights for the Tarheel Negro's Right to an Education," *N.C. Hist. Rev.* 41 (July 1964): 360–69.

administering of public policy save the good will and paternalism of white moderates. *"Something* must be done," Edgar Gardner Murphy exclaimed in 1904. "I have never seen so much sentiment against the Negro."[38]

As the southern education movement gained momentum, the temptation increased among whites to take the Negro's share of the new funds for white schools. The extent of the racial discrimination varied among the southern states and within individual states. In South Carolina, to take an extreme, the white child of school age in 1915 received twelve times as much as the black child. In North Carolina the discrimination in favor of white children increased from about 50 percent in 1900 to 300 percent in 1915. While the amounts spent for black schools rose during the progressive era, the disparity in the expenditures for white and black schoolchildren grew steadily larger.[39] A recent study of reform in North Carolina suggests that the distribution of taxes as well as educational funds discriminated against blacks and, to a lesser extent, poor whites.[40] One reason for the impressive growth of local school support in Virginia was that a strict construction of the Old Dominion's constitution might have required whites to share equally with blacks in the expenditure of state money.

Philanthropic interest in Negro education represented by such foundations as the Peabody Education Fund and the Slater Fund did not disappear from the South after 1900. But the support of black education during the early years of the century was strongly affected by the interregional accord embodied in the Conference for Education in the South. The GEB's early grants went largely to schools emphasizing agricultural and industrial training in the Hampton-Tuskegee mold, although by 1915 the board was beginning to support black high schools. In 1907 the Anna T. Jeanes Fund introduced its program of employing specially qualified teachers to work in black elementary schools, and the Phelps-Stokes Fund, established in 1910, inaugurated its fellowship program for study of the Negro question. Between 1912 and 1920 the Rosenwald Fund aided in the construction of many black school buildings. Disappointed in the limited support they received from private foundations and the penurious treatment accorded them by public authorities, black educators were largely dependent upon their own meager resources. They, too, were commit-

[38]Murphy to Robert C. Ogden, March 8, 1904, Robert C. Ogden Papers, Manuscripts Division, Library of Congress.

[39]Harlan, *Separate and Unequal*, 11, 15–16, 95, 106, 109, 116, 131, 133, 144–45, 165, 204–205, 210, 246–47, 258; Horace Mann Bond, *Negro Education in Alabama: A Study in Cotton and Steel* (Washington, D.C., 1939), 160–63, 192; H. Leon Prather, Sr., *Resurgent Politics and Educational Progressivism in the New South: North Carolina, 1890–1913* (Rutherford, N.J., 1979).

[40]J. Morgan Kousser, "Progressivism—For Middle-Class Whites Only: North Carolina Education, 1880–1910," *JSH* 46 (May 1980): 169–94. See also Glenn Sisk, "The Educational Awakening in Alabama and Its Effect Upon the Black Belt, 1900–1917," *Jour. Negro Edu.* 25 (Spring 1956): 191–96, and Irving Gershenberg, "The Negro and the Development of White Public Education in the South: Alabama, 1880–1930," ibid. 39 (Winter 1970): 50–59.

Adult education class, Central Colored High School, Louisville, Kentucky, 1920.
University of Louisville Photographic Archives.

ted to the philosophy of self-help, and they were imbued with a conviction that educational uplift was indispensable to the economic and social progress of the race. Hundreds of Hampton and Tuskegee graduates spread out over the South, organizing schools and engaging in demonstration work. Yet the obstacles that confronted these struggling projects were indescribably great. As late as 1915, 70 percent of the black teachers in the southern states had received less than six years of elementary education. According to the Slater Fund report of 1910, fewer than fifty public schools for blacks in the South offered any secondary work.[41] But in spite of poverty and discrimination, the black community's struggle to create an adequate system of education represented its most impressive organized social endeavor during these years. "Looking backward on black education in Georgia," John Dittmer concludes, "one is impressed not so much by its shortcomings as by its achievements against overwhelming odds."[42]

Writing in 1909, Philander P. Claxton of the University of Tennessee observed that in the South's first attempt at universal education "we made the usual mistake of supposing the education of the schools to be something foreign in its nature, with little direct relation to the everyday life and interests of the masses of the people, the purpose of which is to lift children out of this life into a life more or less like that of the professional and leisure classes . . . which we have fancied was in some way very superior to the life of the farmer, the mechanic and the tradesman."[43] By the early part of the twentieth century, however, local and state school authorities, as well as businessmen, chambers of commerce, and spokesmen for the various educational campaigns, were stressing the need for vocational training. Industrial education promised to contribute to the material uplifting of a poverty-stricken and undeveloped region, and it reflected the New South vision of economic development through industrialization, commercial enterprise, and agricultural diversification. The great task of the South was "to convert the raw materials of ore, timber, and cotton into finished products." The "business of the school," one of the southern reformers declared in 1908, was "to develop the practical intelligence and technical skill necessary to exploit the natural resources in this extensive domain."[44]

[41]Harlan, *Separate and Unequal*, 253–54; Dabney, *The Southern Education Movement*, 186–87, 378, 432–78; Fosdick, *Adventure in Giving*, 80–98; James H. Dillard, "Fourteen Years of the Jeanes Fund," *SAQ* 22 (July 1923): 193–201. See also Henry Allen Bullock, *A History of Negro Education in the South: From 1619 to the Present* (Cambridge, Mass., 1967), 124–39, and Henry Snyder Enck, "The Burden Borne: Northern White Philanthropy and Southern Black Industrial Education, 1900–1915" (Ph.D. diss., Univ. of Cincinnati, 1970).

[42]Dittmer, *Black Georgia in the Progressive Era, 1900–1920* (Urbana, Ill., 1977), 162. Also see ibid., 142–62; I.A. Newby, *Black Carolinians: A History of Blacks in South Carolina from 1895 to 1968* (Columbia, S.C., 1973), 82–109; Lester C. Lamon, *Black Tennesseans, 1900–1930* (Knoxville, 1977), 59–87; and W.E.B. Du Bois, "The Training of Negroes for Social Power," *Outlook* 75 (Oct. 17, 1903): 409–14.

[43]Claxton, "Educational Ideals and Tendencies in the South," 417–18.

[44]S.C. Mitchell, "Phases in the Educational Movement of the Day," *Sewanee Review* 16 (Jan.

Some city schools in the South began to experiment with modest programs of manual arts in the 1890s, and a few notable schools with industrial education work had been established by that time. One of the best known of the latter type was the Miller Manual Labor School in Albermarle County, Virginia, an endowed school for orphans. Under the leadership of Captain Charles E. Vawter, later one of the founders of the Conference for Education in the South, the school developed an outstanding program of manual training for elementary and secondary school students.[45] The growth of industrial education in the early twentieth-century South can be illustrated with three examples from Georgia. In Columbus, a city of 25,000 people, twelve textile mills, and other industries, an innovative schoolman named Carleton B. Gibson established, with support from the financier George Foster Peabody, the Primary Industrial School. The school substituted tools and benches for textbooks, and offered instruction in some twenty handicraft lines. Gibson then turned to the high school level, and with financial aid from local manufacturers organized the Secondary Industrial School for boys and girls fourteen and older. The public schools for blacks in Columbus also emphasized practical industrial training. Under the leadership of Lawton B. Evans, Augusta, another factory town in Georgia, undertook a similar program of industrial training.[46] Meanwhile, in the mountains of northwest Georgia near Rome, Martha Berry had begun an industrial school for poor white boys. A few years later she added a school for girls. As Miss Berry wrote in 1911, "We are located in a region where we can reach an unlimited number of needy people from the rural districts of Georgia, Alabama, Tennessee and N. C. . . . We try to urge the overflow to go to the State schools, but they claim that they cannot get the industrial and Christian training which they want and need."[47]

Northern philanthropists, church mission boards, and both white and black educators supported the idea of industrial education for Negroes in the early twentieth century. This emphasis, they hoped, would lead to the development of character, manual skill, and industry among southern blacks. In 1898, for instance, the Slater Fund proposed that Booker T. Washington and his wife make an extensive speaking tour of the South over a two-year period to promote

---

1908): 25. See also Few, "Some Educational Needs of the Day," 201–11; Berenice M. Fisher, *Industrial Education: American Ideals and Institutions* (Madison, Wis., 1967), 85–86; and Sol Cohen, "The Industrial Education Movement, 1906–17," *Amer. Quar.* 20 (Spring 1968): 95–110.

[45]"Captain Vawter," *Outlook* 81 (Nov. 11, 1905): 586; Dabney, *The Southern Education Movement*, 167–70. For the promotion of industrial training in Tennessee, see William F. Donovan, Jr., "The Growth of the Industrial Spirit in Tennessee, 1890–1910" (Ph.D. diss., George Peabody College for Teachers, 1955), 189–226.

[46]Carleton B. Gibson, "The Secondary Industrial School of Savannah, Georgia," *Annals* 33 (Jan. 1909): 42–49; Dabney, *The Southern Education Movement*, 170–74.

[47]Martha Berry to Robert C. Ogden, Sept. 14, 1911, Ogden Papers. For the origin and development of the Berry Schools, see Martha Berry, "Uplifting Backwoods Boys in Georgia," *World's Work* 8 (July 1904): 4986–92; Berry, "The Growth of the Berry School Idea," *Survey* 27 (Dec. 16, 1911): 1382–85; and Dabney, *The Southern Education Movement*, 175–76.

industrial education and the Slater program. Washington's primary concern was reform of the Negro home and community life, but the industrial and agricultural training at Tuskegee, as at Hampton, was enormously influential during this period. In 1898 the Tuskegean reported that twenty-six different industries were being operated at the school, and "each student is taught some trade or industry." Tuskegee was emulated by institutions like Penn School in South Carolina. The public schools for blacks, once they were established, usually stressed vocational training. Birmingham, Alabama, started an industrial high school for black students as early as 1899, and by 1921 it claimed 19 teachers and 615 pupils. Nevertheless, there was far more talk than accomplishment. As Washington wrote in 1899, "The great trouble now is that almost every little school that starts up in the South calls itself an industrial school because they find that the matter of industrial education has become popular in the North and in the South." Yet careful examination would show that "few of these schools are doing anything along industrial lines."[48]

Inadequate public support was the main reason that industrial education for blacks did not make more rapid progress in the South. But there were other limiting factors as well. The debate between advocates of higher education and the supporters of industrial education among black leaders proved enervating. The growing support of industrial training for white children was also costly to black programs. Booker T. Washington pointed to one aspect of the problem in 1898, when he warned that "the only way that we can prevent the industries slipping from the Negro in all parts of the South, as they have already in certain parts of the South, is for all the educators, ministers, and friends of the Negro to unite to push forward, in a whole-souled manner, the industrial or business development of the Negro either in school, or out of school, or both."[49] In 1904, Edgar Gardner Murphy expressed his concern over the racial rivalry in this area of southern education: "Many of the same men who assured us, ten years ago, that industrial education is the only education the negro should have, are now ready with the assurance that for fear the industrial development of the negro will clash with that of the white man, this form of negro training is the most dangerous contribution that has thus far been made to the solution of our Southern problems."[50]

---

[48]Washington to Emily Howland, April 4, 1899, in Louis R. Harlan and associates, eds., *The Booker T. Washington Papers*, vol. 5 (Urbana, Ill., 1976), 72. See also ibid., 64; J.L.M. Curry to Booker T. Washington, June 3, 1898, ibid., vol. 4 (Urbana, Ill., 1975), 428; Fisher, *Industrial Education*, 158; Dabney, *The Southern Education Movement*, 406; Claude H. Nolen, *The Negro's Image in the South: The Anatomy of White Supremacy* (Lexington, Ky., 1967), 139–52; Elizabeth Jacoway, "Education for Life: The Penn School Experience," *South Atlantic Urban Studies* 2 (1978): 89–103; August Meier, *Negro Thought in America, 1880–1915: Racial Ideologies in the Age of Booker T. Washington* (Ann Arbor, Mich., 1963), 85–99; and Henry S. Enck, "Black Self-Help in the Progressive Era: The 'Northern Campaigns' of Smaller Southern Black Industrial Schools, 1900–1915," *Jour. Negro Hist.* 61 (Jan. 1976): 73–87.

[49]Harlan and associates, eds., *The Booker T. Washington Papers*, vol. 4, p. 370.

[50]Quoted in Fisher, *Industrial Education*, 163. Also see *Annals* 22 (Dec. 1903): 269.

There was a rural side to the industrial education movement which reflected a broader interest in "practical education" as a key vehicle in the uplift of the countryside. Vocationalism as an emphasis in rural education was not always centered in the school system. Booker T. Washington's conferences at Tuskegee and Seaman A. Knapp's farm demonstration work, for example, were not directly related to the schools. By 1913, demonstration programs were being carried out in all the southern states and in over half the counties of the South. The club movement for boys and girls, developing independently but informally allied with the farm demonstration program, constituted another type of practical education for rural dwellers. Boys' corn clubs, girls' canning clubs, and various other youth organizations were dedicated to the acquisition of skills in agriculture and domestic science. Training in agriculture and domestic science was also being introduced into the public schools. Several states, led by Georgia and Alabama, created agricultural high schools.[51]

Despite the increasing popularity of vocational training in the South, the traditional school curriculum was not displaced in most of the region's school systems. Some educators frowned on the uncritical enthusiasm for practical education. As the president of Wofford College wrote in 1910, "it will be a sad day for the best educational interests of the South if we let a catch-word like the 'People's College,' meaning the high school, narrow our conception of its mission, or if we press too far in practical application that other phrase, 'the high schools do not exist to prepare boys and girls for college.'"[52] At the other extreme, the progressive era witnessed the establishment of a few experimental schools in southern communities. One of these was founded by Marietta Pierce Johnson, an able teacher from Minnesota who organized a free school in the single-tax community of Fairhope, Alabama. By 1915 this child-centered experimental school had begun to attract national attention. Here and there one could find other progressive educators such as the young William H. Kilpatrick, who taught at Blakely Institute in southwest Georgia in the 1890s.[53]

In 1907, Samuel Chiles Mitchell, professor of history at Richmond College and a leader in Virginia's campaign for public education, set down his ideas on "The Task of the College in the South." In the reconstruction of the region, Mitchell wrote, the college and university must assume a vital role. Their task

[51]Lawrence A. Cremin, *The Transformation of the School: Progressivism in American Education, 1876–1957* (New York, 1961), 79. See also Dabney, *The Southern Education Movement*, 177–204; GEB, *The General Education Board*, 18–70; Fosdick, *Adventure in Giving*, 39–57; Linda O. McMurry, *George Washington Carver: Scientist and Symbol* (New York, 1981), 112–29; and Woodward, *Origins of the New South*, 409–12.

[52]Henry N. Snyder, "A Little Experiment in Enforcing a Fourteen-Unit Entrance Standard," *SAQ* 9 (Apr. 1910): 142.

[53]Cremin, *The Transformation of the School*, 147–53; Paul E. and Blanche R. Alyea, *Fairhope, 1894–1954: The Story of a Single Tax Colony* (University, Ala., 1956), 146–47, 153–58; Donald D. Chipman, "Young Kilpatrick and the Progressive Idea," *History of Education Quarterly* 17 (Winter 1977): 407–15.

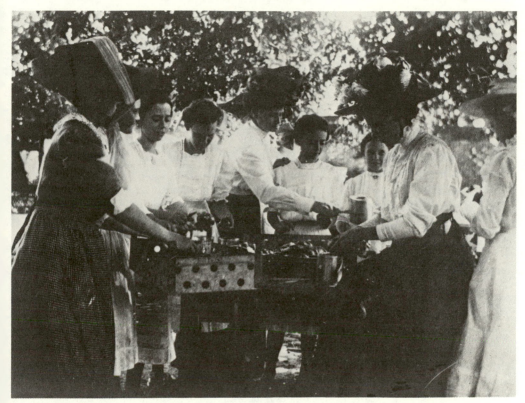

Members of a tomato club at work, Aiken County, South Carolina, 1910. *National Archives and Records Service.*

was nothing less than "to create and to energize the idea of social progress, of national integrity, of industrial justice, and of spiritual power."[54] Although these lofty ideals were never realized, southern colleges were an integral part of a reform structure that included superintendents of public instruction, state departments of education, philanthropic foundations, and friendly political leaders. The college, in Mitchell's view, was "a pioneer" in the struggle for universal education in the South. "Its teachers have stumped the state for the common school; its students have energized in behalf of education the communities to which they have gone; its spirit has been a powerful factor in molding public opinion in the interest of popular enlightenment."[55] Most of the educational leaders were state university men, but there were influential reformers in private institutions, including James H. Kirkland of Vanderbilt University. There were also notable educators in black schools, such as Hollis B. Frissell of Hampton Institute and Booker T. Washington of Tuskegee Institute.

For all their poverty and provincialism, the southern institutions of higher learning were affected by many of the trends that were reshaping colleges and universities in other parts of the country. They, too, came under the sway of the elective system, broadened their curricula, increasingly reflected a more secularized atmosphere, and aspired to be universities rather than mere colleges. They benefited not only from the direction of able administrators such as Chancellor Walter B. Hill of the University of Georgia but also from the leavening influence of a stream of young doctors of philosophy coming out of the graduate schools at Johns Hopkins, Columbia, and other universities in the North and abroad. The idea of the modern university caught the fancy of many southern educators, and the example of the dynamic state universities in the Midwest inspired many southern leaders. In 1904, for example, forty Georgians, including the governor and the chancellor and trustees of the University of Georgia, visited Madison to examine the innovations that were making the University of Wisconsin "a model northern state university."[56] By the time the war in Europe began in 1914, higher education in the South had made genuine progress, particularly among state institutions. Enrollments had grown, new state colleges had been established, a professional professoriat had started to develop, and the university had begun to conceive of its social role in far broader terms than had been true a decade and a half earlier.[57]

[54]Mitchell, "The Task of the College in the South," *SAQ* 6 (July 1907): 259–62; quotation on p. 262.

[55]Ibid., 259–60.

[56]Cremin, *The Transformation of the School*, 168. Also see Daniel W. Hollis, "Samuel Chiles Mitchell: Social Reformer in Blease's South Carolina," *S.C. Hist. Mag.* 70 (Jan. 1969): 28; Ray Mathis, "Walter B. Hill and the Savage Ideal," *Ga. Hist. Quar.* 60 (Spring 1976): 23–34; and "Chancellor Hill," *Outlook* 82 (Jan. 6, 1906): 11.

[57]See, for example, Daniel Walker Hollis, *University of South Carolina*, vol. 2: *College to University* (Columbia, S.C., 1956), 160–220, 239–82; Earl W. Porter, *Trinity and Duke, 1892–1924: Foundations of Duke University* (Durham, N.C., 1964), 140–96; and James Riley

Improvements were limited and far from universal, however, and most of the section's colleges remained poor, parochial, and often dominated by sectarianism. Black colleges, while numerous, suffered from discrimination in the allocation of state appropriations and from private neglect in the wake of the decision by northern philanthropists to support the southern education movement for whites and programs of vocational education. Writing in 1903, William E. B. Du Bois warned that "the best of the Negro colleges are poorly equipped and are today losing support and countenance. . . ." Without a few strong, well-equipped black colleges, Du Bois wrote, "the forces of social regeneration will be fatally weakened, for the college to-day among Negroes is, just as truly as it was yesterday among whites, the beginning and not the end of human training, the foundation and not the capstone of popular education."[58] Such fears were well grounded, and the slow process of developing black colleges and universities would not gather much vitality for more than a decade after Du Bois wrote.

Women were also marginal beneficiaries of the movement to develop higher education in the South during the progressive era. Stereotyped by regional tradition, discriminated against in the state universities, and denied admission to many of the professional schools, southern women found their greatest opportunities in the teacher training and domestic science programs of the state-supported normal schools and women's colleges. The prejudice against admitting women to colleges and universities was strong, and not even a determined struggle could open the gates of institutions such as the University of Virginia.[59] Still, there was a stirring of interest in higher education among southern women, and their reform endeavors included freer access to the broadening programs of the colleges and universities. One champion of women's rights, Lilian W. Johnson, wrote in early 1907 of her efforts to interest clubwomen in making a real study of education and to organize college graduates into chapters of the Southern Association of College Women with programs of local educational work. While making twenty-five addresses in one month, she found "the club women eager to take up a definite programme on education; the college women longing for some organization through which they could reach each other and the young girls of their communities; and I found hundreds of girls planning for a college course."[60] There was, in fact, a

---

Montgomery, *The Volunteer State Forges Its University: The University of Tennessee, 1887–1919* (Knoxville, 1966), 50–129, 203–10.

[58]Du Bois, "The Training of Negroes for Social Power," 414.

[59]Mary Cooke Branch Munford and other feminists were able to secure the establishment of Mary Washington College, a "coordinate institution" located in Fredericksburg, seventy miles from the university in Charlottesville. See Anne Hobson Freeman, "Mary Munford's Fight for a College for Women Co-ordinate with the University of Virginia," *Va. Mag. Hist. and Biog.* 78 (Oct. 1970): 481–91. Also see Sara Bertha Townsend, "The Admission of Women to the University of Georgia," *Ga. Hist. Quar.* 43 (June 1959): 156–69.

[60]Lilian W. Johnson to Robert C. Ogden, Feb. 28, 1907, Ogden Papers.

fresh and zestful quality about the educational activities of middle-class women in the South. Their contributions, through literary clubs and other organizations, to the discussion of informal education for women went well beyond formal study in the colleges and universities.[61]

The stronger universities in the South reflected the service ideal that characterized so many American universities during the progressive period. This ideal, with its faith in equality of opportunity and in material and moral progress, was a manifestation of the larger progressive ferment of the early twentieth century. Thus the new universities busied themselves in establishing a variety of public services in such fields as teacher training, agricultural and domestic science programs, public health work, creation of libraries, and the founding of state historical societies and journals.[62] The service ideal among college students in the South was encouraged by the Young Men's Christian Association and the Young Women's Christian Association. The campus chapters of the YMCA in particular expressed the developing service rationale and the mood of progressivism. The Y's in the South also worked to popularize the idea of higher education. "College sentiment is growing among us," the general secretary of the Mobile YMCA wrote in 1903, "and each year more of our young men are going to college."[63] Still other campus organizations promoted social service programs. At the University of Virginia, for example, undergraduates in 1911 directed the attention of the Civic Club to the spiritual and moral needs of the Virginia mountain people.[64]

One of the most important state services performed by the region's colleges and universities was the professional training of the growing body of public school teachers. This function was a basic element in the widespread commitment to education as a redemptive force in southern life. The Summer School of the South, inaugurated at the University of Tennessee in 1902 as an instrument of the southern education movement, demonstrated the need for and the potential role of teachers' colleges in the state universities. Most of the state institutions in the South soon established such schools; the states also created new

[61]See, for example, John M. McBryde, Jr., "Womanly Education for Woman," *Sewanee Review* 15 (Oct. 1907): 467–84; Anne Firor Scott, *The Southern Lady: From Pedestal to Politics, 1830–1930* (Chicago, 1970), 114–17; Barbara Kuhn Campbell, *The "Liberated" Woman of 1914: Prominent Women in the Progressive Era* (Ann Arbor, Mich., 1979), 30–36, 38, 41–42, 57, 161–62; Lloyd C. Taylor, Jr., "Lila Meade Valentine: The FFV as Reformer," *Va. Mag. Hist. and Biog.* 70 (Oct. 1962): 471–87; and Curt Porter, "Chautauqua and Tennessee: A Study of the Chautauqua Movement in Tennessee" (Honors essay, Vanderbilt Univ., 1963).

[62]Frederick Rudolph, *The American College and University: A History* (New York, 1962), 355–72; John P. Kennedy, Jr., "The Value of a State Library Commission," *SAQ* 5 (July 1906): 275–87; Louis R. Wilson, "The Use of Books and Libraries in North Carolina," *Jour. Soc. Forces* 1 (Jan. 1923): 78–86; Roger D. Tate, Jr., "Franklin L. Riley and the University of Mississippi (1897–1914)," *Jour. Miss. Hist.* 42 (May 1980): 99–111.

[63]Archibald Clinton Harte to Woodrow Wilson, Sept. 18, 1903, in Arthur S. Link and associates, eds., *The Papers of Woodrow Wilson*, vol. 15 (Princeton, N.J., 1973), 3–4.

[64]Clarence B. Wallace, "The Moral Influences of College Life and Training," *SAQ* 7 (Jan. 1908): 78; Rudolph, *The American College and University*, 366.

normal schools apart from the existing universities as a means of helping train public school teachers. Under the leadership of Bruce R. Payne, George Peabody College for Teachers, founded in Nashville in 1909, became a kind of regional center for the promotion of education.[65] The teachers' colleges and normal schools, working with the departments of education, made a major contribution to the emergence of a uniform system of public education in the various southern states. The colleges and universities also played an important part in the organization and professionalization of teachers by supporting the activities of educational associations and journals, school improvement groups, and the parent-teacher movement.[66]

Most of the state universities cooperated with the General Education Board and other foundations in implementing the latter's school programs. The Southern Education Board, with GEB funds, appointed rural school supervisors in all southern states. Usually associated with the state universities and departments of education, these educators sought to promote better county school supervision, to establish parent-teacher organizations, to introduce agricultural and industrial programs, and to increase school support generally. One of the most effective of the rural supervisors was William Knox Tate, who served four years in South Carolina before becoming professor of rural education at George Peabody College in 1914. Tate traveled 25,000 miles during his first year as a supervisor, addressing educational meetings, supervising schools, and encouraging such reforms as school consolidation. Beginning with Virginia in 1905, the GEB provided money to pay the salary of a secondary school specialist in every state university in the South. These professors, in effect "high school evangelists," worked for the passage of state legislation to support high schools, traveled over their respective states, and tried to popularize secondary schools.[67]

The development of the university was closely associated with the southern progressives' longing for economic progress, industrialization, and "material uplifting." The university would be an indispensable instrument in this economic transformation. Thus a professor at the University of Arkansas sug-

[65]Dabney, *The Southern Education Movement*, 114–22; W.F. O'Donnell, "Five Decades of Teacher Education in Kentucky," *Filson Club Hist. Quar.* 30 (Apr. 1956): 115–24.

[66]Mabel Maxwell Jones, "Georgia and the PTA," *Georgia Review* 4 (Winter 1950): 346–52; Frank B. Williams, Jr., "The East Tennessee Education Association, 1903–1954," *East Tenn. Hist. Society's Pubs.* 27 (1955): 49–76; Clara B. Kennan, "Educational Journals in Arkansas," *Ark. Hist. Quar.* 19 (Winter 1960): 325–47; Oscar W. Davison, "Early History of the Oklahoma Education Association," *Chron. Okla.* 29 (Spring 1951): 42–60; Willard Badgette Gatewood, Jr., "Eugene Clyde Brooks: Educator-Journalist in North Carolina, 1906–1923," *N.C. Hist. Rev.* 36 (July 1959): 307–29; Bettersworth, *Mississippi*, 480–89; Wayne Urban, "Organized Teachers and Educational Reform During the Progressive Era: 1890–1920," *History of Education Quarterly* 16 (Spring 1976): 35–52; Ernest J. Middleton, "The Louisiana Education Association, 1901–1970," *Jour. Negro Edu.* 47 (Fall 1978): 363–78.

[67]Fosdick, *Adventure in Giving*, 26–38, 64–74; Dabney, *The Southern Education Movement*, 222–27; GEB, *The General Education Board*, 79–90; S.L. Smith, *Builders of Goodwill: The Story of the State Agents of Negro Education in the South, 1910 to 1950* (Nashville, 1950).

gested in 1912 that the state university should promote democracy, social service, and economic efficiency and research. "The state university professor," according to this writer, "is a public officer and is imbued with the spirit of service." In addition to his professional duties, "he may be serving as an expert on a commission on railroad rates, currency, banking, the tariff; or he may be conducting a geological survey, a farmers' institute, an agricultural survey, determining the water power of the state, or acting as the director of a legislative reference bureau or of a state history commission."[68] Graduates of the university presumably would also be "imbued with the spirit of service." But even if they were, how could the quality of higher education in the region be elevated?

Raising standards concerned some college and university leaders in the South. A contemporary observer pointed out in 1909 that the southern education movement had followed two main lines: "a public impetus in the nature of wide-spread interest and enthusiasm in things educational" and a "private and more personal struggle for efficient standards."[69] Although the two themes were not necessarily incompatible, the emphasis upon popular education and numbers of schools, pupils, and programs threatened, in the opinion of thoughtful educators, to sacrifice quality for quantity. Other southern school leaders were afraid that the educational awakening in the South, with its emphasis upon the needs of the "average man" and the promotion of industrial and vocational training, would severely damage higher education in the region. "The whole atmosphere of the state university," a Kentucky professor lamented in 1912, "tends strongly toward the side-tracking of the undergraduate academic student at an early age into some vocational course."[70]

A few college and university leaders waged an unremitting battle to raise the standards for admission to and graduation from southern institutions. Chancellor Kirkland of Vanderbilt was perhaps the most zealous champion of such reforms. Under his leadership the Southern Association of Colleges and Secondary Schools was founded in 1895 "to elevate the standards of scholarship and to effect uniformity of entrance requirements." Cooperating institutions agreed to abandon preparatory classes, to hold written examinations, and to establish definite entrance requirements. By 1913 the Southern Association claimed twenty-eight members, though few of them required the completion of a four-year program for a bachelor's degree. Meanwhile, several other agencies sought to lift the standards of southern colleges and universities. In 1898 the Southern Methodist church created an education commission with authority to

---

[68]John H. Reynolds, "The State University and a National System of Education," *SAQ* 11 (Apr. 1912): 158–69; quotation on p. 165.

[69]John Bell Henneman, "The South's Opportunity in Education: The Problem of the Application of Standards," *Sewanee Review* 17 (Jan. 1909): 89. Also see William E. Dodd, "Another View of Our Educational Progress," *SAQ* 2 (Oct. 1903): 325–33.

[70]Thomas Lindsey Blayney, "The Liberal Arts College and the New South," *SAQ* 11 (Apr. 1912): 121. Also see Blayney, "The Renascence of the Liberal Arts College," *Sewanee Review* 20 (Apr. 1912): 175–90, and Wallace, "The Moral Influences of College Life and Training," 79.

Vanderbilt University class of 1903, junior year. *Photographic Archive, Vanderbilt University.*

fix minimum requirements for admission and graduation for all of its affiliated colleges and secondary schools. The Carnegie Foundation for the Advancement of Teaching had some effect, since it rated colleges according to admission requirements, made grants only to institutions that adhered to its standards, and published the results of its investigations. The General Education Board's college-aid program also served to make higher education in the South more rigorous. By 1914 the GEB had given thirty-two southern institutions some $3 million.[71]

The school, the region's educational reformers believed, was "the epitome of the South's problem." Social progress depended upon the organization and development of a strong school system. As the southern education movement gained support, the optimism of the progressive educators increased. Thus one of them asserted in 1908 that the South had "found in the school the latent potency that will create industries, uphold the masses, adjust racial differences, and regain political prestige."[72] It was an inspired vision of regional transformation. But the burden of progress rested squarely on the school, for it was assumed that "through education the people would become not only literate and economically productive but racially tolerant."[73] Although many other southern progressives were more restrained in their expectations of social improvements through education, the school was almost always regarded by the reformers as a redemptive force in the development of a better South.

[71]James H. Kirkland, "The High Schools and the University," *SAQ* 6 (July 1907): 223–35; William P. Few, "The Standardizing of Southern Colleges," ibid. 7 (Jan. 1908): 1–10; Edwin Mims, *Chancellor Kirkland of Vanderbilt* (Nashville, 1940), 129–43.

[72]S.C. Mitchell, "The School as the Exponent of Democracy," *Sewanee Review* 16 (Jan. 1908): 18. Also see Mitchell, "The Ethics of Democracy," *University of Tennessee Record* 15 (Aug. 1912): 19–24.

[73]Clayton, *The Savage Ideal*, 110.

9   *Efficiency and Modernization*

SOUTHERN PROGRESSIVES ASSUMED THAT social distress could be ameliorated or prevented through economic development. Keenly aware of their section's pervasive poverty and of its dependence on outside developers and capital, they embraced the New South creed of industrial growth and economic diversification. This led them to emphasize efficiency, rationality, and the potential benefits of science. Thus a North Carolina professor, eager to find evidence of regional progress, reported in 1911 that practically every southern industry was being put on a more "substantial basis" as a result of "better organization, expert management, or technical skill." He cited, as illustrations of the contribution of science to southern development, the work of Charles H. Herty in transforming the turpentine industry and the application of technical knowledge by George G. Crawford in improving the iron and steel business of the Birmingham district.[1] The objective was material progress, for it would provide the key not only to the South's economic well-being, but also to the amelioration of its social problems and to its cultural enlightenment. The notion of an industrialized South, moreover, was essentially "a blueprint for southern economic and cultural independence" as well as freedom from the "chains of mercantile subservience to the North."[2]

Accepting the claims of science and technology, the progressives tended to rely upon objective information, the "facts," and the desirability of using experts in public administration and in dealing with social problems. This tendency became more obvious as "the campaigning era" in behalf of various reforms ended and as concern shifted to effective administration and the provision of public services.[3] The middle-class innovators, themselves products of

[1] Edwin Mims, "The South Realizing Itself: Remakers of Industry," *World's Work* 23 (Dec. 1911): 203–19. Also see "Changing Methods in the South," ibid. 14 (July 1907); 9055–56.

[2] James E. Brittain and Robert C. McMath, Jr., "Engineers and the New South Creed: The Formation and Early Development of Georgia Tech," *Technology and Culture* 18 (Apr. 1977): 175–201; quotation on p. 179.

[3] For an example, see Bruce R. Payne to Edwin Mims, Dec. 24, 1907, quoted in Leah Marie

the New South economy, moved instinctively to staff the reform organizations and newly created public agencies with experts and trained professionals. Without having clearly analyzed the matter, they were, in a measure at least, environmentalists with an implicit confidence in social improvement through economic and institutional innovation.

MODERNIZING THE SOUTHERN CITY

Municipal reform made up an essential part of southern progressivism. While it reflected all of the progressive tendencies of the age, the most significant aspect of municipal reform in the South was the movement to modernize the organization and administration of the city. Part of the reform impetus was a desire for stability in the midst of rapid change in the region's larger cities. But at a deeper level municipal reform was closely related to the South's obsession with industrialization, economic development, and material progress. Businessmen, professionals, and members of the new middle class provided much of the leadership for organized efforts to reform the city. This goes far to explain the moderate character of the southern progressives: their essential conservatism, their suspicion of the masses, and the limited nature of their social reforms.

The urban South was, in considerable part, a product of the region's recent urbanization. The growth of interior railroad and manufacturing centers was especially notable. Birmingham's population increased from 38,415 in 1900 to 178,806 in 1920, Atlanta's increased from 89,872 to 200,616 and Richmond's from 85,050 to 171,667 in the same period, while the populations of Houston, Dallas, and San Antonio more than tripled during the same two decades. Spindletop made Beaumont the "Queen of the Neches," causing its population to surge up from 10,000 to 30,000 within a few months. To the north, Oklahoma City grew from 10,037 in 1900 to 91,295 in 1920. Indeed, the rate of urbanization in the South was proceeding at a faster pace than that of the country as a whole, though not as fast as in the years after 1920.[4]

Despite the growth of southern cities, the section remained overwhelmingly rural during the first part of the twentieth century. In 1900 only about 16 percent of the South's inhabitants resided in towns or cities of 2,500 or more, as compared with 40 percent for the entire nation. The urbanism of the individual southern states ranged from Mississippi's 7.7 percent to Louisiana's 26.5 percent. Only three southern cities—New Orleans, Louisville, and Memphis— had a population of more than 100,000. Although the rate of urbanization in the

---

Park, "Edwin Mims and *The Advancing South* (1894–1926): A Study of a Southern Liberal" (M.A. thesis, Vanderbilt Univ., 1964), 29–30.

[4]Walter J. Matherly, "The Urban Development of the South," *South. Econ. Jour.* 1 (Feb. 1935): 19; Robert Wickliffe Woolley, "The Development of Our Gulf Ports," *American Monthly Review of Reviews* 33 (Feb. 1906): 190–99; Solomon S. Huebner, "The Development of Foreign Commerce of the South," in *The South in the Building of the Nation*, vol. 6, pp. 351–56; Carl Coke Rister, *Oil! Titan of the Southwest* (Norman, Okla., 1949), 60.

TABLE 11. *Largest Southern Cities, 1900, 1910, and 1920*

1900		1910		1920	
New Orleans	287,104	New Orleans	339,075	New Orleans	387,219
Louisville	204,731	Louisville	223,928	Louisville	234,891
Memphis	102,320	Atlanta	154,839	Atlanta	200,616
Atlanta	89,872	Birmingham	132,685	Birmingham	178,806
Richmond	85,050	Memphis	131,105	Richmond	171,667
Nashville	80,865	Richmond	127,628	Memphis	162,351
Charleston	55,807	Nashville	110,364	San Antonio	161,379
Savannah	54,244	San Antonio	96,614	Dallas	158,976
San Antonio	53,321	Dallas	92,104	Houston	138,276
Norfolk	46,624	Houston	78,800	Nashville	118,342
Houston	44,633	Fort Worth	73,312	Norfolk	115,777
Covington	42,938	Norfolk	67,452	Fort Worth	106,482
Dallas	42,638	Savannah	65,064	Jacksonville	91,558
Augusta	39,441	Oklahoma City	64,205	Oklahoma City	91,295
Mobile	38,469	Charleston	58,833	Savannah	83,252

SOURCES: *Twelfth Census of the United States . . . Population*, part 1 (Washington, D.C., 1901), pp. lxix–lxx; *Thirteenth Census of the United States . . .* , vol. 1: *Population, 1910 . . .* (Washington, D.C., 1913), 84–87; *Fourteenth Census of the United States . . .* , vol. 1: *Population, 1920 . . .* (Washington, D.C., 1921), 80–86.

region, especially in the Southwest, increased faster than that of the whole country during the following decades, the South was only about one-fourth urban in 1920 as compared with more than one-half for the nation as a whole.[5] Much of the South's urban expansion, moreover, resulted from migration into the cities and larger towns from the surrounding countryside and villages, creating what one scholar has described as a "rural lag" on southern cities.[6]

The impressive growth of the South's larger cities created a pressing need for an expansion of municipal services such as public utilities, transportation systems, schools, and health facilities. Primitive water and sewer systems constituted a continuing health hazard in many towns and cities. A majority of city residents in the South at the turn of the century still relied on cisterns and wells for water. In 1902 twelve southern cities with a population of 25,000 or more people had no public library.[7] Vagrancy, violence, vice, and political corrup-

[5]Matherly, "The Urban Development of the South," 3–25; Walter J. Matherly, "The Emergence of the Metropolitan Community in the South," *Social Forces* 14 (Mar. 1936): 311–25; Blaine A. Brownell, "Urbanization in the South: A Unique Experience?" *Mississippi Quarterly* 26 (Spring 1973): 105–20.

[6]Gerald M. Capers, "The Rural Lag on Southern Cities," *Miss. Quar.* 21 (Fall 1968): 253–61. Also see William D. Miller, "Rural Ideals in Memphis Life at the Turn of the Century," *West Tenn. Hist. Soc. Papers* 4 (1950): 41–49, and "Rural Values and Urban Progress: Memphis, 1900–1917," *Miss. Quar.* 21 (Fall 1968): 263–74.

[7]Howard N. Rabinowitz, "Continuity and Change: Southern Urban Development, 1860–

The Urban South: Birmingham as seen from the northwest in 1914. *Alvin W. Hudson Collection, Birmingham.*

tion flourished in many of the region's cities. Memphis, for instance, had acquired a well-deserved reputation as a "sin-center." The high percentage of newcomers contributed to the disorder and conflict in the urban South. An educational census of 1918 revealed that less than 2 percent of the 11,781 white parents of schoolchildren in Memphis had been born in that city. While rural values remained pervasive in southern cities during the progressive era, the process of urbanization undoubtedly heightened the contrast between older customs and newer habits, thereby contributing to the conflict over many of the reform campaigns.[8]

Municipal reformers in the South tended to stress expansion, order, and efficiency as major objectives in the improvement of their individual cities. Much of the impetus for reform came from business and professional elements, which dominated the voluntary civic organizations and were usually zealous supporters of city-building. In city after city they led the drive for urban growth, expanded services, more honest and efficient government, and clean-up campaigns in the interest of order, morality, and a good name. These early twentieth-century progressives were somewhat similar to the good-government reformers in New Orleans and a few other southern cities in the 1890s. But there was an important difference. The "commercial-civic elite" of later years, particularly in the dynamic new transportation centers and manufacturing cities, included many "new men" and possessed a marked bourgeois character.[9] Whatever their social aspirations, these men could hardly be compared with New Orleans' "silk-stocking" reformers or the leaders of its Mardi Gras festival.

A recent study of Birmingham demonstrates the close correlation between economic power and political influence in the late nineteenth and early twentieth centuries. In Birmingham, as in most other American cities at the turn of the century, economic power was concentrated in a small minority made up of

---

1900," in Blaine A. Brownell and David R. Goldfield, eds., *The City in Southern History: The Growth of Urban Civilization in the South* (Port Washington, N.Y., 1977), 111–12.

[8]Capers, "The Rural Lag on Southern Cities," 260–61; Martha Mitchell Bigelow, "Birmingham's Carnival of Crime, 1871–1910," *Ala. Rev.* 3 (Apr. 1950): 123–33; William D. Miller, *Memphis During the Progressive Era, 1900–1917* (Memphis, 1957), 88–103; Joy Jackson, "Crime and the Conscience of a City," *La. Hist.* 9 (Summer 1968): 229–44; Brownell, "The Urban South Comes of Age, 1900–1940," in Brownell and Goldfield, eds., *The City in Southern History*, 142–46; L.E. Fredman, *The Australian Ballot: The Story of an American Reform* (n.p., 1968), 78, 102, 114–15.

[9]Don Harrison Doyle, "Urbanization and Southern Culture: Economic Elites in Four New South Cities (Atlanta, Nashville, Charleston, Mobile), c. 1865–1910," in Orville Vernon Burton and Robert C. McMath, eds., *Toward a New South? Studies in Post-Civil War Southern Communities* (Westport, Conn., 1982), 11–36. Also see Doyle, "Leadership and Decline in Postwar Charleston, 1865–1910," in Walter J. Fraser, Jr., and Winfred B. Moore, Jr., eds., *From the Old South to the New: Essays on the Transitional South* (Westport, Conn., 1981), 93–106, and Howard L. Preston, "The Automobile Business in Atlanta, 1909–1920: A Symbol of 'New South' Prosperity," *Ga. Hist. Quar.* 58 (Summer 1974): 262–77.

industrialists, corporation executives, bankers, and the wealthiest commercial and professional people. Political power—the relative pressure that individuals or groups were able to exert in the city's decision-making process—was concentrated in the top 20 percent of the population in terms of economic position. Although these upper- and middle-ranking economic groups were not politically monolithic, they were heavily favored in municipal tax policy, in the allocation of services, and in social, economic, and utility regulation. They dominated the most important commercial and civic organizations and were closely associated with city officials.[10]

Economic interests ranged from railroads and utilities to manufacturing industries, real estate companies, and wholesale and retail merchants involved in the functional sectors of the local economy. Many of these industrial and commercial concerns were well organized at the state and local levels.[11] There were also other elements having common interests, including trade union councils in most southern cities and numerous professional associations and social interest groups like the Anti-Saloon League. But the top economic groups generally enjoyed the most success in determining municipal decisions. Although poor whites and blacks were not without political influence, their role in the making of municipal policy was very limited. Since most black southerners had been disfranchised, along with many poor and illiterate whites, the southern urban electorate was relatively homogeneous and increasingly middle- and upper-class in makeup.[12]

None of the economic interest groups or civic organizations controlled by business elements was more instrumental in shaping municipal reform in the South than local chambers of commerce. Organized in the late nineteenth century or early in the twentieth, in many cases on the basis of older merchant associations, the chambers embodied the commercial-civic passion for urban growth and order. They called for efficiency in government, as in private business, and were inclined to define the concept in terms of economic growth and development. The individual chamber worked to develop the economy of its own city, to extend municipal services, to reorganize governmental authority at the local level, and to eliminate waste, inefficiency, and immorality. In Houston, for example, the chamber organized the Clean-Up Movement League and sponsored an educational campaign to support its activities. Chambers of commerce and other associations of businessmen were almost always in the van of efforts to revise city charters and to introduce such innovations as civil service and budgetary reform. Of thirty-two city-manager systems

[10]Carl V. Harris, *Political Power in Birmingham, 1871–1921* (Knoxville, 1977), 3, 6–7, 38–40, 95–96, 175–76, 185, 216, 243, 268–71, 275–76. For another example of the relationship between economic and political power in southern cities, see Eugene J. Watts, *The Social Bases of City Politics: Atlanta, 1865–1903* (Westport, Conn., 1978).

[11]See Harris, *Political Power in Birmingham*, 39–56.

[12]See, for example, Samuel M. Kipp III, "Old Notables and Newcomers: The Economic and Political Elite of Greensboro, North Carolina, 1880–1920," *JSH* 43 (Aug. 1977): 393–94.

adopted in Oklahoma by the 1920s, twenty-nine were initiated by chambers of commerce or by community committees dominated by businessmen.[13]

Some of the municipal reform campaigns, in the 1890s and early in the new century, were directed at entrenched political organizations identified with corruption, vice, and inadequate services. These efforts, frequently involving good-government leagues and clean-up drives, were highly moralistic. They were often identified with demands for civil service reform, electoral innovations like the direct primary and the Australian ballot, and opposition to boss rule. In 1896, for example, a Citizens' League organized by well-to-do and socially prominent New Orleanians undertook a reform campaign that overthrew the political "machine" in that city. In the Birmingham mayoral race of 1904, George B. Ward, an investment broker, was elected on a "good-government" and "antimachine" platform. During the following year a coalition of reform groups attempted to oust the entrenched Democratic organization of John H. Whallen in Louisville, an effort that eventually produced a reform mayor named Robert W. Bingham.[14] The reformers in these assaults on urban bosses were seldom able to stay in power long or to accomplish all their objectives, but "reform" mayors represented a characteristic aspect of southern progressivism in the cities. As John M. Parker of Louisiana declared in 1912, "I am still an enthusiast in the fight to down the bosses, and believe their being absolutely routed, is necessary to prevent the seventeen bosses of the City of New Orleans, and the bosses of the Free State of Jefferson, St. Bernard, and a few other Parishes from uniting and dictating every office, from constable to Supreme Court, on the State Ticket."[15]

Important features of municipal reform in the South at the turn of the century were included in the program of the National Municipal League (NML), which

[13]Jerome H. Farbar, "The Houston Chamber of Commerce," *National Municipal Review* 2 (Jan. 1913): 104–107; Tom M. Deaton, "The Chamber of Commerce in the Economic and Political Development of Atlanta from 1900 to 1916," *Atlanta Historical Bulletin* 19 (1975): 19–33; Samuel P. Hays, "The Politics of Reform in Municipal Government in the Progressive Era," *Pacific Northwest Quarterly* 55 (Oct. 1964): 159; Martin J. Schiesl, *The Politics of Efficiency: Municipal Administration and Reform in America, 1880–1920* (Berkeley, Calif., 1977), 2–3, 138–40, 177; Lawrence L. Graves, "Lubbock: An Epitome of Urbanization," *West Texas Historical Association Year Book* 36 (1960): 3–17; Burton I. Kaufman, "New Orleans and the Panama Canal, 1900–1914," *La. Hist.* 14 (Fall 1973): 333–46; Charles Garofalo, "The Atlanta Spirit: A Study in Urban Ideology," *SAQ* 74 (Winter 1975): 34–44; Carl Abbott, "Norfolk in the New Century: The Jamestown Exposition and Urban Boosterism," *Va. Mag. Hist. and Biog.* 85 (Jan. 1977): 86–96.

[14]Edward F. Haas, "John Fitzpatrick and Political Continuity in New Orleans, 1896–1899," *La. Hist.* 22 (Winter 1981): 7–29; Martha Carolyn Mitchell, "Birmingham: Biography of a City of the New South" (Ph.D. diss., Univ. of Chicago, 1946), 89–96; Bennett H. Wall, "Louisville Politics, 1880–1910," paper presented at annual meeting of the Mississippi Valley Historical Association, Louisville, April 1960; William E. Ellis, "Robert Worth Bingham and Louisville Progressivism, 1905–1910," *Filson Club. Hist. Quar.* 54 (Apr. 1980): 169–95; Brownell, "The Urban South Comes of Age," 152–53; Evan Marcus Anders, "Bosses under Siege: The Politics of South Texas during the Progressive Era" (Ph.D. diss., Univ. of Texas at Austin, 1978).

[15]Parker to W.F. Millsaps, March 25, 1912, John M. Parker Papers, Southern Historical Collection, University of North Carolina.

had been organized in 1894. The league soon began to receive reports on conditions in southern cities, and at its annual meeting in Baltimore in 1896 it gave special attention to the government of municipalities in the South. The NML met in Louisville in 1897 and in Richmond in 1911. It adopted a model charter in 1900 that proposed such reforms as limited home rule, an increase in the powers of the mayor, a council-appointed auditor or comptroller, limits on city indebtedness, restrictions on the granting of long-term franchises, and the separation of local from state and national elections.[16] Just as the commercial-civic leaders promoted such improvements as harbor and river development, better transportation links, and an image of their own city as an entity of dynamic, purposeful growth, so did they endeavor to enlarge their respective municipalities by annexing the surrounding areas. Annexation promised not only to advertise a city's growth, but also to raise the local tax base and make possible more adequate and better integrated urban services. Economic elites were sometimes divided over the merits of annexation, with outlying industrialists and suburban residents in opposition and the central business community in support. But the expansionists frequently triumphed. Atlanta more than doubled its land area between 1900 and 1920; Birmingham added approximately 72,000 people to its population by means of annexation in 1910; and many other southern cities legally incorporated their rapidly growing fringes during the first years of the century.[17]

Southern municipal reformers devoted much of their attention to the task of extending and modernizing urban services. Most of the region's cities made some progress in this endeavor, although their wealth and per capita tax levies remained significantly below the national average during this period. City authorities and civic groups stressed street development, transportation, public utilities, and police and fire protection. By 1900 every large city in the South had acquired a functioning streetcar system. The high rates charged by private utility companies caused several Dixie cities to build or buy their own utility plants. In 1902, Richmond had one of the five municipally owned gasworks in the nation. Several southern cities owned their own electric light plants (including Nashville, Jacksonville, and Fort Worth), and a larger number operated their own waterworks. The threat of disease encouraged most towns and cities to run fresh water and sewer lines into outlying areas and neglected districts within their boundaries. Seeking to attract new residents and business enterprises and to make life in the city generally more attractive, southern progres-

[16]Frank Mann Stewart, *A Half Century of Municipal Reform: The History of the National Municipal League* (Berkeley, Calif., 1950), 24–25, 50, 73–74, 196; Bradley Robert Rice, *Progressive Cities: The Commission Government Movement in America, 1901–1920* (Austin, Tex., 1977), pp. xii–xiii.

[17]Rabinowitz, "Southern Urban Development, 1860–1900," p. 115; Brownell, "The Urban South Comes of Age," 135–36; Carl V. Harris, "Annexation Struggles and Political Power in Birmingham, Alabama, 1890–1910," *Ala. Rev.* 27 (July 1974): 163–84; William D. Miller, "J.J. Williams and the Greater Memphis Movement," *West Tenn. Hist. Soc. Papers* 5 (1951): 14–30.

sives worked to develop schools and libraries, to provide more adequate utilities, and to establish parks and amusement facilities. But the major bene-neficiaries of such expanded services were usually the commercial elites and the new middle class. White working-class neighborhoods were rarely af-forded such services until the downtown districts and the more affluent residen-tial sections were taken care of. Black areas shared even less equitably in the expansion of municipal services. Large parts of the growing southern cities, white as well as black, were accustomed to inferior housing, unsanitary facilities, poor schools, unpaved streets, and little fire or police protection.[18]

Structural changes in municipal government also appealed to southern re-formers, particularly those from business and professional groups. Elements of this kind had supported charter reform efforts in the late nineteenth century to strengthen city government by making municipalities more independent of state legislatures, by giving mayors greater power, and by improving local adminis-tration. But charter reform made relatively little progress until 1901, when Galveston, Texas, devised an entirely new system of government in an effort to cope with the emergency created by a severe hurricane and tidal wave. With the city in havoc, Galveston's business leaders formulated an emergency plan based on the assumption that "a municipality is largely a business corporation" and should apply business methods to public service.[19] The Galveston plan, legitimized by a special act of the state legislature in 1901, provided for a five-member commission with the combined powers of mayor and aldermen. Each commissioner was responsible for a city department and functioned as both legislator and administrator. The commission dealt with all of the city's business. Although businessmen took the initiative in establishing commission government in Galveston, organized labor and various other groups supported the innovation. The new administration seemed to work well. Schools were built, the water plant was improved, the sewer system was extended, streets were cleaned and repaved, the costs of city government were reduced, and the city's credit was restored.[20]

[18]Rabinowitz, "Southern Urban Development, 1860–1900," pp. 110–13, 116, 119; Brownell, "The Urban South Comes of Age," 135, 140, 150–51, 153–55; Simon J. McLean, "City Govern-ment in Arkansas," *Annals* 17 (May 1901): 132–33; Solomon Wolff, "Public Service Corporations of New Orleans," *Annals* 31 (May 1908): 96–104; Morris Knowles, "Water and Waste: The Sanitary Problems of a Modern Industrial District," *Survey* 27 (Jan. 6, 1912): 1485–1500; John Ihlder, "Housing, Health and Morals in Richmond, Virginia," *National Municipal Review* 1 (Apr. 1912): 228–30; William Kenneth Boyd, *The Story of Durham: City of the New South* (Durham, N.C., 1925), 298–319; William D. Miller, "The Progressive Movement in Memphis," *Tenn. Hist. Quar.* 15 (Mar. 1956): 3–16; Durward Long, "The Making of Modern Tampa: A City of the New South, 1865–1911," *Fla. Hist. Quar.* 49 (Apr. 1971): 333–45; Paul E. Isaac, "Munici-pal Reform in Beaumont, Texas, 1902–1909," *Southwestern Hist. Quar.* 78 (Apr. 1975): 409–30.

[19]James Weinstein, "Organized Business and the City Commission and Manager Move-ments," *JSH* 28 (May 1962): 168.

[20]Ibid., 169; H.J. Haskell, "The Texas Idea: City Government by a Board of Directors," *Outlook* 85 (Apr. 13, 1907): 839–43; William O. Scroggs, "Commission Government in the South," *Annals* 38 (Nov. 1911): 17; Bradley R. Rice, "The Galveston Plan of City Government by

The commission form of municipal government spread to the nearby city of Houston, where it was operating by 1905. Two years later five other Texas cities shifted to commission government, including Dallas and Fort Worth, and the scheme was soon labeled "the Texas idea." After Des Moines, Iowa, introduced the new structure in 1908, it received increasing national publicity and came to be identified as "the Des Moines plan." Meanwhile, it was attracting attention in other parts of the South, especially after 1910. One of the leaders of the National Municipal League reported in 1910 that "the most important development in municipal affairs in Alabama cities is the growth of the movement for commission government."[21] By the end of 1912 no fewer than eighty-eight southern cities and towns were functioning under commission government. Thirty of these were in Texas, nineteen in Oklahoma, and eleven in Alabama. Only Virginia among the thirteen southern states failed to include at least one city commission government at that time. Many of these governments existed in towns and small cities, but there were a number of large municipalities in the list, among them Memphis and Birmingham. By 1912 more than half of the southern states had enacted general laws permitting their municipalities to conduct elections on the question of introducing commission government.[22]

Despite its increasing vogue, commission government was not always successful. The commissioners were sometimes incompetent, the distribution of administrative functions among several elected officials made central direction difficult, and commissioners occasionally resorted to logrolling tactics in an effort to augment the resources under their particular jurisdiction. Coherent leadership was often lacking. A modification of the commission system known as the city-manager plan seemed to offer greater efficiency in municipal government. Under this scheme the actual administration of city affairs was turned over to a professional "expert," who would apply the principles of sound

---

Commission: The Birth of a Progressive Idea," *Southwestern Hist. Quar.* 78 (Apr. 1975): 365–408; George Kibbe Turner, "Galveston: A Business Corporation," *McClure's Magazine* 27 (Oct. 1906): 610–20; E.R. Cheesborough, "Galveston's Commission Plan of City Government," *Annals* 38 (Nov. 1911): 221–30.

[21]Clinton Rogers Woodruff, "The New Municipal Idea," in *Proceedings of . . . the National Municipal League . . . 1910 at Buffalo, New York* (n.p., 1910), 97 (cited hereafter as *National Municipal League Proceedings*).

[22]Scroggs, "Commission Government in the South," 18–25; Rice, *Progressive Cities*, 19–71, 113–23; Carl Dehoney, "Commission Government and Democracy," *American City* 2 (Feb. 1910): 76–78; Jerome H. Farbar, "Results of Commission Government in Houston, Texas," *Annals* 38 (Nov. 1911): 231–35; A.P. Wooldridge, "The Commission as It Operates in Austin, Texas," ibid., 236–37; Walker Percy, "Birmingham under the Commission Plan," ibid., 259–64; "The Growth of Commission Government," *World's Work* 23 (Jan. 1912): 262–63; Joseph Flake Steelman, "The Progressive Era in North Carolina, 1884–1917" (Ph.D. diss., Univ. of North Carolina, 1955), 465–68; Sheldon Hackney, *Populism to Progressivism in Alabama* (Princeton, N.J., 1969), 310; Dan E. Kilgore, "Corpus Christi: A Quarter Century of Development, 1900–1925," *Southwestern Hist. Quar.* 75 (Apr. 1972): 434–43; Richard G. Miller, "Fort Worth and the Progressive Era: The Movement for Charter Revision, 1899–1907," in Margaret Francine Morris and Elliott West, eds., *Essays on Urban America* (Austin, Tex., 1975), 89–121.

management, budgetary restraint, and objectivity. The elected commissioners would serve as a sort of board of directors and as the legislative branch of city government.[23] Staunton, Virginia, appointed a city manager in 1908, but the "commission-manager" plan adopted by Lockport, New York, in 1910 provided for a more fully developed city-manager system. The innovation came to be associated with Dayton, Ohio, which adopted it in 1913 and received national publicity during the next few years. Knoxville, Tennessee, shifted from commission to manager government in 1909; Sumter, South Carolina, secured a commission-manager charter in 1912; and a number of other southern cities and towns introduced the new system before 1920. Business interests once again took the lead in promoting the new form of municipal administration.[24]

Advocates of structural reform in municipal government emphasized efficiency, economy, "honest nonpolitical" administration, and the analogy of the private corporation. As one writer declared of commission government in Houston, "The increased efficiency to-day may be traced directly to the simplicity and centralization of the new plan of government, in which the Mayor and four Aldermen elected at large are left practically untrammeled to work out the city's salvation."[25] Commenting on the "Staunton plan," another observer noted that the new system's watchwords, like those of a business corporation, were "economy and efficiency" in place of "politics and spoils."[26] Executive efficiency should not be sacrificed through the elective choice of "a multitude of only slightly responsible officials." Citing the advantages of at-large elections, one analyst of commission government in Texas, writing in 1907, pointed out that the "desire on the part of Aldermen to make a showing for their home wards is a familiar and sinister phenomenon in American cities."[27]

The southern cities that experimented with the commission and manager systems did realize tangible benefits. Some of them boasted of financial savings and reduced tax rates, others reported greater cooperation on the part of local utility corporations, and most of them expanded and modernized public services. Charles E. Ashburner, Staunton's first city manager, succeeded within three years in placing that city on a sound financial basis, in lifting it from "mud to asphalt" by paving streets at ten times the former rate, and in greatly improv-

[23]Weinstein, "Organized Business and the City Commission and Manager Movements," 169; Brownell, "The Urban South Comes of Age," 151–52.

[24]Weinstein, "Organized Business and the City Commission and Manager Movements," 169–72; Hays, "The Politics of Reform in Municipal Government in the Progressive Era," 159; Schiesl, *The Politics of Efficiency*, 172–74, 180; Robert B. Highsaw, "City and County Manager Plans in the South," *Journal of Politics* 11 (Aug. 1949): 497–517; John Crosby, "Municipal Government Administered by a General Manager—The Staunton Plan," *Annals* 38 (Nov. 1911): 207–13; "The 'City Manager' Plan Adopted by Sumter, S.C.," *American City* 7 (July 1912): 38.

[25]Haskell, "The Texas Idea," 840.

[26]Henry Oyen, "A City with a General Manager," *World's Work* 23 (Dec. 1911): 220.

[27]Haskell, "The Texas Idea," 842. See also "A Municipal Experiment," *Outlook* 82 (Jan. 6, 1906): 5.

ing the local water supply, sewerage, and street lighting. Thus business and civic groups were successful in using this type of municipal reform as an instrument for the expansion of public functions. They also enlarged their own role in municipal affairs as a result of these and other reforms. The money saved through administrative innovation was frequently used to the advantage of businessmen. In Beaufort, South Carolina, for example, the offices of city manager and secretary of the board of trade were combined, with the city and the board each providing half of the salary.[28] "Before we adopted the commission form of government for our city," a North Carolinian wrote in 1911, "Raleigh was classed as somewhat unprogressive, but since the adoption of . . . [this plan] every person will have to admit that Raleigh has been progressive."[29]

Although the commission and manager forms of municipal government received broad support in many southern cities, there was criticism of the new designs. Most of the region's cities retained the mayor-council type of government. A goodly number of municipalities soon abandoned the commission system and introduced the city-manager plan.[30] An Atlanta skeptic called attention to the "strange illusion" of urban reformers who imagined that commission government would eliminate politics from municipal affairs. While conceding the efficiency of the commission plan, this observer pointed to the powerful political voice of public utility corporations, liquor dealers, and other organized interests whose influence, he predicted, would actually be augmented under the new scheme.[31] Some southerners suspected that the business-oriented city authorities under the new dispensation would pursue a narrow and discriminatory approach in handling the essential functions of city government. Socialists, labor organizations, and local politicians sometimes objected to the concentration of power in the hands of the commissioners, to the favoritism shown to business groups, and to the undemocratic implications in the elimination of ward representation. Houston's commission government adopted a $2.50 poll tax, thereby removing 7,500 "irresponsible" voters from a potential electorate of 12,000. One scholar has also suggested that the nonparti-

[28]Weinstein, "Organized Business and the City Commission and Manager Movements," 167–68, 172–74, 178; Schiesl, *The Politics of Efficiency*, 180; *National Municipal League Proceedings, 1910*, pp. 562–63, 565; Charles W. Eliot, "Municipal Government by Commission," *SAQ* 8 (Apr. 1909): 174–83.

[29]William R. Smith to Josiah W. Bailey, April 22, 1911, Bailey Papers.

[30]See, for example, Irby Roland Hudson, "Nashville's Experience with Commission Government," *Nat. Mun. Rev.* 10 (Mar. 1921): 156–60, and "Nashville Plays Politics," ibid. (Sept. 1921): 452–53.

[31]Walter G. Cooper, "Objections to Commission Government," *Annals* 38 (Nov. 1911): 183–91. In Atlanta a long struggle over charter revision, including adoption of commission government, usually found a prorevision business and professional group opposed by an antirevision city council group. The antirevisionists prevailed. See Thomas Mashburn Deaton, "Atlanta During the Progressive Era" (Ph.D. diss., Univ. of Georgia, 1969), 410–28, and Willie Miller Bolden, "The Political Structure of the Charter Revision Movements in Atlanta during the Progressive Era" (Ph.D. diss., Emory Univ., 1978).

san ballot, often considered a "reform," probably made it more difficult for minority candidates to win, in view of their limited access to the press and to campaign funds.[32]

Reform campaigns in the cities and larger towns were far more characteristic of the South's municipal politics in the early twentieth century than was the resort to new forms of city government. Though these campaigns often involved little more than competition between local factions for municipal control, they sometimes revolved around the struggle between a "reform ticket," usually identified with "advanced municipal ideas," and "the officeholding organization ticket." These contests inevitably included proposals for better public services, more economical and efficient administration, and more stringent control of special interests and organized vice. Many southern cities were able to improve public services, regulate public utility companies more adequately, and prohibit conflict of interest practices by municipal officials.[33] Almost all elements of the urban population, including organized labor and the poor, consistently supported public education. Public health measures, recreation facilities, and special protection for women and children elicited backing from labor, women's clubs, and various other economic and social groups. Organized groups undertook numerous reforms. In Louisville, for instance, a tenement reform movement led to the establishment of a Tenement House Commission, to an investigation and report, and with the help of other Kentucky progressives, to the passage of a state tenement house law in 1910. Meanwhile, Louisville reformers were trying to take the city's schools out of politics. The reform leaders persuaded the state legislature to abolish the old school board and authorize the election of a new one with clearly defined powers. The board of trade, commercial club, women's club, and other groups then collaborated in nominating "a citizens' ticket of competent men irrespective of politics."[34]

In some cases urban reform came in the guise of city boss and local organization leadership. Such leaders were not inclined to be enthusiastic about clean-government campaigns, the enforcement of prohibition laws, and the like. But several of them were strong advocates of expanded public services, greater efficiency in city government, and lower utility costs for the masses. Municipal reform of this kind was evident in New Orleans under Martin Behrman, in

[32]Weinstein, "Organized Business and the City Commission and Manager Movements," 175–79.

[33]Woodruff, "The New Municipal Idea," 89–90; Richard H.L. German, "The Queen City of the Savannah: Augusta, Georgia, during the Urban Progressive Era, 1890–1917" (Ph.D. diss., Univ. of Florida, 1971); James R. McGovern, *The Emergence of a City in the Modern South: Pensacola, 1900–1945* (Pensacola, Fla., 1976), 33–47; Edward L. Ayers, "Northern Business and the Shape of Southern Progress: The Case of Tennessee's 'Model City,'" *Tenn. Hist. Quar.* 39 (Summer 1980): 208–22.

[34]Woodruff, "The New Municipal Idea," 96; William E. Ellis, "Tenement House Reform: Another Episode in Kentucky Progressivism," *Filson Club Hist. Quar.* 55 (Oct. 1981): 375–82.

Charleston under John P. Grace, and in Memphis under Edward H. Crump, to name but three. Mayor Crump reorganized the administration of Memphis along lines of efficiency and responsibility, making use of nonpartisan experts, tightening up the tax system, improving services, and reducing waste in municipal purchasing.[35]

Among the most prevalent reform endeavors in southern towns and cities were clean-up and local improvement campaigns. In traveling through the South, a contemporary wrote in 1907, "the need for a different point of view in civic life continually makes itself felt. Towns are ill arranged, streets are too narrow, dust is too plentiful, green spaces and trees are far too few, and too little pride is taken in the appearance of the business part of the city at least." Why, the secretary of the Atlanta chamber of commerce asked at about the same time, should the city be "ugly, dirty, noisy, unhealthy, and immoral?"[36] As a matter of fact, efforts had been under way for several years to improve the appearance of southern towns and cities. These campaigns were sponsored by women's clubs, civic leagues, and local affiliates of the American Civic Association. In a sense, these volunteer activities were an aesthetic expression of urban reform and a manifestation of increasing interest throughout the country in the "city-beautiful idea." Spokesmen for this cause maintained that attractive cities would regenerate civic life, revitalize local economies, and bring beauty, order, and cleanliness to the urban environment.[37]

The city-beautiful idea was popular in many southern cities and towns during the years 1900–13. The Federation of Women's Clubs in the individual states and cities assumed a prominent role in launching a host of projects. In North Carolina, where the movement made notable progress, the Woman's Association for the Betterment of Public School Houses advanced the work of village improvement, as did the state Federation of Women's Clubs, local civic groups, and even some of the textile mill owners. Local clean-up days became the vogue throughout the South. In Louisville, Kentucky, for example, the women's club was inspired to undertake a campaign to secure passage of an antiexpectoration ordinance, after which it moved on to consider such issues as tree

[35]Ethel Hutson, "New Orleans' Experience under Commission Government," *Nat. Mun. Rev.* 6 (Jan. 1917): 73–79; George M. Reynolds, *Machine Politics in New Orleans, 1897–1926* (New York, 1936), 39–198; Robert Webb Williams, Jr., "Martin Behrman, Mayor and Political Boss of New Orleans, 1904–1926" (M.A. thesis, Tulane Univ., 1952); Williams, "Martin Behrman and New Orleans Civic Development, 1904–1920," *La. Hist.* 2 (Fall 1961): 373–400; John Joseph Duffy, "Charleston Politics in the Progressive Era" (Ph.D. diss., Univ. of South Carolina, 1963), 206–63; Miller, *Memphis During the Progressive Era*, 148–79; William D. Miller, *Mr. Crump of Memphis* (Baton Rouge, 1964), 60–103; Thomas Harrison Baker, *The Memphis Commercial Appeal: The History of a Southern Newspaper* (Baton Rouge, 1971), 196–245.

[36]Harold A. Caparn, "The Question of Civic Improvement," *Sewanee Review* 15 (Oct. 1907): 501; W.G. Cooper, "The Beautification of Cities," *SAQ* 7 (July 1908): 275.

[37]Jon A. Peterson, "The City Beautiful Movement: Forgotten Origins and Lost Meanings," *Journal of Urban History* 2 (Aug. 1976): 415–34.

planting, street wires, smoke pollution, and vacant lots. A number of cities began to develop systematic plans for their own improvement and beautification.[38] Memphis created a bureau of municipal research in 1909. Several other municipalities were soon considering the possibility of introducing comprehensive and professional city planning. Advocates of this innovation emphasized its scientific, businesslike, and economical character.[39]

Municipal reform, for many urban dwellers, was primarily a matter of an organized campaign against immorality. It was manifested in a wide range of moral crusades: in the early good-government clubs versus political bossism and corruption, in some of the social justice movements, in the antivice campaigns, and especially in the prohibition drive against the city saloon. Reform efforts against immorality were also identified with the new forms of city government. Thus one writer noted that only after Galveston and Houston adopted commission government did those cities close their "worst dives" and bring saloons and "the disreputable element" under control. In Houston, bucket shops, poolrooms, gambling houses, and "the objectionable variety theatres" were closed, and saloonkeepers were forced to comply with the closing law. New Orleans passed an ordinance in 1909 prohibiting the showing of "indecent" motion pictures, and in 1911, Forth Worth appointed a board of movie censors. The effects of this reformism gradually transformed the social centers for gentlemen which had served as male sanctuaries in some cities.[40] Strong moral sentiment was a factor in the legal ouster of several southern mayors for failing to enforce prohibition statutes. The moralism that infused many reform campaigns also mirrored the persistence of traditional values and the determination to prescribe "proper" standards. It rested as well on a foundation of fundamentalist religion. As one historian has remarked, religion "in one way or another, was an ever-present referral point in the lives of Southerners."[41]

Southern municipal reformers, like the national urban progressives characterized by Roy Lubove, "straddled two worlds." They sought to "insure a safe

[38]Ibid., 423–24; William H. Glasson, "Working for the Common Good: Rural and City Improvement in the South," *SAQ* 8 (July 1909): 201–206; Koleen Alice Haire Huggins, "The Evolution of City and Regional Planning in North Carolina, 1900–1950" (Ph.D. diss., Duke Univ., 1967), 1–43; Huggins, "City Planning in North Carolina, 1900–1929," *N.C. Hist. Rev.* 46 (Oct. 1969): 377–97.

[39]Brownell, "The Urban South Comes of Age," 156; Huggins, "The Evolution of City and Regional Planning in North Carolina," 45–81; E.H. Hyman, "The Women's Auxiliary to the Business Body," *American City* 6 (Feb. 1912): 476–78; "Civic Work of Commercial Organizations," ibid. (Mar. 1912): 572–73.

[40]Haskell, "The Texas Idea," 842; Turner, "Galveston: A Business Corporation," 615–16; Scroggs, "Commission Government in the South," 18; Brownell, "The Urban South Comes of Age," 146–50; Eugene J. Watts, "The Police in Atlanta, 1890–1905," *JSH* 39 (May 1973): 165–82; Philip Thomason, "The Men's Quarter of Downtown Nashville," *Tenn. Hist. Quar.* 41 (Spring 1982): 48–66.

[41]Miller, "Rural Values and Urban Progress," 273.

and orderly transition from the old order to the new—from rural, agrarian America to urban, industrial America. . . ."[42] This was evident in the southern progressives' apprehension over the immorality of the city and in their uplift activities. But it was even more apparent in their work for efficiency, order, and economic growth. Municipal reform in the South was, to a considerable extent, the embodiment of the values and objectives of industrial and business leaders, producers, managers, and technicians associated with the modern corporation. It was also an expression of the goals and values of a dynamic professional class and of an expanding and increasingly assertive middle class. These elements were motivated by more than narrow self-interest, fundamental as that was. They were also impelled by broader social, community, and regional concerns. Those who became reformers generally agreed that the urban setting provided the most favorable milieu for economic and social efficiency in the South. Progress, in other words, was heavily dependent upon the modern city.

THE LABOR MOVEMENT AND SOCIAL REFORM

Organized labor constituted another force in the shaping of southern progressivism, though its role was limited in the region. Efforts to organize southern laborers before World War I were largely unsuccessful except for skilled workers in a few crafts, and the number of union members in the South during the progressive period was never very large. The Knights of Labor made the first noteworthy drive to organize southern industrial workers in the 1880s. With the decline of the Knights, the American Federation of Labor in the 1890s consolidated a goodly number of local unions in the South and incorporated some craftsmen into its affiliates. By 1900 most of the section's major cities had central labor unions (trades and labor assemblies), and a majority of the southern states soon were represented by state Federations of Labor associated with the AFL. Memphis, a fairly typical city, had forty-five labor unions with a total membership of 2,650 at the turn of the century, while Pensacola, a community with a population of no more than 20,000, had twenty-two identifiable unions in 1908.[43] Organized labor in the South, like many business and professional groups, was primarily concerned with the protection of its own vocational interests. But labor unions were of some significance as a factor in state and municipal politics and as a part of broader coalitions working for various social reforms.

A number of distinctive circumstances and attitudes slowed the development of the labor movement in the South. One of the principal determinants was the

[42]Lubove, "The Twentieth Century City: The Progressive as Municipal Reformer," *Mid-America* 41 (Oct. 1959): 199.
[43]F. Ray Marshall, *Labor in the South* (Cambridge, Mass., 1967), 24; Kate Born, "Organized Labor in Memphis, Tennessee, 1826–1901," *West Tenn. Hist. Soc. Papers* 21 (1967): 60–79; Wayne Flynt, "Pensacola Labor Problems and Political Radicalism, 1908," *Fla. Hist. Quar.* 43 (Apr. 1965): 317.

section's ruralism and the dominance of agriculture in its economy, coupled with the fact that its industrial expansion was long concentrated in the basic processing of raw materials. Attitudes were even more important. Lacking industrial experience and formal education, the new mill and factory workers held fast to the agrarian traditions and values of their rural backgrounds. They tended to be members of evangelical churches whose ministers preached a fervent gospel of personal sin and salvation, with little room for social coopera-tion and social reform. They accepted the widely held idea that industrialization would enable the South to escape its economic backwardness and achieve a prosperous and healthy society. As C. Vann Woodward has written, "Probably no class of Southerners responded to the vision of the New South more hope-fully than those who almost overnight left the old farm for the new factory."[44] The notion that industrial development was being promoted as a public service made it difficult for workers to challenge the organizers of the new industries, particularly when labor unions could be viewed as attacking the community itself. Most members of organized labor in the early twentieth-century South, moreover, were affiliated with conservative craft unions, whose primary objec-tive was to monopolize their jobs and restrict access to the skilled trades. Finally, the pervasive competition and mounting hostility between whites and blacks weakened labor organizations in the southern states. Black strikebreak-ers helped defeat many union efforts and further frustrated the embryonic labor movement.[45]

The most impressive gains made by organized labor in the South in the late nineteenth and early twentieth centuries took place among construction work-ers, railroad employees, coal miners, and longshoremen. The number of or-ganized workers in the building trades grew rapidly between 1897 and 1904, mainly in cities and larger towns. Of the twenty locals represented in the Louisiana Federation of Labor in 1912, for example, seven were building-trades groups. By 1920 the United Brotherhood of Carpenters and Joiners claimed 502 locals and 58,673 members in the South. Skilled railroad workers were relatively well organized in the southern states by the turn of the century, particularly in the various railroad brotherhoods. Negro railroad employees, often discriminated against by the brotherhoods, eventually attempted to or-ganize their own unions, such as the Colored Locomotive Firemen's Associa-tion in the early 1900s. Coal miners were among the first noncraft workers to

---

[44]Woodward, *Origins of the New South, 1877–1913* (Baton Rouge, 1951), 222. Also see Michael J. Cassity, "Southern Workers and Social Change: Concepts and Prospects," *Ga. Hist. Quar.* 62 (Fall 1978): 200–12.

[45]See Marshall, *Labor in the South*, 29, 36, 86–87, 311–12; Melton Alonza McLaurin, *Paternalism and Protest: Southern Cotton Mill Workers and Organized Labor, 1875–1905* (Westport, Conn., 1971), 52–58; Woodward, *Origins of the New South*, 360–65; Jerome Dowd, "Cheap Labor in the South," *Gunton's Magazine* 18 (Feb. 1900): 113–21; and Constantine G. Belissary, "Behavior Patterns and Aspirations of the Urban Working Classes of Tennessee in the Immediate Post-Civil War Era," *Tenn. Hist. Quar.* 14 (Mar. 1955): 24–42.

join labor unions in large numbers. There were perhaps as many as 19,000 organized miners in Kentucky at the peak of the movement in 1912. The United Mine Workers also made some progress in Alabama, especially at the turn of the century. The percentage of organized mine workers in that state increased from about one-fourth in 1899 to nearly two-thirds in 1902, when the movement began to lose strength. About half of the union's members in 1904 were blacks. UMW District 21—Texas, Oklahoma, and Arkansas—had about 16,000 members in 1912. Longshoremen who stowed cotton and tobacco aboard ship in the southern ports were also among the earliest workers in the region to join labor unions. Membership for longshoremen continued to be important in the twentieth century, though troubled by racial conflict and technological changes.[46]

In cotton textiles, the South's major industry, the Knights of Labor made some temporary inroads in the 1880s. By 1886 the Knights had established twenty local textile trade assemblies in the region. The unionization movement among southern textile workers soon collapsed, however, in the face of management's "implacable resistance" and such tactics as the discharge of union members and their eviction from company housing. Nevertheless, as one scholar has pointed out, these early union efforts familiarized workers with the concept of labor organization and gave them some experience in union activities.[47] In the late 1890s the American Federation of Labor launched an organizing drive among southern textile workers. Scores of local unions were brought into the AFL's National Union of Textile Workers (NUTW), and by 1900 there were several thousand members of the union in the South. During the next two or three years these organizing efforts were attended by a series of strikes in the southern Piedmont, virtually all of which were lost by the unions, which were vigorously opposed by the American Cotton Manufacturers' Association and numerous state and local organizations of cotton mill owners. The NUTW lacked strong leadership and adequate financial resources, and neither the AFL nor the newly organized United Textile Workers of America did much to support the southern movement after 1902. Union membership dropped

[46]Marshall, *Labor in the South*, 46–47, 50–53, 59–69; George Sinclair Mitchell, "Organization of Labor in the South," *Annals* 153 (Jan. 1931): 182–87; Ruth Allen, *Chapters in the History of Organized Labor in Texas* (Austin, Tex., 1941), 91–99, 173–200; "The Negro and the Trade Unions," *Nation* 76 (Mar. 5, 1903): 186–87; Herman D. Bloch, "Labor and the Negro, 1866–1910," *Jour. Negro Hist.* 50 (July 1965): 163–84; Claude H. Nolen, *The Negro's Image in the South: The Anatomy of White Supremacy* (Lexington, Ky., 1967), 161–86; Keith L. Bryant, Jr., "Labor in Politics: The Oklahoma State Federation of Labor during the Age of Reform," *Labor Hist.* 11 (Summer 1970): 260–61.

[47]Melton A. McLaurin, "Early Labor Union Organizational Efforts in South Carolina Cotton Mills, 1880–1905," *S.C. Hist. Mag.* 72 (Jan. 1971): 44–59; McLaurin, *Paternalism and Protest*, 68–119.

sharply in the South, and for a decade there was little evidence of organized labor's presence among southern textile workers. Another brief surge of labor activity took place in 1912 and 1913, but no real advance occurred until the years of American involvement in World War I.[48]

The episodic and ephemeral nature of the labor movement in the South is nowhere better illustrated than in the case of lumber workers. Although the Knights of Labor had made an effort to organize southern timber workers, the most substantial union activity in this early period came during the years 1910–13, when the South was emerging as the leading regional producer of lumber. Supporters of the International Workers of the World took the lead in organizing the Brotherhood of Timber Workers (BTW), which affiliated with the IWW in 1912. Led by Arthur Lee Emerson, who had spent several years in the lumber camps of the Northwest, the brotherhood made impressive gains, including at one point about 30,000 black and white members. Disgruntled by reduced wages, layoffs, scrip systems, and dangerous working conditions, the union undertook a series of confrontations and strikes in 1912 and 1913. But the BTW faced determined opposition from the labor operators, and it was weakened by internal division over its radical demands. The brotherhood soon crumbled. A few radicals such as Covington Hall, a Louisiana socialist and editor of an IWW journal, tried to organize agricultural and forestry workers, advocated interracial trade unionism, and sought to advance the principles of "Industrial Democracy."[49] Some unionists, particularly in Louisiana and other southwestern states, supported the Socialist party of America, and there were a few other labor elements with radical proclivities in the South. An example was the Tampa cigar industry, which employed 10,500 workers in 1908, most of whom were of Cuban, Spanish, and Italian background. In a setting of intense

[48]Marshall, *Labor in the South*, 80–83; McLaurin, *Paternalism and Protest*, 120–95; Herbert J. Lahne, *The Cotton Mill Worker* (New York, 1944), 184–90; George E. Barnett, "Labor Organization in the South," in *The South in the Building of the Nation*, vol. 6, pp. 36–40; Dennis R. Nolan and Donald E. Jonas, "Textile Unionism in the Piedmont, 1901–1932," in Gary M. Fink and Merl E. Reed, eds., *Essays in Southern Labor History: Selected Papers, Southern Labor History Conference, 1976* (Westport, Conn., 1976), 48–79; Dale Newman, "Textile Workers in a Tobacco County: A Comparison Between Yarn and Weave Mill Villages," in Edward Magdol and Jon L. Wakelyn, eds., *The Southern Common People: Studies in Nineteenth-Century Social History* (Westport, Conn., 1980), 345–68.
[49]Marshall, *Labor in the South*, 93–98; Philip S. Foner, "The IWW and the Black Worker," *Jour. Negro Hist.* 55 (Jan. 1970): 45–64; Ruth A. Allen, *East Texas Lumber Workers: An Economic and Social Picture, 1870–1950* (Austin, Tex., 1961), 167–90; James R. Green, *Grass-Roots Socialism: Radical Movements in the Southwest, 1895–1943* (Baton Rouge, 1978), 176–227; Green, "The Brotherhood of Timber Workers, 1910–1913: A Radical Response to Industrial Capitalism in the Southern U.S.A.," *Past and Present* 60 (Aug. 1973): 161–200; James E. Fickle, "The Louisiana-Texas Lumber War of 1911–1912," *La. Hist.* 16 (Winter 1975): 59–85; Bernard A. Cook, "Covington Hall and Radical Rural Unionization in Louisiana," ibid. 18 (Spring 1977): 227–38.

industrial competition and recurring labor strife, radical ideologies appealed to a minority of the cigar workers.[50]

Strikes and other forms of labor-management conflict in the late nineteenth and early twentieth centuries reflected the basic weakness of organized labor in the South and also provided opponents with a strategic weapon in undermining the actual and potential strength of the labor movement. Though labor disturbances were important and were widely publicized, they were relatively uncommon in southern industries. There were only thirty-two strikes by cotton textile workers between 1887 and 1905, involving 9,274 workers. Strikes in the South failed more often than those in other sections of the country and were concentrated in fewer industries. In the period 1887 to 1904, for example, 61.3 percent of the southern strikes were unsuccessful as compared with 43.8 percent in the rest of the United States.[51]

Among the more notable work stoppages during this period were those involving textile mills in Augusta, Georgia (1898 and 1902), Danville, Virginia (1901), and Atlanta (1913). All of these strikes were defeated through such tactics as the use of strikebreakers, lockouts, and eviction of workers from company houses.[52] A strike of Alabama coal miners was broken in 1908, in part by the state militia, and afterward many of the union miners were blacklisted and replaced with black workers. Membership in District 20 of the UMW dropped as a result from 18,000 to 700. A stoppage precipitated by nonoperating railroad workers spread over much of the Illinois Central Railroad system in 1911, only to be frustrated by strikebreakers, legal injunctions, and state militia. Many of the strikers were never able to return to their jobs. Competition between southern railroad brotherhoods and black workers resulted in several labor disputes, including union strikes over use of Negro firemen by the Georgia Railroad Company in 1909 and the New Orleans and Texas Pacific Railroad in 1911.[53] A large-scale strike by lumber workers in East Texas and western Louisiana in 1907 resulted in the formation of the Southern Lumber Operators' Association to war against unionization. When the

[50]David A. Shannon, *The Socialist Party of America* (New York, 1955), 34, 36–37; Durward Long, " 'La Resistencia': Tampa's Immigrant Labor Union," *Labor Hist.* 6 (Fall 1965): 193–213; Long, "Labor Relations in the Tampa Cigar Industry, 1885–1911," ibid. 12 (Fall 1971): 551–59; George E. Pozzetta, "Cigar Smoke and Radical Ideologies: The Italian Radicals of Tampa, Florida, 1890–1910," unpublished manuscript in possession of its author.

[51]Marshall, *Labor in the South*, 27–28.

[52]Ibid., 80–83; McLaurin, *Paternalism and Protest*, 137–51, 183–95; Lahne, *The Cotton Mill Worker*, 184–90.

[53]Marshall, *Labor in the South*, 53–54, 57–59, 71–75; Richard A. Straw, "The Collapse of Biracial Unionism: The Alabama Coal Strike of 1908," *Ala. Hist. Quar.* 37 (Summer 1975): 92–114; Mitchell, "Birmingham," 117–41; Paul B. Worthman, "Black Workers and Labor Unions in Birmingham, Alabama, 1897–1904," *Labor Hist.* 10 (Summer 1969): 375–407; "The Georgia Railroad Strike," *Outlook* 92 (June 5, 1909): 310–12; John Michael Matthews, "The Georgia 'Race Strike' of 1909," *JSH* 40 (Nov. 1974): 613–30; Hugh B. Hammett, "Labor and Race: The Georgia Railroad Strike of 1909," *Labor Hist.* 16 (Fall 1975): 470–84.

Brotherhood of Timber Workers was organized four years later, the association, headed by a Texas lumber entrepreneur named John H. Kirby, conducted a fierce counterattack. Using strikebreakers, lockouts, and appeals to public opinion, the association soon stymied BTW activities.[54] One scholar has observed that this union effort, like the Socialist party and the IWW, failed because the basic structure of society "was middle class at its core, progressive or conservative, and hence hostile to any movements that would alter property or power arrangements except in its own favor."[55]

The political concerns of most labor organizations in the early twentieth-century South were limited and quite compatible with the AFL injunction against formal involvement in politics. The state federations and local trade assemblies usually framed their legislative agendas in terms of job protection and vocational advantages. Yet even the AFL affiliates constituted a political element of some importance, and organized labor as a whole, while minuscule in size, frequently helped define economic issues for workingmen generally and was probably the main agent in the enactment of labor legislation during the progressive era. By the turn of the century, a significant number of southern workers had rejected laissez-faire capitalism, were looking to the state for intervention, and had come to regard organization as an acceptable method of advancing their interests.[56] In some cases southern labor bodies were quite active in state and local politics. Labor journals exerted considerable influence, particularly in municipal politics. The Texas State Federation of Labor surrendered its AFL charter, for example, because of its desire to form political alliances with other organizations. Labor unions in Muskogee, Oklahoma, formed the "Organized Labor Political Club" even before Oklahoma statehood in order to enter politics against the Citizens' Alliance, a businessmen's group. The Escambia County (Pensacola) Workingmen's Protective Association and similar labor groups in other Florida cities played an important role in the outcome of state elections in 1908. The State Federation of Labor was a major force in the adoption of the initiative and referendum in Arkansas.[57]

[54]George T. Morgan, Jr., "No Compromise—No Recognition: John Henry Kirby, the Southern Lumber Operators' Association, and Unionism in the Piney Woods, 1906–1916," *Labor Hist.* 10 (Spring 1969): 193–204; Morgan, "The Gospel of Wealth Goes South: John Henry Kirby and Labor's Struggle for Self-Determination, 1901–1916," *Southwestern Hist. Quar.* 75 (Oct. 1971): 186–97; Merl E. Reed, "The IWW and Individual Freedom in Western Louisiana, 1913," *La. Hist.* 10 (Winter 1969): 61–69; Reed, "Lumberjacks and Longshoremen: The IWW in Louisiana," *Labor Hist.* 13 (Winter 1972): 41–59; George Creel, "The Feudal Towns of Texas," *Harper's Weekly* 60 (Jan. 23, 1915): 76–78.

[55]Reed, "Lumberjacks and Longshoremen," 59.

[56]See, for example, Melton A. McLaurin, "The Southern Laborer in the Late Nineteenth Century," paper presented at the annual meeting of the Southern Historical Association, New Orleans, Nov. 1977.

[57]Marshall, *Labor in the South*, 36; Bryant, "Labor in Politics," 262; Flynt, "Pensacola Labor Problems and Political Radicalism, 1908," 326–32; *Arkansas Gazette*, Nov. 29, Dec. 2, 1914;

In 1900 the Texas State Federation of Labor (TSFL) and the railroad brotherhoods in the state established the Joint Labor Legislative Board of Texas. The board, which later entered into an alliance with the Texas Farmers' Union, was instrumental in the passage of much favorable labor legislation during the next decade and a half, including a law outlawing the issuance of company checks or tickets redeemable only in merchandise at company stores; child labor restrictions; establishment of an eight-hour day for railroad telegraphers, state employees, and persons working on government contracts; a law fixing maximum limits of nine hours per day and fifty-four hours per week for women in manufacturing; a measure outlawing blacklisting and establishing mine safety codes; a full-crew law for passenger trains; workmen's compensation for railroad employees and industrial workers; abolition of the convict-lease system; and creation of a bureau of labor statistics to strengthen enforcement of protective labor legislation. The labor coalition that worked for this legislation lost strength after 1911. Labor opposed a measure supported by the Farmers' Union to establish a textile mill in the Rusk penitentiary, and in 1913 the farm organization lobbied against a full-crew bill sponsored by the railroad brotherhoods. There was also a split between the railroad unions and the state federation, leading the brotherhoods to withdraw from the TSFL in 1914.[58]

The political role of organized labor in the neighboring state of Oklahoma was for a time even more successful than it was in Texas. The Twin Territories Federation of Labor took part in the movement for Oklahoma statehood. Labor leaders in the territories joined with the railroad brotherhoods and with the Farmers' Union in creating a Joint Legislative Board, which drafted a series of reform demands for action by the constitutional convention. Members of the farmer-labor coalition worked energetically to secure the election of constitutional delegates favorable to their program, and the convention incorporated virtually all of these proposals into the new constitution. The coalition also entered actively into the campaign for the election of the state's first governor and legislature, and in the initial session of the newly elected legislature fourteen of the eighteen measures it sponsored were enacted. This labor legislation included provisions for mine and factory inspection, the regulation of working conditions in shops and factories, an eight-hour day for all state, county, and municipal workers, the outlawing of "yellow dog" contracts, child labor restrictions, compulsory education, and the establishment of free state employ-

L.H. Moore to David Y. Thomas, Dec. 3, 1914, June 17, 1916, David Y. Thomas Collection, University of Arkansas Library.

[58]The Texas Farmers' Union observed labor boycotts, contributed to unions during strikes, and adopted a union label for farm products, which the State Labor Federation asked its members to honor. Marshall, *Labor in the South*, 36–37, 90–92; Allen, *Chapters in the History of Organized Labor in Texas*, 123–41; James Aubrey Tinsley, "The Progressive Movement in Texas" (Ph.D. diss., Univ. of Wisconsin, 1953), 135–49; Alwyn Barr, *Reconstruction to Reform: Texas Politics, 1876–1906* (Austin, Tex., 1971), 229; Thomas B. Brewer, "State Anti-Labor Legislation: Texas—A Case Study," *Labor Hist.* 11 (Winter 1970): 58–60.

ment bureaus. Labor's early success in Oklahoma was based on several factors: its membership of almost 20,000, its effectiveness in uniting a variety of unions and in forming an alliance with farm leaders, and its influence with social reformers and liberal Democrats. Oklahoma unions were also fortunate in having able leaders, some of whom assumed important public positions. Peter Hanraty of the UMW became chief mine inspector, while the social worker and labor champion Kate Barnard was elected commissioner of charities and corrections. The situation became less favorable for labor within a few years as rivalry intensified in the Democratic party and as the farmer-labor coalition was weakened because of differences over legislative proposals.[59]

Organized labor in North Carolina and one or two other southern states enjoyed some success in cooperating with farm groups and reform organizations, though on a smaller scale than in Texas and Oklahoma. An effort was eventually made to create a regionwide organization of industrial and agricultural workers. In 1912, representatives of several southern labor unions and farmers' organizations met in Atlanta and formed the Southern Labor Congress, in order to "unite the farmer, railroad and working man to bring about certain reforms so sadly needed in the south." The 188 delegates from twelve states at the Atlanta meeting envisaged a regional and largely advisory adjunct of the American Federation of Labor, but they also sought to form an alliance with the railroad brotherhoods and the Farmers' Union. While the Southern Labor Congress met in Nashville in 1913, in Birmingham in 1914, and in Chattanooga in 1915, it never amounted to more than a paper organization and soon passed from the scene.[60]

Trade unionism's most important contribution to southern progressivism was the influence it exerted in the enactment of labor reform legislation and the adoption of state codes intended to ameliorate working conditions in mines, workshops, and factories. As one historian has written about organized labor in Oklahoma, a "vibrant union movement" in that state, by working with farm organizations, middle-class reformers, and social progressives, obtained an impressive array of "advanced labor" legislation.[61] Although no other southern state duplicated Oklahoma's progressive record, certainly not before World War I, all the other commonwealths enacted an assortment of labor statutes. These enactments included requirements for the use of safety devices and the maintenance of sanitary and healthful working conditions; restrictions on child labor and regulation of the hours and working conditions of women; establishment of bureaus of labor statistics; modifications in the common law doctrine of employee liability for industrial accidents; provisions for mine and factory

[59]Bryant, "Labor in Politics," 262–76; J.H. Reynolds, "The Oklahoma Constitution," *SAQ* 7 (July 1908): 238–39.

[60]Marshall, *Labor in the South*, 37–38; Harley E. Jolley, "The Labor Movement in North Carolina, 1880–1922," *N.C. Hist. Rev.* 30 (July 1953): 354–75; Steelman, "The Progressive Era in North Carolina," 683–712.

[61]Bryant, "Labor in Politics," 260.

inspection and for the reporting of industrial accidents; regulation of labor contracts and the manner of wage payments (requiring that wages be paid in "lawful money" and the guarantees of mechanics' lien laws); prohibitions against interference by employers with the voting rights of workers; and stipulations for racial segregation in certain kinds of employment.[62]

Nevertheless, the southern states were backward in the passage of strong protective legislation for workers. Some of the states enacted no legislation at all governing labor unions as such. Others adopted restrictive statutes such as a Tennessee anticonspiracy act of 1897, which made it a felony for two or more persons to conspire to take or plan to take human life or to injure or harm property of classes or individuals. Tennessee, in common with other southern states, feared that the adoption of progressive labor legislation would place it at a competitive disadvantage.[63] Many of the regulatory laws were very mild. In the case of the textile industry, for example, as late as 1910 Alabama had no maximum hour law, while Virginia retained a ten-hour per day statute passed twenty years before. The two Carolinas had limits of eleven hours a day and sixty hours per week, while Georgia stipulated a daily maximum of ten and a weekly one of sixty hours. Enforcement was seldom adequate, and the regulatory and inspection machinery was essentially preventive, with little attempt to provide for occupational accidents or to ensure against occupational diseases. There was virtually no minimum wage legislation passed in the South before the 1920s. Workmen's compensation systems, where introduced at all, were rudimentary. Tennessee, for instance, adopted workmen's compensation in 1919, but the system was elective rather than compulsory.[64]

The legislative interests and social policy preferences of the state labor federations, railroad brotherhoods, and labor councils were largely in harmony with the tenor of southern progressivism. Labor spokesmen were basically conservative, sharing with businessmen and middle-class professionals in the vision of a New South emerging on the foundations of industrialization, economic growth, and social efficiency. When southern union leaders tried novel approaches, such as interracial cooperation among miners and longshoremen or militant industrial unionism and radical politics among work-

---

[62]See, for example, Virginia Holmes Brown, *The Development of Labor Legislation in Tennessee* (Knoxville, 1945); Hackney, *Populism to Progressivism in Alabama*, 239–40, 248, 263, 315–20; Alton DuMar Jones, "Progressivism in Georgia, 1898–1918" (Ph.D. diss. Emory Univ., 1963), 69–81; Robert A. Leflar, "Labor Legislation in Arkansas," in David Y. Thomas, ed., *Arkansas and Its People: A History, 1541–1930*, 4 vols. (New York, 1930), vol. 1, pp. 346–53; and William Orestus Penrose, "Political Ideas in Arkansas, 1880–1907" (M.A. thesis, Univ. of Arkansas, 1945), 46–57.

[63]Brown, *The Development of Labor Legislation in Tennessee*, 24; William F. Donovan, Jr., "The Growth of the Industrial Spirit in Tennessee, 1890–1910" (Ph.D. diss., George Peabody College for Teachers, 1955), 121–56.

[64]Lahne, *The Cotton Mill Worker*, 139–42; Brown, *The Development of Labor Legislation in Tennessee*, 49; Royal Meeker, "Lacks in Workmen's Compensation," *American Labor Legislation Review* 9 (Mar. 1919): 35–46.

ers and farmers in the Southwest, their efforts came to grief.[65] Such ventures
became increasingly rare. Southern trade unionists generally had no quarrel
with the middle-class orientation of their local communities. This reflected the
fact that a significant number of industrial workers in this period rose in occupational status, accumulated some property, and moved to more desirable residen-
tial neighborhoods.[66]

Organized labor and the "labor problem" constituted a significant feature of
southern progressivism. This was true not so much because of the contributions
of organized workers to social reform as because of the response of the progressives themselves. The progressives, particularly those concerned with social
justice causes, did lend support to the protection of workers and to the improvement of their living conditions.[67] Reformers in state and municipal politics sought to incorporate labor groups into their campaigns. Labor participated, in other words, in the new interest-group politics of the progressive era.
The more advanced progressives gradually developed reform agendas that
included various labor measures, the enactment of which would necessitate
greater governmental intervention. Governor Ben W. Hooper reminded the
general assembly of Tennessee in 1913, "It is the duty of the State to maintain a
strict supervision of shops, factories, and other enterprises which employ large
bodies of laboring men and women, in order that the lives and health of the
employees may be safeguarded against bad sanitation, dangerous machinery,
unreasonable hours, and other conditions that are unjust and hazardous to
labor."[68]

Most significant, perhaps, in the progressives' view of industrial workers
were their definition of the "labor problem" and their perception of the social
environment in which organized labor should operate. Though many southern
progressives approved of labor unions, their conception of its proper function
was narrow, and the rationale they developed for the labor situation in general
was heavily freighted with such incentives as economic development, effi-

[65]Green, *Grass-Roots Socialism*, 270–315; Worthman, "Black Workers and Labor Unions in
Birmingham," 375–407; Samuel A. Sizer, "'This Is Union Man's Country': Sebastion County,
1914," *Ark. Hist. Quar.* 27 (Winter 1968): 306–29; Margaret Ripley Wolfe, "Aliens in Southern
Appalachia, 1900–1920: The Italian Experience in Wise County, Virginia," *Va. Mag. Hist. and
Biog.* 87 (Oct. 1979): 455–72.

[66]A study of 1,500 workers in Birmingham during the period 1880–1914 suggests that social
and geographic mobility may have inhibited the development of a "working class consciousness"
and even functioned to promote "social order and cohesion in a rapidly industrializing society." See
Paul B. Worthman, "Working Class Mobility in Birmingham, Alabama, 1880–1914," in Tamara
K. Hareven, ed., *Anonymous Americans: Exporations in Nineteenth-Century Social History*
(Englewood Cliffs, N.J., 1971), 172–213.

[67]See, for example, Harold A. Shapiro, "The Labor Movement in San Antonio, Texas,
1865–1915," *Southwestern Soc. Sci. Quar.* 36 (Sept. 1955): 160–75, and Robert E. Zeigler, "The
Limits of Power: The Amalgamated Association of Street Railway Employees in Houston, Texas,
1897–1905," *Labor Hist.* 18 (Winter 1977): 71–90.

[68]Quoted in James A. Hodges, "Meliorative Legislation in Tennessee, 1900–1920," unpublished paper dated April 1957, in possession of its author.

ciency, and social order. Many of the reformers accepted the widely held notion that the South suffered from an industrial labor shortage, that black workers were inefficient and unreliable, that foreign immigration ought to be actively promoted, and that industrial training was a prerequisite for economic and social progress.[69]

In the end southern progressives fell back on the native white population as the best means of supplying their section's labor needs. They shared the basic assumptions of industrial boosters such as Richard H. Edmonds, who argued that the South's white workers represented one of its greatest economic assets. According to Edmonds and many others, these southern men and women, imbued with Anglo-Saxon instincts and character, were eager for employment, would work for low wages, and were not given to strikes. Their background prepared them to enter into friendly and harmonious relations with their employers.[70] Despite their acceptance of labor unions, at least in principle, southern progressives were highly paternalistic in their approach to industrial labor. Their paternalism was related to their confidence in the South's emerging industrial entrepreneurs. Like Samuel C. Mitchell in South Carolina, they were inclined to regard the more enlightened industrialists as the "foremost leaders in the well-being and progress of our state." They admired the welfare programs of corporation executives such as Caesar Cone of North Carolina and George G. Crawford of Alabama, and they applauded the efforts of such leaders to secure a healthy, efficient, and reliable working force.[71] The progressives feared that labor organizers would disrupt the stability of the labor force, make the South less attractive as an area of investment, and inhibit the economic transformation of the region.

[69]The campaign to attract immigration, which elicited great publicity during the years 1905–1907, lost ground rapidly during the next few years. For the South's interest in this question, see Walter L. Fleming, "Immigration to the Southern States," *Political Science Quarterly* 20 (June 1905): 276–97; Robert DeCourcy Ward, "Immigration and the South," *Atlantic Monthly* 96 (Nov. 1905): 611–17; "Immigration to the South," *World's Work* 14 (June 1907): 8959–60; Bert James Loewenberg, "Efforts of the South to Encourage Immigration, 1865–1900," *SAQ* 33 (Oct. 1934): 363–85; Rowland T. Berthoff, "Southern Attitudes Toward Immigration, 1865–1914," *JSH* 17 (Aug. 1951): 326–60; John Higham, *Strangers in the Land: Patterns of American Nativism, 1860–1925* (New Brunswick, N.J., 1955), 73–74, 113–14, 164–76; 179–80; Robert L. Brandfon, "The End of Immigration to the Cotton Fields," *Miss. Valley Hist. Rev.* 50 (Mar. 1964): 591–611; Charles Shanabruch, "The Louisiana Immigration Movement, 1891–1907: An Analysis of Efforts, Attitudes, and Opportunities," *La. Hist.* 18 (Spring 1977): 203–26; Arnold Shankman, "The Menacing Influx: Afro-Americans on Italian Immigration to the South, 1880–1915," *Miss. Quar.* 31 (Winter 1977): 67–88; and David J. Hellwig, "Black Attitudes toward Immigrant Labor in the South, 1865–1910," *Filson Club Hist. Quar.* 54 (Apr. 1980): 151–68.

[70]Yoshimitsu Ide, "The Significance of Richard Hathaway Edmonds and His *Manufacturers' Record* in the New South" (Ph.D. diss., Univ. of Florida, 1959), 141–70.

[71]Daniel W. Hollis, "Samuel Chiles Mitchell, Social Reformer in Blease's South Carolina," *S.C. Hist. Mag.* 70 (Jan. 1969): 26–27; Marlene Hunt Rikard, "George Gordon Crawford: Man of the New South," *Ala Rev.* 31 (July 1978): 163–81; Truman S. Vance, "How a Man Went to Meet His Labor Problems," *Independent* 68 (Mar. 17, 1910): 563–68.

Nonetheless, many civic leaders, urban ministers and church laymen, women's groups, and other reform-minded southerners criticized the treatment of industrial workers by management, advocating shorter hours, safety appliances, factory inspectors, and minimum wage laws, and working to provide kindergartens, night schools, and other social services for workers. Yet they feared aggressive unions and strikes, which they linked with violence and dangerous assaults on the integrity of the community.[72] Their sympathy for working men and women was tempered by their commitment to social order and by their faith in economic efficiency. Though profoundly conditioned by their own middle-class and professional place in society, they often identified labor-management friction with class conflict and the subversion of southern traditions. That explains, in good part, the tendency of progressive governors to resort to use of the state militia in quelling labor disputes, as well as the frequent appearance of citizens' alliances in opposition to local strikes and union demands. Thus the southern progressives wanted to improve the conditions of workers, but their broader economic and social motivations limited their reformism in this area.

THE EXPANSION OF STATE SERVICES

Organized efforts on behalf of municipal efficiency and industrial workers contributed to the growth of state functions in the South and to the emphasis on knowledge, expertise, and effective administration in the public sphere. The knowledge and skill of the expert, it was assumed, were necessary to deal effectively with the complex conditions of twentieth-century life. The expert, moreover, would be "disinterested" and could be counted on to promote the general interest. Thus the strengthened railroad commissions hired rate experts, state boards of examiners employed mining engineers, and professional specialists were increasingly relied on by state and local governments in such areas as education, road construction, public health, vocational training, urban services, agricultural development, and social work. Public authority was being centralized in the state governments. Commenting on this tendency, a student of state government in Virginia wrote in 1912: "A realization of the greater efficiency that central state departments have over county officers who devote only a portion of their time to public duties has, during the past decade,

[72]For southern Protestantism and the "labor question," see Hunter Dickinson Farish, *The Circuit Rider Dismounts: A Social History of Southern Methodism, 1865–1900* (Richmond, Va., 1938), 333–36; John Lee Eighmy, "The Social Conscience of Southern Baptists from 1900 to the Present as Reflected in Their Organized Life" (Ph.D. diss., Univ. of Missouri, 1959), 65–67; Wayne Flynt, "Dissent in Zion: Alabama Baptists and Social Issues, 1900–1914," *JSH* 35 (Nov. 1969): 532–37; Flynt, "Alabama White Protestantism and Labor, 1900–1914," *Ala. Rev.* 25 (July 1972): 192–217; and Harry G. Lefever, "The Involvement of the Men and Religion Forward Movement in the Cause of Labor Justice, Atlanta, Georgia, 1912–1916," *Labor Hist.* 14 (Fall 1973): 521–35.

caused the people to delegate all new functions, and some old ones, to state departments or commissions instead of to county officers."[73]

The most dramatic development of state services in the South during the progressive period took place in education. Along with the sharp increase in appropriations for public schools came a pronounced trend toward educational specialization and professionalization, in which the states played a central role. This was evident in the widespread provision for teacher institutes and normal schools, in the move toward more rigorous teacher certification, in school consolidation and administrative reorganization, and in the passage of compulsory attendance laws. The expansion of public services and the introduction of modern techniques also occurred in other fields, though in a slower and less systematic fashion.

There was much talk during the early years of the twentieth century about "scientific agriculture" and how it could be used to regain soil fertility, to repopulate thousands of abandoned farms in the South, and to guard against further loss of the region's natural resources. Most rural reformers stressed the possibilities of up-to-date agricultural education, along with the work of the U. S. Department of Agriculture (USDA), the agricultural colleges and experiment stations, farmers' institutes, and the teaching of agriculture in colleges and secondary schools.[74] Virginia provides an excellent illustration of the "science fetish" in agriculture. In 1904 the state department of agriculture and immigration, which had served little purpose in earlier years, began to cooperate with the Virginia Polytechnic Institute and the experiment station at Blacksburg. The result was an important contribution to the "new agriculture": a thorough soil study of Virginia, the preparation and distribution of numerous bulletins containing information about the work done at the institute and the experiment station, and support of institute trains featuring exhibits and lectures.[75] The states made greater use of their experiment stations in an effort to regulate the quality of commercial feed, seed, and fertilizer, and to ensure pure food, water, and drugs. A Kentucky pure food act of 1898, for example, gave the experiment station, under the direction of Melville A. Scovell, responsibility for enforcing the provisions of the statute. In 1901, Scovell created a division

[73]F. A. Magruder, *Recent Administration in Virginia* (Baltimore, 1912), 193–94. Increasing state functions did not necessarily result in unified and effective administration. A contemporary political scientist, while noting the democratic features of the Oklahoma constitution of 1907 and its framers' response to the demands for "multifarious governmental activities," also called attention to the way in which administrative responsibilities were parceled out among "many independent departments and commissions . . . with no visible relation to each other, each working for itself, and each fighting for existence." See J. H. Reynolds, "The Oklahoma Constitution," *SAQ* 7 (July 1908): 237.

[74]John H. Reynolds, "The Relation of Agricultural Education to Conservation," *SAQ* 9 (Apr. 1910): 177–88; Jane M. Porter, "Experiment Stations in the South, 1877–1940," *Agricultural History* 53 (Jan. 1979): 84–101.

[75]Jack Temple Kirby, *Darkness at the Dawning: Race and Reform in the Progressive South* (Philadelphia, 1972), 147–48.

of food and drug enforcement headed by Robert M. Allen, who later became an influential advocate of federal food and drug legislation. The division was notably successful during the next few years. A Tennessee measure enacted in 1907 prohibited the adulteration or misbranding of "any article of food and drugs" and established a pure food and drug inspector to enforce the law. Lucius Polk Brown, the first inspector, proved to be a dynamic and resourceful administrator of this program, often against great odds.[76]

The handling of water resources was another area of rising state involvement. The southeastern and Gulf states, which contained large areas of swamp and marsh, made sporadic efforts at reclamation, though most of the success in this realm resulted from private enterprise. North Carolina passed an innovative drainage law in 1909, and most of the other southern states created drainage districts and commissions. These measures were usually designed to encourage landowner cooperation in reclamation projects. In Florida, Governor Napoleon B. Broward pursued an audacious dream of draining the Everglades. He persuaded the legislature to establish an Internal Improvement Fund to carry on the work and managed to save about two million acres of Everglades land claimed by railroads and other corporations. "The politicians who authorized the digging of an ambitious system of canals and ditches," a recent scholar has written, "saw themselves as champions of the people redeeming millions of acres of soil from wealthy monopolists and transforming these swampy tracts into an agricultural paradise for small farmers."[77] But Broward and his supporters were also inspired by hope of rapid economic development. "Ultimately," the governor asserted in 1905, "about 6,000,000 acres of the finest land in the country would be rendered cultivable—an area capable of producing the entire tonnage of cane sugar used in this country, a crop which alone would be of untold value to the State."[78] Although the reclamation program in Florida eventually enjoyed some success, it was surrounded by recurrent crises, financial exigencies, and reorganizations.[79]

In Louisiana the overflow areas along the Mississippi River were divided

[76]Margaret Ripley Wolfe, "The Agricultural Experiment Station and Food and Drug Control: Another Look at Kentucky Progressivism, 1898–1916," *Filson Club Hist. Quar.* 49 (Oct. 1975): 323–38; Wolfe, *Lucius Polk Brown and Progressive Food and Drug Control: Tennessee and New York City, 1908–1920* (Lawrence, Kans., 1978), 8–81; Mark Sullivan, *Our Times: The United States, 1900–1925*, vol. 2: *America Finding Herself* (New York, 1927), 518–49; David M. Moyers, "From Quackery to Qualification: Arkansas Medical and Drug Legislation, 1881–1909," *Ark. Hist. Quar.* 35 (Spring 1976): 3–26; Mrs. Walter McNab Miller, "Report of Pure Food Committee," *Annals* 28 (Sept. 1906): 296–301.

[77]Nelson Manfred Blake, *Land into Water—Water into Land: A History of Water Management in Florida* (Tallahassee, 1980), 88. Also see John T. Thompson, "Governmental Responses to the Challenges of Water Resources in Texas," *Southwestern Hist. Quar.* 70 (July 1966): 44–64, and Robert L. Brandfon, *Cotton Kingdom of the New South: A History of the Yazoo Mississippi Delta from Reconstruction to the Twentieth Century* (Cambridge, Mass., 1967), 125–27.

[78]Quoted in Blake, *Land into Water—Water into Land*, 96.

[79]For the Broward program and subsequent reclamation developments in Florida, see ibid., 88–140, and Samuel Proctor, *Napoleon Bonaparte Broward: Florida's Fighting Democrat*

into fifteen levee districts, and in 1911 the state government spent $336,930 in levee construction, plus a large sum derived from local taxes. The disastrous floods of 1912 and 1913 strengthened the demands of residents along the lower Mississippi for greater federal assistance, and southern congressmen such as Joseph E. Ransdell of Louisiana began to press for a national flood control program.[80] This was one of the objectives of the Southern Commercial Congress, an organization formed in 1908 by John M. Parker and other reform-minded developers.[81]

State governments in the South were slow in developing conservation programs during the progressive era. The absence of public regulations and the obsession with economic advancement led to widespread abuse of land and exploitation of timber, minerals, and waterways.[82] Nonetheless, the first decade and a half of the twentieth century witnessed a transition from almost complete reliance on local efforts at conservation to a growing dependence upon statewide legislation and agencies. All of the states in the region established departments of fish and game or conservation commissions, though none of these agencies was adequately staffed or supported. Laws were passed to protect exotic birds and other wildlife, and a few state parks were created, usually in response to pressure by women's organizations, Audubon societies, and other conservation groups.[83] According to a Texas conservationist in 1910, the conservation movement "is a live one and is more talked of than any other. . . ." But he went on to say, "You of course know the terrible condition of our Texas forests and that they are being cut down and turned into money as quickly as possible, and that after the forest comes the desert."[84]

Writing in 1909, the famous forester Gifford Pinchot noted the rapid

(Gainesville, Fla., 1950), 210–11, 216–24, 240–60, 293–95. See also Sledge Tatum, "Reclamation and Drainage," *Annals* 35 (Jan. 1910): 77–80; Dunbar Rowland, *History of Mississippi: The Heart of the South*, vol. 2 (Chicago, 1925), 533–38; and George Brown Tindall, *The Emergence of the New South, 1913–1945* (Baton Rouge, 1967), 127–28.

[80]William O. Scroggs, "Parish Government in Louisiana," *Annals* 47 (May 1913): 44; Donald C. Swain, *Federal Conservation Policy, 1921–1933* (Berkeley and Los Angeles, 1963), 103–104; Bobby Joe Williams, "Mid-South Views the Floods of 1912 and 1913," *West Tenn. Hist. Soc. Papers* 29 (1975): 71–85; Ide, "The Significance of Richard Hathaway Edmonds and His *Manufacturers' Record*," 286–88.

[81]"The Key to Southern Development," *World's Work* 21 (Feb. 1911): 13954–55; Matthew James Schott, "John M. Parker of Louisiana and the Varieties of American Progressivism" (Ph.D. diss., Vanderbilt Univ., 1969), 151–57.

[82]See, for example, Thomas D. Clark, *Three Paths to the Modern South: Education, Agriculture, and Conservation* (Athens, Ga., 1965), 62–82.

[83]Theodore S. Palmer, "Game and Game Protection in the South," in *The South in the Building of the Nation*, vol. 6, pp. 170–74; Theodore Roosevelt, *A Book-Lover's Holidays in the Open* (New York, 1923), 274, 280, 284, 313–15; Earl M. McGowin, "History of Conservation in Alabama," *Ala. Rev.* 7 (Jan. 1954): 42–52; Wilson K. Doyle, Angus McKenzie Laird, and S. Sherman Weiss, *The Government and Administration of Florida* (New York, 1954), 281–82, 285; Blake, *Land into Water—Water into Land*, 167.

[84]W. Goodrich Jones to T.M. Campbell, Sept. 26, 1910, Thomas M. Campbell Papers, Texas State Archives.

emergence of the South as the regional leader in lumber production (44.3 percent of the national output in 1907), but he warned of the terrible devastation resulting from forest fires, of the damage to land and streams from overcutting in upland areas, and of the need for state and federal intervention to guarantee the permanent retention of southern forests.[85] In the judgment of the secretary of the Appalachian National Forest Association, only about 1 percent of the South's 125 million acres of privately owned lands in 1910 was "in any way being conserved or wisely handled." There were no state or federal laws respecting their "use or abuse," no state enforcement officials to prevent forest fires, no "state forests," and no taxing policy to encourage the preservation of timberlands.[86] Between 1900 and 1920, when the South's vast timber stands were swiftly falling to the ax and the saw, a few noteworthy attempts were made to introduce forestry and reforestation to the region. Gifford Pinchot and Carl A. Schenck, working in the Biltmore and Pisgah forests of western North Carolina, established one of the first scientific forestry projects in the United States. Several states, including Alabama, tried to promote reforestation by offering lumber companies subsidies in the form of tax exemptions. A few southern industrialists, along with foresters, geologists, and conservation groups, worked for reforestation, fire control, and greater care in lumbering and turpentining operations. Among the notable advocates of forest conservation in the South were Henry Hardtner of Louisiana—the "father of southern forestry"—Charles H. Herty of Georgia, Posey Howell of Mississippi, and W. Goodrich Jones of Texas. In several states forestry associations with representatives from business, industry, and agriculture encouraged effective means of controlling forest fires. These associations were primarily responsible for setting up state fire services in Virginia, North Carolina, Louisiana, and Texas by 1918.[87]

Mounting alarm over the rapid disappearance of the rich timber stands in the southern Appalachians, along with destructive forest fires, terrible erosion of hills and slopes, and floods in the valleys, helped inspire a concerted drive for the creation of a national park. Conservationists like Pinchot and Joseph A. Holmes, state geologist of North Carolina, supported the idea. The Asheville

---

[85]Pinchot, "Southern Forest Products and Forest Destruction and Conservation since 1865," in *The South in the Building of the Nation*, vol. 6, pp. 151–56.

[86]John H. Finney, "Forest Resources and Conservation," *Annals* 35 (Jan. 1910): 67–76. Also see James W. Silver, "Paul Bunyan Comes to Mississippi," *Jour. Miss. Hist.* 19 (Apr. 1957): 93–119; Nollie W. Hickman, "The Lumber Industry in South Mississippi, 1890–1915," ibid. 20 (Oct. 1958): 211–23; and Fred H. Lang, "Two Decades of State Forestry in Arkansas," *Ark. Hist. Quar.* 24 (Autumn 1965): 208–19.

[87]Harold T. Pinkett, "Gifford Pinchot at Biltmore," *N.C. Hist. Rev.* 34 (July 1957): 346–57; Roy Ring White, "Austin Cary and Forestry in the South" (Ph.D. diss., Univ. of Florida, 1960), 84–90, 114–16; Hackney, *Populism to Progressivism in Alabama*, 308–309; Frank Bedingfield Vinson, "Conservation," in David C. Roller and Robert W. Twyman, eds., *The Encyclopedia of Southern History* (Baton Rouge, 1979), 289–90; Vinson, "Conservation and the South, 1890–1920" (Ph.D. diss., Univ. of Georgia, 1971).

Portable sawmill operating in a Virginia forest. *Photo by U.S. Forest Service*.

board of trade, keenly aware of the resort and tourist possibilities, sparked the movement. In 1899 the Appalachian National Park Association launched an intense campaign to secure congressional action. After many delays and in the face of considerable opposition, the Weeks Act of 1911 authorized a national park in western North Carolina and eastern Tennessee, as well as one in the White Mountains of New England.[88]

The good-roads movement provides a more important example of the growth of public services and the employment of experts by the southern states. The movement was intimately related to the section's enthusiasm for industrialization, urbanization, and agricultural revitalization. It was also stimulated by the rivalry between cities, localities, and states, as well as by several of the reform movements. The consolidation and improvement of public schools, for example, depended on better roads, while the abolition of convict leasing in some states diverted prison labor to public works and fostered interest in good roads. "What better work can a convict be employed in doing," the state geologist of North Carolina asked rhetorically, "than in the construction of public roads, considering it first from the standpoint of the greatest good to the citizens of the state?"[89] The economic development of many parts of the South became a possibility for the first time with plans for the building of public highways. Yet most of the roads in the South at the turn of the century were incredibly bad. The director of the USDA Office of Public Roads reported 790,284 miles of public roads in the southern states in 1904, only 31,780 miles (just over 4 percent) of which were "improved."[90] The expense of building and maintaining roads was largely borne by the counties and municipalities. State legislation in the early years of the century was primarily concerned with the authorization of direct taxes by counties for road construction and extending aid to local governments in the form of convict labor.

This situation soon began to change, however, and during the second decade of the twentieth century state governments in the South assumed an increasingly significant part in the development of more adequate networks of public roads. Good-roads associations were organized in all the southern states, and Virginia, the Carolinas, Georgia, and Tennessee were represented in the Southern Appalachian Good Roads Association. These organizations used publications, lectures, and demonstration work to promote improved roads. Commercial

[88]Charles Dennis Smith, "The Appalachian National Park Movement, 1885–1901," *N.C. Hist. Rev.* 37 (Jan. 1960): 38–65; Willard Badgette Gatewood, Jr., "North Carolina's Role in the Establishment of the Great Smoky Mountains National Park," ibid. 37 (Apr. 1960): 165–84; Gatewood, "Conservation and Politics in the South, 1899–1906," *Georgia Review* 16 (Spring 1962): 30–42.

[89]Joseph Hyde Pratt, "Convict Labor in Highway Construction," *Annals* 46 (Mar. 1913): 78–87; quotation on p. 79. Also see Hilda Jane Zimmerman, "Penal Systems and Penal Reforms in the South Since the Civil War" (Ph.D. diss., Univ. of North Carolina, 1947), 321–33.

[90]Logan Waller Page, "The Necessity for Road Improvement in the South," *SAQ* 9 (Apr. 1910): 156–60. See also Joseph Hyde Pratt, "The Construction of Good Roads in the South," ibid. (Jan. 1910): 56–62.

organizations and chambers of commerce worked to link their communities with towns and cities in an expanding radius. Farmers, denied rural free delivery of mail until year-round roads were built in their locality, added substantial weight to the movement. Newspapers and journals like the *Manufacturers' Record* became ardent backers of state and regional highway systems. Meanwhile, southern politicians such as John H. Bankhead of Alabama campaigned for good roads with great zeal.[91] "The people of Alabama, and the entire country, are demanding better roads," Bankhead wrote in 1908, "and I believe it is a duty the Government owes to the people to co-operate for the improvement and maintenance of post-roads. . . ." According to the Alabamian, "This is not a subject of politics, but is one in which every citizen is interested, and is far more reaching than any question of political policy."[92] Another advocate declared that good roads "build up the social and moral tone of the community, improve school conditions, increase property values, and encourage a spirit of progressiveness along all lines."[93]

The increasing state involvement in support of public roads was evident in the North Carolina legislature of 1909, which passed no fewer than 131 bills having to do with public roads. Many of these authorized the issuance of bonds or the levying of special taxes for roads by local civil divisions, but some provided state aid or established state standards. One statute appropriated $5,000 to enable the state geological board to send a road engineer to counties and townships in order to advise local authorities on road and bridge construction.[94] Even so, the age of state highways in the South, while in some respects the progeny of the region's progressivism, did not emerge until the 1920s. Although southern legislatures and highway commissions were becoming steadily more involved in the consideration of public road construction and maintenance, there was scarcely any statewide planning or comprehensive coordination of highway development before 1916. Texas, for instance, did not establish a state highway department until 1917. The Federal Highways Act of 1916 gave new impetus to state road programs and proved to be an important

[91]See Thomas Ewing Dabney, *One Hundred Great Years: The Story of the Times-Picayune from the Founding to 1940* (Baton Rouge, 1944), 359–61; Thomas D. Clark, "The Country Newspaper: A Factor in Southern Opinion, 1865–1930," *JSH* 14 (Feb. 1948): 17–18; Clark, *The Southern Country Editor* (Indianapolis, 1948), 32, 322–24; Ide, "The Significance of Richard Hathaway Edmonds and His *Manufacturers' Record*," 76, 238–44; Howard L. Preston, *Automobile Age Atlanta: The Making of a Southern Metropolis, 1900–1935* (Athens, Ga., 1979), 17–44; Wayne E. Fuller, *RFD: The Changing Face of Rural America* (Bloomington, Ind., 1964), 178–97; William Larsen, *Montague of Virginia: The Making of a Southern Progressive* (Baton Rouge, 1965), 170–81; and Tindall, *The Emergence of the New South*, 254–57.

[92]Bankhead to W.A. Morris, May 4, 1908, John H. Bankhead Papers, Alabama Department of Archives and History.

[93]Page, "The Necessity for Road Improvement in the South," 160.

[94]William H. Glasson, "Working for the Common Good: Rural and City Improvement in the South," *SAQ* 8 (July 1909): 202–203. See also Joseph Hyde Pratt, "Good Roads Movement in the South," *Annals* 35 (Jan. 1910): 105–13, and Steelman, "The Progressive Era in North Carolina," 581–603.

Smoothing a sand-clay road with drag after rain, Aransas Pass, Texas, 1912.
National Archives and Records Service.

factor in the formulation of genuine highway systems by the various southern states during and immediately after the First World War.[95]

Public health was another field in which the southern states enlarged their functions. Much of the South experienced recurring epidemics of yellow fever, typhoid fever, smallpox, and other infectious diseases in the latter part of the nineteenth century and the early years of the twentieth. In November 1897, for example, the Montgomery board of health reported 121 cases of yellow fever and 9 deaths from that disease in the city. Soon after that it was faced with an epidemic of 387 cases of smallpox.[96] The secretary of the Georgia board of health disclosed in 1911 that smallpox was "prevalent in every part of the State and nothing is being done to check its ravages." Typhoid fever was a constant menace in the Deep South; Georgia reported 17,000 cases of the disease and 1,766 deaths resulting from it in 1900. Malaria, while often unreported, was responsible for more illness among southern whites than any other disease. One public health official noted that "chills and fever" retarded the growth and economic development of many sections of Georgia "more than any other one disease with which health forces had to contend."[97] The U.S. Department of Agriculture's Bureau of Entomology found, in a detailed study of seventy-four tenant families on Louisiana plantations in 1913 and 1914, that 1,066 days, or an average of 14.4 adult days per family, were lost because of malaria.[98] Pellagra, after its identification was established in 1906, was increasingly cited as a cause of illness and death. It was listed as the cause of 432 deaths in Georgia in 1920.[99]

Gradually, a public health movement took shape in southern cities and states,

[95]For examples of highway development in individual southern states, see Thomas, ed., *Arkansas and Its People*, vol. 2, pp. 436–39; Thomas D. Clark, *A History of Kentucky* (New York, 1937), 546–48; Frank M. Stewart, "The Development of State Control of Highways in Texas," *Southwestern Soc. Sci. Quar.* 13 (Dec. 1932): 211–33; Allen W. Moger, *Virginia: Bourbonism to Byrd, 1870–1925* (Charlottesville, Va., 1968), 258–63; Jones, "Progressivism in Georgia," 37–40; Doyle, et al., *The Government and Administration of Florida*, 291–93, 300; Marsha Perry Hataway, "The Development of the Mississippi State Highway System, 1916–1932," *Jour. Miss. Hist.* 28 (Nov. 1966): 286–303; Leland R. Johnson, *Memphis to Bristol: A Half Century of Highway Construction: A History of the Tennessee Road Builders Association* (Nashville, 1978), 27–33; and William P. Corbett, "Men, Mud and Mules: The Good Roads Movement in Oklahoma, 1900–1910," *Chron. Okla.* 58 (Summer 1980): 132–49.

[96]Glenn N. Sisk, "Diseases in the Alabama Black Belt, 1875–1917," *Ala. Hist. Quar.* 24 (Spring 1962): 54, 56. See also "Yellow Fever and the South," *Independent* 59 (Sept. 21, 1905): 683–87, and Jo Ann Carrigan, "Impact of Epidemic Yellow Fever on Life in Louisiana," *La. Hist.* 4 (Winter 1963): 5–34.

[97]T.F. Abercrombie, *History of Public Health in Georgia, 1733–1950* (Atlanta, 1951), 62, 65, 67.

[98]D.L. Van Dine, "The Relation of Malaria to Crop Production," *Scientific Monthly* 3 (Nov. 1916): 431–39. See also Glenn W. Herrick, "The Relation of Malaria to Agriculture and Other Industries of the South," *Popular Science Monthly* 62 (Apr. 1903): 521–25, and D. Clayton Brown, "Health of Farm Children in the South, 1900–1950," *Agric. Hist.* 53 (Jan. 1979): 170–87.

[99]James J. Wolfe, "Pellagra—The Causative Agent and the Method of Infection," *SAQ* 9 (Jan. 1910): 43–55; "Throwing Light on Pellagra Problems," *Survey* 35 (Nov. 27, 1915): 201–202; Abercrombie, *History of Public Health in Georgia*, 89.

based on the diffused efforts of social reformers and pressure groups. These efforts were supported by charity organizations, social workers, labor unions, civic groups, and many doctors and nurses. The incentive behind such activities ranged from narrow professional concerns to social justice considerations, and they touched on themes as disparate as labor efficiency, the protection of children, and the city-beautiful ideal. The American Medical Association, intent upon changing the poor public image and low economic status of physicians, made an important contribution to the public health movement, in the South as in other sections. Dr. Joseph N. McCormack, who had served as secretary of the Kentucky board of health, was a key figure in the AMA's new emphasis on the promotion of strong local and state medical organizations, the development of better medical schools, and leadership by doctors in public health work. In general those physicians who became public health doctors or who were closely associated with the public health movement were more likely to develop broad social reform interests and objectives than were their counterparts in private practice.[100] Medical societies, like most other professional groups, were successful in using public authority to restrict access to their profession. A South Carolina law of 1900, for instance, allowed homeopathic physicians to have their own examining board, and an osteopath in the same year successfully petitioned the Kentucky court of appeals to grant an injunction restraining the state board of health from interfering with his practice.[101]

Faced with changing social conditions and newly organized interest groups, the states responded with a notable broadening of public services relating to health and sanitation. The various state legislatures in the region established uniform licensing standards for doctors, nurses, pharmacists, dentists, and the like. They created state boards of public health, operated public health laboratories, and built hospitals for the insane and the tubercular. They enacted pure food and drug laws, set up food and milk inspection systems, and eventually required the medical examination of schoolchildren. The states also established bureaus of vital statistics. And by the second decade of the century they were making regular, if still small, appropriations for a variety of public health functions.[102]

[100]See James G. Burrow, *Organized Medicine in the Progressive Era: The Move Toward Monopoly* (Baltimore, 1977), 6–70; Walter I. Trattner, *From Poor Law to Welfare State: A History of Social Welfare in America* (New York, 1974), 118–35; and John H. Ellis, "Businessmen and Public Health in the Urban South During the Nineteenth Century: New Orleans, Memphis, and Atlanta," *Bulletin of the History of Medicine* 44 (July–Aug. 1970): 346–71.

[101]Morton Keller, *Affairs of State: Public Life in Late Nineteenth Century America* (Cambridge, Mass., 1977), 411–12.

[102]See, for example, Magruder, *Recent Administration in Virginia*, 118–42; C.W. Garrison, "The Development of Medicine and Public Health," in Thomas, ed., *Arkansas and Its People*, vol. 2, pp. 555–61; Doyle, et al., *The Government and Administration of Florida*, 28–29, 218–27; John K. Bettersworth, *Mississippi: A History* (Austin, Tex., 1959), 490–91; J.N. Baker, "Alabama's Contribution to Public Health," *American Journal of Public Health* 30 (Aug. 1940): 859–65; Howard L. Holley, "Medical Education in Alabama," *Ala. Rev.* 7 (Oct. 1954): 245–64;

The most important administrative vehicle for this work was the state board of health. Although several of the southern states established boards of health in the last quarter of the nineteenth century, usually as a consequence of yellow fever and other epidemics, these bodies had little authority or financial support. Most of them soon disappeared or became inactive. In this early period municipal health officers and boards sometimes made worthwhile contributions, and a number of southern cities began to improve their waterworks and sewer systems and to establish charity hospitals. During the early years of the twentieth century, state boards of health were reorganized or reestablished in the South, and their responsibilities, powers, and support were gradually expanded. All of the southern states had created such agencies by 1913.[103]

Physicians, acting in concert through state and local medical societies, were the single most important force in the establishment of these early twentieth-century boards. While many doctors distrusted or opposed public health programs, the professionalization of medical practice and the growing faith in medical science encouraged a significant number of them to join the public health movement. One student of the movement in the South has written that it was largely suggested, sponsored, and effected by physicians. It was, this writer concludes, a "constructive, nonrevolutionary movement postulated on an orderly transition to the desired reform within the framework of the existing social structure and in obedience to the prevailing mores."[104] In Arkansas, the last southern state to create a board of health, the state medical society became interested in organizing such an agency about 1910. The society appointed a committee to study the health laws of other states, and that group drafted a bill to establish a state board of health. After failing to pass the general assembly in 1911, the measure was enacted in 1913.[105]

The new boards of health extended their supervision over quarantines, water supplies, and outbreaks of rabies within their jurisdictions. They set up laboratories for systematic analysis, disseminated health bulletins, produced and distributed vaccines, and took part in the organized campaign against tuberculosis. The Louisiana board, led by Dr. Oscar Dowling, undertook an energetic campaign to promote public health and sanitation. One feature of this

---

Shirley G. Schoonover, "Alabama Public Health Campaign, 1900–1919," ibid. 28 (July 1975): 218–33; Grady F. Mathews, "History of the Oklahoma State Department of Health, 1890–1907," *Chron. Okla.* 28 (Summer 1950): 132–42; John A. Ferrell, "The Need of Medical Inspection in Southern Schools," *SAQ* 11 (Oct. 1912): 295–300; and Mabel Parker Massey, "Vital Statistics in North Carolina," *SAQ* 13 (Apr. 1914): 129–33.

[103]Francis R. Allen, "Development of the Public Health Movement in the Southeast," *Social Forces* 22 (Oct. 1943): 67–75; Ellis, "Businessmen and Public Health in the Urban South," 346–71; Schoonover, "Alabama Public Health Campaign," 218–33.

[104]Allen, "Development of the Public Health Movement in the Southeast," 73. Also see John Duffy, "One Hundred Years of the *New Orleans Medical and Surgical Journal*," *La. Hist. Quar.* 40 (Jan. 1957): 3–24, and Burrow, *Organized Medicine in the Progressive Era*, 88–102.

[105]Allen, "Development of the Public Health Movement in the Southeast," 73; Garrison, "The Development of Medicine and Public Health," 555–61.

Demonstration of the sanitary privy, Kentucky State Fair, 1913. *Rockefeller Archive Center*.

program was a "health train," equipped with exhibits and a corps of lecturers, that toured the state.[106] Forceful reformers and administrators like Dowling inevitably aroused resentment and opposition, in some instances because they sought to keep public health programs clear of politics. Vested interests resisted the new standards and regulations. Lucius Polk Brown, Tennessee's able food and drug inspector during the years 1908–15, encountered determined opposition to his enforcement efforts by such groups as the Retail Grocers and Merchants' Association of Nashville.[107]

Georgia's board of health, established in 1903, was probably typical in its development. The board began its work in a small basement room of the state capitol with an appropriation of $3,000. Its annual budget in 1917 was only $30,000. Meanwhile, however, it had opened a bacteriological laboratory, launched an antirabic treatment program, begun the manufacture and distribution of diphtheria antitoxin and typhoid vaccine, prepared and disseminated health information, and taken part in the battle against hookworm and tuberculosis. The antituberculosis campaign had resulted in the establishment of a sanatorium for the treatment of tubercular patients. In 1914 the state legislature provided for the creation of a board of health in every Georgia county, but only four counties had complied with the law by 1916. The general assembly also enacted a vital statistics law in 1914; lack of funds prevented its operation until 1919, however, and Georgia was not admitted to the U.S. Registration Area for deaths until 1922. Indeed, public health remained a new term in Georgia before World War I, and many doctors and public officials were suspicious of it and doubted its value.[108]

State boards of health exerted some influence over municipal and county boards, where the latter existed, but these agencies were usually dominated by the local medical societies. The work of the city and county boards left much to be desired, though there were some noteworthy exceptions. "There have been enough ordinances to make Birmingham a paragon among cities," the secretary of the Associated Charities asserted in 1912, "if 50 per cent of them had been enforced."[109] Still, public health in Birmingham had made progress. This was evident in the local antituberculosis campaign. Beginning in 1910, the city

[106]Scroggs, "Parish Government in Louisiana," 45; "The Gospel of Health on Wheels," *World's Work* 22 (May 1911): 14313–14; Henry Oyen, "Cleaning up a State," ibid. 23 (Mar. 1912): 510–21.

[107]"Politics and Public Health in Louisiana," *Survey* 36 (July 1, 1916): 377–78; Margaret Ripley Wolfe, "Lucius Polk Brown: Tennessee Pure Food and Drug Inspector, 1908–1915," *Tenn. Hist. Quar.* 29 (Spring 1970): 62–78.

[108]Abercrombie, *History of Public Health in Georgia*, 38–46, 54–63, 74–75, 83–86, 97–98, 104; Frank K. Boland, "History of the Medical Association of Georgia, 1881–1949," *Journal of the Medical Association of Georgia* 39 (Mar. 1950): 89–113. For the experience of another state, see J.W.R. Norton, "State and Local Health Department Services in North Carolina," *North Carolina Medical Journal* 17 (June 1956): 250–52.

[109]W.M. McGrath, "Conservation of Health," *Survey* 27 (Jan. 6, 1912): 1506.

health officer and a committee of the county medical society began an energetic battle against the disease, with the help of the Red Cross, the Graduate Nurses' Association, the women's antituberculosis auxiliary, the city commissioners, and other groups.[110] The Memphis board of health, which was reorganized with the adoption of commission government by that city in 1909, carried on an impressive range of public health activities. A newcomer to Wilmington, North Carolina, Dr. Charles T. Nesbitt, began a movement to clean up that city in 1910. His efforts as city superintendent of health, supported by the Wilmington *Dispatch* and a new city government, resulted in better sanitation, an improved water system, and plans for more adequate sewage disposal.[111] Meantime, far to the south in the vicinity of Tampa, Florida, a progressive plan of cooperative medicine had been in operation for years among thousands of immigrant cigar workers. Members of the American Medical Association and the state medical society in the area opposed these cooperative programs as "socialistic" and "un-American."[112]

A highly publicized campaign against hookworm disease gave additional impetus to the public health movement in the South. The campaign, which began in 1909 and lasted until 1914, combined many of the elements of social uplift in the region during this period: a pervasive southern ill, northern philanthropy, the application of a scientific solution, and the involvement of southerners in organized efforts to deal with the problem. The hookworm, an intestinal parasite, infected and chronically debilitated a great many southerners, perhaps as many as two million persons. The director of the hookworm eradication program in North Carolina reported in 1912, for instance, that the disease was "more or less prevalent" in ninety-nine of the state's one hundred counties. The existence of the disease in the South was revealed as early as 1902 by Dr. Charles Wardell Stiles of the United States Public Health and Marine Hospital Service. Stiles subsequently opened a clinic in Columbia, South Carolina, and demonstrated the prevalence of the infection and a practical remedy for it. He eventually won the support and cooperation of Walter Hines Page and other influential advocates of southern rehabilitation. Page helped persuade John D.

[110]Ibid., 1501–14; Ethel Armes, "The Alabama Coal Operators on Health Problems," *Survey* 28 (Sept. 7, 1912): 717–22; Mitchell, "Birmingham," 158–76.

[111]Miller, *Memphis During the Progressive Era*, 113–19; Frank Parker Stockbridge, "A City Health Pilot," *World's Work* 25 (Mar. 1913): 527–39; Walter Hines Page to Charles T. Nesbitt, Sept. 26, 1910, Feb. 17, June 3, Sept. 14, Nov. 28, 1911, Apr. 29, Sept. 17, 1912, and Nesbitt to Page, Apr. 20, May 2, May 21, Aug. 27, Sept. 3, 1911, July 29, 1912, Mar. 15, 1913, Page Papers. Also see "A City's Fight against Mosquitoes," *Outlook* 99 (Sept. 9, 1911): 60–61; W.F. Brunner, "A Southern Health Officer on the Negro Health Problem in Cities," *Survey* 34 (Apr. 17, 1915): 67; and Stella O'Conner, "The Charity Hospital of Louisiana at New Orleans: An Administrative and Financial History, 1736–1941," *La. Hist. Quar.* 31 (Jan. 1948): 5, 72–85.

[112]Durward Long, "An Immigrant Co-operative Medicine Program in the South, 1887–1963," *JSH* 31 (Nov. 1965): 417–19, 423–28.

Rockefeller in 1909 to commit up to a million dollars for a regional campaign to wipe out hookworm infection.[113]

The Rockefeller Sanitary Commission for the Eradication of Hookworm Disease, as the administrative agency was called, made allocations to the various state boards of health, which supervised the actual work. The money was used for sanitary surveys, demonstrations, and organizational efforts, and the campaign elicited the cooperation of many local health officers and boards. Between 1909 and 1914 the clinics supported by the Sanitary Commission examined more than a million people and treated more than 440,000 infected persons in the South. By 1914, for example, ninety-two hookworm dispensaries were distributed through the Alabama black belt. By the end of that year the Rockefeller Sanitary Commission had appropriated $55,918.96 for the campaign in Alabama; the state board of health had spent $4,500, and fifty-seven counties had expended $7,863.21 for hookworm work. Free clinics had examined 52,742 Alabamians and treated 43,519 of them.[114] There was some suspicion in southern quarters of the northern philanthropy and modernizing spirit embodied in this spectacular campaign to eradicate the hookworm. One of the most stinging critics of the program was Bishop Warren A. Candler, who spoke of the Rockefeller Commission's "officious disposition" to single out the South "for all sorts of reforms, remedies, and enlightenments" and who was afraid its activities would undermine southern institutions and traditions.[115]

But it was hard to deny the positive results of the undertaking. It gave a boost to the region's public health activities, encouraged the establishment of county health programs, and was partly responsible for larger state appropriations for public health. "Perhaps the Commission's most important legacy in the South," its historian concludes, "was the network of state and local public health agencies it left in its wake."[116] The antihookworm campaign also helped pave the way for Dr. Joseph Goldberger's long investigation of pellagra, although the conquest of that mysterious and debilitating disease was delayed for many years.[117]

Surveying recent public health accomplishments in the South, *World's Work*

---

[113]John A. Ferrell, "The North Carolina Campaign against Hookworm Disease," *SAQ* 11 (Apr. 1912): 129; James H. Cassedy, "The 'Germ of Laziness' in the South, 1900–1915: Charles Wardell Stiles and the Progressive Paradox," *Bulletin of the History of Medicine* 45 (Mar.–Apr. 1971): 159–69; Mark Sullivan, *Our Times, 1900–1925*, vol. 3: *Pre-War America* (New York, 1930): 291–332; Charles William Dabney, *Universal Education in the South*, vol. 2: *The Southern Education Movement* (Chapel Hill, N.C., 1936), 246–63; John Ettling, *The Germ of Laziness: Rockefeller Philanthropy and Public Health in the New South* (Cambridge, Mass., 1981).

[114]"A New Emancipation for the South," *World's Work* 19 (Dec. 1909): 12316–17; Walter H. Page, "The Hookworm and Civilization," ibid. 24 (Sept. 1912) 504–18; William H. Glasson, "The Rockefeller Commission's Campaign against the Hookworm," *SAQ* 10 (Apr. 1911): 142–48; Sisk, "Diseases in the Alabama Black Belt," 60.

[115]Alfred M. Pierce, *Giant Against the Sky: The Life of Bishop Warren Akin Candler* (New York and Nashville, 1948), 195–98.

[116]Ettling, *The Germ of Laziness*, 220.

[117]See Elizabeth W. Etheridge, *The Butterfly Caste: A Social History of Pellagra in the South*

Clinic for the treatment of hookworm disease. *Rockefeller Archive Center*.

observed with a note of satisfaction in the spring of 1912 that a health officer in Wilmington, North Carolina, "has cleaned up a city," "that one in Louisiana has cleaned up a state," and that the Rockefeller Sanitary Commission "has rid thousands upon thousands of people of the hookworm." Page's journal exulted at the prospect of future progress: "We are at the beginning of the era of health—not merely personal health, but community, state, and national health."[118] Five years later a Louisiana congressman expressed concern over "sanitary conditions in the country districts" but emphasized the "great progress" being made in the cities: "Effective health departments have been organized, and the effect of measures, such as the supervision of water and milk supplies, the visiting nurse, and the tuberculosis dispensary, medical inspection of schools, and the control of contagious diseases has been so pronounced as to place their work on a firm foundation. . . . The solution of many of the problems of municipal sanitation are taking place every day."[119]

The growing role of state regulations and state agencies in the development of good roads and public health programs was part of a larger trend in American public affairs toward expanded public services, more standardized and reliable procedures, and greater efficiency in dealing with social problems. These tendencies were promoted by numerous pressure groups and specialized organizations representing farmers, businessmen, industrial workers, and professional men and women. They all sought to use organizational leverage to advance their particular interests, and many of them wanted to help fashion an environment in the community, marketplace, or profession in which objective knowledge, science, and rational processes would determine decision-making and policy. Agriculture was a major area of concentration in this modernizing process, and the improvement of the rural South was one of the principal objectives of the region's progressives.

(Westport, Conn., 1972), and Willford I. King, "Pellagra and Poverty," *Survey* 46 (Sept. 1, 1921): 629–32.

[118]"A Health Competition for $100," *World's Work* 24 (May 1912): 19.

[119]*Rural Sanitation: Speech of Hon. Ladislas Lazaro of Louisiana in the House of Representatives, February 24, 1917* (Washington, D.C., 1917), copy in Ladislas Lazaro Papers, Louisiana State University Archives.

A county health department in operation, Texas, 1921. *Rockefeller Archive Center.*

THE PRECARIOUS AGRICULTURAL ECONOMY and the tenuousness of rural life at the turn of the century attracted their full share of attention from southern progressives. This is not surprising, since the South remained predominantly agricultural, despite the quickening pace of industrialization and the growth of cities and towns. The countryside, more than any other sector of southern life, contained the harshest and most concentrated evidence of the section's poverty, ignorance, and injustice. The agricultural reformer Seaman A. Knapp, who was thoroughly familiar with farm life in the South, captured the bleakness of agrarian prospects in this description written in 1906:

> Rural conditions . . . in the Southern States have changed little in thirty years. The houses are a little more dilapidated; the fences give evidence of more decay; the highways carry more water in the wet season, and are somewhat less easily traveled in the dry; but the environments are about the same; no paint, and slight evidence of thrift. The same old mule stands at the door with his rope end on the ground, hitched to a plow that Adam rejected as not up-to-date; the same old bushes are in the fields, and the same old weeds are in the fence corners; no strange sights disturb the serenity of Rip Van Winkle. . . .[1]

These conditions were rooted in the agricultural system that developed in the post-Appomattox years as a substitute for the plantation regime. The characteristic features of the postwar system—mounting sharecropping, the crop lien as the basis of credit, and commercialization of production—contributed along with a long period of economic deflation to the widespread poverty, itinerancy, and loss of independence experienced by millions of southern farmers. Only slightly more than half of the South's farmers in 1900 owned the land they worked, and a sharp rise in land values made it increasingly difficult to acquire farm land. In Georgia, for example, the percentage of farms operated by owners dropped from 55.1 in 1880 to 34.6 in 1910. The average sharecropper moved from farm to farm, every year or two, always in search of "something

---

[1]Quoted in Roy V. Scott, *The Reluctant Farmer: The Rise of Agricultural Extension to 1914* (Urbana, Ill., 1970), 207.

better."[2] Small wonder that John Lee Coulter, an agricultural agent for the U.S. Census Bureau, should conclude in 1913 that the southern countryside constituted the nation's "most complete social problem." The result of the section's tenant system, Coulter wrote, was "poor agriculture, exhausted soils, small crops, poor roads, decaying bridges, unpainted homes, and unkept yards."[3]

Nevertheless, in some respects the outlook for southern farmers at the beginning of the new century was encouraging. The long depression of the 1890s had ended, and farm prices were improving. Land values rose, agricultural credit eased, and farm bankruptcies declined. The improvement of agricultural prices lifted rural hopes, in the South as in other regions, and the diagnosis and treatment of southern farm woes proceeded with renewed vigor. Farm journals, agricultural societies, and other groups had long urged the need for diversification of the region's agricultural economy, citing overproduction and low prices of staple crops, the expense of producing such crops, the southern farmer's lack of self-sufficiency, and misuse of the land and bad farming practices resulting from overreliance on staple-crop agriculture. But the tradition of growing cotton and a few other commercial crops was strong, and the rise in commodity prices at the turn of the century reinforced the devotion to staple-crop agriculture. In Georgia, for instance, cotton cultivation rose from three and a half million acres in 1900 to more than five million acres in 1914.[4] Observing this trend, the historian Ulrich B. Phillips expressed a sarcastic lament in 1904: "Let the agricultural organization degenerate and small farms replace the remarkably efficient plantation system, let the soil be worn out, let the people move to Texas for fresh lands, let disorder reign and the planters be driven to town, leaving the negroes to lapse back toward barbarism—let almost anything happen provided all possible cotton is produced each year."[5]

Agricultural reform in the South during the progressive period took a variety of forms, most of which involved some type of farm organization and cooperation. One approach sought to employ economic pressure through the application of production and price controls, thereby bringing higher commodity prices and greater farm incomes. On occasion, when economic leverage failed, desperate

[2]Robert Preston Brooks, *The Agrarian Revolution in Georgia, 1865–1912* (Madison, Wis., 1914), 57; Willard Range, *A Century of Georgia Agriculture, 1850–1950* (Athens, Ga., 1954), 159; George Washington Carver, "The Need of Scientific Agriculture in the South," *Amer. Rev. of Reviews* 25 (Mar. 1902): 320; Enoch Marvin Banks, "Tendencies Among Georgia Farmers," *SAQ* 3 (Apr. 1904): 109–16; Benjamin H. Hibbard, "Tenancy in the Southern States," *Quarterly Journal of Economics* 27 (May 1913): 482–92; Lewis H. Haney, "Farm Credit Conditions in a Cotton State," *American Economic Review* 4 (Mar. 1914): 47–67; Harold D. Woodman, "Sequel to Slavery: The New History Views the Postbellum South," *JSH* 43 (Nov. 1977): 523–54; William N. Parker, "The South in the National Economy, 1865–1970," *South. Econ. Jour.* 46 (Apr. 1980): 1019–48. For an example of the yeoman farmer's decline, see Grady McWhiney, "The Revolution in Nineteenth-Century Alabama Agriculture," *Ala. Rev.* 31 (Jan. 1978): 27–30.

[3]Coulter, "The Rural Life Problem of the South," *SAQ* 12 (Jan. 1913): 61, 63.

[4]Range, *A Century of Georgia Agriculture*, 91–101, 169–72.

[5]Phillips, "Conservatism and Progress in the Cotton Belt," *SAQ* 3 (Jan. 1904): 5.

farmers resorted to violence. Another pattern of farmer activity emerged in the form of a comprehensive farm organization, which spread over the South and committed itself to a broad program of agricultural reform. In the meantime, rural reform found still another focus in the movement for agricultural education and demonstration programs. It also exhibited growing interest in the passage of new legislation in the state capitols and in Washington.

The most conspicuous organized effort to raise farm prices by adjusting production to demand involved the South's major cash crop, cotton. For years there had been talk of voluntary crop limitation in the cotton belt, rising and falling with fluctuations in the price of the staple. Several conferences and ephemeral associations of cotton growers in the late 1890s called for acreage reduction and a mechanism for holding existing cotton off the market. Meanwhile, cotton production increased as newer land was planted in the Southwest and as fertilizers were applied to the growing of the plant in older areas. Prices dropped precipitously in 1904, in the wake of U.S. Department of Agriculture predictions of a banner cotton crop. Amid talk of cotton dropping to five cents a pound, farmers and their leaders demanded action. During the autumn of 1904, the Texas Cotton Growers' Association encouraged farmers in that state and in nearby Oklahoma and Indian territories to arrange mass meetings in which they could work out methods of holding their cotton off the market until prices rose. Concern over the depressed cotton market soon spread to bankers, railroads, and other business interests with a stake in the production and sale of the crop. Many farm leaders and businessmen began to advocate the agricultural equivalent of an industrial combination to influence prices, a kind of "countertrust" or "benevolent trust" that would reduce production, regularize the marketing of cotton, and raise the prices paid to producers.[6]

A well-publicized convention was convened in New Orleans on January 24, 1905, in an effort to deal more comprehensively with the cotton crisis. The three-day meeting was presided over by Harvie Jordan, a professional farm organizer and lobbyist who had headed the short-lived Southern Cotton Growers' Protective Association of 1900. Like countless farm meetings in the past, the cotton convention of 1905 was characterized by a flood of oratory and exhortation. In formally organizing the Southern Cotton Association (SCA), the New Orleans meeting created elaborate machinery and agreed upon an

[6]Theodore Saloutos, *Farmer Movements in the South, 1865–1933* (Berkeley, Calif., 1960), 153–54; Gilbert C. Fite, "Voluntary Attempts to Reduce Cotton Acreage in the South, 1914–1933," *JSH* 14 (Nov. 1948): 481; Yoshimitsu Ide, "The Significance of Richard Hathaway Edmonds and His *Manufacturers' Record* in the New South" (Ph.D. diss., Univ. of Florida, 1959), 109–31; Ulrich Bonnell Phillips, "The Overproduction of Cotton and a Possible Remedy," *SAQ* 4 (Apr. 1905): 148–58; Clarence H. Poe, "Economic Wastes in Our Cotton Farming," ibid. 5 (Apr. 1906): 128–33; Matthew Brown Hammond, "Cotton Production in the South," in *The South in the Building of the Nation*, vol. 6, pp. 87–104; Harvie Jordan, "Cotton in Southern Agricultural Economy," *Annals* 35 (Jan. 1910): 1–7.

ambitious program.[7] The association set its sights on a voluntary acreage reduction of 25 percent in 1905. By the early spring of 1905 the SCA claimed to have a dozen or more state organizations in the South, and the work of the association was being supported by local meetings, farm journals, bankers and merchants, and several agricultural organizations. At its second convention, in January 1906, association leaders announced that the organization had succeeded in limiting cotton acreage, reducing production by about 14 percent, causing cotton prices to go up, and generally improving the condition of southern farmers. They drew up pretentious plans for the new year, including the development of stronger local associations, a fifteen-cent-per-pound minimum price, the promotion of diversified farming, a thorough investigation of foreign markets, and the organization of a chartered corporation to buy, sell, and warehouse cotton. The last two objectives never got much beyond the talking stage. Nor did the more basic acreage-limitation and pooling efforts achieve conspicuous success. Enthusiasm for the SCA program evaporated in 1906, and the association declined rapidly thereafter.

The reasons for the failure of the Southern Cotton Association are apparent. The loose structure of the association virtually ruled out any disciplined and effective program of common action. But cotton farmers were a heterogeneous lot, and any attempt to make cooperation compulsory would no doubt have brought division and withdrawal. Many farmers considered the association a "mongrel" organization working primarily in the interest of bankers, merchants, and the cotton exchanges. The question of how to bring black farmers into the association was never resolved. The association lacked storage facilities, failed to develop feasible credit arrangements, and raised doubts in some quarters about the legality of its pooling scheme under the Sherman Antitrust Act. There were also pressures of another kind that led to continued overproduction: cotton expansion in the Southwest and the mounting interest in more efficient cultivation. Finally, farm prices were reasonably good, fluctuating between ten and fourteen cents a pound during the period 1900–14. Looking at cotton production over the past half-century, a discerning scholar observed in 1929 that every "bad year is the occasion . . . of social unrest and innumerable panaceas for relief. All these are forgotten upon the next good price year, and so the cycle goes. Campaigns for restriction of cotton acreage follow upon the wake of every disaster. Agreements to cut acreage 10, 15, or 20 per cent are cheerfully made, and in many instances as cheerfully broken. . . ."[8]

[7] Voting power was distributed among the delegates on the basis of 1 vote for every 100,000 bales of cotton produced. Thus Texas led with 26 votes, followed by Georgia and Mississippi with 14 votes, and so on. This discussion of the SCA relies heavily on Theodore Saloutos, "The Southern Cotton Association, 1905–1908," *JSH* 13 (Nov. 1947): 492–510, and Saloutos, *Farmer Movements in the South*, 153–66.

[8] Rupert B. Vance, *Human Factors in Cotton Culture: A Study in the Social Geography of the American South* (Chapel Hill, N.C., 1929), 113.

While the unsuccessful movement to limit production and raise staple prices in the cotton belt was running its course, a more dramatic campaign of protest and concerted action was unfolding in the tobacco region of western Kentucky and middle Tennessee. This tobacco area, like other farm regions, had suffered from overproduction and recurrent hard times during the latter part of the nineteenth century. Even though most farm prices improved during the early years of the new century, dark-leaf tobacco prices dropped to an average of four cents per pound, less than it cost the toilworn farmer to produce it. Farm leaders in the tobacco belt had long advocated united action by tobacco farmers; they urged the repeal of discriminatory federal taxes, the adoption of an acreage restriction plan, and an investigation by the government of the "Tobacco Trust"—the monopoly of the tobacco business created by the American Tobacco Company. In the fall of 1904 a well-to-do Tennessee planter named Felix G. Ewing took the lead in organizing the Dark Tobacco District Planters' Protective Association.[9]

The leaders of the Planters' Protective Association hoped to persuade tobacco raisers in the Black Patch—the dark-tobacco district of western Kentucky and north-central Tennessee—to pool their tobacco, that is, pledge it to the association and store it in association warehouses until the entire crop could be sold by the organization. The new association launched a vigorous campaign to win the support of the dark-leaf growers. Speakers and organizers toured the Black Patch lambasting the American Tobacco Company and painting a glowing picture of the new era the association would usher in. The response was encouraging. By September 1906, when 25,000 people attended an association rally at Guthrie, twenty-five counties in Kentucky and Tennessee were affiliated with the organization. Ultimately, the membership in the two states reached 30,000, with an additional 5,000 members in the dark-leaf region of Virginia. Meanwhile, a similar association had been formed at Henderson, Owensboro, and Bowling Green, with approximately 20,000 members, and the American Society of Equity had established the Burley Tobacco Society with the same objectives in the burley belt of central Kentucky. It had a membership of about 35,000.[10]

[9]Saloutos, *Farmer Movements in the South*, 167–83; James O. Nall, *The Tobacco Night Riders of Kentucky and Tennessee, 1905–1909* (Louisville, Ky., 1939); John G. Miller, *The Black Patch War* (Chapel Hill, N.C., 1936); Dewey W. Grantham, "Black Patch War: The Story of the Kentucky and Tennessee Night Riders, 1905–1909," *SAQ* 59 (Spring 1960): 215–25; Harry Harrison Kroll, *Riders in the Night* (Philadelphia, 1965); Meyer Jacobstein, "The Condition of Tobacco Culture in the South," in *The South in the Building of the Nation*, vol. 6, pp. 66–72; Anna Youngman, "The Tobacco Pools of Kentucky and Tennessee," *Jour. Pol. Econ.* 18 (Jan. 1910): 34–39.

[10]Theodore Saloutos, "The American Society of Equity in Kentucky: A Recent Attempt in Agrarian Reform," *JSH* 5 (Aug. 1939): 347–63; John L. Mathews, "The Farmers' Union and the Tobacco Pool," *Atlantic Monthly* 102 (Oct. 1908): 482–91. For resentment against the American Tobacco Company in North Carolina, see Nannie May Tilley, *The Bright-Tobacco Industry, 1860–1929* (Chapel Hill, N.C., 1948), 271–74, 396, 405–46.

Despite this progress, the Planters' Protective Association was in a tenuous financial condition, was strongly opposed by the tobacco "trust," and encountered stubborn resistance from some producers. Ironically, when prices began to rise as a result of the association's pooling agreements, the nonsigning tobacco growers became the chief beneficiaries of the movement against the tobacco monopoly. During the latter part of 1905, there were reports of secret meetings in the dark-leaf area and rumors of a secret society being organized to force farmers to cooperate. Acts of violence were soon reported in various parts of the Black Patch, and the term "night riders" came into general use. These anonymous bands probably numbered ten thousand men at the height of their influence in 1907 and 1908. The night-rider assaults led to uncontrolled violence and terror in the Black Patch. Valuable tobacco plantbeds of nonassenting farmers were "scraped." Barn-burnings and floggings became almost nightly occurrences in some counties. The marauders also attacked hostile tobacco dealers and "trust" agents, and they eventually went so far as to raid and terrorize entire towns and villages.[11] The night-riding practice soon spread beyond the tobacco belt. A national periodical reported in the autumn of 1908 that "night riders are becoming a menace throughout many parts of the South."[12]

By this time, the original night riders had fallen on difficult times. A new Kentucky governor, Augustus E. Willson, proved more determined than his predecessor in working to eliminate night riding. Willson and Governor Malcolm R. Patterson of Tennessee sent state troops to various parts of the Black Patch, and these units slowly began to curb the "Silent Brigade." The press grew hostile, and a Law and Order League was organized with branches in all the tobacco counties. Finally, the night riders, who had exerted almost com-

---

[11]Charles V. Tevis, "A Ku-Klux of To-day: The Red Record of Kentucky's 'Night Riders,'" *Harper's Weekly* 52 (Feb. 8, 1908): 14; Martha McCulloch-Williams, "The Tobacco War in Kentucky," *Amer. Rev. of Reviews* 37 (Feb. 1908): 168–70; Edward A. Jonas, "The Night-Riders: A Trust of the Farmers," *World's Work* 17 (Feb. 1909): 11213–18; Saloutos, "The American Society of Equity in Kentucky," 356–57; Albin Lee Reynolds, "War in the Black Patch," *Reg. Ky. Hist. Soc.* 56 (Jan. 1958): 1–10; Rick Gregory, "Robertson County and the Black Patch War, 1904–1909," *Tenn. Hist. Quar.* 39 (Fall 1980): 341–58.

[12]"The Night Riders," *Outlook* 90 (Oct. 31, 1908): 462. Also see William F. Holmes, "Whitecapping: Agrarian Violence in Mississippi, 1902–1906," *JSH* 35 (May 1969): 165–85. One of the most notorious areas of night riding activity outside the tobacco belt was the Reelfoot Lake country in the extreme northwestern section of Tennessee. The poor fishermen and hunters who inhabited this wild region, made reckless by their bitter controversies with the West Tennessee Land Company and the Reelfoot Lake Fish Company over fishing and grazing rights, turned to night riding. These men and others in nearby counties committed more than a hundred crimes before their assaults came to a climax on an October night in 1908, when a band of riders seized two prominent lawyers at a lodge near the lake and ruthlessly killed one of them. This incident aroused public opinion and brought the governor and state troops of Tennessee to Reelfoot Lake. The night riders were rounded up, more than 100 indictments were obtained, and eight men were tried and found guilty of murder. See Paul J. Vanderwood, *Night Riders of Reelfoot Lake* (Memphis, 1969), and Hillsman Taylor, "The Night Riders of West Tennessee," *West Tenn. Hist. Soc. Papers* 6 (1952): 77–86.

plete control over local officials and courts in many tobacco counties, began to encounter legal problems. In the spring of 1908, they were suddenly confronted with civil suits in the federal courts, brought by victims who had left Kentucky to establish residence in other states. The night riders lost many of these damage suits. Sporadic night riding continued for a time, but by early 1909 law and order had returned to the Black Patch. The Planters' Protective Association, which disclaimed responsibility for the violence, faded away, as did the Burley Tobacco Society. Still, the "tobacco strike" was not a total failure: it helped raise prices, introduced some marketing reforms, and demonstrated for the first time that the tobacco growers could achieve a measure of cooperation.

A larger and more sustained movement in the interest of southern agriculturists was the Farmers' Union, a general farm organization that came into existence early in the twentieth century. Eschewing party politics, the new organization concentrated on the price and marketing problems of farmers, particularly those of cotton producers. During the decade before the United States entered the Great War, the Farmers' Union constituted a powerful pressure group in the legislative arena and an important force in the progressive politics of the South.

Like the Farmers' Alliance, whose experience greatly influenced the new association, the Farmers' Educational and Cooperative Union of America was born in Texas. It was begun in Rains County in 1902, the brainchild of a newspaperman and former Alliance organizer named Isaac Newton Gresham. The times were propitious for a renewed effort to improve farm conditions through cooperation. There was a strong residue of agrarian discontent in Texas, a compound of James S. Hogg's reformism, the program of the Farmers' Alliance, the impact of populism, and a pervasive apprehension about monopoly in transportation and finance. At the same time, Texas was the scene of rapidly developing commercial agriculture, including the production of cotton. The behavior of the cotton market, meanwhile, was frustratingly ambiguous. While prices tended to improve from the low point they had reached in the mid-nineties, they failed to rise steadily, fluctuating between seven and eleven cents per pound. Reacting to these conditions, Newton Gresham and nine associates, most of whom were his friends and neighbors, obtained a charter from the state of Texas. The purpose of the Farmers' Union, it said, was to assist subordinate unions in "marketing and obtaining better prices for their products . . . and to co-operate with them in the protection of their interests. . . ."[13]

Gresham's organization had a genuine appeal for many farmers in northeast Texas. They approved the idea of concerted action and could afford an initiation fee of a dollar and monthly dues of five cents. Organizers were sent into other states, and an active campaign to expand the movement was soon under-

---

[13] Carl C. Taylor, *The Farmers' Movement, 1620–1920* (New York, 1953), 350.

taken. As the organization spread over the South, plans were made to establish a National Farmers' Union. Despite some friction between the Texas Farmers' Union and a national organization created in late 1905, the latter body began to operate effectively in 1906. The National Farmers' Union experienced a phenomenal growth during the years 1906–1908, particularly in Arkansas, Mississippi, and Alabama. The organization claimed more than 1,000 local chapters and 80,000 members in Georgia alone. More than 200 locals were established in Florida in 1907, while 226 were organized in Kentucky in 1908. By the latter year the union had expanded into every southern state except Virginia, where it first appeared in 1910.[14]

The most important stimulus to the growth of the Farmers' Union was the depressed and erratic behavior of the commodity market, especially of cotton, and the heightened anxiety in the countryside over the fate of individual producers in an economy that was increasingly organized and seemingly manipulated by middlemen and financiers. But there were also other incentives. "In effect," one historian has written, "union membership offered the producers the benefits of agrarian evangelism, fraternal fellowship, and the prospects of higher prices for the goods they sold and lower prices for those they purchased."[15] During the early years membership in the union was secret, an operational safeguard designed to prevent the association from falling into the hands of its enemies. Although blacks were not eligible for membership, locals of a Colored Farmers' Union were organized as early as 1905. A national union representing blacks soon appeared and shortly afterward a rival association emerged with headquarters in Texas. There was no organic connection between these Negro groups and the NFU, and the white union was unable to resolve the thorny question of opening its doors to blacks. Even so, some efforts were made in a few states, notably Texas and Oklahoma, to permit black farmers to store their cotton in union warehouses on the same basis as white members.[16]

In the South the National Farmers' Union and the state unions affiliated with it concentrated on the problems of low cotton prices. Various tactics were employed by union leaders: fixing a minimum price for the staple, withholding cotton from the market, reducing the acreage under cultivation, and even a "plow-up" campaign in 1908, when cotton prices dropped to eight cents a pound following the financial panic of the previous year. In 1904, for example, the Texas union sponsored a plan that called for its members to withhold from the market one out of every five bales, disposing of the other four bales slowly as their needs required. When cotton prices rose to their demanded level of ten cents per pound in June 1905, Farmers' Union spokesmen claimed credit for the

[14]Ibid., 335–64; Saloutos, *Farmer Movements in the South*, 184–212; Range, *A Century of Georgia Agriculture*, 240.

[15]Saloutos, *Farmer Movements in the South*, 188.

[16]For these developments and those discussed in the following three paragraphs, see the sources cited in note 14.

improvement, asserting that they had saved producers $160 million. In May 1906 the Farmers' Union and the Southern Cotton Association participated in a highly advertised conference of cotton farmers, brokers, and spinners. While failing to agree upon a definite plan of action, the assemblage did endorse the

Higher prices finally come to the cotton belt. The southern farmer's jubilation is portrayed by cartoonist Lewis Gregg, Atlanta *Constitution*, November 1, 1909. *Courtesy Atlanta Newspapers, Inc.*

building of warehouses and certain other reforms in the marketing of cotton. In 1906 and 1907 the NFU called for a minimum price of eleven cents a pound, and in the following year union leaders demanded fifteen cents.

One of the organization's major objectives was the establishment of warehouses for the storing and marketing of cotton, a revised version of the

Farmers' Alliance scheme. A warehouse plan was unveiled as early as 1904. The idea was to enable producers to store their cotton in union warehouses for which they would receive negotiable certificates of deposit, which could serve as collateral for bank loans until prices rose. More than three hundred of these warehouses had been built in Texas by 1906. Through the warehouse system, the president of the Oklahoma union declared in 1907, "we can revolutionize the present system and enthrone the farmer as absolute master in fixing the price upon his own products."[17] Other state unions in the cotton belt undertook similar programs. The National Farmers' Union created a standing "committee on warehouses," and in 1908 this committee recommended that "every town that markets as much as 500 bales of cotton should have a warehouse of sufficient capacity to accommodate the people."[18] The warehouse system never produced the hoped-for results. Many of the states lacked the necessary cooperative legislation, and frequently the local unions lost control of their warehouses to businessmen. Nevertheless, the warehouse facilities promoted by the Farmers' Union gradually became more adequate in states like Texas, and by 1913 the NFU claimed some 1,600 warehouses in the cotton region.

In spite of its emphasis on cotton withholding and price-fixing plans, the Farmers' Union assumed a variety of other functions. Like the Grange and the Farmers' Alliance, the union sponsored numerous cooperative business ventures. Several state unions attempted to sell cotton directly to domestic and foreign textile mills. Most of the state organizations established business departments and tried to operate business agencies of one kind or another. The Georgia union started a farm implement company and built a fertilizer plant. The Mississippi union organized the Farmers' Union Bank and Trust Company as a means of aiding its members in marketing their cotton crop. Local unions formed hundreds of cooperative arrangements, including the purchasing of fertilizer and other supplies in carload lots, the operation of warehouses, elevators, gins, terminal facilities, and produce exchanges, and the ownership of banks, newspapers, and factories. These enterprises encountered resistance from established businessmen and frequently failed for want of adequate capital and efficient management. Some of them enjoyed momentary success, and such activities did serve to foster the Farmers' Union ideal of farmer cooperation. The union also promoted better farming practices, crop diversification, and greater self-sufficiency on the part of its members. Its literature stressed the importance of improved educational facilities for farmers and supported agricultural journals, fairs, and demonstrations. There were social activities as well, and the local unions enhanced their appeal by arranging rallies, picnics, and barbecues as the setting for their meetings and programs.

The new farmer organization, recalling the fate of the Farmers' Alliance,

[17]Quoted in Taylor, *The Farmers' Movement*, 352.
[18]Ibid., 353.

was almost obsessively determined to avoid being drawn into party politics. Newton Gresham made this clear in the first constitution of the Farmers' Union: "This is in no degree a political party, and shall forever abstain from even so much as a discussion of partyism." In his first presidential address, in 1907, Charles S. Barrett emphasized this point when he declared: "I trust in the Almighty God that we shall never see a time when the Farmers' Union shall be fretted by political demagogues within its ranks . . . [or] contaminated by an affiliation with any political party."[19] The Texas state charter was revoked for a time by the NFU because of that union's political activities, and in at least a few instances local unions had their charters suspended because of their political involvement.

Nevertheless, the Farmers' Union was clearly intended to sway public opinion and shape political decisions. Indeed, its role as an organized pressure group was probably more important than its efforts to raise prices in the cotton market. The state unions, like the NFU, soon appointed committees on legislation. The North Carolina union, which had a noticeable effect upon political affairs in the Old North State, created a special committee to attend to the legislative needs of the organization, conducted a lobby in Raleigh and Washington, questioned candidates for public office about their stands on issues, and urged its members to sign petitions advocating certain reforms. Southern politicians were quick to sense the benefits to be derived from identification with the farmer organization, and the weight of the Farmers' Union soon became evident in political conventions, platforms, and candidates. Speaking of the North Carolina union, the *Progressive Farmer* asserted in 1916 that "the Farmers' Union has been the most potent factor that has ever been brought to bear in legislative matters that affect the life and business of agriculture" in the state.[20] The Mississippi union successfully lobbied for the creation of a state department of agriculture, for the establishment of agricultural high schools, and for legislation restricting the ownership of land by corporations.[21]

The National Farmers' Union was influential in Washington, where Charles S. Barrett of Georgia, the long-time president of the NFU, became an effective publicist and lobbyist. His close relations with the southern congressional delegations enhanced his role as an advocate of national agricultural measures such as banking and currency reform. In 1910, for instance, Barrett was trying to persuade individual congressmen to abolish "gambling on farm products," to enact a parcel post bill, to set up a system of postal savings banks, to restrict foreign immigration, to vote against "the proposed central bank," and to dem-

---

[19] Quoted in Taylor, *The Farmers' Movement*, 358.

[20] Quoted in ibid., 360. See also Louis Bernard Schmidt, "The Role and Technique of Agrarian Pressure Groups," *Agric. Hist.* 30 (Apr. 1956): 51.

[21] For activities of the Mississippi Union, see George L. Robson, Jr., "The Farmers' Union in Mississippi," *Jour. Miss. Hist.* 27 (Nov. 1965): 373–89.

onstrate greater "liberality" in national appropriations for agricultural projects.[22]

During the years of the movement's greatest strength in the South, a period that ended about 1915, the North Carolina union was the largest and most effective state organization in the region. The North Carolina association was formed in the spring of 1908, when some 5,000 Farmers' Union members from twenty-one counties were reported for the state. By 1912 the state organization claimed 33,688 paid-up members and 1,783 local unions. The union's greatest strength was centered in the cotton region of the east and the tobacco belt of the Piedmont. In addition to various cooperative ventures, the state union attempted to set up a warehouse system.[23] The organization also began a campaign to reduce the acreage of staple crops and to diversity agricultural production. There was a militant cast to the North Carolina union not apparent in most other states; it spoke out against Wall Street, cotton speculators, and the American Tobacco Company trust. It also condemned the crop-lien system, agitated for freight-rate reductions, endorsed the initiative and referendum, and worked to secure the passage of credit union legislation and a Torrens system of land title registration. Dr. H. Q. Alexander, an energetic and somewhat eccentric farm publicist, was president of the NCFU from 1908 to 1919. Other leaders included Clarence Poe of Raleigh, whose *Progressive Farmer* absorbed the *Carolina Union Farmer* in 1913. "The fact that the important leaders were prosperous farmers, physicians, and teachers with experience in other farm organizations," one authority has noted, "partly explains why the North Carolina Division of the Union played the important part in public affairs that it did."[24]

The Farmers' Union in most other southern states was less active and less influential than it was in North Carolina, and throughout the South the organization lost ground in the immediate prewar years. In Mississippi, for example, union membership dropped from a reported 65,000 early in 1908 to 7,500 in March 1912.[25] The poor showing of union business endeavors, dissatisfaction with the campaigns to alter production and marketing practices, and the absence of a common bond between poorer and more substantial farmers contributed to the movement's decline. The upward trend in farm prices also sapped the organization's strength. Still, the Farmers' Union was the most important agricultural organization in the region during the first part of the century, and its impact upon the course of southern politics and progressive legislation was

[22]Barrett to Senator John H. Bankhead, Feb. 21, 1910, Bankhead Papers.

[23]For the early years of the North Carolina Union, see Charles P. Loomis, "The Rise and Decline of the North Carolina Farmers' Union," *N.C. Hist. Rev.* 7 (July 1930): 305–25, and "Activities of the North Carolina Farmers' Union," ibid. (Oct. 1930): 443–62.

[24]Loomis, "The Rise and Decline of the North Carolina Farmers' Union," 320. See also copy of the 11-point platform adopted by the state council of the North Carolina Union on Mar. 28, 1916, Benjamin Rice Lacy Papers, North Carolina Department of Archives and History.

[25]Robson, "The Farmers' Union in Mississippi," 378, 387.

striking. Its experiments in cooperative enterprises and market controls, while largely unsuccessful, were significant precursors of later organizational and legislative actions.

A more important emphasis in progressive efforts to rehabilitate the southern farmer was the widespread support of practical education and efficient methods in agriculture. As one of the southern reformers declared after visiting Denmark in 1906, "If Georgia were cultivated with the same kind of intensity, diversity, and skill that are put into these Danish areas, we would raise twenty-five billion dollars worth of agricultural products annually, or enough to maintain a population three times as great as the present population of the entire United States."[26] There was much talk of better cultivation, increased productivity, and more economical handling of cotton and other crops. Agricultural reformers such as Clarence Poe, who dreamed of raising the earning power of the average southern farm by $500 a year, proclaimed the absolute necessity of increasing the efficiency and earning ability of the region's farmers.[27] Rural leaders, agricultural educators, and business interests had earlier advocated scientific farming, and attempts had been made to inform the section's farmers of new approaches and techniques. Among the legacies of the farmers' upheaval of the late nineteenth century was the idea of a more practical type of education for southern agriculturalists. The Farmers' Alliance and other farm organizations had been instrumental in the establishment of new agricultural, vocational, and women's colleges in the late 1880s and the 1890s. The early twentieth-century farmer societies also made education a primary objective. Thus the preamble of the Farmers' Educational and Cooperative Union stated that one of its purposes was to "educate the agricultural class in scientific farming."[28]

Notable among promoters of agricultural education and rural change in the early years of the century was the farm journal. In 1903 some twenty-five agricultural periodicals were being published in the South, and by 1911 the circulation of southern farm journals was estimated at 636,000. The leading regional journals were the *Southern Planter* (Richmond), the *Progressive Farmer* (Raleigh), the *Southern Agriculturalist* (Nashville), the *Southern Cultivator* (Atlanta), and the *Southern Ruralist* (Atlanta). Several of the major newspapers in the South were confirmed advocates of agricultural improvement, such as the Memphis *Commercial Appeal* under C.P.J. Mooney. Walter Hines Page's *World's Work* became a champion of rural rehabilitation through

[26]Eugene C. Branson, quoted in Lanier Branson, *Eugene Cunningham Branson: Humanitarian* (Charlotte, N.C., 1967), 11.

[27]Clarence H. Poe, "Agricultural Revolution a Necessity," *Annals* 35 (Jan. 1910): 42–51; Jordan, "Cotton in Southern Agricultural Economy," 1–7; S.A. Knapp, "The Value of Agricultural Instruction in the Secondary Schools," *SAQ* 6 (Apr. 1907): 135–46; David Y. Thomas, "The Need for Agricultural Education," *Annals* 35 (Jan. 1910): 150–55.

[28]Scott, *The Reluctant Farmer*, 46.

practical education and modern methods.[29] None of the farm journals was more dedicated to the transformation of southern agriculture than the *Progressive Farmer*. Founded in 1886 by the Alliance leader Leonidas L. Polk, the magazine was revitalized and expanded by Clarence Poe, a young North Carolinian who joined its staff in 1899. Under Poe's energetic direction, the *Progressive Farmer* spread throughout the South, absorbing numerous other farm papers and achieving a circulation of more than 100,000 by 1911. Poe established editorial and business offices in Birmingham, Memphis, and Dallas as well as Raleigh, and he employed experts in the various facets of agriculture. The *Progressive Farmer* persistently urged the need to increase southern farm incomes through better methods of cultivation, diversification, the introduction of livestock, and greater self-sufficiency. Poe was an ardent supporter of educational reform, practical schooling for farmers, and home economics. He introduced a "Home Department" in his magazine in which matters of family and community life were discussed.[30]

Agricultural colleges in the various southern states were also agents of innovation and greater efficiency in the rural areas. By 1912 most of the land-grant colleges had set up extension departments and were distributing literature, providing agricultural instruction through direct correspondence, and offering short courses for farmers, frequently away from the campus. Schools of agriculture played a vital role in the conduct of farm institutes, a species of agricultural program that became highly popular in the South during the progressive era. The University of Georgia, for example, created a special department in 1903 to hold farm institutes. Forty-four institutes were conducted in the state that year, and in 1913 no fewer than 109 were held, with an estimated attendance of 32,000 people. The state agricultural college, which was reorganized in 1907, developed a farm extension program. During the years 1908–11 the college sent an "educational train" through the state, with special exhibits that were viewed at 150 stops.[31] The state departments of agriculture in the South also became more active during this period. Encouraged by federal support authorized in the Hatch Act of 1887 and the Adams Act of 1906, the states established agricultural experiment stations, usually in conjunction with their colleges of agriculture. The experiment stations and substations played an important part in the discovery and dissemination of scientific knowledge about plant and animal life.[32]

[29]Ibid., 20–22; George C. Osborn, "The Southern Agricultural Press and Some Significant Rural Problems, 1900–1940," *Agric. Hist.* 29 (July 1955): 115–22; James W. Silver, "C.P.J. Mooney of the Memphis *Commercial Appeal*, Crusader for Diversification," ibid. 17 (Apr. 1943): 81–89; H.L. Meredith, "The Agrarian Reform Press in Oklahoma, 1899–1922," *Chron. Okla.* 50 (Spring 1972): 82–94.

[30]Clarence Poe, *My First 80 Years* (Chapel Hill, N.C., 1963), 87–105, 129–42, 146–50. Also see Joseph A. Cote, "Clarence Hamilton Poe: The Farmer's Voice, 1899–1964," *Agric. Hist.* 53 (Jan. 1979): 30–41.

[31]Range, *A Century of Georgia Agriculture*, 234–37.

[32]Charles E. Rosenberg, "Science, Technology, and Economic Growth: The Case of the

The institute movement, whether managed by state departments of agriculture or land-grant colleges and experiment stations, made rapid headway in the South between 1900 and 1914. More than three thousand institutes were conducted in 1913–14 in southern and border states. Some of the institutes were exclusively for black farmers. Some were highly specialized, organized for producers of such commodities as fruits and vegetables. Institutes for farm women were also held, usually in conjunction with those arranged for men. North Carolina, which developed the best system of women's institutes, sponsored more than two hundred in 1912. Beginning in 1908, the Southern Railway Company provided a domestic science demonstration car for a number of institutes. There were also institutes for farm boys and girls, held in connection with the various types of youth clubs and supported by school officials and agricultural colleges. By 1910, institute managers in several states were cooperating with newly established agricultural high schools in offering short-term courses for farmers. Although the institute movement touched only a minority of southern farmers, it stimulated interest in scientific agriculture, brought many farmers into contact with the agricultural colleges and experiment stations, and encouraged the idea that the colleges had something useful to offer the farmer.[33]

Farm institutes, as well as the broader campaign to promote efficiency and diversification in southern agriculture, received support from many business firms. Railroads, farm machinery manufacturers, and fertilizer companies were active boosters of improved agriculture in the South. Railroads were particularly important, and the "educational" or "demonstration" train was one of the most popular features of the farm extension movement. Business firms aided in the conduct of agricultural institutes, sponsored farm exhibits, distributed scientific literature, supported the club movement for farm youths, and established model farms. The economic development of the section would obviously serve the long-range interests of these businesses. Boards of trade, chambers of commerce, and regional groups like the Southern Soil Improvement Committee similarly endorsed many of the efforts to modernize southern agriculture.[34]

Agricultural Experiment Station Scientist, 1875–1914," *Agric. Hist.* 45 (Jan. 1971): 1–20; Jane M. Porter, "Experiment Stations in the South, 1877–1940," ibid. 53 (Jan. 1979): 84–101; Samuel Proctor, "The Early Years of the Florida Experiment Station, 1888–1906," ibid. 36 (Oct. 1962): 213–21; Scott, *The Reluctant Farmer*, 138–69; William Warren Rogers, "Reuben F. Kolb: Agricultural Leader of the New South," *Agric. Hist.* 32 (Apr. 1958): 109–19; Jack Temple Kirby, *Darkness at the Dawning: Race and Reform in the Progressive South* (Philadelphia, 1972), 147–49.

[33]Scott, *The Reluctant Farmer*, 65–102, 105–30; Roy V. Scott, "Farmers' Institutes in Louisiana, 1897–1906," *JSH* 25 (Feb. 1959): 73–90.

[34]Scott, *The Reluctant Farmer*, 170–205; Roy V. Scott, "American Railroads and Agricultural Extension, 1900–1914: A Study in Development Techniques," *Bus. Hist. Rev.* 39 (Spring 1965): 74–98; Jesse C. Burt, Jr., "Railroad Promotion of Agriculture in Tennessee," *Tenn. Hist. Quar.* 10 (Dec. 1951): 320–33.

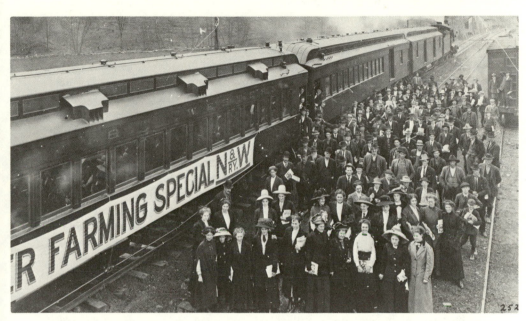

Teaching sanitation by farmers' train, Scott County, Virginia, 1912. *Rockefeller Archive Center*.

The growing interest in the status of the farmer, in and out of the South, was spotlighted in the work of Theodore Roosevelt's Country Life Commission. The commission, created by the president in 1908, undertook an extensive investigation, including the holding of public hearings throughout the country. Two of the commission members were southerners: Charles S. Barrett, president of the Farmers' Union, and Walter Hines Page, editor and publisher of *World's Work*. The commission's report, submitted early in 1909, warned of the threatened loss of the nation's celebrated agrarian values while stressing the need for greater use of scientific knowledge and "business" methods on the farm. The report elicited widespread comment. "Farmers' Weeks" were held in several southern states, providing an occasion for discussions of scientific farming and the rehabilitation of rural life. Late in 1908, for example, the University of Virginia sponsored a Country Life Conference, with delegates in attendance from a number of southeastern states.[35] The spirit of the country life movement was reflected in Page's desire to turn his journal into "an experiment to induce people to go to the land, and to acquire land—and to stay on the land—of course, not primarily nor mainly for speculative purposes, but for the sounder economic reason of continuous ownership and improvement."[36]

Advocates of rural reform dwelt on the inherent virtues of farm life and the urgent need to relieve the isolation and cultural limitations of the countryside. They wanted to arrest the decline of the rural community. But the task was formidable. Writing in 1912, the chairman of the General Education Board described what he called "a story unmatched in pathos," a story of "worn out soil, inefficient cultivation, scanty crop, abandoned field overgrown with bushes, deeply washed and gullied hillside, rotten orchard, sprawling fence, tumble-down houses, with unkempt and littered surroundings." Was there, he wondered, "aught of remedy for this neglect of rural life?"[37] Southern progressives were hopeful. Joseph D. Eggleston, superintendent of public instruction in Virginia, called attention in 1905, for example, to the "blessings" that would enrich community life in his state: "good schools, good roads, good churches,

---

[35]Kirby, *Darkness at the Dawning*, 132–35; Clayton S. Ellsworth, "Theodore Roosevelt's Country Life Commission," *Agric. Hist.* 34 (Oct. 1960): 155–72; William L. Bowers, *The Country Life Movement in America, 1900–1920* (Port Washington, N.Y., 1974), 24–29, 63–85, 92–93; Wayne E. Fuller, *RFD: The Changing Face of Rural America* (Bloomington, Ind., 1964), 259–83; Fuller, "The South and the Rural Free Delivery of Mail," *JSH* 25 (Nov. 1959): 499–521.

[36]Page to Edwin Mims, Aug. 18, 1911, in possession of Mims family, Nashville, Tenn. See also John Milton Cooper, Jr., *Walter Hines Page: The Southerner as American, 1855–1918* (Chapel Hill, N.C., 1977), 224–30.

[37]Frederick T. Gates, "The Country School of To-Morrow," *World's Work* 24 (Aug. 1912): 461. For illustrations of the decline of rural life in the early twentieth-century South, see Herman Clarence Nixon, *Possum Trot: Rural Community, South* (Norman, Okla., 1941), 58–74; Clifton Paisley, *From Cotton to Quail: An Agricultural Chronicle of Leon County, Florida, 1860–1967* (Gainesville, Fla., 1968); and J. Wayne Flynt, "Southern Baptists: Rural to Urban Transition," *Baptist History and Heritage* 16 (Jan. 1981): 24–34.

rural telephones, rural free delivery of mails and traveling libraries."[38] In Clarence Poe's opinion the "fullest and freest training of the average man" would bring an increase in efficiency, earning power, and prosperity. Then, indeed, would "the South blossom as the rose." Farm homes would be supplied "with all the conveniences our city brethren now enjoy." Rural dwellers would have good roads and telephones, and "fine stock and fat acres" would greet "the glad eyes of an awakened people."[39]

Despite the invocation of rural values, the movement to rehabilitate the southern farmer was basically concerned with programs to improve agricultural techniques, increase production, and raise farm incomes. Most of the agricultural improvers at the turn of the century sought, in one way or another, to accomplish their goal by telling farmers how to better themselves. This included the U.S. Department of Agriculture, which had become involved in a number of efforts to deal with the general malaise that affected southern agriculture. The USDA's Bureau of Plant Industry, for instance, established five government farms in Texas and Louisiana as a means of demonstrating that the region's farm difficulties could be surmounted by better management, the use of good seed, crop rotation, and the like. In 1902 the USDA selected Seaman A. Knapp as special agent for the promotion of agriculture in the South.[40]

Knapp was a remarkable figure who had an extraordinary effect upon the agricultural reform movement in the South. A native of New York State, he had become an expert agriculturist in Iowa, where he was a teacher, farmer, farm editor, and professor of agriculture. In the mid-1880s he was employed by an English syndicate which was trying to develop extensive agricultural holdings in southwest Louisiana. By subsidizing a farmer in each township to demonstrate the area's agricultural potential, Knapp and his associates helped make Louisiana the nation's leading rice producer. In 1898, Knapp began to work for the USDA; during the next few years he undertook a study of agricultural practices and crops in the Far East and Puerto Rico. Knapp's contemporaries were invariably struck by his exceptional personal qualities as well as his vast agricultural knowledge. He laid great stress on the idea of self-help. The farmer, he often insisted, had to solve his problems "on his own farm and with his own hands and find the answer in the crib or granary." Seaman Knapp never told a farmer that he had come to teach him something. Instead, Knapp would ask: "Will you take some of this seed and plant it? I want you to prepare the soil and make a good seed-bed, to cultivate it many times, to plant it wide in the rows so that it may have light and air, and then we will see if between us we can show your neighbors how to make cotton."[41]

---

[38]Quoted in Allen W. Moger, *Virginia: Bourbonism to Byrd, 1870–1925* (Charlottesville, Va., 1968), 253.

[39]Poe, "Agricultural Revolution a Necessity," 46–47.

[40]Scott, *The Reluctant Farmer*, 206–36.

[41]Quoted in Raymond B. Fosdick, *Adventure in Giving: The Story of the General Education*

Initially Knapp's work as a special agent was concentrated in Texas, where the alarming spread of the boll weevil had resulted in USDA efforts to help save cotton farmers. Knapp soon realized that in contrast to the problem he had faced in the Louisiana rice belt, his task in Texas was to persuade farmers to adopt new methods on land they had cultivated for long periods of time. The situation called for a new approach. Early in 1903 the special agent persuaded a group of local farmers and businessmen in Terrell, Texas, to undertake a novel type of farm demonstration. Following Knapp's recommendations, community leaders selected a suitable farm and raised money to compensate the owner for any losses that might be suffered during the test period. The farm owner agreed to operate a designated plot under the supervision and technical guidance of the USDA, through Knapp. The 800-acre farm of Walter C. Porter was chosen for the Terrell demonstration in 1903, and a 70-acre plot was planted in corn and cotton, well fertilized, and carefully cultivated under Knapp's supervision. The results were very encouraging. Unlike most of his neighbors, Porter made a profit in 1903. The government had provided nothing except information and guidance. The lesson was that with similar methods, any farmer apparently could do what Porter had done. The Terrell experiment had shown, as one historian has written, that "a community demonstration farm conducted by the farmer himself was a highly effective teaching device."[42]

The results of the Terrell demonstration attracted great attention in the vicinity because it seemed to offer a way of combating the boll weevil, which had moved across the southern half of Texas by the autumn of 1903, creating widespread fear and panic. Department of Agriculture officials in Washington, though at first unenthusiastic about Knapp's innovation, agreed to provide federal funds for community demonstration work. In late 1903, Congress appropriated $250,000 for boll weevil control programs. Knapp, early in 1904, established his office in Houston and made preparations for an expanded demonstration program. He conferred with agricultural representatives of the railroads serving Texas and began appointing special agents to organize the work. Within a few months he had twenty agents in the field.[43]

Knapp's agents usually approached a community's leading businessmen in an effort to have them arrange a general meeting at which the cooperative demonstration work could be explained. Then, if sufficient interest existed, a guarantee fund was raised and a committee chosen to decide upon one or more

Board, a Foundation Established by John D. Rockefeller (New York, 1962), 42–43. For Knapp's career, see Joseph Cannon Bailey, *Seaman A. Knapp: Schoolmaster of American Agriculture* (New York, 1945). Also see Seaman A. Knapp, "An Agricultural Revolution," *World's Work* 12 (July 1906): 7733–38, and "Farmers' Cooperative Demonstration Work in the Southern States," in *The South in the Building of the Nation*, vol. 10, pp. 603–13.

[42]Scott, *The Reluctant Farmer*, 211.

[43]This paragraph and those that follow are based on Scott, *The Reluctant Farmer*, 206–52, and Bailey, *Seaman A. Knapp*, 169–231.

demonstrators among the better farmers in the locality. A plot of approximately ten acres was used to carry out the experiment on each demonstration farm. The special agents also sought to enlist a second class of demonstrators. These so-called cooperators agreed to follow such instructions as might be given them, usually by mail, and to report the results at the end of the crop year. Knapp's famous ten commandments stressed proper cultivation and drainage, careful seed selection, sensible crop rotation, use of fertilizers to rebuild fertilizer and humus content, the production of livestock, more efficient use of labor, and greater self-sufficiency on the part of the farmer. Little of this was new; the important thing was the way these methods were taught. Although the immediate purpose of the demonstration program was to control the boll weevil through an application of the USDA's cultural technique, Knapp's larger goal was to overcome the backwardness and poverty of the average farmer.

Interest in the demonstration approach grew as the boll weevil moved eastward and as the program's effectiveness was publicized. The demonstrations of 1904 encouraged many farmers to believe that cotton could be grown successfully in spite of the boll weevil. Within a few years southern agricultural leaders like Clarence Poe were referring to Knapp's demonstration system as "the most striking educational innovation of this generation."[44] In 1905, Knapp gave more attention to Louisiana, where demonstration work had been started the previous year, and his agents began preliminary efforts in Arkansas, Mississippi, and West Tennessee. But congressional appropriations limited demonstration work to areas that were suffering from weevil infestation, even though interest in the new program had spread widely through the South. A partial solution was found early in 1906, when the General Education Board agreed to help finance an enlarged demonstration program. The GEB, which had already made important contributions to the southern education movement, had concluded that schools in the South could best be encouraged by improving southern agriculture, the foundation of the section's economic life. An arrangement was worked out in January 1906 whereby the GEB would finance Knapp's work in southern states not yet threatened by the boll weevil, while the USDA concentrated on the weevil-infested areas.

The continuing success of the demonstration work facilitated a steady increase in funds for its support. Federal appropriations amounted to $335,856 a year in 1912, and by 1914 the GEB was contributing $187,000 a year to the program. Local support was indispensable, however, and southern businessmen were strong backers of the new approach from the start. By about 1910, moreover, the states and counties had begun to allocate public money as a means of expanding demonstration work. In Georgia, for example, there were 50 demonstration agents, plus 28 home demonstration agents, at work in seventy counties in 1913. Alabama in 1911 had at least one demonstration agent in

---

[44]Poe, "Builders of an Agricultural Commonwealth," *SAQ* 8 (Jan. 1909): 8.

every county, and the term "county agent" had already come into general use.[45] As the program expanded, agents were increasingly made responsible for only one county, rather than six or eight, as in the beginning of the work. State agents were also appointed to coordinate the demonstration efforts in individual commonwealths. By 1912 there were approximately 700 demonstration agents in the South, and more than 100,000 southern farmers participated in the program that year as demonstrators and cooperators. By the time of Seaman A. Knapp's death in 1911, Farmers' Co-operative Demonstration Work, as it was officially known, had attracted nationwide attention as the most promising technique yet developed for agricultural improvement.

Meanwhile, the demonstration work was being elaborated in several significant respects. In line with Knapp's broader interest in the rehabilitation of southern agriculture, the demonstration program soon came to encompass almost every crop and type of farming in the region. Knapp realized that in order to transform farm practices it would be necessary to reach the farm wife and farm children. Thus he encouraged the embryonic movement, initially supported by private funds, to reach the rural housewife through home demonstration agents. Believing that adults could be instructed through their children, he helped make the rural youth program a valuable adjunct of his demonstration work. Boys' and girls' clubs, using demonstration techniques and various kinds of competition, impressed Knapp as a practical means of interesting farm youths in agriculture, showing them the value of improved farming, stimulating agricultural diversification, and helping undermine prejudice among adult farmers against instructions coming from outside agencies. Writing in 1910, an employee of the USDA noted that "Boys' Corn Clubs" had been organized in nearly every southern county. "It is only about five years since this movement started," he wrote, "but it seems to have swept the whole southern country and has won the respect and support of all progressive planters."[46] With the financial assistance of the General Education Board and the cooperation of the agricultural colleges, the boys' club movement was expanded and standardized in the years after 1908. By 1912 some 70,000 boys were enrolled in corn clubs. There were also clubs for the production of other crops and livestock. A similar though less significant movement involved farm girls in the South. An estimated 30,000 girls were members of tomato clubs in 1913, by which time some 200 agents were promoting various types of clubs for girls in the region. The movement was especially strong in Alabama, Georgia, Mississippi, Oklahoma, and Texas. [47]

[45]Range, *A Century of Georgia Agriculture*, 234–37; Charles S. Davis, "Early Agricultural Demonstration Work in Alabama," *Ala. Rev.* 2 (July 1949): 176–88.

[46]S.M. Tracy, "New Farm Crops for the South," *Annals* 35 (Jan. 1910): 55.

[47]Scott, *The Reluctant Farmer*, 237–52; Bailey, *Seaman A. Knapp*, 230–37. For an illuminating treatment of a young agricultural educator and leader in the boys' club movement, see Roy V. Scott and J.G. Shoalmire, *The Public Career of Cully A. Cobb: A Study in Agricultural Leadership* (Jackson, Miss., 1973), 36–112.

Field meeting of boys' corn club. *Rockefeller Archive Center*.

Although Negro farmers had participated to a limited extent in the demonstration program from the first, they were not extensively involved during the early years, in part because Knapp opposed the use of black agents. He eventually changed his mind, influenced by the arguments of GEB representatives at Tuskegee Institute. Washington and his associates had long held annual conferences at Tuskegee to discuss better farm methods. In May 1906 the institute began sending a wagon with tools, seeds, fertilizer samples, and the like through Macon County and the surrounding countryside. This Jesup Wagon—financed by the New York banker Morris K. Jesup—seemed to fit well into the demonstration approach, and Knapp and Tuskegee worked out a cooperative arrangement whereby Thomas M. Campbell operated the wagon and also served as a demonstration agent. A similar arrangement was made between Knapp and Hampton Institute, with John B. Pierce becoming the second black agent. By 1912 there were 32 Negro agents in the demonstration program, with 3,500 black farmers enrolled as demonstrators. Tuskegee Institute sponsored several other programs to help black farmers, including annual farm conferences, short courses, institutes, county fairs, and the only all-black agricultural experiment station in the South. Under the direction of George Washington Carver, thousands of black farmers were being taught the benefits of scientific farming.[48]

One of the most important aspects of the agricultural scene during the early part of the twentieth century was the farmers' altered approach to politics and legislative policy. Much of the reform sentiment and progressive political action in the South rested on rural support, including the efforts to regulate railroads and insurance companies, the campaigns for public education, and the prohibition movement. Some of these political campaigns attracted support from rural inhabitants in a broad, amorphous fashion. But as farmers organized in new associations and new campaigns involving particular crops and programs, they increasingly emphasized specific agricultural interest objectives. Thus southern farm journals and farm organizations urged the expansion of federal appropriations for Knapp's demonstration work. The same tendency was evident in the state capitals. These legislative demands reflected the nar-

[48]Felix James, "The Tuskegee Institute Movable School, 1906–1923," *Agric. Hist.* 45 (July 1971): 201–209; Lewis W. Jones, "The South's Negro Farm Agent," *Jour. Negro Edu.* 22 (Winter 1953): 38–45; Allen W. Jones, "The Role of Tuskegee Institute in the Education of Black Farmers," *Jour. Negro Hist.* 60 (Apr. 1975): 252–67; Allen W. Jones, "The South's First Black Farm Agents," *Agric. Hist.* 50 (Oct. 1976): 636–44; Barry Mackintosh, "George Washington Carver: The Making of a Myth," *JSH* 42 (Nov. 1976): 512–16; Linda O. Hines, "George W. Carver and the Tuskegee Agricultural Experiment Station," *Agric. Hist.* 53 (Jan. 1979): 71–83; Linda O. McMurry, *George Washington Carver: Scientist and Symbol* (New York, 1981), 112–44; A. Lee Coleman and Larry D. Hall, "Black Farm Operators and Farm Population, 1900–1970: Alabama and Kentucky," *Phylon* 40 (Dec. 1979): 387–402; James D. Anderson, "The Southern Improvement Company: Northern Reformers' Investment in Negro Cotton Tenancy, 1900–1920," *Agric. Hist.* 52 (Jan. 1978): 111–31.

Thomas M. Campbell, the first black demonstration agent, and the Jesup Wagon. *Rockefeller Archive Center*.

rowing political concerns and the more specialized needs of organized farmers, in the South as in other regions.

On paper, at least, a mass of farm legislation was passed by the various state legislatures during the progressive era. State commissioners of agriculture were authorized and usually made elective. Special boards were established to serve as veterinary examiners, livestock sanitary inspectors, and so on. Provision was made for inspecting, grading, and labeling commercial fertilizer, seed, and feedstuffs. Speculation in commodity futures was outlawed. Pure food and drug laws were passed, and inspectors were provided. State funds were appropriated for agricultural high schools, extension programs in agriculture and domestic science, and such things as boll weevil control and tick eradication.[49]

In Virginia a long controversy over lime led, despite the opposition of fertilizer manufacturers, to the passage of a farmers' bill in 1912 that provided for the construction of two state plants. Westmoreland Davis, president of the Farmers' Institute (a private organization dedicated to the promotion of scientific agriculture), was instrumental in the formation in 1914 of the Agricultural Conference, a farm-problem caucus. During the same year Governor William Hodges Mann created the United Agricultural Board as a liaison between federal programs and Virginia farmers. The commissioner of agriculture in Georgia inaugurated a rudimentary marketing service in 1914 by hiring a marketing expert whose responsibility was to assist farmers in selling their crops. In 1917, Georgia established a bureau of markets and began publishing the *Georgia Market Bulletin*.[50] There was clearly an expansion of state agencies and services concerned with the needs of farmers during this period. While many of these state agencies were overlapping and poorly coordinated, the functions they undertook were increasingly centralized in state governments.

But there were limits to this state intervention, and several proposals for fundamental changes in southern agriculture were defeated. The Farmers' Union of North Carolina, for instance, made no progress in its efforts to abolish the sharecropping and crop-lien system. The *Southern Cultivator* was no more successful in its campaign against the supply credit system in Georgia. In Texas a radical group organized the Land Renters' Union of North America in 1911,

        [49]See, for example, Joseph Flake Steelman, "The Progressive Era in North Carolina, 1884–1917" (Ph.D. diss., Univ. of North Carolina, 1955), 651–82; Danney Goble, *Progressive Oklahoma: The Making of a New Kind of State* (Norman, Okla., 1980), 158–65; and Walter Pittman, "Chemical Regulation in Mississippi: The State Laboratory (1882–)," *Jour. Miss. Hist.* 41 (May 1979): 133–53.
        [50]F. A. Magruder, *Recent Administration in Virginia* (Baltimore, 1912), 129–45; Kirby, *Darkness at the Dawning*, 147–49, 151–53; Range, *A Century of Georgia Agriculture*, 201–202, 214, 231–32, 243; Alton DuMar Jones, "Progressivism in Georgia, 1898–1918" (Ph.D. diss., Emory Univ., 1963), 110–24. Also see Dunbar Rowland, *History of Mississippi: The Heart of the South* (Chicago, 1925), vol. 2, pp. 316, 326–31, 336–37, 342; Loomis, "Activities of the North Carolina Farmers' Union," 443–55; Saloutos, *Farmer Movements in the South*, 206–208; James Aubrey Tinsley, "The Progressive Movement in Texas" (Ph.D. diss., Univ. of Wisconsin, 1953), 150–55; and Sheldon Hackney, *Populism to Progressivism in Alabama* (Princeton, N.J., 1969), 307–308.

demanding heavy taxation of lands held out of cultivation for speculation and "use and occupancy" as the valid way to secure title to land. Despite the worsening plight of the tenant class, these demands were never seriously considered by the Texas legislature.[51] A reform of a different type was Clarence Poe's scheme for the racial segregation of the rural population of the South. Poe was influenced by the example of European rural community organizations he had observed in his overseas travels and by Maurice S. Evans, a South African leader and author of *Black and White in the Southeastern United States* (1915). A determined advocate of rural values, the North Carolina editor had grown worried by what appeared to be a steady trend toward greater Negro farm occupancy and ownership in the Carolinas. Poe began to talk about the "black peril," and in 1913 he unveiled a comprehensive reform program for the southern countryside. The heart of Poe's plan was a mechanism for segregating farmers along racial lines. Although he received support from Farmers' Union leaders in the state and the recently organized North Carolina Conference for Social Service, the editor's efforts proved unavailing. The state legislature took no action on his proposal, he encountered opposition from some businessmen and landlords, and many North Carolinians seemed to think that rural segregation was not really needed.[52]

In the meantime, southern farm pressure was being applied with greater effect in Washington. The recession and banking crisis of 1907–1908 provoked renewed demands among southern farm groups for a reorganization of the nation's banking system, for stronger governmental controls, and for more liberal credit arrangements, including loans on staple crops. The popularity of Knapp's demonstration work brought growing southern support for the idea that federal appropriations were needed to establish a national system of agricultural extension. Regional groups such as the Association of Southern Agricultural Workers did their best to make sure that the South received its share of federal research funds. The Farmers' Union and other farm pressure organizations contributed to the passage of the federal parcel post law in 1912. Southern farm interests found much to approve in the Democratic platform of 1912, and farm leaders turned with eager anticipation to the new Wilson administration as a source of national legislation. As Charles S. Barrett declared in his address to the 1913 convention of the NFU, "The National Congress is waking up and is giving heed more and more to the voice of the agriculturist."[53]

[51]Loomis, "Activities of the North Carolina Farmers' Union," 449; Range, *A Century of Georgia Agriculture*, 254; Tinsley, "The Progressive Movement in Texas," 172. For the manifestation of agrarian radicalism in Texas and other southwestern states, see James R. Green, *Grass-Roots Socialism: Radical Movements in the Southwest, 1895–1943* (Baton Rouge, 1978), 228–69, and "Tenant Farmer Discontent and Socialist Protest in Texas, 1901–1917," *Southwestern Hist. Quar.* 81 (Oct. 1977): 133–54.

[52]Kirby, *Darkness at the Dawning*, 119–30.

[53]Quoted in Taylor, *The Farmers' Movement*, 363. The parcel-post movement is described in Fuller, *RFD: The Changing Face of Rural America*, 199–257.

No well-informed contemporary went so far as to claim that the average southern farmer had been rehabilitated by 1913. Millions of poor and itinerant farmers, without property, political rights, or education, were hopelessly involved in the sharecropping and crop-lien system. As Eugene C. Branson declared in 1912, in presenting a report on Bartow County, Georgia, the growth of farm tenancy was "appalling." During the first decade of the twentieth century, the percentage of farm owners in the county had dropped from 40 to 30, with "the inevitable small average yield per acre, and large illiteracy ratios." Tenancy in the South, Branson noted, "means cotton growing, and cotton growing calls for women and children in the fields, with the constant interruption of interest in and attendance upon the schools."[54] Traditional in outlook, isolated, often illiterate, and extremely individualistic, many a small farmer was "his own executive and technical expert."[55] The new agriculture hardly touched such farmers, who were inclined to distrust books and science and even schools and progress. This attitude mirrored the class division among rural southerners, who were increasingly separated into what Rupert B. Vance labeled the banker-merchant-landlord class and the tenant-small landowner class.[56] There was also the complicating factor of racial animosity, which was heightened by the intense competition that affected millions of tenants and workers in the agricultural economy.[57]

The ferment of agricultural reform was most compelling in its appeal to farm leaders, editors, scientists, and the more successful producers. Speaking in 1913, an agricultural expert characterized cooperative marketing and purchasing associations as "the salvation of the rural South." Yet he was profoundly discouraged by prospects for change in the region: "I might as well try to move the earth as to advocate co-operation, because the great mass of the farm operators are shifting tenants."[58] A majority of the southern farmers seemed to take the existing system for granted. In the words of one scholar, "they have not characterized it at all."[59] Farm protests and farm organizations, new educational methods, and the application of scientific techniques probably had little effect on the condition of the vast southern peasantry. "The whole tendency of agricultural education," a critic of the extension system charged in 1915, "is to

[54]Branson to A.P. Bourland, Jan. 9, 1912, Eugene C. Branson Papers, Southern Historical Collection, University of North Carolina.

[55]Vance, *Human Factors in Cotton Culture*, 315.

[56]Ibid., 312. See also Range, *A Century of Georgia Agriculture*, 119, and John Gould Fletcher, *Arkansas* (Chapel Hill, N.C., 1947), 335–53.

[57]See, for example, Poe, "Agricultural Revolution a Necessity," 42–51; R.P. Brooks, "A Local Study of the Race Problem: Race Relations in the Eastern Piedmont Region of Georgia," *Pol. Sci. Quar.* 26 (June 1911): 193–221; and William F. Holmes, "Labor Agents and the Georgia Exodus, 1899–1900," *SAQ* 79 (Autumn 1980): 436–48.

[58]Coulter, "The Rural Life Problem of the South," 64–65.

[59]Edgar T. Thompson, "The Natural History of Agricultural Labor in the South," in David Kelly Jackson, ed., *American Studies in Honor of William Kenneth Boyd by Members of the Americana Club of Duke University* (Durham, N.C., 1940), 111.

benefit the man who is already progressive. It does not reach the man who is in most need, the neglected man, who neglects himself, who does not seek knowledge, and to whom the colleges and the department [of agriculture] . . . should go as a missionary."[60] Nor did rising farm prices do much to ease the plight of depressed rural southerners. By the 1920s it had become apparent that a more efficient and productive agriculture geared to landlords and independent farmers would not, even with the aid of public policies that provided generous credit, agricultural extension, and governmental regulation, remedy the fundamental ills of the southern farmers.

Yet the winds of change had begun to blow across the southern countryside during the first two decades of the twentieth century. Organization, education, and improved methods brought increases in production, income, and general well-being to many farmers in the South, particularly those whose holdings were large enough to permit benefits from agricultural innovations. These elements, from the middle and upper ranks of the region's farmers, took advantage of an emerging agricultural structure that included agricultural colleges and high schools, experiment stations, extension programs, farm agents, and farm organizations. Their farm operations benefited from the introduction of new crops, fruits, and livestock. The reorganization of farm life brought new educational and professional opportunities for a large number of farm youths. It quickened the imagination of many rural families, relieved the cultural barrenness of farm life, and for a brief period promised a golden era of unexcelled production, efficiency, and prosperity. "Let us keep on building factories," Ulrich B. Phillips urged in 1905, "and take away all the profit we can from the outside districts, which are parasites upon the South, and let us plant more orchards and vineyards and broad fields of varied crops; let us raise the best sorts of grasses and forage crops, and cover the land with lowing herds and thrifty creameries. . . ."[61] Southern progressives spoke admiringly of agricultural innovators, of "great farmers at work," of "redeemers of the soil," of "builders of agricultural commonwealths."[62]

Southern reformers idealized rural life and found in the agrarian mythology an important source of cherished values. While they were usually identified

[60]Unidentified speaker quoted in Sidney Baldwin, *Poverty and Politics: The Rise and Decline of the Farm Security Administration* (Chapel Hill, N.C., 1968), 31.

[61]Phillips, "The Overproduction of Cotton and a Possible Remedy," 158.

[62]See, for example, Harry Hodgson, "A Great Farmer at Work," *World's Work* 9 (Jan. 1905): 5723–33; Clarence Poe, "Little Stories of Big Successes," ibid. 23 (Nov. 1911): 55–59; Poe, "Builders of an Agricultural Commonwealth," 1–11; Edwin Mims, "The South Realizing Itself: Hartsville and Its Lesson," *World's Work* 22 (Oct. 1911): 14972–87; Mims, "The South Realizing Itself: Redeemers of the Soil," ibid. 23 (Nov. 1911): 41–54; E.C. Branson, "A Way to Better Country Living," ibid. 24 (July 1912): 354–57; Hugh MacRae, "Vitalizing the Nation and Conserving Human Units through the Development of Agricultural Communities," *Annals* 63 (Jan. 1916): 278–86; George Lee Simpson, Jr., *The Cokers of Carolina: A Social Biography of a Family* (Chapel Hill, N.C., 1956), 132–70; and James L. McCorkle, "Mississippi Truck Crops: An Exercise in Agrarian Organization," *Miss. Quar.* 33 (Winter 1979/1980): 55–77.

with the city, many of the progressives grew up on farms or in small towns. "Circumstances have brought me to town and kept me here thus far," John J. McMahan of South Carolina wrote in 1904, "but my heart is so much in the country and on the farm that I must be trying to work out some of my ideals there."[63] As the efforts to modernize farm life continued, there were signs of progress. Thus a Baptist leader asserted in 1917 that "the farmer's ultra-conservatism" was crumbling.

> His home is now open at last to "paper" information about farming, and so is his mind. [H]is son goes to the farmers' college, and perhaps he himself attends the special summer lectures at the school or at the farmer's institute train on the sidetrack at the nearest town. Rural delivery of mail, good roads, the automobile, farm machinery, and the rural telephone, have worked wonders for him. Into his environment have entered things which change it from that which his father faced more than his father's surroundings differed from those of the first frontiersmen who hewed down the forests.[64]

Even so, this writer remarked, country youths continued to regard the city as "the door of opportunity and adventure." He deplored the fact that the rural community frequently made a hero of the boy who succeeded in the city: "Oh, the pity of it, that the big, toilsome, honest, deliberate, frank, kindly, country community should thus sell its soul to the alert, self-seeking, money-gathering, complacent, cold, calculating city!"[65] There was irony as well in the movement to improve southern farm life, for the new agriculture the progressives envisaged, with its emphasis on scientific techniques and commercial success, seemed likely in the long run to destroy the yeoman farmer and undermine the values most treasured by the reformers.

Few of the reformers recognized this paradox at the time. They remained hopeful about the various farm improvement projects. They wanted both to modernize southern agriculture and to preserve the best traditions of the village and countryside. Meanwhile, they were looking to the state and national governments for appropriations and services that would meet their needs and advance their causes.

[63]McMahan to Senator Archer, Nov. 29, 1904, John J. McMahan Papers, South Caroliniana Library, University of South Carolina. On this theme, also see Kirby, *Darkness at the Dawning*, 131, and Wayne E. Fuller, "The Rural Roots of the Progressive Leaders," *Agric. Hist.* 42 (Jan. 1968): 1–13.

[64]Victor L. Masters, *Country Church in the South: Arranged to Meet the Needs of Mission Study Classes and also of the General Reader* (2d ed., Atlanta, 1917), 44.

[65]Ibid., 38–40; quotation on p. 40.

BY THE END OF THE FIRST DECADE of the twentieth century, a pattern was discernible in the development of social reform in the South. The most important reform movements had acquired a regional focus and organization by about 1910, and the reformers were turning more frequently to Washington and the possibility of national action. This tendency was evident in two of the southern progressives' major regulatory movements: the campaign to control railroads and the prohibition crusade. The barriers to effective regulation of railroads by state legislatures and commissions, including the inherent problem of dealing with large companies that were often interstate in their operation and the restraints imposed by federal court decisions and Interstate Commerce Commission rulings, encouraged a move from reliance on state regulation to national control. Meanwhile, the vexatious task of enforcing state and local prohibition in dry areas, not to mention the defeat of the antiliquor cause in Florida, Texas, and Alabama, led many southern reformers to fall in with the American Anti-Saloon League's call for national prohibition. The inclination to look for national solutions was also apparent in other progressive campaigns such as the child labor movement, in the demand by the Farmers' Union and other agricultural pressure groups for federal legislation, and in the desire of the Southern Commercial Congress and similar organizations to obtain federal aid in dealing with problems like flood control. This shift from state to federal solutions was hastened by the activities of such groups as the National Child Labor Committee, the American Anti-Saloon League, the Commission on Country Life, and the National Association of Charities and Correction.

Southern politics also showed signs of increasing involvement in the debate over national issues and elections. In 1910 the Democrats won control of the House of Representatives, and when the House organized for business in 1911, the seniority rule brought a group of southerners to prominence as chairmen of important committees. By that time the movement to nominate Woodrow Wilson for the presidency was getting under way, and in that endeavor the South was to play a vital part. With Wilson's election in 1912, the South assumed an influence in Washington which it had not enjoyed for half a century. The Wilson era coincided with and gave impetus to the coalescence of progressive currents in the South and to the drive toward the nationalization of reform. Wilson himself embodied the ideals and hopes of the region's progressives, and it was altogether fitting that the years of his presidency should have witnessed the elaboration of a reform synthesis in the South and the culmination of southern progressivism.

THE SOUTH IN NATIONAL POLITICS

During the early years of the twentieth century there was little evidence that the South would play a larger role in national politics. Writing in 1910, one perceptive observer called attention to the section's continuing obsession with the race question, lack of free thought as compared with other regions, and long-time political isolation within the nation. Save for the ill-fated Andrew Johnson, no southerner had occupied the White House since the Civil War, nor had any southern leader been nominated for president or vice-president in that period. The region had seldom been represented in the cabinet or on the Supreme Court, and relatively few men from the South had served in the diplomatic and consular services during those years. As for Congress, one contemporary wrote, "If for fifty years there has been a single great general law or policy initiated by Southerners or by a Southerner, or which goes or should go by any Southerner's name, the fact has escaped me."[1] Although William Jennings Bryan, the foremost Democratic leader in national politics during the early years of the twentieth century, had a large following in the South, most of the party organizations in the region were racked by continuing struggles between the Bryanites and more conservative factions.

In one respect the South's participation in national politics was substantial during the first decade of the new century: it dominated the Democratic party in Congress. The realignment of national parties in the 1890s severely weakened the Democratic party outside the South, thereby enhancing the role of its southern members, particularly in Congress. The Fifty-seventh Congress (1901–1903), for example, contained ninety-five Democratic representatives and twenty-two Democratic senators from southern states, as against fifty-six Democratic representatives and nine Democratic senators from other regions.[2] Not only were southerners more numerous than other Democrats in the minority party's congressional ranks; the seniority they achieved as a result of

[1] William Garrott Brown, "The South in National Politics," *SAQ* 9 (Apr. 1910): 103–15; quotation on p. 106. See also James W. Garner, "Southern Politics since the Civil War," in *Studies in Southern History and Politics Inscribed to William Archibald Dunning* (New York, 1914), 367–87.
[2] *Official Congressional Directory*, 57th Cong., 1st sess. (Washington, D.C., 1901). Also see Numan V. Bartley, "The South and Sectionalism in American Politics," *Jour. Politics* 38 (Aug. 1976): 239–57.

habitual reelection usually made them the ranking members of the standing committees.[3] The contributions of these southern congressmen were greater than might be thought. They provided strong support for railroad regulation, tariff and tax revision, and a variety of agrarian reforms during the administrations of Theodore Roosevelt and William Howard Taft.[4] Yet they struck many observers as being peculiarly undisciplined, quixotic, and anachronistic.

One reason for this impression was the way in which the Negro and racial considerations seemed to color every political issue in the South. Another factor was the fierce factional struggles that developed at the state level throughout the region. Perhaps the most important ideological referent in these struggles, except for a vague differentiation between "progressives" and "conservatives," was the complex of reforms identified with William Jennings Bryan. The division among southern Democrats was reflected in Bryan's presidential nomination in 1900 and 1908, as well as in the nomination of the conservative Alton B. Parker in 1904. Although Bryan was resented and opposed by numerous politicians and newspaper editors in the South, the Nebraskan exerted a telling effect on southern political attitudes. As a leading historian has written, the South became "the most thoroughly Bryanized region in the country."[5] In the opinion of the Chicago *Chronicle,* a Republican newspaper, the southern Democratic leadership during this period was just as "wrong-headed and fanatical on economic questions and as strong in its socialistic tendencies as the Bryan and Hearst Democracy in the northern states."[6] William Jennings Bryan's appeal among southerners was related to the revival of Jeffersonian principles, especially the agrarian side of Jefferson, but it was centered even more solidly in Bryan's advocacy of currency and banking reform, railroad regulation, democratic innovations, and the like.[7]

A minor but persistent refrain in the political discourse of the early twentieth-century South was the call for a more independent and nationally oriented politics. Voiced by a group of latter-day mugwumps, this view was a manifestation of the new social criticism in the South and in a broad sense was a product of the emerging professions and growing middle class in the cities. The

---

[3]Incumbency was a decided advantage in most primary elections for congressional seats in the South. The lack of Republican opposition in general elections was if anything even more significant in the long tenure of the average congressman from the South.

[4]See Anne Firor Scott, "A Progressive Wind from the South, 1906–1913," *JSH* 29 (Feb. 1963): 53–70, and "The Southern Progressives in National Politics, 1906–1916" (Ph.D. diss., Radcliffe College, 1957), 1–16.

[5]C. Vann Woodward, *Origins of the New South, 1877–1913* (Baton Rouge, 1951), 469.

[6]Quoted in "A Southern Democratic Leader?" *Public Opinion* 40 (Mar. 31, 1906): 393.

[7]See, for example, John Callan O'Laughlin, "The Next President," *Outlook* 85 (Apr. 6, 1907): 793–800; "Bryan's Strength," *Nation* 86 (May 21, 1908): 458; Josephus Daniels, "Mr. Bryan's Third Campaign," *Amer. Rev. of Reviews* 38 (Oct. 1908): 423–31; Paul W. Glad, *The Trumpet Soundeth: William Jennings Bryan and His Democracy, 1896–1912* (Lincoln, Nebr., 1960); and Merrill D. Peterson, *The Jefferson Image in the American Mind* (New York, 1960), 253–64.

critics contrasted the economic advances and bright industrial prospects of their section with its political intolerance, lack of influence in national affairs, and loss of "the old time southern force and character." They longed for an end to the Solid South, for the expulsion of its "narrow and sectional spirit," for greater independence of thought, and for discussion of national issues. The Solid South had proven a misfortune, the young historian Ulrich B. Phillips wrote in 1904. "It has prevented her having due influence upon national legislation and administration, and what is worse it has proved perhaps a greater check to freedom of thought than slavery was."[8] "We have been told for years," complained Walter Hines Page in December 1900, "that if the negro vote were eliminated, the Southern white vote would be divided on National questions." Yet there was little indication of such political competition in the aftermath of disfranchisement. The political trouble with the South, Page wrote a few years later, could be summed up in five words: "small men in public life." The region desperately needed new political leaders. This leadership must "leave the war alone—and the Negro question," must not be afraid of "Mr. Bryan, nor of the backward Southern press," must "speak the language of Tilden and Cleveland," and must be "national" in thought.[9]

Some of the independents hoped that the South's political emancipation would be effected through presidential leadership. They spoke kindly of William McKinley, were alternately encouraged and disappointed by Theodore Roosevelt, and for a brief time placed their confidence in William Howard Taft. "Roosevelt," a North Carolinian predicted in October 1901, "is going to break the back bone of the old moss back democratic ring rule in the South, as sure as fate."[10] Such wistful expectations were never realized, of course, and the twenty-sixth president's racial contretemps and controversial appointments

[8]Phillips, "Conservatism and Progress in the Cotton Belt," *SAQ* 3 (Jan. 1904): 4. Also see "New Political Sentiment in the South," *World's Work* 1 (Dec. 1900): 134–35; S.S.P. Patteson, "The Political Isolation of the South," *Sewanee Review* 9 (Jan. 1901): 94–96; "Is the Solid South to Yield at Last?" *World's Work* 2 (June 1901): 797–98; John L. McLaurin, "Breaking Up the Solid South," ibid. 2 (July 1901): 985–86; "Why Not Southern Democratic Leadership?" ibid. 4 (Aug. 1902); 2367; "A Southern Democratic Leader?" *Public Opinion* 40 (Mar. 31, 1906): 392–93; "A Southern Presidential Candidate," *World's Work* 12 (May 1906): 7479–80; "The National Spirit of the South," ibid. 14 (Aug. 1907); 9175; Walter H. Page, "Breaking the Solid South," *Outlook* 90 (Dec. 19, 1908): 874–75; Hannis Taylor, "The Solid South a National Calamity," *North American Review* 189 (Jan. 1909): 1–10; Enoch Marvin Banks, "The Passing of the Solid South," *SAQ* 8 (Apr. 1909): 101–106; and William F. Mugleston, "An Attempt to Break the 'Solid South,' " *Ala. Hist. Quar.* 38 (Summer 1976): 126–36.

[9]"New Political Sentiment in the South," 134; "The Sorrow of the South," *World's Work* 9 (Dec. 1904): 5563–64; "Sectional Self-Consciousness," ibid. 14 (Sept. 1907): 9277. Also see Bruce L. Clayton, "Southern Critics of the New South, 1890–1914" (Ph.D. diss., Duke Univ., 1966), 260–64, and "An Intellectual on Politics: William Garrott Brown and the Ideal of a Two-Party South," *N.C. Hist. Rev.* 42 (July 1965): 319–34.

[10]Henry A. Page to Walter Hines Page, Oct. 8, 1901, Walter Hines Page Papers. For McKinley, see B.J. Ramage and John Bell Henneman, "President McKinley," *Sewanee Review* 9 (Oct. 1901): 483–93.

provoked an outpouring of scorn and condemnation below the Potomac and the Ohio. Still, southerners could not resist the effervescent Roosevelt entirely, even though few of them were ever willing to vote for him. Professor Edwin Mims of Trinity College noted early in 1905, for example, that many southerners were drawn to Roosevelt because of his "intense Americanism" and his "disinterested public service." Mims also thought that the president, who boasted that his ancestry was half southern, acted like a southerner in displaying "a certain quality of enthusiasm, demonstrativeness, and cordiality."[11] William Garrott Brown, who followed Roosevelt's southern maneuvers with close attention, suggested that TR had brought "a new democratic impulse" to politics throughout the country, while Alexander J. McKelway declared that the New Yorker's advocacy of progressive measures like pure food, meat inspection, and railroad regulation had made him many friends in the South. During the Roosevelt years, McKelway remarked, southerners began for the first time since the Civil War to consider the federal government as possibly a "beneficent agency."[12]

"Hurrah for Bill Taft!" Edwin A. Alderman exuberantly wrote a friend following Taft's election as president in November 1908.[13] Other southern independents shared Alderman's enthusiasm. Taft had increased the Republican percentage of votes in most of the southern states, and after his election he attracted attention in the region with several sympathetic speeches and felicitous statements designed to appeal to the sensibilities of white southerners. "I did not carry South Carolina or, indeed, any Southern State," Taft wrote a Charleston editor, "unless you call Delaware, Missouri and Maryland Southern States. But I shook up the old bones of the South and got a good many more votes than most of my predecessors, and have the consciousness that there are many who did not vote for me who are glad that I am elected."[14] Perhaps the new president could revitalize the Republican party in the South, transform it into a respectable alternative to the Democratic party, and end the section's isolation in national politics. That was the wish of men like Walter Hines Page, who persuaded Taft to address a meeting of the North Carolina Society of New York in December 1908. Page described the affair as "a bugle call to all

[11]Mims, "President Theodore Roosevelt," *SAQ* 4 (Jan. 1905): 48–62.

[12]William Garrott Brown, "President Roosevelt and the South," *Independent* 59 (Nov. 9, 1905): 1086–89; Brown, "The New Politics: Parties and Men," *North American Review* 92 (Nov. 1910): 630–44; Alexander J. McKelway, "The Progressive South," unpublished manuscript (1914), Alexander J. McKelway Papers, Manuscripts Division, Library of Congress. Also see "The President and the Southern People," *World's Work* 11 (Dec. 1905): 6917–18; Willard B. Gatewood, Jr., "Theodore Roosevelt and Arkansas, 1901–1912," *Ark. Hist. Quar.* 32 (Spring 1973): 3–24; and several of the essays in Gatewood, *Theodore Roosevelt and the Art of Controversy: Episodes of the White House Years* (Baton Rouge, 1970).

[13]Alderman to Walter Hines Page, Nov. 9, 1908, Page Papers.

[14]Taft to J.C. Hemphill, Nov. 30, 1908, James Calvin Hemphill Papers, Duke University Library.

progressive Southerners."[15] As Edgar Gardner Murphy surveyed the scene, he concluded that the South was no longer "a section with a single problem and an exclusive issue." It seemed to Murphy that "all the questions of American life are becoming southern questions, just as our southern questions have become broadly and humanly American."[16]

Whatever hopes men like Page may have had for William Howard Taft's southern policies were soon obliterated by the disruption of the Republican party and the controversy surrounding the Taft administration. But as the fortunes of the Taft presidency declined, prospects for the Democratic party rose. Confirmation of these possibilities first came in the mid-term congressional elections of 1910, when the Democrats won control of the House of Representatives. Southern congressional leaders began to come to the fore in 1911, most conspicuously in the person of Oscar W. Underwood of Alabama, chairman of the Ways and Means Committee and majority leader in the lower house.[17] This southern leadership in Washington aroused pride and anticipation among southerners, many of whom were revealing an unaccustomed interest in national legislation such as tariff reduction, railroad regulation, aid to agriculture,

---

[15]See Page to Taft, Nov. 7, 1908, Jan. 5, 1909, Page Papers; *Speeches Delivered at the Dinner of the North Carolina Society of New York at the Hotel Astor, December 7, 1908,* undated pamphlet, ibid.; "Mr. Taft and the South," *World's Work* 17 (Feb. 1909): 11187–88; and John Milton Cooper, Jr., *Walter Hines Page: The Southerner as American, 1855–1918* (Chapel Hill, N.C., 1977), 230–34. Also see Silas McBee, "The South and Mr. Taft," *Sewanee Review* 16 (Oct. 1908): 486–94; Silas McBee to William Howard Taft, Jan. 20, 1909, Silas McBee Papers, Southern Historical Collection, University of North Carolina; Henry Litchfield West, "President Taft and the South," *Forum* 41 (Apr. 1909): 289–96; William Garrott Brown, "President Taft's Opportunity," *Century Magazine* 78 (June 1909): 252–59; Joseph F. Steelman, "Jonathan Elwood Cox and North Carolina's Gubernatorial Campaign of 1908," *N.C. Hist. Rev.* 41 (Oct. 1964): 436–47; and Steelman, "Republicanism in North Carolina: John Motley Morehead's Campaign to Revive a Moribund Party, 1908–1910," ibid. 42 (Apr. 1965): 153–68.

[16]Murphy, "Backward or Forward?" *SAQ* 8 (Jan. 1909): 19–38; quotations on pp. 20–21.

[17]Scott Bone, "Democrats in Congress Making Good," *Amer. Rev. of Reviews* 44 (Aug. 1911): 209–10; Burton J. Hendrick, "Oscar W. Underwood: A New Leader from the New South," *McClure's Magazine* 38 (Feb. 1912): 404–20; Evans C. Johnson, *Oscar W. Underwood: A Political Biography* (Baton Rouge, 1980), 118–69; Monroe Lee Billington, *The Political South in the Twentieth Century* (New York, 1975), 20–22; John B. Wiseman, "Racism in Democratic Politics, 1904–1912," *Mid-America* 51 (Jan. 1968): 38–58; Claude E. Barfield, " 'Our Share of the Booty': The Democratic Party, Cannonsim, and the Payne-Aldrich Tariff," *Jour. Amer. Hist.* 57 (Sept. 1970): 308–23; James S. Fleming, "Re-establishing Leadership in the House of Representatives: The Case of Oscar W. Underwood," *Mid-America* 54 (Oct. 1972): 234–50; John J. Broesamle, "The Democrats from Bryan to Wilson," in Lewis L. Gould, ed., *The Progressive Era* (Syracuse, N.Y., 1974), 83–113; George O. Carney, "Oklahoma's House Delegation in the Sixty-first Congress: Progressive or Conservative?" *Chron. Okla.* 55 (Summer 1977): 190–210; Karl Rodabaugh, "Congressman Henry D. Clayton, Patriarch in Politics: A Southern Congressman During the Progressive Era," *Ala. Rev.* 31 (Apr. 1978): 110–20; Thomas W. Ramage, "Augustus Owsley Stanley: Early Twentieth Century Kentucky Democrat" (Ph.D. diss., Univ. of Kentucky, 1968), 64–90, 100–29; Emmett B. Fields, Jr., "The Senate Career of James P. Clarke of Arkansas, 1903–1916" (M.A. thesis, Vanderbilt Univ., 1949), 57–89.

and constitutional amendments providing for an income tax and direct election of U.S. senators.[18]

Southern interest in national politics rose to new heights with the nomination and election of Woodrow Wilson as the nation's twenty-eighth president. Southerners were quick to claim Wilson, who had been born and reared in the South, as one of their own, and his spectacular rise as a reform governor of New Jersey was followed with keen interest by newspaper editors, educators, and public leaders all over the South. Richard Evelyn Byrd, speaker of the Virginia house of delegates, wrote Wilson after the latter's election as governor in 1910: "I regard you as the best & most available candidate for the Presidency on the democratic ticket of 1912."[19] There were numerous messages of this kind, and Wilson's campaign in 1911 and 1912 for his party's presidential nomination evoked an enthusiastic response throughout the South. Even so, the New Jersey governor was forced to divide the southern delegations to the national Democratic convention with two other popular candidates: Representative Underwood and Representative Champ Clark of Missouri.[20]

The spirited preconvention contest for southern support in the national Democratic convention was itself a factor in stimulating regional thinking about national issues. The fact that two native southerners—Wilson and Underwood

[18]The prospect of federal intervention was disturbing to many southerners. Thus the president of a Georgia textile firm, concerned over the likely passage of federal labor legislation, declared that "We are rapidly drifting towards paternalism. . ." (G. Gunby Jordan to John H. Bankhead, Jan. 22, 1912, Bankhead Papers). In opposing ratification of the federal income tax amendment in Virginia, Richard Evelyn Byrd warned that "a hand from Washington will be stretched out and placed upon every man's business; the eye of the federal inspector will be in every man's counting house.—The law will of necessity have inquisitorial features, it will provide penalties, it will create complicated machinery. . . . I do not hesitate to say that the adoption of this amendment will be such a surrender to imperialism that has not been seen since the Northern states in their blindness forced the fourteenth and fifteenth amendments upon the entire sisterhood of the Commonwealth" (Richmond *Times-Dispatch,* Mar. 3, 1910).

[19]Byrd to Wilson, Nov. 10, 1910, in Arthur S. Link and associates, eds., *The Papers of Woodrow Wilson,* vol. 22: *1910–1911* (Princeton, N.J., 1976), 20. For similar expressions, see Charles Robert Hemphill to Wilson, Nov. 10, 1910; Joseph R. Wilson, Jr., to Wilson, Nov. 25, 1910; Thomas Bell Love to Wilson, Dec. 1, 1910; Philip Alexander Bruce to Wilson, Dec. 23, 1910; and Clarence Hamilton Poe to Wilson, Feb. 17, 1911, ibid., 21, 95, 122–23, 254, 437.

[20]Underwood was a formidable contestant in the Deep South, while Clark was very strong in Kentucky and the Southwest. Wilson won Texas and South Carolina, three-fourths of the North Carolina delegates, half of the Louisiana delegation, one-third of the Virginia delegates, and about one-fourth of Tennessee's. See Arthur Stanley Link, "The South and the Democratic Campaign of 1912" (Ph.D. diss., Univ. of North Carolina, 1945); Link, *Wilson: The Road to the White House* (Princeton, N.J., 1947), 311–16, 327–29, 332–35, 339–40, 357, 373–75, 406–408, 415–17, 526; Link, "The Wilson Movement in Texas, 1910–1912," *Southwestern Hist. Quar.* 48 (Oct. 1944): 169–85; Link, "The Democratic Pre-Convention Campaign of 1912 in Georgia," *Ga. Hist. Quar.* 29 (Sept. 1945): 143–58; Link, "The Wilson Movement in North Carolina," *N.C. Hist. Rev.* 23 (Oct. 1946): 483–94; Willard B. Gatewood, Jr., "James Calvin Hemphill: Southern Critic of Woodrow Wilson, 1911–1912," *Ga. Rev.* 13 (Winter 1959): 378–92; C. Richard King, "Woodrow Wilson's Visit to Texas in 1911," *Southwestern Hist. Quar.* 65 (Oct. 1961): 184–95; Cooper, *Walter Hines Page,* 235–41; and George N. Green, "The Florida Press and the Democratic Presidential Primary of 1912," *Fla. Hist. Quar.* 44 (Jan. 1966): 169–80.

—were genuine candidates for the Democratic presidential nomination heightened southern interest. Both Wilson and Underwood, moreover, were pictured as reformers: the former as a progressive bent on liberating a corporation-dominated and machine-ridden state, the latter as a congressional leader using his position as chairman of the House Ways and Means Committee to reform the tariff system and bring about other changes in national policy. "It is good to be a Democrat in this year of our Lord," exclaimed the president of the University of Virginia, who went on to assert: "The leaders of the party that bears the great name in the Federal Congress are going about the tasks imposed upon them by the nation with a sobriety and an intelligence, a self-sacrifice and a calmness, very disappointing and surprising to their enemies and very heartening to their friends."[21] Theodore Roosevelt's strenuous campaign as the Progressive party's nominee for president in 1912 added to the excitement in the South.[22]

The Wilson movement was closely identified with progressive politics in the South, and its impact upon the diffused currents of social reform in the region was profound. In short, Woodrow Wilson's nomination and election marked an important stage in the evolution of various reform movements in the South. Arthur S. Link has argued that the most significant thing about the Wilson movement in the South was that the region's progressives "seized upon it as a weapon to use against the conservatives in order to gain control of their own state governments."[23] Although Wilson's campaign for the presidential nomination in the South did not invariably lead to a progressive-conservative cleavage, it was generally the case that his strongest support came from the so-called reform factions, from the old Bryan elements, from anticorporation and antiboss Democrats. Editors, educators, and civic leaders were prominent among the southerners who first rallied to Wilson's leadership. Of course, southerners of different ideological persuasions were no doubt attracted to the New Jersey governor because, in Link's words, they "saw in him the South's great hope for

[21]Edwin A. Alderman, "A Virginia Democrat," *Harper's Weekly* 55 (May 6, 1911): 7. See also Arthur S. Link, "The Underwood Presidential Movement of 1912," *JSH* 11 (May 1945): 230–45, and Johnson, *Oscar W. Underwood,* 170–92.

[22]George E. Mowry, "The South and the Progressive Lily White Party of 1912," *JSH* 6 (May 1940): 237–47; Arthur S. Link, "Theodore Roosevelt and the South in 1912," *N.C. Hist. Rev.* 23 (July 1946): 313–24; Howard W. Smith, "The Progressive Party and the Election of 1912 in Alabama," *Ala. Rev.* 9 (Jan. 1956): 5–21; G.N. Green, "Republicans, Bull Moose, and Negroes in Florida, 1912," *Fla. Hist. Quar.* 43 (Oct. 1964): 153–64; Lewis L. Gould, "Theodore Roosevelt, William Howard Taft, and the Disputed Delegates in 1912: Texas as a Test Case," *Southwestern Hist. Quar.* 80 (July 1976): 33–56; William F. Mugleston, "The 1912 Progressive Campaign in Georgia," *Ga. Hist. Quar.* 61 (Fall 1977): 233–45; Paul D. Casdorph, *Republicans, Negroes, and Progressives in the South, 1912–1916* (University, Ala., 1981), 1–153; Edith Snyder Evans, "The Progressive Party in Tennessee in 1912" (M.A. thesis., Univ. of Tennessee, 1933).

[23]Link, "The Progressive Movement in the South, 1870–1914," *N.C. Hist. Rev.* (Apr. 1946): 180–81.

presidential preferment."[24] There was a connection between the national campaign of 1912, with its strong infusion of progressivism, and a number of local and state reform movements in the South. In Louisiana, for example, statewide agitation against boss rule reached a climax in the gubernatorial campaign that year. The Good Government League, organized in August 1912, elected its candidate for governor, the first reform candidate to win the office in the twentieth century.[25]

THE SOUTH AND THE NEW FREEDOM

Woodrow Wilson's election to the nation's highest office seemed to mark the end of an era in southern politics and the beginning of a new phase in the development of the region's progressivism. Millions of southerners experienced an unaccustomed excitement—a thrill of pride and exhilaration—in the knowledge that one of their own had at last ascended to the presidency. Wilson, editors and public speakers repeated throughout the South in 1912 and 1913, was a man of southern birth, upbringing, and culture, a man who understood and exemplified the section's finest traditions. He was, his more enthusiastic supporters contended, a man of destiny who would end the South's long political isolation and respond generously to the region's political and economic needs. Southern representation in the new president's cabinet, in Congress, and in the Democratic party strengthened the South's expectations.[26] There was "a fine justice," Edwin A. Alderman had observed in presenting Woodrow Wilson to a Norfolk audience in the spring of 1911, "in the turning southward of the eyes of all the [American] people for help and guidance at this decisive hour . . . when the supremest need of the nation's life is the leadership of a patriotic national-minded man whose eyes are clear to see the whole blessed truth about things, who has stomach for the fight, who will not falter before difficulties, nor swerve backward nor be made afraid."[27]

Southern progressives looked to the new administration for recognition, political support, and beneficial legislation. "I have a stronger confidence in government now as an instrument of human progress," Walter Hines Page remarked during the first week of Wilson's presidency, "than I have ever had before." In a memorandum written soon after the November election, Page pinpointed the most promising opportunities: "To use the Government, especially the Department of Agriculture and the Bureau of Education, to help

[24]Link, *The Road to the White House,* 171.

[25]Matthew J. Schott, "John M. Parker of Louisiana and the Bull Moose Progressive Party in State and Nation" (M.A. thesis, Tulane Univ., 1960), 24–30.

[26]Arthur S. Link, *Woodrow Wilson and the Progressive Era, 1910–1917* (New York, 1954), 25–30. Also see Link, "Woodrow Wilson: The American as Southerner," *JSH* 36 (Feb. 1970): 3–17.

[27]"A Virginia Democrat," *Harper's Weekly* 55 (May 6, 1911): 32.

actively in the restoration of country life—that's the great chance for Woodrow Wilson."[28] Whatever their role or cause as reformers, progressives in the South were quick to identify their own situations with the Wilson administration. The response of the region's congressional delegations was also highly favorable. Few among the southern congressmen had ever enjoyed the kind of power and patronage that came to them during the Wilson era. Their seniority enabled them to dominate the standing committees in both houses of Congress. Most of them were in general agreement with Wilson's reform proposals in 1913 and 1914, and they firmly supported the major legislative features of the New Freedom. Indeed, experienced southern leaders such as Underwood of Alabama and Furnifold M. Simmons of North Carolina skillfully guided the administration's tariff, banking, and business-regulation measures through Congress.[29]

Wilson's election led many of his southern adherents to anticipate presidential assistance in their continuing struggles with opposing Democratic factions for state and local control. A Texas progressive warned the president-elect soon after the election, however, that "the Democratic Party is now in a most perilous situation. The danger lies largely in the Southern States and arises out of the fact that a large element of the Party in those states are not Democrats in reality, but stand-pat Republicans, sailing under the colors of Democracy, and others who, having no political convictions, are machine gangsters."[30] Indeed, the hopes of many reform-minded southerners were soon dashed by what Arthur S. Link describes as "the realities and necessities of practical politics."[31] Wilson, determined to enact the New Freedom and to make his party a disciplined instrument for that purpose, was confronted with a situation in which conservative Democrats, particularly from the South, held powerful positions in Congress and were established solidly in their constituencies. The president soon capitulated, deferring to the recommendations of Postmaster General Albert S. Burleson and other conservatives and permitting much of the federal patronage to go to the old-line Democrats in the South. In one south-

[28]Burton J. Hendrick, *The Life and Letters of Walter H. Page,* 3 vols. (New York, 1921–25), vol. I, pp. 110, 128–29.

[29]Dewey W. Grantham, "Southern Congressional Leaders and the New Freedom, 1913–1917," *JSH* 13 (Nov. 1947): 439–59; Johnson, *Oscar W. Underwood,* 193–225; Martin Torodash, "Underwood and the Tariff," *Ala. Rev.* 20 (Apr. 1967): 115–30; Paschal Reeves, "Thomas S. Martin, Committee Statesman," *Va. Mag. Hist. and Biog.* 68 (July 1960): 344–64; Richard L. Watson, Jr., "Furnifold M. Simmons: 'Jehovah of the Tar Heels'?" *N.C. Hist. Rev.* 44 (Spring 1967): 166–87; Burton J. Hendrick, "A New Leader and a New Trust Policy," *World's Work* 27 (Mar. 1914): 499–504; Rodabaugh, "Congressman Henry D. Clayton, Patriarch in Politics," 110–20.

[30]Cone Johnson to Woodrow Wilson, Dec. 17, 1912, in Arthur S. Link and associates, eds., *The Papers of Woodrow Wilson,* vol. 25 (Princeton, N.J., 1978), 603. Also see Thomas Bell Love to Wilson, Dec. 27, 1912, ibid., 624–26.

[31]Link, "Woodrow Wilson and the Democratic Party," *Review of Politics* 18 (Apr. 1956): 148.

ern state after another—Virginia, Kentucky, Alabama, and so on—the result was to disappoint and weaken the insurgent factions.[32]

In Virginia, Wilson's campaign was paralleled by a struggle between the dominant faction led by Senator Thomas S. Martin and antiorganization Democrats, who supported the New Jersey governor. Wilson's decision to work with the Martin regulars marked what one scholar has described as "the final demise of the anti-organization faction in Virginia politics."[33] The independents fought on for a time. In 1914 they organized the Virginia Progressive League, with a renewed attack on the state "machine" and an effort to popularize a broad reform program.[34] The results were disappointing, and the factional division based on the Wilson movement of 1911–12, never clear-cut, became steadily less distinct in the face of the new president's wide appeal in the state and region. Meanwhile, North Carolina progressives, inspired by Wilson's New Freedom and disheartened by the conservative character of the state legislature, set about the formulation and adoption of an ambitious program of social reform, including a statewide primary, revision of the state tax system, more stringent regulation of business, new child labor legislation, a minimum school term of six months, and a series of constitutional amendments. They arranged a progressive convention in 1914 and publicized their demands widely through the state, only to have their proposals repudiated by the next state Democratic convention.[35] Progressives in Virginia and North Carolina—and in other southern states—achieved a number of their legislative objectives over the course of the next few years, but these successes were not the result of presidential intervention in the factional politics of the region.

Despite their state-rights tradition and instinctive distrust of federal activism, southern congressmen during the Wilson period were forceful advocates of national assistance, especially in the field of agriculture. Thus they provided large majorities for long-term rural credits, a federal warehouse statute, an agricultural extension program, vocational education, and more effective regulation of commodity exchanges.[36] Among the southern congressmen, particularly in the House of Representatives, a group of agrarian reformers expressed a

[32]Ibid., 146–56; Scott, "The Southern Progressives in National Politics," 181–82; Adrian Anderson, "President Wilson's Politician: Albert Sidney Burleson of Texas," *Southwestern Hist. Quar.* 77 (Jan. 1974): 339–54; Wythe W. Holt, Jr., "The Senator from Virginia and the Democratic Floor Leadership: Thomas S. Martin and Conservatism in the Progressive Era," *Va. Mag. Hist. and Biog.* 83 (Jan. 1975): 3–21.

[33]Burton Ira Kaufman, "Virginia Politics and the Wilson Movement, 1910–1914," *Va. Mag. Hist. and Biog.* 77 (Jan. 1969): 16.

[34]Ibid., 3–21; Allen W. Moger, *Virginia: Bourbonism to Byrd, 1870–1925* (Charlottesville, Va., 1968), 276–96.

[35]Joseph F. Steelman, "The Progressive Democratic Convention of 1914 in North Carolina," *N.C. Hist. Rev.* 46 (Apr. 1969): 83–104, and "Origins of the Campaign for Constitutional Reform in North Carolina, 1912—1913," ibid. 56 (Oct. 1979): 396–418.

[36]Theodore Saloutos, *Farmer Movements in the South, 1865–1933* (Berkeley, Calif., 1960), 213–35; Dewey W. Grantham, *Hoke Smith and the Politics of the New South* (Baton Rouge,

kind of neopopulism and Bryanism that looked to Washington both for antitrust action and federal assistance to farmers and small businessmen. Their ranks included Robert Lee Henry and Rufus Hardy of Texas, Otis T. Wingo of Arkansas, J. Willard Ragsdale of South Carolina, and Claude Kitchin of North Carolina. These southern agrarians helped secure progressive changes in the Glass banking and currency bill, urged more rigorous antitrust legislation, worked for more democratic tax schedules, and championed a system of rural credits and other agricultural aid.[37] Southern backers of new federal programs also contributed to the metamorphosis of the Wilsonian program into a series of broader and more vigorous federal policies in 1915 and 1916.[38]

Nevertheless, southern congressmen objected to many of the more advanced progressive proposals considered during Wilson's first term. There was marked southern opposition to the Alaskan Railroad bill, the La Follette Seamen's bill, workmen's compensation for federal employees, the Keating-Owen child labor bill, and a constitutional amendment to enfranchise women. Southern lawmakers were more inclined to support certain measures of social control. They took the lead in the passage of a measure to restrict foreign immigration in 1914 and 1915, and in the successful repassage of a literacy requirement for immigrants early in 1917.[39] Southern leaders were even more ardent in the advocacy of Negro proscription in Washington and the federal service. Indeed, southern pressure, in and out of Congress, was the most important influence in the Wilson administration's thoroughgoing segregation of government workers and denial of federal appointments to blacks, as well as the flood of Jim Crow bills introduced in the Sixty-third Congress (1913–15).[40] "Between 1913 and

---

1958), 238–67; Howard W. Allen, "Geography and Politics: Voting on Reform Issues in the United States Senate, 1911–1916," *JSH* 27 (May 1961): 216–28; Wayne Flynt, *Duncan Upshaw Fletcher: Dixie's Reluctant Progressive* (Tallahassee, 1971), 59–95.

[37] Link, *Woodrow Wilson and the Progressive Era,* 48–50, 70–71, 194–95, 225–28; John W. Davidson, "The Response of the South to Woodrow Wilson's New Freedom, 1912–1914" (Ph.D. diss., Yale Univ., 1953), 150–79; Jack E. Kendrick, "Alabama Congressmen in the Wilson Administration," *Ala. Rev.* 24 (Oct. 1971): 243–60; George O. Flynn, "A Louisiana Senator and the Underwood Tariff," *La. Hist.* 10 (Winter 1969): 5–34; Philip A. Grant, Jr., "Tennesseans in the 63rd Congress, 1913–1915," *Tenn. Hist. Quar.* 29 (Fall 1970): 278–86; Richard N. Sheldon, "Richmond Pearson Hobson as a Progressive Reformer," *Ala. Rev.* 25 (Oct. 1972): 243–61; "Hon. Robert Lee Henry, Member of Congress from Texas," *Independent* 74 (May 22, 1913): 1134; *Cosmopolitan* 55 (Nov. 1913): 797–99.

[38] Arthur S. Link, "The South and the 'New Freedom': An Interpretation," *American Scholar* 20 (Summer 1951): 314–24. For an interpretation that minimizes southern reformism and the liberal role of congressmen from the South, see Richard M. Abrams, "Woodrow Wilson and the Southern Congressmen, 1913–1916," *JSH* 22 (Nov. 1956): 417–37.

[39] Scott, "The Southern Progressives in National Politics," 186–92, 195–99.

[40] Link, *Woodrow Wilson and the Progressive Era,* 63–66; George Brown Tindall, *The Emergence of the New South, 1913–1945* (Baton Rouge, 1967), 143–46; Kathleen Long Wolgemuth, "Woodrow Wilson's Appointment Policy and the Negro," *JSH* 24 (Nov. 1958): 457–71; George C. Osborn, "Woodrow Wilson Appoints a Negro Judge," ibid., 481–93; Nancy J. Weiss, "The Negro and the New Freedom: Fighting Wilsonian Segregation," *Pol. Sci. Quar.* 84 (Mar. 1969): 61–79; Morton Sosna, "The South in the Saddle: Racial Politics during the Wilson Years," *Wisconsin Magazine of History* 54 (Autumn 1970): 30–49.

1917," one historian has concluded, "the direct impact of race consciousness upon national politics stemmed largely from the reinvigorated influence of southern Democrats in Washington. . . ."[41]

Two of the most controversial issues of the early Wilson years were national prohibition and federal legislation to outlaw child labor. The South was divided in its reaction to federal intervention in these two areas. Yet the limitations of state action, in the South as elsewhere, persuaded more and more southerners to join the movement for reform at the national level.

The accelerating movement for national prohibition was accompanied by a new prohibition surge in the South. This antiliquor wave was first manifested in Virginia, where favorable action in 1914 climaxed a long and complex struggle. Relatively unimportant before the turn of the century, the temperance movement in the Old Dominion began to acquire greater vitality in 1901 with the organization of the Virginia Anti-Saloon League. The state's first significant prohibition law—the Mann Act of 1903—supplemented the local-option statute of 1886 by prohibiting the manufacture or sale of liquor without a license. Another regulatory measure—the Mann-Byrd Act—was adopted in 1908; it forbade the manufacture or sale of alcoholic beverages in towns of fewer than five hundred people. By 1909 the number of dry counties had risen to eighty-six. The pivotal figure in the development of the modern prohibition movement in Virginia was James Cannon, Jr., who became president of the state ASL in 1904. Cannon, a Methodist minister, editor, and educator, was a man of extraordinary force and ability. He saw the necessity of making the league a compelling factor in Virginia politics, and under his leadership the organization moved away from its early policy of avoiding political involvement. The best approach, Cannon believed, lay in cooperating with the dominant political faction in Virginia politics. Cannon endeavored to cooperate with the Martin "machine," and he worked closely with such Martin lieutenants as William Hodges Mann and Richard Evelyn Byrd.[42]

Confronted with the Martin faction's opposition to statewide prohibition, Cannon and other ASL leaders pursued a local-option approach until 1910. Cannon set out to convert the Martin organization, while the Anti-Saloon League began an intensive campaign in behalf of a legislative enabling act that would permit Virginians to vote on the question of statewide control. "It is hard," one organization leader lamented in February 1910, ". . . to hold a Legislature when preachers and women inject a moral issue in a proposi-

---

[41]Sosna, "The South in the Saddle," 30.

[42]For a comprehensive account of the prohibition movement in Virginia, see C. C. Pearson and J. Edwin Hendricks, *Liquor and Anti-Liquor in Virginia, 1619–1919* (Durham, N.C., 1967). For Cannon's role see Virginius Dabney, *Dry Messiah: The Life of Bishop Cannon* (New York, 1949); Richard L. Watson, Jr., ed., *Bishop Cannon's Own Story: Life As I Have Seen It*, by James Cannon, Jr., (Durham, N.C., 1955); and Robert A. Hohner, "Bishop Cannon's Apprenticeship in Temperance Politics, 1901–1918," *JSH* 34 (Feb. 1968): 33–49.

tion."[43] Despite Cannon's pleas and the rising tide of prohibition sentiment, the Democratic organization opposed the enabling act, which was buried in the house of delegates and voted down in the senate. But Cannon persisted. He supported the reelection of Senators Martin and Claude A. Swanson in 1911, when Virginia independents waged a furious campaign against the regulars. He and other prohibitionist leaders worked hard that year to elect dry legislators, and they enjoyed some success.

During the legislative session of 1912, the enabling act easily passed the lower house, only to fail in the senate by a vote of 16 to 24. The organization had apparently decided not to oppose the enabling legislation, but it was not yet prepared to put pressure on its supporters in the general assembly to pass the measure. The attitude of the regular Democrats changed during the next two years, partly because of ASL success in campaigning in the districts of recalcitrant senators in 1913. Even more important in explaining the organization's change of heart was the threatened alignment of the ASL and the Virginia Progressive Democratic League, a recently organized group of anti-Martin Democrats intent upon restoring "popular government in Virginia." When the legislature met in 1914, Martin and his allies persuaded enough senators to vote for the enabling bill for that measure to clear the senate as well as the house.[44] Cannon's strategy had worked.

The campaign that followed was unparalleled in the history of the temperance movement in Virginia. The Anti-Saloon League, led by the indefatigable Cannon, organized the dry forces all over the state for the referendum on September 22, 1914. The required number of petitioners was quickly obtained, and the ASL, the WCTU, the Woman's Prohibition League of America, and other dry organizations labored to convince the electorate to vote in favor of statewide prohibition. A massive volume of prohibition literature poured out of Anti-Saloon League headquarters in Richmond; the ASL's newspaper, the *Virginian*, lashed out at the Demon Rum in daily editorials and feature stories; the WCTU sponsored numerous parades and public meetings; ministers spoke out for the cause from their pulpits; and famous out-of-state leaders such as Alabama's Richard Pearson Hobson visited Virginia to urge approval of statewide control. The state was swept during that hectic summer by an evangelical mood. The antiprohibitionists fought back, led by such groups as the Virginia Association for Local Self-Government, the State Liquor Dealers' Association, and the Brewers, Wine and Spirit Merchants' Association. Emphasizing local self-government and the alleged economic losses portended by prohibition, such "antis" as Henry St. George Tucker and several of Virginia's

---

[43]Quoted in Hohner, "Bishop Cannon's Apprenticeship in Temperance Politics," 39.

[44]For the impact of prohibition on state politics in Virginia during this period, see Henry C. Ferrell, Jr., "Prohibition, Reform, and Politics in Virginia, 1895–1916," in *East Carolina College Publications in History*, vol. 3: *Studies in the History of the South, 1875–1922* (Greenville, N.C., 1966), 175–242, and Moger, *Virginia: Bourbonism to Byrd*, 297–319.

leading newspapers struggled to stem the prohibition tide. But the struggle was to no avail: prohibition carried by 30,000 votes.[45]

Far to the south the prohibition campaign won another victory with the redemption of Alabama, whose statewide law had been repealed in 1911 following the election of Emmett O'Neal as governor. Prohibition became a central point of debate in the Democratic primaries of 1914, but in the runoff election for the party's gubernatorial nomination the explosive issue of "Comerism" emerged as the dominant bone of contention in the struggle. Braxton B. Comer was narrowly defeated by a combination of local optionists, railroad interests, and anti-Comer Democrats identified with Governor O'Neal. Representative Richmond P. Hobson's vigorous campaign for the United States Senate was turned back in the same year by Representative Underwood, a local optionist. Nonetheless, the dry forces more than held their own in the legislative contests, and a staunch prohibitionist was elected lieutenant governor. When the legislature met in January 1915, prohibition leaders organized both houses. Brooks Lawrence of the Anti-Saloon League worked steadily to advance the passage of a new statewide law, both by using the influence of his organization and by helping to devise legislative strategy. The mounting pressure from organized church groups and ministers such as Washington B. Crumpton was also having an effect, as was an advertising campaign launched by the WCTU. A statewide enforcement measure was quickly passed by the general assembly, and subsequently easily repassed over Governor Charles Henderson's veto. The legislature of 1915 took another step by prohibiting liquor advertisements in newspapers that circulated in the state.[46]

Arkansas also entered the prohibition column in 1915. Following their setback in a special referendum of 1912, the state's prohibitionists succeeded the next year in securing passage of the so-called Going Law. This statute, drafted by the Anti-Saloon League, provided that liquor licenses could be issued only after a favorable local vote in a general election and after a petition requesting such a license had been signed by a majority of the relevant community's adult white population. The Going Act survived a serious constitutional challenge in 1914, and the Arkansas ASL undertook a number of "clean-up campaigns" in various parts of the state to enforce the law. On the eve of the legislative session of 1915, the league organized a determined campaign in behalf of statewide prohibition. With the governor also calling for adoption of prohibition, the

---

[45]The turnout was large, resulting in a prohibition victory of 94,251 to 63,886. See *"The Saloon Must Go": Proceedings Sixteenth National Convention of the Anti-Saloon League of America, Atlantic City, New Jersey, July 6–9, 1915, with State Reports* (Westerville, Ohio, n.d.), 527–31, and Robert A. Hohner, "Prohibition Comes to Virginia: The Referendum of 1914," *Va. Mag. Hist. and Biog.* 75 (Oct. 1967): 473–88.

[46]*ASL Proceedings, 1915*, pp. 287–88; James Benson Sellers, *The Prohibition Movement in Alabama, 1702 to 1943* (Chapel Hill, N.C., 1943), 176–85; Albert Burton Moore, *History of Alabama* (University, Ala., 1934), 753–56; James F. Doster, *Railroads in Alabama Politics, 1875–1914* (University, Ala., 1957), 222; Johnson, *Oscar W. Underwood*, 226–44.

general assembly responded in January 1915 by passing the ASL's bill, 74 to 22 in the house and 32 to 2 in the senate. Opponents of prohibition initiated a measure in 1916 to repeal statewide regulation and return to a policy of local option, but this proposal was defeated in the ensuing referendum by more than 50,000 votes.[47]

The third southern state to embrace prohibition in 1915 was South Carolina, which had permitted both publicly owned dispensaries and privately owned saloons on a local-option basis following the disestablishment of the state dispensary system in 1907. Although the abolition of the dispensary was regarded by many South Carolinians as a necessary temperance "reform," the question of how best to regulate the traffic in alcoholic beverages continued to agitate the state's voters. It was a perennial issue with wide political ramifications. "The liquor business seems inseparable from politics," the Columbia *State* observed in 1915, "and—politics is the worse for it."[48] The question became more acute during Governor Coleman L. Blease's administration, and a series of legislative investigations and liquor-related controversies contributed to the heightening of interest in the matter. When the general assembly met early in 1915, it refused to heed either the governor, who recommended a return to the license system, or the advocates of statutory prohibition. Instead, the lawmakers passed a measure calling for a popular vote on statewide prohibition. Both sides mounted active campaigns, but the referendum gave the prohibitionists a sweeping victory. The legislature of 1915 had already enacted an antishipping law, and two years later it passed an antiliquor advertising statute.[49]

With the adoption of prohibition by South Carolina in 1915, the southern march under the white flag of temperance slowed, though the movement toward more stringent public regulation continued. The frustrations of southern prohibitionists were nowhere greater than in Texas, where the movement had been on the verge of success for years. Following the defeat of their candidate for governor and the failure of a popular vote on constitutional submission in 1914, Texas prohibitionists redoubled their efforts to secure a statewide law. The Texas Anti-Saloon League was reorganized and strengthened early in 1915, and the dry forces began an aggressive campaign to elect favorable candidates in the elections of 1916. The revelations growing out of a suit brought

---

[47]*ASL Proceedings, 1915*, pp. 386–87; Ernest H. Cherrington, *The Evolution of Prohibition in the United States of America: A Chronological History of the Liquor Problem and the Temperance Reform. . .* (Westerville, Ohio, 1920), 302, 310–11, 332, 342, 349; George Murrell Hunt, "A History of the Prohibition Movement in Arkansas" (M.A. thesis, Univ. of Arkansas, 1933), 136–49.

[48]Quoted in John Evans Eubanks, *Ben Tillman's Baby: The Dispensary System of South Carolina, 1892–1915* (Augusta, Ga., 1950), 145.

[49]Ibid., 175–78; Robert Milton Burts, *Richard Irvine Manning and the Progressive Movement in South Carolina* (Columbia, S.C., 1974), 98–107; Alan Coleman, "The Charleston Bootlegging Controversy, 1915–1918," *S.C. Hist. Mag.* 75 (Apr. 1974): 77–94.

by the state attorney general against seven brewery companies for violating election and antitrust laws also reinforced the demand for prohibition. Although Governor James E. Ferguson, no friend of state prohibition, was renominated in the Democratic primary of 1916, the electorate narrowly approved the question of submitting a constitutional amendment for statewide prohibition to the voters. But then came another of the Texas prohibitionists' recurrent setbacks. Governor Ferguson managed to keep prohibition out of the party platform in 1916, and he was able to prevent action by the next general assembly in early 1917.[50]

The progress of the campaign for state prohibition, coupled with the difficulties of enforcing the statewide statutes and strong court challenges in several cases, caused a growing number of prohibitionists to support federal action. The American ASL took the lead in this quickening movement, and as early as 1913, Congress passed the Webb-Kenyon Act making it illegal to transport alcoholic beverages from a wet state to a dry one. Congressmen from the South were, by and large, enthusiastic supporters of the Webb-Kenyon bill and of the ASL prohibition amendment to the federal constitution, which was introduced in the two houses by Representative Hobson and Senator Morris Sheppard of Texas. Hobson became a full-time campaigner for national prohibition in 1915. James Cannon of Virginia headed the Anti-Saloon League's legislative committee, and such southerners as Secretary of the Navy Josephus Daniels became zealous champions of the movement. The prohibitionists won scores of endorsements in the congressional races of 1916, and the impetus provided by the war enabled them to win congressional approval of the prohibition amendment in 1917. Southern congressmen voted overwhelmingly in favor of the amendment.[51]

Southern congressmen were generally much less enthusiastic about federal child labor legislation. The most important measure of this kind was a bill introduced in 1914 by Representative A. Mitchell Palmer of Pennsylvania and Senator Robert L. Owen of Oklahoma. The National Child Labor Committee soon decided to work for the enactment of the Palmer-Owen bill. The committee's endorsement of federal action was largely a consequence of the slow progress the child labor movement had made in securing adequate state statutes. In 1914 the NCLC had been in existence for a decade, but only nine states could then meet all the standards set forth by the organization in 1904. Only three of

[50]Lewis L. Gould, *Progressives and Prohibitionists: Texas Democrats in the Wilson Era* (Austin, Tex., 1973), 150–84; Seth Shepard McKay, *Texas Politics, 1906–1944, with Special Reference to the German Counties* (Lubbock, Tex., 1952), 63–72; Cherrington, *The Evolution of Prohibition*, 343, 351; *ASL Proceedings, 1915*, pp. 524–25.

[51]Charles Merz, *The Dry Decade* (Garden City, N.Y., 1931), 15–42; Andrew Sinclair, *Era of Excess: A Social History of the Prohibition Movement* (New York, 1964), 152–66; Richard L. Watson, Jr., "A Testing Time for Southern Congressional Leadership: The War Crisis of 1917–1918," *JSH* 44 (Feb. 1978): 7–8, 24–29.

these—Arkansas, Kentucky, and Oklahoma—were southern states, and the repeated failure to achieve stronger legislation in the South was a major reason for the decision to seek a federal solution. The uneven course of state action and the great diversity among state laws also influenced the committee, as did the flagrant violations of the legal requirements that were established. As Alexander J. McKelway said of the southern regulations in 1908, "it is a matter of common knowledge that these laws have been almost universally violated, both in letter and in spirit. . . ."[52]

Most southerners were slow to concede the necessity for uniform regulatory standards—and thus to embrace the desirability of national legislation. Even the reformers were divided, especially during the early years. Although Edgar Gardner Murphy recognized that industrial child labor had become a national problem, he stoutly opposed the idea of a federal law. Murphy questioned the proposed federal statute on constitutional grounds. He also argued that such legislation would be "contrary to sound public policy," would retard effective action by the states and divide the reform forces, and would have a harmful effect upon public opinion.[53] McKelway did not share these doubts. He was a strong supporter of the bill introduced by Senator Albert J. Beveridge in 1906, directed the NCLC's Washington office after its establishment in 1908, and worked assiduously with southern congressmen in behalf of the committee's federal program. In 1911, McKelway observed that after three regional conferences on child labor, many southern reformers had learned that there were no peculiar reasons for a different standard of legislation in the South and the rest of the country, that as a practical matter the states below the Potomac needed the "same standards and the best standards of the whole country."[54]

The Palmer-Owen bill provoked resolute opposition in the southern textile states. Southern manufacturing interests were well represented at congressional hearings held in 1914 on the proposed legislation. The man who led the resistance campaign was David Clark, a fervent defender of the textile manufacturers and editor of the *Southern Textile Bulletin,* a trade journal published in Charlotte. In 1915, Clark and other textile men organized what was known as the Executive Committee of the Southern Cotton Manufacturers, whose raison d'être was the defeat of federal legislation. This committee employed William W. Kitchin, a former governor of North Carolina, to represent its interests in

---

[52]McKelway, "Child Labor and Its Attendant Evils," *Sewanee Review* 16 (Apr. 1908): 220. See also McKelway, "The Evil of Child Labor: Why the South Should Favor a National Law," *Outlook* 85 (Feb. 16, 1907): 360–64, and Harry Tucker, "Federal and State Regulation of Child Labor," *SAQ* 16 (Jan. 1917): 39–43.

[53]Hugh C. Bailey, *Edgar Gardner Murphy: Gentle Progressive* (Coral Gables, Fla., 1968), 94–102, 107–108.

[54]"The Proceedings of the Seventh Annual Conference on Child Labor Under the Auspices of the National Child Labor Committee," in supplement to *Annals* 38 (July 1911): 218. See also Herbert J. Doherty, Jr., "Alexander J. McKelway: Preacher to Progressive," *JSH* 24 (May 1958): 180–82, and Betty J. Brandon, "A Wilsonian Progressive—Alexander Jeffrey McKelway," *Journal of Presbyterian History* 48 (Spring 1970): 2–17.

Washington.[55] Kitchin and other southern critics contended that federal action was unnecessary, that conditions in the South were improving, and that state regulations were effective in preventing the exploitation of youthful workers. Many of the arguments earlier used against state laws were brought forth to do service in the stand against federal legislation. Spokesmen for the millowners insisted that the proposed statute would seriously impede the economic development of the South. They were especially critical of that feature of the Palmer-Owen bill which would limit children under sixteen to an eight-hour day, since, they argued, the long single-shift operation of southern mills could not be adjusted to such a restriction and thus all workers under sixteen would have to be discharged. In reality, David Clark later asserted, the measure was intended "to force the cotton mills of the South to conform to the ideas of agitators and competitors in other states."[56] The major contention of southern opponents was that a federal law would violate state rights and constitute an improper use of the commerce power by the national government.

Alexander J. McKelway attempted to refute the arguments of the southern manufacturers. He and other reformers pointed out the weaknesses of the state laws, cited evidence of growing popular demand for national legislation, and defended the proposed law against the charge of unconstitutionality. McKelway maintained that child labor was not the result of poverty, as many southern conservatives insisted, but was itself the cause of poverty, since it depressed wages to such an extent that many adults were unable to make a living. He reviewed the history of the National Child Labor Committee in order "to lift away the sectional prejudice that its work was directed against the South or one of its industries."[57] There was actually a good deal of support for federal legislation in the South, particularly outside of the textile states. The women's organizations tended to endorse the measure, as did numerous southern newspapers. Many editors shared the view of the New Orleans *Times-Picayune*, which had concluded by the summer of 1916 that "there is no hope of correcting and curing the evils of child labor with the consent of the cotton-manufacturing States of the South; and no way to do so except through the Federal Government and the interstate-commerce clause."[58]

[55]Stephen B. Wood, *Constitutional Politics in the Progressive Era: Child Labor and the Law* (Chicago, 1968), 31, 38–39, 41–45, 48–52, 69–77; Elizabeth H. Davidson, *Child Labor Legislation in the Southern Textile States* (Chapel Hill, N.C., 1939), 255–63; "The Child Labor Bill," *Outlook* 112 (Jan. 26, 1916): 168–69.

[56]Quoted in Wood, *Constitutional Politics in the Progressive Era,* 83. See also Arden J. Lea, "Cotton Textiles and the Federal Child Labor Act of 1916," *Labor Hist.* 16 (Fall 1975): 485–94.

[57]Wood, *Constitutional Politics in the Progressive Era,* 59; A.J. McKelway, "Another Emancipation Proclamation: The Federal Child Labor Law," *Amer. Rev. of Reviews* 54 (Oct. 1916): 423–26; Doherty, "Alexander J. McKelway: Preacher to Progressive," 182–86.

[58]"The President and the Mill-Child," *Literary Digest* 53 (Aug. 5, 1916): 290. See also "The South Against Child Labor," *Survey* 35 (Feb. 19, 1916): 596; "The South and the Child Labor Bill," *Outlook* 112 (Feb. 23, 1916): 404–407; and Mrs. Alex Caldwell, "The Tennessee Federation and Legislation," in Tennessee Federation of Woman's Clubs, *Woman's Work in Tennessee* (Memphis, 1916), 79.

Following favorable action by committee, the House of Representatives passed the Palmer-Owen bill in early 1915 by a vote of 233 to 43. Most of the negative votes came from six southern states, but only in the cases of the Carolinas, Georgia, and Mississippi were a majority of the state delegations from the South recorded in opposition.[59] The Senate failed to act on the measure before the session expired, and a new child labor bill was introduced by Senator Owen and Representative Edward Keating of Colorado when the Sixty-fourth Congress convened. Southern opinion remained divided, but many southerners indicated their willingness to accept a federal law, especially after President Wilson endorsed the bill. The measure was passed by a vote of 337 to 46 in the House and 52 to 12 in the Senate, with the principal opposition coming from the southeastern textile states.[60] The statute required the U.S. Children's Bureau, through a newly established Child Labor Division, to administer the law. The basic federal policy was to cooperate with state administrative officials and not to interfere with or duplicate their work except where standards and practices were too low to be tolerated. In a letter to the secretary of the NCLC, written about the time of the Keating-Owen bill's passage, McKelway observed that he had been "looking forward to partial release from the Washington strain and traveling over the South again, first, in bringing up all the southern legislatures to the proper standard of child labor legislation, with the main opposition from the manufacturers removed by the Federal law."[61] But the law, which went into effect in September 1917, did not remove the opposition of southern textile men, who turned to the courts in what proved to be a successful effort to invalidate the statute.

Despite this example of southern resistance to federal regulation, southerners found much to applaud in Wilson's New Freedom. There were two periods of strain and criticism in the South's reaction to the Wilson administration between 1913 and 1917: the crisis that enveloped the cotton market in the autumn of 1914 and the first part of 1915 and the struggle over neutrality and preparedness in 1915 and early 1916. The two episodes were not unrelated. The beginning of the war in Europe disrupted the normal pattern of cotton exports, brought a sharp drop in the price of the staple, and created a panic throughout the cotton belt. Organizations like the Farmers' Union, chambers of commerce, and banking groups quickly moved into action, formulating such schemes as the "buy a bale of cotton" movement and demanding relief measures by Congress and the Wilson administration. Southern congressmen, led by Senator Hoke

---

[59]*Cong. Record*, 63d Cong., 3d sess., p. 3836 (Feb. 15, 1915). See also William Sidney Coker, "Pat Harrison: The Formative Years," *Jour. Miss. Hist.* 25 (Oct. 1963): 258–59.

[60]*Cong. Record*, 64th Cong., 1st sess., pp. 2035 (Feb. 2, 2916), 12313 (Aug. 8, 1916). The House delegations from North and South Carolina voted solidly against the bill, while both senators from the two Carolinas, Georgia, and Florida opposed it.

[61]McKelway to Owen R. Lovejoy, July 29, 1916, McKelway Papers. Also see McKelway to Lovejoy, Sept. 1, 1917, ibid.

Smith of Georgia, responded by pressing for large-scale government purchases of cotton and other federal aid. The president resisted what he regarded as "class" legislation and, much to the disappointment of many southern lawmakers, managed to head off the more extreme relief proposals.[62] Although the gloom in the cotton areas gradually disappeared, as British purchases and an economic upturn at home caused staple prices to go up, some southern congressmen continued to attack the British blockade and to criticize the administration's neutrality policies. Wilson's decision in late 1915 to launch a preparedness program brought a good deal of opposition from the South, much of it reflecting Bryanite sentiment against involvement in European wars and a latent suspicion of the role of corporations and cartels in the great conflagration. Most southerners were predisposed to take the side of the Allies, however, and they provided impressive support for the president's diplomatic and defense policies.

Becoming more conscious of their nationalism, southern spokesmen were now more inclined to express concern about national problems and to deny that the South was "backward and sectional." As the North Carolina editor Clarence Poe wrote in the fall of 1916, "If the test of a section is 'not where it stands, but how it is moving,' the South is unmistakably progressive, and no section of America is more broadly National or patriotic."[63] Earlier that year Frederick M. Davenport, a New York professor of law and politics, provided evidence to support Poe's claim in articles he wrote for *Outlook* on the basis of a tour of the South. Davenport found many indications in the various southern states that the Wilson administration had "very perceptibly increased and established a new sense of loyalty to the national government." The South, he reported, "feels that during the last two or three years it has come back in leadership and influence toward its own." "If you listen to the old-time Republican in Washington," he continued, "you get an idea that the South during the Wilson Administration has been rather belligerently in the saddle, that the 'rebel yell' echoes from secret chambers in the Capitol. In the South itself, however, I found much evidence of earnest, serious, and concrete thoughtfulness about the condition of the country and its lack of preparedness both for peace and for war."[64]

[62]Arthur S. Link, "The Cotton Crisis, the South, and Anglo-American Diplomacy, 1914–1915," in J. Carlyle Sitterson, ed., *Studies in Southern History* (Chapel Hill, N.C., 1957), 122–38; Link, *Woodrow Wilson and the Progressive Era,* 149–50, 170–72, 180–83, 194–95; Saloutos, *Farmer Movements in the South,* 236–47; Grantham, *Hoke Smith and the Politics of the New South,* 277–91; James L. McCorkle, Jr., "The Louisiana 'Buy-a-Bale' of Cotton Movement, 1914," *La. Hist.* 15 (Spring 1974): 133–52; McCorkle, "Louisiana and the Cotton Crisis, 1914," ibid. 18 (Summer 1977): 303–21; C.T. Revere, "Effect of the War on Cotton," *North American Review* 200 (Oct. 1914): 549–58; Richard Spillane, "The Cotton Crisis at Home and Abroad," *Amer. Rev. of Reviews* 50 (Nov. 1914): 599–605.

[63]Poe, "The South: Backward and Sectional or Progressive and National?" *Outlook* 114 (Oct. 11, 1916): 331.

[64]Davenport, "The Pre-Nomination Campaign: The National South," *Outlook* 112 (Feb. 16,

Speaking to the North Carolina Press Association in June 1914, President Edward K. Graham of the state university remarked that progressivism, in addition to its disruptive efforts upon national politics, had "set off a preliminary explosion or two [in North Carolina], more or less disturbing to the safely dominant party, separating the press and the people into fairly recognizable divisions." Yet he noted that " 'Progress,' on the other hand, was never so conspicuously the master word in the thought of all the people as it is at this moment."[65] During the following year Eugene C. Branson, one of Graham's faculty members, wrote Secretary of Agriculture David F. Houston about his reform activities in the university. He reported that no less than six different surveys of his own county were currently in progress. "They are not investigative alone," he explained, "but stimulative and educative as well. Practically the whole summer is being given to pack social steam behind piston rods. We are fairly certain of pulling off a whole-time health officer for the county, and other progressive steps forward seem possible."[66] Organized and purposeful social improvement efforts had never been so prevalent in the South. They were apparent in the development of the public school system, in the farm demonstration programs, in the club movement among rural youths, in the state university extension work, in the emergence of public health services, in the undertakings of the Federation of Women's Clubs, in the reorganization and expansion of municipal government, and so on. Of course, not all this activity was a manifestation of progressivism. In discussing civic reform, Edward K. Graham pointed out that the term "progressive" was "in danger of becoming confused with motion in any direction, as distinguished from progress which is concerned with only that motion which is in the right direction."[67] Still, Graham could not have doubted the vital presence of a progressive spirit in the South at the time he spoke.

Politics and government at the state and local levels responded, haltingly to be sure, to the many groups demanding innovation and reform. This response was no doubt encouraged by the general mood of reform that prevailed throughout the country, and especially by the Wilsonian example in Washington. It was characterized less by the initiation of new campaigns in the region's states than by continuing efforts to elaborate and strengthen earlier progressive

---

1916): 386–87. See also Davenport, "The Pre-Nomination Campaign: The Southern Renaissance," ibid. (Feb. 23, 1916): 427–30.

[65]Graham, "Civic Service Week, and a State-Wide Campaign for Arousing Civic Consciousness," unpublished address (1914), Eugene C. Branson Papers, Southern Historical Collection, University of North Carolina.

[66]Branson to Houston, May 25, 1915, Branson Papers. See also Branson to Dr. C.W. Thompson, Dec. 22, 1914, ibid.; S.H. Hobbs, Jr., "Developing a State through Student Club Work," *Jour. Soc. Forces* 2 (Nov. 1923): 48–49; and Louis R. Wilson, *The University of North Carolina, 1900–1930: The Making of a Modern University* (Chapel Hill, N.C., 1957), 179–229.

[67]Graham, "Civic Service Week, and a State-Wide Campaign for Arousing Civic Consciousness."

beginnings. The same process was evident in municipal reform. One aspect of this development was the establishment by legislatures and administrative agencies of more rigorous controls and standards for the regulation of public utilities, child labor, prison labor, foods and drugs, and the like. A second emphasis in the state and local progressivism of this period was the steady increase in the provision of public services like education, roads, health facilities, and institutional care of the handicapped and destitute. Finally, a number of the southern states succeeded during the immediate prewar years in putting into effect more efficient and equitable tax systems.

If southern progressivism had evolved from its early organizational and campaigning phase to one of greater concern with institutional needs and development, it was still closely identified with political leadership. Several southern governors made notable contributions to the advance of social reform during the early years of the Wilson era. These governors included Ben W. Hooper of Tennessee, Park Trammell of Florida, Richard I. Manning of South Carolina, Theodore G. Bilbo of Mississippi, and Augustus O. Stanley of Kentucky. Manning, who was descended from a prominent South Carolina family, rescued the state from "Bleaseism" and gave it a genuine taste of progressivism. Under his leadership (1915–19), the tax system was revised and assessments were equalized; educational appropriations were increased and a compulsory attendance law was adopted; child labor and other protective labor legislation was enacted; a state board of charities and corrections and a girls' industrial school were established; a highway commission was created; a statewide system of primary elections was legalized; and more stringent control of fire insurance companies was put into operation.[68]

An even more comprehensive reform program was achieved in Mississippi during the administration of Theodore G. Bilbo (1916–20). Bilbo, who had earlier been a lieutenant of James K. Vardaman, prodded the legislature into revising the state's revenue system, equalizing its taxes, establishing a variety of new agencies, including a commission on illiteracy, and increasing the appropriations for education and other public services. The revision of Mississippi's cumbersome and inefficient tax system was particularly noteworthy, for it reconciled state and local taxing authority and quickly brought a rise in tax assessments.[69] In Kentucky, progressive legislation made impressive gains under the leadership of Augustus O. Stanley (1915–19), a former congressman and a fiery advocate of antitrust measures. Building on the moderate reforms of his Democratic predecessor, James B. McCreary, Stanley presided over an

[68]Burts, *Richard Irvine Manning*, 70–144.
[69]Albert D. Kirwan, *Revolt of the Rednecks: Mississippi Politics, 1876–1925* (Lexington, Ky., 1951), 241–66; Charles Granville Hamilton, "Mississippi Politics in the Progressive Era, 1904–1920" (Ph.D. diss., Vanderbilt Univ., 1958), 298–337; Larry Thomas Balsamo, "Theodore G. Bilbo and Mississippi Politics, 1877–1932" (Ph.D. diss., Univ. of Missouri, 1967), 93–118; Vincent A. Giroux, Jr., "The Rise of Theodore G. Bilbo (1908–1932)," *Jour. Miss. Hist.* 43 (Aug. 1981): 180–209.

outpouring of progressive enactments. The legislative session of 1916 was extremely productive, in spite of an intramural controversy among Kentucky Democrats over the prohibition issue. This legislation included creation of a public utilities corporation commission; an antitrust law; corrupt-practices, antilobbying, and antipass statutes; a workmen's compensation act; establishment of a state tax commission; a "blue sky" law; and several other reform measures.[70]

Thus southern politics and southern progressivism were significantly altered during Woodrow Wilson's first administration. Wilson's leadership of the Democratic party and of a national reform program went a considerable distance in nationalizing southern politics and in making reform more respectable among southerners. It also reinforced the emergent tendency in the region to seek federal legislation and federal assistance, in some cases involving reform objectives. At the same time, the configuration of regional and national reform endeavors stimulated rather than diminished progressivism at the state and local levels, both in politics and government and in the work of private organizations and voluntary agencies.

THE SOUTHERN SOCIOLOGICAL CONGRESS

While the Wilson movement and the New Freedom were absorbing the attention of southerners and orienting the section's politics toward Washington in unaccustomed fashion, another movement, largely outside of politics, was achieving a regional organization and showing greater awareness of social reforms in other parts of the country. The new organization was called the Southern Sociological Congress (SSC), and it was formally established in Nashville in the spring of 1912. The purpose of this regional civic organization was the study, discussion, and amelioration of social problems in the South. Its founders also hoped "to coalesce the influence of sociological specialists and the activities of social welfare workers."[71] Dedicated to service and progress, the congress was envisioned as a medium for the organization and coordination of social reform in the South. It was, in some respects, a regional counterpart of the National Conference of Charities and Correction.

The formation of the SSC reflected the growth of social services in the South during the past decade, particularly in the larger cities. Such reform movements as the public school campaign, the drive for child labor laws, and the prohibi-

---

[70]Ramage, "Augustus Owsley Stanley: Early Twentieth Century Kentucky Democrat," 160–213; Nicholas C. Burckel, "From Beckham to McCreary: The Progressive Record of Kentucky Governors," *Reg. Ky. Hist. Soc.* 76 (Oct. 1978): 297–306; Burckel, "A.O. Stanley and Progressive Reform, 1902–1919," ibid. 79 (Spring 1981): 136–61.

[71]E. Charles Chatfield, Jr., "The Southern Sociological Congress, 1912–1920: The Development and Rationale of a Twentieth-Century Crusade" (M.A. thesis, Vanderbilt Univ., 1958), p. iv (cited hereafter as "The Southern Sociological Congress").

tion crusade also contributed to the burgeoning social consciousness in the southern states. The organized charity movement had made significant gains. Associated charities had been organized in several southern cities. By 1912 a number of state conferences of charities and correction had been established in the South, promoted by family welfare groups, community chests, and state boards of health.[72] These developments all pointed up the desirability of establishing a broad social welfare organization for the region.

Many social reformers in the South recognized the need for such an organization. One of those who wanted an association of this kind was Kate Barnard, the Oklahoma commissioner of charities and corrections, who wrote to Governor Ben W. Hooper of Tennessee in December 1911 urging him to convene a regional conference. Hooper, a Republican governor and leader of the fusionist movement that captured control of Tennessee politics in 1910, was a staunch prohibitionist and an advocate of child labor legislation, penal improvements, and other social reforms. There were also other reasons why Nashville took the lead in creating a Southwide welfare association. Several other organizations had met in the Tennessee capital in 1912, including the Southern Education Board and the Southern Commercial Congress. Numerous civic, religious, and educational leaders lived in Nashville, and several regional organizations were centered there. The Methodist Training School for Religious Workers, operated by the Board of Missions of the Methodist Episcopal Church, South, was located in the Tennessee city. The Biblical Department of Vanderbilt University, another Methodist institution, conducted an annual Biblical Institute which attracted ministers from all over the South. In 1912 the institute's sessions for the first time dealt directly with social and civic applications of religion. The "Men and Religion Forward Movement," recently organized by the national YMCA to develop interest in social service among churchgoing men, held a convention in Nashville in December 1911. The Nashville campaign struck an evangelistic note but also stressed the connection between religion and social concerns.[73]

Governor Hooper discussed Kate Barnard's proposal with several interested persons, among them James E. McCulloch, general secretary of the American Interchurch College for Religious and Social Workers and a former president of

[72]Frank Dekker Watson, *The Charity Organization Movement in the United States: A Study in American Philanthropy* (New York, 1922), 347–58; Margaret E. Rich, *A Belief in People: A History of Family Social Work* (New York, 1956), 177–78; Lyda Gordon Shivers, "Some Variations in State Conferences of Social Work," *Social Forces* 12 (May 1934): 546–50; Foy Lisenby, "The First Meeting of the Arkansas Conference of Charities and Correction," *Ark. Hist. Quar.* 26 (Summer 1967): 155–61.

[73]Chatfield, "The Southern Sociological Congress," 1–10; "Interchurch College for Social Service," *Survey* 26 (Aug. 28, 1911): 749; "Sixteen States in Southern Conference," ibid. 27 (Mar. 23, 1912): 1947–49; A.J. McKelway, "The Southern Sociological Congress," ibid. 28 (June 1, 1912): 359–61; Graham Taylor, "The Southern Social Awakening," ibid. (Sept. 14, 1912): 744–45; Robert Hamlett Bremner, *From the Depths: The Discovery of Poverty in the United States* (New York, 1956), 157.

the Methodist Training School for Religious Workers, both based in Nashville. McCulloch and other Tennesseans interested in social reform urged Hooper to take the responsibility for launching a great Southwide conference, and on February 6, 1912, the governor issued a call for such a meeting to convene in Nashville in the spring. Hooper requested the governors of fifteen other southern and border states to join him in each appointing at least one hundred delegates to the conference and to attend in person if possible. Various civic and social institutions were also requested to send delegates. Hooper appointed an executive committee of prominent businessmen, educators, and professional leaders to plan the conference. The committee met regularly during March and April, working out the details of the meeting and drafting a statement of purpose entitled "The Challenge of the Southern Sociological Congress." James McCulloch, who served as secretary of the executive committee, made a two-week trip through several southern states and to Washington, D.C., and New York City in order to secure pledges of gubernatorial cooperation and to arrange for speakers at the spring convention.[74]

The first session of the conference was held on Tuesday evening, May 7, in Nashville's famous Ryman Auditorium. James H. Kirkland, chancellor of Vanderbilt University, presided over the session. The welcoming address was delivered by Dr. Ira Landrith, a well-known prohibition leader, president of Nashville's Ward Belmont College, and recently chairman of the "Committee of One Hundred" of the local Men and Religion Forward Movement. Another of the opening addresses, "Southern Problems that Challenge Our Thought," was given by Gus W. Dyer, professor of sociology at Vanderbilt and an activist in a number of social reform causes. During the following three days a great variety of topics was discussed, including the liquor traffic, child welfare, care of the feeble-minded, crime and prison reform, public health, the social mission of the church, and race relations.[75] Most of the meetings, which were open to the public, attracted sizable audiences. The general sessions, several of which were held at night, were attended by all delegates. There were also nine departmental conferences on such subjects as temperance, public health and housing, adult dependents and delinquents, charity organization, the church and social service, recreation and medical inspection, and race relations. Speakers and discussion leaders were drawn mainly from the ranks of ministers, educators, and professional social workers. About half of the speakers came from outside the South.

A comprehensive list of objectives was adopted by the participants. These

[74]This account of the SSC is based on E. Charles Chatfield's articles: "The Southern Sociological Congress: Organization of Uplift," *Tenn. Hist. Quar.* 19 (Dec. 1960): 328–47, and "The Southern Sociological Congress: Rationale of Uplift," ibid. 20 (Mar. 1961): 51–64.

[75]For the activities and addresses of the Nashville meeting, see James E. McCulloch, ed., *The Call of the New South: Addresses Delivered at the Southern Sociological Congress, Nashville, Tennessee, May 7 to 10, 1912* (Nashville, 1912).

objectives included abolition of the convict lease and contract systems and the application of modern principles of penology; the extension and improvement of juvenile courts and juvenile reformatories; abolition of child labor by enactment of the uniform child labor law; and passage of school attendance laws in all the southern states. Additional goals were the proper care and treatment of the blind, epileptic, feeble-minded, and other "defectives"; control of alcoholic beverages and education about its contribution to disease, crime, and pauperism; the suppression of prostitution; adoption of uniform laws of "the highest standards" concerning marriage and divorce; and enactment of the uniform law on vital statistics. The delegates also pledged to help solve the race question in a spirit of helpfulness to blacks and equal justice to both races. And they urged cooperation between the church and all social agencies in working for the accomplishment of their program.[76]

The Nashville conference decided to form a permanent organization, despite some initial disagreement over the desirability of creating a distinctly southern body. Nevertheless, the establishment of the Southern Sociological Congress was influenced by the activities and example of the National Conference of Charities and Correction, and the SSC agreed to hold its annual meetings with the NCCC when the latter met in a southern state. The conference also drafted and adopted a constitution for the congress; the purpose of the new organization, according to this document, was to study and improve social, civic, and economic conditions in the South. In addition the SSC was intended to develop the region's social service leadership. The term "sociological" was meant to suggest social services, not academic or theoretical approaches. The congress was basically an organization of individuals—of "persons interested in the work." Governor Hooper was chosen as president of the SSC; Alexander J. McKelway and Kate Barnard were elected vice-presidents. An impressive group of southerners was named to serve on the organization's executive committee, while James McCulloch was appointed full-time executive secretary. The society's permanent office was to be in Nashville. Anna Russell Cole, a philanthropic leader of Nashville, generously provided funds for the administrative expenses of the congress. Plans were made to hold the next annual meeting in Atlanta.[77]

Almost a thousand delegates, including eight-nine Negroes, attended the four-day Atlanta conference in late April 1913. Among the speakers were prominent northerners such as the social gospel minister Walter Rauschenbusch as well as a large number of southern ministers, educators, and social welfare professionals. Nearly a hundred southern specialists in welfare work were present. The Atlanta *Constitution* noted that "the meeting represents the first gathering of the specialists and the actual workers who are trying to solve

---

[76]L. L. Bernard, "Southern Sociological Congress," *Amer. Jour. Soc.* 18 (Sept. 1912): 258–59; McCulloch, ed., *The Call of the New South,* 7–8, 355–57, 361–62.

[77]McCulloch, ed., *The Call of the New South,* 355–81.

for the South those problems in applied sociology which bulk so large in the thought of our day."[78] Seven special conferences were conducted, patterned after the annual meeting of the National Conference of Charities and Correction; they were concerned with organized charities, courts and prisons, public health, child welfare, travelers' aid, race relations, and the church and social service. A number of the participants spoke at the Sunday services of various Atlanta churches. Dr. John E. White, a local minister, said of the meeting: "We have come at last to the conclusion that to rid ourselves of criticism, we must first criticize ourselves. We here propose constructive criticism at the hands of southern men."[79] The departmental conference on the church and social service adopted a series of thirty-five recommendations beginning with: "We would recommend a more aggressive policy on the educational side of civic matters. Such questions as sanitation, the milk supply, meat inspection, social hygiene and other important matters can be taught with tremendous effectiveness by use of the moving picture machine."[80] Alexander J. McKelway characterized the SSC as an organized effort to enlist "the entire South in a crusade of social health and righteousness."[81]

The Southern Sociological Congress remained a going concern for five or six more years. The third annual meeting was convened in Memphis in the spring of 1914.[82] Although the Memphis meeting was held in conjunction with the National Conference of Charities and Correction, the SSC finally decided against merging with the national organization. The theme of the Memphis gathering reflected this decision: "The Solid South for a Better Nation." The congress met in Houston in 1915 and in New Orleans the following year. In the autumn of 1916 the association's headquarters were moved from Nashville to Washington, D.C., and the congress became more centralized during the next few years. The sixth annual meeting was held in the summer of 1917 at the Blue Ridge conference grounds and in nearby Asheville, North Carolina. Birmingham was the site of the next conference, which took place in April 1918. The program that year was dominated by war concerns. By the time the next annual meeting convened in Knoxville in mid-May 1919, the original purpose of the organization had changed significantly. In fact, the congress soon disappeared.

While the SSC was deeply concerned with the prevalence of social injustice

---

[78]Atlanta *Constitution*, April 25, 1913, quoted in Chatfield, "The Southern Sociological Congress," 37. For the program of the Atlanta meeting, see James E. McCulloch, ed., *The South Mobilizing for Social Service: Addresses Delivered at the Southern Sociological Congress, Atlanta, Georgia, April 25–29, 1913* (Nashville, 1913).

[79]"Sociology's Welcome in the New Southland," *Survey* 30 (May 10, 1913): 212.

[80]Ibid., 213. See also Philip Weltner, "Southern Sociological Congress," *Survey* 30 (May 17, 1913): 244–45, and L.L. Bernard, "The Southern Sociological Congress," *Amer. Jour. Soc.* 19 (July 1913): 91–93.

[81]McCulloch, ed., *The South Mobilizing for Social Service*, 13.

[82]See James E. McCulloch, ed., *Battling for Social Betterment: Southern Sociological Congress, Memphis, Tennessee, May 6–10, 1914* (Nashville, 1914).

in the South, it was also an expression of reform directed toward various kinds of social control. Thus prohibition was an important matter for consideration at the annual congresses during the early years. The temperance section of the 1912 conference was well organized, and prohibition leaders such as Henry Beech Carre, a Vanderbilt professor and the president of the Tennessee Anti-Saloon League, made a concerted effort to win support for federal legislation to ban the interstate shipment of alcoholic beverages. Prohibitionists were also active in subsequent meetings of the SSC. The Anti-Saloon League urged temperance leaders in the South to attend the New Orleans meeting of the congress in 1916 for a "council of war" against alcohol. But there was also evidence of the social gospel in the work of the congress. The departmental conference on the church and social service at the Atlanta meeting in 1913 adopted a large number of resolutions reflecting the widening social concerns of religious leaders in the region. In Memphis during the following year's conference attention was given to the relation of the church to such social forces as workingmen, the city, modern industry, and rural life.[83] Indeed, the congress was both a product and a symbol of changing attitudes in the South about the role of the church in society.[84]

Social services constituted a large part of the SSC's discussions and activities. The executive committee of the congress chose "The Conservation of Health" as the theme of the Houston conference in 1915. The meeting featured an idealistic slogan: "The New Chivalry—Health." Leaders of the congress hoped that the campaign they were launching would serve as a model program throughout the South. During the meeting, on Sunday morning, a "health message" was given in many Houston churches, and later in the day a "health parade" was staged. Several "health institutes" were also conducted during the convention. There was more talk than action in support of the health crusade in 1915, but the program became more concrete during the following year. Plans were made at the New Orleans conference to issue a monthly health bulletin, and a campaign was formulated to eradicate malaria, hookworm, typhoid, tuberculosis, and other preventable diseases. Surveys were to be made of ten southern cities. These discussions revealed that the prevention of disease had become a primary object of the Southern Sociological Congress, which stressed

[83]Booker T. Washington and Clarence H. Poe were among the speakers emphasizing the paucity of social opportunities in rural districts. Professor William K. Tate of the Peabody College for Teachers advocated the establishment of rural social centers staffed by teachers, ministers, and visiting nurses, and operated in connection with practice farms. "The Meetings at Memphis: Forty-first National Conference of Charities and Corrections," *Survey* 32 (May 30, 1914): 235–36.

[84]For the growth of social Christianity in the South during the progressive period, see John Lee Eighmy, "Religious Liberalism in the South During the Progressive Era," *Church History* 38 (Sept. 1969): 359–72; Wayne Flynt, "Dissent in Zion: Alabama Baptists and Social Issues, 1900–1914," *JSH* 35 (Nov. 1969): 523–42; and Flynt, "Southern Baptists and Reform: 1890–1920," *Baptist History and Heritage* 7 (Oct. 1972): 211–23.

the idea that health was vital to the well-being of the whole community.[85] There was also an economic dimension to this SSC campaign, one that could be comfortably accommodated within the New South creed. It was the notion that disease and poor health cost the South heavily in material terms—through inefficiency, waste, and retarded economic development.

An extension program was devised as a means of implementing the SSC's health crusade. Following the New Orleans meeting in 1916, the executive officers of the congress created a community extension service. The extension program called for a week's visitation to a dozen smaller cities. Each visit would include a health survey, an exhibit, and a campaign to promote better health. The first of the extension campaigns was carried out in Columbia, Tennessee. Speakers from national and state agencies took part in the program, community meetings were held, and a special exhibit dealt with public health, housing, child welfare, and temperance. Local committees set about investigating all phases of the town's life. Similar extension campaigns were undertaken in about ten other cities—in Virginia, South Carolina, and Tennessee. A railroad car transported SSC speakers and workers, exhibits, and literature from city to city. In each city the extension staff organized a study of social and civic conditions in the community, conducted public meetings, delivered addresses, and presented a definite program of community development to a local group. It also erected exhibits on sanitation, diseases, child welfare, temperance, housing, and pure food. In Chattanooga, for instance, staff members prepared a report that was critical of the city's fee system, poor sanitation, housing for the poor, and bad physical conditions in the public schools. The report contained numerous recommendations for remedial action.[86]

Nothing on the agenda of the Southern Sociological Congress elicited greater interest or more discussion than the place of the Negro and the exigencies of race relations in the southern states. The departmental conference on race relations was probably the most important of the themes considered at the organizational meeting in 1912. That conference was led by Dr. James Hardy Dillard.[87] A permanent committee on race relations was established by the Nashville conference, and the sessions there were partly responsible for the

[85]James E. McCulloch, ed., *The New Chivalry—Health: Southern Sociological Congress, Houston, Texas, May 8–11, 1915* (Nashville, 1915); McCulloch, ed., *Democracy in Earnest: Southern Sociological Congress, 1916–1918* (Washington, D.C., 1918); *Health Crusade Bulletin of the Southern Sociological Congress,* undated pamphlet in Madeline McDowell Breckinridge Papers, University of Kentucky Library. The experiments of Dr. Joseph Goldberger and other efforts sponsored by the United States Public Health Service during this period received some support, as well as heated criticism, in the South. State boards of health and other agencies in the region were generally prepared to cooperate with Dr. Goldberger, but the SSC seems to have paid little attention to his pioneering work. See Elizabeth W. Etheridge, *The Butterfly Caste: A Social History of Pellagra in the South* (Westport, Conn., 1972), 65–145.

[86]Chatfield, "The Southern Sociological Congress," 60–82.

[87]Among the addresses at the Nashville meeting dealing with racial matters were "The Negro and Crime," by William Holcombe Thomas; "The Negro and Public Health," by Oscar Dowling;

founding of a separate group called the Commission of Southern Universities on the Race Question. Racial matters were a major consideration of the 1913 congress in Atlanta, which included no fewer than seventeen addresses dealing with blacks and racial questions. "I want to maintain here and now," declared Willis D. Weatherford, "that every minister of the gospel, every secretary of the Young Men's Christian Association or the Young Women's Christian Association, every teacher in our schools, every social worker in the South has a sacred and solemn obligation to instill into the hearts of all those whom they lead this principle of the value and sacredness of the person."[88] Although blacks were not invited to present papers at the Atlanta meeting, they did meet with white southerners on something approaching intellectual equality to discuss common problems. The 1914 conference in Memphis emphasized racial cooperation and agreed to join with the YMCA in racial work. Booker T. Washington spoke at one of the sessions in 1914. While William E.B. Du Bois and other spokesmen of the National Association for the Advancement of Colored People criticized the SSC during the Memphis meeting, the sessions were moved from the Orpheum Theater to a church so that black members could sit on the main floor with other delegates.[89] The New Orleans congress of 1916 adopted a vigorous statement against lynching and created a new antilynching organization, the Conference on Law and Order. In the immediate postwar period interracial cooperation became an even more pressing concern of the SSC. Several hundred black delegates attended the Knoxville meeting in 1919, and racial problems made up one of the principal topics of discussion at that convention.[90]

The sessions on the "race problem" consistently attracted large audiences at the annual meetings of the congress. An editorial in the *Southern Workman*, a journal published by Hampton Institute, characterized the Atlanta conference of 1913 as one of "honest inquiry and constructive criticism." The writer noted that the two races were present at the Atlanta congress on an equal footing. He was especially impressed by the speeches of the young professors from southern colleges, for they gave "a fair, appreciative estimate" of the Negro and his value to the South, while urging a more liberal white opinion toward blacks, better housing conditions, improved accommodations in public conveyances, greater industrial opportunities, special agricultural training, protection of the black man's human rights, justice in the courts, and the franchise as a reward

"My Experience in Organizing Negro Anti-Tuberculosis Leagues," by C.P. Wertenbaker; and "The Negro and the New South," by W.D. Weatherford. See McCulloch, ed., *The Call of the New South*, 203–25.

[88] McCulloch, ed., *The South Mobilizing for Social Service*, 352.

[89] "The Meetings at Memphis," 234; Chatfield, "The Southern Sociological Congress," 51–58.

[90] See McCulloch, ed., *Democracy in Earnest*, and McCulloch, ed., *"Distinguished Service" Citizenship: Southern Sociological Congress, Knoxville, Tennessee* (Washington, D.C., n.d.).

for intelligence, character, and efficiency.[91] The position of the liberal white southerner was well expressed by the Reverend Arthur J. Barton of Texas. In his speech "The White Man's Task in the Uplift of the Negro" at one of the Atlanta sessions, Barton declared: "The pity is that we have not hitherto recognized our task; the joy is that we are now seeing our duty and undertaking it."[92] The duty that southerners like Barton had in mind was essentially one of noblesse oblige in race relations. They abhorred the practice of lynching, the race-baiting of southern demagogues, the inhumanity of the judicial system's treatment of blacks, and on occasion the inexorable toll of the land-tenure and credit system in the South. But they also accepted the finality of existing social arrangements, and even the boldest among them could scarcely venture beyond the accommodationism of Booker T. Washington and the uplift activities of the Methodist women's missions.[93] Thus a Chicago social worker, who had been reared in the South, expressed disappointment over the results of the Memphis conference of 1914. Noting the conference's unwillingness to confront the consequences of poverty, misery, and racial prejudice, she asserted that it "failed absolutely to carry any message at all to the colored people."[94] And a year or so later a conservative educator from Mississippi declared, with the SSC in mind, that "pious palaver has been the bane of much well-intended study of the Negro Problem. . . ."[95]

SSC members were predominantly urban, middle class, and professional in character. An observer of the Houston conference reported that the participants in that meeting included doctors, teachers, lawyers, preachers, editors, "sanitarians," foreign delegates, clubwomen, "motion-picture experts," jurists, prison reformers, Negro leaders, housing commissioners, federal health officers, and YMCA secretaries.[96] A writer for the NCCC magazine *Survey*, reporting on the SSC's fifth annual conference in New Orleans in 1916, pointed out that the activities of the congress were increasingly being shaped by "a fast-growing group of earnest southern social workers." He also remarked that those affiliated with the organization were coming to regard it as more than an annual assembly that did little else the rest of the year.[97]

The Southern Sociological Congress enjoyed some success. It stimulated interest in attacking social problems, including racial injustice. It spread the

[91]"The Southern Sociological Congress," *Southern Workman* 42 (June 1913): 323–25. See also "The Southern Sociological Congress," ibid. 43 (June 1914): 331–33.

[92]"The Southern Sociological Congress," *Southern Workman* 42 (June 1913): 325.

[93]See, for example, Charles Hillman Brough, "Work of the Commission of Southern Universities on the Race Question," *Annals* 49 (Sept. 1913): 47–57, and W.D. Weatherford, "Race Relationship in the South," ibid., 164–72.

[94]Sophonisba P. Breckinridge to Charles P. Neill, July 30, 1914, Sophonisba P. Breckinridge Papers, Manuscripts Division, Library of Congress.

[95]T.P. Bailey, in *Sewanee Review* 24 (Jan. 1916): 126.

[96]"Conferences," *Survey* 34 (June 12, 1915): 252.

[97]"A Growing Social Effort in the South," *Survey* 36 (May 20, 1916): 196.

social gospel and promoted interest in public health facilities. It gave a boost to the creation of state boards of charities and correction and encouraged the organization of state conferences on prison reform. Its annual meetings served to coalesce the influence of sociological specialists and the activities of social workers. The congress also reported on social welfare programs and experiences in other parts of the country.[98]

Spokesmen for the congress claimed that it was a significant factor in the enactment of "more public welfare legislation" in the individual states.[99] There was some basis for such claims in the legislative programs put forward by conferences of charities and correction, conferences of social workers, and other statewide associations. The Arkansas Conference on Charities and Corrections, for example, was organized in 1912 in order to educate the public about social problems, to stimulate interest in social legislation, and to provide a forum for the discussion of social work. During its early years the conference directed its efforts toward the passage of legislation establishing schools for delinquent children, an institution for the feeble-minded, and a state commission on charities and correction.[100] A *Survey* article on social reform in Florida in early 1917 emphasized the decided change in public opinion during the past five years and the influential role of the Children's Home Society of Florida, the state Federation of Women's Clubs, and "other progressive social agencies." The author also commented on the marked impact of the state's child labor law, juvenile court system, and industrial schools for children. He cited the increasing employment of visiting nurses by private and public agencies, the modernization of Florida's jails and almshouses, the way in which associated charities were "ministering" to the needs of small cities, the "springing up" of YMCA buildings, and the fact that the state's churches and colleges were becoming interested in "social service." Social welfare in Florida, it appeared, was "going ahead by leaps and bounds."[101]

Even so, the influence of the Southern Sociological Congress should not be exaggerated. Other organizations and forces played a part in the emergence of social welfare in the South. Most southerners were probably unaware of the congress and its program. A South Carolina reformer observed in 1920 that although the SSC had made a contribution in earlier years by "arousing Southern public opinion," its usefulness had ended. He explained: "The American Sociological Association looks after the scientific and theoretical sides of social

[98]"Some State Meetings," ibid. 32 (May 30, 1914): 247; "A Survey of Southern Social Problems," ibid. 40 (May 11, 1918): 163–64; Shivers, "Some Variations in State Conferences of Social Work," 547–48.

[99]"Conferences," *Survey* 34 (June 12, 1915): 251–52.

[100]"Some State Meetings," ibid. 32 (May 30, 1914): 247; "Social Gains by the Texas Legislature," ibid. 34 (May 29, 1915): 191–92; "Conferences," ibid. (June 12, 1915): 253; Foy Lisenby, "The Arkansas Conference on Charities and Correction, 1912–1937," *Ark. Hist. Quar.* 29 (Spring 1970): 39–47.

[101]"From Ponce De Leon's Times to Ours," *Survey* 37 (March 24, 1917): 728–29.

progress; the National Conference of Social Work satisfies the needs of the social workers in the various fields; and then we have State Boards of Public Welfare, Development Boards, and a number of other organizations devoted in whole or in part to social betterment, like the Rotary Clubs, the Kiwanis, Focus Clubs, the American Legion, and others. Then too, we have the Interracial Commissions in every Community, Illiteracy Commissions, and the Universities are promoting Public Health work in its various phases."[102]

Writing for the *Journal of Social Forces* in 1923, two women, one of whom was commissioner of public welfare in North Carolina, described the growth of "social consciousness" in the Old North State during the past few years. They gave credit to the North Carolina Conference for Social Service, to the reorganized State Board of Charities and Public Welfare, and to the Child Welfare Commission. They also mentioned the programs of several state agencies in such areas as public health, education, and agriculture, as well as institutions and training schools for the crippled, mentally retarded, and delinquent boys and girls. They called attention to the Library Commission and the hundreds of traveling libraries it sent into isolated parts of North Carolina, and they noted the state university's growing interest in serving the larger population through such means as its extension program, whose *Newsletter* was weekly spreading "the social gospel from one end of North Carolina to the other." Looking farther back, the two writers found the seeds of the current "popular awakening" in the educational crusade at the turn of the century. But they were struck by the perceptible quickening of social awareness and social activism about 1913, when the North Carolina Conference for Social Service, partly inspired by the Southern Sociological Congress, came into being. Earlier social service efforts had usually been local, sporadic, and short-lived. A remarkable cast of leaders also contributed to progress in the second decade of the century: Alexander W. McAlister, Clarence H. Poe, Edward Kidder Graham, William Louis Poteat, Eugene C. Branson, and so on. The North Carolina Federation of Women's Clubs and other voluntary associations were active in the cause of social reform. "Now that North Carolina is pretty well aroused to its social needs," the authors concluded, "the various agencies foster each other and function reciprocally."[103]

The most important contribution of the Southern Sociological Congress was its rationale. Society in the view of these southern reformers was organic, all segments of the community were interdependent, and all conditions had rational causes. In a sense these ideas represented an assault on the notion of extreme individualism, a conviction that the social consciousness of the South

[102]Josiah Morse to Samuel C. Mitchell, June 5, 1920, Mitchell Papers, Southern Historical Collection.
[103]Kate Burr Johnson and Nell Battle Lewis, "A Decade of Social Progress in North Carolina," *Jour. Soc. Forces* 1 (May 1923): 400–403.

must be heightened, that only an enlightened people would act to regulate social conditions and ameliorate social ills. The congress failed in its efforts to become an agent for the coordination of social work in the South, but it was at least partially successful as "a vehicle of challenging social ideas."[104] Its ideas, to be sure, influenced only a limited number of professional and middle-class people in the region, and some southerners considered the organization too religious in orientation, too "damn pious," a sort of "Negro 'big meeting.'"[105] Still, the Southern Sociological Congress is important for an understanding of southern progressivism, though less perhaps for its tangible accomplishments than for the evidence it provides of broader currents that were affecting the outlook and behavior of southerners early in the twentieth century.

The Wilson era—especially the years from 1912 to 1919—was critically important in the evolution of southern progressivism. During this period many of the progressive campaigns for specific reforms achieved statewide organization and substantial legislative success. These years also witnessed the creation of a regionwide organization dedicated to social reform. Even more important, the Wilson administration enabled the progressive currents in southern politics to flow into the channels of national progressivism, gave the section's political leaders an opportunity to contribute to the passage of a remarkable legislative program, and stimulated reform energies in many southern states and municipalities. The war years, somewhat ironically, opened the way for new social services and the introduction of procedures and standards from outside the South, as well as the application of additional social controls.

[104]Chatfield, "The Southern Sociological Congress: Rationale of Uplift," 64.
[105]C.S. Waterfield, "Southern Sociological Congress," *Survey* 32 (May 30, 1914): 244.

THE SOUTH'S INVOLVEMENT in national affairs was stimulated still further by the First World War. The war spirit intensified the patriotism of most southerners and made them more self-conscious about their Americanism. Developments in 1917 and 1918 had a profound effect upon southern society. The war led to an expansion of government, particularly in Washington, and fostered civic cooperation and community programs. It also created new opportunities for social planning and even nourished the progressive belief that "by altering the environment it was possible to reconstruct society."[1]

There was, nonetheless, a divisive and debilitating aspect of the war for southern progressives. Many southerners were critical of the Wilson administration's neutrality policies and of the preparedness program it sponsored in the winter of 1915–16. Some of this criticism was related to the distrust and resentment resulting from the cotton crisis of 1914 and 1915 which, one historian has written, "left deep scars upon the South and a residue of intense anti-British sentiment."[2] Criticism of the administration's policies also embodied the virulent anti-Wilson attacks of a few influential southern spokesmen such as Tom Watson of Georgia and Coleman L. Blease of South Carolina. But the opposition to the Wilson measures was more basic than these sources of irritation; it was rooted in a widespread agrarian fear of international complications, militarism, and monopoly.[3] It was closely identified with the ideas of William

---

[1] Allen F. Davis, "Welfare, Reform and World War I," *Amer. Quar.* 19 (Fall 1967): 516–33; quotation on p. 517. Also see Walter I. Trattner, "Progressivism and World War I: A Reappraisal," *Mid-America* 44 (July 1961): 131–45.

[2] Arthur S. Link, "The Cotton Crisis, the South, and Anglo-American Diplomacy, 1914–1915," in J. Carlyle Sitterson, ed., *Studies in Southern History* (Chapel Hill, N.C., 1957), 138.

[3] See Alex Mathews Arnett, *Claude Kitchin and the Wilson War Policies* (Boston, 1937), 47–239; Arthur S. Link, *Woodrow Wilson and the Progressive Era, 1910–1917* (New York, 1954), 180–96; Dewey W. Grantham, *Hoke Smith and the Politics of the New South* (Baton Rouge, 1958), 281–302; Monroe Billington, "Senator Thomas P. Gore: Southern Isolationist," *Southwestern Soc. Sci. Quar.* 42 (Mar. 1962): 381–89; William F. Holmes, *The White Chief:*

Jennings Bryan and with what a contemporary writer called "the thought that preparedness is a frame-up to keep wealth pouring into the coffers of bankers and munition makers."[4] The president of the North Carolina Farmers' Union argued that "the masses of the people" were opposed to "extensive and expensive preparations for wars." The cry for preparedness, he asserted, came from "the sordidly selfish"—from the army and navy, the shipbuilders, the investment bankers, and the money lenders.[5] Another North Carolinian, the federal judge Henry Groves Connor, admitted at about the same time that he regarded "all militarism as evil and evil only, to be held in the strictest possible limitations."[6] Representative Claude Kitchin, an antipreparedness leader in the House of Representatives, was alarmed as early as August 1915 by the specter of administration involvement in "a big military-naval propaganda." He feared that Congress would "lose its head" and permit "the ammunition and war equipment interests to pile millions of additional burdens upon the people."[7]

Many southern congressmen disliked the Continental Army recommended by Secretary of War Lindley M. Garrison, and various state leaders in the South were afraid that the reorganization of the nation's military forces would jeopardize the decentralized operation of the state militia units. Congressional leaders such as James Hay of Virginia were able to bring about some modifications in President Wilson's program, and in general they proved to be reliable supporters of the key preparedness measures. Indeed, southerners were predisposed to favor the administration's neutrality and preparedness policies because of their loyalty to the Democratic party, the president's great appeal in the section, and the South's ethnic and cultural ties with the British. In any case, despite a dissenting minority, both public opinion and public leaders in the South strongly favored the foreign and military policies of the Wilson administration.[8] As Clarence Poe wrote to Representative Kitchin early in 1916, "I believe

---

James Kimble Vardaman (Baton Rouge, 1970), 294–327; Joseph E. Fortenberry, "James Kimble Vardaman and American Foreign Policy, 1913–1919,"*Jour. Miss. Hist.* 35 (May 1973): 127–40; Richard Leverne Niswonger's "William F. Kirby, Arkansas's Maverick Senator," *Ark. Hist Quar.* 37 (Autumn 1978): 252–63; and Laurence W. Levine, *Defender of the Faith, William Jennings Bryan: The Last Decade, 1915–1925* (New York, 1965), 19.

[4]"Preparedness and the South," *Current Opinion* 60 (Mar. 1916): 208.

[5]H. Q. Alexander to Claude Kitchin, Nov. 3, 1915, Claude Kitchin Papers, Southern Historical Collection, University of North Carolina. "It appears," another southerner wrote, "that the town and city people are inclined to approve of the Presidents [*sic*] policy with Germany, but the country people are a unit in opposing him" (W. J. Olive to Kitchin, March 15, 1916, ibid.).

[6]Connor to Claude Kitchin, Dec. 1, 1915, ibid.

[7]Kitchin to Warren Worth Bailey, Aug. 3, 1915, ibid.

[8]"The South and the Nation," *Outlook* 115 (Mar. 21, 1917): 495–96; Link, *Woodrow Wilson and the Progressive Era,* 184–96; Timothy Gregory McDonald, "Southern Democratic Congressmen and the First World War, August 1914–April 1917: The Public Record of Their Support for or Opposition to Wilson's Policies" (Ph.D. diss., Univ. of Washington, 1962), 65–257; George C. Herring, Jr., "James Hay and the Preparedness Controversy, 1915–1916," *JSH* 30 (Nov. 1964): 383–404; Sarah McCulloh Lemmon, *North Carolina's Role in the First World War* (Raleigh, N.C., 1966), 13–17; Milton L. Ready, "Georgia's Entry into World War I," *Ga. Hist.*

the people of North Carolina want you to stand with President Wilson in the present diplomatic crisis."[9] After the passage of the administration's preparedness proposals in modified form and the easing of the submarine crisis in the spring and summer of 1916, southerners turned to the presidential campaign in a spirit of unity and enthusiasm for the Democratic ticket.

Southern support of the Wilson administration after the United States entered the war was even more pronounced. There was some resistance to the draft in the Appalachian South and among isolated elements like the radicalized sharecroppers of Oklahoma, but the dominant theme throughout the region was patriotic backing of the war effort.[10] When President Wilson addressed the Confederate Veterans' reunion in 1917, he reminded the old soldiers that the South was now "part of a nation united, powerful, great in spirit and in purpose," a nation that could be "an instrument in the hands of God to see that liberty is made secure for mankind."[11] Southern churches committed themselves to Wilson's definition of the war as a holy crusade. The symbol of nationalism was taken up easily by southern leaders. "I thank God that one flag now floats over an indissoluable Union of indestructable [*sic*] States," Representative Robert L. Doughton of North Carolina declared to a northern audience on July 4, 1918, and that "the grandsons of the men who wore the blue and the grandsons of the men who wore the gray are now marching with locked shields and martial step to the mingled strains of Dixie and the Star Spangled Banner."[12]

Despite some quibbling and uneasiness over federal controls and the determined opposition of a handful of southern congressmen such as James K. Vardaman and Thomas P. Gore, most of the region's congressmen stood with the president on all of the major war measures. They did so even though the war legislation increased the functions and powers of the federal government and

Quar. 52 (Sept. 1968): 256–64; John Carver Edwards, "Georgia Guardsmen and the Politics of Survival, 1915–1916," ibid. 60 (Winter 1976): 344–55; Richard Glen Eaves, "Pro-Allied Sentiment in Alabama, 1914–1917: A Study of Representative Newspapers," *Ala. Rev.* 25 (Jan. 1972): 30–55; Theodore A. Thelander, "Josephus Daniels and the Publicity Campaign for Naval and Industrial Preparedness before World War I," *N.C. Hist. Rev.* 43 (July 1966): 316–32; Robert D. Ward, "Stanley Hubert Dent and American Military Policy, 1916–1920," *Ala. Hist. Quar.* 33 (Fall and Winter 1971): 177–89.

[9]Poe to Kitchin, Mar. 1, 1916, Kitchin Papers. Also see Harold T. Pulsifer, "The South and the War," *Outlook* 115 (Apr. 11, 1917): 648.

[10]See, for example, David A. Shannon, *The Socialist Party of America: A History* (New York, 1955), 106–108; Garin Burbank, "The Disruption and Decline of the Oklahoma Socialist Party," *Journal of American Studies* 7 (Aug. 1973): 133–52; Robert W. Dubay, "The Opposition to Selective Service, 1916–1918," *South. Quar.* 7 (Apr. 1969): 301–22; and Judith Sealander, "Violent Group Draft Resistance in the Appalachian South during World War I," *Appalachian Notes* 7 (1979): 1–12.

[11]Quoted in Charles Reagan Wilson, *Baptized in Blood: The Religion of the Lost Cause, 1865–1920* (Athens, Ga., 1980), 179–80.

[12]Unpublished address, delivered at Trenton, N.J., July 4, 1918, Robert L. Doughton Papers, Southern Historical Collection, University of North Carolina.

Preparedness parade, Mobile, Alabama, July 4, 1916. *Erik Overbey/Mobile Public Library Collection, University of South Alabama Photographic Archives.*

thus tended to undermine state-rights principles. Those who persisted in opposing the administration's war policies found themselves denounced in the southern press and confronted with grass-roots petitions demanding that they either work with the administration or resign. For the most part southern congressional leaders, entrenched in powerful committee positions, provided constructive and indispensable legislative assistance in the enactment of the administration's wartime program.[13]

State and local leaders, in and out of government, were equally responsive in behalf of mobilization measures. A host of war-related agencies, emanating from federal bodies in Washington, devoted themselves to the endless tasks of organizing and coordinating the war effort on the home front. Thus the state and local councils of defense carried out an energetic campaign of patriotic education, food conservation, health protection, persecution of "slackers" and "radicals," and public support of labor recruitment, bond drives, and so on. The councils of defense, middle class in outlook and under business leadership, manifested a keen interest in creating greater order and stability in society. They expressed in large measure the prewar progressive faith in the value of efficiency and social control.[14]

Preoccupation with the war effort was evident in virtually every aspect of southern life. Even the social agencies sought to do their part in mobilizing men and materials for the cause. One of the officers of the Southern Sociological Congress described the organization's Birmingham meeting in April 1918 as an attempt "to mobilize the leadership of the South for a win-the-war campaign."[15] An observer of the Birmingham congress reported that "the consciousness of the war was in the background of every meeting, and every speaker spoke with peculiar earnestness because of the pressure of war needs."[16] Nevertheless, the mobilization of community resources for military

[13]I. A. Newby, "States' Rights and Southern Congressmen during World War I," *Phylon* 24 (Spring 1963): 34–50; Richard L. Watson, Jr., "A Testing Time for Southern Congressional Leadership: The War Crisis of 1917–1918," *JSH* 44 (Feb. 1978): 3–40; Watson, "Principle, Party, and Constituency: The North Carolina Congressional Delegation, 1917–1919," *N.C. Hist. Rev.* 56 (July 1979): 298–323; Monroe Billington, "Thomas P. Gore and Oklahoma Public Opinion, 1917–1918," *JSH* 27 (Aug. 1961): 344–53; Holmes, *James Kimble Vardaman,* 319–27; Seward W. Livermore, *Politics Is Adjourned: Woodrow Wilson and the War Congress, 1916–1918* (Middletown, Conn., 1966), 50–58, 136–40.

[14]See Austin L. Venable, "The Arkansas Council of Defense in the First World War," *Ark. Hist. Quar.* 2 (June 1943): 116–26; Gerald Senn, *"Molders of Thought, Directors of Action:* The Arkansas Council of Defense, 1917–1918," ibid. 36 (Autumn 1977): 280–90; David O. Demuth, "An Arkansas County Mobilizes: Saline County, Arkansas, 1917–1918," ibid. 211–33; O. A. Hilton, "The Oklahoma Council of Defense and the First World War," *Chron. Okla.* 20 (Mar. 1942): 18–42; James H. Fowler II, "Tar and Feather Patriotism: The Suppression of Dissent in Oklahoma During World War One," ibid. 56 (Winter 1978–79): 409–30; Harry L. Coles, Jr., "The Federal Food Administration of Tennessee and Its Records in the National Archives, 1917–1919," *Tenn. Hist. Quar.* 4 (Mar. 1945): 23–57; William J. Breen, "The North Carolina Council of Defense during World War I, 1917–1918," *N.C. Hist. Rev.* 50 (Jan. 1973): 1–31.

[15]"Southern Sociological Congress," *Southern Workman* 47 (June 1918): 260.

[16]"A Survey of Southern Problems," *Survey* 40 (May 11, 1918): 163. For other examples of

Liberty Loan parade in New Orleans, October 1918. *National Archives and Records Service*.

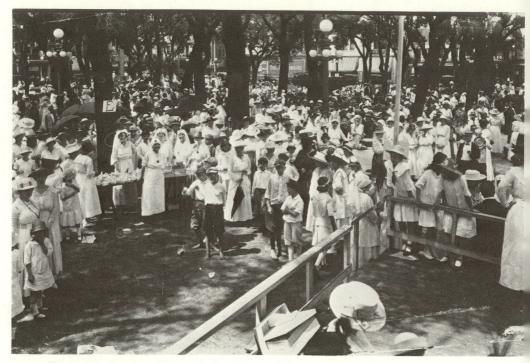

World War I scene, Bienville Square, Mobile, Alabama. *Erik Overbey/Mobile Public Library Collection, University of South Alabama Photographic Archives.*

purposes had important consequences for the development of new social services in the South. As a representative of the Russell Sage Foundation wrote during the war, in reporting on the social agencies and institutions of South Carolina, the state's war activities were "necessarily and inseparably involved with its social activities." Furthermore, he added, South Carolina had an opportunity "so to direct its war work in production and food conservation, in guarding the health and morals of the soldier, in the care of invalid, crippled, and insane soldiers, and in the training of youth for patriotic service as greatly to improve the quality and efficiency of the social work of the State for all future time."[17]

Hastings H. Hart, who carried out surveys of social conditions in Alabama, Florida, and South Carolina during the war, gave an address, "Social Reconstruction in the South," at the annual meeting of the Southern Sociological Congress in the spring of 1919. Hart cited the impact of economic prosperity on the southern states and the war's "amazing effect upon the morale" of southerners, which he thought had "set them forward in their social progress twenty-five years at a single bound." He also emphasized the recent changes in the region's social conditions, agencies, and institutions, resulting in good part from "the practical measures" taken by the government and voluntary organizations to overcome southern weaknesses. These steps, Hart thought, were "already bearing fruit in the reorganization of state boards of health, with vastly increased appropriations, in the building of state sanatoria for tuberculosis patients, in the enlargement and improvement of hospitals, in the establishment of reformatories for women and girls, in the development of state and county farm schools, and in increased state appropriations and local taxes for public schools."[18]

All of this represented a far cry from the prewar situation when, as one social worker recalled, social work in the South was only "a washed out, broken down, sour, dilapidated field."[19] The war's demands on the home front threw a revealing light on many of the social evils and inadequacies of the South. It brought more social workers—especially women—into southern communities,

the war's pervasive effect, see William Hurd Hillyer, "The South on Easy Street," *Independent* 93 (Feb. 23, 1918): 320, 326; R. B. House, "The Influence of War Travel on One Rural State: From the Letters of Quincy Sharpe Mills to Laconic Illiteracy," *Jour. Soc. Forces* 2 (Nov. 1923): 121–24; Jean M. Palmer, "The Impact of World War I on Louisiana's Schools and Community Life," *La. Hist.* 7 (Fall 1966): 323–32; and Lester D. Stephens, ed., "A Righteous Aim: Emma LeConte Furman's 1918 Diary," *Ga. Hist. Quar.* 62 (Fall 1978): 213–24.

[17]Hastings H. Hart, *The War Program of the State of South Carolina: A Report Prepared at the Request of Governor Richard I. Manning, the State Council of Defense, and the State Board of Charities and Corrections* (New York, 1918), 14.

[18]J. E. McCulloch, ed., *"Distinguished Service" Citizenship: Southern Sociological Congress, Knoxville, Tennessee* (Washington, D.C., n.d.), 49–50.

[19]"What the Southern Division Did for the South," *Survey* 53 (Mar. 15, 1925): 760. Also see "The South and the New Citizenship," ibid. 44 (Apr. 3, 1920): 35–41.

contributed to the professionalization of social workers in the section, and made them more acceptable to other southerners. It promoted the coordination and federated financing of social services. And it made the standards and procedures of social work in other parts of the country increasingly relevant to the amelioration of southern problems.

The major focus of the wartime social agencies was the task of protecting and entertaining servicemen and responding to the needs of their families. As the Reverend Kirkman G. Finlay of Columbia, South Carolina, put the matter, in addressing the 1917 meeting of the SSC, "We must clean up our town, stop the sale of liquor, and close up the houses of prostitution and other dens of iniquity." Military leaders contributed by bringing pressure to bear on local authorities to do away with prostitution around army and navy camps, and antivice campaigns were launched by a number of cities in the region. But wartime service to the soldier had to do more than that. The YMCA and the churches must "give him something else to do, and we must try to give him at least some of the refining and restraining influences of home."[20] This task was facilitated by the War Camp Community Service, which sought to mobilize community recreational facilities, and the Commission on Training Camp Activities, which tried to coordinate the work of the YMCA and other civilian service organizations.

Programs sponsored by the Red Cross were particularly important. The organization's southern membership grew rapidly during the war. The Atlanta chapter, for example, reported more than twenty-five thousand members by the end of 1917. In addition to operating dozens of canteens for soldiers and sailors throughout the South, the Red Cross provided various other services to men in the armed forces. Its southern and Gulf divisions brought social work to many of the region's towns and villages as well as to its cities. Its Home Service Bureau became a vital agency in many southern communities, serving as a liaison between the soldier and his family and often assuming much of the responsibility for the care of servicemen's dependents at home. Home Service Institutes, sponsored by the Red Cross, provided six-week courses for the training of workers in the Home Service program.[21] The YMCA also con-

---

[20]"Social Problems of the Southland," ibid. 38 (Aug. 11, 1917): 428. See also "Zones of Safety: Texas Cantonment Cities Made Safe for Health and Decency," ibid. 38 (July 21, 1917): 349–50; Raymond B. Fosdick, *Chronicle of a Generation: An Autobiography* (New York, 1958), 142–54; James R. McGovern, "'Sporting Life on the Line': Prostitution in Progressive Era Pensacola," *Fla. Hist. Quar.* 54 (Oct. 1975): 131–44; and Garna L. Christian, "Newton Baker's War on El Paso Vice," *Red River Valley Historical Review* 5 (Spring 1980): 55–67.

[21]Henry P. Davison, *The American Red Cross in the Great War* (New York, 1919), 40, 42–45; Nathan Edward Cohen, *Social Work in the American Tradition* (New York, 1958), 134–35; Howard Jensen, "The County as a Unit for Public Welfare," in Howard W. Odum and D. W. Willard, eds., *Systems of Public Welfare* (Chapel Hill, N.C., 1925), 228–29; G. P. Wyckoff, "Louisiana Notes," *Jour. Soc. Forces* 1 (May 1923): 411; Hart, *The War Program of South Carolina*, 17–18; Mildred Gregory Mullins, "Home-Front Activities of Atlanta Women during World War I" (M.A. thesis, Emory Univ., 1947), 67–69; Lemmon, *North Carolina's Role in the First World War*, 32–33, 39–40.

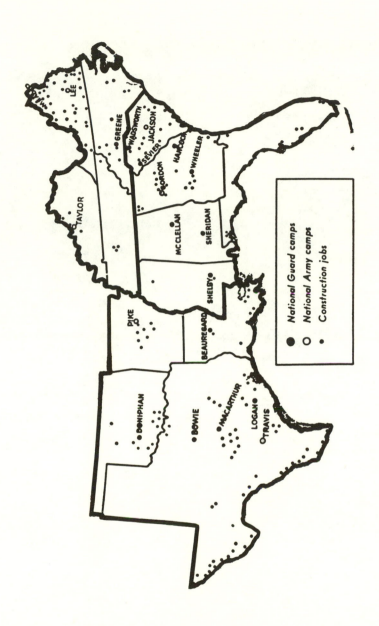

4. THE SOUTH IN WORLD WAR I: TRAINING CAMPS AND CONSTRUCTION PROJECTS. Adapted from Clifford L. Lord and Elizabeth H. Lord, *Historical Atlas of the United States*, rev. ed. New York: Holt, 1953.

War Camp Community Service, Kentucky State Fair, Louisville. *University of Louisville Photographic Archives.*

ducted training schools for its workers during the war. The success of these schools in the South led to the organization in the spring of 1919 of the "Southern Y.M.C.A. College" in Nashville, with Willis D. Weatherford as president.[22]

Social work by private concerns also seems to have been encouraged by the war. Hastings Hart, in his wartime survey of Alabama, reported that a number of that state's industrial firms were "gradually developing social work for their employees." Some of these efforts were crude and imperfect, and most of them were paternalistic in spirit. But Hart was impressed with the program of the Tennessee Coal and Iron Company, whose department of social science contained divisions of welfare, education, recreation, and horticulture. In its company towns TCI had built parks and playgrounds, community houses, public baths, and churches. It supplemented the salaries of the public school teachers in these towns, provided social workers for both races, and arranged for regular dental clinics. Hart concluded that the corporation was making "a sincere and earnest effort to promote the social welfare of the workers."[23]

Southern women made a notable contribution to the mobilization of community resources for the war effort. In Atlanta and Fulton County, for example, some 73,000 women participated in war work, including 31,000 church women.[24] The National League for Women's Service had organizations in several southern states by the fall of 1917, and agencies like the American Red Cross and the Food Administration involved women in their programs. But the most important support organizations among southern women were the committees in each state established at the urging of the Committee on Women's Defense Work of the Council of National Defense. Although their role was not clearly defined and their work was inhibited by inadequate financial support and the fact that the councils of defense were the official mobilizing agencies at the state level, the state women's committees organized county and community branches throughout the region and undertook a wide range of war-related activities. These efforts were most successful in areas such as food production and home economics, public health, and child welfare. In connection with the last of these, the committees endeavored against stubborn opposition to promote compliance with the national child labor law of 1916, and most of them took part in the National Children's Year campaign of 1918. Thus the war brought new opportunities for southern women to promote social reform.

[22]C. Howard Hopkins, *History of the Y.M.C.A. in North America (New York, 1951), 612–* 13.
[23]Hastings H. Hart, *Social Problems of Alabama: A Study of the Social Institutions and Agencies of the State of Alabama as Related to Its War Activities Made at the Request of Governor Charles Henderson* (Montgomery, Ala., 1918), 81–85.
[24]Mullins, "Home-Front Activities of Atlanta Women during World War I," 12–13.

North Carolina women, one authority has recently written, "were very much alive to the possibilities for domestic reform that the war had created."[25]

Black women in the South also responded patriotically to the mobilization drive, and many of them saw possibilities for social reform in the wartime situation. The war ended, however, before many of these possibilities could be pursued. The national women's committee, like the Council of National Defense, sought to persuade the southern states to integrate Negroes into the civilian war work. But progress was slow, since the state women's committees usually opposed an independent organizational structure for black women. Only in Florida and one or two other states did a complete black women's organization emerge. Thus the war work of black women in the South tended to be sporadic and unorganized, largely the result of efforts by the Federation of Colored Women's Clubs and local war service groups. Nevertheless, southern black women waged a quiet struggle for a more effective wartime organization, and they achieved some success, particularly in the cities and larger towns, in aiding black soldiers and their families, in food conservation programs, and in improving the general social conditions of their communities, especially with respect to public health and child welfare.[26]

Wartime concerns were largely responsible for what one investigator described as a series of "studies of social work and progress" in the South.[27] These social surveys were undertaken by a number of states and cities during and immediately after the war. In Jackson, Tennessee, for instance, the local chapter of the Red Cross set out "to discover the actual conditions as they exist, to secure real facts, and on the basis of these facts to build a program which will make for community welfare and progress." The project was endorsed by "all of the leading civic and social agencies of the city and the county." A central committee was created and subcommittees were appointed to report on "social and living conditions" in such areas as health, recreation, education, industry, and religion. Special committees reported on conditions in the black community. The findings and recommendations of the survey were published as a book in the spring of 1920.[28]

The war years also created a milieu that was favorable to the passage of more

[25]William J. Breen, "Southern Women in the War: The North Carolina Woman's Committee, 1917–1919," *N.C. Hist. Rev.* 55 (July 1978): 251–83; quotation on p. 281. Also see Lemmon, *North Carolina's Role in the First World War*, 39–43; Senn, *"Molders of Thought, Directors of Action,"* 289–90; and Mullins, "Home-Front Activities of Atlanta Women during World War I."

[26]William J. Breen, "Black Women and the Great War: Mobilization and Reform in the South," *JSH* 44 (Aug. 1978): 421–40; Breen, "The North Carolina Council of Defense during World War I," 25–29; Senn, *"Molders of Thought, Directors of Action,"* 288.

[27]Hastings H. Hart, "Peonage and the Public," *Survey* 46 (Apr. 9, 1921): 43. Also see "Florida Surveyed for War and Peace," *Survey* 39 (Mar. 2, 1918): 598, and "Making Social Surveys 'On High,'" ibid. (Mar. 16, 1918): 659.

[28]A. F. Kuhlman, *Social Survey of the City of Jackson and Madison County, Tennessee* (Jackson, Miss., 1920), 5–7 and passim.

advanced social welfare legislation. The social requirements of the mobiliza-tion drive, the activities of social service leaders and organizations, and the cooperation of political leaders all contributed to the enactment of welfare measures in most of the southern states. North Carolina, which reorganized its public welfare program during the years 1917–19, was the regional leader in this sphere. The efforts of such reform advocates as Alexander W. McAlister and of the North Carolina Conference for Social Service resulted in the enactment of a statewide public welfare law in 1917. The new statute established a state board of charities and public welfare with greater responsibilities and powers than the old board of public charities. It authorized county commissioners to establish a board of public welfare and appoint a county superintendent of public welfare. In 1919 the legislature made mandatory the provision of public welfare facilities and the creation of a juvenile court in every county.[29] Ken-tucky, Tennessee, and several other southern states expanded their welfare programs and reorganized their administrative systems during this period.[30]

In Tennessee, the legislature of 1917 passed a general child welfare act which increased the responsibilities and functions of the state board of charities and brought all private child-caring institutions under the supervision of the board. Arkansas, Tennessee, and Virginia enacted mothers' pension bills during the war.[31] Other southern states adopted "reform" measures having to do with child and family care, reformatories, juvenile courts, prisons, health, and public schools. During and immediately after the war, several states reor-ganized their public schools and strengthened their departments of public health.[32] "Both the war effort and the new prosperity," one authority con-cludes, "had spurred activity in social work and public health, and the in-

[29]Howard W. Odum, "The North Carolina Plan," in Odum and Willard, eds., *Systems of Public Welfare,* 172–73; Roy M. Brown, *Public Poor Relief in North Carolina* (Chapel Hill, N.C., 1928), 100–101, 157; William Foy Lisenby, "An Administrative History of Public Pro-grams for Dependent Children in North Carolina, Virginia, Tennessee, and Kentucky, 1900–1942" (Ph.D. diss., Vanderbilt Univ., 1962), 14–18; Andrew Dobelstein, "The Effects of the Reform Movement on Relief Administration in North Carolina: The Contributions of Alexander Worth McAlister," *SAQ* 75 (Spring 1976): 245–57.

[30]See, for example, G. P. Wyckoff, "Louisiana Notes," *Jour. Soc. Forces* 1 (May 1923): 409–11; Virginia Ashcraft, *Public Care: A History of Public Welfare Legislation in Tennessee* (Knoxville, 1947), 20–23, 43, 48–49; John M. Glenn and others, *Russell Sage Foundation, 1907–1946,* 2 vols. (New York, 1947), vol. 1, pp. 245–63; and Constantine William Curris, "State Public Welfare Developments in Kentucky," *Reg. Ky. Hist. Soc.* 64 (Oct. 1966): 309–10.

[31]Lisenby, "An Administrative History of Public Programs for Dependent Children," 94–95, 108–10, 134–38, 145–47; "Social Legislation," *Survey* 38 (May 19, 1917): 183; "Making over Arkansas in Sixty Days," ibid. (Apr. 14, 1917): 43; Burr Blackburn, "Mileposts of Progress in Georgia," *Jour. Soc. Forces* 1 (May 1923): 404.

[32]See, for example, "A Department on the Job," *Survey* 42 (Aug. 16, 1919): 728–29; N. B. Bond, "The Physician and Mental Ills in Mississippi," *Social Forces* 4 (Dec. 1925): 325–30; D. J. Whitener, "Education for the People," *N.C. Hist. Rev.* 36 (Apr. 1959): 192–93; Willard B. Gatewood, Jr., "Eugene Clyde Brooks and Negro Education in North Carolina, 1919–1923," ibid. 38 (July 1961): 362–79; and Alton DuMar Jones, "Progressivism in Georgia, 1898–1918" (Ph.D. diss., Emory Univ., 1963), 259–60.

creased revenues of state governments inspired the development of highways, public schools, and other state services in the new decade."[33]

In June 1918, the United States Supreme Court upheld the decision of a lower court invalidating the Child Labor Act of 1916 as an improper use of the commerce power.[34] The child labor reformers returned to the attack, and a new measure, based on the federal taxing power, was introduced in Congress in the autumn of 1918. There was great popular support for a national law by this time, and the bill passed both houses early the next year by overwhelming majorities.[35] Once again, textile interests under David Clark's leadership moved to kill the law in the courts. The act of 1919 was enjoined by the same North Carolina judge who had ruled against the first statute, and in 1922 the Supreme Court declared the second law unconstitutional.[36] The reformers then sought to amend the constitution, but although their amendment was approved by Congress, it was never ratified by the required number of states. It enjoyed little success in the South.[37]

Still, the movement to enact a federal child labor law during the Wilson period had contributed to the passage of better state regulatory statutes. In Alabama the reformers conducted an organized drive for a stronger law during the legislative session of 1915, following an extensive investigation carried out with the help of the NCLC during the previous year. The result was the enactment of a compromise measure, establishing a minimum age of fourteen after September 1916 and instituting a system of employment certificates. Before the legislature met in 1919, a statewide child welfare investigation was made under the direction of Edward N. Clopper, an NCLC agent. The legislature proceeded to strengthen the child labor regulations in several ways: by establishing a forty-eight-hour week, by requiring every employed minor under seventeen to have either an employment certificate or a certificate of age, and by creating a child welfare department and making it responsible for enforcing the child labor laws. The neighboring state of Georgia adopted a factory inspection law in 1916, enacted its first compulsory school attendance statutes in 1916 and 1919, and established a children's code commission in the early 1920s. South Carolina established a fourteen-year age standard in 1917 and improved its child

[33]George Brown Tindall, *The Emergence of the New South, 1913–1945* (Baton Rouge, 1967), 69.

[34]*Hammer* v. *Dagenhart*, 247 U.S. 251 (1918); Stephen B. Wood, *Constitutional Politics in the Progressive Era: Child Labor and the Law* (Chicago, 1968), 119–69; Elizabeth H. Davidson, *Child Labor Legislation in the Southern Textile States* (Chapel Hill, N.C., 1939), 263–65.

[35]*Cong. Record*, 65th Cong., 3d sess., pp. 621, 3035; Wood, *Constitutional Politics in the Progressive Era*, 185–217. Congressional opponents of the bill knew that they could not defeat it, and consequently their resistance was rather token. They pinned their hopes on another court decision.

[36]*Bailey* v. *Drexel Furniture Co.*, 259 U.S. 20 (1922); Wood, *Constitutional Politics in the Progressive Era*, 255–99.

[37]Only three southern states had ratified the amendment as late as 1937. Tindall, *The Emergence of the New South*, 322.

labor legislation in other ways. North Carolina, the other major textile state in the region, was the slowest to act. But after several setbacks in earlier years, North Carolina reformers were rewarded in 1919 when the general assembly adopted a fourteen-year age limit, provided for compulsory school attendance, and created a new child welfare commission to enforce the child labor regulations.[38]

Most of the other southern states also improved their child labor laws between 1914 and 1920. Tennessee, for example, strengthened its law in 1917 to meet the requirements of the Keating-Owen Act. In 1918 and 1920, Virginia raised its standards by extending the fourteen-year minimum to additonal occupations and by adopting the eight-hour day for working children under sixteen. The growing interest in the codification of child labor and other welfare laws was reflected in the completion of several statewide surveys, usually with the assistance of the National Child Labor Committee.[39] Thus, since the reform movement's initial successes in the South, the various states had slowly raised age limits, reduced hours, established inspection and employment certificate systems, and begun to recognize in their statutes the relationship between child labor and illiteracy. The effects of this state action were clearly evident by the end of the progressive era. "Ten years ago," wrote a representative of the NCLC in 1923, "nobody was paying any serious attention to the enforcement of the very poor child labor law; now, we have [in North Carolina] a State Commissioner with a staff for this very purpose and a designated enforcing agency in every county."[40] Almost 4,000 inspections were made and 738 violations were reported in 1920 by North Carolina's child welfare commission. In Alabama the percentage of children under sixteen among the state's industrial wage earners declined from 16.7 in 1914 to 1.8 in 1919.[41]

Finally, the war brought to fruition three major reform movements in which southern progressives had long struggled. One of these was national prohibition, an achievement that owed a great deal to southern congressmen, legislators, and public opinion. Another was the adoption of the Nineteenth Amendment enfranchising women. Although a majority of southern congressmen voted against the amendment and it encountered powerful opposition in the state legislatures of the region, it was supported by an increasing number of southerners. During the war the woman suffrage movement in the South emerged as a reform cause that could no longer be dismissed with rhetoric and

---

[38]Davidson, *Child Labor Legislation in the Southern Textile States,* 168–76, 190–93, 210–11, 228–37.

[39]Ibid., 243–44, 246; "Child Welfare Studied in Oklahoma," *Survey* 39 (Mar. 30, 1918): 713–14.

[40]Wiley H. Swift, "Child Labor in North Carolina, 1912–1922," *Jour. Soc. Forces* 1 (Mar. 1923): 253.

[41]Davidson, *Child Labor Legislation in the Southern Textile States,* 273; Tindall, *The Emergence of the New South,* 322–23.

ridicule. The third movement was the search for progress in race relations. The attention given this perennial question by the Southern Sociological Congress and the efforts of progressives like Willis D. Weatherford, James H. Dillard, and Will W. Alexander helped pave the way for tangible action in this field. Furthermore, the exigencies and opportunities of the war and its aftermath seemed to make such action imperative.

Prohibition had become an accepted Democratic principle in most southern states well before the United States entered the war in April 1917. Nevertheless, some southern prohibitionists considered federal intervention a mistake, a violation of state rights and an infringement upon personal liberties and property rights. But most of these antisaloon people were advocates of rigorous state regulation, and as a rule the local optionists of earlier years shifted to the support of statewide prohibition as the strength of the national movement increased. This was one reason for the success of "bone dry" laws and other rigid enforcement proposals in various legislatures during the years 1917–19. The Wilson administration's enthusiasm for wartime prohibition as a conservation device also stimulated the passage of tighter antiliquor laws in the South. But the identification of prohibition with patriotism and the war effort proved to be an even greater influence in the continuing crusade against alcohol in the region. Texas, Florida, and Kentucky joined the prohibition ranks in 1918 and 1919. Only Louisiana resisted statewide control. Mississippi was the first state to ratify the Eighteenth Amendment, and all of the thirteen southern states approved it in 1918 and early 1919. The majorities for ratification in the southern legislatures were lopsided, except in Louisiana, where the state senate voted in favor of the amendment by a single vote.[42]

Southerners were more divided over woman suffrage, particularly the question of enfranchisement by federal action. A majority of the southern congressmen opposed the so-called Susan B. Anthony Amendment to the Constitution, despite President Wilson's endorsement of it and mounting support for the amendment as a result of women's war work. Although the House of Representatives approved the amendment in January 1918, 90 of the 101 Democratic votes against the measure came from the South. When the Senate narrowly rejected the amendment, on October 1, 1918, only seven senators from the former Confederate states voted in the affirmative. Both houses approved the amendment by the necessary two-thirds majority in 1919, with stubborn resistance from most of the southern delegations. In the House all six of the Arkansas representatives voted for the measure, however, as did three of the four Florida representatives and ten of the seventeen Texas members. In general, congressional support was greatest in the Upper South and border states.

---

[42]Charles Merz, *The Dry Decade* (Garden City, N.Y., 1931), 307–308, 315–316; Andrew Sinclair, *Era of Excess: A Social History of the Prohibition Movement* (New York, 1964), 152–66; Watson, "A Testing Time for Southern Congressional Leadership," 7–8, 24–29.

Only five southern states ratified the Nineteenth Amendment—Arkansas, Kentucky, Oklahoma, Tennessee, and Texas. Southern legislators, like the region's congressmen, tended to regard the proposal as a radical scheme which would subvert traditional cultural patterns, jeopardize state rights, and open the gates to federal intervention in race relations. "If you submit to this amendment," Representative Robert L. Henry of Texas had warned his colleagues in 1914, "the next request will be for a law to prohibit the States from passing 'Jim Crow' laws, separate-coach laws, separate schools, [and] separate churches. . . . The next demand will be to place a Federal ban on the States where the intermarriage of the white and black races is prohibited."[43] Few southerners seemed to give much thought to the irony involved in their lawmakers' overwhelming approval of federal prohibition.

While these formal legislative decisions provide evidence of the South's basic conservatism, they fail to illuminate a significant aspect of southern progressivism. This was a robust movement for woman suffrage that had gained momentum in the region during the Wilson era. Between 1912 and 1914, suffragist leaders in virtually all of the southern states organized state associations or strengthened existing ones. These state groups usually became affiliates of the National American Woman Suffrage Association (NAWSA), and they sought to promote the formation of local suffrage bodies. By 1916, for example, the Equal Suffrage League of Virginia reported more than a hundred local affiliates. Statewide movements for woman suffrage were under way all over the South by 1914 or 1915, and by that time the question had become a serious issue in almost every southern legislature. The enfranchisement of women was receiving support from federations of women's clubs and the Women's Christian Temperance Union, from labor organizations, from an increasing number of newspapers, and from a variety of reform groups.[44]

The National Suffrage Association was not alone in its efforts to promote the

[43]Quoted in Morton Sosna, "The South in the Saddle: Racial Politics During the Wilson Years," *Wisconsin Magazine of History* 54 (Autumn 1970): 48. Also see Newby, "States' Rights and Southern Congressmen during World War I," 46–47; Watson, "A Testing Time for Southern Congressional Leadership," 29–34; Watson, "Principle, Party, and Constituency," 319–22; and Anne F. Scott and Andrew M. Scott, *One Half the People: The Fight for Woman Suffrage* (Philadelphia, 1975), 24–46.

[44]See, for example, A. Elizabeth Taylor, *The Woman Suffrage Movement in Tennessee* (New York, 1957), 15–93; Taylor, "The Woman Suffrage Movement in Arkansas," *Ark. Hist. Quar.* 15 (Spring 1956): 17–41; Taylor, "The Woman Suffrage Movement in Mississippi, 1890–1920," *Jour. Miss. Hist.* 30 (Feb. 1968): 1–21; Taylor, "The Woman Suffrage Movement in North Carolina," *N.C. Hist. Rev.* 38 (Jan. 1961): 45–62 (Apr. 1961): 173–89; Taylor, "South Carolina and the Enfranchisement of Women: The Later Years," *S.C. Hist. Mag.* 80 (Oct. 1979): 298–310; Lee N. Allen, "The Woman Suffrage Movement in Alabama, 1910–1920," *Ala. Rev.* 11 (Apr. 1958): 83–99; Kenneth R. Johnson, "Florida Women Get the Vote," *Fla. Hist. Quar.* 48 (Jan. 1970): 299–312; Lloyd C. Taylor, Jr. "Lila Meade Valentine: The FFV as Reformer," *Va. Mag. Hist. and Biog.* 70 (Oct. 1962): 471–87; Annette Shelby, "The Southern Lady Becomes an Advocate," in Waldo W. Braden, ed., *Oratory in the New South* (Baton Rouge, 1979), 204–36; and Lemmon, *North Carolina's Role in the First World War*, 25.

enfranchisement of women in the South. In 1913, Kate Gordon of Louisiana had set out to create a southern wing of the suffrage movement by working for state legislation rather than a federal amendment. The Congressional Union (later called the National Woman's Party), on the other hand, devoted itself exclusively to working for federal action. It began to organize in the South as early as 1915, though with limited success.[45] Forced to choose between Gordon's state-rights approach and NAWSA's increasing emphasis upon the desirability of amending the national Constitution, southern suffragists moved steadily toward the latter position. "I am a progressive, and often radical *thinker,*" a North Carolina feminist wrote in 1913, while adding that she was "a conservative *actor*" because it was better "to strive for a little and *get it,* than to ask *much* and get *nothing.*"[46] By the time the war ended, a growing number of southern women were becoming less conservative actors.

Support for a federal amendment among suffragists in the South developed noticeably in 1918 and 1919. Carrie Chapman Catt and other NAWSA leaders influenced southern moderates, as did Woodrow Wilson's endorsement of the suffrage amendment in January 1918. More important still was the suffragists' failure to make more progress with southern legislators and voters. Only one of the thirteen southern states—Oklahoma in 1918—had adopted woman suffrage. Arkansas and Texas permitted women to vote in primary elections, Kentucky had authorized its female citizens to participate in school elections, and Tennessee had enacted legislation in 1919 allowing women to vote in presidential and municipal elections. Otherwise, the suffrage movement had been stymied, losing critical contests time after time in state legislatures and statewide referenda. Perhaps the most telling example of such setbacks occurred in Kate Gordon's Louisiana, where a suffrage amendment was rejected by the voters in 1918 following a hard-fought campaign.[47] Yet woman suffrage had become a significant issue in southern politics. And when the general assembly of Tennessee in August 1920 became the thirty-sixth state to ratify the Nineteenth Amendment, most southern suffragists probably looked with satisfaction on the

[45]Kenneth R. Johnson, "Kate Gordon and the Woman-Suffrage Movement in the South," *JSH* 38 (Aug. 1972): 365–92; Loretta Ellen Zimmerman, "The National Woman's Party and the South, 1914–1920," paper presented at the annual meeting of the Southern Historical Association, Atlanta, Nov. 1980. Also see Louise B. James, "Alice Mary Robertson—Anti-Feminist Congresswoman," *Chron. Okla.* 55 (Winter 1977): 454–61, and Bill Sumners, "Southern Baptists and Women's Right to Vote, 1910–1920," *Baptist History and Heritage* 12 (Jan. 1977): 45–51.

[46]Sallie Southall Cotten to Walter Clark, Mar. 27, 1913, Walter Clark Papers, North Carolina Department of Archives and History.

[47]Ida Husted Harper, ed., *The History of Woman Suffrage,* vol. 6: *1900–1920* (New York, 1922), 520–37; Aileen S. Kraditor, *The Ideas of the Woman Suffrage Movement, 1890–1920* (New York, 1965), 185–91, 205, 267; Taylor, *The Woman Suffrage Movement in Tennessee,* 91–104; Paul E. Fuller, *Laura Clay and the Woman's Rights Movement* (Lexington, Ky., 1975), 145–61; Johnson, "Kate Gordon and the Woman-Suffrage Movement in the South," 378–92; Grace Elizabeth Prescott, "The Woman Suffrage Movement in Memphis: Its Place in the State, Sectional and National Movements," *West. Tenn. Hist. Soc. Papers* 18 (1964): 87–106; Anne Firor Scott, "After Suffrage: Southern Women in the Twenties," *JSH* 30 (Aug. 1964): 298–318.

Women register to vote for the first time, Mobile, Alabama. *Erik Overbey/Mobile Public Library Collection, University of South Alabama Photographic Archives.*

culmination of a process of nationalization in which they had been willing participants. The vote had become a symbol of something larger than the exercise of the franchise; for many southern women it embodied the image of the "new woman," with all that term suggested in the way of greater freedom and independence.

One of the areas of war-spawned change that seemed most portentous to contemporary southerners was that of race relations. The mass movement of blacks out of the region during the war years disturbed white southerners, while the upsurge of lynchings in 1918 and 1919, the widespread rumors of black uprisings after the Armistice, reports of black participation in organized labor activities, and the wave of race riots in 1919 heightened the uneasiness in the white mind.[48] The reformer Will W. Alexander called attention in the summer of 1919, for example, to what he described as "a small group of radical Negroes" in the United States who were trying "to drive a wedge between Negroes and whites based on the assumption that the white man is autocratic and that he means to dominate everything himself." Alexander suggested that "a great sane group" of black southerners was just as afraid of this radical threat as were the region's whites. "The most important thing that can be done for this racial situation," he declared, "is the promotion of closer contacts between the right sort of Negroes in our communities and the right sort of white men."[49]

A subtle alteration was discernible in the bearing and outlook of many black southerners, who had begun to demonstrate a new assertiveness and independence. This new spirit was sometimes revealed in black protest and resistance during the postwar riots. Although black Americans had been loyal supporters of the war effort, their responses to racial discrimination in the selective service and the military forces were tinged with dissent and impatience. The outbreak of antiblack violence in 1919, the strengthening of segregation laws in the

[48]See, for example, Dewey H. Palmer, "Moving North: Migration of Negroes during World War I," *Phylon* 28 (Spring 1967): 52–62; Robert Higgs, "The Boll Weevil, the Cotton Economy, and Black Migration, 1910–1930," *Agric. Hist.* 50 (Apr. 1976): 335–50; Jerrell H. Shofner, "Florida and the Black Migration," *Fla. Hist. Quar.* 57 (Jan. 1979): 267–88; T. J. Woofter, Jr., "The Negro on a Strike," *Jour. Soc. Forces* 2 (Nov. 1923): 84–88; Wayne Flynt, "Florida Labor and Political 'Radicalism,' 1919–1920," *Labor Hist.* 9 (Winter 1968): 73–90; Richard A. Straw, "The United Mine Workers of America and the 1920 Coal Strike in Alabama," *Ala. Rev.* 28 (Apr. 1975): 104–28; James A. Burran, "Labor Conflict in Urban Appalachia: The Knoxville Streetcar Strike of 1919," *Tenn. Hist. Quar.* 38 (Spring 1979): 62–78; J. W. Butts and Dorothy James, "The Underlying Causes of the Elaine Riot of 1919," *Ark. Hist. Quar.* 20 (Spring 1961): 95–104; Lester C. Lamon, "Tennessee Race Relations and the Knoxville Riot of 1919," *East Tenn. Hist. Society's Pubs.* 41 (1969): 67–85; William Cohen, "Riots, Racism, and Hysteria: The Response of Federal Investigative Officials to the Race Riots of 1919," *Massachusetts Review* 13 (Summer 1972): 373–400; Robert V. Haynes, "The Houston Mutiny and Riot of 1917," *Southwestern Hist. Quar.* 76 (Apr. 1973): 418–39; and Arthur I. Waskow, *From Race Riot to Sit-In, 1919 and the 1960's: A Study in the Connections Between Conflict and Violence* (Garden City, N.Y., 1966), 12–37, 105–109, 121–74.

[49]Minutes of interracial conference at Blue Ridge, N.C., July 17, 1919, Commission on Interracial Cooperation Papers, Atlanta University Library.

postwar South, and the frustration of Negro hopes for a larger role in politics combined to reinforce the mood of dissatisfaction and resentment in the black community.[50] Meanwhile, the major black organizations were growing rapidly and were sharpening their demands. By December 1918, for instance, the National Association for the Advancement of Colored People had branches in every southern state and a southern membership of more than 18,700.[51] A more militant temper was also evident among Negro women in the South, particularly in the activities of the Federation of Colored Women's Clubs and in the efforts of black women to obtain equality and greater autonomy within the predominantly white YWCA.[52]

The riots of 1919 and the new militancy among blacks galvanized southern progressives into action. In Nashville and several other cities, law and order leagues were formed in 1918 and 1919. But the most notable step was the organization, in Atlanta in April 1919, of the Commission on Interracial Cooperation. The establishment of this body followed a series of discussions by leaders of both races in Atlanta. The distinguishing feature of the commission was its emphasis on the need to facilitate interracial contact among community leaders throughout the South. Plans were soon perfected for a Southwide organization, and by 1920 more than five hundred state, county, and local interracial committees had been created. The Woman's Committee of the Interracial Commission came into existence in 1920.[53]

Social control was an important consideration in the minds of the commission's white founders. "It is quite evident to me," a Tennessee member declared in 1920, "that the war has created a situation that has given the extreme negro his opportunity for leadership. . . . The only way in the world to keep

---

[50]Robert R. Moton, "The South and the Lynching Evil," *SAQ* 18 (July 1919): 191–96; William Pickens, "The Woman Voter Hits the Color Line," *Nation* 111 (Oct. 6, 1920): 372–73; Andrew Buni, *The Negro in Virginia Politics, 1902–1965* (Charlottesville, Va., 1967), 69–89; John Dittmer, *Black Georgia in the Progressive Era, 1900–1920* (Urbana, Ill., 1977), 186–210; Carl S. Matthews, "The Decline of the Tuskegee Machine, 1915–1925: The Abdication of Political Power," *SAQ* 75 (Autumn 1976): 460–69; Theodore Kornweibel, Jr., "Apathy and Dissent: Black America's Negative Responses to World War I," ibid. 80 (Summer 1981): 322–38.

[51]Charles Flint Kellogg, *NAACP: A History of the National Association for the Advancement of Colored People*, vol. 1: *1909–1920* (Baltimore, 1967), 134–37, 209–63; Nancy J. Weiss, "From Black Separatism to Interracial Cooperation: The Origins of Organized Efforts for Racial Advancement, 1890–1920," in Barton J. Bernstein and Allen J. Matusow, eds., *Twentieth-Century America: Recent Interpretations* (2d ed., New York, 1972), 52–87.

[52]Jacquelyn Dowd Hall, *Revolt Against Chivalry: Jessie Daniel Ames and the Women's Campaign Against Lynching* (New York, 1979), 77–88.

[53]Edward Flud Burrows, "The Commission on Interracial Cooperation, 1919–1944: A Case Study in the History of the Interracial Movement in the South" (Ph.D., diss., Univ. of Wisconsin, 1954), 45–240; George Peter Antone, Jr., "Willis Duke Weatherford: An Interpretation of His Work in Race Relations, 1906–1946" (Ph.D. diss., Vanderbilt Univ., 1969), 92–136; Wilma Dykeman, *Prophet of Plenty: The First Ninety Years of W. D. Weatherford* (Knoxville, 1966); Wilma Dykeman and James Stokely, *Seeds of Southern Change: The Life of Will Alexander* (Chicago, 1962), 43–81; Hall, *Revolt Against Chivalry*, 94–106; Tindall, *The Emergence of the New South*, 170–81.

this type of leader from completely dominating his race is to give the conservative man an opportunity to point to and defend the concrete achievements of the best Southern white men."[54] The Interracial Commission would serve this purpose, among other worthy objectives. The new organization was also the product of a growing concern for greater justice and fair play in the treatment of southern blacks. The roots of this concern reached back to the church missions of white women, to the YWCA and neighborhood work of black women, to the racial activities of the YMCA, and to the work of dedicated reformers such as Willis D. Weatherford, Lily Hammond, and Lugenia Hope. "For many years," Weatherford explained in 1920, "there has been a growing determination on the part of southern white men to see to it that the southern Negro had justice, fair play, and a chance for development." Weatherford also referred to another factor: "Parallel with this determination on the part of the white people there has been a similar determination on the part of the colored people to continue knocking at the door of opportunity until it was opened wide."[55]

The war nourished the seeds of both social control and social justice in race relations. It also suggested new possibilities for social progress in areas like race relations through the application of better techniques and scientific knowledge. Some of the interracial reformers were impressed by the methods of organization, rational planning, publicity, and efficient management they had seen demonstrated in the mobilization of the home front, particularly in the social service activities of agencies such as the YMCA and the Red Cross. They had also found unaccustomed opportunities to work with black leaders in some of the wartime social programs. There was still another ingredient in this reform movement: the financial support of the Phelps-Stokes Fund, the National War Work Council, and other foundations that promoted the uplift of blacks. Thus the sources of the interracial movement were quite diverse. But it was the war that provided the context and the imperatives that brought the movement to life.

In many respects, then, the First World War provided a favorable setting for southern progressivism. The war generated strong currents of change in the South, loosening some of the regional restraints on experimentation and innovation. It intensified the process of nationalization, expanding the role of the federal government, spreading the effect of national regulations and standards, and bringing southerners more fully into the arena of national affairs. It resulted in an extraordinary mobilization of resources—private as well as public—some of which were used for social purposes. These developments helped create new avenues of efficiency, public service, social control, and social justice. Social reform was thereby encouraged, although it was frequently constrained, in the

[54]Quoted in Leah Marie Park, "Edwin Mims and *The Advancing South* (1894–1926): A Study of a Southern Liberal" (M.A. thesis, Vanderbilt Univ., 1964), 143–44.
[55]Weatherford, "Growing Race Cooperation," *Survey* 45 (Oct. 16, 1920): 88.

South as elsewhere, by an attitude of intolerance and coercive conformity.[56] But for the most part southern progressives were able to accommodate their objectives to the realities of wartime. Indeed, the war brought several of their campaigns to a successful culmination and momentarily, at least, promised further progress in the new era of the 1920s.

[56]See, for example, H. C. Peterson and Gilbert C. Fite, *Opponents of War, 1917–1918* (Madison, Wis., 1957), 24, 28, 38–41, 63–64, 86–91, 99, 106–107, 141, 151–55, 171–76, 191, 196, 200, 213–14, 217, 219, 223–35, and Alan B. Bromberg, "Free Speech at Mr. Jefferson's University: The Case of Professor Leon Whipple," *Va. Mag. Hist. and Biog.* 88 (Jan. 1980): 3–20.

13   *The Reconciliation of Progress and Tradition*

SOUTHERN PROGRESSIVISM lost much of its vitality with the end of the war and the breakdown of the Wilson administration. By that time the regional focus of the reformers had been disrupted, and they were no longer united by a common program of social reforms and values. They had also lost much of their élan and optimism as progressives. The dispersion of reform energies was related to the progressives' success in obtaining national prohibition and woman suffrage. The organizations that had supported these reforms were disbanded or reorganized, while broad regional groups such as the Southern Sociological Congress declined or redefined their purposes. Social change, accelerated by the war, created new tensions, and the postwar years were exacerbated by sharp conflicts between the South and other regions and among southerners. The milieu was no longer conducive to the progressive campaigns of earlier years. But progressivism in the South, as in other parts of the country, was far from dead. Its major constituent elements remained surprisingly virile, and their impact on the politics and social thought of the South in the 1920s—and afterward—was substantial.

The South entered the 1920s on a rising tide of economic diversification and urbanization. The region's industrial progress and urban growth led many of its leaders to assume that the economic transformation would steadily alleviate social problems. In short, the prosperity of the twenties promised to remove what constituted, in progressive eyes, the most formidable barrier to regional progress and social well-being. There was, however, a more somber aspect of the economic situation: the depressed agricultural economy that began with the new decade and stubbornly persisted in the midst of overproduction, low commodity prices, heavy farm mortgages, and a mass of sharecroppers and tenant farmers. The perilous condition of the rural South, where a majority of the section's inhabitants still lived, seriously weakened the progressives' long-held vision of a healthy economy and society dominating the southern countryside.

Contrasting economic conditions in the city and on the farm no doubt contributed to urban-rural tension in the postwar years. Even though most south-

410

erners continued to appreciate traditional agrarian virtues, rural dwellers tended to take a more conservative position on questions like child labor legislation, the enforcement of prohibition, and the teaching of evolution in the schools.[1] This urban-rural dichotomy, while seldom clear-cut, illustrates a more general problem progressives confronted during the 1920s in organizing campaign coalitions to support social reforms. The earlier equilibrium between the forces of modernization and those of cultural tradition could no longer be sustained. One of the chief reasons for this failure was the growing cultural conflict that developed with the South's continuing social alteration. "The United Daughters of the Confederacy and the Kiwanis Club flourished side by side," one observer later wrote. "Mule-wagon and automobile, fundamentalism and liberalism, education and illiteracy, aristocratic pride and backwoods independence disproved the axiom that two bodies cannot occupy the same space. Cities that preserved the finest flavor of the old regime had to be approached over brand-new roads where billboards, tourist camps, filling stations, and factories broke out in a modernistic rash among the white oaks and Spanish moss."[2] Yet innovation, secularism, and novel beliefs seemed to jeopardize traditional values, evangelical Protestantism, and individual piety.[3] Change itself, for many erstwhile progressives, had acquired a dubious and often threatening appearance. The result in many cases was a politics of cultural conflict rather than of cultural consensus.

Social divisions in the South following World War I were evident not only in the campaigns to preserve traditional values by such groups as the Ku Klux Klan and religious fundamentalists, but also in the ideas of a new generation of social critics. These southern critics—journalists, writers, and scholars in the developing universities—produced a body of self-criticism that proved to be more challenging and sometimes more penetrating than that of the progressives. Underlying the Southern Literary Renascence that began in the twenties, one scholar writes, was "a new critical vision that challenged the old assumptions and the old gods."[4] This critical vision owed a good deal to outside critics

---

[1] See, for example, Clifford B. Anderson, "Agrarian Attitudes toward the City, Business, and Labor in the 1920's and 1930's," *Miss. Quar.* 14 (Fall 1961): 183–89.

[2] Donald Davidson, *The Attack on Leviathan: Regionalism and Nationalism in the United States* (Chapel Hill, N.C., 1938), 141–42.

[3] See Blaine A. Brownell, "A Symbol of Modernity: Attitudes Toward the Automobile in Southern Cities in the 1920s," *Amer. Quar.* 24 (Mar. 1972): 20–44. For an example of contrasting contemporary views of conditions in a rural Arkansas county and a progressive mill village, see Frances Sage Bradley, "A Survey of Conditions Affecting Children of Bradley County, Arkansas," *Jour. Soc. Forces* 1 (Mar. 1923): 296–99, and M. W. Heiss, "The Southern Cotton Mill Village: A Viewpoint," ibid. 2 (Mar. 1924): 345–50.

[4] Fred C. Hobson, Jr., *Serpent in Eden: H. L. Mencken and the South* (Chapel Hill, N.C., 1974), 80. See also ibid., 33–120; Gerald W. Johnson, "Critical Attitudes North and South," *Jour. Soc. Forces* 2 (May 1924): 575–79; Johnson, "Southern Image-Breakers," *Va. Quar. Rev.* 4 (Oct. 1928): 508–19; C. Hugh Holman, "Literature and Culture: The Fugitive-Agrarians," *Social Forces* 37 (Oct. 1958): 15–19; and George B. Tindall, "The Significance of Howard W. Odum to Southern History: A Preliminary Estimate," *JSH* 24 (Aug. 1958): 285–307.

like the Baltimore writer Henry L. Mencken, though the general effect of northern indictments was to provoke defensiveness and recrimination among southerners. Unlike the intersectional accord of the progressive period, the 1920s witnessed mounting attacks from other parts of the country on lynching, peonage, racial brutality, and other practices associated with the South. This produced what one historian has described as "a kind of neo-abolitionist image of the benighted South."[5] This, too, weakened the progressive synthesis of earlier years.

Changes in politics also undermined the position of southern progressives. The South's hour of leadership in national politics had ended, and the inspiring figure of Woodrow Wilson no longer occupied the White House. Furthermore, the bitter struggle that racked the national Democratic party in the 1920s was, to a large extent, a sectional conflict over cultural values, with the South being identified with the rural, Protestant, and nativist faction of the party. While southerners dominated the Democratic party in Congress, their leadership of the congressional minority was generally cautious and conservative.[6] The divisive election of 1928 did, however, elicit a brand of southern liberalism that emphasized individual liberty and toleration and supported an Irish-Catholic presidential candidate. Meanwhile, the nature of the state party systems in the South was changing. The vigorous bifactionalism that characterized the Democratic party in most of the southern states early in the century had been superseded by new factional alignments, new leaders, and new issues. The role of reform elements in the old party groupings was no longer as apparent or as significant as it had been in the progressive era.

Other factors also impaired the strength of southern progressivism. Its earlier successes may have contributed in some cases to its loss of vigor in the twenties. There were signs that the progressives had about reached the limits of their concept of reform. A new generation of leaders was coming to the fore. In addition, many professional groups were making the transition from "the missionary era to one of institutionalization and professionalism."[7] Caught up in the struggle to develop effective agencies and services in their particular fields and in their professional growth and recognition, they found the old kinds of social reform increasingly irrelevant and unsatisfying. Southern social workers, for example, like their counterparts in the rest of the country, now seemed more concerned with procedure and the adjustment of the individual to the

---

[5]George B. Tindall, "The Benighted South: Origins of a Modern Image," *Va. Quar. Rev.* 40 (Spring 1964): 281–94; quottion on p. 281. See also Hobson, *Serpent in Eden* , 11–32, and Frank Tannenbaum, *Darker Phases of the South* (New York, 1924).

[6]David Burner, *The Politics of Provincialism: The Democratic Party in Transition, 1918–1932* (New York, 1967); Philip A. Grant, Jr., "Southern Congressmen and Agriculture, 1921–1932," *Agric. Hist.* 53 (Jan. 1979): 338–51.

[7]George Brown Tindall, *The Emergence of the New South, 1913–1945* (Baton Rouge, 1967), 254.

environment than in transforming the social environment in which the individual lived.[8]

Despite its loss of strength and unity, progressivism in the South did not disappear in the 1920s. Instead, as George B. Tindall has shown, it was "transformed through greater emphasis upon certain of its tendencies and the distortion of others."[9] One of the altered strains of southern progressivism took shape as a reform movement in race relations. This new venture in racial reform—the Commission on Interracial Cooperation—reflected the white South's continuing interest in order, stability, and harmony in race relations. The commission was careful not to challenge segregation or to be portrayed as subversive of southern traditions. It was intent upon stamping out lynching and attacking other forms of racial injustice. Commission members hoped, through regional, state, and local organizations, to improve communication between the races, to foster law and order at the community level, and to publicize constructive achievements in race relations.[10]

Social justice as well as social control was a central theme in the origins and activities of the Commission on Interracial Cooperation. Religious conviction was a powerful motivating factor in the leadership of Will W. Alexander, who became the executive director of the commission, and others involved in its work. The Interracial Commission appealed not only to liberal sentiment in the South but also to progressives in other regions and to northern philanthropists, who provided much of the financial support for CIC activities. Another notable feature of the interracial movement in the 1920s and 1930s was the vital part played by southern women, black as well as white. The Woman's Committee of the Interracial Commission was, as its perceptive interpreter has recently noted, the earliest attempt in the South to build a women's organization "explicitly devoted to overcoming the barriers of race."[11] Unlike earlier white reformism in the field of race relations, the Interracial Commission could point to a concrete and realistic mode of action. It sought to avert racial violence and to secure specific improvements in community life.[12] The very concept of interracial organization, although anticipated in some of the wartime community programs, represented a sharp break with the past. The interracial movement

[8]See Clarke A. Chambers, *Seedtime of Reform: American Social Service and Social Action, 1918–1933* (Minneapolis, 1963), 93.

[9]Tindall, *The Emergence of the New South*, 219.

[10]Edward Flud Burrows, "The Commission on Interracial Cooperation, 1919–1944: A Case Study in the History of the Interracial Movement in the South" (Ph.D. diss., Univ. of Wisconsin, 1954); Wilma Dykeman and James Stokely, *Seeds of Southern Change: The Life of Will Alexander* (Chicago, 1962), 52–164; George Peter Antone, Jr., "Willis Duke Weatherford: An Interpretation of His Work in Race Relations, 1906–1946" (Ph.D. diss., Vanderbilt Univ., 1969), 92–136.

[11]Jacquelyn Dowd Hall, *Revolt Against Chivalry: Jessie Daniel Ames and the Women's Campaign Against Lynching* (New York, 1979), 106.

[12]See, for example, Morton Sosna, *In Search of the Silent South: Southern Liberals and the Race Issue* (New York, 1977), 20–41.

slowly began to reverse the trend toward increasing separation between white and black southerners. Finally, the commission's approach was different from previous reform movements in its interest in the scientific study of race relations, which was manifested in its emphasis on education, research, and publication. Thus, while its approach was cautious and its reforms largely superficial, the Interracial Commission was nonetheless a bolder and more liberal social experiment than the racial uplift of prewar progressives.

Other kinds of progressivism also survived into the 1920s, though usually in a different form. The humanitarian and social justice motif, while somewhat muted, was still a significant factor in voluntary endeavors and public welfare programs. The drive to improve the world in which they lived, for example, was one of the most important underlying motivations in the political and social-action efforts of newly enfranchised southern women.[13] A more conspicuous manifestation of the reform spirit in the twenties was the series of campaigns to protect moral standards and traditional cultural values. The prohibition movement and other antivice efforts of the progressive era were expressions of this widespread southern concern over immoral behavior, as well as an aspect of the reformers' commitment to more effective means of social control. The zeal that many southerners displayed for the attacks on trusts and the campaigns to overthrow political "machines" drew upon the springs of this morality. It was closely identified with evangelical Protestantism, with rural and small-town life, with agrarian reformism, and with the politics of William Jennings Bryan. Wartime dislocations and rapid social change in the postwar years heightened the social concerns of southern moralists and strengthened their resolve to defend the traditional culture.

Prohibition absorbed much of the energy of southern reformers during the 1920s. Although the enforcement of prohibition statutes was interpreted by many southerners as a social reform, the issue was no longer an integral part of a progressive program of social action, as had often been the case in earlier years.[14] The recently organized Ku Klux Klan, which enjoyed spectacular

[13]Nellie Roberson, "The Organized Work of Women in One State," *Jour. Soc. Forces* 1 (Sept. 1923): 613–15; Anne Firor Scott, "After Suffrage: Southern Women in the Twenties," *JSH* 30 (Aug. 1964): 298–318; Mary E. Swenson, "To Uplift a State and Nation: The Formative Years of the Alabama League of Women Voters, 1920–1921," *Ala. Hist. Quar.* 37 (Summer 1975): 115–35; Burr Blackburn, "Mileposts of Progress in Georgia," *Jour. Soc. Forces* 1 (May 1923): 403–406; "The State Conferences at Work in 1923: A Symposium of Forward-Looking Plans," ibid., 421–29; Joseph C. Logan, "Relation of Layman and Expert in Social Work," ibid. 2 (May 1924): 492–97; Mrs. L. B. Bush, "A Decade of Progress in Alabama," ibid., 539–45; Foy Lisenby, "The Arkansas Conference on Charities and Correction, 1912–1937," *Ark. Hist. Quar.* 29 (Spring 1970): 42–44.

[14]See, for example, James Benson Sellers, *The Prohibition Movement in Alabama, 1702 to 1943* (Chapel Hill, N.C., 1943), 190–232; Daniel Jay Whitener, *Prohibition in North Carolina, 1715–1945* (Chapel Hill, N.C., 1945), 184–200; Virginius Dabney, *Dry Messiah: The Life of Bishop Cannon* (New York, 1949); Andrew Sinclair, *Era of Excess: A Social History of the Prohibition Movement* (New York, 1964); and Arthur F. Howington, "John Barley Corn Subdued: The Enforcement of Prohibition in Alabama," *Ala. Rev.* 23 (July 1970): 212–25.

growth in the region, also attracted support from southerners worried about the decline of moral standards and alienated by relentless social change. The Klan, for all its prejudice and violence, was in part a reform movement with a heritage from prewar progressivism. Community morals were an overriding concern of the organization's members, whose activities represented, among other things, a general quest for moral and social conformity.[15] A similar insistence upon moral conformity was embodied in the antievolution crusade and especially in the efforts of Protestant fundamentalists to stamp out "the specter of infidelity."[16] The region's defensive temper in the twenties was intensified by what its moral custodians interpreted as challenges to southern orthodoxies. One result was a kind of "political fundamentalism," in which defenders of traditional morality sought to deny divisions in southern society by appealing to regional loyalties and coercing a sense of unity. This fundamentalism contained an element of popular democracy, since it reflected the belief of many southerners that their society was being reshaped by a diverse but powerful economic group that seemed to disregard historic tradition and the idea of popular consent.[17]

In any case, the compulsion to preserve cultural values, a basic characteristic of southern progressivism, became more defensive and negative in the 1920s. The region's churches, particularly in the cities, continued to be concerned with social issues, for example, but now they tended to work for what one historian has described as "a restrictive, enforced community based on its own standards."[18] The same tendency was evident in several of the redoubtable progressive newspapers such as Josephus Daniels's Raleigh *News and Observer*. Daniels's newspaper, in the words of a new-style critic, rolled "a soft-boiled eye" at the Ku Klux Klan and the fundamentalists. "It professes high respect for

[15]Charles C. Alexander, *The Ku Klux Klan in the Southwest* (Lexington, Ky., 1965), 20–32. Also see David M. Chalmers, *Hooded Americanism: The First Century of the Ku Klux Klan, 1865–1965* (Garden City, N.Y., 1965), 56–84, 92–118, 225–35; Kenneth T. Jackson, *The Ku Klux Klan in the City, 1915–1930* (New York, 1967), 25–87; Robert Moats Miller, "A Note on the Relationship between the Protestant Churches and the Revived Ku Klux Klan," *JSH* 22 (Aug. 1956): 356–68; and Roger K. Hux, "The Ku Klux Klan in Macon, 1919–1925," *Ga. Hist. Quar.* 62 (Summer 1978): 155–68.

[16]Kenneth K. Bailey, "The Antievolution Crusade of the Nineteenth-Twenties" (Ph.D. diss., Vanderbilt Univ., 1953); Norman F. Furniss, *The Fundamentalist Controversy, 1918–1931* (New Haven, Conn., 1954); Laurence W. Levine, *Defender of the Faith, William Jennings Bryan: The Last Decade, 1915–1925* (New York, 1965), 248–355; Willard B. Gatewood, Jr., *Preachers, Pedagogues, & Politicians: The Evolution Controversy in North Carolina, 1920–1927* (Chapel Hill, N.C., 1966); Gatewood, ed., *Controversy in the Twenties: Fundamentalism, Modernism, and Evolution* (Nashville, 1969). Also see Robert F. Sexton, "The Crusade Against Pari-Mutuel Gambling in Kentucky: A Study of Southern Progressivism in the 1920's," *Filson Club Hist. Quar.* 50 (Jan. 1976): 47–57.

[17]Robert A. Garson, "Political Fundamentalism and Popular Democracy in the 1920's," *SAQ* 76 (Spring 1977): 219–33. See William E. Leuchtenburg, *The Perils of Prosperity, 1914–32* (Chicago, 1958), 204–23, for a discussion of political fundamentalism in the context of national politics.

[18]Wayne Flynt, "Religion in the Urban South: The Divided Religious Mind of Birmingham, 1900–1930," *Ala. Rev.* 30 (Apr. 1977): 125–28.

Thomas Jefferson, but obviously doubts that he intended the Bill of Rights to apply to Republicans, bootleggers, college professors and Socialists."[19]

But if the postwar era changed the content and the spirit of progressivism in the South, it failed to dampen the enthusiasm of southern businessmen and professional people for economic development. Indeed, the war stimulated the region's economic expansion and heightened the yearnings and expectations southerners had for further "progress." The preoccupation with economic growth, the institutionalization of state services, and the achievement of administrative efficiency and professional standards, like the crusades for morality, represented an elaboration of older progressive themes. Southern progressives had always been strongly committed to the need to "modernize the region through transforming its economic base."[20]

"Good government" and more adequate public services, southern leaders increasingly assumed, were as vital to economic progress as natural resources, abundant labor, and resourceful entrepreneurs. This ingredient in prewar progressivism reached early fruition during the 1920s in the politics and policies of several southern states and municipalities. It was evident in the leadership of a number of forceful and effective governors such as Cameron Morrison of North Carolina, Austin Peay of Tennessee, Bibb Graves of Alabama, and Harry Flood Byrd of Virginia. These exemplars of "business progressives" stressed economy and efficiency. They reorganized and modernized the structure of their state governments, devised new administrative and tax systems, and expanded state services.[21]

The development of public services, a significant but somewhat inchoate part of earlier progressivism, was one of the most notable features of state and municipal government in the twenties. In the South dramatic advances were made in the construction of highways, the support of education, the expansion of public health facilities, and the growth of social welfare programs. All of these functions were associated with the themes of economic growth, efficiency, and modernization, and they elicited strong backing from businessmen, professional groups, and the urban middle class generally. Chambers of commerce and other business organizations, for instance, were devoted advocates of good roads; they increasingly identified the automobile as a vehicle of commercial development and urban growth.[22] Professionals such as teachers,

[19]Gerald W. Johnson, "Journalism Below the Potomac," *American Mercury* 9 (Sept. 1926): 77–82; quotation on p. 81.

[20]See Daniel Joseph Singal, "Broadus Mitchell and the Persistence of New South Thought," *JSH* 45 (Aug. 1979): 356.

[21]George B. Tindall, "Business Progressivism: Southern Politics in the Twenties," *SAQ* 62 (Winter 1963): 92–106; Tindall, *The Emergence of the New South*, 224–38; Allen W. Moger, *Virginia: Bourbonism to Byrd, 1870–1925* (Charlottesville, Va., 1968), 333–44; Joseph T. Macpherson, "Democratic Progressivism in Tennessee: The Administrations of Governor Austin Peay, 1923–1927" (Ph.D. diss., Vanderbilt Univ., 1969).

[22]Tindall, *The Emergence of the New South*, 254–84; Blaine A. Brownell, *The Urban Ethos in*

engineers, public health doctors and nurses, and social workers were also champions of the expanding role of government in providing what they regarded as essential services. With the growth of these governmental functions came, slowly and hesitantly, a conception of greater state responsibility for social welfare.

In 1926, Edwin Mims, a participant in many of the progressive campaigns of the past quarter-century, published *The Advancing South*. Mims was responding to the disturbing trends symbolized by the trial of John T. Scopes in 1925 for teaching evolution in a Tennessee high school. The book was a spirited and hopeful account of "progress and reaction," of what the author called a "war of liberation" and a long struggle "for emancipation from outworn traditions" in the South.[23] Although Mims was not a representative progressive, he captured the idealism of the reformers, their hopefulness, their moderation, and their middle-class values. He instinctively understood their almost compulsive reliance on the South as an idea and on the region as an arena for reform, and he appreciated their ardent desire to reconcile tradition with progress, to mediate between classes, races, and sections, to bring stability, harmony, and enlightenment to southern society. Yet *The Advancing South* was curiously limited as a characterization of southern progressivism. The interpretation gave short shrift to populism, the antitrust movement, and political insurgency and factionalism in the Democratic party. Nor did it make sufficient allowance for prohibition and other campaigns to enforce morality in the early twentieth-century South. Mims was correct in asserting that organized action had brought progressive advances to the South during this era: in economic development, social welfare programs, more adequate public services, and the modernization of institutions. But his portrayal scarcely did justice to the comprehensiveness and complexity of southern progressivism.

Certain attributes of the southern progressives need to be emphasized. In the first place, these reformers were in no sense involved in the promotion of fundamental social change. Nor were they, as a rule, democrats with an implicit faith in the masses or a concrete program for assisting the poor and disadvantaged, although their social reformism did embody a sort of popular elitism. Their racial attitudes and practices were carefully restricted by the bounds of orthodoxy. They accepted or accommodated themselves to a system whose major institutions were dominated by powerful economic and political interests. Representing the emerging professional and bourgeois elements of the South's social structure, they shared many of the assumptions and goals of southern businessmen and entrepreneurs. They found much to admire in an urban ethos whose central theme was "the necessity for growth and order,

---

the South, 1920–1930 (Baton Rouge, 1975), 157–89; Charles Paul Garofalo, "The Sons of Henry Grady: Atlanta Boosters in the 1920s," *JSH* 42 (May 1976): 187–204.

[23] Mims, *The Advancing South: Stories of Progress and Reaction* (Garden City, N.Y., 1926), pp. vii–viii.

change and stability, progress and preservation."[24] While their social compassion was genuine and their uplift activities extensive, much of the progressives' reformism was essentially "preventive social work" designed to provide a stabilizing effect on society.[25] In their eyes stability, tradition, and class structure were indispensable requirements for a strong social system. In other words, the progressives were cultural traditionalists, bent on maintaining the best of their section's habits and values.

There was, however, a less conservative, less traditional side of southern progressivism. After all, the progressives were reformers. They were advocates of change. They were believers in the efficacy of social action, governmental intervention, and scientific knowledge. Even a cursory examination of their social thought, reform causes, organizations, campaigns, and leadership will suggest the impressive range of their endeavors and the fervor and commitment of their involvement. Many of these men and women were profoundly moved by social injustice and zealous in their efforts to ameliorate the plight of the weak and unfortunate. Though paternalistic, they believed, as one scholar has written of the educator James H. Kirkland, not only in "the stewardship of wealth" but also in "the stewardship of talent and energy."[26] Other reformers were less interested in social justice undertakings than in regulatory measures, developmental projects, and new public services. A large number of those who joined reform organizations or supported reform movements were primarily concerned with their own professions, businesses, and communities. Still, the notion of advancing the public good was widely endorsed; it was an ideal firmly woven into the fabric of progressivism. But above all, southern progressives wanted to define a more satisfactory concept of regional community and to create a new and more harmonious social balance for the South.

Progressivism in the South had a marked effect on the region's politics, social action, and social thought during the early twentieth century. This was true in large part because the progressives brought together in tolerable equipoise a number of assumptions and ideas about the nature and development of the South. There was room in this complex of ideas for material progress, efficiency, ethical standards, social order, a more vigorous regulatory state, social justice, public services, and especially the vision of a revitalized southern community. The progressives were able to effect a synthesis of the antithetical approaches of the Bourbons and Populists.[27] They attracted support from diverse social elements, including the section's civic-commercial elites and up-

[24]Brownell, *The Urban Ethos in the South*, 40.
[25]See, for example, Raymond H. Pulley, *Old Virginia Restored: An Interpretation of the Progressive Impulse, 1870–1930* (Charlottesville, Va., 1968), 132–51.
[26]See Timothy C. Jacobson, "Medical Center: A History of Science in Medicine" (unpublished manuscript in possession of its author), 13.
[27]George B. Tindall, *The Persistent Tradition in New South Politics* (Baton Rouge, 1975), pp. xii, 48–72.

wardly mobile urban groups. But southern progressivism also drew on the swirling protest of the 1890s, and agrarian radicalism flowed in a somewhat attenuated but distinct current into the politics of the progressive era, helping to account for the anticorporation sentiment, party insurgency, and morality-oriented campaigns that followed. In the early twentieth-century setting the progressives were able to function both as agents of modernization and as guardians of southern tradition.

The setting in which southern progressives operated presented them with a uniquely favorable opportunity for the creation of a broadly based social synthesis. The early twentieth century brought the South greater social and political stability, exciting economic prospects, and an exhilarating sense of new possibilities, along with an awareness on the part of many southerners of their own emergence as members of an increasingly important rank in society. In this milieu the progressives took the materials that lay around them and fashioned an inviting reform structure. They brought into this gestalt a broadened and humanized version of the New South creed, a component of agrarian tradition and rural uplift, a substantial part of the region's antitrust outlook, and a commitment to the protection of traditional values and patterns of life. For all their emphasis on interregional accord and national involvement, they frequently resorted to sectional appeals in their reform campaigns. Their success in developing a workable synthesis and a harmony of interests in behalf of their major reforms owed a great deal to politics. Relatively few of the progressives were professional politicians, but many of them were successful in working with political leaders, in helping construct reform coalitions, and in campaigning for popular support and legislative action. Southern progressives were inclined to think that reform was relative, that it could sometimes serve conservative functions, and that it should take place "within the framework of the established society."[28]

Southern progressivism's legacy was also important. Thus tradition and modernization, both encompassed in southern progressivism, strongly influenced the region's political culture during the 1920s. One aspect of southern progressivism looked toward intersectional accommodation, national involvement, and national solutions to regional problems, and most of those southerners who held this view welcomed the New Deal and later liberal administrations in Washington. More conservative and sectional-minded southerners were upset and increasingly alienated by this kind of national social action. Southern liberals themselves were, characteristically, cautious reformers. Keenly aware of the South's pressing social problems and of the many regional barriers to progress as well as the fragility of their own strength and resources, they were, in Gunnar Myrdal's words, "inclined to stress the need for patience

[28]The quoted phrase is from Carl N. Degler, *The Other South: Southern Dissenters in the Nineteenth Century* (New York, 1974), 368.

and to exalt the cautious approach, the slow change, the organic nature of social growth."[29] The reform tradition in the South survived in the antitrust and consumer protection politics of men such as Hugo L. Black, Claude Pepper, and Estes Kefauver.[30] Yet most southern liberals, like the South's political leaders generally, continued to emphasize the essential role of economic development in the rehabilitation of the region. They also continued to stress the need to broaden and unite the middle class in order to deal with contemporary social problems.

There were, as might be expected, inconsistencies and contradictions in the progressive synthesis. This goes far to explain the decline of the progressive balance following World War I, as well as the controversy that surrounded the activities of southern liberals in subsequent years. For one thing, the reformers underestimated the extent of the South's deficiencies. As Hastings H. Hart wrote after surveying Alabama's public facilities in 1918, "Notwithstanding the general fine spirit and the excellent work which most of those institutions are doing, I was met everywhere by the cry of poverty, insufficient appropriations and inadequate equipment."[31] The progressives also discovered that economic development did not automatically lead to social progress. Edwin Mims once remarked that he and other progressives had assumed that material progress, along with educational betterment sure to follow in its wake, would result in "freedom of opinion and action, real culture, and a critical intelligence applied to all problems." But progress at one point did not mean "progress at all points," and Mims singled out "a great mass of uneducated people" as one explanation.[32] As a matter of fact, the relationship between economic development and cultural continuity in the South was more complex than the progressives realized. If cultural change lagged behind the region's economic alteration, as seemed to be true at the time Mims wrote, later scholars sometimes explained the limited transformation of the southern economy in terms of cultural drags, including racial prejudice and segregation.[33] Progress and tradition were not easily reconciled. No matter what expedients he tried, one historian has said of a southern liberal who came to maturity during the progressive era, "the values underlying paternalism could not be reconciled with the modernization of southern society, nor could the goal of Americanization be coupled with the preservation of a distinctive regional identity."[34]

[29]Myrdal, with Richard Sterner and Arnold Rose, *An American Dilemma: The Negro Problem and Modern Democracy*, 2 vols. (New York, 1944), vol. 1, p. 470.

[30]See, for example, Richard E. McFadyen, "Estes Kefauver and the Tradition of Southern Progressivism," *Tenn. Hist. Quar.* 37 (Winter 1978): 430–43.

[31]Hart, *Social Problems of Alabama: A Study of the Social Institutions and Agencies of the State of Alabama as Related to Its War Activities Made at the Request of Governor Charles Henderson* (Montgomery, Ala., 1918), 22–23.

[32]Mims, "Why the South is Anti-Evolution," *World's Work* 50 (Sept. 1925): 548–52.

[33]See, for example, William H. Nicholls, *Southern Tradition and Regional Progress* (Chapel Hill, N.C., 1960).

[34]Singal, "Broadus Mitchell and the Persistence of New South Thought," 371.

Even so, the southern progressives were innovators. They were committed to the industrialization, economic development, and urbanization of the South. They promoted the modernization of their region's institutions, including more efficient government and the expansion of public services. They sought to integrate the South more fully into the economic and political life of the nation, and they were eager for southerners to play a more constructive role in national affairs. In this respect their ideas contrasted sharply with the critique of American material progress and the vision of an agrarian South contained in the collection of essays published in 1930 under the title *I'll Take My Stand*.[35]

In the final analysis, however, the progressives and their ideological descendants were no more prepared than were the agrarians to embrace "progress," if it meant rejecting southern tradition. William H. Nicholls, an economist interested in the effect of cultural factors on economic performance, later singled out what he regarded as the principal elements in the southern tradition: the persistence of agrarian values, the rigidity of the social structure, the undemocratic political structure, the weakness of social responsibility, and conformity of thought and behavior.[36] The progressives were critical of various aspects of this cultural complex, but at the same time they accepted in some degree and were partly responsible for every one of the regional characteristics identified by Nicholls. This becomes clear when one recalls the progressives' moderation as reformers, their nostalgia for rural virtues, their paternalistic and hierarchical view of society, their class consciousness, distrust of the masses, and acceptance of racial stereotypes, and their search for social consensus and social stability.

The passage of time did confirm some of the southern progressives' hopes and aspirations. The region's industrial and urban growth, the slow modernization of its institutions, and its increasing though frequently painful integration into national patterns of behavior were based at least in part on southern progressivism. But in certain other areas the progressive effort to reconcile progress and tradition became steadily more anachronistic, particularly in the realm of social control. This was true of the progressives' approach to racial reform. Pressures from outside the South, coalescing to force federal intervention, and the remarkable leadership of Martin Luther King, Jr., and other southern blacks brought the Second Reconstruction to culmination. Although southern progressivism may have conditioned an older generation of white southerners to accept drastic changes in race relations, it was the black freedom movement that ironically made the greatest southern contribution to progress in the field of civil rights.[37]

[35]Twelve Southerners, *I'll Take My Stand: The South and the Agrarian Tradition* (New York, 1930). Also see Louis D. Rubin, Jr., *The Wary Fugitives: Four Poets and the South* (Baton Rouge, 1978).

[36]Nicholls, *Southern Tradition and Regional Progress*, 17–153.

[37]See F. Garvin Davenport, Jr., *The Myth of Southern History: Historical Consciousness in Twentieth-Century Southern Literature* (Nashville, 1970), 186–98.

Whatever its limitations, contradictions, and failures, southern progressivism was perhaps the most significant venture in social reform undertaken thus far in the twentieth-century South. The progressives were the first southerners to make a concerted attempt to cope with social problems growing out of the modern industrialized and urbanized system. Convinced of the benefits to be derived from economic progress and modern institutions but still self-conscious defenders of southern values, they set out to reconcile progress and tradition. The spirit and energy they demonstrated were remarkable. Their achievements, under the circumstances, were impressive. Although many of their reforms were modest and even barren, the fundamental problems they identified and tried to remedy—the problems of a complex, differentiated, and segmented society—have continued to challenge and perplex southerners and other Americans ever since.

WHEN I FIRST BECAME INTERESTED in southern progressivism, many years ago, there were neither many readily available sources for its study nor an extensive scholarly literature devoted to its nature and impact. The situation has changed dramatically during the last two decades. State and local archives, university libraries, and other institutions throughout the South, in Washington, D.C., and in other parts of the country have undertaken the systematic collection of manuscript sources, newspaper files, public records, and printed materials concerned with southern history in the early twentieth century. That period has become the focus of great interest among historians, and the southern experience between the Populist revolt of the 1890s and the New Deal of the 1930s has been subjected to an impressive historiographical assault. This scholarly investigation shows no signs of slackening in the near future, as the continuing outpouring of books and articles makes clear.

So massive are the primary sources for the progressive era in the South and so far-reaching is the historical literature on southern progressivism that one might devote a lifetime to its study. This book, while the product of a long-sustained inquiry, represents a more modest endeavor. Although the study is based on extensive research in primary sources, it rests heavily upon the work of other scholars. It offers a synthesis and a tentative interpretation of social reform in the early twentieth-century South.

The commentary that follows is intended to suggest the broad dimensions of the research undertaken for this project. Since the notes identify all sources directly used in the study, no attempt is made here to provide a comprehensive listing of works consulted for the project. The purpose is to reveal the major types of materials used, to illustrate the nature of the large body of monographic scholarship, and to comment on the most significant historical contributions and interpretations.

MANUSCRIPTS

Most of the manuscript research for this study was devoted to the papers of southern political leaders. The letterbooks and official papers of southern governors during the progressive period were systematically examined in the various state libraries and archives. Few records exist for some governors, but for others, such as John M. Slaton of Georgia and Thomas M. Campbell of Texas, large and revealing collections of official documents have been preserved. Valuable papers of other southern political leaders, of social reformers, and of educators and intellectuals in this period are also available to the researcher. The principal manuscript materials used in this investigation are listed below. Important collections of several progressive governors have been acquired by university libraries. Among such collections consulted for this project were the papers of Napoleon B. Broward of Florida (University of Florida), Braxton B. Comer of Alabama (University of North Carolina), Jeff Davis and Charles Hillman Brough of Arkansas (University of Arkansas), and Oscar B. Colquitt of Texas (University of Texas).

A number of other manuscript holdings proved useful, including the following listed by state. *Alabama:* John H. Bankhead and William B. Bankhead (Alabama Department of Archives and History), Henry De Lamar Clayton (University of Alabama), and Oliver D. Street (University of Alabama). *Arkansas:* Harmon L. Remmel (University of Arkansas) and George B. Rose (Arkansas Historical Commission). *Florida:* James B. Hodges (University of Florida). *Georgia:* Thomas E. Watson (University of North Carolina). *Kentucky:* Augustus O. Stanley (University of Kentucky). *Louisiana:* John M. Parker (University of North Carolina). *North Carolina:* Josiah W. Bailey (Duke University), Henry Groves Connor (University of North Carolina), Josephus Daniels (University of North Carolina and Library of Congress), and John Bryan Grimes (University of North Carolina). *South Carolina:* William Watts Ball (Duke University) and Mendel L. Smith (University of South Carolina). *Tennessee:* Edward Ward Carmack (University of North Carolina and Tennessee Department of Archives and History) and Jacob McGavock Dickinson (Tennessee Department of Archives and History). *Texas:* James S. Hogg (University of Texas). *Virginia:* Allen Caperton Braxton (University of Virginia), John W. Daniel (University of Virginia and Duke University), John T. Ellyson (University of Virginia), Henry D. Flood (Library of Congress), and Henry St. George Tucker (University of North Carolina).

The Theodore Roosevelt and Woodrow Wilson collections, in the Manuscripts Division of the Library of Congress, are indispensable for the South's involvement in national politics during the first two decades of the twentieth century. The papers of several southern congressmen are notable for the light they throw on the Wilson era, including the collections of Alben W. Barkley (University of Kentucky), Albert Sidney Burleson (University of Texas), Edward J. Gay (Louisiana State University), Carter Glass (University of Virginia), James Hay (University of Virginia), Claude Kitchin (University of North Carolina), Ladislas Lazaro (Louisiana State University), Jeff: McLemore (University of Texas), Hoke Smith (University of Georgia), Oscar W.

Underwood (Alabama Department of Archives and History), and John Sharp Williams (Library of Congress).

Political and social currents in the early twentieth-century South are illuminated in the papers of William Garrott Brown (Duke University), James Calvin Hemphill (Duke University), Silas McBee (University of North Carolina), Thomas Nelson Page (Duke University), and Jesse F. Stallings (University of North Carolina). The Warren A. Candler Papers at Emory University throw light from a conservative perspective on southern politics as well as southern religion. The Walter Hines Page Papers at Harvard University, one of the most valuable collections for the period, is rich in its coverage of education, agriculture, and other aspects of southern reform. Among the best sources for the southern education movement are the papers of Edwin A. Alderman (University of Virginia), Eugene C. Branson (University of North Carolina), James H. Kirkland (Vanderbilt University), John J. McMahan (University of South Carolina), Samuel Chiles Mitchell (University of North Carolina and University of South Carolina), and Robert C. Ogden (Library of Congress).

The movement to restrict child labor in the South, as well as certain other reform causes, is illuminated in the papers of Alexander J. McKelway (Library of Congress) and Edgar Gardner Murphy (University of North Carolina). The Richmond P. Hobson Papers in the Library of Congress are valuable for the prohibition crusade. Information on the campaigns for woman suffrage and women's rights in the South is contained in the papers of the Breckinridge family (Library of Congress), Laura Clay (University of Kentucky), Judith Hyams Douglas (Louisiana State University), Rebecca Latimer Felton (University of Georgia), and Ethel Hutson (Tulane University). The progress of black southerners and developments in race relations are revealed in the collections of Oswald Garrison Villard (Harvard University) and Booker T. Washington (Library of Congress). The Committee on Interracial Cooperation Papers, located at Atlanta University, are useful for racial currents in the years immediately following the First World War. The papers of Benjamin Rice Lacy (North Carolina Department of Archives and History) throw light on politics and organized labor in the Old North State.

CONTEMPORARY PRINTED SOURCES

The *South Atlantic Quarterly* is an invaluable source for the study of progressive thought in the South. The *SAQ* published hundreds of articles during the years 1902–20 on education, industrialization, race relations, religion, social problems, and politics. In 1910, for example, the *Quarterly* carried more than a dozen articles pertaining to social reform in the South, on such topics as education, science, industry, good roads, conservation, and politics. *World's Work*, a monthly magazine published by Walter Hines Page in New York, was scarcely less interested in southern developments. During the years of Page's editorship, between 1900 and 1913, the journal carried numerous articles on education, agriculture, industrialization, and political affairs in the South. "The March of Events," a regular feature of the magazine, included many notes dealing with the South. The *Sewanee Review,* while emphasizing literary and cultural themes, is another important source for an understanding of southern progressivism. The *Review* occasionally published articles on race relations, economic issues, and politics during the period surveyed for this study (1898–1919). Several magazines published outside the South devoted a good deal of attention to southern matters. The *Nation* (1900–17), *Outlook* (1898–1916), and *Harper's Weekly* (1913–17) contain many items on southern blacks, race relations, child labor, peonage, and education. The *Survey* (1909–22) is very useful for such topics as child labor, public health, prison reform, race relations, conferences of social workers, and surveys of social legislation. Municipal reform, public health activities, the work of commercial clubs and women's organizations, and other civic developments are reported in the *American City* (1909–20) and the *National Municipal Review* (1912–20). Another important source is the *Annals of the American Academy of Political and Social Science* (1900–20), a bimonthly publication with useful supplements. It contains many articles on southern politics, race relations, state and municipal government, child labor, prohibition, and the like.

Although newspapers constitute an indispensable source for progressive campaigns, particularly at the local and state levels, it was impossible to carry out a systematic search of southern papers on a state-by-state basis for this study. I have attempted to use a few of the major journals published in the region and to sample others. The Atlanta *Constitution,* Atlanta *Journal,* and New York *Times* were carefully surveyed for the period beginning in the 1890s and extending into the 1920s. The Richmond *Times-Dispatch* (1905, 1908, 1911, 1913), Jacksonville *Florida Times-Union* (1907, 1909, 1912, 1914), and New Orleans *Times Democrat* (1904, 1906, 1910, 1912) were used on a selective basis. Among other journals examined less systematically were the Raleigh *News and Observer,* Columbia (S.C.) *State,* Macon (Ga.) *Telegraph,* Montgomery *Advertiser,* *Arkansas Gazette,* Nashville *Banner,* Nashville *Tennessean,* Memphis *Commercial Appeal,* Dallas *Morning News,* and Oklahoma City *Oklahoman.*

Annual proceedings and reports of various organizations and movements throw light on certain aspects of southern progressivism. One example is the *Proceedings* of the annual meeting of the National Municipal League for 1908 (in Pittsburgh) and 1910 (in Buffalo). Even more important are the addresses and reports contained in James E. McCulloch, ed., *The Call of the New South: Addresses Delivered at the Southern Sociological Congress, Nashville, Tennessee, May 7 to 10, 1912* (Nashville, 1912), and in the annual volumes published by the congress in 1913, 1914, 1915, 1918, and 1919. Several of the volumes in Julian A.C. Chandler, et al., eds., *The South in the Building of the*

Nation, 13 vols. (Richmond, 1909–13), contain information on southern life early in the twentieth century. A detailed treatment of the campaign for woman suffrage in the southern states, consisting of contemporary reports, is given in Ida Husted Harper, ed., *The History of Woman Suffrage*, vols. 5 and 6 (New York, 1922). Some use has been made of *The American Year Book: A Record of Events and Progress* for the years 1910 and 1915.

Contemporary analyses provide one of the best sources for social thought in the early twentieth-century South. Among the more instructive publications in this genre are Walter Hines Page, *The Rebuilding of Old Commonwealths* (New York, 1902); W.E. Burghardt Du Bois, *The Souls of Black Folk* (Chicago, 1903); Edgar Gardner Murphy, *Problems of the Present South* (New York, 1904), and *The Basis of Ascendancy: A Discussion of Certain Principles of Public Policy Involved in the Development of the Southern States* (New York, 1909); Philip A. Bruce, *The Rise of the New South* (Philadelphia, 1905); Alfred H. Stone, *Studies in the American Race Problem* (New York, 1908); Ray Stannard Baker, *Following the Color Line: An Account of Negro Citizenship in the American Democracy* (New York, 1908); Charles S. Barrett, *The Mission, History and Times of the Farmers' Union* (Nashville, 1909); William Archer, *Through Afro-America: An English Reading of the Race Problem* (London, 1910); William Garrott Brown, *The New Politics, and Other Papers* (Boston, 1914); Lily H. Hammond, *In Black and White: An Interpretation of Southern Life* (New York, 1914); General Education Board, *The General Education Board: An Account of Its Activities, 1902–1914* (New York, 1915); Victor I. Masters, *Country Church in the South: Arranged to Meet the Needs of Mission Study Classes and Also of the General Reader* (2d ed., Atlanta, 1917); Hastings H. Hart, *The War Program of the State of South Carolina: A Report Prepared at the Request of Governor Richard I. Manning, the State Council of Defense and the State Board of Charities and Corrections* (New York, 1918); and Emmett J. Scott, *Negro Migration During the War* (New York, 1920).

Two documentary series have been of central importance to this study: Arthur S. Link and associates, eds., *The Papers of Woodrow Wilson* (Princeton, N.J., 1966–), now into Wilson's second administration, and Louis R. Harlan and others, eds., *The Booker T. Washington Papers* (Urbana, Ill., 1972–), which is nearing completion. Other helpful documentary works include Aubrey Lee Brooks and Hugh Talmage Lefler, eds., *The Papers of Walter Clark, 1857–1924*, 2 vols. (Chapel Hill, N.C., 1948–50); Burton J. Hendrick, *The Training of an American: The Earlier Life and Letters of Walter H. Page, 1855–1913* (Boston, 1928); and Robert C. Cotner, ed., *Addresses and State Papers of James Stephen Hogg* (Austin, Tex., 1951).

Numerous memoirs and personal accounts deal with this period, a few of which are valuable historical documents. Among the most illuminating for southern progressivism are Everett Robert Boyce, ed., *The Unwanted Boy: The Autobiography of Governor Ben W. Hooper* (Knoxville, 1963); Aubrey

Lee Brooks, *A Southern Lawyer: Fifty Years at the Bar* (Chapel Hill, N.C., 1950); E. David Cronon, ed., *The Cabinet Diaries of Josephus Daniels, 1913–1921* (Lincoln, Nebr., 1963); Josephus Daniels, *Editor in Politics* (Chapel Hill, N.C., 1941) and *The Wilson Era: Years of Peace, 1910–1917* (Chapel Hill, N.C., 1944); Katherine DuPre Lumpkin, *The Making of a Southerner* (New York, 1947); Samuel Chiles Mitchell, "An Aftermath of Appomattox: A Memoir" (unpublished manuscript, South Caroliniana Library); Clarence Hamilton Poe, *My First 80 Years* (Chapel Hill, N.C., 1963); *Washington Wife: Journal of Ellen Maury Slayden from 1897–1919* (New York, 1963); Henry Nelson Snyder, *An Educational Odyssey* (Nashville, 1947); Richard L. Watson, Jr., ed., *Bishop Cannon's Own Story: Life as I Have Seen It* (Durham, N.C., 1955).

GENERAL STUDIES

Scholarly literature on southern progressivism began to appear as early as 1946, when Arthur S. Link published a pioneering article on "The Progressive Movement in the South, 1870–1914," *N.C. Hist. Rev.* 23 (Apr. 1946): 172–95. Link provided evidence to show that the southern states were the scene of "a far-reaching progressive movement." A fuller treatment of reform in the early twentieth-century South appeared five years later with the publication of C. Vann Woodward's *Origins of the New South, 1877–1913* (Baton Rouge, 1951). In a chapter entitled "Progressivism—For Whites Only" and elsewhere in his book, Woodward described the various manifestations of progressivism in the South, which he characterized as "a pretty strictly indigenous growth, touched lightly here and there by cross-fertilization from the West." Although Link and Woodward viewed progressivism in the South as an outgrowth of the agrarian upheaval of the 1890s, they emphasized its urban and middle-class character.

A decade and a half elapsed before another broad interpretation of southern progressivism appeared. It was contained in George Brown Tindall's *The Emergence of the New South, 1913–1945* (Baton Rouge, 1967). Focusing on the Wilson era and after, Tindall described southern progressivism as "an amalgam of agrarian radicalism, business regulation, good government, and urban social justice reforms." He dealt with the effects of World War I on this reformism and made a notable contribution in analyzing the remnants of the region's progressivism in the 1920s. Hugh C. Bailey's *Liberalism in the New South: Southern Social Reformers and the Progressive Movement* (Coral Gables, Fla., 1969), while informative, is less impressive as an interpretation of southern progressivism as a regional phenomenon. A more vigorous and challenging interpretation was advanced by Jack Temple Kirby in *Darkness at the Dawning: Race and Reform in the Progressive South* (Philadelphia, 1972). Concentrating on the interaction of the race issue with reform in the South, Kirby argues that "the great race settlement of 1890–1910"—black disfranchisement and segregation—was itself the seminal "progressive" reform of the period. Equally provocative is the thesis advanced by George B. Tindall in *The Persistent Tradition in New South Politics* (Baton Rouge, 1975). In a reconsideration of southern Bourbons, Populists, and progressives, Tindall concluded that the progressives were the "legitimate heirs of the Bourbons." They developed "a synthesis which governed southern politics through the first half of the twentieth century."

Several interpretive state studies offer appraisals of southern progressives. The oldest of these is Albert D. Kirwan's *Revolt of the Rednecks: Mississippi Politics, 1876–1925* (Lexington, Ky., 1951), a revealing analysis of the complicated struggle for political power in a social context of class, race, and party. Kirwan describes the long conflict that resulted in the triumph of the "wool hat boys" early in the twentieth century and their control of Mississippi politics for almost two decades after 1903. Unlike Kirwan's interpretation of agrarian reform in Mississippi, Raymond H. Pulley's *Old Virginia Restored: An Interpretation of the Progressive Impulse, 1870–1930* (Charlottesville, Va., 1968) portrays progressivism in the Old Dominion as "a direct reaction" against populism. Pulley's provocative study emphasizes "the conserving tendencies of progressivism" and the effort "to resurrect and rebuild the Old Virginia system of controls over society and politics." Allen W. Moger's *Virginia: Bourbonism to Byrd, 1870–1925* (Charlottesville, Va., 1968) is less interpretive and less concerned with progressivism than Pulley's *Old Virginia Restored,* but it is noteworthy for its treatment of Virginia politics in the progressive era. *Populism to Progressivism in Alabama* (Princeton, N.J., 1969), by Sheldon Hackney, is perhaps the most significant analysis of progressivism in a southern state published thus far. Hackney's work is distinguished not only by its analysis of the progressive coalition in Alabama but also by its exploration of the nature of and the relationship between populism and progressivism in that state. Progressivism, the author concludes, was an alternative to populism; it represented "a substantially different reaction by a separate set of men to the same enemy Populism faced—the dominant industrial wing of the Democratic Party."

The late nineteenth-century background of southern progressivism is made clearer by several recent state studies. Alwyn Barr, in *Reconstruction to Reform: Texas Politics, 1876–1906* (Austin, Tex., 1971), finds considerable continuity between Texas politics in the 1890s and twentieth-century progressivism. Barr also stresses the flexibility and adaptability of the Democratic party in Texas, the consequences of new election laws adopted early in the twentieth century, and the role of organizations and pressure groups that appeared about the turn of the century. Another important state study is William Ivy Hair's *Bourbonism and Agrarian Protest: Louisiana Politics, 1877–1900* (Baton Rouge, 1969), a balanced treatment of "a repressive Bourbon oligarchy" and "impotent agrarian reformers" in the Pelican State. Roger L. Hart's revisionist work, *Redeemers, Bourbons, & Populists: Tennessee, 1870–1896* (Baton Rouge, 1975), minimizes the significance of economic interests and emphasizes "a status-anxiety framework of explanation" in analyzing late nineteenth-century Tennessee politics. By contrast, William Warren Rogers, *The One-Gallused Rebellion: Agrarianism in Alabama, 1865–1896* (Baton Rouge, 1970), reasserts the importance of economic problems in that state as well as the positive, rational goals of the agrarian reformers in Alabama. Among other state political histories that survey this period are William J. Cooper, *The Conservative Regime: South Carolina, 1877–1890* (Baltimore, 1968); Edward C. Williamson, *Florida Politics in the Gilded Age, 1877–1893* (Gainesville, Fla., 1976); and Danney Goble, *Progressive Oklahoma: The Making of a New Kind of State* (Norman, Okla., 1980). Cooper's volume is helpful in understanding the relationship between Bourbonism, agrarian reformism, and the Tillman movement in South Carolina. Finally, Jonathan M. Wiener, in *Social Origins of the New South: Alabama, 1860–1885* (Baton Rouge, 1978), and Dwight B. Billings, Jr., in *Planters and the Making of a "New South": Class, Politics, and Development in North Carolina, 1865–1900* (Chapel Hill, N.C., 1979), seek to explain the process of modernization and argue that the upper classes headed by the old landed elite imposed an industrial society on Alabama and North Carolina.

The historiography of southern progressivism includes a large number of valuable unpublished state studies. These monographs, along with certain of the published works already mentioned in this essay, are important sources for the content of southern progressivism. The most impressive of these studies is Joseph Flake Steelman, "The Progressive Era in North Carolina, 1884–1917" (Ph.D. diss., Univ. of North Carolina, 1955). Progressivism in other states is considered in James Aubrey Tinsley, "The Progressive Movement in Texas" (Ph.D. diss., Univ. of Wisconsin, 1953); Charles Granville Hamilton, "Mississippi Politics in the Progressive Era, 1904–1920" (Ph.D. diss., Vanderbilt Univ., 1958); Alton DuMar Jones, "Progressivism in Georgia, 1898–1918" (Ph.D. diss., Emory Univ., 1963); David Alan Harris, "Racists and Reformers: A Study of Progressivism in Alabama, 1896–1911" (Ph.D. diss., Univ. of North Carolina, 1967); Matthew James Schott, "John M. Parker of Louisiana and the Varieties of American Progressivism" (Ph.D. diss., Vanderbilt Univ., 1969); Lester M. Salamon, "Protest, Politics, and Modernization in the American South: Mississippi as a 'Developing Society'" (Ph.D. diss., Harvard Univ., 1971); and J. Michael Shahan, "Reform and Politics in Tennessee, 1906–1914" (Ph.D. diss., Vanderbilt Univ., 1981). Two other unpublished studies are useful for their comprehensive treatment of party politics at the state level during this period: Herman L. Horn, "The Growth and Development of the Democratic Party in Virginia Since 1890" (Ph.D. diss., Duke Univ., 1949), and James Ralph Scales, "Political History of Oklahoma, 1907–1949" (Ph.D. diss., Univ. of Oklahoma, 1949).

A few specialized studies are important for the broader implications of their account of particular reform movements at the state level. Thus James F. Doster's monograph, *Railroads in Alabama Politics, 1875–1914* (University, Ala., 1957), reveals the significant role of the campaigns for railroad regulation in bringing Alabama progressivism into focus. *Prohibition and Politics: Turbulent Decades in Tennessee, 1885–1920* (Knoxville, 1965), by Paul E. Isaac, illuminates party politics and social reform efforts in the Volunteer State. Lewis L. Gould, *Progressives and Prohibitionists: Texas Democrats in the Wilson Era* (Austin, Tex., 1973), is virtually alone in providing a comprehensive treatment of reform politics in a southern state during the latter part of the progressive era. Gordon B. McKinney's *Southern Mountain Republicans, 1865–1900: Politics and the Appalachian Community* (Chapel Hill, N.C., 1978) examines the origins of Appalachian Republicanism and follows the course of the GOP to the turn of the century in Virginia, West Virginia, North Carolina, Tennessee, and Kentucky. James R. Green's *Grass-Roots Socialism: Radical Movements in the Southwest, 1895–1943* (Baton Rouge, 1978) offers a revealing perspective for an examination of progressivism in Texas, Oklahoma, Louisiana, and Arkansas. Although Green finds a close relationship between populism and socialism in the Southwest, he concludes that the two movements represented "significantly different constituencies on the basis of rather different ideologies."

Another helpful source for reform politics in the individual southern states during the progressive period is a shelf of biographies. Several of these biographical studies are concerned with political leadership and the coalescence of progressivism in particular states. These include William E. Larsen, *Montague of Virginia: The Making of a Southern Progressive* (Baton Rouge, 1965); Oliver H. Orr, Jr., *Charles Brantley Aycock* (Chapel Hill, N.C., 1961); Samuel Proctor, *Napoleon Bonaparte Broward: Florida's Fighting Democrat* (Gainesville, Fla., 1950); William F. Holmes, *The White Chief: James Kimble Vardaman* (Baton Rouge, 1970); and Dewey W. Grantham, *Hoke Smith and the Politics of the New South* (Baton Rouge, 1958). Other political biographies that deal with aspects of southern progressivism are Henry Clifton Ferrell, Jr., "Claude A. Swanson of Virginia" (Ph.D. diss., Univ. of Virginia, 1964); Jack Temple Kirby, *Westmoreland Davis: Virginia Planter-Politician, 1859–1942* (Charlottesville, Va., 1968); Charlotte Jean Shelton, "William Atkinson Jones, 1849–1918: Independent Democracy in Gilded Age Virginia" (Ph.D. diss., Univ. of Virginia, 1980); Joseph L. Morrison, *Josephus Daniels Says . . . . : An Editor's Political Odyssey from Bryan to Wilson and F.D.R., 1894–1913* (Chapel Hill, N.C., 1962); Robert Milton Burts, *Richard Irvine Manning and the Progressive Movement in South Carolina* (Columbia, S.C., 1974); Wayne Flynt, *Duncan Upshaw Fletcher: Dixie's Reluctant Progressive* (Tallahassee, 1971), and *Cracker Messiah: Governor Sidney J. Catts of Florida* (Baton Rouge, 1977); Edward Everett Dale and James D. Morrison,

Pioneer Judge: The Life of Robert Lee Williams (Cedar Rapids, Iowa, 1958); and Keith L. Bryant, Jr., *Alfalfa Bill Murray* (Norman, Okla., 1968).

REGULATION AND SOCIAL CONTROL

The scholarly writings on southern blacks, race relations, and disfrachisement in the late nineteenth and early twentieth centuries have reached staggering proportions. Among the more significant works that analyze racial ideas and attitudes during this period are Thomas F. Gossett, *Race: The History of an Idea in America* (Dallas, 1963); Rayford W. Logan, *The Negro in American Life and Thought: The Nadir, 1877–1901* (New York, 1954); Idus A. Newby, *Jim Crow's Defense: Anti-Negro Thought in America, 1900–1930* (Baton Rouge, 1965); Claude H. Nolen, *The Negro's Image in the South: The Anatomy of White Supremacy* (Lexington, Ky., 1967); and Lawrence J. Friedman, *The White Savage: Racial Fantasies in the Postbellum South* (Englewood Cliffs, N.J., 1970). C. Vann Woodward's *The Strange Career of Jim Crow* (2d rev. ed., New York, 1966) illuminates the complexities of the shifting racial scene in the South and other parts of the country during the progressive era. *Negro Thought in America, 1880–1915: Racial Ideologies in the Age of Booker T. Washington* (Ann Arbor, Mich., 1963), by August Meier, is indispensable for that subject. Northern reactions to southern initiatives in race relations, among other things, are revealingly explored by George M. Fredrickson, *The Black Image in the White Mind: The Debate on Afro-American Character and Destiny, 1817–1914* (New York, 1971), and James M. McPherson, *The Abolitionist Legacy: From Reconstruction to the NAACP* (Princeton, N.J., 1975). Jack Temple Kirby's *Darkness at the Dawning,* mentioned above, is a suggestive consideration of the interaction of race and reform in the early twentieth-century South.

Negro disfranchisement is analyzed anew by J. Morgan Kousser in *The Shaping of Southern Politics: Suffrage Restriction and the Establishment of the One-Party South, 1880–1910* (New Haven, Conn., 1974). A comprehensive and critical reevaluation of the disfranchisement campaigns and legislation, this work also advances a provocative interpretation of the effect of suffrage limitation on the politics and governance of the southern states in later years. Two older books are still useful for certain aspects of the disfranchisement movement: Paul Lewinson, *Race, Class & Party: A History of Negro Suffrage and White Politics in the South* (New York, 1932), and William Alexander Mabry, *Studies in the Disfranchisement of the Negro in the South* (Durham, N.C., 1938). Among the best state studies of suffrage restriction are George B. Tindall, *South Carolina Negroes, 1877–1900* (Columbia, S.C., 1952); Allie Bayne Windham Webb, "A History of Negro Voting in Louisiana, 1877–1906" (Ph.D. diss., Louisiana State Univ., 1962); Helen G. Edmonds, *The Negro and Fusion Politics in North Carolina, 1894–1901* (Chapel Hill, N.C.,

1951); Malcolm Cook McMillan, *Constitutional Development in Alabama, 1798–1901: A Study in Politics, the Negro, and Sectionalism* (Chapel Hill, N.C., 1955); Ralph Clipman McDanel, *The Virginia Constitutional Convention of 1901–1902* (Baltimore, 1928); and Charles E. Wynes, *Race Relations in Virginia, 1870–1902* (Charlottesville, Va., 1961). One of the disfranchising devices is discussed in Frederic D. Ogden, *The Poll Tax in the South* (University, Ala., 1958).

The rising walls of Jim Crow are described in several books and numerous articles on individual states. The more valuable state studies include John Dittmer, *Black Georgia in the Progressive Era, 1900–1920* (Urbana, Ill, 1977); Idus A. Newby, *Black Carolinians: A History of Blacks in South Carolina from 1895 to 1968* (Columbia, S.C., 1973); Andrew Buni, *The Negro in Virginia Politics, 1902–1965* (Charlottesville, Va., 1967); and Lester C. Lamon, *Black Tennesseans, 1900–1930* (Knoxville, 1977).

A comprehensive and authoritative treatment of southern penal conditions and penal reform in the late nineteenth and early twentieth centuries is provided by Hilda Jane Zimmerman, "Penal Systems and Penal Reforms in the South Since the Civil War" (Ph.D. diss., Univ. of North Carolina, 1947), and "The Penal Reform Movement in the South during the Progressive Era, 1890–1917," *JSH* 17 (Nov. 1951): 462–92. Two brief but useful regional interpretations are Blake McKelvey, "A Half Century of Southern Penal Exploitation," *Social Forces* 13 (Oct. 1934): 112–23, and Fletcher Melvin Green, "Some Aspects of the Convict Lease System in the Southern States," in Green, ed., *Essays in Southern History Presented to Joseph Gregoire de Roulhac Hamilton . . .* (Chapel Hill, N.C., 1949), 112–23. Mark T. Carleton's *Politics and Punishment: A History of the Louisiana State Penal System* (Baton Rouge, 1971) is an exemplary state study. Most of the general works cited earlier in this essay devote some attention to penal conditions as well as other reform movements manifested in southern progressivism. For other specialized studies, see Malcolm C. Moos, *State Penal Administration in Alabama* (University, Ala., 1942); Jesse Crawford Crowe, "Agitation for Penal Reform in Tennessee, 1870–1900" (Ph.D. diss., Vanderbilt Univ., 1954); Thomas L. Baxley, "Prison Reforms during the Donaghey Administration," *Ark. Hist. Quar.* 22 (Spring 1963): 76–84; Robert G. Crawford, "Degradation by Design: Punishment in Kentucky Penitentiaries," *Border States: Journal of the Kentucky-Tennessee American Studies Association* 1 (1973): 72–84; and A. Elizabeth Taylor, "The Convict Lease System in Georgia, 1866–1908" (M.A. thesis, Univ. of North Carolina, 1940).

Use of convicts in road construction and other public work is illustrated in Jesse F. Steiner and Roy M. Brown, *The North Carolina Chain Gang: A Study of County Convict Road Work* (Chapel Hill, N.C., 1927), and Carl V. Harris, "Reforms in Government Control of Negroes in Birmingham, Alabama, 1890–1920," *JSH* 38 (Nov. 1972): 567–600. Pete Daniel's scholarly study of peonage, *The Shadow of Slavery: Peonage in the South, 1901–1969* (Urbana, Ill, 1972), concentrates on Alabama, Florida, and Georgia in the early twentieth century. Forced black labor is also examined in a useful essay by William Cohen, "Negro Involuntary Servitude in the South, 1865–1940: A Preliminary Analysis," *JSH* 42 (Feb. 1976): 31–60.

The drive to regulate railroads and other large corporations in the South should be approached within the larger context of national attitudes and policy. Several scholarly works throw light on the national scene and the South's involvement in efforts to regulate big business: Hans B. Thorelli, *The Federal Antitrust Policy: Origination of an American Tradition* (Baltimore, 1955); Robert H. Wiebe, *Businessmen and Reform: A Study of The Progressive Movement* (Cambridge, Mass., 1962); Gabriel Kolko, *Railroads and Regulation, 1877–1916* (Princeton, N.J., 1965); and Louis Galambos, with the assistance of Barbara Barrow Spence, *The Public Image of Big Business in America, 1880–1940: A Quantitative Study in Social Change* (Baltimore, 1975). Railroad regulation as a political issue and reform rallying point is cogently described in Woodward's *Origins of the New South*. An older work by Maxwell Ferguson, *State Regulation of Railroads in the South*, previously cited, is still valuable. The complexities of southern freight rates are made understandable by David M. Potter, "The Historical Development of Eastern-Southern Freight Rate Relationships," *Law and Contemporary Problems* 12 (Summer 1947): 416–48, and William H. Joubert, *Southern Freight Rates in Transition* (Gainesville, Fla., 1949).

The best state study is James F. Doster, *Railroads in Alabama Politics*, mentioned above. Doster is notably successful in showing the relationship between railroad regulation and reform politics in Alabama. The previously cited studies of progressivism in North Carolina and Texas by Joseph F. Steelman and James A. Tinsley, respectively, are also helpful in this respect. Two other significant monographs are Albert Neely Sanders, "State Regulation of Public Utilities by South Carolina, 1879–1935" (Ph.D. diss., Univ. of North Carolina, 1956), and Robert Lewis Peterson, "State Regulation of Railroads in Texas, 1836–1920" (Ph.D. diss., Univ. of Texas, 1960). Other examples of business regulation in the southern states are provided by James A. Tinsley, "Texas Progressives and Insurance Regulation," *Southwestern Soc. Sci. Quar.* 36 (Dec. 1955): 237–47; Morton Keller, *The Life Insurance Enterprise, 1885–1910: A Study in the Limits of Corporate Power* (Cambridge, Mass., 1963); and Cedric B. Cowing, *Populists, Plungers, and Progressives: A Social History of Stock and Commodity Speculation, 1890–1936* (Princeton, N.J., 1965).

Prohibition as a manifestation of progressivism in the United States is well described by James H. Timberlake in *Prohibition and the Progressive Movement, 1900–1920* (Cambridge, Mass., 1963). Two other general studies are helpful in understanding prohibition in the South: Andrew Sinclair, *Era of*

Excess: A Social History of the Prohibition Movement (New York, 1964), and Joseph R. Gusfield, *Symbolic Crusade: Status Politics and the American Temperance Movement* (Urbana, Ill., 1963). The latter, a sociological interpretation stressing conflict between rival social systems, cultures, and status groups, is suggestive in terms of an approach to prohibition in the South as an instrument of social control. Robert A. Hohner throws light on a central question in an essay entitled "The Prohibitionists: Who Were They?" *SAQ* 68 (Autumn 1969): 491–505.

Although there is not a good history of the modern prohibition movement in the South, there are several first-rate state studies. Two of these are especially important for their analysis of prohibition as an issue in state politics during the progressive period: Isaac, *Prohibition and Politics: Turbulent Decades in Tennessee*, and Gould, *Progressives and Prohibitionists: Texas Democrats in the Wilson Era*, cited earlier in this essay. Among other useful state histories are Henry C. Ferrell, Jr., "Prohibition, Reform, and Politics in Virginia, 1895–1916," in *East Carolina College Publications in History*, vol. 3: *Studies in the History of the South, 1875–1922* (Greenville, N.C., 1966), 175–242; C.C. Pearson and J. Edwin Hendricks, *Liquor and Anti-Liquor in Virginia, 1619–1919* (Durham, N.C., 1967); Daniel Jay Whitener, *Prohibition in North Carolina, 1715–1945* (Chapel Hill, N.C., 1945); John Evans Eubanks, *Ben Tillman's Baby: The Dispensary System of South Carolina, 1892–1915* (Augusta, Ga., 1950); James Benson Sellers, *The Prohibition Movement in Alabama, 1702 to 1943* (Chapel Hill, N.C., 1943); George Murrell Hunt, "A History of the Prohibition Movement in Arkansas" (M.A. thesis, Univ. of Arkansas, 1933); Seth Shepard McKay, *Texas Politics, 1906–1944, With Special Reference to the German Counties* (Lubbock, Tex., 1952); and Jimmie Lewis Franklin, *Born Sober: Prohibition in Oklahoma, 1907–1959* (Norman, Okla., 1971).

SOCIAL JUSTICE

Organized efforts to promote social justice in the South during the early years of the twentieth century were strongly influenced by religion. The relationship between social reform and the major churches has received a good deal of scholarly attention. The best general work in this connection is Kenneth K. Bailey, *Southern White Protestantism in the Twentieth Century* (New York, 1964). Samuel S. Hill, Jr., *Southern Churches in Crisis* (New York, 1967), is also useful, though not directly concerned with the progressive era. Two older works deal with the rural church in the early twentieth-century South: Masters, *Country Church in the South*, cited above, and Edmund deS. Brunner, *Church Life in the Rural South: A Study of the Opportunity of Protestantism Based upon Data From Seventy Counties* (New York, 1923). Important studies of particular denominations include Hunter Dickinson Farish, *The Circuit Rider*

Dismounts: A Social History of Southern Methodists, 1865–1900 (Richmond, Va., 1938); Rufus B. Spain, *At Ease in Zion: A Social History of Southern Baptists, 1865–1900* (Nashville, 1967); John Lee Eighmy, *Churches in Cultural Captivity: A History of the Social Attitudes of Southern Baptists* (Knoxville, 1972); Henry Y. Warnock, "Moderate Racial Thought and Attitudes of Southern Baptists and Methodists, 1900–1921" (Ph.D. diss., Northwestern Univ., 1963); Wayne Flynt, "Dissent in Zion: Alabama Baptists and Social Issues, 1900–1914," *JSH* 35 (Nov. 1969): 523–42; and Flynt, "Southern Baptists and Reform: 1890–1920," *Baptist History and Heritage* 7 (Oct. 1972): 211–24. The profound influence of racism upon religion in the South is shown in H. Shelton Smith, *In His Image, But . . . Racism in Southern Religion, 1780–1910* (Durham, N.C., 1972). Charles Reagan Wilson's *Baptized in Blood: The Religion of the Lost Cause, 1865–1920* (Athens, Ga., 1980) is an interesting study of civil religion that illuminates the relationship between the South's Christian churches and its secular culture.

The role of the church was vitally important in developing social reformism among southern women, as is evident in Noreen Dunn Tatum, *A Crown of Service: A Story of Woman's Work in the Methodist Episcopal Church, South, from 1878–1940* (Nashville, 1960), and Anne Firor Scott, "Women, Religion, and Social Change in the South, 1830–1930," in Samuel S. Hill, Jr., et al., *Religion and the Solid South* (Nashville, 1972), 92–121. Two other publications by Anne Scott deal more broadly with the role of southern women in social justice activities during the progressive era: "The 'New Woman' in the New South," *SAQ* 61 (Autumn 1962): 473–83, and *The Southern Lady: From Pedestal to Politics, 1830–1930* (Chicago, 1970). For helpful studies of individual social reformers, see Sophonisba Preston Breckinridge, *Madeline McDowell Breckinridge: A Leader in the New South* (Chicago, 1921); John E. Talmadge, *Rebecca Latimer Felton: Nine Stormy Decades* (Athens, Ga., 1960); Anne Gary Pannell and Dorothea E. Wyatt, *Julia S. Tutwiler and Social Progress in Alabama* (University, Ala., 1961); and Edward T. James and others, eds., *Notable American Women, 1607–1950: A Biographical Dictionary,* 3 vols. (Cambridge, Mass., 1971).

Woman suffrage campaigns in the South have been studied intensively by A. Elizabeth Taylor. She is the author of *The Woman Suffrage Movement in Tennessee* (New York, 1957) and a series of valuable articles on other southern states. Another outstanding monograph is Paul E. Fuller's *Laura Clay and the Woman's Rights Movement* (Lexington, Ky., 1975). Other aspects of the feminist movement are dealt with by Kenneth R. Johnson in "The Woman Suffrage Movement in Florida" (Ph.D. diss., Florida State Univ., 1966) and "Kate Gordon and the Woman-Suffrage Movement in the South," *JSH* 38 (Aug. 1972): 365–92. Andrew Sinclair's *The Emancipation of the American Woman* (New York, 1965) is a useful general treatment. The influence of the national suffrage movement on the South and vice versa is analyzed by Aileen

S. Kraditor, *The Ideas of the Woman Suffrage Movement, 1890–1920* (New York, 1965). She argues that the woman suffrage movement in the United States "was essentially from beginning to end a struggle of white, native-born, middle-class women for the right to participate more fully in the public affairs of a society the basic structure of which they accepted."

The growth of social criticism in the South in the late nineteenth and early twentieth centuries is revealed by Bruce Clayton, *The Savage Ideal: Intolerance and Intellectual Leadership in the South, 1890–1914* (Baltimore, 1972); William Baskerville Hamilton, "Fifty Years of Liberalism and Learning," in Hamilton, ed., *Fifty Years of the South Atlantic Quarterly* (Durham, N.C., 1952), 3–27; and Herbert J. Doherty, Jr., "Voices of Protest from the New South, 1875–1910," *Miss. Valley Hist. Rev.* 42 (June 1955): 45–66. Intellectual background is supplied by Carl N. Degler's *The Other South: Southern Dissenters in the Nineteenth Century* (New York, 1974), which emphasizes the continuity of the South's self-consciousness and the comparative scarcity of its dissenters, and Paul M. Gaston's *The New South Creed: A Study in Southern Mythmaking* (New York, 1970), which points up the mythic qualities of the New South creed and suggests its instrumental role in the social thought and politics of the modern South. Wayne Mixon, *Southern Writers and the New South Movement, 1865–1913* (Chapel Hill, N.C., 1980), is a good analysis of the literary side of the New South movement. A perspicacious biography by John Milton Cooper, Jr., *Walter Hines Page: The Southerner as American, 1855–1918* (Chapel Hill, N.C., 1977), limns the career of the best-known southern expatriate and intersectional ambassador.

Child labor reform in the South is covered in a solid study by Elizabeth H. Davidson, *Child Labor Legislation in the Southern Textile States* (Chapel Hill, N.C., 1939). The activities of two of the preeminent child labor reformers are described in Hugh C. Bailey, *Edgar Gardner Murphy: Gentle Progressive* (Coral Gables, Fla., 1968), and Betty Jane Brandon, "Alexander Jeffrey McKelway: Statesman of the New Order" (Ph.D. diss., Univ. of North Carolina, 1969). Child labor reform in particular states is dealt with in many of the general studies cited above and in a number of scholarly articles such as "The 1913 Campaign for Child Labor in Florida," *Fla. Hist. Quar.* 35 (Jan. 1957): 233–40, by Emily Howard Atkins, and "Kate Barnard, Organized Labor, and Social Justice in Oklahoma During the Progressive Era," *JSH* 35 (May 1969): 145–64, by Keith L. Bryant, Jr. Two new social classes are examined in David Lee Carlton's "Mill and Town: The Cotton Mill Workers and the Middle Class in South Carolina, 1880–1920" (Ph.D. diss., Yale Univ., 1977). The author is perceptive in his treatment of the response of the middle class to the "mill problem." He emphasizes the conservative, paternalistic, and self-interested character of this middle-class reform. Two other pertinent studies are broader in focus: Walter I. Trattner, *Crusade for the Children: A History of the National Child Labor Committee and Child Labor Reform in*

America (Chicago, 1970), and Stephen B. Wood, *Constitutional Politics in the Progressive Era: Child Labor and the Law* (Chicago, 1968).

The southern crusade for the support of education is described by Charles William Dabney, one of the movement's leaders, in an informative but uncritical account entitled *Universal Education in the South,* vol. 2: *The Southern Education Movement* (Chapel Hill, N.C., 1936). There are several good biographies of the region's educational reformers, including Dumas Malone, *Edwin A. Alderman: A Biography* (New York, 1940); Charles Lee Lewis, *Philander Priestley Claxton: Crusader for Public Education* (Knoxville, 1948); Rose Howell Holder, *McIver of North Carolina* (Chapel Hill, N.C., 1957); and Willard B. Gatewood, Jr., *Eugene Clyde Brooks: Educator and Public Servant* (Durham, N.C., 1960). State studies of education are numerous but often of limited value to the student of southern progressivism. Three exceptions are Andrew David Holt, *The Struggle for a State System of Public Schools in Tennessee, 1903–1936* (New York, 1938); Frank L. McVey, *The Gates Open Slowly: A History of Education in Kentucky* (Lexington, Ky., 1949); and Dorothy Orr, *A History of Education in Georgia* (Chapel Hill, N.C., 1950). Lawrence A. Cremin's *The Transformation of the School: Progressivism in American Education, 1876–1957* (New York, 1961) provides a national frame for the analysis of regional reform in education.

Northern philanthropy in the field of southern education is discussed in *The General Education Board: An Account of Its Activities, 1902–1914,* a chronicle by the GEB cited above; Raymond B. Fosdick, *Adventure in Giving: The Story of the General Education Board, a Foundation Established by John D. Rockefeller* (New York, 1962); Ullin Whitney Leavell, *Philanthropy in Negro Education* (Nashville, 1930); and Henry Snyder Enck, "The Burden Borne: Northern White Philanthropy and Southern Black Industrial Education, 1900–1915" (Ph.D. diss., Univ. of Cincinnati, 1970). Two useful studies of educational trends among southern blacks in this period are Horace Mann Bond, *Negro Education in Alabama: A Study in Cotton and Steel* (Washington, D.C., 1939), and Henry Allen Bullock, *A History of Negro Education in the South: From 1619 to the Present* (Cambridge, Mass., 1967). The widespread discrimination by southern white authorities against blacks in the allocation of educational funds, and the acquiescence of northern philanthropists in the emphasis on the development of white schools in the region, is made clear in Louis R. Harlan, *Separate and Unequal: Public School Campaigns and Racism in the Southern Seaboard States, 1901–1915* (Chapel Hill, N.C., 1958), and J. Morgan Kousser, "Progressivism—For Middle Class Whites Only: North Carolina Education, 1880–1910," *JSH* 46 (May 1980): 169–94. The place of industrial education in the thinking of southern educational reformers is suggested by Berenice M. Fisher in *Industrial Education: American Ideals and Institutions* (Madison, Wis., 1967). The concern for higher academic standards felt by some southern educators is evident in Guy E. Snavely, *A Short History of the Southern Association of Colleges and Secondary Schools* (Durham, N.C., 1945).

One has to search carefully to discern the faint stirrings of a more sensitive and ameliorative approach to the "race question" among southern whites early in the twentieth century. The powerful sway of southern racial orthodoxy over well-meaning reformers is illustrated in Hugh C. Bailey's biography of Edgar Gardner Murphy, referred to earlier in this essay. The dissenting view that gradually found expression, usually among church groups, included Lily H. Hammond's compassionate treatment of southern Negroes, *In Black and White: An Interpretation of Southern Life*, previously mentioned. Noreen D. Tatum's *A Crown of Service*, cited above, provides other examples. One of the white reformers in the sphere of race relations is discussed in Wilma Dykeman, *Prophet of Plenty: The First Ninety Years of W.D. Weatherford* (Knoxville, 1966), and George Peter Antone, Jr., "Willis Duke Weatherford: An Interpretation of His Work in Race Relations, 1906–1946" (Ph.D. diss., Vanderbilt Univ., 1969). Uplift activities in the South's black communities are described in Kirby, *Darkness at the Dawning;* Dittmer, *Black Georgia in the Progressive Era;* Lamon, *Black Tennesseans;* and Newby, *Black Carolinians,* all cited previously. August Meier and Elliott Rudwick have analyzed a wave of black protest against segregated streetcars in "The Boycott Movement Against Jim Crow Streetcars in the South, 1900–1906," *Jour. Amer. Hist.* 55 (Mar. 1969): 756–75, and a series of articles dealing with boycotts in individual southern states.

Public welfare and social work in the early twentieth-century South have not yet received much scholarly investigation. J. Wayne Flynt, *Dixie's Forgotten People: The South's Poor Whites* (Bloomington, Ind., 1979), places southern poverty in historical perspective. Some of the essays contained in Edward Magdol and Jon L. Wakelyn, eds., *The Southern Common People: Studies in Nineteenth-Century Social History* (Westport, Conn., 1980), are informative in this respect. Two useful general studies—Lyda Gordon Shivers, "The Social Welfare Movement in the South: A Study in Regional Culture and Social Organization" (Ph.D. diss., Univ. of North Carolina, 1935), and Elizabeth Wisner, *Social Welfare in the South: From Colonial Times to World War I* (Baton Rouge, 1970)—are sketchy on the progressive era. Frank Dekker Watson, *The Charity Organization Movement in the United States: A Study in American Philanthropy* (New York, 1922), throws light on one manifestation of social welfare in the South. National developments are traced in Robert Hamlett Bremner, *From the Depths: The Discovery of Poverty in the United States* (New York, 1956); Frank J. Bruno, *Trends in Social Work, 1874–1956: A History Based on the Proceedings of the National Conference of Social Work* (2d ed., New York, 1957); Nathan Edward Cohen, *Social Work in the Ameri-*

can Tradition: Field, Body of Knowledge, Process, Method, and Point of View
(New York, 1958); and Roy Lubove, *The Professional Altruist: The
Emergence of Social Work as a Career, 1880–1930* (Cambridge, Mass., 1965).

The role of the settlement house in the United States—and in the South—is
described in Robert A. Woods and Albert J. Kennedy, eds., *Handbook of
Settlements* (New York, 1911); Allen F. Davis, *Spearheads for Reform: The
Social Settlements and the Progressive Movements, 1890–1914* (New York,
1967); Milton D. Speizman, "The Movement of the Settlement House Idea into
the South," *Southwestern Soc. Sci. Quar.* 44 (Dec. 1963): 237–46; Edyth L.
Ross, "Black Heritage in Social Welfare: A Case Study of Atlanta," *Phylon* 37
(Dec. 1976): 297–307; and Dittmer, *Black Georgia in the Progressive Era,*
cited above.

The fullest treatment of social welfare activities in a southern state during this
period is Arthur W. James, *Virginia's Social Awakening: The Contribution of
Dr. Mastin and the Board of Charities and Corrections* (Richmond, 1939).
Other state studies, some of which are quite restricted in scope, include Roy M.
Brown, *Public Poor Relief in North Carolina* (Chapel Hill, N.C., 1928);
Howard W. Odum and D.W. Willard, *Systems of Public Welfare* (Chapel Hill,
N.C., 1925), which deals with several southern states; Harriet L. Herring,
*Welfare Work in Mill Villages: The Story of Extra-Mill Activities in North
Carolina* (Chapel Hill, N.C., 1929); Elizabeth Wisner, *Public Welfare Admin-
istration in Louisiana* (Chicago, 1930); Virginia Ashcraft, *Public Care: A
History of Public Welfare Legislation in Tennessee* (Knoxville, 1947); and
William Foy Lisenby, "An Administrative History of Public Programs for
Dependent Children in North Carolina, Virginia, Tennessee, and Kentucky,
1900–1942" (Ph.D. diss., Vanderbilt Univ., 1962). The work of an important
state organization in the South is described in Virginia Wooten Gulledge, *The
North Carolina Conference for Social Service: A Study of Its Development and
Methods* (Chapel Hill, N.C., 1942). Benevolence in one subregion is consid-
ered in Henry D. Shapiro, *Appalachia on Our Mind: The Southern Mountains
and Mountaineers in the American Consciousness, 1870–1920* (Chapel Hill,
N.C., 1978). The Southern Sociological Congress is examined in E. Charles
Chatfield, Jr., "The Southern Sociological Congress, 1912–1920: The De-
velopment and Rationale of a Twentieth-Century Crusade" (M.A. thesis,
Vanderbilt Univ., 1958), and in two articles by the same author cited in chapter
11.

EFFICIENCY AND MODERNIZATION

Efficiency as a major theme in reform during the progressive era was first
broadly asserted by Samuel P. Hays in *The Response to Industrialism, 1885–
1914* (Chicago, 1957) and *Conservation and the Gospel of Efficiency: The
Progressive Conservation Movement, 1890–1920* (Cambridge, Mass., 1959),

and by Robert H. Wiebe in *The Search for Order, 1877–1920* (New York, 1967). The concept has not received much attention in general interpretations of southern progressivism, although it has been identified as a strong force in particular reform campaigns and programs. The results of modernization were not always salutary, as is shown by Ronald D. Eller in *Miners, Millhands, and Mountaineers: Industrialization of the Appalachian South, 1880–1930* (Knoxville, 1982).

Agricultural reform in the South was clearly an area in which the drive for greater economic and social efficiency played a conspicuous part. Changes in various sectors of southern agriculture are discussed by Robert Preston Brooks, *The Agrarian Revolution in Georgia, 1865–1912* (Madison, Wis., 1914); Rupert B. Vance, *Human Factors in Cotton Culture: A Study in the Social Geography of the American South* (Chapel Hill, N.C., 1929); J. Carlyle Sitterson, *Sugar Country: The Cane Sugar Industry in the South, 1753–1950 (Lexington, Ky., 1953);* Willard Range, *A Century of Georgia Agriculture, 1850–1950* (Athens, Ga., 1954); and Clifton Paisley, *From Cotton to Quail: An Agricultural Chronicle of Leon County, Florida, 1860–1967* (Gainesville, Fla., 1968). Theodore Saloutos's *Farmer Movements in the South, 1865–1933* (Berkeley, Calif., 1960) is the basic work on agricultural organizations, pressure groups, and movements in the late nineteenth and early twentieth centuries. Carl C. Taylor's *The Farmers' Movement, 1620–1920* (New York, 1953) is also useful in this respect. The development of agricultural extension programs and the instrumental role of Seaman A. Knapp are illuminated in Roy V. Scott, *The Reluctant Farmer: The Rise of Agricultural Extension to 1914* (Urbana, Ill., 1970), and Joseph Cannon Bailey, *Seaman A. Knapp: Schoolmaster of American Agriculture* (New York, 1945). The career of one of the new agricultural specialists in the South is described by Roy V. Scott and J.G. Shoalmire in *The Public Career of Cully A. Cobb: A Study in Agricultural Leadership* (Jackson, Miss., 1973). Other aspects of southern agricultural reform are dealt with by William L. Bowers, *The Country Life Movement in America, 1900–1920* (Port Washington, N.Y., 1974); Wayne E. Fuller, *RFD: The Changing Face of Rural America* (Bloomington, Ind., 1964); and John Milton Cooper, Jack Temple Kirby, and Clarence Poe in works previously cited. Linda O. McMurry, in *George Washington Carver: Scientist and Symbol* (New York, 1981), adds to our understanding of black education, scientific farming, and agricultural extension work as well as Tuskegee Institute.

The best brief survey of urban development in the South during the late nineteenth and early twentieth centuries is Howard N. Rabinowitz, "Continuity and Change: Southern Urban Development, 1860–1900," in Blaine A. Brownell and David R. Goldfield, eds., *The City in Southern History: The Growth of Urban Civilization in the South* (Port Washington, N.Y., 1977), 92–122, and Blaine A. Brownell, "The Urban South Comes of Age, 1900–1940," ibid., 123–58. Bradley Robert Rice's *Progressive Cities: The Commis-*

sion Government Movement in America, 1901–1920 (Austin, Tex., 1977) is a key study of structural reform in municipal government in the South and other parts of the country. Other features of southern urban reform are dealt with in Frank Mann Stewart, *A Half Century of Municipal Reform: The History of the National Municipal League* (Berkeley, Calif., 1950); James Weinstein, "Organized Business and the City Commission and Manager Movements," *JSH* 28 (May 1962): 166–82; and Koleen Alice Haire Huggins, "The Evolution of City and Regional Planning in North Carolina, 1900–1950" (Ph.D. diss., Duke Univ., 1967).

Scholarly interest in the study of individual southern cities in the twentieth century is growing. A significant example is Carl V. Harris's *Political Power in Birmingham, 1871–1921* (Knoxville, 1977), an illuminating analysis of the influence wielded by economic and social interest groups. Urban politics and reform are considered in George M. Reynolds, *Machine Politics in New Orleans, 1897–1926* (New York, 1936); William D. Miller, *Memphis During the Progressive Era, 1900–1917* (Memphis, 1957), and *Mr. Crump of Memphis* (Baton Rouge, 1964); James R. McGovern, *The Emergence of a City in the Modern South: Pensacola, 1900–1945* (Pensacola, Fla., 1976); John Joseph Duffy, "Charleston Politics in the Progressive Era" (Ph.D. diss., Univ. of South Carolina, 1963); Richard H.L. German, "The Queen City of the Savannah: Augusta, Georgia, During the Urban Progressive Era, 1890–1917" (Ph.D. diss., Univ. of Florida, 1971); Samuel M. Kipp III, "Urban Growth and Social Change in the South, 1870–1920: Greensboro, North Carolina as a Case Study" (Ph.D. diss., Princeton Univ., 1974); and Thomas Mashburn Deaton, "Atlanta during the Progressive Era" (Ph.D. diss., Univ. of Georgia, 1969).

The contributions of organized labor to progressive campaigns and legislation in the South were limited, but the precise extent and character of labor's involvement in the region's reform politics during this period still await careful study. There is no adequate history of the labor movement in the South during the progressive era. Nor is there a good treatment of organized labor in an individual southern state early in the twentieth century. But for Texas see Ruth A. Allen, *Chapters in the History of Organized Labor in Texas* (Austin, Tex., 1941), and *East Texas Lumber Workers: An Economic and Social Picture, 1870–1950* (Austin, Tex., 1961). Scholarly histories of the various state federations of labor and of the more important labor councils at the local level would probably be illuminating. F. Ray Marshall's general account, *Labor in the South* (Cambridge, Mass., 1967), throws some light on the progressive period. Gary M. Fink and Merl E. Reed, eds., *Essays in Southern Labor History: Selected Papers, Southern Labor History Conference, 1976* (Westport, Conn., 1977), presents examples of recent scholarship. Two other works are useful for textile mill workers: Herbert J. Lahne, *The Cotton Mill Worker* (New York, 1944), and Melton Alonza McLaurin, *Paternalism and Protest: Southern Cot-*

ton Mill Workers and Organized Labor, 1875–1905 (Westport, Conn., 1971). One of the few studies of labor legislation is Virginia Holmes Brown, *The Development of Labor Legislation in Tennessee* (Knoxville, 1945). The last decade has witnessed the publication of numerous articles on various aspects of the labor movement in the South, particularly on radical unions in the Southwest. Examples are Keith L. Bryant, Jr., "Labor in Politics: The Oklahoma State Federation of Labor During the Age of Reform," *Labor Hist.* 11 (Summer 1970): 259–76; George T. Morgan, Jr., "The Gospel of Wealth Goes South: John Henry Kirby and Labor's Struggle for Self-Determination, 1901–1916," *Southwestern Hist. Quar.* 75 (Oct. 1971): 186–97; and James R. Green, "The Brotherhood of Timber Workers, 1910–1913: A Radical Response to Industrial Capitalism in the Southern U.S.A.," *Past and Present* 60 (Aug. 1973): 161–200.

The relationship between efficiency and the expansion of state services is pointed up in Tindall's *The Emergence of the New South*. This theme is also developed in some of the previously cited works dealing with reform movements in such areas as agriculture, public education, and municipal government, as well as several of the state studies cited above. One sphere in which southern states assumed a larger role during the progressive era was public health. Francis R. Allen, "Development of the Public Health Movement in the Southeast," *Social Forces* 22 (Oct. 1943): 67–75, provides a brief introduction, but there is no scholarly treatment of the movement at the regional level. Among the more useful studies bearing on the development of public health are T.F. Abercrombie, *History of Public Health in Georiga, 1733–1950* (Atlanta, 1951); Elizabeth E. Etheridge, *The Butterfly Caste: A Social History of Pellagra in the South* (Westport, Conn., 1972); John Ettling, *The Germ of Laziness: Rockefeller Philanthropy and Public Health in the New South* (Cambridge, Mass., 1981); Shirley G. Schoonover, "Alabama Public Health Campaign, 1900–1919," *Ala. Rev.* 28 (July 1975): 218–33; and Margaret Ripley Wolfe, "The Agricultural Experiment Station and Food and Drug Control: Another Look at Kentucky Progressivism, 1898–1916," *Filson Club Hist. Quar.* 49 (Oct. 1975): 323–38. James G. Burrow, *Organized Medicine in the Progressive Era: The Move Toward Monopoly* (Baltimore, 1977), is revealing on the emergence of public health and on national and regional trends in medical reform and professionalism.

Enthusiasm for good roads contributed to the expansion of state services during the early years of the twentieth century. Systematic study of this development has focused on the movement within individual states and cities. Three examples are Cecil Kenneth Brown, *The State Highway System of North Carolina: Its Evolution and Present Status* (Chapel Hill, N.C., 1931); Leland R. Johnson, *Memphis to Bristol: A Half Century of Highway Construction: A History of the Tennessee Road Builders Association, 1928–1978* (Nashville, 1978); and Howard L. Preston, *Automobile Age Atlanta: The Making of a*

Southern Metropolis, 1900–1935 (Athens, Ga., 1979). Beginnings were also made during the progressive period in the reclamation and conservation of natural resources. The most valuable study yet published is Nelson Manfred Blake, *Land into Water—Water into Land: A History of Water Management in Florida* (Tallahassee, 1980). Two useful unpublished works are Roy Ring White, "Austin Cary and Forestry in the South" (Ph.D. diss., Univ. of Florida, 1960), and Frank Bedingfield Vinson, "Conservation and the South, 1890–1920," (Ph.D. diss., Univ. of Georgia, 1971).

THE NATIONALIZATION OF SOUTHERN REFORM, 1912–1920

The movement in the South to nominate and elect Woodrow Wilson to the presidency has been described in impressive detail by Arthur S. Link in "The South and the Democratic Campaign of 1912" (Ph.D. diss., Univ. of North Carolina, 1945); *Wilson: The Road to the White House* (Princeton, N.J. 1947); and *The Higher Realism of Woodrow Wilson and Other Essays* (Nashville, 1971). The South's participation and influence in early twentieth-century national politics are also dealt with by Anne Firor Scott in "A Progressive Wind from the South, 1906–1913," *JSH* 29 (Feb. 1963): 53–70, and "The Southern Progressives in National Politics, 1906–1916" (Ph.D. diss., Radcliffe College, 1957), and by Willard B. Gatewood, Jr., *Theodore Roosevelt and the Art of Controversy: Episodes of the White House Years* (Baton Rouge, 1970).

George B. Tindall's *The Emergence of the New South* contains the most authoritative treatment of the interrelationship between the South and the administration of Woodrow Wilson. This relationship is also clarified in Arthur S. Link's *Woodrow Wilson and the Progressive Era, 1910–1917* (New York, 1954) and in Link's biography of Wilson: *Wilson: The New Freedom* (Princeton, N.J., 1956); *Wilson: The Struggle for Neutrality, 1914–1915* (Princeton, N.J., 1960); *Wilson: Confusions and Crises, 1915–1916* (Princeton, N.J., 1964); and *Wilson: Campaigns for Progressivism and Peace, 1916–1917* (Princeton, N.J., 1965). Aspects of the South's role in the New Freedom are described in John M. Blum, *Joe Tumulty and the Wilson Era* (Boston, 1951), and John J. Broesamle, *William Gibbs McAdoo: A Passion for Change, 1863–1917 (Port Washington, N.Y., 1973)*. Saloutos, *Farmer Movements in the South,* includes two valuable chapters on Wilson's New Freedom and southern agriculture. An older, unpublished study by John W. Davidson, "The Response of the South to Woodrow Wilson's New Freedom, 1912–1914" (Ph.D. diss., Yale Univ., 1953), remains useful.

The role of the southern congressional delegations is given some attention in the works by Link and Tindall. A number of biographies explore this topic in greater detail, including Evans C. Johnson, *Oscar W. Underwood: A Political Biography* (Baton Rouge, 1980); Monroe Billington, *Thomas P. Gore: The Blind Senator from Oklahoma* (Lawrence, Kans., 1967); George Coleman Osborn, *John Sharp Williams: Planter-Statesman of the Deep South* (Baton

Rouge, 1943); Francis B. Simkins, *Pitchfork Ben Tillman: South Carolinian* (Baton Rouge, 1944); Edward Elmer Keso, *The Senatorial Career of Robert Latham Owen* (Gardenvale, Canada, 1938); and the studies of Duncan U. Fletcher, Hoke Smith, and James K. Vardaman mentioned above. The reaction of southern congressmen to the difficult problems of American neutrality are examined in Alex Mathews Arnett, *Claude Kitchin and the Wilson War Policies* (Boston, 1937), and Timothy Gregory McDonald, "Southern Democratic Congressmen and the First World War, August 1914–April 1917: The Public Record of Their Support for or Opposition to Wilson's Policies" (Ph.D. diss., Univ. of Washington, 1962).

Political and social reform in the South during the Wilson era is considered in several state studies. The most informative of these are the works on Westmoreland Davis, Richard I. Manning, Robert L. Williams, and Sidney J. Catts, previously cited, and Larry Thomas Balsamo, "Theodore G. Bilbo and Mississippi Politics, 1877–1932" (Ph.D. diss., Univ. of Missouri, 1967).

Southern politics and reform during the war years are interpreted by Tindall in *The Emergence of the New South,* and some light is thrown on the South's reaction to wartime developments by David M. Kennedy's *Over Here: The First World War and American Society* (New York, 1980). The pressures for conformity in the South and other regions are described by H.C. Peterson and Gilbert C. Fite in *Opponents of War, 1917–1918* (Madison, Wis., 1957). The contributions of southern congressmen to the demands of the American war effort are analyzed in two valuable articles by Richard L. Watson, Jr.: "A Testing Time for Southern Congressional Leadership: The War Crisis of 1917–1918," *JSH* 44 (Feb. 1978): 3–40, and "Principle, Party, and Constituency: The North Carolina Congressional Delegation, 1917–1919," *N.C. Hist. Rev.* 56 (July 1979): 298–323. The broader congressional context is provided by Seward W. Livermore, *Politics Is Adjourned: Woodrow Wilson and the War Congress, 1916–1918* (Middletown, Conn., 1966). Wartime mobilization, welfare programs, and voluntary activities to relieve social distress are beginning to receive scholarly scrutiny, although no large-scale study of such efforts has yet been published. Sarah McCulloh Lemmon's *North Carolina's Role in the First World War* (Raleigh, N.C., 1966) is a short but informative survey. Examples of the growing list of journal articles are two essays by William J. Breen: "Southern Women in the War: The North Carolina Woman's Committee, 1917–1919," *N.C. Hist. Rev.* 55 (July 1978): 251–83, and "Black Women and the Great War: Mobilization and Reform in the South," *JSH* 44 (Aug. 1978): 421–40.

THE 1920S AND AFTER

The close relationship between southern progressivism and political trends in the South during the 1920s is illuminated by Tindall in *The Emergence of the New South.* One of the elements of continuity between the progressive era and the postwar period in the South was an intense search for moralistic solutions to many social problems, including the traffic in alcoholic beverages. The prohibition campaigns of the 1920s are discussed in Peter H. Odegard, *Pressure Politics: The Story of the Anti-Saloon League* (New York, 1928); Sinclair, *Era of Excess;* Virginius Dabney, *Dry Messiah: The Life of Bishop Cannon* (New York, 1949); Watson, ed., *Bishop Cannon's Own Story: Life As I Have Seen It;* and several of the state studies of prohibiiton mentioned above.

Another manifestation of crusading moralism found an outlet in the antievolution movement in the South, aspects of which are examined in Norman F. Furniss, *The Fundamentalist Controversy, 1918–1931* (New Haven, Conn., 1954); Willard B. Gatewood, Jr., *Preachers, Pedagogues, & Politicians: The Evolution Controversy in North Carolina, 1920–1927* (Chapel Hill, N.C., 1966); Laurence W. Levine, *Defender of the Faith, William Jennings Bryan: The Last Decade, 1915–1925* (New York, 1965); and Kenneth K. Bailey, "The Antievolution Crusade of the Nineteen-Twenties" (Ph.D. diss., Vanderbilt Univ., 1953). For the Ku Klux Klan, see Charles C. Alexander, *The Ku Klux Klan in the Southwest* (Lexington, Ky., 1965); David Mark Chalmers, *Hooded Americanism: The First Century of the Ku Klux Klan, 1865–1965* (Garden City, N.Y., 1965); and Kenneth T. Jackson, *The Ku Klux Klan in the City, 1915–1930* (New York, 1967). Still another example of moralistic reform in the 1920s is described by Robert F. Sexton, "The Crusade Against Pari-Mutuel Gambling in Kentucky: A Study of Southern Progressivism in the 1920's," *Filson Club Hist. Quar.* 50 (Jan. 1976): 47–57. Outside criticism of southern institutions in the twenties is revealed in Frank Tannenbaum, *Darker Phases of the South* (New York, 1924), and Fred C. Hobson, *Serpent in Eden: H.L. Mencken and the South* (Chapel Hill, N.C., 1974).

The "metamorphosis" of southern progressivism following World War I led to greater emphasis on reorganization, efficiency, and public services in state government. George Tindall has analyzed this phenomenon in *The Emergence of the New South* and in an essay entitled "Business Progressivism: Southern Politics in the Twenties," *SAQ* 62 (Winter 1963): 92–106. There are only a handful of scholarly state studies for this period of southern politics. For the treatment of one state, see David D. Lee, *Tennessee in Turmoil: Politics in the Volunteer State, 1920–1932* (Memphis, 1979), and Joseph T. Macpherson, "Democratic Progressivism in Tennessee: The Administrations of Governor Austin Peay, 1923–1927" (Ph.D. diss., Vanderbilt Univ., 1969). Business progressivism is also clarified by Blaine A. Brownell's *The Urban Ethos in the South, 1920–1930* (Baton Rouge, 1975).

Developments in race relations and the major southern reform effort in this sphere are treated in Wilma Dykeman and James Stokely, *Seeds of Southern Change: The Life of Will Alexander* (Chicago, 1962); Jacquelyn Dowd Hall, *Revolt Against Chivalry: Jessie Daniel Ames and the Women's Campaign Against Lynching* (New York, 1979); Edward Flud Burrows, "The Commission on Interracial Cooperation, 1919–1944: A Case Study in the History of the Interracial Movement in the South" (Ph.D. diss., Univ. of Wis., 1954); Antone, "Willis Duke Weatherford: An Interpretation of His Work in Race Relations, 1906–1946"; Morton Sosna, *In Search of the Silent South: Southern Liberals and the Race Issue* (New York, 1977); and Lamon, *Black Tennesseans, 1900–1930*.

The liberalism of modern white southerners was indelibly marked by early twentieth-century progressivism. This remained true until mid-century, when the civil rights movement and other powerful currents of change began to transform some of the old liberal assumptions and expectations in the region. The nature of southern liberalism during the first half of the century is one of the concerns in Tindall, *The Emergence of the New South*, in Gunnar Myrdal, *An American Dilemma: The Negro Problem and Modern Democracy* (New York, 1944), and in V.O. Key, Jr., with the assistance of Alexander Heard, *Southern Politics in State and Nation* (New York, 1949). The relationship between the South and the New Deal needs more scholarly investigation, but some light is shed on the question by Frank Freidel, *F.D.R. and the South* (Baton Rouge, 1965); James T. Patterson, *Congressional Conservation and the New Deal: The Growth of the Conservative Coalition in Congress, 1933–1939* (Lexington, Ky., 1967); Thomas A. Krueger, *And Promises to Keep: The Southern Conference for Human Welfare, 1938–1948* (Nashville, 1967); and Elmer L. Puryear, *Democratic Party Dissension in North Carolina, 1928–1936* (Chapel Hill, N.C., 1962). The limitations and regenerative possibilities of liberal politics in the post-World War II South are set forth, respectively, in Numan V. Bartley and Hugh Davis Graham, *Southern Politics and the Second Reconstruction* (Baltimore, 1975), and Jack Bass and Walter DeVries, *The Transformation of Southern Politics: Social Change and Political Consequence since 1945* (New York, 1976). The continuing influence of the South's most pronounced cultural values and traditions is stressed in William H. Nicholls, *Southern Tradition and Regional Progress* (Chapel Hill, N.C., 1960). Daniel Joseph Singal's *The War Within: From Victorian to Modernist Thought in the South, 1919–1945* (1982), an imaginative and insightful analysis of the region's cultural transition in the period between the two world wars, appeared too late for me to make use of in this study.

Index

Abbott, Edward, 247
Adams Act (1906), 333
Addams, Jane, 201, 223
Adler, Felix, 191
Advancing South, The (Mims), 417
Agrarian radicalism, 13, 36, 111; in
   Alabama, 46, 47; in Tennessee, 80; in
   Kentucky, 85; in the Southwest, 87; in
   Arkansas, 93; in Louisiana, 94
Agrarian revolt, 26, 116, 143, 147; in
   Mississippi, 45; in Texas, 100; in Okla-
   homa, 103–104
Agricultural Conference (1914), 344
Agricultural economy: in Mississippi,
   37–41; in Louisiana, 93
Agricultural organizations. *See* Agricul-
   tural reform movement. *See also*
   Farmers' Alliance; Farmers' Union
Agricultural reform movement: as a
   progressive reform movement, xx,
   321–48; agricultural organizations of,
   8; production and price controls of,
   320–31; and comprehensive farm organizations, 322; education and demonstration programs of, 322, 332;
   legislation of, 322; and crop production adjustments, 322; in cotton industry, 322–23; in tobacco industry,
   324–26; farm journals of, 332–33;
   and farm institute movement, 333–34;
   experiment stations and extension
   programs of, 333, 334; and Seaman
   A. Knapp, 337–41; politics and legislative policies of, 342
Alabama: Constitutional Convention of

1901, 46, 48; child labor act (1903),
   50, 185; General Assembly of, 50,
   151; primary election law (1915), 50;
   vagrancy law (1903), 137; Constitu-
   tion of 1901, 150
Alabama Anti-Saloon League, 163, 169,
   365
Alabama Black Belt. *See* Black Belt
Alabama Child Labor Committee, 182,
   183, 184, 195
Alabama Citizen (American Anti-Saloon
   League), 163
Alabama Educational Association, 253
Alabama Federation of Women's Clubs,
   185, 195, 253
Alabama Sociological Congress (1913),
   229
Alaskan Railroad bill, 362
Alderman, Edwin A., 77, 234, 249,
   250, 259, 355, 359
Aldrich plan, 155
Alexander, H. Q., 331
Alexander, Will W., 402, 406, 413
Allen, Robert M., 303
Almshouses, 217–18
American Anti-Saloon League, 172,
   280, 351, 367, 379
American Bankers' Association, 155
American Book Company, 84
American Civic Association, 288
American Cotton Manufacturers' Asso-
   ciation, 154, 155, 292
American Federationist, 189
American Federation of Labor, 181, 185,
   186, 290, 292, 297

449

〜 Twentieth-Century America Series
DEWEY W. GRANTHAM, GENERAL EDITOR

Each volume in this series focuses on some aspects of the politics of social change in recent American history, utilizing new approaches to clarify the response of Americans to the dislocating forces of our own day—economic, technological, racial, demographic, and administrative.

THE UNIVERSITY OF TENNESSEE PRESS : KNOXVILLE